Introducing World Religions

Introducing World Religions offers an exciting new approach to the study of world religions. Taking its inspiration from performance studies and using an innovative dramatic metaphor, it enables students to explore religious ideas and culture in terms of the players (key figures), the script (foundational texts), and performance (religious practices). The discussion of key players treats human and non-human figures on the world stage, including the principle (God, Dharma, Dao), imaginal figures (angels, ba'alim, bodhisattvas), exceptional persons (founders, prophets, gurūs), and historical persons (significant players in the drama of religions). The discussion of the script addresses foundational texts, also examining materials that balance or challenge mainstream texts with an alternative perspective. The section on performance explores non-verbal religious activities such as pilgrimage, icon painting, dance, divination, and meditation.

Those concerned with introducing "postcolonial" discourse to students without losing the classic category of "the sacred" should find this textbook to be balanced and evocative. It presents workable concepts from the camps of both "religionists" and "reductionists," and students are challenged to move between "inside" and "outside" positions as they survey what have been called (controversially) "world religions."

Specially designed textbook features include:

- chapter timelines showing key persons, events, and dates
- themed boxes to encourage methodological enquiry
- key point chapter summaries to support understanding and revision
- study questions to assist classroom discussion
- glossary of key concepts and terms
- key reading, a comprehensive bibliography, and index
- a support website at www.routledge.com/textbooks/9780415772709 with additional discussion questions, podcast interview with author, and many other support features.

Ideal for one-semester or modular introductory survey courses, *Introducing World Religions* will be essential reading for any student of religions, worldwide.

Victoria Kennick Urubshurow is Associate Professor at the University of Maryland University College, where she was given a "Teaching Excellence Award" in 2007. She has taught courses in world religions and culture for over twenty years, including graduate seminars at the Catholic University of America, and undergraduate classes at George Washington University and Coe College.

Introducing World Religions

Victoria Kennick Urubshurow

Routledge
Taylor & Francis Group
NEW YORK AND LONDON

The author and Routledge would like to thank consultants Professor Charles Prebish, Pennsylvania State University and Editor Emeritus, *Journal of Buddhist Ethics*, and Professor Damien Keam, Goldsmith's College, University of London.

First published 2008 by Routledge
711 Third Avenue, New York, NY 10017

Simultaneously published in the UK
by Routledge
2 Park Square, Milton Park, Abingdon, Oxon OX14 4RN

Routledge is an imprint of the Taylor and Francis Group, an informa business

Typeset in Garamond and Univers by
Keystroke, 28 High Street, Tettenhall, Wolverhampton

British Library Cataloguing in Publication Data
A catalogue record for this book is available from the British Library

Library of Congress Cataloging in Publication Data
Urubshurow, Victoria Kennick, 1950–
Introducing world religions / Victoria Kennick Urubshurow.
p. cm.
Includes bibliographical references and index.
1. Religions. I. Title.
BL80.3.U78 2008
200—dc22 2007041884

ISBN 10: 0–415–77269–9 (hbk)
ISBN 10: 0–415–77270–2 (pbk)

ISBN 13: 978–0–415–77269–3 (hbk)
ISBN 13: 978–0–415–77270–9 (pbk)

Contents

Illustrations

PLATES

TIMELINES

FIGURES

BOXES

TABLES

Illustration acknowledgments

The publishers and author would like to thank the following individuals and archives for permission to reproduce illustrations:

Louisa Gould for plates 1.1 and 8.3; The Library of Congress for plates 2.1, 2.2 and 2.3; Behram Pantaki for plates 3.1 and 3.3; Freer Gallery of Art, Smithsonian Institution, Washington, D.C. for plate 3.2; Freer Gallery of Art, Smithsonian Institution, Washington D.C., purchase F1955.11 for plate 5.1; Freer Gallery of Art, Smithsonian Institution, Washington, D.C., purchase F1997.33 for plate 8.1; Freer Gallery of Art, Smithsonian Institution, Washington, D.C., purchase F1949.9 for plate 9.2; Freer Gallery of Art, Smithsonian Institution, Washington, D.C., gift of Charles Lang Freer, F1907.537 for plate 9.3; Freer Gallery of Art, Smithsonian Institution, Washington, D.C., purchase F1984.42 for plate 10.1; Freer Gallery of Art, Smithsonian Institution, Washington, D.C., purchase F1930.84 for plate 10.4; Freer Gallery of Art, Smithsonian Institution, Washington, D.C., collected by Seymour J. Janow and gifted in his memory by his family, F2003.5.11 for plate 13.2; Freer Gallery of Art, Smithsonian Institution, Washington, D.C., gift of Charles Lang Freer, F1898.508 for plate 13.3; Mark Levoy and the Polo Museale fiorentino for plate 4.1; Laura Cornelius for plates 4.2, 5.2 (a) and (b), 6.3 (a) and (b), 7.1, 12.1 and 12.2; the Dorot Jewish Division, The New York Public Library, Astor, Lenox and Tilden Foundations for plate 4.4; Slavic and Baltic Divison, The New York Public Library, Astor, Lenox and Tilden Foundations for plate 5.4; Picture Collection, The Branch Libraries, The New York Public Library, Astor, Lenox and Tilden Foundations for plate 6.1; The Dorot Jewish Division, The New York Public Library, Astor, Lenox and Tilden Foundations for plate 6.4; The New York Public Library, Astor, Lenox and Tilden Foundations for plate 8.2; AKG-images for plate 5.3; Howard Lafranchi II for plate 6.2; US Bahai National Center for plate 7.2; John Schumacher for plate 10.2; Vrinda Arangetram for plate 10.3; The Asian Art Museum of San Francisco, gift of the Kapany Collection, 1998.58.14 for plate 11.1; The Asian Art Museum of San Francisco, gift of the Kapany Collection for plate 11.2; Nian-zu Li for plate 12.4; the University of Virginia Library for plate 14.1; The Metropolitan Museum of Art, gift of J. Pierpont Morgan, 1917 (17.190.724), image © The Metropolitan Museum of Art for plate 14.2; The Metropolitan Museum of Art, purchase, Buckeye Trust and Mr. and Mrs. Milton Rosenthal Gifts, Joseph. Image © The Metropolitan Museum of Art for plate 2.4; David Baasch for plate 13.1; Joginder Kaur courtesy of Gobind Sadan for plate 11.3; Vance Hyndman for plate 12.3.

Preface

RELIGIONS IN OUR WORLD TODAY

Our world now has around 6.1 billion people on it. Of those almost 85 percent are thought to be religious in some way or other. Table 0.1 shows members of various world religions in terms of their demographic visibility on the planet. Here the religions are named more or less according to current designations in demographic listings. The world religions are listed in descending order of total adherents.

Some religions boast a great many adherents, while others have a modest membership. Yet despite the variation in numbers this book aims to represent (if not include) all religious peoples around the globe. The world religions are surveyed roughly in geographical order around the globe beginning and ending in the "circum Pacific," which includes land on the Asian and American sides of the Pacific Ocean. There is no perfect way to arrange world religions in a sequence. Yet there is a kind of geographical and even cultural logic in moving from Oceania "eastward" around the globe winding up finally in Japan. This Asian Pacific point of origin and return reinforces Japan's ancestral connections to both mainland Asians and Malayo-Polynesians. It also traces the Africans of Latin America to their roots on the African continent, exposes the

Table 0.1 Religions in our world today*

Religion	*Daily increase*	*Total population*	*% world population*	*% yearly increase*
Christian	69,000	2.0 billion	33.0	1.4
Muslim (Islamic)	68,000	1.2 billion	19.6	
Hindu	37,000	811.0 million	13.4	1.7
Chinese folk	10,700	384.8 million	6.4	1.0
Buddhist	10,600	360.0 million	5.9	1.1
Tribal ethnic	8,200	228.4 million	3.8	1.3
New Religions of Asia	2,800	102.4 million	1.7	1.0
Sikh	1,100	23.3 million	<1	1.9
Jewish (Judaic)	350	14.4 million	<1	0.9
Non-Christian spiritist	600	12.3 million	<1	2.0
Bahá'í	400	7.1 million	<1	2.3
Confucian	120	6.4 million	<1	?
Jain	100	4.2 million	<1	0.9
Shintō	– 90	2.8 million	<1	– 1.0
Daoist	70	2.7 million	<1	?
Zoroastrian (Mazdean)	160	2.7 million	<1	?

*Statistics are from the *World Christian Encyclopedia*, except for the Confucian, Daoist, and Zoroastrian total population figures, which are rounded from the *World Almanac* report. The figures are basically corroborated by the *World Almanac 2005* for populations, and www.adherents.com for percentages.

cultural link between the Zoroastrian and Vedic (early Hindu) traditions, follows the spread of Buddhism along the Silk Roads, and observes the outflow of Chinese culture into Korea and Japan.

A WORD ABOUT PROBLEMATIC TERMS

In 1963 Wilfred Cantwell Smith wrote, "I seriously suggest that terms such as Christianity, Buddhism, and the like must be dropped, as clearly untenable once challenged" (Smith [1963] 1991: 194). He argued that the world had Buddhists but not Buddhism, Christians but not Christianity, and so forth. Smith suggested that the word "religion" be dropped as well, claiming that monolithic terms such as "religion," "Christianity," "Hinduism" obscure the dynamic and personal quality of religious traditions.

> "Hinduism" refers not to an entity; it is a name that the West has given to a prodigiously variegated series of facts. It is a notion in men's minds – and a notion that cannot but be inadequate. To use this term at all is inescapably a gross oversimplification. There is an inherent contradiction between history and this order of idea.
>
> (Smith [1963] 1991: 144)

One day W. C. Smith even wrote, "I am bold enough to speculate whether these terms will not in fact have disappeared from serious writing and careful speech within twenty-five years." (Smith [1963] 1991: 195) Yet habits die hard, as does language.

Now over forty-five years after W. C. Smith called for an end to the word "religion" it shows little sign of expiring, and "-isms" are as convenient as ever. Due to problems with the "-isms" and monolithic terms that sanitize the messiness of culture, the terminology of this book minimizes their use. Thus "Judaic tradition" generally is used in place of "Judaism" and so forth. Here the word "tradition" should carry a *holistic sense* that conveys the fact that traditions are ongoing with multiple strands that intertwine with many aspects of people's lives. A religious tradition may be thought of as a cultural heritage that is both: (1) kept alive through participation (what W. C. Smith calls "faith"), and (2) continually challenged by ongoing cultural circumstances. At this point it is still not practical to dispense with the word "religion." Thus stuck with the word, one is advised to think of particular religions as dynamic cultural complexes, not as static monolithic entities.

Nowadays, the trope "world religions" is often avoided due to its original connection with European colonialism. Consequently the status of a "world religion" was given only to traditions that somehow dominated the world stage. (See pages 8–12.) To dispense with such embarrassing and annoying political baggage many people now use the expressions "the world's religions" or "religions *of* the world." These tropes (words or expressions used in a figurative, non-literal sense) seem to be more inclusive and politically correct. However, the term "world religions" is retained in this book because it allows for a richer set of meanings than the two possessive expressions. The trope "world religions" *may incorporate* the possessive sense of "the world's religions" or "religions of the world." But the grammatically simple expression "world religions" allows for a larger spectrum of meanings. For example, it may carry the sense that religions are *in* the world, not possessed by the world. "In" carries an active connotation: we are all *in* the world together; religions are *in* the world together. Moreover, the terms "the world's religions" and "religions *of* the world" are problematic because they force all religions into a single world. And while religious cultures all develop on the same terrestrial globe each one also creates its own world (of meaning). Therefore the trope "world religions" captures the sense that religions are on our globe – *each with a world of meaning.*

EDITORIAL FORMALITIES

Dates

Dates are rendered according to contemporary Western conventions. The designations BCE and CE are used to mark the years of historical time. BCE means "Before the Common Era" and CE means "Common Era" – where "common" refers to what is common to Western culture. BCE replaces BC (Before Christ), while CE replaces AD. AD stands for *Anno Domini,* which is Latin for "in the year of our Lord [Jesus Christ]." Although the actual dates rendered as BCE or CE are exactly those of the Gregorian Christian calendar, the newer abbreviations introduce a modicum of cultural even-handedness. It is important to realize a calendar can never be value free. Calendars always embody cultural interpretations of time, regardless of whether they "objectively" measure it by means of the sun, moon, or something else.

In the history of religions the dates of an overwhelming number of events cannot be pinpointed. Moreover, traditional dates provided within religions often contradict dates suggested by modern historians. To further complicate matters, scholars often disagree among themselves as to when something happened. Traditional dates may be historically accurate, but differ from Western dates because they start from their own points of reference. An example is the start of the Islamic calendar, which dates from Prophet Muḥammad's migration (hijra) from Mecca to Medina in 622 CE. The year 622 CE (Common Era) corresponds to the year 1 AH (*Anno Hegirae*, in the year of the hijra) – but not for the whole time because the CE date is measured by the sun, while the AH date is measured by the moon's shorter year! Sometimes dates are reported on the basis of both lunar and solar calendars, resulting in two sets of dates for a single event. It also happens that scholars provide a range of dates within which something is supposed to have occurred. A prolonged event might have actually taken several centuries. For example, dates for the Hindu *Mahābhārata* epic may be given as "ca. 400 BCE–ca. 400 CE." This range indicates that the written rendering of the ancient oral tradition happened over many years. Here "ca." stands for the Latin *circa* (from *circum* meaning "around") and means that the date is approximate. A range of dates can also be given because the exact year of an event is unknown, but is accepted as having occurred within that specified range of time.

When a set of dates ascends in number it is understood that the time frame is the Common Era, so the designation CE is often omitted. For example, Augustine's dates of 354–430 are CE, as opposed to Buddha's dates of 566–486, which are BCE. If two sets of dates have been proposed for an event (such as Buddha's life, also given as 448–368 BCE) both dates *may* be provided here. If a person's life spans two centuries, the earlier century is used to mark the date. Thus Augustine's date might simply be rendered as "b. 300s CE" or "b. fourth c. CE." When placed before dates, "b." means born, "d." means died, "fl." means flourished, and "r." means reigned. In cases where traditional dates are at odds with dates given by modern scholars, the designation "traditional" or "expert" is appended to the date.

Treatment of terms

Transliterations generally follow the editorial choices of the *Encyclopedia of Religion*, second edition, and *The Oxford Dictionary of Religions.* Diacritical marks are preserved even when a word has made it into *The Oxford English Dictionary.* Upon first use in a chapter, glossary terms are printed in boldface, and non-*OED* terms are printed in italics. Definitions of boldfaced terms are provided at the end of each chapter, as well as in a comprehensive Glossary located at the end of the book. Proper names are capitalized; other terms occur in lower case unless capitalized in their original context or commonly in translation. When contemporaneous place names are used, modern locations are indicated in parentheses. Book titles are italicized, except for major religious scriptures whose names have become commonplace in the English language.

CHAPTER ENHANCEMENTS

Each chapter that treats a world religion includes a timeline, and four boxes. Each timeline is divided into three columns, with players on the left, major events on the right, and dates in the middle. Boxes involve these subjects: (1) "A Spiritual Path" treats some form of religious discipline; (2) "Symbols" explores key symbols; (3) "Culture Contrast" compares items from two cultural contexts; and (4) "Interpretations" provides an example of how the tradition defines its own religious categories. The chapters end with features to enhance study: Key points, Study questions, Glossary and Key reading. Key reading contains a handful of titles that represent different types of books, normally including key scriptures or anthologies, historical surveys, anthropological studies of a living population, modern interpretations, and a dictionary or encyclopedia. A comprehensive bibliography is provided at the back of the book. A companion website for this textbook to be found at www.routledge.com/textbooks/9780415772709 includes: (1) self-test questions; (2) discussion questions; (3) essay questions for each chapter; and other materials as they become available.

The use of websites to complement this textbook is helpful. Yet students of religion must keep in mind that the authors of websites (as the authors of books, films, and so on) speak from a point of view (i.e., a bias). It is important to keep authors' assumptions and research methods in mind when evaluating information presented in their work. A wide range of views is available on the World Wide Web. For example, searching through Google for material on contemporary Islam brings up links from diverse political perspectives. To wit, a link for "Salafiyya" (which defines Islamic fundamentalism) seems to be associated with the US military, while a link for "Islamic Cultural Revolution" is maintained by the SCCR (Secretariat of Supreme Council of Cultural Revolution). Normally, for a deep understanding of any given subject matter consideration of several points of view is recommended.

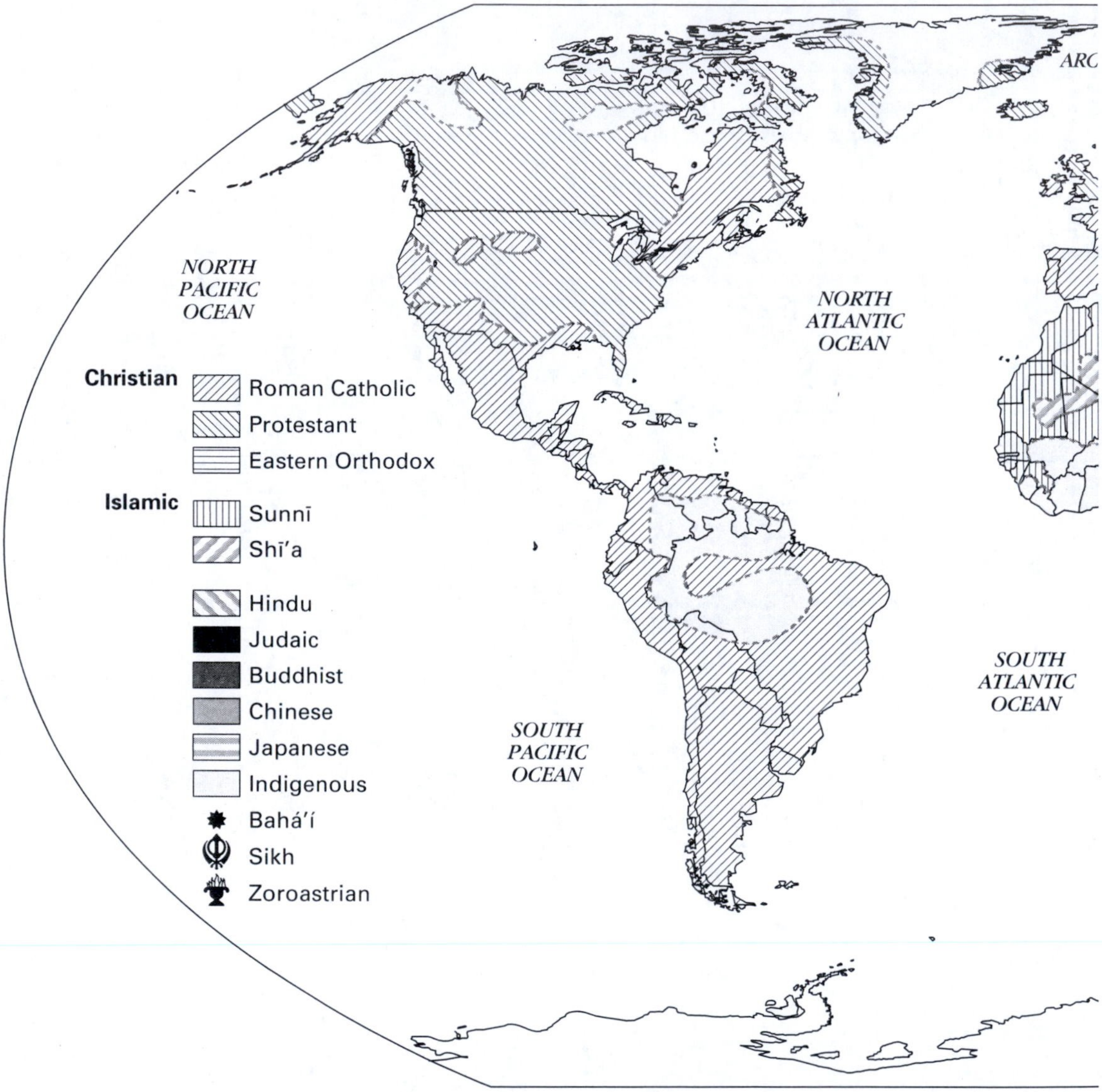
ARC
NORTH PACIFIC OCEAN
NORTH ATLANTIC OCEAN
SOUTH ATLANTIC OCEAN
SOUTH PACIFIC OCEAN
Christian
Roman Catholic
Protestant
Eastern Orthodox
Islamic
Sunnī
Shī'a
Hindu
Judaic
Buddhist
Chinese
Japanese
Indigenous
Bahá'í
Sikh
Zoroastrian

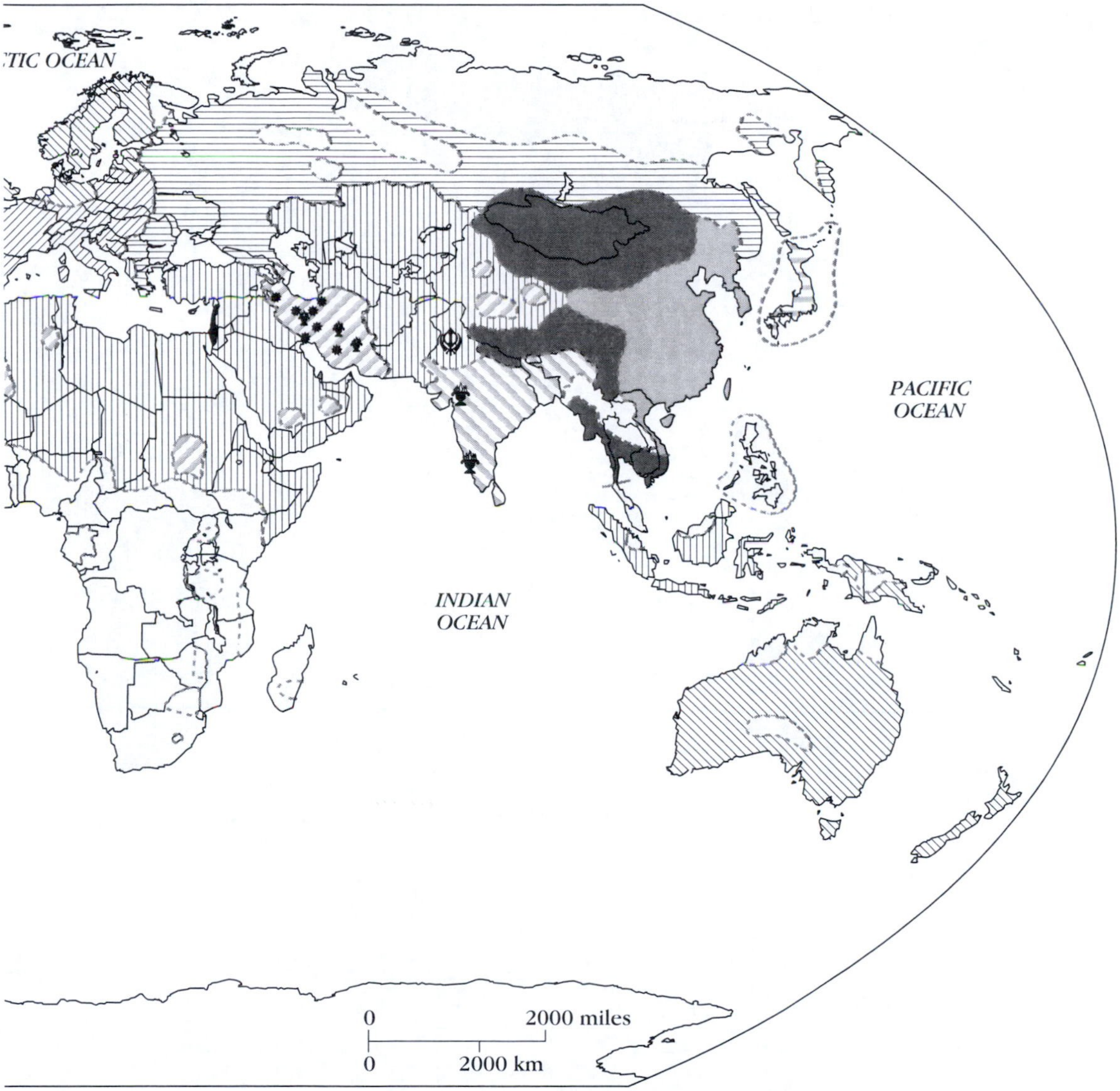
TIC OCEAN
PACIFIC OCEAN
INDIAN OCEAN
0 2000 miles
0 2000 km

CHAPTER 1

Approaching religious traditions

Plate 1.1 "Gaṇeśa, a Hindu deity." How did you feel when you first saw this image? Hindus invoke Gaṇeśa at the start of new ventures because he removes obstacles to success with his trunk. The svastika is an ancient religious symbol from India that hearkens well-being. (In the Sanskrit language *su* means "well," while *asti* is the verb "to be.")

Ouch! A **religious symbol** is a powerful tool . . . and the figure of Gaṇeśa bringing good fortune is no exception. To see an elephant-faced deity greeting you at the start of this textbook might feel peculiar, and the *svastika* beneath Gaṇeśa might call up sad feelings. But Gaṇeśa is sacred to Hindus, and the svastika is intended as a symbol of good fortune on the statue of the Hindu deity. Gaṇeśa is invoked at the start of new ventures to clear away obstacles with his trunk and bestow well-being. The image of a deity with a trunk for a nose may stir up uncomfortable thoughts of idolatry for people who refrain from depicting the divine. And because Nazis used the svastika, the ancient Indian symbol took on the unfortunate associations of fascism and genocide in twentieth-century Western culture. From Gaṇeśa's example it becomes clear that religious symbols are powerful communicators – and can stir up a wide range of reactions in people. It also becomes clear that a religious symbol must be considered in its own cultural context.

THE INSIDER–OUTSIDER CHALLENGE

All of us in one way or another grapple with the insider–outsider problem. With the fabulous cross-cultural contact provided by travel and the Internet we are challenged both to empathize with others from an insider's perspective and to see ourselves from an outsider's perspective. Scholars in many fields of study argue about the extent to which one can: (1) *know the experience of another person*, and (2) *view objectively the acts of another person.* In the end it appears that no one can *totally* do either due to cultural conditioning and personal bias. Yet historians of religions, anthropologists, sociologists and other people continue to welcome the **insider–outsider challenge** in spite of recognized human limitations.

Studying religions is a "challenge" because it is not easy to leave one's own inside position – even considering that empathizing with others does not mean personally adopting their points of view. For the sake of understanding, historians of religions bracket (leave aside) their personal views as much as possible and aim to: (1) appreciate the **existential value** of other people's religious experience, and (2) critically analyze (without hostility or favoritism) acts done in the name of religions. The difficulty of taking an inside position is especially clear with respect to people who have in one way or another become our "enemies." But generating empathy from an inside position for another person (especially an enemy) is not the only difficulty presented by an insider–outsider challenge. Taking an outside position to evaluate – as fairly as possible – the positive and negative impacts of religious acts also can be emotionally or intellectually demanding. It is not always easy to give credit where credit is due, and to impartially evaluate things one would rather ignore. Nevertheless, intellectual honesty demands that students of world religions be what Russell T. McCutcheon calls culture critics who are "not in the business of nurturing, enhancing, or . . . criticizing the communities" they study. And while culture critics do not discount the viewpoints of believers, they are not caretakers of religions. That is, they "do not see the participant as setting the ground rules for how his or her behavior ought to be studied by scholars" (McCutcheon 2001: 239, x–xi).

Students of world religions are challenged to move back and forth between inside and outside positions more intensively than people who practice religion in a narrow cultural setting. Pious people who stay within the worldview of their own religion tend to be thoroughly identified with one particular inside position. But once a second religion is encountered they automatically become students of world religions – by even slightly seeing their own religion from the outside in comparison to the other. Scholars of religion are basically divided into two camps according to which position they emphasize in research. **Religionists** see the inside position as indispensable, and tend to focus on it. **Reductionists** contend that the real meaning of religion can only be understood by examining the subject from an outside position. Both contribute valuable insights on religion. Religionists are expert in the nature of religion, while reductionists must be credited with exposing the way religion functions, particularly in the socio-political aspects of human life.

TWO APPROACHES TO THE STUDY OF RELIGIONS

Religion interpenetrates many dimensions of our lives including social institutions, law, and the art world. In light of the fact that religious ideas and practices seem to show up just about everywhere, scholars have wondered whether or not there is actually something *in itself* that should be called "religion." They ask: *Can "religion" be understood purely as a social phenomenon without reference to any form of deity or transcendent principle?* Scholars who answer *Yes* to this question are called reductionists because they view religion as a thoroughly human creation. Reductionists analyze religion in terms of its social, biological, political, economic, or historical components. They say that nothing is inherently religious, and thus "religion" can be *reduced* to component parts within studies of human beings in society. On the other hand, scholars who claim that religion is something unique are called religionists. Religionists say that religion is ***sui generis*** – in a class by itself. They contend that *experience of the sacred* makes religion unique, and argue that it cannot be studied *only* in terms of social structures, political movements, historical trends, and so forth. They say that religion should be studied as *religion.*

The "truth" question in the study of religions

The study of religions revolves around four basic topics: origin, function, meaning, and truth. Scholars have asked: (1) What is the starting point of religion? (2) How does religion work? (3) What does religion mean to those who practice it? and (4) Are the claims of religion true? Both reductionists and religionists feel free to address the issues of function and meaning because their research pertains to the *academic study of religions.* And though they typically respond quite differently to the second and third questions, they agree *on principle* not to make a judgment on the truth-value of religion. Since the question of truth is closely tied to the question of the *ultimate* origin of religions, they often leave that question aside as well.

Thinkers who deal with the *question of truth* and *ultimate origins* fall into a separate class. All people who study religions can have their own personal beliefs. But scholars who engage in the academic study of religions make a distinction between research and *praxis* (practice, action). They attempt to minimize the *distortion* that undisclosed personal beliefs have on research. As scholars in the academic study of religions they make an effort to disclose their assumptions, and become as explicit as possible about how personal beliefs guide their research. (It is generally agreed that no scholar can dispense totally with personal bias. Yet responsible scholars strive to remain alert to the impact of personal biases on their research.) By contrast, thinkers who take up the truth question tend to engage in *praxis* and involve personal beliefs in their life work. For this reason, such practical thinkers may be called *believers*, regardless of whether they think religious claims are true or false.

Practical thinkers (who are "believers") fall into two camps that reflect the basic views of reductionist and religionist academic scholars. Some contend that religion is a purely human creation, and others contend that the origins of religion are connected to a deity or transcendent principle. Marxists (communists) are a prime example of reductionist-type believers who judge the truth-value of religion, and act according to their views. On the other hand, theologians are a prime example of religionist-type believers who take up the issue of truth. Typically, Marxists do not believe in a transcendent principle, and judge religious claims about God to be ultimately false. Typically, theologians do believe in God. They generally identify with one particular religious tradition, and thus labor to clarify the truth of their particular religion. Thus Marxists and theologians tend to argue about the falsity or truth of religion according to their personal convictions. By contrast, scholars engaged in the academic study of religions do not build their theories on the basis of the truth question. They bracket personal beliefs and study religions based on the data they collect – though their choice of data may reflect personal beliefs.

Some (not all) reductionist scholars engaged in the academic study of religions are in fact Marxists. Their atheism may guide the kinds of questions they ask about religion; but they do not build theories based on the hypothesis that God does not exist. Likewise, some (not all) religionist scholars believe in God. Their monotheism may guide the kinds of questions they ask about religion; but they do not build theories based on the hypothesis that God exists. Religionist and reductionist scholars engaged in the academic study of religions are called historians of religions. This has become a problematic term for reductionists because they do not believe that "religion" is *sui generis*. But because their interest is in religious aspects of culture (i.e., aspects of culture that make key references to God or other ultimate principles) many reductionists still affiliate with the discipline called history of religions or comparative religions.

The orientation of this book

This survey of world religions falls within the framework of the academic study of religions. It does not take up the truth question. It discusses neither the *ultimate* origin nor the *ultimate* truth of religions. Deciding on the ultimate origin or ultimate truth of any given religion would involve statements about whether or not God, angels, ancestors, and other spiritual forces actually exist. Such judgments are not relevant to the discussions in this book; they are left entirely up to readers in their own personal explorations of religions. Yet this book does *speak seriously* about angels, God, ancestors, and spiritual forces "as if they exist" when the inside position of a religion presents them as real. This book *leans* toward the religionist approach to accommodate an insider's perspective. (Religionists tend to speak a lot about what is held sacred in a tradition.) It attempts to present each religion in large measure as the religion presents itself. This is because it is important for readers of an "introduction" to world religions to learn what members of each religion take seriously. However, in this book the outsider's perspective is not ignored. Questions and categories developed by reductionist scholars *deepen* a reader's understanding of a religion by focusing attention beyond the "what" to the "how." Accordingly, this discussion goes beyond "what" each religion teaches, and attempts to provoke thought about "how" each religion developed historically and functioned as a social force. It also attempts to provoke thought about the "so what" (i.e., the meaning) of religious beliefs and practices.

This book primarily takes up questions (2) and (3) among the four questions (on origin, function, meaning, and truth) asked by people who study religions.

Beyond presenting some content of each religion it considers: How does religion work? What does religion mean to those who practice it? To prepare the ground for a fruitful reading of the "what," "how," and "so what" of the world religions it is useful to become familiar with some key concepts developed by both reductionists and religionists. Here a "religionist primer" comes first. This is because many reductionist arguments developed in response to perceived shortcomings of religionist methods. Whether or not a reader subscribes to the *sui generis* view of religion, she or he can benefit from key concepts developed by religionists. Their work is useful for exploring the existential value of religious symbols, myths, and rituals. Subsequently, the section on "reductionist warnings" provides tools for gaining an outside perspective – along with a healthy dose of skepticism. The strength of reductionist research is in its insistence that there is more to religion than meets the eye. . . . And to find that "more" one must look to the fruits of human ambition rather than through a looking glass in search of the supernatural.

A RELIGIONIST PRIMER

Rudolph Otto (1869–1937), Gerardus van der Leeuw (1890–1950), and Mircea Eliade (1907–1986) were three thinkers who regarded religion as *sui generis.* By the force of this bias they helped to establish religion as a distinct field of study. Their research was heavily influenced by **phenomenology** as they tried to understand the existential meaning religious experiences had for believers. Eliade in particular worked to distinguish the field of history of religions from theology, psychology, and other academic disciplines.

Creating religious symbols

Eliade used the term *homo religiosus* (the religious human) to indicate the fundamentally religious nature of human beings. He also recognized that meaning for *homo religiosus* is generated through religious symbols. Thus Eliade further designated the human being as a *homo symbolicus* (the human symbol maker). The symbol-making instinct of *homo symbolicus* is so profound that Eliade basically equated the study of religions with the study of religious symbols. He noted that there is hardly anything that has not at some point in history been regarded as sacred. Anything from an ant, a tree, a rock, an eye, the moon, and the universe itself may be regarded as a sacred object – depending upon cultural context. And such sacred objects help define sacred spaces, which range from the simple cordoning off of a rock with a rope in the creation of a Shintō shrine, to the labor-intensive and economically taxing construction of Chartres cathedral. Sacred time can involve something as quick as the mind can act, conceived in Indian meditation as the *kṣana,* which lasts an instantaneous 1/84th of a second, or in terms of cycles of cosmic creation and destruction. Sacred time can also be measured in terms of religious actions that mark out a daily, yearly, or jubilee cycle.

The power of Religious Impressions

Human beings create religious symbols in response to perceiving something highly unusual and extraordinarily powerful. The phenomenological research done by Gerardus van der Leeuw provides a framework for understanding how *homo symbolicus* creates symbols. He analyzed the content of religious experience in terms of four components: Religious Subject, Religious Object, Religious Impression, and Religious Expression. A **Religious Subject** is a person (the subject) who attains religious faith or understanding through an encounter with something that is experienced as sacred. An object becomes a Religious Object to a person when it manifests divine Power. It makes a **Religious Impression**. After being struck with a Religious Impression, the person is then impelled to act in a creative manner to express the content of his or her experience. A Religious Expression is that creative act. Religious Expressions include creations of sacred objects, actions, spaces, and times that can be simple or complex.

Not every object becomes a Religious Object. That is to say, not every encounter or event creates a Religious Impression. Only the deepest – and often the most sudden, dangerous, and frightful – experiences make Religious Impressions on people. Rudolph Otto identified two emotions stirred up by encounters with what he called the Holy (a concept akin to van der Leeuw's Power). Otto said that experience of the Holy is so radical or Wholly Other that people are smitten with the dual impulse both to run away from it, and run to it – to escape it, and embrace it. Otto used two Latin tropes to describe the ambiguous way that the Holy manifests: ***mysterium tremendum*** and ***mysterium fascinans.*** Feeling the *mysterium tremendum* a person experiences the deep emotion of terror or trepidation. Otto noted that Jesus Christ experienced this *mysterium tremendum* during his Night of Agony in the Garden at Gethsemane. When he realized he would soon die a violent death, Jesus sweated blood. Empathizing with this awesome event, Otto wondered about the biblical passage that told the story.

> What is the cause of this "sore amazement" and "heaviness", this soul shaken to its depths, "exceeding sorrowful even unto death", and this sweat that falls to the ground like great drops of blood? Can it be ordinary fear of death in the case of one who had had death before his eyes for weeks past and who had just celebrated with clear intent his death-feast with his disciples? No, there is more here than the fear of death; there is the awe of the creature before the *mysterium tremendum*, before the shuddering secret of the numen.
>
> (Otto [1923] 1970: 84–85)

Experience of the Wholly Other generates not only terror, but also fascination. In facing the Holy, people experience the *mysterium fascinans.* They feel themselves in the presence of a mystery so fascinating that they are pulled toward it, as if to take it in, embrace it, or become absorbed into it. The Wholly Other appears as tantalizing and irresistible. Religious Subjects who become immersed in the *mysterium fascinans* are overwhelmed by the expansive emotion of astonishment, amazement, and seizure. They find the Holy to be wondrous and beauteous. Sometimes a religious experience seems to be characterized more heavily by one or another of the two emotions of terror and fascination. At other times their paradoxical mixture is felt in an emotional confusion.

Hierophany and kratophany

Eliade developed two new terms to designate the bursting forth of foreign energy into the profane world: **hierophany** and **kratophany.** A hierophany is a manifestation of the sacred into the profane world of history. A kratophany is like a hierophany, except that its sacredness has yet to be established, because it shows itself as something "monstrous" or "foreign," such as the "roar of a waterfall [that] is louder than usual," an "earthquake," "the body of a lion or snake," and so on (Eliade [1958] 1996: 27). Hierophanies and kratophanies have impelled human beings to develop a great variety of spiritual traditions. Smitten by powerful eruptions of sacred energy into the profane world, people were inspired to create symbolic rituals to reconnect with sacred forces, stories to describe sacred events, treatises to render their meaning into words, objects of art to imitate or embody the divine, and architectural structures to house it. Prophets, shamans, artisans, poets, musicians, and philosophers have contributed to the cultural history of humankind in response to experiences of the Religious Object.

Religious symbols stand in for hierophanies and kratophanies. They are Religious Expressions that follow on from Religious Impressions. Symbols are the key to understanding the existential value that religion has for people because they preserve what human beings feel has been a profound encounter with the sacred dimension of existence. According to Eliade, an actual hierophany is the ultimate expression of a religious symbol. As autonomous forms of revelation, religious symbols serve to restore or recapitulate the original hierophany for which they stand in. As extensions of hierophanies, religious symbols are put in place by *homo symbolicus* to prolong the sacred manifestations.

The *sui generis* nature of religion

Rudolph Otto affirmed the *sui generis* nature of religion. To illustrate what he thought was a distinctly religious perspective on life, he imagined three people going to a cathedral, each with a different relationship to the building. One person approached the structure with a "theoretic relationship," and tried to calculate its dimensions. A second person had a "practical relationship" to the building, and considered how it should be changed for particular purposes. A third person had a "religious relationship" with the cathedral. Such a person might sit in the cathedral without any theoretical or practical considerations, but gain a profound experience of its space as sacred. Otto illustrated the person's particularly *religious* mindset this way:

> [S]itting quietly in a corner, [a person with a religious relationship will] "experience" the cathedral in receptive contemplation. It may be half ruin, or it may be an unfinished building, but he will be seized of its essential idea, which in the execution may even be concealed rather than expressed; to this spirit [i.e., the religious person] it will be revealed in its entirety and unity, in its mystery and sublimity, in its profound symbolism – all those unspeakable impressions which escape the man of pure theory and practice, and in which alone the real inner meaning and nature of the building is manifest.
>
> (Otto 1931: 75–76)

Otto's example of someone sitting quietly in the corner of a cathedral illustrates the religious person's relationship to life, in which a person grasps the "underlying ideal essence" of the universe, transcending analysis of the parts. When this essence makes itself felt, it gives "unspeakable impressions" that involve the *mysterium tremendum* and *mysterium fascinans*. In Otto's view this essence that gave rise to such impressions is what made religion special. In defining the Holy, Otto coined the term *numen* (from Latin) to stand for "this 'extra' in the meaning of 'holy' above and beyond the meaning of goodness" (Otto [1923] 1970: 6). He then argued that religious experience was based on numinous encounters:

> I shall speak, then, of a unique "numinous" category of value and of a definitely "numinous" state of mind, which is always found wherever the category is applied. This mental state is perfectly *sui generis* and irreducible to any other; and therefore, like every absolutely primary and elementary datum, while it admits of being discussed, it cannot be strictly defined.
>
> (Otto [1923] 1970: 7)

REDUCTIONIST WARNINGS

Reductionists reject the religionist claim that religion is *sui generis*. They are wary of the religionists' tendency to frame the study of religious symbols around the human relationship with some undefined and unproved sacred power. Reductionists tend to view symbols, myths, and rituals as socio-rhetorical tools (tools for social communication or manipulation) originating from human need. They do not mind "reducing" the religious data of symbols, myths, and rituals to their social components because they recognize that people have been subject to social manipulation based on their beliefs in the efficacy of the so-called numinous powers. Reductionists are culture critics who contribute to the health of a society by exposing abuses to which people have been subject in the name of religion. Reductionist research delves into the social sciences, and warns us that religious data should not be automatically taken at face value. They seek to expose the latent (hidden, source) content or motive that lies beneath the manifest (obvious, declared) content. An example of manifest content might be a religious teaching that suggests women are less pure than men. The latent motive of that teaching might be that men seek to control women. Reductionists reject all presumptions about the reality of the sacred. They often look for the function and meaning of religion in the political domain where values are shaped according to the views of prevailing authorities.

The kind of phenomenological analysis undertaken by Rudolph Otto in the 1920s came under critical attack by reductionist historians of religions after the field had more than half a century to mature. Notions such as "underlying ideal essence" and "unspeakable impressions" seemed fuzzy, and did not sit well with scholars who wanted to bring unquestioned assumptions into the light of day. For reductionists there is no place in the history of religions for a category of the *numinous* because it was presumed, but neither proved nor defined. While Otto defined the Holy as a "category of interpretation and valuation peculiar to the sphere of religion" (Otto 1970 (1923): 5) the reductionists consider nothing peculiar to the sphere of religion. They aim to study religion as a "purely human activity with no metaphysical distillate left over"

(McCutcheon 2001: xi). Their research on religion is informed by the methods of various academic disciplines, including psychology, sociology, economics, anthropology, political science, and more.

THREE FUNCTIONS OF RELIGION IN SOCIETY

Reductionist writings on religion range widely through the social sciences. From a reductionist perspective, Bruce Lincoln, a contemporary American historian of religions, took an interest in the way religions serve to maintain, challenge, or overturn cultural values. Based on these functions, he classified religion into three types: (1) religions of the status quo, (2) religions of resistance, and (3) religions of revolution (Lincoln 1985: 268–281). These three categories of religion help clarify the relationship between religion and political power. From Lincoln's discussion a student of religions can better understand the dynamics of how various world religions exist in relation to each other today.

Religions of the status quo

Religion is a cultural force that can stabilize society, and exert a powerful effect on people over many generations. Religions of the status quo perpetrate a way of life that can be experienced as positive by some and negative by others. A religious institution is fairly successful at preserving itself when it gives people a sense of identity and hope in the midst of suffering, prepares them for critical life cycle events such as death, provides ethical guidelines, and so forth. Often religious institutions manage to inculcate a religious worldview through the force of authority that comes from political power, wealth, and psychological manipulation. In this case, those who lack power may become dissatisfied with the religion of the status quo if they feel their needs are not being met, or their worldview conflicts with prevailing ideologies.

Religions of resistance

Religions of resistance are considered as "heterodox" in relation to religions of the status quo. They resist the religions of the status quo due to values, beliefs, and practices that are at odds with those prevailing in society. Leaders of religions of resistance may encourage fanatical or socially deviant behavior among followers to set them apart from adherents to the religion of the status quo. Religions of resistance may be catalyzed into religions of revolution if members are subject to unjust treatment, economic depression, or other oppressive conditions – and find sufficient motivation, numbers, resources, and leadership to set up an organized campaign. Until then, even the daily acts done by members of a religion that lacks power can be interpreted as resistance to the status quo.

Religions of revolution

Religions of revolution actively challenge religions of the status quo through some form of militant or rebellious action. Leaders of religions of revolution seek to wrest control of current political structures, and install their own worldview to replace that of the religion of the status quo. In other words, members of religions of revolution seek proactively and forcefully to become religions of the status quo. Religions of resistance turn into religions of revolution when their members become intensely motivated by coherent convictions, and gain sufficient resources to exert their collective will.

Keeping in mind the three categories of religion in society will help us to understand the dynamics of religions within single societies. In reading about the historical development of various world religions, it is possible to see how traditions split, grow, and sustain themselves.

ROOTS OF THE MODERN STUDY OF RELIGIONS

The modern study of world religions has three roots: (1) the academic discipline of Christian theology, (2) the **European Enlightenment**, and (3) **European colonialism**. These formed the prevailing concept of "world religions," and the very enterprise of *studying world religions*.

- ***Christian theology.*** Christian theology was the central discipline of the early European universities:

Plate 1.2 "Shoes." These shoes represent the historically obscure, pious individuals who constitute the bulk of religious heritage. Their stories remain largely untold. What meaning do you find in this photographic image taken on the pavement in front of a small outdoor market in India? Adopt both inside and outside positions as you talk about these shoes.

University of Bologna in Italy, Paris University in France, and Oxford University in England. During the High Middle Ages (1000–1300) it was regarded as "Queen of the Sciences." The scholastic theologians asked questions about the nature of the divine, and the relationship between revelation and reason.

- ***The European Enlightenment.*** Thinkers of the European Enlightenment in the late 1700s began to separate out reason from faith in their approach to religion. Reason as the key value of Enlightenment thinkers produced individualism and empiricism. The value of the individual was upheld, because people were considered able to reason on their own without dependence on religious authorities. And empirical evidence based on what could be perceived by the senses was valued over metaphysical religious speculation that produced no scientific proof.
- ***European colonialism.*** The development of science not only gave birth to rational attitudes toward religion for those who were philosophically inclined. It also gave birth to European colonialism, which involved the large-scale exploitation and domination of human beings for those who were ambitious. As science progressed, new opportunities for travel arose with the knowledge of how to calculate longitude, and to build seafaring vessels suitable for lengthy journeys. Thus as Enlightenment thinkers were one by one expanding their mental horizons, seafaring businessmen with deep Christian convictions were moving people and goods across oceans, and colonizing ever new territories.

These days reductionists are very critical of the impact of European colonialists on religious culture. They speak of "invisibility" of peoples whose cultures were "erased" under the force of **cultural imperialism.**

CULTURAL IMPERIALISM AND "WORLD RELIGIONS"

Early lists of world religions mentioned only religions of the status quo. Only politically powerful traditions with world missions were thought to qualify. Jonathan Z. Smith, a contemporary historian of religions, observed:

> "Religion" is not a native category. It is not a first-person term of self-characterization. It is a category imposed from the outside on some aspect of native culture. It is the other, in these instances colonialists, who are solely responsible for the content of the term.
>
> (Smith 2004: 179)

Russell T. McCutcheon, a contemporary theorist, noted further:

BOX 1.1 CULTURE CONTRAST: A DEBT TO THE EUROPEAN ENLIGHTENMENT

European Enlightenment thinkers of the 1700s and 1800s developed an outsider perspective on religions. They emphasized intellectual freedom, and sought to bring into open discussion their culture's assumptions about the nature of things – God included. They extolled the power of human rationality, and used philosophy (broadly conceived) to analyze matters that later formed the disciplines of natural sciences, humanities, and social sciences.

Baruch Spinoza. Spinoza (1632–1677) set the agenda for modern biblical criticism by insisting that religious scriptures should be studied in their historical context – including consideration of who wrote, when they wrote, why they wrote, and for whom they wrote. Spinoza was ostracized from his Jewish community in Amsterdam for expressing such radical ideas. His unconditional excommunication at the age of 23 meant that Spinoza could not attend synagogue services, or socialize with other Jews – including members of his own family. Spinoza's writings were banned in his community.

François-Marie Arouet de Voltaire. Voltaire (1694–1778) visited England from his native France and was impressed by the diversity of religions. He became dedicated to religious toleration – defending victims of fanatical intolerance both in his novels and in real life. Voltaire felt that religion was a strictly personal affair that called for no social rituals. He was critical of Roman Catholicism, and considered the call to uncritical faith as a tool of priests and the religious establishment. He spoke of the Supreme Being as a universal intelligence, and thought that human reason could lead a person to the worship of God as the cause of all that occurs.

David Hume. Hume (1711–1776) was a Scotsman who thought that religions were mired in superstition. As a religious skeptic he applied human reason to the subject of morals. Hume argued that moral standards arise from natural human sentiments, and need not be grounded in religious revelation. He claimed that revealed religion could not be justified on rational grounds, because revelations cannot be clarified in relation to experience. Yet, Hume suggested that religion could be useful if it shed matters that exceeded the bounds of reason, namely prophetic, and other miraculous claims.

Moses Mendelssohn. Mendelssohn (1729–1786) was a German-born Jewish philosopher who refined the classical philosophical proofs for God's existence. He regarded the Judaic traditions as a body of revealed legislation whose practice led people to realize universal truths. Mendelssohn argued that adherence to the law of Moses does not require blind acceptance of dogma, and emphasized the role of reason in applying Jewish law to historically changing circumstances. He advocated the separation of church and state, and called for religious toleration in both spheres – including equal civil rights for Jews.

Immanuel Kant. Kant (1724–1804) was born in East Prussia of Scottish ancestors. He disclosed logical failures of the classical philosophical proofs for the existence of God – without becoming an atheist. Kant advanced a moral proof for God's existence. He demonstrated that ethical categories function within the structure of human thought. In effect, this autonomy grounded the proof of God's existence in the experience of personal moral conviction. Kant had a deep appreciation of the scientific advances of Isaac Newton – and also realized that ethical challenges were posed by such triumphs of human reason.

Historians of religions in our own day resemble the European Enlightenment thinkers because they attempt to: (1) view religion with a scientific mindset as one among many cultural phenomena, (2) use human reason to assess the content of religious teachings, and (3) promote tolerance of differing views.

> *[M]any of the peoples that we study by means of this category [religion] have no equivalent term or concept whatsoever.* . . . So, right off the bat, we must recognize that, in using this Latin-derived term [religion] as a technical, comparative category, even the most ardently sympathetic religious pluralist is, from the outset, deeply embedded in the act of intellectual, if not cultural imperialism or theoretical reduction.
>
> (McCutcheon 2001: 10)

European colonialists considered a world religion as one that "centered around notions of salvation . . . in opposition to national or ethnic religions" (Smith 1995: 1140). Thus in the nineteenth century only three traditions qualified as world religions: Christianity, Islam, and Buddhism. And from a European colonialist perspective, Christianity was the superior tradition. Gradually Judaism, Hinduism, Confucianism/Daoism, and Shintō were added. It seemed absurd to omit Judaism in spite of its relatively few adherents, because the tradition had spread widely, and provided the Christians with their Old Testament. And, with the British colonization of India, it was convenient to lump together several religious perspectives under the heading of "Hinduism," and so create a religion that could be both conceived and managed (King 1999: 100). It then made sense to include that monolithic Indian tradition on the list of world religions.

Colonization is the process of one political entity taking political and economic control of a foreign territory. Motives for colonization include the desire for: (1) *resources* such as land and wealth, (2) *freedom* of religious or cultural expression, (3) *economic opportunity* such as gaining trading partners, and (4) *spreading culture*, for example, religious or political ideology. In modern times European colonialism began with the efforts of Portugual and Spain to gain control of maritime trade starting in the sixteenth century. They were soon rivaled by the Dutch, British, and French. After 1870 other countries (Russia, Japan) also acquired colonial possessions. European colonialism was tied in with a Christian religious mission. Both Roman Catholic and Protestant forms of Christianity spread widely under the impact of European colonial rule in the Americas, Africa, the Middle East, South Asia, and the Far East. European colonialists (as all colonialists) tended to erase the religions of colonized peoples. Jonathan Z. Smith remarked facetiously on the culture-bound nature of the "dubious category of 'World Religions'" that attends a colonialist mentality:

> A World Religion is a religion like ours; but it is, above all, a tradition which has achieved sufficient power and numbers to enter our history, either to form it, interact with it, or to thwart it. All other religions are invisible. . . . All "primitives" . . . may be simply lumped together as may so-called "minor religions" because they do not confront our history in any direct fashion. They are invisible.
>
> (Smith 1978: 295)

In taking the **postcolonial turn** it remains important to note how research, regardless of the motive, may also have a positive impact on visibility of non-dominant religions. For example, a handful of European colonialist missionaries created detailed accounts of the culture and language of native peoples in the Americas, and, though some of their accounts were purposely destroyed once the missionary effort was complete, other accounts and linguistic works have survived. Nowadays tremendous research is being done on peoples of Africa and the Americas who were subjects of European colonialism. Colonialist writings on these indigenous peoples are highly valued today by scholars of religions, along with other data including transatlantic shipping records and material recovered from archeological digs. Yet the legacy of European colonialism remains.

THE FALLOUT FROM COLONIALISM

Communism emerged as fallout from the Industrial Revolution, which was sustained by economic exploitation of native peoples by European colonialists. This was a new form of secular authoritarian rule – with fascism as its alternative. In the modern world, communist, fascist, as well as colonialist and theocratic rule all work in the context of the nation-state. The design of nation-states tends to make religions as well as ethnic groups seem monolithic – as though peoples and their traditions were static, homogeneous entities. This way of lumping people together and labeling them helps governments to identify specific groups and target them for various ends. While European colonialists aimed to convert colonized people to the Christian religion, communist leaders in the Soviet Union and China basically forbade the practice of religion, while fascist leaders sought ethnic cleansing that was closely tied in with religious prejudice.

Today what is called Islamic fundamentalism (Islamism) may be viewed – in part – as a response to European colonialism. Following the distintegration of the Ottoman Empire, Muslims sought to establish a religious identity that stood in contradistinction to the West.

> The Muslim response to the European [colonial] assault on the Dar al-Islam, as well as to centuries of deprivation, took a number of forms. During the nineteenth century, these were largely limited to reformism. . . . Of course, there were also outbreaks of fundamentalist revolt as well. . . .
>
> In the twentieth century, as the depth and intention of the Great Power assault on Islam became more evident, Muslims responded with an even wider range of alternatives.
>
> (Lundin and Lundin 1996: 159)

The role of religion in the modern world is complicated by the fact that the impulse toward colonization shows itself in the twenty-first century as several world powers vie with each other to control peoples and territories. When religions of resistance that oppose powers of oppression gain sufficient strength they often aim to themselves become religions of the status quo.

SUBTLE ERASURES

Religious traditions can be erased by persecution, debasement, and forced conversion. They can also be ignored due to cultural imperialism. Beyond that, more "subtle" erasures occur based on the very *choice of data* used by scholars in their research. Unwittingly (or with the best of intentions) scholars can reinforce elitism, sexism, and racism in cultures that are foreign to them, making marginalized people of that religious culture even less visible. Here are three observations on how subtle erasures can occur based on choice of research data:

1. Scholars who bring a "literary bias" to their research pay more attention to religions with well-developed bodies of written literature than to expressive traditions based in oral culture. In doing so, they may seriously underestimate the value of non-literary cultural contributions.
2. Even within highly literary cultures, the voices of people with little access to education and power are difficult to hear. For example, in their research on Tibetan women, Janet Gyatso and Hanna Havnevik recognize the problem of "finding 'genuine' women's voices, or female perspectives, in the accounts of women's lives" since "[v]irtually all the information we have from traditional textual sources about Tibetan women is written by men, operating in the ambit of andocentric institutions and textual traditions" (Gyatso and Havnevik 2005: 6).
3. Scholarly attention given to specific texts tends to reinforce the cultural values of those texts. Leila Ahmed, an Egyptian Muslim scholar, noted the power of Western scholarship to shape Muslim women's views of themselves:

> Ironically, therefore, literacy has played a baneful part both in spreading a particular form of Islam and in working to erase oral and living forms of the religion. For one thing, we all automatically assume that those who write and who put their knowledge down in texts have something more valuable to offer than those who simply live their knowledge and use it to inform their lives. . . . Even the Western academic world is contributing to the greater visibility and legitimacy of textual Islam and to the gradual silencing and erasure of alternative oral forms of lived Islam.
>
> (Ahmed 1999: 128–129)

A more representative view of players in the drama of world religions will emerge through the efforts of diligent scholars and wise readers who keep in mind that bias operates not only within data, but also in choice of data.

THE EAST–WEST DIPTYCH

Some contemporary scholars of religions are fighting deep-held prejudices that pit the West against the rest of the world. According to a simplistic view, the world resembles an **East–West diptych**, where the geographic regions flatly oppose each other as two monolithic cultural plates. The literary theorist and founder of postcolonial theory Edward W. Said (1935–2003) remarked on the intellectual harm caused by such flat and over-generalized divisions between peoples.

> When one uses categories like Oriental and Western as both the starting and the end points of analysis, research, public policy . . . the result is usually to polarize the distinction – the Oriental becomes more Oriental, the Westerner more Western – and limit the human encounter between different cultures, traditions, and societies.
>
> (Said 1978: 45–46)

Edward Said used the term **orientalism** to characterize a racist attitude harbored by scholars and politicians of the "Occident" (West) with reference to people of the "Orient" (East). The orientalist sense of superiority was associated with the greater economic well-being, and industrialization of Western nations that were built up through European colonial exploitation. The term "orientalism" also connoted a Western superiority complex in the intellectual sphere, based on the European Enlightenment and the Newtonian revolution. (The cultural association of these movements exclusively with the West tends to ignore the role played by Islamic philosophers in preserving classical Greek thought before the rise of European universities, and the African presence in early Greek thought.) Orientalism was linked to cultural imperialism, and the pride of bringing Western civilization into non-Western territories. It also undergirded (and still does) justifications for political conquest.

DEFINING RELIGION

By now it should be obvious that the word "religion" is difficult to define – as are all generic terms that attempt to classify aspects of human culture. Yet if we are to use the word it should have at least a provisional definition. Thus a concise **definition of religion** to consider is the following:

> A religion is a dynamic cultural complex with positive or negative impact that stakes a claim to legitimacy based on a foundational connection to reports of hierophany.

The definition takes into account both religionist and reductionist perspectives. It can be unpacked in this way: (1) *Religion is a dynamic cultural complex with positive or negative impact.* This is to say: Religion interfaces with many aspects of culture including social institutions, the arts, and so forth. In the context of cultural interaction, religion can have a constructive or deleterious effect on people. (2) *Religion stakes a claim to legitimacy based on a foundational connection to reports of hierophany.* This is to say: Religions are closely tied to political authority, and take advantage of their grounding in a superior authority derived from connections to hierophanies. Reports of hierophany thus become the religious cornerstones of culture.

DRAMA: A ROOT METAPHOR FOR WORLD RELIGIONS

The Greek-speaking crowd of Athenians in the fifth century BCE saw the same old myths presented in the amphitheater year after year. Yet they awaited the new twists and turns given to the material by Sophocles, Euripides, and others to gain insights into human nature, history, and current politics. Dramatists portray players along with their words and actions to provoke new insights and, though this work is not written as a play, the root metaphor of a *drama* guides the arrangement of its material. Here a spotlight illuminates a host of religious players, their thoughts, and their activities to show how religion is filled with personal and cultural meaning in the theater of world religions. In this book each chapter is divided into three parts organized in terms of: (1) A slate of players, (2) Religious texture, and (3) Meaningful performance.

1 *A slate of players* treats both non-human and human figures on the world stage, including the **ultimate principle** that governs the universe, subtle beings, founders, and key historical people. Discussions target players in religiously transformative personal and cultural moments so that the history of each religion may be told.
2 *Religious texture* covers foundational works, commentarial texts that validate the foundational works, and material that in some way reaches out beyond the core. These can be innovative (sometimes controversial) works that challenge the core texts, or commentaries that bridge the tradition to the outside.
3 *Meaningful performance* examines in detail a custom, ritual, or artistic form that shaped the non-verbal backdrop of the tradition. The various "performances" are not necessarily the most widespread or popular activities found in the religious traditions. Rather they were selected to stimulate an appreciation of the *power of religion to create culture.*

This three-part dramatic organization allows for a **thick description** of the material in which both insider and outsider perspectives may be considered: (1) The biographical emphasis on players allows for considerable attention to an insider's perspective that shows how people in the religion understand the characters in their traditional story. (2) Exploration of a religion's texture (key scriptures and other literature) allows for considerable attention to an outsider's perspective that shows how texts shape attitudes and social institutions. (3) Examining the symbolism of key rituals and spiritual disciplines readily exposes both insider and outsider perspectives as religious experience and social impact are considered. A thoughtful reading will allow readers to apply concepts from both religionist and reductionist scholars.

PLAYERS IN THE DRAMA OF WORLD RELIGIONS

"All the world's a stage, and all the men and women merely players," observed William Shakespeare (1564–1616) in *As You Like It* (act 2, scene 7). As the players parade across the world stage of human cultures, we might observe further that some are more colorful than others. Among the most colorful players on the world stage are those enacting the drama of world religions. This is so because the drama includes a wider variety of figures than any other drama of human history. Many of these players are **liminal beings**. They live betwixt-and-between our ordinary world and a subtler world we can call the **imaginal realm**. These are spiritual or mind-based entities of various sorts such as angels (even fallen angels like Satan of the Christian and Islamic traditions), gods, goddesses, demons, and so forth. It seems that all the world religions speak of these kinds of subtle entities – even though some might be disparaged or minimized in their views. Often liminal beings play significant roles in the performance.

Claims about the kinds of beings that populate the universe can stretch far beyond what historians can demonstrate as reliable. But religious communities often form their collective identities around stories that involve extraordinary experiences in relation to such beings – even when historical proof is lacking. For adherents, a *religiously meaningful memory* of the past does not have to bear historical certainty. Biographical accounts of extraordinary events become meaningful through ritual activity that clarifies their "truth." For example, the Christian ritual of communion brings meaning to the event of the last supper that Jesus shared with his disciples. Historical details about the event cannot be known. Yet the *religious value* of the story stands.

Sociologists use the term "actors" to recognize that society comprises human beings who exercise their wills, or are deprived from so doing. The notion of **agency** emphasizes the fact that society is not an abstract, monolithic entity, but is composed of people who make choices, or are prevented from so doing. Thus "actor" is a powerful word to use. But the notion of **play** lends added significance. Anthropologists make reference to *homo ludens* (the human player) to indicate that people are *creatively* involved in their lives. Play is a spontaneous element that brings insight, while interfacing with the willful agency of human life. Thus "player" conveys the double sense that those who participate in the drama of world religions are both social agents and creators of culture. There are four basic types of players involved in religious traditions: (1) the ultimate principle, (2) imaginal players, (3) exceptional players, and (4) historical players.

The ultimate principle

The term "ultimate principle" applies to *that beyond which nothing greater can be conceived* within the tradition. Because they tend to be amorphic (without form), the abstract term "principle" best describes them. Ultimate principles may be transcendent (existing above and beyond the cosmos) or immanent (infused within things that exist in the cosmos). Traditions sometimes define their ultimate principle as an omniscient consciousness, a cosmic creator, or a life force. At other times, names are used to indicate its qualities, such as Compassionate, or Majestic. Examples of ultimate principles in the world religions are: Allāh, Dharma, Sat Nām, YHVH, Wakan-Tanka, and Brahman.

Imaginal players

Imaginal players are normally from an ahistorical realm of "reality." They tend to appear in accounts of **hierophanic history** rather than conventional history. Some people claim to perceive these figures through the **creative imagination** and, though the existence of imaginal players cannot be verified through scientific methods, *they live in the worlds of meaning* of religious people. Imaginal players may be anthropomorphic (with human form), theriomorphic (with animal form), or polymorphic (with multiple forms). For instance: (1) the Hebrew patriarch Jacob wrestled with an angel who looked like a man; (2) a buffalo may appear in the visions of Native Americans performing the Sun Dance; and (3) Hindu Arjuna saw Kṛṣṇa display countless heads and arms in an astounding panoramic vision of "time itself" while in his chariot on the battlefield. Sometimes religious traditions consider beings from the imaginal realm as real, but they refrain from worshipping them. Here are two examples: (1) Asherah, the Canaanite *ba'al*, played a role in the religious life of ancient Israel, but later was rejected from Judaism; (2) Buddhism speaks about godlings as though they exist in the universe, but considers them to be unenlightened.

Exceptional players

Exceptional players participate in both the imaginal and historical realms. They shape religious traditions based on teachings that may include: (1) reports of hierophanic experience (sometimes involving a revealed text); (2) ethical guidelines; and (3) plans for community life. Traditional accounts of exceptional players tend to be filled with extraordinary claims of their experiences in relation to imaginal players or the ultimate principle. Therefore, to understand more fully the contributions of exceptional players, it is helpful to look at their lives from two frames of reference: (1) in accord with the teachings of their traditions, including reports of hierophanic experiences; and (2) in light of historical developments. Many founders of religious traditions are exceptional players – though their religious experiences tend to be quite distinctive. Examples include Prophet Muḥammad, Gautama Buddha, Bahá'u'lláh, and the ten Sikh Gurūs.

Historical players

Historical religious players are human beings who play a critical role in developing religious traditions. Often they do so by articulating ideas, promoting rituals, presenting artworks, or skewing the course of history through conquest. Historical players are cultural contributors such as authors, saints, sages, artists, and rulers. Beyond that, historically obscure pious individuals should be recognized as players in the drama of world religions. Exceptional players could also be considered as historical players in their own right. For example, even without reports of their extraordinary encounters, founders often have shrewd leadership and excellent organizational abilities that change the course of history.

THE RELIGIOUS TEXTURE OF WORLD RELIGIONS

The word "texture" describes the songs, stories, scriptures, commentaries and other words used by players in the drama of world religions. As strands of fabric woven together give cloth its texture, so strands of verbal culture create the texture of a religion. The word "text" comes from the Latin *textus*, meaning literally "that which is woven." A text is a "web" of ideas and expressions that forms the theme or starting point of a discussion. To convey a dynamic sense, the "-ure" suffix denotes an action or process, and its results. For example, a *closure* is something that closes, or allows something to close. *Texture* is something that embodies texts, or webs of meaning. It allows something to be known and discussed. The word *texture* (like the word *legislature*) further has the sense of a collective body. Thus the texture of a religion is the body of its oral and written texts. Elements of material culture are also included as part of the texture of a religious tradition because they are carriers of meaning. For example, food, hair, and costume have all become great significators in the history of religions. Based on how they function, there are three categories of material that make up the texture of a religious tradition: foundational, supportive, and cross-over.

Foundational texture

A tradition's most sacred teachings are generally set apart in a canon that forms its foundation. Once they are selected and vetted the canon typically is closed. These canonized works are frequently considered as revealed by a transcendent being – possibly through the agency of an imaginal player, such as an angel. When the sound vibrations of the words are considered spiritually potent great care is taken to keep them unaltered. Examples of such powerful revealed texts are the Hebrew Torah and the Arabic Qur'ān. Due to their extraordinary status, texts of the sacred canon are normally surrounded by taboos that govern their use. For example, the authority to recite sacred words or touch books that embody them may be restricted to priests, shamans, augurs, or initiates. Foundational texture often forms the oldest layer of text in a tradition – representing the decision to commit strands of oral tradition to writing.

Supportive texture

Once the foundational texture of a religion has been established, a major portion of subsequent work serves to reinforce that foundation. Types of supportive texture include: (1) legal works that codify a body of law or tradition; (2) historical works that record events and shape the selective memory of a people; (3) philosophical or theological commentaries that aim to clarify or enhance the foundational message; and (4) exemplary works such as sermons and biographies that provide models for behavior. In various ways, supportive texture tends to validate the status quo represented by the foundational texture. For example, commentaries that clarify meaning may be used to legitimate the power associated with particular people, social institutions, or territorial entities. This legitimation of power need not be viewed as negative. The very creation of culture depends upon supportive texture.

Cross-over texture

Cross-over texture is work that crosses cultural boundaries, adopts a comparative perspective, orients itself toward alternative philosophies, or in some way extends beyond the mainstream channels of supportive texture. It is often associated with folk wisdom or marginal groups in society (such as the poor or women). Cross-over texture can put a new spin on officially sanctioned religious worldviews. Such innovation can prompt a religion to split by establishing a powerful alternate perspective. Yet cross-over texture need not oppose the status quo. It could help validate the status quo by developing new lines of argument in the face of challenge, or it might simply rethink religious ideas in terms of theory from another context such as science. The broad cross-over category could also include such material as: jokes, recipes, spells, folksongs, and other works that convey religious insights or pertain to simple "everyday" levels of religious practice.

MEANINGFUL PERFORMANCE IN WORLD RELIGIONS

The performative aspects of religious life involve ritual actions of one sort or another, including: sacrifice, healing, rites of passage, dramatic recitations, divination, pilgrimage, gestural arts (e.g., dancing, making music), and so forth. In some religious traditions the performative aspects of religious life predominate. These may be called **expressive traditions** as opposed to literate traditions. People practicing expressive traditions tend to express religious ideas through their bodies rather than through written scriptures. Written scriptures serve as a respository of knowledge and doctrine in literate traditions. Using van der Leeuw's terms, one can say that the religious expressions of literate traditions (e.g., sacrifice, rites of passage) relate back to the written texts for an explanation. In literate traditions written texture also stands as a key factor in the creation of religious impressions (e.g., as when experience is interpreted in terms of doctrine). Written texts allow a body of material to be transported over larger distances and preserve their uniformity across cultures. Thus large-scale religions tend to rely on written scriptures. By contrast, expressive traditions rely on oral delivery of sacred texture. Expressive traditions tend to operate on a small scale where it is feasible to rely on oral transmission of sacred lore to preserve religious ideas. Both literate and expressive traditions make use of meaningful performance. Yet in the absence of written texture, ritual actions tend to dominate the religious culture of small-scale traditions. This very fact (i.e., a preponderance of meaningful performance) is the defining feature of expressive traditions.

Meaningful performance can be understood in terms of: (1) what actions are done and (2) in what context those actions are done. Sacrifice, rites of passage, healing, and so forth are *actions* done in the *context* of a ritual time and ritual place with ritual objects. With this distinction in mind, performance can be classified in terms of seven expressive functions and three expressive aspects. Together these comprise ten elements of performance.

Three expressive aspects

The expressive aspects pertain to the *when*, the *where*, and the *things used* in religious performance. Ritual brings time, place, and things to life. Thus the three expressive aspects are called *lived* time, place, and object. The word "sacred" could apply to many instances of these lived elements. But the designation of sacred time, sacred place (or space), or sacred objects is suited especially to *religionist* interpretations of performance. But the word "sacred" carries too many extraordinary connotations for *reductionists.* Reductionists think of dynamic times, places, and objects that become symbolically meaningful (in politics, society, and so forth) without reference to a divine dimension of existence. Thus reductionist interpretations tend to lay the word "sacred" to rest. Yet reductionists still come upon cultural phenomena that are politically potent (for better or for worse) and charged with symbolic value. An example would be objects whose use is restricted to rulers or elite members of society. People who control their use might call those objects "sacred," while an outside observer could see them as tools of class oppression. Thus, for example, a reductionist might avoid the term "sacred objects" with reference to royal insignia. The term "lived objects" better serves to distinguish royal insignia from ordinary objects. Thus in defining the expressive aspects, the term "lived" is used to designate the specially potent and symbolic character of time, place, and object. Here each element is called "lived" because of its dynamic, powerful, and symbolic character that brings meaning to people in the context of rituals regardless of whether they are focused on a transcendent being or society.

Lived time

Lived time can be created in two basic ways: (1) breaking up an uncharted duration into meaningful units, or (2) making it bend, stretch, shrink, layer, or disappear. In the first instance, lived time can be demarcated in terms of special occasions or cycles that periodically repeat (e.g., by the day, week, month, year, lifespan). These meaningful units can be experienced in the context of rites of passage, agricultural cycles, and so forth. In the second instance, lived time can be manipulated into unusual experiences through altered states of consciousness. Lived time can be marked to commemorate, re-enact or re-create hierophanic events, in which case the events might be called "sacred." Lived time may also be used to manage social order and views of human potential.

Lived place

Lived place can be experienced in two basic ways: (1) as an arena created for particular ritual activities, or (2) as a large living space that defines the borders of the life of a person or community. In the first instance, a lived place might link an area in the physical world with a corresponding imaginal space. Symbolically some form of **axis mundi** would then bridge these levels in a vertical dimension. Permutations of ordinary places can be experienced in a ritual arena, where space is bent, shrunk, layered, or made to disappear. Such extraordinary manifestations of lived place are linked to the performance of meditation, chanting, dancing, pilgrimage, and so forth. These may be called instances of "sacred space." In the second instance, nondescript territory might become a lived place as it is mapped out. Territory becomes religiously meaningful as people experience hierophanies in particular places, give inspired names to things, create ritual spaces, and so forth. For example, paths along which medicinal plants are found, sacred rivers used for purification, boulders that manifest spiritual energy, can all become significant markers that define territorial contours. Of course, lived territory can be robbed of religious meaning – just as rituals and symbols are subject to degeneration. The religious meaning of a lived territory degenerates when materialistic concerns override the existential value of a place. This can happen when: (1) borders are moved to incorporate land for purely economic gain, (2) people are forced into resettlement, or (3) foreign constructions are placed on land that disrupt its sacred ecology. Lived places (like lived times and lived objects) can be defined in order to exert authoritative control over people.

Lived objects

Lived objects play a key role as carriers of symbolic meaning and ritual efficacy in performance. There are three main types: (1) supernatural objects, which are obtained through extraordinary means; (2) natural objects, which are things from the physical world that acquire religious meaning or power; (3) cultural artifacts, which are humanly created objects such as ritual implements, clothing, food, buildings, and so forth that acquire meaning or power. All lived objects may be associated with hierophanic events. In such cases they could be called "sacred."

Seven expressive functions

Lived times, places, and objects provide a context for numerous actions that are performed to create religious meaning. A great number of actions are performed as religious expressions, including sacrifice, healing, and so forth. These many expressive actions can be classified into seven expressive functions that are distinguished according to their function. Performance thus includes donation, restoration, enactment, symbolization, transformation, accession, and transmission. For convenience these may be called the DRESTAT functions. All of these performative activities can be analyzed from both religionist and reductionist perspectives. In other words, they can be viewed as operating in the context of hierophany or kratophany (that is, some extraordiary or supernatural event) or as cultual activities. These seven expressive functions should not be considered to be "airtight" categories. There is overlap between them. In addition, any particular ritual will involve several elements of performance.

- ***Donation.*** Refers to the ritual act of giving. A key form of donation is sacrifice, whereby something of high value is given to achieve a religiously significant goal. Other forms include alms giving, potlach (ceremonial distribution of property among the Native peoples living on the northwest coast of North America), and so forth.
- ***Restoration.*** Refers to the ritual act of re-establishing a former condition that was somehow damaged in the course of non-religious acts, the breaking of taboos, and so on. Healing generally involves acts of restoration whereby what is off balance, incomplete, or somehow disturbed is set right. Other forms include creation of structures that symbolize the cosmos, such as altars, cities, temples.
- ***Enactment.*** Refers to the ritual act of re-creating an event of religious significance (which could

involve hierophanies and kratophanies). Pilgrimage is a key form of enactment, whereby a person lives through a situation of striking importance by sharing lived place, time, and objects of high value. Other forms include rituals of commemoration, and so forth.

- *Symbolization.* Refers to the ritual act of capturing a religiously significant matter (hierophanic event, transcendent energy) in artistic terms. Dance performances stand as a key example of symbolization insofar as they make use of colors, gestures, and narratives that dynamically represent a person, place, or thing that is normally inaccessible to the imagination. Symbolization pervades the arts, rituals, and myths where form is given to something transcendent, abstract, or otherwise difficult to define.
- *Transformation.* Refers to the ritual act of changing something from one condition to another. All rites of passage involve such transformations. For example, puberty rites, marriage rites, and funeral rites all involve a religiously significant change of condition. A **vision quest** stands as another example.
- *Accession.* Refers to the ritual act of gaining access or getting in touch with something ordinarily inaccessible. Prayer is a prime example of accession, whereby a person devises a way to communicate with imaginal beings or gain wisdom. Other forms of accession include divination, shamanic journeys to the other world, acting as a trance medium, and so forth.
- *Transmission.* Refers to the ritual act of passing on a body of knowledge that is religiously or culturally significant. A key means of transmission is the recitation of epic poems, songs, stories, and so forth. Other forms include the transfer of authority through coronation rites, initiation into a lineage, and so forth.

The material chosen to illustrate "meaningful performance" (in all but Chapter 2) was selected for its value in raising issues of cross-cultural relevance. Here are two examples: (1) "Holy death" is explored as a Jain performance. And while relatively few Jains elect to undergo the ritual of *saṃlekhanā*, treatment of this unusual custom may stimulate discussions on cross-cultural ethics. (2) Icon painting is treated as a Christian performance. In the course of Christian history many arguments have been advanced for and against figural representation of sacred beings. Thus the discussion of icons may provoke thought about the function of sacred art and the attitude toward images across cultures. The discussions of "meaningful performance" in Chapters 3 through 13 do not analyze the material explicitly in terms of ten elements of performance. Rather, part 3 of each chapter is subdivided by headings that pertain specifically to the subject matter. By contrast, Chapter 2 is dedicated wholly to expressive traditions and the ten elements of performance are treated one by one through an extended example for each.

KEY POINTS

- Scholars of religions adopt inside and outside positions to find out how people experience their religions, as well as how religions shape societies and alter the course of history. Students of world religions face the challenge of taking both insider and outsider perspectives.
- Historians of religions can be distinguished according to whether they are religionists or reductionists. Religionists argue for the *sui generis* position of religion, while reductionists argue against it.
- Three types of religion in society are: religions of the status quo, religions of resistance, and religions of revolution. Religions may shift categories over time depending upon historical circumstances.
- The roots of the modern study of religions are Christian theology, the European Enlightenment and European colonialism. These forces proved to be both creative and destructive for our understanding of world religions, as certain groups were "erased," while others became highly visible and powerful.
- Religion may be defined *as a dynamic cultural complex that stakes a claim to legitimacy based on a foundational connection to reports of hierophany.* This means that every religion is grounded in events that people consider to be manifestations of the sacred.

- The root metaphor of a "drama" frames the world religions in terms of players, texture, and performance. This allows for a detailed look at a wide range of data organized around the notion that religion comprises: (1) people creating culture based on ideas of extraordinary events; (2) ideas shifting cultural values; and (3) customs shaping the physical environment.
- The ten elements of performance help describe the expressive aspects of religious traditions, which rely largely on transmission of sacred lore. These ten elements include the three expressive aspects: lived time, lived place, and lived objects, and the seven expressive functions: donation, restoration, enactment, symbolization, transformation, accession, and transmission. (For convenience these seven may be called the DRESTAT functions.)

STUDY QUESTIONS

1. What is the insider–outsider challenge?
2. Distinguish between the religionist and the reductionist approaches to the study of religions.
3. Name and define five main concepts developed by religionists to do research in the phenomenology of religion. Include the concepts of Rudolph Otto, Gerardus van der Leeuw, and Mircea Eliade.
4. Name the three ways religions function in society. How do religions change their role in society over time?
5. Name three cultural roots of the modern study of religions. What did some of the European Enlightenment thinkers contribute to the Western way of studying religions?
6. Summarize the attitudes and oversights that contributed to the "erasure" of people from consideration in the study of world religions.
7. List the four types of "players," three types of "religious texture" in world religions, and state what distinguishes them from one another. Then name the ten elements of performance and think about their relation to each other.

GLOSSARY

agency Term used by social scientists to emphasize the element of will (or political deprivation of will) in the lives of human actors who comprise and create society.

axis mundi (Latin) World pole. Term used by historians of religions for any symbol that vertically connects the realms of existence, and represents the center of the world.

creative imagination A human way of perceiving beings or forms in mystical visions of the imaginal realm. In Hindu and Buddhist yoga this is called the "divine eye" (Sanskrit = *divya-cakṣu*). In Islamic mysticism the term in Arabic for this imagination is *quwwat al-khāyal.*

cultural imperialism The cultural domination that results from the spread of values, customs, and so on associated with a politically or economically powerful nation or civilization – often accompanied by an attitude of triumphalism.

definition of religion A religion is a dynamic cultural complex with positive or negative impacts that stakes a claim to legitimacy based on a foundational connection to reports of hierophany.

East–West diptych A metaphor that emphasizes the orientalist view of the world as divided into two opposing flat plates (a diptych) with the West on one side and the East on the other.

European colonialism Europeans in modern times (sixteenth to twentieth centuries) taking political and economic charge of foreign territories to gain control of maritime trade and to spread Christianity. This began with Portugual and Spain, followed by the Dutch, British, and French.

European Enlightenment A European cultural movement spanning the late 1600s to the late 1700s that emphasized the role of human reason in thinking about religion, and championed intellectual freedom and tolerance.

existential value The intellectual or emotional weight of an experience that bears on a person's very existence. Term taken from existentialist philosophy.

expressive traditions Performance-based traditions that rely on oral transmission of sacred lore, and many non-verbal expressions to build religious meaning.

hierophanic history Accounts of religious experiences of hierophany, as opposed to accounts based in conventional history. Many spiritual (auto)biographies may be considered as such.

hierophany (Greek: *hieros* + *phainein* = sacred + to manifest) Manifestation of the sacred. Hierophanic events are unique, but people attempt to recapitulate them in the ritual arena of space–time using power objects.

imaginal realm (Arabic: *'alam al-khayāl*; Latin: *mundus imaginalis*) The ahistorical realm of "reality" where immaterial beings abide. Most religions make reference to such beings, whether or not they accept these figures.

insider–outsider challenge The challenge for people to adopt both inside and outside positions in their study of religions. This means to empathize with a religious worldview while maintaining a critical (analytic, not hostile) perspective.

kratophany (Greek: *kratos* + *phainein* = power + manifest) Manifestations of power that have yet to be counted as sacred, such as a terrific tsunami storm.

liminal beings Beings that move betwixt-and-between two realms of existence or experience. Players in the drama of world religions that inhabit the imaginal realm.

mysterium fascinans (Latin) A mystery that draws people toward it because it evokes the emotion of religious fascination.

mysterium tremendum (Latin) A mystery that frightens people away because it evokes the emotion of religious awe.

orientalism A racist attitude running through Western scholarship and politics (leaking to the general public) that lumps all peoples of the "Orient" (East) together without distinguishing their specific characteristics. Concept developed by Edward Said, postcolonial theorist.

phenomenology A philosophical school that originated in the early 1900s with Edmund Husserl in Germany. Applied to religion, it becomes a field of study that aims to describe and understand the religious experience of sacred phenomena, especially through sense experience that occurs prior to rational thought.

play Term used by anthropologists with reference to the activity of *Homo ludens* (the human player) whose creative, spontaneous activity is central to the creation of culture.

postcolonial turn Phase of modern cultural criticism that can involve a wide range of issues including challenging Western ethnocentrism, exposing the nation-state mentality established by colonialists for ease of subjugation, and deconstructing feminine identity in light of colonialism.

reductionist In the context of religious studies, scholars rejecting the *sui generis* view of religions, and therefore working largely in the social sciences; they explain religious data without presuming the existence of anything irreducibly religious.

religionist A term coined by contemporary scholar Robert A. Segal with reference to scholars in religious studies who hold a *sui generis* view of religions, including both theologians and historians of religions who claim that something irreducibly *religious* exists.

Religious Impression The experience of a Religious Subject being deeply moved (impressed) in the moment when an object is perceived as religiously meaningful, which gives rise to a creative act called a Religious Expression that tends to have symbolic meaning.

Religious Subject A person (the subject) who attains religious faith or understanding through an encounter with something experienced as sacred. Religious Subject and Religious Object come into existence at the same existential moment, and give rise to Religious Impressions and Religious Expressions.

religious symbol An object that represents or reconstitutes a sacred entity. The stand-in for a hierophany, which is its ultimate expression. The term is ambiguous, and needs more scholarly attention.

sui generis (Latin) "Belong to its own kind," or in a class of its own.

thick description Complex description that suggests the significance of an action or thing, as opposed to the "thin" portrayal of its obvious outward aspect; term coined by English philosopher Gilbert Ryle, and applied to the interpretation of culture by anthropologist Clifford Geertz.

ultimate principle Term for the highest, greatest, or deepest aspect of the cosmos conceived by a human being. A word such as "God" is often used with reference to (in the words of Christian Saint Anselm) "that greater than which nothing can be conceived."

vision quest A form of prayer used by Native Americans in which an individual spends time alone, fasting, in an isolated place to appeal to the cosmic powers for guidance, protection, and greater personal ability.

KEY READING

Appadurai, Arjun, Korom, Frank, and Mills, Margaret (1991) *Gender, Genre, and Power in South Asian Expressive Traditions*, Philadelphia, PA: University of Pennsylvania Press.

Corbin, Henry (1969) "Theophanic Imagination and Creativity of the Heart," pp. 216–245, in *Creative Imagination in the Sūfism of Ibn 'Arabī*, Princeton, NJ: Princeton University Press.

Deming, W. (2005) *Rethinking Religion: A Concise Introduction*, New York/Oxford: Oxford University Press.

Eliade, M. ([1958] 1996) *Patterns in Comparative Religion*, trans. Rosemary Sheed, Lincoln and London: University of Nebraska Press.

Idinopulos, T. A. and Wilson, B. C. (eds) (1998) *What is Religion? Origins, Definitions, and Explanations*, Leiden, The Netherlands: Brill.

Lincoln, B. (ed.) (1985) *Religion, Rebellion, and Revolution*, New York: St. Martin's Press.

McCutcheon, R. T. (2001) *Critics Not Caretakers, Redescribing the Public Study of Religion*, Albany, NY: State University of New York Press.

Otto, Rudolph ([1923] 1970) *The Idea of the Holy*, trans. John W. Harvey, London: Oxford University Press.

Gennep, Arnold van (1960) *The Rites of Passage*, trans. Monika B. Vizedom and Gabrielle L. Caffe, London: Routledge & Kegan Paul.

Turner, Victor W. (1969) *The Ritual Process: Structure and Anti-structure*, Chicago, IL: Aldine Publishing.

CHAPTER 2

Expressive traditions of Oceania, America, and Africa

TIMELINE

	CE	
	ca. 1240–1500	Mali Empire in West Africa
La Malinche (Doña Marina)	ca. 1496–ca.1529	
	1580s	Portuguese establish slave trade in Dahomey (Benin)
	1519	Hernán Cortés in Mexico
Moctezuma	d. 1520	
Cuauhtémoc	1502–1525	
Martín Cortés	1523–1568	
	1530s	First Africans in Brazil
	1531	Indian Juan Diego's vision of the Virgin of Guadalupe
	1600	25,000 Portuguese settlers in Brazil
	1606	Nine Dutch crew members eaten by cannibals in New Guinea
	8 October 1769	First Maori with moko shot by British crew member
	1770s	British claim New Guinea, New Zealand, and Australia
	1800s	Migrant workers carry Candomblé to urban centers in Brazil
	1821	Mexico's independence from Spain
	1846	US military moves into Navajo territory
Black Elk (Hehaka Sapa)	1863–1950	
	1865–1900	Moko virtually disappears among New Zealand Maori
	1888	Slavery abolished in Brazil
	29 December 1890	Massacre of Sioux at Wounded Knee Creek, SD
	1890s (late)	French control of Dahomey, Mali, Burkina Faso, etc.
	1904–1934	Sun Dance banned in USA
	1946	Candomblé legalized
Malidoma Somé	b. 1956	
	1986	Wole Soyinka wins Nobel Prize for Literature
	1990	Octavio Paz wins Nobel Prize for Literature
	1994	Disney's "Lion King"

This chapter highlights ten traditions from the indigenous peoples of Oceania, America, and Africa. One chapter of a book such as this can provide only a glimpse into the religious lives of the many distinctive peoples who live in these three vast areas. Yet despite their variety, the **indigenous peoples** of these regions are alike in two culturally significant ways: (1) They created expressive traditions that center on the performative aspects of religious life rather than on a corpus of sacred literature. (2) They became vulnerable to the powerful economic ambitions of European colonizers – many of whom worked hard to convert **aboriginals** to the Christian faith. Because the indigenous peoples of Oceania, America, and Africa emphasize the expressive (non-literate) aspects of religion, they are treated here in terms of the ten elements of performance. Three Oceanic traditions are explored in terms of the three expressive aspects (lived place, lived time, and lived objects), while four American and three African traditions illustrate the DRESTAT functions: donation, restoration, enactment, symbolization, transformation, accession, and transmission (see pages 16–18).

Each Element of Performance is illustrated by one religious practice that represents a key value from its religious culture. To aid in thinking about these indigenous traditions in comparative terms, the examples were chosen to highlight aspects of religious life in five complementary sets: (1) Ceremonial Gardening and Fon divination deal with *cosmic patterns* they find in the world that relate to the human situation. (2) Aboriginal dreaming and the Lion King story both deal with *key myths* that shape their religious identities. (3)

Plate 2.1 "Prayer." The ceremonical cottonwood tree is regarded as a living being that sustains those who sacrifice themselves in the Sun Dance. In the intense heat the tree transmits the cooling moisture it collected at the stream while it grew. This scene captures the spirit of Native American prayer.

Table 2.1 Overview of chapter contents

Category	*Focus*	*Illustration*	*Location*
Lived time	cosmic patterns	Trobriand gardening	Papua New Guinea – Oceania
Lived place	key myths	Aboriginal dreaming	Australia – Oceania
Lived object	human body	Maori tattoos	New Zealand – Oceania
Donation	human body	Sioux Sun Dance	USA – North America
Restoration	healing	Navajo sandpainting	USA – North America
Enactment	personal view	Mexican identity	Mexico – Central America
Symbolization	healing	Candomblé dance	Brazil – South America
Transformation	personal view	Dagara initiation	Burkina Faso – West Africa
Accession	cosmic patterns	Fon divination	Benin – West Africa
Transmission	key myths	The Lion King story	Mali – West Africa

Candomblé dance and Navajo sandpainting treat aspects of *healing* that use the expressive arts of dance and painting. (4) Maori tattoos and Sioux Sun Dance involve use of the *human body* as the focal point of religious expression. (5) Mexican identity and Dagara initiation present two *personal accounts* about experiences and values of the Mexican and West African cultures.

Although the indigenous traditions of Oceania, America, and Africa are presented thematically in this chapter, it is critical to remember that they were all subject to the European colonial experience. The ten religious ideas and practices explored here are inseparable from the trauma of early modern world history. Needless to say, world history shows that many brutal regimes and "civilized societies" have committed unspeakable atrocities. Here some negative acts of the Europeans come to the fore because *at this cultural moment* many indigenous peoples seek to define themselves in response to their experience of European colonialism. Colonialism is very much on the minds of **native** peoples who wish to prevent the erasure of their traditional collective memories.

LIVED TIME: CEREMONIAL GARDENING

Ceremonial gardening done by Melanesian people who live on the Trobriand Islands of Papua New Guinea illustrates the expressive function of lived time. Ceremonial gardening creates a lived time whose cyclic rhythm of two seasons brings meaning to all aspects of life. Trobrianders do two types of gardening: (1) ceremonial *taytu* (yam) gardening and (2) secondary gardening to produce sweet potatoes, bananas, squash, beans, greens, taro, and other crops. Taytu gardening is accompanied by extensive ritual that is divided into ten lunar months – five sunny unripe moons and five rainy ripe moons. This is because yams (*dioscorea*) grow only where dry and wet seasons are distinct.

- ***The unripe moons.*** This is the sunny time (starting around July) when a space for the year's garden is cleared and the taytus are planted. This is men's work. The planting of a taytu requires clearing holes. Thus each man squats and digs with a stick (*dayma*) that could be anywhere from about two meters in length (for a strong man) to a short stick (for a child). A whole taytu is placed in the hole.
- ***The ripe moons.*** This is the rainy time during which the taytu gestates in the ground. Men may not approach women during this phase. Women's work is taking care of the growing tubers by weeding. The **towosi** (ritual garden specialist, sometimes called the garden magician) utters verses of fertility to promote growth of the taytus. During this time villagers tell stories (some of a ribald nature) to encourage the growth of the tubers. This is a time when careful nurturing is needed.

The two phases of the ceremonial gardening cycle parallel the process of impregnation and gestation. Thus Trobrianders view the production of food and the production of life itself according to the same cycle. The symbolism of the sunny phase of yam gardening done by the men is of opening the way and planting the embryos. After men have planted the embryo of the taytu the women see to its gestation. And just as men do not approach women during the rainy moons, so a pregnant woman separates from her husband and male company after her fifth month of pregnancy.

The towosi chants sacred verses said to have been passed down from the legendary ancestor who brought ceremonial gardening to the Trobriand Islands. Knowledge of these verses carries political as well as religious power. Although people always hear the songs, their use is restricted to specialists. Verses are sometimes purchased or recited for special favors. The taytus are supposed to imbibe the vibrational energy of the words and respond by moving in the soil without being blocked by stones. The key song used in ceremonial gardening is the *vatuvi* (show the way). Similar incantations are sung during the time of a woman's gestation. A portion of the *vatuvi* goes like this (Malinowski [1935] 1966: 97):

> The belly of my garden leavens,
> The belly of my garden rises,
> The belly of my garden reclines,
> The belly of my garden grows to the size of a
>   bush-hen's nest,
> The belly of my garden grows like an anthill; . . .

* repetition

The belly of my garden lies down,
The belly of my garden swells,
The belly of my garden swells as with a child,
I sweep away.

The parallel between gestation and taytu cultivation is just one of many symbolic patterns found in ceremonial gardening among Trobrianders. For example, a man will bring his axe to the ritual garden specialist to empower it. Thus the tool will become more effective in cutting roots to prepare garden soil if the towosi spreads a herbal mixture on the axe and wraps it in banana leaf. After he has sensed the arrival of the ancestral spirits the towosi sings a song whose words are

BOX 2.1 CULTURE CONTRAST: THE WORLD STAGE IN 1500 CE

The year 1500 is often chosen to mark the start of the modern period of world history. At that moment in world history, "it was by no means obvious to the inhabitants of Europe that their continent was poised to dominate much of the rest of the earth" (Kennedy 1987: 3). According to historian Paul Kennedy's analysis, these "power centers" were at play with the following strengths and weaknesses:

Ming China. Ming China was heir to a long-standing civilization – one of the oldest and most cultured in the world. It was fertile, well populated and efficiently run by its organized Confucian bureaucracy. In 1500 China's cities had already grown large due to vibrant industry and trade, and they far overshadowed European urban centers. In addition, the Chinese were technologically advanced in arms with gunpowder (which they invented), cannons, a huge standing army, and a sophisticated navy in possession of the magnetic compass (which they invented). But China seemed to retreat from the world stage.

Muslim cultures. In the 1500s Muslim cultures were immensely successful in several arenas of the world stage. The Ottoman Empire (1301–1922) bumped up against Europe, the Safavids in Persia (1502–1736) prospered, and Emperor Akbar (1556–1605) ruled the Mughal Empire in India. Besides those great Islamic empires, a significant Muslim presence was felt along the Silk Road, and in West Africa. But overextension of the Ottomans and overindulgence of the Mughals proved to be crippling.

Tokugawa Japan. After a hundred years of clan feuding, the Japanese became unified under the Tokugawa clan. The great potential they had begun to develop in terms of international trade came to an abrupt halt with a new policy of isolationism. No Japanese was allowed to sail, and foreign trade was all but cut. Internal economic conditions were not bad, but there was a radical break in economic and cultural contact with the outside.

Muscovy. The Russian czars would someday grow to become rulers of a world power. In the 1500s the Kingdom of Muscovy possessed the arms (muskets and cannons) that put them in the running (along with the other "gunpowder empires" named above) for extended economic and political influence. Besides their relative military might, however, the Russians were economically underdeveloped. As they expanded, internal disputes had a stifling impact on economic success.

Europe. Europe paled in comparison to India and China in population; it was not the most fertile of lands; its borders were vulnerable to attack by both land and sea; and it was disunited. But what allowed the cluster of independent territories to succeed seems to have been an entrepreneurial spirit, a drive for innovation, and the absence of a single authority whose policies could control, homogenize, and regulate commercial activity.

Among all the world powers in 1500 the Europeans found a combination of social and economic factors that brought them to the forefront. The fantastic success of Europe in trade led to colonization, and colonization led to cultural domination.

supposed to penetrate the blade and herbs. The herbal mixture is composed of various items that function as **symbols**. Each contributes something to the production of an ideal taytu crop: (1) Coconut leaves and the areca nut have a dark green color like a healthy taytu plant. (2) Three items are gathered because they have a good round shape like a bulging taytu, namely earth from a mound created by a bush-hen, chalk scraped from a large coral boulder with a musselshell, and a part of a large hornet's nest that was made in the ground. (3) Leaves from several creepers are crushed up and mixed in because their foliage is luxurious like healthy taytu foliage. (4) A small white tuber with white fragrant petals is used to obtain pleasant-smelling beautiful white taytus, and so forth (Malinowski 1935, 1966: 105–106). These symbols illustrate the principle of **homology** in the practice of religion. Each symbolic item is *like* the object it is meant to affect. They have the same *structure* and therefore a change in one effects a change in the other. (In religious studies this type of operation is sometimes called sympathetic magic.)

LIVED PLACE: ABORIGINAL DREAMING

The Dreaming (*Altjeringa*) is a key tradition among Australia's Aboriginal people. It gives religious meaning to the land on which they live – and by extension to everything associated with that lived place. The Dreaming connects people to each other through associations with family territory. Aboriginal genealogy is not passed down as a memory because saying the name of ancestors is forbidden. Thus relationships are based upon shared Dreaming. A connection to a grandfather or grandmother is made on the basis of the particular area in which those relatives lived. The living and deceased members of families are related through their common affiliation with the Eternal Beings of the Dreaming (*Altjeringa Mitjina*) who awakened at the beginning of time.

Aboriginal tradition says that the Eternal Beings of the Dreaming dreamed land, rivers, mountains, and living creatures into existence. They did this by walking across the land that had no features and doing things for the first time. The Dreaming beings used tools and did things that Aborigines do today. They camped, made fire, engaged in combat, and performed rituals. Their Dreaming started the culture of human beings. At some point the Dreaming ended, but stories about it survived through retellings and ritual enactments. Aboriginal elders pass on the sacred body of Dreaming myths, songs, and rites. Based on the memories passed down about the Dreaming, Aboriginal people discuss details of what the Eternal Ones did at every place. They also base tribal laws on examples of social relationships shown in the Dreaming, and keep the laws alive through the performance of rituals. As ritual articles are prepared the Dreaming stories about them are always recited.

The Aborigines tell stories about the origins of many things and customs, such as the first kangaroo, death, fire, children, and so forth. Here is a story about the travels of Yam Dreaming as told by Paddy Japaljarri Sims (Warlukurlangu Artists 1987: 47):

> He moved with his feet dragging along the ground at Yumurrpa. He was walking along and he noticed, at a distance from Yumurrpa, the flower of a yam plant standing all alone. He kept going . . . [and] dug into the earth there [at Jupurrurla and Jakamarra] and followed the roots deep down into the earth. He dug and found yams and made them into a pile. Having dug deep down and dug out the yams and made them into a pile, he left them and went on his way. Yamaparnta is near the road to the east of Pikilyi. It too belongs to Jupurrurla-Jakamarra. He moved off, dragging his feet along the surface of the earth. He went south, and kept walking a long way. . . . As the yam roots spread out to the east the Dreaming travelled in the same direction and he came to be in the eastern country. Keeping to the south he travelled through Warnipiyi to Kuurrpa, which is a hill. From there the Dreaming, who was originally a person, spread out like yam roots and became them. Thus the yams which the Dreaming carried with him spread out into the country. . . . Then a fire burnt the country and burnt the yam roots into many pieces. White ants ate them bit by bit. The Dreaming travelled and was burnt at that place. The Dreaming finished at that place and entered into the earth, going no further.

Aborigines must have Dreaming knowledge of the land and their connection with it. For example, people might be associated with particular places if their mothers first felt them move in their belly at that spot, or if they were born at that spot, or if their grandparents lived there. They use land and objects only when they can tell Dreaming stories pertaining to them. Circumstances have changed with the European colonization of Australia. The Aboriginal people no longer live by hunting and gathering in small bands. Rather they live in large settlements, towns, and cities. But no matter where they live, traditional Aborigines always have Dreaming myths associated with their place of residence as well as people, creatures, and objects involved in their lives at that place. Elders find evidence of the Dreaming if the group moves to a new area, and new objects obtained at stores are brought into use through recitation of Dreamings.

LIVED OBJECT: MAORI TATTOOS

Among the Maori people of New Zealand the tattooed body is a sacred object. It is a religious symbol that bridges two realms of reality: (1) the world of light in which humans dwell, and (2) the world of *atuas* (spirits) who dwell in twelve heavens and an underworld. The Maori feel the presence of atuas in powerful manifestations of the weather (thunder, lightning) or in uncharacteristic mental states such as fear in the case of a brave warrior or mental illness. Atuas also manifest in the growth energy of plant life and can work through human beings who skillfully carve wood or etch a tattoo. The Maori consider anything under stimulation from the non-human realm as **tapu**. This means that every circumstance of encounter with atuas requires ritual care. The process of **ta moko** (applying a tattoo) is tapu, and thus both artist and subject need protection. Maori have the sense that while something is being ornamented with a pattern under tapu conditions it becomes invested with power (*ihi*), awe (*wehi*), and authority (*wana*). A word, message, or living iconography (*kupu*) is built into the sacred object as well. The sacred object created through this artistry gives access to the spiritual realm.

Traditional Maori full moko designs are created as follows: (1) six lines on each side of the chin, (2) lines on the chin, (3) six lines below nostrils, (4) a curved line on cheekbone, (5) lines between cheekbone and ear, (6) lines below cheekbone and ear, and (7) lines on each side of the lower part of nose (Robley [1896] 2003: 68). The patterns are etched as negatives with the design on the uncolored skin. An untattooed vertical line runs from forehead to chin that divides a symmetrical pattern. Spirals are etched on the nose and cheeks, while arched bands are carved into the forehead. The eyelids are also tattooed and lips are black. Each buttock has a large spiral and the thighs are covered with tattoos resembling foliage down to the knees. A Maori woman traditionally had moko on her upper lip and chin with deep lip coloring. A Maori myth tells how ta moko originated in the underworld (Robley [1896] 2003: 116):

> Tama-nui-a-raki visited his ancestors. When they asked what brought him there he said, "To obtain your services to make on my face the lines I now see marked on yours." He wanted markings that would not wash off when he bathed. The ancestors referred him to another group of ancestors to undergo the procedure but warned that it was painful. Tama-nui-a-raki said, "It cannot be death, as you have borne it and live." Coming to the right place Tama shut his eyes as an ancestor cut lines into his face. Tama fainted three times during the operation. On recovering the first time he cried out thinking he would die, but the ancestors sang words of comfort. After a second faint, Tama bathed and rested facedown on the earth, whereupon an ancestor knelt on him to press blood from the wounds. When Tama fainted a third time the ancestors laid him near a fire. In three days he could see again, rising from the "black darkness" that had covered him. When he could again walk and bathe Tama bid his ancestors farewell: "I will now return home to my children."

The method of applying the Maori tattoo involves piercing the skin with a bone chisel. The bone has a serrated edge that holds the pigment. These are finely made implements with decorations that make them look like miniature adzes. While applying the pigment, the bone is tapped rhythmically with a small mallet made of wood. The pigment is made from a mixture

BOX 2.2 INTERPRETATIONS: OBSTACLES TO UNDERSTANDING ORAL CULTURES

It would be naive to think that a student of religions could immediately find out all there is to know of the religions of indigenous peoples. Because their traditions have been largely expressive there are several factors that make understanding them difficult.

Problems with translation. Relatively few people have good knowledge of the language of small groups of people. Expressive cultures are largely oral. Their religious specialists do not commit their body of wisdom to writing. Those who first studied the languages of the people of Oceania, America, and Africa were largely missionaries. Over time the field of anthropology developed, and their accounts provided a view of tribal cultures. Thus some information emerges when reports of the customs of indigenous tribal peoples were written by outsiders.

Biased reports. Written accounts of oral traditions have not always been sensitive to cultural nuances and religious values of people who do not use writing to transmit their religious rituals and beliefs. Therefore what is translated and recorded may not have captured an accurate sense of the oral religions.

Faulty or partial information. Some missionaries may have tried to be accurate, and within the field of anthropology much thought has been given over time to the most suitable ways of gaining information and transmitting it. Yet the willingness of indigenous people to convey especially their most sacred lore is variable. Anthropologists have discussed problems of paid informants relating what they think the anthropologist wants to hear, or providing only partial information for religious or other reasons. And there is always the problem of communication – understanding through language and cultural barriers. An anthropologist may ask questions that pertain to his or her worldview, but miss out on the most important aspects of the informant's worldview. Answers come in response to questions, and questions frame reality in such a way that much of a worldview may be ignored.

Obscured or devastated traditions. Often the traditions of small-scale societies become obscured or devastated when the people encounter cultures that are more politically and economically powerful. Sometimes a superior ruling power purposely attempts to wipe out earlier traditions. Other times the indigenous traditions become mixed with the newer traditions. This process of **syncretism** makes it difficult to learn about traditions that existed prior to the onset of a new ruling power.

of soot with a liquid substance to make it smooth. Artists keep the sticky indigo blue-black or greenish-black substance in specially decorated ink-pots that traditionally were passed down from one generation to the next. Pigment was continually added to the pot and over time it made a precious mixture. Between 1865 and 1900 the tradition of ta moko virtually disappeared. But today the Maori are taking an interest in their traditional arts including ta moko.

DONATION: SIOUX SUN DANCE

The **Sun Dance** illustrates the expressive function of donation because some dancers give their flesh as a sacrifice to **Wakan-Tanka** for the sake of the people. It is typically (but not always) an annual large-scale ceremonial made by members of about three dozen Native American **People**. Practices vary according to the tribe, the individual, and the time period under consideration. Black Elk (1863–1950), a holy man of the Oglala Sioux, said that the Sun Dance first came to his tribe in a vision. The Sioux call it a "dance looking at the sun" (*wiwanyag wachipi*) and for them Wakan-Tanka, the Great Spirit, is associated with the sun, life, and light. The man to whom the vision was given explained, "Long ago *Wakan-Tanka* told us how to pray with the sacred pipe, but we have now become lax in our prayers, and our people are losing their strength" (Brown 1953: 68). Thus the vision was interpreted as Wakan-Tanka's gift to the Sioux to help them recover their intensity of prayer.

The Sun Dance evolved into an annual gathering where thousands of tribal bands came together to distribute goods and engage in communal prayer. A handful among the thousands of participants came as Sun Dance pledgers. This meant that they had already undertaken a vow to perform the Sun Dance at a higher level of intensity. The most intense prayer involved being attached to a pole by hide thongs that skewered the body above each nipple on the chest. Black Elk said, "when we tear ourselves away from the thongs, it is as if the spirit were liberated from our dark bodies" (Brown 1953: 92). The pole (typically) was a ritually prepared cottonwood tree (*wagachun*), and the dancer pulled back against the pole until the flesh tore so he could be released. (This intensive torture was not done by women. However, another option for Sun Dancers, including women, was the donation of small pieces of flesh.) Anthropologist Alice C. Fletcher, an eyewitness of a Sun Dance performed by the Oglala Sioux in 1882, described its culmination as follows:

> At this time all the dancers are painted according to the visions of their respective priests. Scarifications are next performed. After noon, the leader is led to the pole, when according to certain ceremonies the flesh is punctured a little above the nipples by a wedge-shaped knife, and a stick having one end embroidered with porcupine quills is inserted. To this skewer the raw hide rope fastened to the pole is secured, and the man is led out toward the east until the rope is taut. A large amount of goods are then given away, and many ceremonies take place to insure him a speedy release. When a certain song is started, he must put his whistle in his mouth and bracing himself pull with all his force, until he shall tear the flesh loose. When one side gives way he raises his hand, palm upward to the sky, as a sign of thanks for the deliverance. With one man the struggle lasted nearly twenty minutes. When these tortures are completed the festival is over.
>
> (Fletcher 1883: 584)

The Sun Dance is held during the hottest part of the summer – namely late June or early July. The highpoint of the ceremony typically is a span of three days during which pledgers abstain from food and drink. During these days the weather should be scorching hot. One can say "should be" because the weather is thought to

Plate 2.2 "Sun Dance pledgers." The Sun Dance ceremony is led by someone who has received authority through a vision quest or transmission from an elder medicine person. These two men have prepared themselves to deal with the awesome power of the sacred, which by nature is dangerous. To cope with danger, they should have undergone certain dangerous trials themselves. It is possible that participation in war (in modern times as a member of the United States armed forces) could provide this qualification. Participants in the Sun Dance go without food and water for several days.

be a reflection of the intensity and sincerity of the dancers' sacrifice. Cool weather or a cloudy sky is considered inauspicious becauase the dancers obtain spiritual power from being dried out and cannot do so in case of rain or clouds. Their lament is deepened through the ordeal of staring at the sun and refraining from water. On the other hand, after the Sun Dance, rain is thought to be an auspicious cosmic response to the sacrifices made.

Although the Sun Dance pledgers do not drink water, it is said that they might get a taste of sacred water under extraordinary circumstances. In some versions of the Sun Dance a buffalo head hangs from the cottonwood pole. From this buffalo comes soothing water that the pledgers may find dripping through their eaglebone whistles. "Dancers say, 'Just as when the buffalo is thirsty he can dig water out of the dust where no one can see it, *nuc* [Indian] can get water from Buffalo when he is thirsty'" (Jorgensen 1972: 209). Sometimes they are granted moisture from the sacred cottonwood pole itself – which is one of the "standing peoples" (i.e., trees) chosen to be at the center (Brown 1953: 69).

> Stories circulate that during the dance the center pole opens, and water comes out. It is spiritual water that blesses the dancers but only can be seen by some. Dancers may drink it through their whistles.
>
> (Hultkrantz 1981: 251)

At some point a dancer may be hit with a vision. This becomes evident from the outside as the dancer is literally knocked down by the force of something sacred, such as the buffalo or the pole, and would lie unconscious for three to four hours. During the time of the vision the Sun Dancer gains new knowledge that includes such things as songs, a dance step, techniques for healing, and so forth. The Sun Dancer is instructed during this time as his (or her) spiritual body leaves the physical body. The experience of vision can involve drinking water with holy beings. Thus the dancers may return from such shamanic journeys with moistened throats and dance effortlessly without experiencing hunger or thirst. Later the Sun Dancers share details of their visions with the other Sun Dancers, chiefs, and family. Many symbolic objects, words, songs, movements, and so forth patterned on events in the visions are incorporated into future Sun Dances. The relatively small number of Sun Dancers who undergo the most intensive practice of ripping their flesh offer themselves as a sacrifice to Wakan-Tanka so that "much strength would be given to the life of the nation" (Brown 1953: 100).

RESTORATION: NAVAJO SANDPAINTING

The Navajo religion centers on healing, based on the assumption that illness is caused by interference with the life force of a person. Thus healing is a form of restoration. Illness can arise from contact with the dead or things associated with blood, excessive behavior, witches, and contact with specific animals, a pre-natal incident or even Holy People (i.e., supernaturals who pose danger due to their power). The Navajo classify their healing into ceremonials called "ways," such as Enemyway, Beautyway, and Uglyway. Each healing way is associated with one branch of a vast story network. Navajo songs are a form of wealth and no cure is possible without them. Sacred songs link the healer, patient, medicine, and ritual objects to the supernatural world. Singers specialize in healing ways and must learn the songs (many hundreds), stories, iconography, and medicines associated with them. A Navajo curing chant invokes supernatural beings who set things right. Through the ritual, the healer makes contact with the supernatural counterpart of an earthly cause of trouble. The cure applies a kind of "homeopathic" remedy whereby ritual contact with the source of trouble restores health. Physical diseases and other ailments are linked to problematic associations with the earthly counterparts of characters in the Navajo stories. The supernatural counterpart of the character must be called to undo the effect of the improper act.

In the Navajo system, a sore throat, stomach trouble, or skin disease is attributed (sometimes) to an inappropriate act involving snakes. Thus the healer must use a story about snakes in the cure. Navajo sandpaintings depict various "people" that exist in the sacred stories. The healing power of the paintings comes from the (hierophanic) fact that supernaturals invest energy in their symbols. The holy people become present after corn pollen is sprinkled on the sandpainting and patient. A painting might be six feet across, made on the floor of a hogan (ceremonial lodge) around 15–20 feet across. The sick person sits in the middle of the painting facing east, in line with the hogan entryway. Sand from specific areas of various "people" is picked up with moistened hands and "pressed" on to corresponding parts of the patient's body. As part of the remedy, the sick person is fed a ceremonial stew in a prescribed manner:

> At dawn, after the stew has been kept boiling all night long the pot is placed before the patient. With his fingers the singer takes a pinch from the east side and inserts this into the patient's mouth. He repeats this feeding with a pinch from the west, south and north and concludes with a pinch from the center of the dish.
>
> (Haile 1947: 29)

Medicines are also fed to the patient, bringing the container to the patient's lips. Usually they drink it four times when the appropriate song words are sung. At dawn following the closing songs the patient goes outside and inhales dawn's breath four times, facing east toward dawn and drawing hands toward the mouth and inhaling.

In the sandpaintings supernatural beings are always portrayed in human form, whereas plants, animals, and natural phenomena might look like people or be depicted in their own shape (e.g., curvy snake, straight snake, weasel) or in abstract form (e.g., rainbow lines, zigzag thunder). Usually the protagonist of a healing story is represented as human. Circular paintings have the place of the episode depicted in the center. Some symbols, represented in multiples of two and four, are put in cardinal directions or in a line with heads pointing east. Symbols in the sandpaintings include: snakes, people, water creatures, thunder, corn, and guardians. For example, one painting of a corn myth includes corn rooted in a cloud symbol standing above a mountain symbol (all of the same color). The corn plant has six leaves on each side with a bird perched on each leaf, and two more birds hovering over the corn. In addition, two human figures one above the other stand on each side of the corn. The birds have sacred pollen on their bills and feet, and the corn tassels also have pollen (Wyman 1957: 181). Most circular paintings have the four Navajo sacred domesticated plants marking the four quadrants: corn, beans, squash, and tobacco. A male or female rainbow guardian in the form of an elongated figure encircles most Navajo sandpaintings – leaving an opening to the east.

ENACTMENT: MEXICAN IDENTITY

In the study of religions it is common to find people ritually "enacting" wondrous hierophanic events in order to relive them. But "enactment" can also occur in response to kratophanies that came as traumatic events of irresistible power. The persistent Mexican enactment of the trauma of the Spanish Conquest is an example of the latter. In *The Labyrinth of Solitude*, Ocatvio Paz (1918–1998) contemplates his Mexican identity (*mexicanidad*) as it embodied the trauma of long-passed events. Paz says that the history of the Spanish Conquest of Mexico should begin with an understanding that Hernán Cortés encountered Moctezuma, leader of the Aztec Empire, who was already defeated by the expectation that Mexico's gods were dead. According to the Aztec calendar one cycle was ending and a new cosmic age was starting. Many warnings and bad omens had been seen. The Aztecs felt "suicidal" with a kind of death-wish because the gods had abandoned Moctezuma who was "so fascinated by the Spaniards that he experienced a vertigo which it is no exaggeration to call sacred – the lucid vertigo of the suicide on the brink of abyss" (Paz 1961: 93). Since the trauma of the Conquest, Mexicans await the redemption of history – and the power of a new cycle. Thus they still look for the tomb of Cuauhtémoc, the young hero who went out to meet Cortés alone without his woman, "separated from the curved breast of the Empress," Moctezuma's daughter (Paz 1961: 84). Mexicans call Cuauhtémoc the "young grandfather" and await his resurrection.

An intense solitude followed the death of the gods and the leaders of Mexico after the Conquest. This defeat of the indigenous gods prompted a turn to the feminine. The Spanish conquistadors introduced a new empire and a new cosmic cycle with a new vision of the Divine wrapped around the goddesses of vegetation and agriculture. Catholicism in Mexico centered on

BOX 2.3 A SPIRITUAL PATH: PRESERVING CULTURAL MEMORIES

Efrain Tomas Bó, an Afro-Brazilian social critic, observed that the "clouding of memory" was a powerful colonialist weapon.

> A noun, an apparently simple neologism – civilization – coined, curiously, as recently as the middle of the eighteenth century, simultaneously in France and England, derived itself into a verb, to civilize, would become, within a century and a half, a weapon and a tool, a powerful ideology of conquest. From this weapon or tool or ideology would emerge colonialism, the African and Asian colonial wars, entire peoples' enslavement for their economic and human exploitation. And what form did the instrumental violence of this weapon or ideology take? It sought, first, to cloud the memory, and then to implant the civilizing powers' own cultural forms among the conquered peoples.
>
> (Efrain Tomas Bó in Nascimento 1995: 133)

Nowadays the restoration of traditional values is a kind of spiritual path for many indigenous peoples. The American Indian Movement (AIM) was formalized about thirty years ago as a reaction to unjust treatment of native nations with this vision:

> The movement was founded to turn the attention of Indian people toward a renewal of spirituality which would impart the strength of resolve needed to reverse the ruinous policies of the United States, Canada, and other colonialist governments of Central and South America. At the heart of AIM is a deep spirituality and a belief in the connectedness of all Indian people.
>
> (Whittstock and Salinas accessed online 7 February 2007)

Yet even in resisting the effects of colonization, some indigenous peoples acknowledge the benefits of colonization and recognize the difficulties of governing without the Europeans.

Octavio Paz, winner of the 1990 Nobel Prize for Literature, notes in *The Labyrinth of Solitude* that in spite of the trauma of the Spanish Conquest of Mexico, the Spaniards brought a rich cultural heritage of universality – including "almost all the artistic forms of the Renaissance: poetry, the novel, painting and architecture," along with well-developed philosophical and political ideas (Paz 1961: 98). Furthermore, the conquistadors brought a living faith in Christ along with a universal openness that made room for indigenous peoples. Notwithstanding "the religious pretensions of colonial society" the Roman Catholic Church provided a place for the disillusioned and defeated Indian – a place in the cosmos, even though it was at the bottom of the social order (Paz 1961: 101). Paz expresses gratitude that Mexico did not have to endure what the indigenous people in the English colonies endured at the hands of Protestants in the North American colonies. Paz also acknowledges social difficulties faced by Mexico after independence from Spain. In his view no ideal government has been able to replace the colonial rule, noting that the independent governments were beset with corruption and unable to solve many social problems. Paz argues that Mexicans have been unable to transcend their deep-set ambivalence about being "mixed" with the Spanish because they tried to get rid of the past by canceling themselves out and adopting the identity of the universal man.

The examples of self-assertion and introspection among indigenous peoples could be multiplied. In today's creative atmosphere of restoration, two questions run deep in the hearts of many indigenous peoples: (1) How much traditional cultural memory can or should be restored? and (2) How much memory of colonization should be erased?

the Virgin of Guadalupe who appeared to the Indian Juan Diego in 1531 on a hill sacred to Tonantzin, the Aztec fertility goddess. But despite the Virgin's association with fertility, "the worshipers do not try to make sure of their harvests but to find a mother's lap. The Virgin is the consolation of the poor, the shield of the weak, the help of the oppressed. In sum, she is the mother of orphans" (Paz 1961: 85). The deep thirst for a compassionate deity is seen also in the way villagers express their love of Christ, the "victimized Redeemer," in villages. Paz notes, "The village churches have a great many images of Jesus – on the cross, or covered with thorns and wounds – in which the insolent realism of the Spaniards is mingled with the tragic symbolism of the Indians" (Paz 1961: 83).

La Malinche (Doña Marina to the Spanish) was Hernán Cortés' Indian lover-mistress. La Malinche (Náhuatl-Māyā) was drawn to Cortés and loved by him – and then abandoned. She and Hernán had a son, Martín, who became known as the first **mestizo** (Spanish-Indian). La Malinche became a Mexican symbol of the woman who sold out, who was violated and discarded. She is called **La Chingada**. The term Chingada is so powerful a word that it is normally taboo. La Chingada is the violated one. La Chingada embodies the ambivalence of attraction to the stranger – and the subsequent violation or seduction. Cortés' violation of La Malinche/La Chingada became the foundation of Mexican identity. The trauma of the rape of Mexico is reflected in the words shouted by its people on every Mexican Independence Day, September 15: "¡Viva México, hijos de la Chingada!" (Paz 1961: 74). This cheer (that borders on a curse) is highly colloquial, meaning something like "Go Mexico, sons of the tramp!" or "Long live Mexico and the children of the Chingada!" The Chingada is the woman-mother who was violated and passive to the point of nothingness. And Mexicans are drawn to her with deep ambivalence as their mother, from whose womb the illegitimate mestizo people were born.

> Paz uses the hated *Chingada*/Malinche to explain the cult of the Virgin in Mexico. He maintains that the specific nature of Mexican Catholicism revolves around the cult of the Virgin of Guadalupe. . . . She constitutes the very antithesis of *la Chingada* whom Mexicans simply cannot forgive and they, the bastard race, the orphans, turn toward their Virgin mother for comfort and solace.
>
> (Davies 2000: http: //www.cf.ac.uk/euros/newreadings/volume6/davisl.html)

Paz suggests that Mexican goddesses (and women) are symbols of passivity. The immense passivity of the divine figures in Mexico gave birth to a strange and disturbing social polarity that pits the violator against the violated. The violence of Mexican society is seated in the opposite side of the Chingada. One either inflicts actions "implied by *chingar* on others, or else he suffers them himself at the hands of others" (Paz 1961: 78). Thus Mexican society became divided between strong and weak. In a move of identification with the oppressor, Paz notes that the figure of the Mexican "macho" took up the role of the conquistador. The macho Mexican male knows only the drive for power. The macho becomes the model for those in power in Mexican society – in relation to the powerless, including women. Paz claims that Mexicans continually relive the Spanish Conquest of the Aztec Empire. They seem unable to reconcile their self-hatred and ambivalence toward a powerful oppressor who still lives as a figment of the Mexican imagination. In Mexico the term *malinchistas* applies to those who want Mexico to open up to the outside world. Thus rather than chance another humiliation, Mexicans retreat into a "labyrinth of solitude."

SYMBOLIZATION: CANDOMBLÉ DANCE

The Afro-Brazilian religion **Candomblé** centers on the worship of **orishas**, who are spiritual beings that represent many aspects of life. The deepest influence in Candomblé comes from the Yoruba people of West Africa who were brought as slaves to the Americas. Yoruba tradition associates some orishas with historical persons while others are connected with features of the land or the cosmos, such as rivers, thunder, and so forth (see Box 2.4). The **babalawô**, priests of Ifá, pass along sacred lore about the orishas – such as these lines about Shangô, the warrior orisha who is associated with iron:

BOX 2.4 SYMBOLS: A WEEKLY CYCLE OF ORISHAS IN CANDOMBLÉ

The orishas of Yoruba-based religions have many symbolic associations (with variants) – including characteristic functions and specially colored beads worn by those who seek their protection. Here is a description of several orishas, listed according to the weekday with which they are typically linked (see especially Verger 1993).

Monday. Eshu brings order to the world and travels between cosmic zones to facilitate divine–human communication. All Candomblé ceremonies open with an invocation to Eshu to open up a channel to the other orishas. He is a **trickster** associated with crossroads (which is the best place to leave him offerings). Eshu is felt to be the most human among the orishas. People wear black and white beads for Eshu.

Tuesday. Oshun is the goddess of love. She is associated with the Oshun River in West Africa, and devotees (even from Brazil) make pilgrimages there to honor her. Oshun dances voluptuously, looking brightly at herself in a mirror, graciously waving a fan and wearing lots of jewelry. People wear golden yellow glass beads and many bracelets made of brass for Oshun.

Wednesday. Shangô was a former African king who manifests as a forceful character and dances to warlike rhythms. His insignia is a two-sided axe. A long dried gourd filled with small seeds is used as an instrument to sound like rain in his honor because lightning is associated with his administration of justice. People wear red and white beads for Shangô.

Thursday. Ogun is the god of iron and blacksmiths. Those whose work involves metal seek his protection, such as farmers, hunters, butchers, carpenters, and machinists. He wears a metal helmet and bracelets, and carries a shield and sword or war axe. In Brazil due to the enslaved position of Africans, the original association of Ogun with farming was lost. People wear dark-blue or green beads for Ogun.

Friday. Obatala is perhaps the greatest orisha. He descended from the heavens to fulfill the mission of his father, Olorun. Obatala was entrusted with the act of making humans out of clay. Because the clay took on many shapes, people with hunched backs or crippled limbs worship him. Obatala is associated with the crucified Christ of Christian teachings and walks with a dignified presence among the people. Obatala always wears white, as do his followers (including white beads). All Candomblé ceremonies close with reverence to Obatala, who is offered white rice.

One of the customers of Ogun, the blacksmith, was Shangô,
Who liked to dress elegantly,
To the point of braiding his hair like that of a woman.
Having pierced the lobes of his ears,
He always wore earrings.
He wore necklaces of beads.
He wore bracelets.
What elegance!!!
This man was equally powerful through the use of his talismans.
He was a warrior by trade.
He never took prisoners during his battles.
(He killed all of his enemies.)
For that reason, Shangô is saluted as
King of Kosô who acts with independence!

(Carybé 1993: 251)

Candomblé makes intensive use of symbolism. Specially trained people known as Orisha Children serve as channels through which the orishas manifest to the Candomblé community. The person "mounted" by an orisha *becomes* a living religious symbol. A person who seeks protection from the orishas need not become such a trance medium, however. One must be *called by an orisha* to become an Orisha Child. This calling may be indicated in several ways, including: (1) falling into a trance during a drumming ceremony, (2) having an illness that does not respond to normal treatment, (3) having an unusual dream, (4) discovering a strange object, or (5) having a series of life setbacks (Verger 1993: 242). Those called to the spiritual vocation go through a seventeen-day period of ritual training during which they become a vehicle for the orisha that will be special to them for the rest of their lives.

In the course of initiation, sacred lore is transmitted about the orisha's greeting, gestures, rhythms, favorite foods, colors, clothes, medicinal plants, and other matters. An initiate learns to serve the orisha who mounts her or him, showing its personality through distinctive dance moves, expressions, vestments, and so forth. The vestments include insignia such as a double-headed axe, a fan, a broom, a bow and arrow, or other insignia depending on what item is associated with the orisha. The dance moves are performed along with specific rhythms and are accompanied by gestures that convey the nature of the orisha. For example, a person mounted by the feminine warrior Oya-Yansan would press forward the palms of the hands as though stirring up wind because the orisha is associated with storms and spirits of the dead. After the seventeen-day period the new Orisha Child consciously remembers nothing about the initiation, but continues to serve the orisha and gain deeper knowledge of its ways of helping people.

Candomblé is a healing religion. During a public ceremony non-members may join worshipers in seeking advice and personal help from the Orisha Children, who prescribe remedies. Each medicinal plant is associated with a particular orisha. Herbal baths serve as medicine for weight loss, menopause and reduction of fever or inflammation. In addition, herbs are used for illnesses such as rheumatism, liver and stomach ailments, anxiety, diabetes, hemorrhage, and whooping cough (see Voeks 1997: 170–191). Illness is interpreted as a symptom of being out of harmony with the spiritual realm. Orisha worshipers feel that one source of illness is neglect of one's duty to the ancestors. Thus the orishas are called upon for help in resisting political oppression that prevents people from practicing their traditional rites. Abdias do Nascimento (b. 1914), the Brazilian-born African artist and activist, appealed to Eshu for powerful speech to help him resist the violence perpetrated against Afro-Brazilians by death squads:

I implore you Eshu
to plant in my mouth
your verbal axé [vital force]
restoring to me the language
that was mine
and was stolen from me
blow Eshu your breath
to the bottom of my throat
down where the voicebud
sprouts so the
bud may blossom
blooming into the flower of
my ancient speech
returned to me by your power
mount me on the axé of words . . .
we are murdered
because they judge us orphans
scorn our humanity
not knowing we are
African men
African women
proud sons and daughters of
Orun's Lord . . .
O Eshu
one and omnipresent
in all of us
take to our Father
in your shredded flesh . . .
the news of our devotion . . .
overflowing with tears.

(Nascimento 1995: 15, 17)

As Eshu is associated with freedom fighters and communication, so each orisha has a specific function. No matter when or where an orisha mounts a person, the spiritual personality is said to come out looking the same. Orisha Children hone the beauty and power of these manifestations through ever-deepening experience in managing the protective energies of the orishas.

TRANSFORMATION: DAGARA INITIATION

The process of transformation during a rite of passage may be seen in the personal account given by Malidoma Patrice Somé (b. 1956), who was born in a village in Burkina Faso, West Africa among the Dagara people. Malidoma was taken against his family's will to a Jesuit mission boarding-school where he lived for fifteen years. One day he ran away and returned to his village. There he underwent a traditional Dagara six-week initiation. He went with five elders and some sixty-three boys (13 to 14 years old) from five villages. All the initiates were naked through their many trials, allowed only to cover themselves with leaves while sleeping on the ground.

> Nakedness is very common in the tribe. It is not a shameful thing; it is an expression of one's relationship with the spirit of nature. To be naked is to be open-hearted. Normally, kids stay naked until puberty and even beyond. It was only with the introduction of cheap cloth from the West, through Goodwill and other Christian organizations, that nakedness began to be associated with shame.
>
> (Somé 1994: 193)

Malidoma's initiation began with an exercise on vision. The elder had told the initiates the first night, "Tomorrow we will begin working with your sight . . . . When you have learned to see well, you will journey one by one to your respective places in this world and find every piece of your self" (Somé 1994: 203). The seeing exercise involved choosing a tree and staring at it. The initiates were not told what they were supposed to see, but they were to continue with the exercise until they had seen something. Malidoma chose a *yila* tree about ten meters high with thin and straight branches and a trunk less than a meter in diameter. He stared at the tree for five hours and nothing happened. The heat of the sun beating on his back began to disturb him. He began to feel helpless. Even after the whole day had passed Malidoma still did not see anything. One or two elders (who at times sang songs that penetrated his whole body) were watching him. Yet he could not see anything but the tree, and went back to the camp for the night. He resumed the tree-gazing exercise the following day. With four of the five elders watching him, Malidoma felt pressured to experience something, so he lied about seeing an antelope shape in the tree. The elders knew he lied and Malidoma began crying with humiliation. He began to speak to the tree sincerely and respectfully. His body suddenly felt cool and all the trees around were "glowing like fires or breathing lights." Then he had an experience of the *yila* tree that broke through his ordinary vision. Malidoma's *yila* tree began to look like a green lady who lifted a veil from her face. Malidoma described her this way:

> She was green, light green. Even her eyes were green, though very small and luminescent. She was smiling and her teeth were the color of violet and had light emanating from them. The greenness had nothing to do with the color of her skin. She was green from the inside out, as if her body were filled with green fluid. I do not know how I knew this, but this green was the expression of immeasurable love.
>
> (Somé 1994: 221)

Malidoma felt an intense, overwhelming love from the green lady. Only after the experience ended did he realize he was embracing the tree. He had been doing so for several hours, but the time felt very short. The immense happiness he felt from the energy of the tree was almost too much to bear. It taught Malidoma that there is a part in us that yearns for these kinds of feelings, but that part is not human. Reflecting on the experience in his account, Malidoma concluded: "If we ever understood the genuine desires of our hearts at any given moment, we might reconsider the things we waste our energy pining for" (Somé 1994: 222). That experience with the green lady of the *yila* tree opened Malidoma's sight and gave him knowledge that differed from Jesuit learning.

> It seemed to me that Dagara knowledge was liquid in the sense that what I was learning was living, breathing, flexible, and spontaneous. . . . It was not fixed, even when it appeared to be so. For example trees are not immobile, they travel like us from place to place. . . . The learning one gets from a book . . . is very different from the living, breathing knowledge that an elder has to offer – and different from the knowledge that comes from within, from the soul.
>
> (Somé 1994: 203–204)

The Dagara elders determined that Malidoma should re-enter the white man's world to transmit some Dagara knowledge. They said: "The white man needs to know who we really are, and he needs to be told by someone who speaks his language and ours. Go. Tell him" (Somé 1994: 307).

Plate 2.3 "Witch doctor." In the 100 years since this picture was taken how far have we come in dealing with stereotypes? Perhaps Malidoma Somé's story will help people of European extraction and others overcome preconceptions and see in this "witch doctor" just a human being who has a job to do. *Malidoma* means roughly "Be friends with the stranger/enemy" – and he was sent by his elder to the West to live up to that name. The Dagara chief told Malidoma: "The white man needs to know who we really are" (Somé 1994: 307).

ACCESSION: FON DIVINATION

Divination is a tradition common to many indigenous African peoples. Divination is a means to gain access to the unseen dimension of existence; hence it illustrates the expressive function of accession. The Fon people of Dahomey (now called Benin) in western Africa have three kinds of divination, ranked according to their level of reliability: (1) augury, (2) trance, and (3) wisdom divination, known as **Fá** (or **Ifá**) divination (see Zuesse 1985: 206–222, and 1995).

- ***Augury.*** Augury is typically performed by Fon heads of families and is the least reliable. It employs nonhuman agents for divination, including kola nuts, fowl entrails, mirror-gazing, water-gazing or spinning eggs. The diviner expects that minor local spirits can be called to dwell in the nuts, entrails, or eggs. A sign is revealed as the kola nuts are cast down, the entrails of a chicken "read," or eggs are spun around. The use of kola nuts is common among diviners in West Africa. Several stories are told to justify their special status: (1) they came from the "first" kind of tree, (2) they were originally the sacrificed body of a primal being, or (3) they were a divine gift to humanity. Nowadays, European-made playing cards are used for augury as well.
- ***Trance divination.*** Fon priests act as mediums for the purpose of divination. Ritual specialists are the "wife" of only one **vodú** (spirit). There are different types of spirits: (1) vodú of nature who can affect the weather, (2) spirits of specific localities that affect the condition of people according to their range of influence, and (3) spirits of ancestors. Across the countryside are shrines dedicated to various vodú. If people ignore them, suffering will come in the form of bad luck, mental or physical illness, and even death. Fon priests enter trances to find out from the vodú, or from ghosts (*gbô*), about the cause of people's illness and death. The diviner

might discover that a witch was responsible for a person's difficulties. (Witchcraft accusations sometimes pit one family or person against another.)

- *Fá wisdom divination.* Fá divination is the most highly respected form of divination among the Fon. The Fon ultimate divinity is Mawu-Lisa. Fá (Ifá) is Mawu-Lisa's messenger, and so is understood as the voice of divinity that brings harmony and wisdom. Fá is sometimes thought of as a weakling without arms and legs who cannot stand up. This amorphous Fá is superior to the vodú. Fá knows the fate of all creatures – even the vodú. The Fon ritual specialist is a **bokónô**. The bokónô are highly trained in sacred lore, medicine, and divination techniques. They learn proverbs and stories that help give the meaning of each sign revealed during the divination ritual. The most masterful bokónô have memorized some 600 verses per sign. The most accomplished African diviners who are involved in systems of wisdom divination travel throughout Africa to learn from other diviners.

  The Fá diviner uses sixteen palm kernels. In front of the bokónô is a rectangular wooden tray sprinkled with white powdered clay or meal. This is used to record the signs determined by the diviner from the palm kernels in the following manner:

  > In one hand he holds his sixteen palm-kernels, and with great rapidity brings the hand which holds them into the palm of the other one, leaving either one or two seeds for an instant before they are once more picked up and the process is repeated. As soon as he has glimpsed one or two kernels in his left hand, the right, with the palm-kernels, closes down upon it and the two clasp the seeds. The index and the second fingers of the right hand are, however, left free, and with these he describes marks in the white powder on the board in front of him.
  > (Herskovitz 1967: 210)

The result is a set of sixteen combinations of lines, each of which is associated with a vodú or group of vodú. The lines are interpreted along with a person's individual configuration of eight marks that serve as a life reading. Thus there are 240 major combinations of lines and the possibility for more permutations. After reading the signs the bokónô recites stories associated with the lines and sends the client to find various articles related to the prognosis. These will serve as the basis for a sacrificial offering and ritual healing. The articles may include such things as small stones, snakeskin, pieces of wood, and chickens. African wisdom diviners sometimes provide quarters where people needing attention for physical or mental ills can come for healing. They even exert a calming influence on the vodú themselves.

TRANSMISSION: THE LION KING STORY

In expressive traditions the history of a people is generally transmitted through stories. **Griots** are the oral historians in the African Republic of Mali who pass on the history associated with different social groupings including families, villages, and clans. The griots play a key role in shaping the identity of their people. A key story that griots have told for some 400 years is about Sundiata, the founding hero of the Mali Empire (ca. 1240–1500). The story of Sundiata reinforces the Muslim identity of the people of Mali by speaking of Sundiata as a descendant of Bilāl, the son of an Ethiopian slave. Bilāl was the first black African whose heart was moved by the qur'ānic message delivered by Prophet Muḥammad in Arabia in the early 600s CE. The griots say that Mali is linked to the Keita clan, which traces back to Bilāl. He had a voice so rich that the Prophet asked him to offer the Muslim calls to prayer. Thus he forever has the distinction of being the first muezzin. Tradition states that Bilāl had seven sons – and the one named Lowalo left Mecca in Arabia to settle in Mali. Tradition also states that just prior to the founding of the Mali Empire there were sixteen African leaders descended from Bilāl (Thobhani 1998: 5). Here follows the story of Sundiata in whose veins ran the blood of Bilāl's lineage.

> There was once a king of the Keita clan named Nare Maghan, who had several sons and daughters. One day a hunter from Do (a neighboring region) came to offer the king meat from an antelope he had killed in the king's domain. The hunter was

Plate 2.4 "Art from the Mali Empire." This sculpture was created around 1300 CE while Mali was at the height of its power – about 200 years before the start of the modern age of exploration. The Mali Empire (ca. 1240–1500) covered territory close to the size of Western Europe, and Timbuktu became a key center for the study of Muslim law. Today the Republic of Mali is among the poorest of countries. Most of its people farm without agricultural machinery and produce just enough to feed their families. Yet this statue dates from a time when Mali was the source of nearly half the gold known in the Old World. Gold was so plentiful that gold dust was the currency, and trade with gold nuggets was illegal. France gained control of Mali in 1895, and the country won independence in 1960.

invited to remain in the capital for some days – and in the course of conversation he told the king many things about Sumanguru, a neighboring ruler. This Sumanguru had obtained power through the **mantic** arts. He kept human skulls, sat on a carpet of human skin and used body parts from his enemies for black magic. The hunter said that Sumanguru was planning to extend his territory and thus would threaten the domain of the Keita clan. But after telling all these things, the hunter uttered a prophecy that gave Nare Maghan confidence. The hunter gave the following information: (1) Nare Maghan's successor was not among his living sons, but was yet to be born. (2) A hunchbacked young woman with bulging eyes from the kingdom of Do would come to visit with two young men who appeared to be hunters. (3) The king should marry her. (4) Their son would begin a great dynasty and make the Manlinke name live forever. (5) The king should sacrifice a red bull so that all this might come to pass.

The hunters of Do were renowned for their ability to predict the future by reading the patterns shown by cowrie shells thrown on a mat. Thus Nare Maghan believed in the prophecy and made the appropriate sacrifice. Several years passed before a young hunchback named Sogolon Kedjou arrived in the capital. Two hunters brought her as a gift to Nara Maghan, informing him of an old woman's prediction that the ruler of Do's ugly daughter would become the mother of a great king. They had chosen her (among the ruler of Do's daughters) as a prize for killing a terrible buffalo. Nare Maghan took the girl as his second wife. Soon she had a son – and because Nare Maghan's guardian animal was the lion he named the child Mari Diata, which meant "Lion King." (The boy was later called Sundiata.) The king's first wife was resentful and cruel to both the hunchbacked Sogolon and the little Lion King who was still crawling at the age of 7 because his legs were so weak. She mocked the boy for his bulging eyes, large head, and crippled state. When it came time to appoint a successor, Nare Maghan chose Dankara Touman, the son of his first wife. But it so happened that after his father died the little Lion King was gradually able to stand on two legs. He began to excel at hunting and quickly learned all the Keita traditions about plants and animals. Fearing that Mari Diata (Lion King) would take power from her son, Dankara Touman's mother plotted to kill the boy. Thus the hunchbacked Sogolon Kedjou escaped from the royal capital with her family in search of a safe haven. They finally settled at the court of Moussa Tounkara in a country north of Mali. The ruler adopted the Lion King as his own son and educated him in the ways of a chief. After many adventures Mari Diata defeated Sumanguru in a bloody battle and became the first king of the Mali Empire.

The story of Sundiata is a culturally rich oral text which preserves elements of Mali's culture and history. As always, stories like the one about the founding of the Mali Empire by the Lion King are a challenge to interpret because they mix legend and history.

BETWEEN OLD AND NEW

Modern Western culture has had a penetrating (and often devastating) influence on indigenous traditions of Oceania, Africa, and America. Yet it would be a mistake to think that any culture is purely "indigenous." Human beings are creative agents of culture. They do not rest – and their stories are filled with dynamic moments of culture contact due to migrations, business with neighboring peoples, encounters with foreign powers, and even worldwide electronic communications. Nigerian poet Wole Soyinka (b. 1934), winner of the 1986 Nobel Prize for Literature, noted, "There is a charge often raised against African poets, that of aping other models, particularly the European" (Soyinka 1975: 14). In defense he said, "I believe that society at all times is perpetually fluctuating and I don't think that any society at any given time has ever been without the old and the new" (Jeyifo 2001: 71). Each of the indigenous peoples treated in this chapter continues to grow and change. Some have lost many traditions, while others are reviving traditions.

Colonization of Oceania, America, and Africa by the Europeans had a devastating effect on all indigenous traditions from all three cultural areas. The European encounters resulted in a disproportionate loss of non-European life in the early modern period due to starvation, disease, forced relocation, enslavement, and armed conflict. Beyond enduring such tragedies, the indigenous peoples of Oceania, America, and Africa were subject to heavy-handed (though sometimes "goodwilled") Christian missionizing. As a result of religious conversions and intentional cultural destruction, a great portion of their expressive heritage was lost. In return Christian converts gained education, social welfare, and (arguably) other benefits. However ironic it may be, the early modern spread of English, French, or Spanish languages into European colonies now serves to link indigenous peoples with one another and with the rest of the postcolonial world. Ever new opportunities for communication may prove to be a "silver lining" in the cloud of past tragedies.

Table 2.2 Where are they now?

Group/Person	*Current situation*
Trobriand Islanders (Boyowans)	They famously adapted the British game of "cricket" to their own style. The tropical rainforest region is in need of conservation. There are four main islands: Kiriwina, Kaileuna, Vakuta, and Kitava. Ceremonial gardening is still practiced.
Aboriginal peoples	These comprised many different groups that went through massive depopulation through disease and shootings in the 1800s. In 1788 the British started settling. In the 1940s almost all were missionized and assimilated; they still face much discrimination.
Maori	Maori have pride in traditional culture. Some people are undergoing ta moko (traditional tattooing) and have interest in woodcarving; Maori are pursuing land rights legislation with hundreds of claims going back to 1840.
Sioux (Dakota)	A confederation of seven tribes that live mainly on reservations in Minnesota, Nebraska, North Dakota, South Dakota, and Montana. They perform the Sun Dance and other rites. In 2002 they took steps to save the Lakota language.
Navajo (Diné)	The largest group of Native Americans in the USA with 17.5 million acres (beneath which are tons of uranium, coal, oil, and gas). The Navajo language and traditions are active, and they are expanding territory due to growth.
Octavio Paz (1918–1998)	This Mexican writer, poet, and diplomat received the 1990 Nobel Prize for Literature. *The Labyrinth of Solitude* (1950) explored the Mexican identity. Paz studied Marxism, but was disaffected with it. Leftist Mexicans criticize him.
Candomblé	This has been called a "syncretic" religion with Yoruba and Roman Catholic components. Presently some practitioners are trying to go back to the African roots and remove Christian influences. The membership is growing.
Malidoma Somé (b. 1956)	Somé teaches Western people about his tribal rituals and makes necessary adaptations. The official language of Burkino Faso (Somé's country) is French. Religion is 40 percent indigenous, 50 percent Muslim, 10 percent Christian.*
Fon peoples	The Fon lived in Dahomey, now Benin. In 1892 the French conquered the Dahomean kingdom. In 1960 the country won independence. Religion is 50 percent indigenous, 30 percent Christian, 20 percent Muslim.* Belief in Fá divination is widespread.
Mali storytellers	Traditionally the Sundiata story was recited in marketplaces. French is the official language. Religion is about 90 percent Muslim, 9 percent indigenous, 1 percent Christian.*

* Figures from *CIA World Factbook.*

* could be important

KEY POINTS

- Starting around 1500 CE for about 400 years the traditions of indigenous peoples around the globe were deeply impacted by European colonialism. Nowdays many native peoples of Oceania, America, and Africa wish to reclaim portions of their heritage that were disrupted through economic, religious, and political domination.
- The ten elements of performance play a pervasive role in the creation of religious and social meaning in expressive traditions. Thus the religious practices of small-scale oral traditions may be understood through looking at their use of lived time, lived place, and lived objects as well as the seven expressive functions of donation, restoration, enactment, symbolization, transformation, accession, and transmission.
- Oceania is home to many indigenous peoples each with local religious variants. Among the religious practices in this cultural area are: ceremonial gardening on the Trobriand Islands of Papua New Guinea, ta moko (now stirring a new interest) and wood carving among the Maori of New Zealand, and myth-making about Eternal Beings of the Dreaming among the Aboriginal peoples of Australia.
- Although Native American peoples were relocated to reservations by the United States government in the 1800s, many are resurrecting or strengthening aspects of their traditional religions. Among practices that survived their political defeat are the Sioux Sun Dance and Navajo sandpainting.
- Sometimes even seemingly small historical events create a huge psychological and cultural impact on a people. Octavio Paz sees La Malinche (mother of the "first" mestizo) who was abandoned by Hernán Cortés as a decisive figure in the formation of the modern Mexican identity.
- Indigenous Yoruba-based traditions from West Africa impacted upon neighboring Africans such as the Fon of Benin as well as New World cultures in Brazil, the Caribbean, and elsewhere. Candomblé, for example, resulted from the transatlantic slave trade (which affected mostly West Africans).
- Some indigenous cultural elements are finding their way into non-indigenous populations. Examples are non-African Brazilians involved in orisha worship, North Americans fascinated with Native American rituals, and even Disney borrowing stories from Mali and elsewhere.

STUDY QUESTIONS

1 Name two culturally significant ways in which the indigenous peoples of Oceania, America, and Africa are alike. How would you expect them to differ?

2 Who held significant powers on the world stage in 1500 CE? How did Europe manage to "dominate much of the rest of the earth," according to historian Paul Kennedy's assessment?

3 Describe religious practices found among the indigenous Oceanic peoples of Papua New Guinea, Australia, and New Zealand.

4 Name four obstacles to understanding oral cultures faced by the student of world religions. How might a student of world religions deal with the problems created by these obstacles?

5 Describe religious practices found among the Sioux and Navajo Native American Nations.

6 Name some issues faced by indigenous peoples in the midst of defining their identities following the period of European colonialism.

7 Describe religious practices found among indigenous West African peoples. Describe some New World developments of Yoruba-based West African traditions.

GLOSSARY

aboriginal One who was there "from the beginning"; term refers to native peoples of a region, used interchangeably with the term "indigenous."

babalawô "Father of the secret," a priest of Ifá divination practiced among the Yoruba ethnic peoples of West Africa and people elsewhere (e.g., the Caribbean, America) who practice Yoruba-based traditions. Also known as *bokónô*, those who "repel" danger.

bokónô A ritual specialist (among the Fon people of West Africa) trained in sacred lore, medicine, and divination techniques.

Candomblé A Yoruba-based tradition in Brazil, related to other African diaspora traditions including Santería, Umbanda, and others. The West African spiritual system is known as Vodú(n), which incorporates the Ifá tradition of divination.

divination Foretelling future events or interpreting current circumstances through ritual methods that make use of signs and frequently involve supernatural communications.

Eternal Beings of the Dreaming Supernatural beings discussed in the sacred lore of the Australian Aboriginal peoples.

Fá Fon term for the orisha associated with divination, who is known also as Ifá, Orunmila, and Orunla. Fá refers to the Fon divination system.

griot A storyteller or oral historian among the Dogon people of Mali in West Africa.

homology (n.) A likeness between two or more things that have the same structure; e.g., Mircea Eliade speaks of the moon, the snail, and the bear as homologous because they all appear and disappear (Eliade 1996: 157).

Ifá System of divination that originated among the Yoruba peoples of West Africa, and is practiced by related groups including diviners among the Fon people of Dahomey (Benin), Candomblé diviners in Brazil, and others.

indigenous peoples Early inhabitants of a place who have a long-standing cultural association with their geographical region prior to its colonization or annexation as a modern nation-state.

La Chingada Culturally packed (nearly unspeakable) term meaning the violated woman, used by Mexicans with reference to La Malincha, the mother of Martín Cortés (sixteenth century CE) who is considered to be the first mestizo.

mantic (adj.) General term for practices related to divination.

mestizo Term of Spanish origin for a person of mixed blood, used with reference to Mexicans of Spanish and Indian descent, for example.

moko Term used by the indigenous Maori people of New Zealand for a tattoo.

native (n., adj.) Used with reference to indigenous, aboriginal people (i.e., people are native whose family line is traced to a certain place). No value judgment should mark this word, although in the past it (as also the word primitive) carried connotations suggesting that the native was uncultured, hence inferior.

orisha The spiritual beings of the indigenous Yoruba tradition of West Africa, and related traditions such as Candomblé, Santería, Umbanda, Vodú(n), and others.

People English translation of the term in various Native American languages, used with reference to themselves.

Sun Dance Native American ceremony including a dance in which participants face the hot sun for several days, and offer their flesh to the divine for the sake of their community.

symbol (n.) An object or act that effectively represents something else because it has a common structure; a symbol is the visible form that stands in for – or makes present – an invisible or abstract entity in need of a concrete representation. Religious symbols are distinguished from signs because they are associated with spiritual power and are generally created on the basis of hierophanic events.

syncretism (n.) The combining of elements from different traditions. Syncretism implies a thorough fusion, but the extent to which each element is destroyed in the process of syncretism remains a matter of debate. A "syncretic" culture might better be called "mixed" or "varied."

tapu (taboo) Term used by the Maori of New Zealand with reference to powerful (hence dangerous) things or situations that must only be encountered through ritual.

towosi Ceremonial gardener of the indigenous people of the Trobriand Islands (Papua New Guinea).

trickster A type of mythical character who plays on the border between the world of humans and the unseen world of the spirits or godlings; often a messenger; known for playing tricks, hence the name trickster.

vodú (vodoo, vodoun) West African term for spirit.

Wakan-Tanka Sioux term for "Great Mystery." It pervades and energizes the cosmos.

KEY READING

Best, Elsdon ([1924] 1977) *Maori Religion and Mythology*, Wellington, NZ: W. A. G. Skinner, Government Printer.

Carybé, Jorge Amado (1993) *Os Deuses Africanos no Canbomblé da Bahia* (African Gods in the Candomblé of Bahia), 2nd edn, Salvador: Bigraf.

Hultkrantz, Ake (1981) *Belief and Worship in Native North America*, ed. Christopher Vecsey, Syracuse, NY: Syracuse University Press.

Malinowski, Bronislaw ([1935] 1966) *Coral Gardens and Their Magic: Soil-tilling and the Agricultural Rites in the Trobriand Islands*, vol. 1, 2nd edn, introduction by Edmund R. Leach, London: George Allen and Unwin.

Warlukurlangu Artists (1987) *Kuruwarri: Yuendumu Doors*, Canberra: Australian Institute of Aboriginal Studies.

CHAPTER 3

Zoroastrian tradition

TIMELINE

	BCE	
	2nd–1st millennium	Āryans split to Iranian plateau and India*
Zarathushtra	1800–1500 range	Based on Bronze Age cultural hints**
Zarathushtra	1500–600 range	Based on *Gāthas'* Old Avestan language**
Zarathushtra	?628–?551	Based on date of Alexander's conquest**
Cyrus (Kūrush)	r. 550–530	
	550–330	Achaemenid era
	274 BCE–224 CE	Parthian era
	CE	
Kirdīr	200s	
	226–651	Sassanid era (used Pahlavi language)
	636 +	Arabs begin conquest of Iran
	936	Parsis arrive in India
	ca. 1300	Iranis withdraw to desert areas in Iran
	1858–1947	Parsis under British rule in India
Behramshah Shroff	1858–1927	
	1906	Iran Constitution allows religious freedom
	1925–1979	Pahlavi era in Iran
	1979	Islamic Cultural Revolution in Iran
	1980	Worldwide Zoroastrian Organization established

*Theories of Indo-European migrations are still evolving. See Box 3.1 and Box 10.1.
**See Box 3.2 for a discussion of Zarathushtra's life on the basis of this evidence.

People who worship **Ahura Mazdā** are the **Mazdeans** or Zoroastrians. Zoroastrians trace their religion back to Zarathushtra whose revelation from Ahura Mazdā is recorded in the *Avesta*. This revelation began what Zarathushtra called the **Good Religion**. The Zoroastrian religion stems from an older Āryan (Indo-Iranian) tradition that also formed the basis of Vedic religion in India. Mazdā worship spread from Central Asia across the Iranian plateau, and was adopted by two ethnic Iranian groups: Medes and **Persians**. The Mazdean tradition persisted in Iran and neighboring areas for over a thousand years under three Persian dynasties: Achaemenid, Parthian, and Sassanid (ca. 500s BCE–600s CE). Zoroastrians split into two groups during the 900s CE: **Iranis** (Zardushtis) who stayed in Iran, and **Parsis** who left Iran and settled in India.

PART 1
ZOROASTRIAN PLAYERS

THE ULTIMATE PRINCIPLE

Ahura Mazdā (Wise Lord)

Ahura Mazdā is the ultimate principle in the Zoroastrian religion. In the beginning Ahura Mazdā thought forth two parallel worlds: (1) the *mēnōg* or world of thought, and (2) the *gētīg* or world of bones (i.e., living beings). These are often called the spiritual and physical worlds. The first is apprehended by thought, the second by the senses. Together the world of thought and the world of bones make up the order of the universe. The Wise Lord is the eternal source of light in two worlds. Thus Zoroastrians pray in front of a fire or other source of light (e.g., the sun, a lamp) to activate the connection between *gētīg* where the fire exists and *mēnōg* where inner illumination occurs. The name Ahura Mazdā means Wise Lord. This name indicates a close connection between wisdom (symbolized by light) and Zoroastrian worship (centering on light). Fire worship of Ahura Mazdā enhances the human faculty of wisdom. Empowered with wisdom, people use free will to *wisely choose* to act according to the Good Religion by means of body, speech, and mind. Thinking good thoughts, speaking good speech, and doing good deeds help maintain order in this world, and spread the Wise Lord's illumination.

IMAGINAL PLAYERS

Cosmic twins

Two forces came into existence when Ahura Mazdā fashioned the world: a Holy Entity and a Hostile Entity. They are called **Spenta Mainyu** and **Angra Mainyu**. In the world of bones these twins represent the Truth and the Lie. These twins continually oppose each other in the *gētīg*, and at every moment a human being can exercise his or her freedom of choice to affiliate with either of them. Angra Mainyu is the chief force of cosmic and psychological darkness, while Spenta Mainyu is the prime manifestation of Ahura Mazdā's cosmic and psychological illumination.

Spenta Mainyu has beneficent entities called **Amesha Spentas** (Holy Immortals) who aid in the struggle against the Lie. These positive forces are associated with features of the (spiritual) world of thought, as well as things in the (physical) world of living beings. Zoroastrians contemplate and revere these Amesha Spentas. This means that people who worship Ahura Mazdā try to develop the characteristics of the Amesha Spentas, and help protect the aspects of creation over which they have charge. Zarathushtra named six Amesha Spentas who assist Spenta Mainyu, the twin of Truth (see Table 3.1).

Angra Mainyu has wicked *daivas* fighting with him. They are associated with things called *dregvant* (deceitful, wicked), such as: desire, wrath, bad thoughts, idolatry, and pollution. *Daivas* were confused about the true nature of the world, and made a wrong choice in becoming allied with Angra Mainyu. Likewise, human beings who use their free will to fight on Angra Mainyu's side are thought to be confused.

Table 3.1 Amesha Spentas (Holy Immortals)

Name	*In* mēnōg *(world of thought)*	*In* gētīg *(world of bones)*
Vohu Manah	Good Thought (Mind)	animals (cattle)
Asha Vahishta	Best Order	fire
Khshathra Vairya	Desirable Dominion	sky (metal)
Spentā Ārmaiti	Life-giving Humility	earth
Haurvatāt	Wholeness	waters
Ameretāt	Rejuvenation	plants (including *haoma*)

Thus the Good Religion counsels all people to gain wisdom, and to ally themselves with Spenta Mainyu the life-giving twin instead of with the hostile twin. People who ally on the side of Order are called *ashavan* (as opposed to *dregvant*) after the Amesha Spenta named Asha who embodies Best Order (often called Truth). The Amesha Spentas have helpers called *yazatas* who join the battle to defeat the *daivas*. But even more significant is the help given by human beings in resisting deceit, chaos, and confusion.

The *fravashis*

The **fravashis** are mysterious players in the Zoroastrian religion. The precise meaning of the Old Iranian word **fravarti* is obscure. The root *var* has several meanings, including: choose, cover or enclose, make pregnant, and valor (Boyce 1996: 118). One key sense is that they are female protectors, associated with the souls (*urvan*) of the dead. Each truthful person has a fravashi.

> The *fravashi* appears to have been conceived as a winged and warlike being, female, like the Valkyries, and an inhabitant of the air rather than one dwelling beneath the ground, who was swift to fly to the help of those of its kinsmen who had satisfied it with prayers and offerings.
>
> (Boyce 1996: 118 119)

The watch of the night between sunset and midnight is associated with the fravashis. These are the hours of darkness during which the *dregvant* powers seem to gain influence. This is before the forces of good begin gathering strength (between midnight and dawn) to eventually smite them in the light of day. In modern times the fravashis are invoked during marriage ceremonies. They promote the survival of families that are *ashavan* (truthful, orderly).

BOX 3.1 CULTURE CONTRAST: INDO-EUROPEAN TRADITIONS

Zoroastrian tradition derives from tribespeople whom historians call "proto-Indo-Europeans" (the prefix "proto" indicates a people who later became Indians and Europeans). There is controversy about their place of origin, but scholars have thought of them as Central Asians who moved into India, Iran, and Europe (see Box 10.1). In India the group referred to themselves as *ārya*, which connotes nobility or greatness. Other versions of the word *ārya* are the *irān* (after which the country Iran is named) and *eire* (which is the ancient name for Ireland). Many languages derive from the Indo-European people, including English, French, Italian, German, Romanian, Persian, Sanskrit, and many more.

The *Gāthās* sung by Zarathushtra and the hymns of the *Ṛgveda* sung by seers in northwest India are thought to be about the same "age" based on analysis of style, syntax, and meter. Some similar terms are listed in Table 3.2.

Table 3.2 Comparison of terms in Zarathushtra's *Gāthās* and the *Ṛgveda*

Term in the Iranian Gāthās	*Term in the Indian* Ṛgveda	*Meaning (G or RV)*
Haoma	Soma	Name of sacred ritual liquor (*G, RV*)
Mithra	Mitra	Guards cattle (*G, RV*)
daiva	deva	Demon (*G*)/God (*RV*)
Athra	Agni	Fire as the key ritual object (*G, RV*)
Asha	Ṛta	Cosmic truth (*G*)/Cosmic order (*RV*)
Khshathrya	Kṣatriya	Protector of the dominion (*G, RV*)
manthra	mantra	Sacred word (*G, RV*)

Sayoshyant

Zoroastrians believe that our world is in the morally degenerate phase of a great cosmic cycle. The Good Religion is disappearing, and Zoroastrians await the arrival of a savior descended from Zarathushtra's family. Tradition predicts that in the mythic year 11973 **Saoshyant** (Savior) will usher in the last days of the world year by leading a battle against the dark forces of Angra Mainyu. Ahura Mazdā will come to earth with the Amesha Spentas and *yazatas* to destroy the *daivas*. Stars will fall to the earth, and mountains will become molten metal. The dead will be resurrected from heaven, hell, and limbo. Ahura Mazdā will determine any outstanding punishments that are due to people. Those who have not yet paid for all their sins will pass through the molten metal to become purified. The molten metal will then be used to seal off hell after Angra Mainyu is confined to it. A special divine cow will be sacrificed and a drink that bestows immortality will be concocted from the cow's fat. Finally, the cosmos will be renewed. This restoration is called **frashkard** (see page 56).

EXCEPTIONAL PLAYERS

In the study of world religions it is impossible to have much if any historical certainty about the lives (or even the existence) of ancient figures. Many religious founders lived in societies that never recorded their deeds in writing. Moreover, when biographies were finally written they often took the form of archetypal tales that mixed elements of hierophanic and conventional history. The modern historian of religions Mircea Eliade made a comment about Zarathushtra that applies well to discussions of exceptional players from many world religions:

> It was normal for the historical personage Zarathustra to be transformed into a paradigmatic model for the believers who made up the "Mazdean religion." After a few generations the collective memory can no longer preserve the authentic biography of an eminent personage; he ends by becoming an archetype, that is, he expresses only the virtues of his vocation, illustrated by paradigmatic events typical of the model he incarnates. This is true not only of Gautama Buddha or Jesus Christ but also of far less influential personages, such as Marko Kraljevic or Dieudonné de Gozon.
>
> (Eliade 1978: 303)

Zarathushtra Spitāma

Some details about a person who calls himself "Zardusht" are scattered through the five *Gāthās* in the ***Avesta***. Because there are no independent sources of information outside the *Gāthās* from the same time period, some scholars think "Zarathushtra" is only a legendary figure. Yet the content and style of the hymns suggest that a single person composed them, and Zoroastrians attribute these hymns to their founder. Over time, Zoroastrians built on this Avestan core under the influence of literary material from the three Abrahamic religions. This biographical tradition began to develop after the Achaemenid conquest of Babylonia (538 BCE) when Persians were exposed to Hebrew accounts of their patriarchs. Zarathushtra's sacred biography was elaborated in the centuries following the production of Christian writings about Jesus of Nazareth (ca.100 CE), and Muslim traditions about Prophet Muḥammad (after 600 CE). Collective memories of founders are often created through such a lengthy and cumbersome process. Here are some details from the life story of Zarathushtra based first upon the *Gāthās*, and then upon later biographical materials.

Zarathushtra's story based on the Gāthās

Zarathushtra was of the Spitāma clan whose members were involved in horse breeding. They were herders, but Zarathushtra had few flocks and was not powerful or wealthy. Zarathushtra had two older and two younger brothers. He was married to a woman named Hvovi (possessing good cattle). Together they had three daughters and three sons. Zarathushtra's father was a priest named Pourusaspa (of the spotted horse), and Zarathushtra too became a priest. As a priest Zarathushtra would have chanted hymns while performing sacrificial rituals. Through chanting, Zarathushtra may have gone into an ecstatic state of mind, out of which he spoke in praise of Truth (*Asha*). This literal translation of one of his verses gives the sense that his tongue moved according to some form of inspiration:

> (Led thus to) the Best of this Most-Holy Spirit (he speaks) words with-(his)-tongue in-accord-with Vohu Manō, (and) with-(both-his)-hands the tasks of Ārmaiti he-fulfils, (inspired) by-the-one idea (that) Mazdā alone (is) the Father of Aśa.
>
> (*Yasna* 47:2; in Taraporewala 1977: 642)

Zarathushtra's words were transmitted by tradition in the Old Avestan sacred language (preserved in the five *Gāthās*). The *Gāthās* may be thought of as an exchange between Zarathushtra and Ahura Mazdā. Zarathushtra asked burning questions with a Good Mind. In return, he heard announcements from Ahura Mazdā. These inspired responses came through the activity of Zarathushtra's Vohu Manah (Good Thought). Zarathushtra's speech approximates to that of the ancient ṛṣis (seers) of India. Yet the Zoroastrian priest seemed particularly occupied with the tension between what is True and what is False. He asked Ahura Mazdā about good and foul things in this world. He was intent on understanding order, and sought to know the appropriate rewards and punishments associated with good or ill deeds. Zarathushtra was deeply concerned about his own actions, and prayed for guidance from the Wise Lord. He sang:

> Truly in my lifetime I have been condemned as the greatest defiler, I who seek to satisfy with truth those who are poorly protected, O Mazdā! With good apportioning of gifts come to me, support me!
>
> (*Yasna* 49:1; in Boyce 1984: 40)

Vohu Manah (Good Thought) is among the most frequent Amesha Spentas mentioned in Zarathushtra's songs. Vohu Manah is a divine entity that serves to guide the words and actions of human beings in this world. Thus as a priest Zarathushtra was preoccupied with the propriety of his words and ritual gestures. The Zoroastrian *yasna* ritual was supposed to be a replication of the primordial sacrifice made by Ahura Mazdā upon thinking forth the world. Thus the *yasna* included devastating sounds that Ahura Mazdā formed by thought into words of prayer. As the Wise Lord had stunned the foul spirit Angra Mainyu with words formed by thought, so Zarathushtra as a priest of the Good Religion was to help regenerate order in this world by the force of the ritual commands that Ahura Mazdā revealed to him.

Zarathushtra seems to have been a religious reformer. It appears that he redirected the priests and the people toward worship centered on Ahura Mazdā. He was disturbed by priests who sacrificed bulls and overindulged in drinking the intoxicating haoma.

Plate 3.1 "Portrait of Zarathushtra." Nobody knows what Zarathushtra looked like. In Persia the Sassanian ruler Ardeshīr II (*r.* 379–383 CE) commissioned a portrait of the Mazdean priest. In it light radiates from Zarathushtra's head to depict a powerful aura or bright halo. Around 1500 CE during the Renaissance in Italy (some 3,000 years after Zarathushtra lived) Raphael Santi painted a portrait of Zarathushtra. Santi gave the Mazdean priest a golden robe and put a globe into his hands. Sometimes portraits show Zarathushtra pointing his right finger toward heaven – as Plato was doing in Raphael's fresco – to indicate the prophet's interest in the spiritual world. How would *you* portray Zarathushtra? Note the **Fravahar** on top.

(During Zarathushtra's reform, haoma was not eliminated, however. In modern times a version of the drink is pressed from ephedra and pomegranate twigs.) Zarathushtra made enemies for criticizing aspects of the traditional Āryan religion, and urged his followers to take up arms to drive them away. He found an ally in the tribal chieftain named Vishtaspa who was converted to the worship of Ahura Mazdā. It is said that at the age of 77 years and 40 days Zarathushtra was assassinated by members of a rival cult.

Zarathushtra's sacred biography

Zarathushtra's sacred biography was elaborated over the course of centuries. Such is the case with biographical traditions of religious founders in many cultures. In addition, though some incidents associated with an exceptional person's life may not be historically plausible, sacred biographies provide religious meaning to a community and shape its values. Zoroastrian values are reflected in three themes that run through its founder's biographical tradition: Illumination, Struggle, and Devotion. Here follow a few incidents from Zarathushtra's life story that pertain to light, the battle between good and evil, and worship of the Wise Lord.

- ***Illumination.*** After Zarathushtra's mother Dughdōvā conceived, rays of light emanated from her womb. For three days the sides of their house looked as though they were made of fire. And three days prior to the birth, their village shone so brightly that the inhabitants left, thinking it was on fire. At birth Zarathushtra radiated light.
- ***Struggle.*** Wicked beings tried to harm Zarathushtra while he was still in Dughdōvā's belly. He was attacked again after birth, and went through numerous ordeals that nearly took his life. He rejected the *daivas* ("shining ones") worshiped by other priests, favoring their destruction by the *yazatas.*

BOX 3.2 INTERPRETATIONS: WHEN DID ZARATHUSHTRA LIVE?

No one knows when Zarathushtra lived, but people continue to look for clues in a variety of places. Depending on which "evidence" one uses, a person could place Zarathushtra anywhere between the nineteenth and the sixth century BCE.

Literary evidence (628–551 BCE). Zoroastrians say that Zarathushtra lived "258 years before Alexander," based on a literary tradition. This means he was active in 588 BCE. Some scholars propose the dates 628–551 BCE for Zarathushtra's life based on three further details; (1) Alexander burnt down Persepolis in 330 BCE, (2) Zarathushtra became well known at the age of about 40 when he converted Vishtaspa, and (3) Zarathushtra died at the age of 77.

Linguistic evidence (1500–1000 BCE). Judging from the archaic language of the *Gāthās,* scholars suggest that Zarathushtra's date could be moved back four centuries to 1000 BCE, or further still. One *possible* scenario suggests that Zarathushtra was born in the mid- to late second millennium BCE in what is now Kazakhstan/Tajikistan – the Central Asian lands east of the Volga River and north of the Aral Sea from which the Iranian people originated.

Cultural evidence (1800–1500 BCE). References to chariots and aspects of a new lifestyle in the *Gāthās* indicate the onset of a Bronze Age culture. Archaeological evidence suggests that the Bronze Age hit Central Asia between 1800 and 1500 BCE. Thus, by some estimates, Zarathushtra seems to have lived in Central Asia during that period.

The mythic view (b. 8970 of the "world year"). A Zoroastrian tradition dates Zarathushtra's birth to the year 8970 after the Ahura Mazdā's first *yasna* (sacrifice) that initiated a "world year" which lasts for 12,000 human years (see pages 55–6).

- ***Devotion.*** At the age of 20, Zarathushtra left home for a life of wandering. He spent a period of seven years in silence, devoted to contemplation. When he was 30, a revelation of Ahura Mazdā came to Zarathushtra. Eventually he returned to teach about this God, and present a new ethic for humankind. Today followers of the religion he brought add the respectful title *Asho* (Righteous) to Zarathushtra's name.

HISTORICAL PLAYERS

Cyrus the Great (Achaemenid era: 550–330 BCE)

A great man named Kūrush (Cyrus) (r. 550–530 BCE) founded the Achaemenid dynasty in Persia. His greatness was proclaimed even in the Hebrew Bible where Isaiah calls him the Lord's anointed one or messiah:

> Thus says Yahweh to his anointed one, to Cyrus whom, he says, I have grasped by his right hand, to make the nations bow before him and to disarm kings, to open gateways before him so that their gates be closed no more.
>
> (Isaiah 45:1)

The Israelites were living in exile in Babylon when Cyrus II (commonly called Cyrus the Great) came to power. (See pages 70–3.) Cyrus supported the exiled people from Judea, and sanctioned the building of a temple in Jerusalem to replace Solomon's temple, which the Babylonians had destroyed in 586 BCE. Archeological evidence reflects the Achaemenid familiarity with Ahura Mazdā, but not specifically with Zarathushtra. The Achaemenid rulers unified two western Iranian tribes: the Persians, and the Medes (whose hereditary priests were called **magi**). Zoroastrian magi were present at the royal court where they functioned as seers and counselors. There were two kinds of magi: *āthravans* who tended the sacred fire, and *zaotars* who offered libations and chanted invocations. The magi were well trained in fine details of ritual, which they performed at temples.

The three magi (Parthian era: 274 BCE–224 CE)

The Zoroastrian religion thrived under the Achaemenid rulers, but the conquest of the Persian Empire by Alexander the Great opened another chapter of their history. This was a devastating chapter, so the Persians call Alexander the "Accursed." The magi lost royal patronage when Alexander defeated the Achaemenid ruler Darius III, and conquered Iran (334–326 BCE). Zoroastrian tradition claims that Alexander's army slaughtered Ahura Mazdā's priests and set their scriptures ablaze. After Alexander's death, his vast empire was divided among his three foremost generals. General Seleucid got to rule Persia. Thus began the Seleucid era (323–60 BCE). According to Alexander's cosmopolitan value system, beliefs, customs, and peoples of eastern and western lands should be beautifully blended. And while his generals did not hold this view so close to their hearts, the Seleucids had a syncretistic approach to religions. Thus Persia produced a Hellenistic civilization from their culture mixed with **Hellenic** influences. In this environment the deities Ahura Mazdā and Zeus were identified.

The Parthian era began after one century of Greek rule under the Seleucids. The Parthians established their center east of the Caspian Sea in eastern Iran and spread from there. The Parthians favored the deity Mithra over Ahura Mazdā. According to the traditional Zoroastrians, Mithra was one of the *yazatas* in their spiritual universe. He was associated with the sun and with covenants. The figure of Mithra suited their imperial mentality, and worship of Mithra spread among soldiers not only of Persia but later all over the Roman Empire. The Christian Gospel of Matthew relates a story of three magi who traveled from afar to Herod's temple in Jerusalem. They were in search of a new king whose birth – indicated by certain astronomical phenomena – had taken place somewhere nearby (see Plate 3.2). The cult of Mithra was the most serious religious rival to Christianity as it was taking root in Europe during the latter part of Parthian rule. Members of the new Muslim religion in the 600s CE were also aware of the Zoroastrian priests. A passage from their scripture (Qur'ān 22:17) mentions the Magians along with Jews, Christians, and Sabaeans in speaking about the Day of Resurrection.

> Verily, as for those who have attained to faith [in this divine writ], and those who follow the Jewish faith, and the Sabians, and the Christians, and the Magians [on the one hand], and those who are bent on ascribing divinity to aught but God [on the other], verily God will decide between them on Resurrection Day: for, behold, God is witness unto everything.
>
> (Qur'ān 22:17; Asad 1980: 507)

Plate 3.2 "Adoration of the magi." The Christian New Testament scripture tells the story of three Zoroastrian priests who came from the east to pay homage to the Christ child: "After Jesus had been born at Bethlehem in Judaea during the reign of King Herod, suddenly some wise men [Greek: *magi*] came to Jerusalem from the east asking, 'Where is the infant king of the Jews? We saw his star as it rose and have come to do him homage.' . . . [Finding the child in Bethlehem] they offered him gifts of gold and frankincense and myrrh" (Matthew 2:1–2, 11).

Kirdīr (Sassanid era: 226–651 CE)

The old form of the Zoroastrian religion barely survived the force of religious syncretism in the Parthian era, even though large fire temples were constructed. The magi kept Zoroastrian ritual alive by passing on traditions from father to son through almost five hundred years of Parthian rule. When the Sassanids rose to power in 226 CE they aimed to continue the legacy of Cyrus II, and established the seat of their new empire in the old Achaemenid homeland. Sassanid imperial coins pictured their rulers as Mazdā worshipers, and the Zoroastrian religion was institutionalized by the royal court. It soon pervaded Iran and Central Asia. Under the Sassanid rulers, Zoroastrian priests were organized into two ranks: teaching and ritual, and in the seminaries Zoroastrian sacred oral tradition was consolidated into written texts. The Sassanid high priests gathered what had survived of the *Avesta*, and wrote it down using an alphabet based on Aramaic.

The high priest Kirdīr (active in the 200s CE) was in charge of the official Zoroastrian religion, and was committed to its domination over others in the empire. Apostasy (leaving the religion) was outlawed. Beyond that, Jews, Christians, Buddhists, and Hindus were persecuted. Kirdīr rooted out heresy, and condemned the prophet Mani (b. 216 CE). Mani was 10 years old when the Sassanids first came to power. His thinking was steeped in Zoroastrian traditions, but he wanted to found a universal religion open to all people on the basis of a new scripture. This approach represented a rejection of the official Zoroastrian institution. It also threatened Christians who saw Mani as undermining their teachings and influence. Mani was supposed to be the final prophet in the course of history, who supplanted Zarathushtra, the Hebrew prophets, and Jesus. When King Varahan came to power in 276 CE he ordered that Mani be crucified. The high priest Kirdīr was behind this move.

Iranis and Parsis

The Persian Sassanids gave way to the Arabs who began their conquest of Iran around 636 CE. From the establishment of the Umayyad dynasty in 661 CE to this day, Iran has been largely under Muslim rule.

Around the year 700 CE, Arabic officially replaced the **Pahlavi** language, and Islam spread. In the early 900s CE life became difficult for Zoroastrians in Iran, and many converted to Islam. Sassanid nobles and other Zoroastrians went into self-imposed exile to India, Egypt, China, and elsewhere. In 936 CE a core group arrived at Div, on India's western coast. After 19 years they settled in nearby Sanjan. For the next century groups of Zoroastrian families continued to migrate out of Iran. By the mid-1300s the Sassanid nobles who had fled through Central Asia to China had become culturally assimilated in those regions. Meanwhile those who stayed in Iran became known as Iranis or Zardushtis, and those who flourished in India were called Parsis (i.e., Persians).

In modern times both Parsis and Iranis have lived intermittently under Muslim and non-Muslim rule. The Iranis experienced economic difficulties in Iran under the Qajars (1796–1925). Meanwhile the Parsis developed a successful working relationship with the British, who replaced a crumbling Mughal Empire in the 1800s. Parsis in Bombay who wished to help their Irani co-religionists founded the Society for the Amelioration of the Zarathustrians in 1854. A member of the organization named Manekji Limji Hataria (1813–1890) helped eliminate the burdensome *jizya* tax from the Iranis in 1882. Thereafter, with British political pressure and Parsi economic support, the Iranis began to build schools and orphanages in Iran. In the late 1800s Irani priests began to go to India for religious education, because they had lagged behind the Parsis in terms of education, wealth, and social opportunities. The Iranian community grew fivefold through the 1900s, and re-established their own organizations to provide traditional instruction for priests. When the British left India in 1947, many Parsis moved from there to other parts of the old British Empire. Parsis who had moved to Africa to engage in trade under the British felt pressure there following the downfall of colonialism. Thus many moved to Western countries from Zanzibar, Mombasa, Nairobi, and Uganda.

The Iranis obtained religious freedom in the 1906 Constitution of Iran. Subsequently under the secular Pahlavi dynasty (1925–1979) the Iranis did well politically, socially, and economically. The Pahlavi rulers were affiliated with Western cultural and political interests on the one hand, and dedicated to Iranian nationalism on the other. They resurrected images of pre-Islamic Persian culture, and associated the Iranis with those ancient times. Following the Iranian Cultural Revolution of 1979, the Zoroastrians in Iran reverted to minority status. At that time, many Iranis left Iran for Western Europe, the USA, and Canada. In the late 1990s it appeared that many Irani priests in Iran lacked education, and none was qualified to perform the most sacred fire rituals. Moreover, not all temples had maintained their sacred fires. Today in Iran many priests and laypersons do not wear religious clothing. Some still flee to Turkey, Pakistan, and India – and then to Europe, Canada, and the USA. In 1980 the World Zoroastrian Organization based in London was founded to assist Zoroastrians worldwide.

Parsi innovators

Modern magi (*mōbads*) trace themselves back to priests in medieval Iran. Traditionally only males from priestly families could become priests. They must be ordained before puberty (around 12 years of age), and are at liberty to follow any profession. Head priests can be nominated or placed on the basis of hereditary family line, and there is no formal law of succession among the leaders. There is no single authority among head priests, but lower level priests consult the high priests. At present there are three levels of priest: a teacher priest (*ostā*), a first-level introduction (*ērvad*), and a high priest (*dastur*). Women cannot become priests in the Zoroastrian religion, although the scriptures do not deny their general status as equal to men. Yet, despite the traditional requirement that the priestly lineage be carried through male members of priestly families, some innovations have come forth from the Parsi community both in India and in North America.

Behramshah Naoroji Shroff (1858–1927) was a Parsi who introduced an esoteric form of Zoroastrian religion in which laypersons exercise religious authority. His teachings are known as the *Ilm-e Khshnum*, which translates as "knowledge of joy," or "science of spiritual satisfaction." Shroff traced his spiritual lineage through some Zoroastrian nomads who secretly taught him the deeper meaning of the *Avesta*. This happened on Mount Damavand in Persia. Shroff was silent for 30 years after his encounter with the sages. He then began to teach the *Ilm-e Khshnum*, which bears some kinship to Hindu values. Practitioners of the "knowledge of joy" believe in reincarnation and maintain a vegetarian diet. They take an interest in the esoteric (non-obvious) meaning of words in the Zoroastrian scriptures – including "joy" (*khshnum*), which appears once in the *Gāthās*.

In 1997 the North American Parsi community instituted a new category of priest, called the *mōbedyār* (semi-*mōbad*). The semi-*mōbads* are men ordained from non-priestly families who function as priests at the rudimentary level. The Parsi priest Behram Panthaki ordained Jamshīd Mistry as the first *mōbedyār* after the candidate underwent training according to a curriculum developed by the North American Mōbad Council. The innovators instituted this new category of priest so that local communities outside of India could benefit from traditional Zoroastrian rituals, such as marriages and funerals. The low number of priestly families among Parsi immigrants to North America had caused a shortage of persons trained to perform much-needed rituals. Thus the training of males from non-priestly families was a creative solution to a modern problem.

All Zoroastrian priests and laypersons are encouraged to live a married life, as traditionally Zoroastrians did not favor renunciation of the world. Iranis and Parsis living in Western cultures tend to recite their prayers in English, from a book called *Daily Prayers of the Zoroastrians*, translated by Framroz Rustomjee (1896–1978), a lay Parsi scholar from Sri Lanka. Zoroastrians date their calendar with the designation A.Y. from the coronation of Yazdegird III (the last Zoroastrian ruler) in the year 632 CE.

PART 2
ZOROASTRIAN TEXTURE

FOUNDATIONAL TEXTURE

The *Avesta*

The name of the Zoroastrian scripture *Avesta* means "Fundamental Utterance." This Fundamental Utterance is divided into five main portions: *Yasna*, *Yashts*, *Vīsperad*, *Vidēvdād*, and *Khorde Avesta*. Tradition states that everything except the *Vidēvdād* was lost when Alexander the Great overthrew the Achaemenid ruler Darius III, and burned his capital Persepolis in 330 BCE. During Sassanid rule in Persia (3–7 c. CE), what survived in the oral tradition was compiled, written, and distributed. The oldest surviving manuscript of the *Avesta* dates from 1323 CE, and the *Avesta* in use today amounts to about a thousand pages, which represents only a quarter of the original.

Linguistic variations in the text reflect material from different eras. The five *Gāthās* (whose seventeen sections in the Old Avestan language make self-reference to "Zardusht" as the author) are the oldest. These are part of the daily Zoroastrian *yasna* ritual in

Table 3.3 The *Avesta*

Text name	*Main contents*	*Comments*
Yasna	Invocations and ritual oblations recited five times per day by the magi	Includes Zarathushtra's divinely inspired seventeen hymns arranged in five *Gāthās*
Yashts	Hymns used in worship; each is dedicated to one divinity	Hymns honor Ahura Mazdā, the Amesha Spentas, and *yazatas*
Vīsperad	Invocations and prayers that supplement the *Yasna*	Recited at Gahambar festivals that honor the seasons
Vidēvdād	Code of ceremonial ablution, penance, and purification	Laws made to protect against visible and invisible impurities and evil forces
Khorde Avesta	Selections from the *Avesta* compiled in Sassanian times	Called the "smaller" (*khorde*) *Avesta*; compiled by Adarbad Marespand

a portion of the *Avesta* called the Yasna. The other Avestan material is anonymous, transmitted over generations by priests and scholars in the Young Avestan language. Avestan is strictly a ritual language. Zoroastrians believe that when properly uttered the *Avesta*'s vibrations create a channel between the world of thought (*mēnōg*) and the world of bones (*gētīg*).

SUPPORTIVE TEXTURE

In the 500 years between 300 CE and 800 CE, the magi produced several key works in a Persian dialect known as Pahlavi. (They are sometimes called the Pahlavi texts.) This body of supportive texture includes supplementary prayers.

The *Bundahishn* creation story

The main source for the Zoroastrian creation story is the *Bundahishn* (Creation). On the basis of this story the Iranians posited the existence of a world year that lasts 12,000 ordinary years. During the world year, Spenta Mainyu and Angra Mainyu contest with each other. Eventually, with the help of human beings, Truth will prevail over the Lie, and time will end. The restoration of happiness and peace comes at the end of this timetable, which is divided into four quarters:

- *1–3000.* Ahura Mazdā made the world of thought, including the souls of beings who later manifest physically in the world of bones. Angra Mainyu emerged from the deep and fashioned the *daivas* to attack the goodness of creation. The

BOX 3.3 A SPIRITUAL PATH: FOUR ZOROASTRIAN VALUES

Truth. The Amesha Spenta who protects fire is associated with Truth. Truth is called Asha, and is the greatest of the virtues. Every Zoroastrian child is taught to have the highest regard for truth. Truth alone brings happiness. There are four levels on which Asha expresses itself: (1) Physical Truth manifests as orderliness in the world; (2) Psychological Truth is Asha as human beings can understand it; (3) Spiritual Truth is a sense of righteousness that comes from deep within one's heart; (4) Divine Truth is harmony among created things, including human beings who recognize the physical world as divinely ordered.

Charity. Charity means to help people in need, and to treat livestock justly. It includes bestowing physical, financial, and spiritual help. A Zoroastrian prayer teaches that double of what is given with a good heart comes back to the charitable person. Zoroastrians build hospitals and schools, and dedicate a portion of their wealth to charity. They also make a point of giving to others on their own birthdays, and on festive occasions such as the six holy days of obligation known as Gambhars. The Gambhars originally marked the coming of new seasons, including mid-spring, mid-summer, harvest season, and time for bringing in the herds. They became associated with an Amesha Spenta, a virtue, and an element of Ahura Mazdā's good creation, linked to skies, waters, earth, plants, cattle, and human life.

Labor. Zoroastrians believe that God wishes for people to work hard and earn an honest living in the context of a married family life. For example, those who work the land should divide their time into thirds, giving one portion each to: (1) studying religion and attending the fire temple, (2) tilling the earth, and (3) eating, resting, and enjoying life.

Cleanliness. Pollution is associated with Angra Mainyu and the *daivas.* The concern for cleanliness shows up in many facets of Zoroastrian life, for example: (1) a bride and groom take a ritual bath before marriage; (2) ablutions are made before praying; (3) priests always wear white (a pure color) garments; and (4) it is a grave sin to pollute fire and earth, which are considered to be especially sacred elements.

Wise Lord (Ahura Mazdā) incapacitated the Hostile Spirit (Angra Mainyu) and the forces of darkness.

- ***3000–6000.*** Ahura Mazdā fashioned the world of bones in seven stages, with seven continents. Then the Wise Lord made one androgynous human being called Gaya-maretan (mortal life), one cow, and one plant.
- ***6000–9000.*** Angra Mainyu polluted the world and thus destroyed Gaya-maretan, the cow, and the plant. From Gaya-maretan's semen came a man named Mashya, and a woman named Mashyāna. Animals came from the cow, and cereals from the plant. This is the time of mythic events remembered by the Iranian people. The era of myth ends with the birth of Zarathushtra in 8970. His role was to bring teachings to the morally degenerate age that would inspire human beings to do four things: (1) desist from the Lie, (2) vanquish the Lie, (3) promote the Truth, and (4) ensure restoration of happiness and peace in the frashkard.
- ***9000–12,000.*** Zarathushtra began his religious work at the age of 30, as the last quarter of finite time began. Thereafter at thousand-year intervals three saviors should enter the world: (1) Ukhshyat-erata, (2) Ukhshyat-nemah, and (3) Astvat-erata. Zoroastrians say that Astvat-erata will be the true savior, and thus call him Sayoshant (savior). Sayoshant will begin the frashkard. Finite time will cease in the year 12000.

CROSS-OVER TEXTURE

Responses to the Abrahamic traditions

A Zoroastrian layperson named Mardan Farrokh wrote a text in Pahlavi called *Shkand-gumānīg Wizār* (Doubt-destroying Exposition). He defended the dualistic Zoroastrian theological position of good versus evil against Jewish and Christian attacks. The author considered the claim that God is all-good and all-seeing as false, because it could not be logically justified. He objected to all theological discussions that went beyond the scope of knowledge.

> So what, pray, is the point of obstinately discussing a thing which one does not know, of disputing and bandying words, and so deceiving the immature and those of immature intelligence? . . . Nothing can be perfectly understood except that which is completely comprehensible to the intellect and within its scope.
>
> (*Shkand-gumānīg Wizār* 102; in Nasr 1999: 60–61)

Beyond that, he treated topics such as free will, which is the key to Zoroastrian ethics. Mardan Farrokh's ninth-century text was considered so important that a scholar-priest in India translated the work into Sanskrit 300 years later. Other Zoroastrian thinkers wrote texts that responded specifically to challenges from Muslim theologians.

PART 3
ZOROASTRIAN PERFORMANCE

LIVING A SACRED HISTORY

The religious life of a Zoroastrian reflects three phases of sacred history: eternity, life in finite time, and restoration. (1) Remembering Truth and eternal goodness the magi tend fire. (2) Recognizing that human beings live on the battleground where good and evil fight, the magi initiate people into the Good Religion. (3) Believing in a restoration of eternity at the end of time, the magi perform funeral rites.

Keeping the fire

Zoroastrians do not worship fire. They worship Ahura Mazdā. Zoroastrians always pray in the presence of fire or light, which is symbolically connected to Ahura Mazdā. For daily worship it is acceptable to face any source of light, including the sun, moon, stars, or a lamp. In places where a fire cannot be maintained by burning wood, Zoroastrians tend to keep a small oil lamp burning. Three ranks of fire are used in Zoroastrian ritual. Each is in a fire temple identified by the rank of fire that burns within it. The three temples are: (1) *ātesh behrām* with the highest ranked fire; (2) *ātesh ādarān* with the middling ranked fire, and (3) *ādurōg ī dādgāh* with the simplest ranked fire. The fires are identified as the fire of Verethraghna, the fire of fires and the hearth fire. The basic Zoroastrian fire temple is a single room with four arched walls topped with a dome. Inside is a stone altar upon which stands a waist-high metal urn in which the fire is tended. Sixteen kinds of flame are required to consecrate a fire of the rank of *ātesh behrām.*

> The different fires now collected in practice are the following: – (1) The fire used in burning a corpse, (2) the fire used by a dyer, (3) the fire from the house of a king or a ruling authority, (4) that from a potter, (5) a brick-maker, (6) a *fakir* or an ascetic, (7) a goldsmith, (8) a mint, (9) an ironsmith, (10) an armourer, (11) a baker, (12) a brewer or distiller or an idol-worshipper, (13) a soldier or a traveler, (14) a shepherd, (15) fire produced by atmospheric lightning, (16) a household fire or fire from the house of any Zoroastrian.
>
> (Modi 1922: 212)

The 16 flames represent light from both the natural and social order of ancient Iranians. Fire is the most potent material in the world of bones – and a flame started from lightning is considered to be the most potent among flames because lightning connects the sky and earth. The consecration ritual for the highest rank of fire requires over 14,000 man hours reciting sacred incantations. It takes a pair of priests 1,128 days (i.e., 37 to 38 months) to complete the ritual. Once burning, it is a sin to let this sacred fire die. In Iran there is one temple for a holy fire of the *ātesh behrām.* There are eight more in India. The fire in Udwada (north of Mumbai) is known as the Irān Shāh. Tradition says it has been burning for a thousand years non-stop, and is relocated when necessary.

Initiation

Each person from a Zoroastrian family must undergo a "new birth" (*navjote*) into the Good Religion. The initiation ritual is normally performed when a girl or boy is between the ages of 7 and 12. The child first bathes, then drinks a purifying drink prepared by the priest. After being purified physically and spiritually, the initiate dons a sacred shirt (Gujarati: *sudre*) called the Garment of Good Mind. The priest then wraps a cord (Gujarati: *kustī*) around the initiate's waist over this shirt, and ties it. The cord is called the Girdle of Righteousness. The shirt and cord are worn beneath the street clothes. The kustī is untied and retied during prayers that occur five times each day: (1) sunrise to noon, (2) noon to 3 p.m., (3) 3 p.m. to sunset, (4) sunset to midnight, and (5) midnight to sunrise. When Zoroastrians retie the sacred cord they reaffirm their commitment to thinking good thoughts, speaking good speech, and doing good deeds.

Funerals

The Zoroastrian funeral ritual takes place within 24 hours of death, during daylight hours. At dawn on the fourth day after death, the corpse of a member of the Good Religion is taken to a tower of silence (*dakhma*) to be quickly devoured by vultures. A dakhma is an above-ground well, situated in a high place, with a paved platform with a circumference measuring 250 to 300 feet. The round tower has a pit in the center with drainage, and it is open to the sky. Males, females, and children each have a separated area around the platform, starting with the outermost concentric ring. The clean-picked bones naturally bleach under the hot sun. Finally, after 30 days, the clean, dry bones are swept into a dry limestone pit in the center of the dakhma. There they turn to dust from the lime's chemical action. Zoroastrians believe that these bones will be reassembled for the resurrection body at the time of the frashkard. To a Zoroastrian, pollution is *dregvant.* A corpse is considered polluting; therefore it must be disposed of carefully. Because both earth and fire are Ahura Mazdā's sacred creations, care must be taken not to pollute these elements. Thus a corpse can be neither burned nor buried.

Zoroastrians believe that their souls go to heaven, hell, or limbo, depending upon the extent to which they have used their free will to choose the side of Asha (Truth) in thought, word, and deed. At dawn on the fourth day after death a person's soul (*urvan*) is led to the Chinvat Bridge (Bridge of the Separator) that connects the world of bones with the world of thought. When souls of the righteous approach, the bridge

BOX 3.4 SYMBOLS: SYMBOLS OF INITIATION

Garment of Good Mind. The Garment of Good Mind is put on a child when he or she is initiated into the Good Religion. It is a white shirt, the body of which is made from a single piece of thin cotton. The white color symbolizes purity. The cotton is a reminder to protect the plant world. The single cloth means unity among good people. The shirt has nine seams, which symbolize the 9,000 years of finite time during which good and evil battle in the physical world. The first five seams stitch the sides, sleeves, and neck. The sixth attaches a semicircular piece of cloth at the back neckline. It is a small pouch that symbolizes a place where potential good deeds are stored. The seventh seam attaches a small rectangular piece of cloth (open in back) at the base of the V-neck at heart level, symbolizing a place for good already done. A straight dart at the bottom side symbolizes the physical world's imperfections. A triangular dart at the opposite bottom side symbolizes the past, present, and future because it unites the front (past) and back (future) of the shirt on the person who wears it (present). The garment gives protection in the midst of the battle, and enables the wearer to generate a Good Mind, comprising good thoughts (*humata*), good words (*hūkhta*), and good deeds (*huvarshta*).

Girdle of Righteousness. A sacred cord called the Girdle of Righteousness is wrapped around the child's waist three times over the white shirt as a reminder of good thoughts, good words, and good deeds. It is then tied with a simple knot at the back and front representing commitment. The cord is woven from lambs' wool from 72 strands that are grouped into 6 sections of 12 threads each. The 72 symbolizes the number of chapters in the *Yasna* text used for the fire ritual. The 12 stands for the 12 words in the *Ashem Vohu* prayer, as well as the number of months in a year. The cord has six tassels (three at each end), which symbolize the seasonal festivals, each of which is associated with one of Ahura Mazdā's creations.

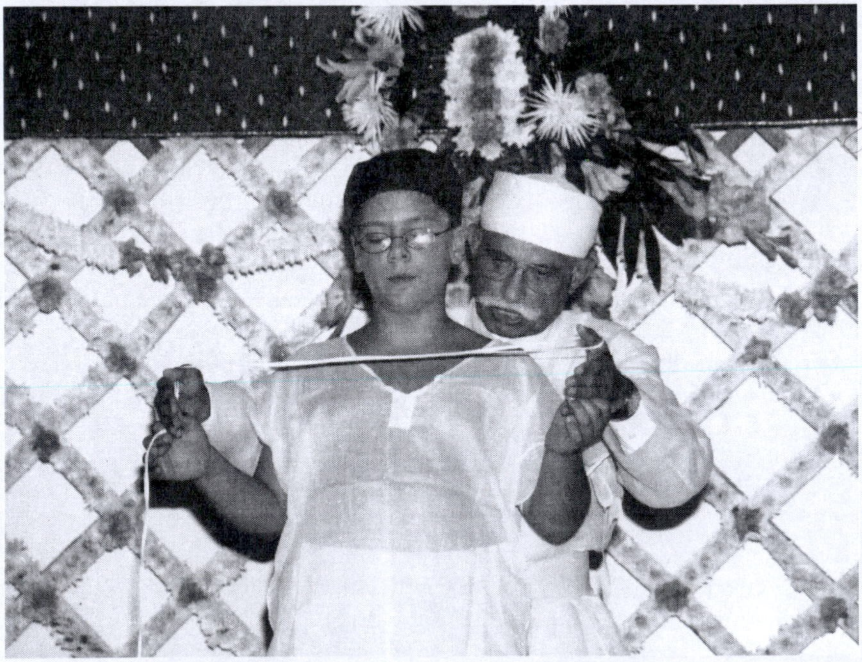

Plate 3.3 "Zoroastrian initiation ritual." Here a Zoroastrian priest puts the sacred cord (kustī) around a young person undergoing the traditional rite of initiation. Note the seams in the Garment of Good Mind worn by the initiate.

widens. But it becomes like a knife's edge for souls of people who have led wicked lives. Souls approaching heaven experience light in three stages of increasing luminosity, associated with stars, the moon, and the sun. In heaven souls experience joy, warmth, light, and virtuous pleasures. Souls in hell are tortured in darkness. Souls of people who have engaged in mixed (both good and evil) thoughts, words, and deeds go to limbo where they experience nothing at all. Souls dwell in their proper places until the end of finite time. All souls will undergo a final purification at the end of the world year when the world is made fresh.

KEY POINTS

- The Mazdean religion is frequently called Zoroastrianism after the founder Zarathushtra (whose name was latinized to Zoroaster). Scriptures call it the Good Religion, or *Mazdāyasna* (worship of Mazdā). Since adherents worship Ahura Mazdā the term *Mazdean* is suitable.
- Ahura Mazdā fashioned two parallel worlds. First came *mēnōg*, which is the world of thought (spiritual world). Next came *gētīg*, which is the world of bones (physical world). In the physical world the Amesha Spentas and *yazatas* battle the *dregvant* forces of evil, namely Angra Mainyu and the hostile *daivas*.
- Based on linguistic and cultural evidence in the *Avesta*, historians suggest that Zarathushtra lived sometime between 1800 BCE and 1000 BCE. Based on a classical literary tradition, some give his dates as 628–551 BCE. The earliest sources of information about Zarathushtra's life are 17 hymns preserved in the *Avesta*.
- For a thousand years the Zoroastrian religion developed in Iran under the Achaemenid (550–330 BCE), Parthian (250 BCE–226 CE), and Sassanid dynasties (226–661 CE). It sustained itself through syncretistic developments under the Parthians, and became an official imperial religion under the Sassanids.
- Zoroastrians split into two groups after around 700 CE: (1) Iranis (Zardushtis) who remained in Iran, and (2) Parsis who migrated to India. Both groups exist today, and have tried to maintain uniform religious beliefs and practices, in spite of separation and cultural changes.
- Fire is the central object of Zoroastrian ritual. It is the holiest aspect of physical creation and acts as the channel of life, protection, and strength from Ahura Mazdā. There are three grades of fire, and Zoroastrians pray five times per day facing a source of light.
- Zoroastrian ethics revolves around four key teachings: (1) truth, (2) charity, (3) labor, and (4) cleanliness. Practice of the Good Religion involves: (1) good thoughts, (2) good words, and (3) good deeds. Human beings have free will to choose between good and evil, and have a responsibility to bring about a cosmic restoration, the frashkard.

STUDY QUESTIONS

1. Name the two worlds fashioned by Ahura Mazdā, and discuss the relationship between them.
2. Who are the cosmic twins and their helpers? What is the relationship of these entities to human beings and to the natural world?
3. When did Zarathushtra live? (Discuss alternative views of Zarathushtra's dates.) What stories are told about his life?
4. Trace the development of the Zoroastrian religion in the Achaemenid, Parthian, and Sassanid eras (between 550 BCE and 651 CE). What happened to the Zoroastrian community after that thousand-year period ended?
5. What core values are set forth in Zoroastrian teachings? How are these tied into the Zoroastrian conception of divinity and the world year?
6. What is the meaning of fire in the Zoroastrian religion? What types of fire are used in Zoroastrian ritual?
7. What happens after death to a Zoroastrian – in this world, in the next world, and ultimately?

GLOSSARY

Ahura Mazdā Wise Lord. The ultimate principle in the Zoroastrian (Mazdean) religion that is associated with sacred fire.

Amesha Spentas Holy Immortals. Beneficent entities in Zoroastrian religion that protect the physical world, and inspire good thoughts, good words, and good deeds.

Angra Mainyu The hostile spirit in Zoroastrian religion who battles the "twin" spirit Spenta Mainyu in this physical world.

Avesta The Zoroastrian scripture; the ancient ritual language from eastern Iran used by worshipers of Ahura Mazdā.

frashkard In the Zoroastrian religion, the restoration or freshening of the cosmos after 12,000 years of finite time.

Fravahar A key Zoroastrian symbol of a figure whose upper body is a bearded man, and whose lower body is a bird with outstretched wings.

fravashi A spiritual being in the Zoroastrian religion who serves as a feminine guardian spirit.

Gāthās Five songs (comprising 17 sections) attributed to Zarathushtra that form the oldest portion of the Zoroastrian *Avesta*.

Good Religion Term for the Zoroastrian religion found in the *Avesta*. The religion is also called Zarathushti or Zoroastrian, after its founder.

Hellenic (adjective) Refers to the culture of the Hellenes (Greeks), as opposed to "Hellenistic," which refers to cultures influenced by Hellenic culture (e.g., fourth-century CE Persian culture).

Iranis Zoroastrians who remained in Persia following the Arab conquest in 636+ CE; also known as Zardushtis.

magi (sing: *magus*) Zoroastrian priests (now called *mōbads*).

Mazdean A person who worships Ahura Mazdā; also called Zoroastrian or Zardushti, and more specifically Irani or Parsi.

Mithra One of the chief *yazatas* in Zoroastrian religion, associated with the sun and contracts; became the focus of a religious sect that spread throughout the Persian and Roman Empires during the Parthian era (250 BCE–226 CE).

Pahlavi Persian language (also called Middle Persian) in which most Zoroastrian theological texts and religious commentaries are written, especially in the 800s and 900s CE; name of the secular dynasty that ruled Iran from 1925 to 1979.

Parsis Zoroastrians ("Persians") who migrated to India in search of religious freedom starting in 936 CE.

Persians A tribe of western Iranians; a name for Iran because the Achaemenids and Sassanids ruled from the southwestern province of Persia (Fārs); all Persians are Iranian, but not all Iranians are Persian.

Saoshyant Zoroastrian savior who will come to usher in the end of time.

Spenta Mainyu The Holy Spirit in Zoroastrian religion who battles the "twin" spirit Angra Mainyu in this physical world.

KEY READING

Boyce, Mary (ed. and trans.) (1984) *Textual Sources for the Study of Zoroastrianism*, Chicago, IL: University of Chicago Press.

Duchesne-Guillemin, Jacques (1973) *Religion of Ancient Iran*, trans. K. M. Jamaspāsa, Bombay: Tata Press.

Mirza, Hormazdyar Dastur Kayoji (1987) *Outlines of Parsi History*, 2nd edn, Bombay: Melhi H. Batliboi of Amalgamated Enterprises.

Mistree, Khojeste, and Shahzadi, Faroborz S. (1998) *The Zarathushti Religion: A Basic Text*, Hinsdale, IL: The Federation of Zoroastrian Associations of North America (FEZANA).

Skjærvø, Prods Oktor (2005) *Introduction to Zoroastrianism*, available online: <http: //www.fas.harvard.edu/~iranian/Zoroastrianism/index.html (accessed 28 June 2007).

Taraporewala, Irach J. S. ([1947]) (1977) *The Gāthās of Zarathushtra: Text with a Free English Translation*, Bombay: Dr. Irach J. S. Taraporevala. Reprinted (1977) New York: AMS Press.

Zaehner, Robert Charles (1961) *The Dawn and Twilight of Zoroastrianism*, London: Weidenfeld & Nicolson.

CHAPTER 4

Judaic tradition

TIMELINE

	BCE	
Patriarchs and matriarchs	ca. 1800*	
	ca. 1200*	Exodus from Egypt
Deborah	ca. 1200s*	
	ca. 1250–1020*	Period of the Judges
David	ca. 1037–967	
Solomon	ca. 986–932	Solomon's temple (ca. 960)
	922	Kingdom of Israel splits
Elijah	800s	
Isaiah and Amos	700s	
	722	Northern kingdom conquered
Jeremiah	b. 600s	
	587	Southern kingdom conquered
	587–ca. 539	Babylonian exile
	559–529	Cyrus II rules Persia
	ca. 516	Zerubbabel's temple built
Ezra and Nehemiah	400s	
	332	Alexander conquers Palestine
	142–63	Jews free under Hasmoneans
	63	Judea comes under Roman rule
	ca. 20–19	Herod enlarges temple

	CE	
Hillel and Shammai	d. ca.10 and 30	
	70	Herod's temple destroyed
	ca. 90	Tanakh completed
	ca. 550	Babylonian Talmud done
	630	Roman rule ended in Palestine
Moses Maimonides	1134–1204	
	1348	Black Death enters Italy
Isaac Luria	1534–1572	
Shabbetai Tzevi	1626–1676	
Baruch Spinoza	1632–1677	

TIMELINE (*continued*)

Ba'al Shem Ṭov	1699–1760	
Moses Mendelssohn	1728–1796	
	1917	Balfour Declaration
	1933–1945	Sho'ah (Holocaust)
	1948	Proclamation of State of Israel
	1972	Ezrat Nashim manifesto

* Current scholarship supposes that Hebrew patriarchs may have lived in the first millennium BCE – later than these dates that had been fairly standard.

Judaic tradition has a long and dynamic history, and what has been called "Judaism" might be better understood as a *collection of Judaisms.* (The following point may hold true for all religions. Religions are cultural complexes – not monolithic entities.)

> There is not now, and never has been, a single Judaism. No Judaic religious system recapitulates any other, and no linear and incremental history of one continuous Judaism is possible. But each Judaism reworks in its own circumstance and context a single paradigmatic and definitive human experience. . . . It is an error to view all Judaisms as a single unitary religion and to ignore the profound differences in belief and behavior among the Judaic faithful in times past as much as in our own day.
>
> (Jacob Neusner quoted in Smith 1995: 598)

Although there is nothing that properly should be called the Judaism, there is something that binds Judaic tradition together. It is a firm commitment to one God, to the Hebrew people who were chosen by God to follow his commandments, and to the land designated for them by God. **Jews** regard themselves as a people bound by covenant to the single deity whose law is contained in the Torah, which was delivered to them by the Prophet Moses. Commandments recorded in the Torah set the foundation for religious behavior, and a bond made with the Lord by covenant established the sense of **Israel** as a people.

PART 1
JUDAIC PLAYERS

THE ULTIMATE PRINCIPLE

Ha-Shem

Shema' Yisrael Adonai Eloheinu Adonai Echad. Every Jew speaks these words from the Hebrew Bible (*Deuteronomy* 6:4) to affirm her or his commitment to the one and only God. These words open a prayer known as the Shema'. The word *shema'* defines a Jew's relationship with the divine. It means *listen.* A Jew must *hear* that the Lord God is the one and only God, and *listen* to the Lord's commands. It is difficult to capture the full and true sense of the words "*Shema' Yisrael Adonai Eloheinu Adonai Echad,*" but they can be rendered into English as: "Listen, Israel: Yahweh our God is the one, the only Yahweh" (Bible 1993: 381).

In the Shema' the word for God is *'el* – who is called **Adonai** (Lord). The Hebrew patriarchs who settled in Canaan seem to have worshiped a "god of the fathers" who became the *'el* of the **Hebrew** people descended from **Abram** (ca. 1800 BCE). The Hebrew scriptures refer to this deity as **Ha-Shem**. But Ha-Shem never revealed a name for itself to Abram. Instead, it provided new names for Abram and his wife Sarai by adding the syllable "ha." The Hebrew patriarch and matriarch thus became Abraham and Sarah. By contrast, the deity did provide a name for itself to the Hebrew patriarch Moses (ca. 1200 BCE).

YHVH

The sacred name revealed to Moses is written as a tetragrammaton. The four Hebrew letters are: *Yud – Hay – Vav – Hay.* Jews never speak the name **YHVH** aloud. While reading the Hebrew scriptures the word Adonai (Lord) is said in place of YHVH. Only the high priest of the temple at Jerusalem would utter "YHVH" aloud – and only on the Day of Atonement. Traditionally, Hebrew was not written with vowels, so this name of the Lord has no vowels. YHVH is more like a breath. But the tetragrammaton is peculiar even in the Hebrew language because each letter can convey a vowel sound.

> The letter *yod* can indicate vowels of the "ay" and "ee" class. *Hey,* those of the "ah" and "aw" sound. And *vav,* the vowel sounds of "oh" and "oo." . . . They are the ether in which consonants linger, and the medium of meaningful sound. . . . [They are] like the universal noises of human emotion [and] the letters of the root of the word for being itself.
>
> (Kushner 2000: 120)

When Moses encountered YHVH on the mountain, he wondered what he should tell his people about the deity. He asked if there was a name he could tell them. The response came in the form of six syllables that tradition recorded as: "*Ehyeh asher Ehyeh*" (Exodus 3:14). This was YHVH speaking about YHVH. The phrase "*Ehyeh asher Ehyeh*" and the tetragrammaton "YHVH" are related through their grammatical roots. Because "*Ehyeh asher Ehyeh*" is in the imperfect tense it carries the sense of an action not yet complete. There are several ways the statement might be translated: (1) "I am who I am." (2) "I will be what I will be." (3) "I am not yet who I am not yet." (4) "I am who I am becoming." (5) "I am becoming who I am." (6) "I am not yet who I am becoming."

IMAGINAL PLAYERS

Angels (*malakhey elohim*)

Malakh is a Hebrew root word meaning "to send." The ***malakhey elohim*** are messengers of *'el,* also known as "angels" (based on a Greek word for messenger). The Hebrew Bible speaks of many such creatures, but only provides names for two: Michael and Gabriel. The **Talmud** adds Uriel and Raphael. The "el" at the end of these names means they portray something that comes from *'el* (i.e., God). Thus each of these four beings (sometimes called archangels) brings something significant to the world: Gabriel brings justice, Michael brings mercy, Uriel brings illumination, and Raphael brings healing. Angels are not worshiped in Judaic tradition. And in modern times the existence of the *malakhey elohim* is largely ignored, except among mystics. Yet their existence is not denied.

The belief in God's messengers seems to have entered Judaic tradition in the 500s BCE, during the Babylonian exile when members of the tribe of Judah were in what is now Iraq. There they had contact with Babylonians who believed in the Amesha Spentas, spiritual entities of the Mazdean religion. Not all Jews were receptive to the notion of *malakhey elohim,* and the level of belief continues to fluctuate. The medieval philosopher Maimonides theorized that *malakhey elohim* have form, but are not made of any material substance. He named ten grades of such beings. Occasionally the Hebrew scriptures state that one of God's messengers appeared in human form to someone. And while Maimonides speculated that such things occurred in dreams, other Jewish thinkers would not deny that *malakhey elohim* could appear physically to people as their scriptures indicate. Thus, for example, it became an open question in Judaic tradition as to whether Genesis 32:25–30 spoke of a dream or a live encounter between the patriarch Jacob and an angel that looked like a man.

Prophet Elijah

Elijah (ca. 800s BCE) was the first prophet not of the ruling class discussed in the Hebrew Bible. Instead of dying, Elijah was taken up to heaven in a chariot of fire. And he has a key role to play on Judgment Day. Elijah will return to mark the coming of the **Messiah** when the world ends. The Hebrew Bible says of this event:

> For look, the Day is coming, glowing like a furnace. All the proud and all the evil-doers will be

> the stubble, and the Day when it comes, will set them ablaze, says Yahweh Sabaoth, leaving them neither root nor branch. But for you who fear my name, the Sun of justice will rise with healing in his rays. . . . Look, I shall send you the prophet Elijah before the great and awesome Day of Yahweh comes. He will reconcile parents to their children and children to their parents, to forestall my putting the country under the curse of destruction.
>
> (Malachi 3:19–20, 23–24)

The prophet is expected to preside at certain Jewish rituals – being in the midst of many gatherings at once. Accordingly, during the **Pesach** celebration a cup for Elijah is put on the table and the door is opened to welcome him. And during the rite of circumcision an empty chair is set for Elijah in expectation of his arrival. Moreover, Jewish mystics claim that Elijah appears spontaneously on occasion to inspire them.

Sephiroth of the cabbala

The Jewish mystical teachings of the **cabbala** state that the divine light of creation has ten manifestations. These are called **sephiroth**. The sephiroth make up a Tree of Life with ten branches. The root of the tree is the first emanation known as Ein-Sof, which has no qualities or characteristics, and thus is equivalent to the principle of the universe. Ein-Sof is the colorless light from which all color emanates in nine sephiroth. Each of the nine manifestations is associated with a different color that reflects an aspect inherent in the unfathomable, limitless, universal energy of Ein-Sof. Jewish mystics contemplate the ten sephiroth as they manifest various qualities in four interpenetrating aspects of existence, namely: (1) the outer cosmos, (2) the human being as a microcosm, (3) the Hebrew scriptures as a microcosm, and (4) history. In all these contexts, they are paired in terms of male and female. Among the sephiroth are wisdom, understanding, loving kindness, judgment, beauty, victory, and splendor. Thus, for example, the cabbalists contemplate loving kindness and judgment as they balance each other in each of those four contexts.

The Canaanite *ba'alim*

The Hebrew scriptures note that while in Canaan the **Israelites** sometimes joined their neighbors in the worship of various *ba'alim*, or godlings. Certain ***ba'alim*** were thought to be helpful in promoting agricultural prosperity. Among them was the female Asherah who was a favorite of some ancient Israelites (2 Kings 21:7). Yet the Hebrew scriptures condemned worship of the *ba'alim* (Deuteronomy 7:5, 12:3; Exodus 34:13). Relating to any god except the single deity revealed to Moses was considered idolatry. Thus cult practices involving the Canaanite godlings were forbidden for the people of Israel.

EXCEPTIONAL PLAYERS

Abraham's lineage

The patriarchs through whom Jews trace their lineage are: Abraham (Abram), Abraham's second son Isaac, Isaac's second son Jacob, and Jacob's twelve sons who formed the twelve tribes of Israel. Abram, his wife Sarai, and their extended family lived in tents set up around the Mesopotamian centers of culture and commerce. They lived a semi-nomadic life, grazing his flocks, and possibly cattle. Abram's forefathers were among waves of Semitic migrants who moved northward into the Fertile Crescent, escaping the deadly heat and harsh nomadic life of the Arabian Desert. The date of Abram's wanderings is unknown, but in considering elements in the biblical narrative such as the domestication of camels, scholars now suppose that the patriarchs lived during the first millennium BCE.

Sarai and Ḥājar

According to the Hebrew Bible, Abram lived in the city of Ur (in present-day Iraq) when he first encountered Ha-Shem. Ur was among the oldest Sumerian urban centers on the Euphrates River, dating back to the third millennium BCE or earlier. The city had a palace, royal tombs, a ziggurat, and numerous dwellings. Abram's family included Terah (father), Sarai (wife), Nahor and Milcah (brother and spouse), and Lot (son of a deceased brother Haran). Terah thought of taking Abram, Sarai, and Lot to Canaan, so they traveled north along the Euphrates River. Upon reaching Haran, Terah decided to settle in that lush grazing territory for their flocks and cattle. After some time Ha-Shem, the Lord, appeared to Abram and instructed him to leave his father's household and set out for a place that would be specified later. Thus when Abram was 75 years old he, Sarai, and Lot left Haran, taking all the possessions and people they had acquired. Upon arriving in Canaan, Ha-Shem indicated that the land would be for his descendants. The Hebrew Bible says:

> Abram passed through the country as far as the holy place at Shechem, the Oak of Moreh. The Canaanites were in the country at the time. Yahweh appeared to Abram and said, "I shall give this country to your progeny." And there, Abram built an altar to Yahweh who had appeared to him.
>
> (Genesis 12:6–7)

After Ha-Shem made a promise of the land, Abram continued moving south. He built another altar near Bethel, and eventually entered Egypt to escape famine. One night Abram contemplated the heavens, and heard from Ha-Shem that his offspring would be as numerous as the stars in the night sky. While Abram and Sarai had no offspring, he was uncertain to whom Ha-Shem was giving the promised land. As Sarai was barren, she dedicated Ḥājar (her Egyptian maidservant) to Abram so that they might build a family through her. Ḥājar conceived, and their son was named Ishmael (Genesis 16:2–5). When Ishmael was 13 years old Ha-Shem appeared again to Abram. During this hierophanic encounter the Lord promised that Sarai would bear a son and become the mother of nations. At that time Abram was 99 years old and Sarai about ten years younger. The Lord renamed the couple "Abraham" and "Sarah," designated their future son's name as "Isaac" – and promised to establish a covenant through the child. Thinking of his first son, Abraham cried out, "If only Ishmael might live under your blessing!" In reply the Lord promised:

> For Ishmael too I grant you your request. I hereby bless him and will make him fruitful and exceedingly numerous. He will be the father of twelve princes, and I shall make him into a great nation. But my covenant I shall maintain with Isaac, whom Sarah will bear you at this time next year.
>
> (Genesis 17:20–21)

At that time, there in Canaan, the Lord also declared:

> And to you and to your descendants after you, I shall give the country where you are now immigrants, the entire land of Canaan, to own in perpetuity. And I shall be their God. . . . You for your part must keep my covenant, you and your descendants after you, generation after generation. . . . As soon as he is eight days old, every one of your males, generation after generation, must be circumcised.
>
> (Genesis 17:8–9, 12)

Following Ha-Shem's order, Abraham and his son Ishmael were both circumcised on the same day. In due time, Abraham's wife Sarah had the son that had been anticipated for many long years. He was named Isaac. And he was welcomed as the person through whom the Lord would bind a relationship with the Hebrew people.

Isaac and Ishmael

Among pastoral nomads each head of the family sacrificed his first-born animals in the springtime. Sacrifices involved pouring the blood and burning the flesh of sheep, goats, or cattle whose essence wafted upward in the smoke. In accord with custom, Abraham was used to making ritual sacrifices. (The custom continued in Judaic tradition for generations until the destruction of Herod's temple in Jerusalem in 70 CE.) But according to the Hebrew scriptures, one day Abraham was told to make a human sacrifice. The Lord commanded Abraham to go to the region of Moriah and sacrifice Isaac there as a burnt offering. It took Abraham three days to arrive at the place. Once on Mount Moriah, Abraham loaded the wood on to Isaac's back while he took the fire and the knife. Seeing that there was no animal for the sacrifice Isaac was puzzled.

> Isaac spoke to his father Abraham. "Father?" he said. "Yes, my son," he replied. "Look," he said, "here are the fire and the wood, but where is the

> lamb for the burnt offering?" Abraham replied, "My son, God himself will provide the lamb for the burnt offering."
>
> (Genesis 22:7–8)

Abraham was at the point of slaying Isaac with the sacrificial knife when an angel commanded him to stop. When Abraham looked up he saw a ram caught by its horns in a thicket. Abraham freed Isaac and sacrificed the ram instead. God's messenger approved. Genesis never says how Isaac felt about all of this, but it reports that Isaac kept in touch with his older brother Ishmael. And when the time came, both Isaac and Ishmael buried their father Abraham in the cave where Sarah already lay.

Jacob and Esau

Isaac and his wife Rebekah had twins, Esau the first-born, and Jacob who followed grasping his brother's heel. Rebekah favored Jacob, and many years later helped him get the family inheritance in spite of being the second son. In his old age Isaac's eyesight was failing, and so he was tricked into passing the birthright to Jacob. After the ruse, Rebekah urged him to flee and take refuge with her brother in Haran to keep him safe from Esau's revenge. On the way Jacob had a hierophanic experience. As he lay to rest with his head on a stone he dreamed of a ladder reaching from earth to heaven with angels coming up and down on it. HaShem stood above and granted Jacob's descendants the land upon which he was lying. The next morning Jacob made the stone into a shrine. Eventually Jacob had a daughter named Dinah and twelve sons by his wives Leah and Rachel, and their maidservants Zilpah and Bilhah (Genesis 29:23–35, 30:1–22). Reuben, Simeon, Levi, Judah, Issachar, Zebulun, and Dinah were born from Leah. Bilhah gave birth to Dan and Naphtali. Gad and Asher were from Zilpah's womb. And finally Rachel (whom Jacob loved best of all) gave birth to Joseph and Benjamin. The twelve sons became patriarchs of the twelve tribes of the Hebrew people. Eventually Jacob was blessed with the name Israel, meaning struggle. This was after he wrestled all night with an angel who appeared in the form of a man. In turn, Jews call themselves *b'nei Yisrael* (children of Israel) after Jacob who was called Israel because he "struggled" with the Lord.

Early Israelite leaders

Moses is the person through whom the Israelite tradition was shaped in detail. Traditionally Jews consider that the Torah contains the literal word of YHVH as transmitted through Moses. After Moses, subsequent leaders had to ensure that Israelite life was carried on according to Mosaic law. There were three kinds of early Israelite leaders: judges, kings, and prophets. Judges and kings governed, while prophets warned them when politics and social life appeared to deviate from religious law.

Moses

Some scholars view "Moses" as a composite figure, stories of whom come from various cultural traditions of West Asia. Moses is known in scripture as the Hebrew prophet of the **Exodus**. The Torah says that the divine name YHVH was revealed to Moses (Exodus 3:13–15), and the Lord instructed Moses to lead the Israelites out of Egypt to escape their servitude under the pharaoh's rule. By some miracles of the Lord, the Israelites escaped. Thereafter Moses (and his siblings Aaron and Miriam) lived with their people in the desert for forty years. According to the Hebrew scriptures, three months after leaving Egypt, Moses encountered the deity on Mount Sinai. The deity impelled Moses to prepare his people to witness YHVH's descent on to the mountain top. At daybreak two days after this command, the Israelites experienced a fierce storm of thunder and lightning. Moses ascended the mountain, and the Lord issued commandments that were to guide the behavior of the Israelites from that point forward (Exodus 20:1–17). Thus Moses was transformed into a law-giver for the Hebrew people. These are the fundamental ten **mitzvoth** issued by YHVH. (In this list the author removed the "o" from the word *God* out of respect for the sanctity of the name, which cannot be pronounced without the vowel.)

1 I am the L-rd your G-d – There is only one G-d, The L-rd.

2 You will have no other gods – neither in belief nor through an act of worship.
3 You shall not pronounce the Holy Name of G-d needlessly.
4 Remember the **Sabbath** day to sanctify it, by ceasing productive labour and dedicating it to spiritual rest.
5 Honour your father and mother.
6 Do not murder.
7 Do not commit any act of adultery.
8 Do not steal.
9 Do not testify as a false witness against your neighbor.
10 Do not covet your neighbor's possessions.

(Altmann 1985: 21)

On the basis of the new law, Moses reorganized the ethical and ritual life of the Israelites. In his attempt to reform Israelite ritual, Moses battled those who would not succumb to the Lord's command to give up idol worship. The ritual known as Pesach (Passover) commemorates the miraculous escape of the Israelites from Egypt.

Judges

Moses himself never entered Canaan. However, before the twelve tribes of Israel settled there, Moses appointed their elders to serve as judges to help clarify the law. Joshua was the successor who led the Israelites into Canaan. He divided the territory they inhabited among the twelve tribes. In that new society, the judges began to administer the Mosaic law. Eventually the function of the judges was passed to a Supreme Court known as the Sanhedrin, which operated for over five centuries as a legal governing body.

A prophet named Samuel organized the Israelite tribes to fight against the Philistines, a sea people who settled in southern Palestine around the 1100s BCE.

BOX 4.1 CULTURE CONTRAST: SCRIPTURAL PARALLELS FROM THE ANCIENT NEAR EAST

Scriptural material from the Hebrew Bible echoes portions of other documents from the ancient Near East (see Pritchard 1950, 1955). Two instances of parallels are: (1) the mitzvoth given to Moses and a list of confessions from the Egyptian *Book of the Dead*; and (2) the flood stories from Genesis and a Babylonian text known as the *Gilgamesh Epic*.

The Ten Commandments. A group of Egyptian mortuary texts (usually written on papyrus) were gathered by modern scholars into a volume called the *Book of the Dead*. The 125th chapter is often called "The Protestation of Guiltlessness" because it outlines sinful acts that the person refrained from doing. The chapter presents a "negative confession" including the following verses to be recited by a deceased person to earn a favorable position in the afterlife:

> (I) have not lied nor sinned against anyone. I have not oppressed dependants. I have not done crookedness instead of truth. I know not sin; I have not done anything evil. . . . I have not done what the gods abominate. . . . I have not caused (anyone) to go hungry; I have not (caused anyone) to weep. I have not killed; I have not {commanded} killing unjustly. I have not done injustice to anyone. I have not {diminished} the food (-offerings) in the temples; . . . I have not copulated (illicitly). . . . I have not increased nor diminished measures. . . . I have not taken milk from a child's mouth.
>
> (*Book of the Dead* 125a, in Allen 1960: 196)

"The Protestation of Guiltlessness" dates from the eighteenth to twenty-first dynasties (1550–950 BCE) – a period during which Moses is thought to have lived. The key Hebrew mitzvoth that are frequently called The Ten Commandments resemble ethical principles found in the Egyptian *Book of the Dead*. Here follow some commandments which Moses presented to the Hebrews after leaving Egypt.

> I am the LORD your God who brought you out of Egypt, out of the land of slavery. . . . Honour your father and your mother, so that you may enjoy long life in the land which the LORD your God is giving to you. Do not commit murder. Do not commit adultery. Do not steal. Do not give false evidence against your neighbour. Do not covet your neighbour's household: you must not covet your neighbour's wife, his slave, his slave-girl, his ox, his donkey, or anything that belongs to him.
>
> (Exodus 20:2, 12–17, from the Revised English Bible)

The flood story. Both the Hebrew Bible and the Babylonian *Gilgamesh Epic* have flood stories with a remarkable number of details in common. The possibility of a historical connection between the texts is suggested by the fact that around 2600 BCE Gilgamesh was a king who built walls around the city of Erech (modern Warka) on the Euphrates River 120 miles from Babylon. This is near Ur, the place where (according to the Hebrew Bible) Abraham originally lived. Erech was one of the oldest Sumerian urban centers dating from the fourth millennium BCE. Both Noah of the Hebrew Bible and Utnapishtim of the *Gilgamesh Epic* were given divine advice to build boats to save themselves and creatures from a devastating flood.

> [The Lord Ea told Utnapishtim:]
> Tear down (this) house, build a ship! . . .
> Aboard the ship take thou the seed of all living things.
> The ship that thou shalt build,
> Her dimensions shall be to measure.
> Equal shall be her width and her length.
>
> (*Gilgamesh tablet XI*, in Pritchard 1950, 1955: 93–95)

> God said to Noah, . . . Make yourself an ark out of resinous wood. . . . [T]he length of the ark is to be three hundred cubits, its breadth fifty cubits, and its height thirty cubits. . . . From all living creatures, from all living things, you must take two of each kind aboard the ark, to save their lives with yours.
>
> (Genesis 6:13–15, 19)

Both Utnapishtim and Noah obeyed their deity and survived the devastating floods with the help of a bird whose disappearance in flight indicated that land was near.

According to the Hebrew scriptures, Samuel anointed a tall, handsome, and popular leader named Saul as the first Israelite king. Historians prefer to think of Saul as a powerful judge rather than as an actual monarch. Judge Saul managed to gain control beyond his local territory, and set the stage for unification under monarchic rule. Due to economic pressures the dispersed Israelite agricultural settlements were becoming less viable, and the time was ripe for a new political structure. Saul recruited members of his own tribe of Benjamin to provide for a successor. Thus one unlikely recruit was his son's close friend David from the tribe of Judah. The young David eventually became king – but only after a series of interpersonal troubles: (1) Samuel became alienated from Saul; (2) Saul became alienated from David; (3) David shifted his allegiance to Samuel, fled into Philistine territory, and attacked the Israelites loyal to Saul; (4) Saul fell on his sword to commit suicide; (5) Saul's fourth son Ishbaal became the next Israelite leader; (6) David defeated Ishbaal, and became the first Israelite monarch.

David and Solomon

David (d. 900s BCE) had been a shepherd. He served as Saul's royal attendant and bearer of arms, and became famous for slaying a giant of a man named Goliath. (Some who take this story as historical fact speculate that Goliath had acromegaly, a glandular dysfunction causing the body to overmanufacture growth hormones.) In a fight of brains over brawn,

Plate 4.1 "King David." Over the centuries artists have been fascinated with the figure of the Israelite King David. This plate shows an ultra-modern rendering of David. It is a computer-generated image of a three-dimensional geometric model of the head of Michelangelo's "David." Michelangelo worked on his sculpture from 1501 to 1504. The computer work has been done as part of "The Michelangelo Project" undertaken at Stanford University.

David shot Goliath in the forehead with his slingshot and cut off his head with the Philistine giant's own sword. Whether or not this incident is historically true, it appears that Saul became jealous of David's popularity. David fled and associated himself with a faction of priests headed by Samuel. As Samuel had anointed Saul, now he anointed David in Saul's place. David gained control over the northern and southern territories of Israel and Judah. But he was a poet as well as a military man. Many psalms in the Hebrew Bible are in David's name. He transferred the **Ark** from Shiloh to Jerusalem, making Jerusalem the political and religious center of a united Israelite kingdom. David danced at the head of the procession wearing the linen garment reserved for priests. His heartfelt wish was to establish a place for worship of the Lord of the Israelites (1 Kings 8:41–43). But it would be left to David's son Solomon to accomplish this.

King Solomon built the temple to YHVH in Jerusalem around 1000 BCE in the period of Israel's glory. According to the Hebrew scriptures, Solomon had 700 wives and 300 concubines. Many of these alliances cemented political ties with neighboring kingdoms such as Egypt and Phoenicia. Like his father, Solomon ruled from Jerusalem for four decades. The Israelite tribes from the north and south remained united under Solomon, and both prospered through the spice trade from southern Arabia and eastern Africa. Certain items that were useful for war and some for peace also exchanged hands under his watch: horses, chariots, iron, copper, gold, ivory, gems, and rare birds. The wisdom of Solomon is legendary. Many proverbs in the Hebrew Bible are attributed to this son of the poet David. After Solomon died, his son Rehoboam became monarch. King Rehoboam was unable to keep the twelve old tribal territories united. Thus in 922 BCE Solomon's internationally renowned kingdom split into the northern kingdom of Israel, and the southern kingdom of Judah. Rehoboam and others of the Davidic lineage maintained control over the kingdom of Judah from their seat in Jerusalem. Meanwhile the northern kingdom of Israel had its own series of rulers for precisely two centuries.

Prophets and a prophetess

The era of Israelite prophecy spanned six centuries from the time of the early judges to the end of the Israelite monarchy (ca. 1250–587 BCE). It ended when the Babylonians destroyed Solomon's temple in 587 BCE. Israelites believed that the Lord had stopped communicating with the people of Israel through human beings. Among the last prophets were Jeremiah and Ezekiel, two men who warned about the destruction of Solomon's temple. Among the prophets, Moses alone had a direct verbal exchange with the deity. Otherwise, the Lord's message was received through dreams, visions, or ecstatic states of consciousness. The Hebrew scriptures mention fifty-five prophetic figures, including seven women. Their stories contain many prophetic warnings – some of which actually "came true" in history. This correspondence between historical reality and the recorded prophecies may indicate that the stories were written down after the historical events came to pass. Regardless of the dates when the texts were collected and written down, traditional Jews accept stories in the Hebrew Bible as divinely inspired. During the 600 years of the prophetic era, there were long stretches when no prophet appeared – particularly between the time of Deborah and Amos.

Deborah

Deborah (ca. 1200s BCE) was the only woman judge in Israelite history. Like the other judges, she played both a political-military and a religious role in serving her people. A poem by this prophetess (the "Song of Deborah") is among the oldest material in the Hebrew Bible. It relates the military venture in which she led an army of 10,000 men against the Canaanite ruler in accordance with divine guidance she received. Deborah used to perform her judicial duties in the open under a palm tree just north of Jerusalem. Tradition claims she did this so as not to be alone with whatever man was referred to her for a legal judgment.

Amos

Amos (700s BCE) may have been a shepherd from Judah (the southern kingdom), but he prophesied in the northern kingdom of Israel. Prophet Amos warned that Israel's king would die by the sword, and that his people would be exiled if they did not change their ways. In fact, the Assyrians conquered the northern kingdom of Israel in 722 BCE. They deported large numbers of its Hebrew inhabitants, and brought in people from diverse parts of their empire to ethnically mix with the remaining Israelites. The Samaritans of today claim to be descended from these ancient Hebrew people.

Isaiah

Isaiah (700s BCE) preached social justice in the southern kingdom of Judah following the fall of Israel in the north. He warned Judah's king to overcome social inequalities, and to take Assyrian threats from the north as the Lord's work. Prophet Isaiah said that disaster would come to both Judah and Assyria, and that the people of Judah would be deported. He further prophesied that a peaceful time would come when natural enemies like the wolf and the lamb would dwell together, and the Israelites would desist from war. A century later the danger presented in the Hebrew scriptures in Isaiah's name came to pass. The Babylonians conquered the southern kingdom of Judah, destroyed Solomon's temple, and sent the elite of the tribe of Judah to exile in Babylon (in present-day Iraq).

Jeremiah

Jeremiah (b. 600s BCE) had a long, prophetic career and was alive for the destruction of Solomon's temple. Jeremiah began his outspoken conduct at age 18. He taught that worship should be more open to the people and not be confined to the Jerusalem temple. He also predicted the temple's destruction. For all this provocative talk about the temple, Jeremiah was barred from entering its grounds. Undeterred, he walked around Jerusalem with a yoke on his shoulders to indicate that the city would come under the yoke of Nebuchadnezzar of Babylon. Jeremiah said the Lord willed that Babylon would overrule the Israelites to ensure that the temple would stay pure. He also predicted an exile of seventy years and a subsequent restoration of the temple. For these views Jeremiah was arrested for sedition. Soon after, the Babylonians actually conquered Jerusalem and destroyed Solomon's temple. Jeremiah was spared and took refuge in Egypt. After sixty years Cyrus the Great (r. 550–530) rose to power in Persia, conquered the Babylonians, and sponsored the rebuilding of Solomon's temple.

HISTORICAL PLAYERS

Temple rebuilders

When King David's royal dynasty came to an end in 587 BCE, people awaited the return of a messiah or "anointed one" born of David's lineage. Three types of people were anointed in ancient Israel: kings, priests, and prophets. Thus the Israelites expected that a man descended from David would distinguish himself as one of these. The general sense was that the messiah would lead the people as a king. Through his actions this anointed one would ensure that the people of Israel could once again abide together in the Holy Land given by Ha-Shem to Abraham and his children. The Prophet Isaiah identified Cyrus II (Hebrew: *Koresh*) as a messiah chosen by the Lord to help the people of Israel (Isaiah 44:24–45:8). Although he was a non-Israelite, Cyrus provided tremendous aid to the people of Israel. The elite families from the tribe of Judah were in the midst of their Babylonian exile when Cyrus II founded the Achaemenian dynasty. He defeated the Babylonians and established the Persian Empire, which covered Asia Minor. Cyrus issued an edict in 538 BCE that gave Jews permission to rebuild the temple. He wanted friendly relations with Palestine to create a buffer zone along the borders of his empire that faced territory governed by the Greeks.

Zerubbabel

It took about two decades for the Jews who returned from captivity in Babylon to rebuild Solomon's temple. The task was finally accomplished under the leadership of Zerubbabel (500s BCE), a man from the lineage of David who was appointed by the Persian King Darius I to serve as governor of Judah. Zerubbabel had led a group of some 44,000 exiled Jews back to Judah. With him was the grandson of the last high priest of Solomon's temple, as well as the prophets Haggai and Zechariah. After Zerubbabel's temple was finished around 516 BCE, nothing more is heard of the governor. Perhaps he began to stir up messianic expectations that proved unwelcome. A number of Zerubbabel's descendants were given political appointments in Judah for some time afterwards. Zerubbabel's temple stood in Jerusalem for 500 years.

Samaritans

When exiled Judeans returned to Jerusalem to rebuild the temple, disputes arose as to who qualified as true followers of the laws of Moses. Those left behind in the former southern kingdom had lived for half a century without Solomon's temple. These Judean peasants and members of lesser families had eked out a living in and around Jerusalem, while the elite of Judah were remaking their tradition in Babylon. Meanwhile a group from Samaria in the ancient northern kingdom of Israel considered themselves as faithful to the Hebrew tradition. The Samaritans claimed descent from the ancient Israelites, and wanted to join in rebuilding Solomon's temple under the auspices of Cyrus the Great.

Ezra was a priest and scribe who led a second wave of Judeans from Babylon for settlement in Jerusalem. He brought the temple vessels, and worked to enforce the law of Torah in the community (ca. 458 BCE). To define the people of Israel, Ezra imposed a policy of family reform whereby mixed marriages were annulled. He insisted that the Jews of exile who had taken foreign wives give them up. Soon, the reformer Nehemiah (ca. 465–424 BCE) reinforced Ezra's stringent marriage laws. According to Nehemiah's ruling, the Jews of Samaria were eliminated from the fold because of their generations of intermarriage with people brought in

Plate 4.2 "A Samaritan with Torah scroll." The Samaritans' temple on Mount Gerizim (near present-day Nablus) housed an ancient Torah scroll. Samaritans base their religion on the Torah, and claim to use an older version of the text than copies of the square Hebrew characters developed by Ezra after the Babylonian exile in the fifth century BCE. Here a Samaritan stands with the Samaritan Torah scroll in a photograph taken in the 1920s. The scroll may date back to the thirteenth century CE.

by the Assyrians after the conquest of the northern kingdom. Thus the Samaritans were not allowed to participate in rebuilding Solomon's temple.

Manasseh, grandson of the chief priest Eliashib, was married to the daughter of the governor of Samaria. Nehemiah rejected him for noncompliance with the marriage ruling. Thus he went north to join the Samaritans. Samaritan tradition claims that Manasseh brought a Torah scroll. Thus an alternative center of Israelite worship was established as the Samaritans built a temple on Mount Gerizim, by ancient Shechem, where Abram first set up an altar to God upon entering Canaan. To this day some 700 Samaritans practice their form of ancient Israelite religion. Many of them live in Nablus, the present-day site of ancient Shechem. Modern Samaritans claim descent from the Hebrews of Samaria, which was located in the ancient northern kingdom of Israel. Jewish tradition based on the Talmud considers the Samaritans as related to non-Hebrews brought in by the Assyrians when they conquered the northern kingdom.

Herod the Great

Alexander the Great conquered Palestine in 332 BCE. After his death, the empire he created was divided up by three of his generals. Palestine was put under the control of Seleucus, who favored Greek culture and began to persecute Jews. In the second century BCE, Jews in Palestine resisted the policies of King Antiochus IV, the Greek ruler of Syria and Judea who forbade Jews to: (1) observe the Sabbath, (2) circumcise their sons, (3) study the Torah, and (4) eat according to their religious customs. The priest Mattathias of Modin murdered a Syrian official. After the incident, Mattathias with his five sons and their followers began a revolt. After Mattathias's death in 166, his son Judah took over the fight. Judah was a fierce man, so people called him the Hammer (Maccabee). Under Judah Maccabee's command, the Jews established an independent Israel. As a crowning act, the Maccabees cleansed the temple of idols. It became customary to commemorate this event with the minor festival known as Ḥanukkah. The Maccabees ruled for some eighty years. Their line is known as the Hasmonean dynasty.

Herod the Great (74–ca. 4 BCE) took as his second wife a women in the line of the Maccabees. He seized power from the independent Jewish Hasmoneans with the backing of the Roman emperor, and ruled Palestine for three decades. Herod "the Great" was from a family that had converted to Judaism several generations earlier. He was a cruel leader, killing members of his own family if he felt politically threatened. But Herod managed to maintain social order in spite of the heavy tax burden he placed on people, and to establish a prosperous and peaceful rule. With tax funds, Herod sponsored huge building projects. For Jews of the diaspora, Herod built places for religious gathering, study, and cleansing. He encouraged Jews to migrate to Jerusalem. Starting in 19 BCE Herod began reconstructing Zerubbabel's temple. He replaced the modest structure. And though Solomon's temple a millennium before had been covered in gold, his building was even more magnificent. Herod's temple is often called the Second Temple – the first being the structure built by Solomon. Zerubbabel's temple was actually second, but because continuity of worship was not interrupted in the course of construction, the second and the third structures are counted as the same. The altar of these temples is said to have been the rock on which Abraham bound his son for sacrifice.

Jews of the Hellenistic era

Herod's close affiliation with the Roman rulers made some Jews feel uneasy due to the cultural as well as political ties. Herod supported the declining Greek Olympic games – and was awarded the title of president for life. He also invited Greek and foreign scholars, poets, musicians, and athletes to his court. To accommodate them he built an open-air stadium for chariot racing and a theater for Greek and Roman dramatic productions in Jerusalem. Over time, affluent Jews absorbed some Hellenic culture, such as language, dress, and education. They participated in Greek games, cooperated with Roman rule, and enjoyed what life in the era of prosperity in the Roman Empire had to offer. Not all Jews were happy with this response to non-traditional ways, however. The more conservative compatriots resisted the challenge of cultural assimilation. Thus, to speak about Jews in the **Hellenistic era**, several factions must be considered.

Sadducees

The oldest group of Palestinian Jews of the Hellenistic era goes by the name Sadducee, named after Zadoq, King David's priest. Members of this elite Zadokite group belonged to the higher orders of the Israelite priestly class, which was aristocratic and wealthy. Sadducees were concentrated in Jerusalem because they were involved in the temple sacrifices. Sadducee men were more likely to participate in the Greek games than Pharisee men, even though they were theologically more conservative. They maintained a strict literal perspective on the books of Moses, and rejected popular belief in angels, the apocalypse, and resurrection of the body in the afterlife. By keeping religious perspectives and requirements contained, they could reduce friction with the Roman authorities. Tensions grew in Palestine despite the general cooperation between the Sadducee elite and the Roman officials. Outbreaks of Jewish activism perpetrated by a group known as the Zealots culminated in the Roman destruction of Herod's temple in 70 CE.

Essenes

A marginal group of Jews resided in the rugged cliffs and stark terrain surrounding Jerusalem, about thirteen miles from the Dead Sea. Dating from the second century BCE this group of Jews known as the Essenes established a monastic community at Qumran. They were opposed to acts of violence, including the animal sacrifice performed regularly by the temple priests in Jerusalem. They had their own ideas of what a temple should be like, which did not match the physical grandeur of Herod's temple. In addition, while King Herod reigned in Jewish Palestine, they lived an isolated life in anticipation of the apocalypse. The Essenes had an oral Torah different from that of the Sadducees. The first bunch of their long-lost texts was discovered in 1947 near the Dead Sea. These "Dead Sea Scrolls" present ideas that were rejected from mainstream Hebrew tradition. The Essenes had radical political expectations for the arrival of a kingly messiah of David's lineage who would appear in the world to lead a violent cosmic struggle in which the children of light would be victorious against the children of darkness. The scrolls taught that the messiah would annihilate evil, and bring our world's injustice to an end in a golden age.

Pharisees

The majority of educated people in Jewish Palestine were Pharisees. They interacted less with the Romans because, unlike the Sadducees, their focus was not international politics. Like the Essenes, many Pharisees awaited a messiah and the end of the world. After the complete destruction of Herod's temple, Jews were made to leave Jerusalem. This event is known as the **diaspora**. In the absence of a temple the priestly knowledge of the Sadducees became outdated. While the Sadducee priests had performed the temple rites, Pharisees had focused on Torah study. Thus Pharisees survived the Roman destruction of Jerusalem in 70 CE. Their religious perspective was carried forward by a new group of religious specialists known as **rabbis**.

Rabbis

After the Romans destroyed Herod's temple, a new religious center for teaching emerged at Jabneh in Palestine. The three annual festivals over which the Sadducee priests used to preside were no longer held, and animal sacrifice was abandoned. In place of the temple, synagogues became the focal point of communal worship in which learned laymen presided instead of priests. The scholars who were Pharisees henceforth were called "teachers," or "rabbis."

Hillel and Shammai

Hillel (d. ca. 10) and Shammai were alive while Jesus of Nazareth was maturing before his three-year ministry. During their lifetimes King Herod constructed the magnificent new temple in Jerusalem that replaced Zerubbabel's temple. Hillel and Shammai were the last of the so-called "five pairs" of famous Jewish teachers. They were part of the Sanhedrin Supreme Court, and headed two opposing schools or "houses." Over three hundred differences of opinion between the house of Hillel and the house of Shammai were recorded. Shammai tended to be stricter in ritual observance than Hillel. An example concerns the type of oil that fed lamps used for the weekly Sabbath. Shammai insisted on olive oil, though it was very expensive. Hillel thought that mustard seed oil (which was cheaper) would do just as well. In most cases the view of the Hillel house prevailed. Thus Hillel may be considered the founder of the rabbinical tradition of Judaism today. Hillel began the tradition that culminated in the compilation of the Talmud. Four centuries of religious leaders were descended from Hillel, many of whom were considered princes (*nasi*).

Johanan ben Zakkai

The youngest of Hillel's students was Johanan ben Zakkai (ca. 15 BCE–105 CE?) – a Pharisee who established a rabbinical school in Jabneh. He survived the siege of Jerusalem by pretending to be a corpse while his disciples carried his shroud-wrapped body out of the city for burial. The "corpse" was captured and imprisoned in Jabneh, but the clever Pharisee convinced the authorities to release him so that he could teach. Johanan ben Zakkai created many substitutes for temple practice in conjunction with a new calendar. He instituted prayer in place of sacrifice, counting it as the ritual act pleasing to the divine. Under his influence, the oral Torah (tradition of living commentary on the written Torah) was integrated into Hebrew scriptural studies. After Johanan ben Zakkai, the work of the rabbis undertaken at Jabneh and Babylon continued to gain influence. Over the next 600 years the Hebrew tradition would consolidate itself by gathering up strands of oral tradition to produce a comprehensive written corpus.

Medieval Jews

Something new happened to Jewish scholarship when the tradition found itself face to face with two other monotheistic religions that suddenly loomed large in their intellectual environment. The small sect of renegade Jews of the first century CE who had considered Jesus of Nazareth to be the awaited messiah had grown beyond anyone's expectations. In the year 800 CE with the crowning of Emperor Charlemagne, Christianity became the backbone of the Holy Roman Empire. Moreover, by that date the new monotheistic tradition that claimed descent from Abraham's first son, Ishmael, informed powerful politics from Spain all the way through the Middle East. Islam, established by the prophet Muḥammad in 622 CE, had spread widely from Arabia in the century following his death.

Moses Maimonides

Moses Maimonides (1135–1204 CE) was among the Sephardic Jews who lived side-by-side with Muslims in the sophisticated Moorish culture centered in Córdoba (in present-day Spain). Reflecting the culture and interests of his times, Maimonides wrote texts in Hebrew as well as Arabic. He systematized aspects of Jewish thought using categories he derived from the philosophical works by Aristotle that Muslims had translated from Greek into Arabic. Maimonides identified thirteen principles that he presumed were common to Jewish thought:

1. The Creator is the Author and Guide of everything that exists.
2. The Creator is a Unity.
3. The Creator is not corporeal.
4. The Creator is first and last.
5. It is right to pray to the Creator, but to no other being.
6. All the words of the prophets are true.
7. The prophecy of Moses is true and he was the father (criterion) for all prophecy.
8. The Torah now in our possession is that given to Moses.
9. The Torah will not be changed, nor will the Creator give any other Torah.
10. The Creator knows the deeds and thoughts of people.
11. He rewards those who keep his commandments and punishes those who disobey.
12. Though the Messiah delay, one must constantly expect his coming.
13. The dead will be resurrected.

(Solomon 2006: 392)

Exhibiting the spirit of the scholastic intellectual movement that was emerging, Maimonides dedicated himself to summarizing all available knowledge. He wrote fourteen volumes known as the *Mishneh Torah*, which comprehensively classified Jewish law (1170–1180). This helped set the stage for the Christian theologian Thomas Aquinas to write his summary of Christian theological knowledge in his massive *Summa Theologiae* one century later (1269–1273).

The Black Death

The Black Death (bubonic plague) should be counted as an historical player in our account of the Judaic traditions. Although not a person, the Black Death was a real presence – a kratophany – in Europe during the Middle Ages. The bubonic plague did not discriminate between Christians and Jews when it killed; yet it seemed to incite Christians to violence against Jews. Already in the late twelfth century the relationship between European Jews and Christians took serious turns for the worse. Attacks by Christian mobs against Jews were based in religious prejudice. When the Black Death entered Europe the situation worsened. Some of the violence against European Jews of the twelfth and thirteenth centuries is noted in Table 4.1.

In 1348 the bubonic plague entered Italy, and within six months spread like wildfire throughout Western Europe. It was called the Black Death because the infection caused bulbous swellings in the armpits and groin that turned the skin dark. By 1350 the plague had devastated a quarter to half of the population. It subsided naturally, but returned to Europe every generation for about three centuries. The Black Death started in the Far East and traversed the silk routes across Central Asia. It was transmitted into Western Europe by fleas on brown rats hiding in merchant vessels. But people did not know the scientific cause of the disease. Some thought mistakenly that it was airborne miasma, and many believed the devastation to be a divine punishment. Ironically, groups of fanatical Christians who went from town to town flagellating themselves in repentance indirectly helped spread the plague as prostitutes and thieves mingled in the crowds that gathered. The years 1348 to 1349 were devastating for Europe's Jewish community because human cruelty compounded the ravaging effects of the Black Death. In the atmosphere of desperation and irrational mistrust, town councils even organized massacres of Jews in territory that today is Spain, Switzerland, and Germany. The Jewish population of Europe was forced to move from one country to another many times from the 1100s through the 1400s.

Table 4.1 Attacks on European Jews during the Middle Ages

Date	*Country*	*Event**
1096	Germany	Jews living along the Rhine were massacred during the First Crusade.
1190	England	Crusaders, townsfolk, and nobility massacred Jews in York; 150 Jews took refuge in a castle, but most committed suicide.
1215	Italy	The Fourth Lateran Council under Pope Innocent III required Jews to wear a yellow badge indicating religious affiliation.
1242	France	A copy of the Talmud was burned publicly in Paris. The complete expulsion of Jews followed shortly thereafter.
1279	England	Jews given the death penalty for blaspheming against Christianity.
1290	England	Jews expelled, and sailed to France and Flanders. Their houses and lands were confiscated. Jews forbidden to settle in England until 1655.
1298	Germany	A rampage started in Roetingen where a nobleman led a mob to round up Jews and burn them at the stake. They moved from town to town in south Germany and Austria and annihilated forty Jewish communities.
1391	Spain	Riots against Jews broke out in Seville, Toledo, Madrid, and Córdoba. Some 100,000 Jews became Roman Catholic; half that number were massacred.
1394	France	Jews expelled.
1492	Spain	Jews expelled.

*This loss of life due to anti-Semitism in the Middle Ages was magnified more than 60-fold between 1933 and 1945 when approximately 6 million European Jews (about 1 in 3 Jews worldwide) were exterminated in Nazi concentration camps.

Conversos

Many Jews in medieval Europe converted to Christianity to avoid being killed or exiled. Jews who converted to Christianity became known as ***conversos***. In time *conversos* became the object of great suspicion as the Church authorities questioned whether or not they had truly abandoned their Judaic traditions. In 1480 King Ferdinand and Queen Isabella set up a commission known as the Inquisition to identify *conversos* who secretely maintained their Jewish practices. These Roman Catholic monarchs were intent on re-establishing Christianity throughout the Iberian Peninsula. They overtook Granada as part of a "re-conquest" in January 1492. Thus after 700 years of Moorish rule, the land that today is part of Spain once again became Christian territory. In March 1492 Ferdinand and Isabella issued an edict of expulsion. Some 250,000 **Sephardim** who did not convert were expelled, taking only what they could carry.

About two in five *conversos* went from Granada to Portugal, but many met the fate of conversion or exile there in 1496. At that time perhaps a hundred thousand Jews were expelled. By 1536 Jewish converts to Roman Catholic Christianity were formally allowed to settle in the Netherlands. And though the Inquisition operated in the Netherlands, it was not as oppressive as in the Iberian Peninsula. Thus, the *conversos* who wished to maintain their Jewish heritage in secret could practice more easily in a place like Amsterdam, a growing commercial center. Under the auspices of the new Protestant Christians, Jews were able to build a synagogue and practice Judaism openly. By 1619 laws supporting religious toleration were passed that allowed city rulers to define the religious rights of its residents. Once Jews were allowed religious freedom, many *conversos* reverted to the open practice of their old faith.

The diaspora Jews of North Africa, the Middle East, Western Asia, and Spain became known as Sephardim because Sepharad is the biblical name for the Iberian Peninsula. Sephardic Jews lived in close proximity to Muslims, while a smaller number who lived in Christian Europe were known as **Ashkenazim**. Exposure to different cultures shaped aspects of Jewish life, such as everyday language, music, foods, and style of dress that continue to distinguish Sephardic and Ashkenazi Jews. After the expulsion of Jews from Spain in 1492, the majority of Sephardim moved to the eastern Mediterranean. From generation to generation, they transmitted their language known as Ladino, which encapsulated medieval Spanish. Meanwhile the Ashkenazim developed the Yiddish language, which mixes Indo-European and Semitic words into a Germanic linguistic base.

Jewish mystics

The roots of Jewish mysticism go back to the earliest years of the Hebrew tradition – as when David prayed: "Open mine eyes that I may behold wondrous things out of thy Torah" (Martin 1974: 41). Yet there was an intensification of mystical Judaism following the tragedies of the twelfth through fifteenth centuries in Europe. The massacres, expulsions, and religious conversions moved Jewish thinkers away from the intellectual life represented by scholastic learning. Exposure to the fears, prejudices, and resentments of Christian neighbors inspired two reactions among pious Jews: (1) to turn to more traditional religious practice, and (2) to delve into mystical experiences. Jewish cabbala theology appeared in Provence and northern Spain during the twelfth and thirteenth centuries.

Isaac Luria

When Jews and *conversos* emigrated from Spain at the end of the fifteenth century many made contact with older established Jewish communities in the Middle East. The town of Safed in the Galilee became the center of a mystical revival. Isaac Luria (1534–1572) developed the idea that each individual has a specific role to play in the restoration and redemption of himself or herself, society, and the cosmos. He taught that when the material world was created, some portions of it could not sustain the shock of the divine light used in the creation process. These portions of the material world were like vessels that shattered. Consequently, sparks of divine light were trapped in the shards of the vessels that shattered under the impact of creation. Luria said that people must repair the shattered vessels. They must release the trapped light, and gather it together. Illness, evil, and chaos are healed through gathering the light from "exile" into its proper place. The word for this mystical repair is *tikkun*. Jews perform the divine mitzvoth to speed up the process of *tikkun* on the level of the individual, the society, and the universe. When the process of *tikkun* is completed, the messiah will enter the world. The messiah's appearance should be taken as confirmation that the divine light has finally been organized in the universe. Thus the messiah will preside over a world that is as it would have been had the vessels not shattered.

Shabbetai Tzevi

The cabbala teachings of Isaac Luria set up expectations for a messiah to come, and in 1648 a person named Shabbetai Tzevi (1626–1676) from Smyrna, Turkey, claimed to be that messiah. Shabbetai Tzevi began attracting attention because he could perform supernatural feats. Local rabbis who had no patience in dealing with any false messiahs kicked him out of Smyrna. But that rejection gave Shabbetai Tzevi the chance to travel and gather disciples in neighboring regions. When he returned to the synagogue in Smyrna in 1665 crowds received him as the messiah. Thereafter enthusiasm for Shabbetai Tzevi spread through Europe and along the eastern Mediterranean. The following year he went with a group of followers to Constantinople. The Muslim sultan put him in prison, and before long Shabbetai Tzevi converted to Islam, and received the title "Effendi." The surprising conversion of their messiah to Islam disappointed large numbers of Shabbetai Tzevi's followers. They thought that the Jewish messiah would never do such a thing and abandoned him, their faith dashed. Other disciples converted to Islam. Their lineage continues even today as the Donmeh sect in Turkey. This sect is a cross between Judaism and Islam, and small numbers continue their spiritual practice to this day, having faith in Shabbetai Tzevi as the messiah who will return.

Ba'al Shem Ṭov

In the mid-1700s when Jews in Europe began to engage in the culture of the European Enlightenment with its rational and scientific thinking, the Jews of Eastern Europe were able to conserve their traditions. A man born in the Ukraine named Israel ben Eliezer (ca. 1699–1760) began the Ḥasidic spiritual movement that gradually permeated Eastern European Jewish life. Israel studied the cabbala from an early age, and regularly had spontaneous ecstatic experiences. Eventually people called him Ba'al Shem Ṭov (Master of the Name) believing that he knew the esoteric names of God based on the cabbala. When he was about 45 years old, Israel founded a house of study where rabbis, scholars, and common people all came to see him. Ba'al Shem Ṭov taught orally using stories, and did not write down any teachings. Later teachers established the theoretical underpinnings of Ḥasidism, calling their approach to Judaism "Ḥabad" – an acronym for the three highest sephiroth.

Although the Ḥasidic movement started among people who still had faith that Shabbetai Tzevi had been the messiah, Israel Ba'al Shem Ṭov did not emphasize the messiah doctrine. He liked to focus on life in the present based on three principles: (1) joyfulness, (2) humility, and (3) enthusiasm. In line with his preference for direct experience, Israel emphasized prayer over the traditional study of Torah. Prayer frees sparks of divine light within a person and negative thoughts brighten up. It purifies those who love God, and removes veils that separate the person from God. As a fringe benefit many wonderful things happen to people through prayer: they can heal illness, avoid obstacles, and even attract wealth. After Ba'al Shem Ṭov passed away, Ḥasidic Jews tended to emphasize the role of the **tsaddik** ("righteous one," spiritual guide) – even though Israel himself encouraged people to rely on their own spiritual capacity.

Jewish thinkers of the European Enlightenment

It seemed to be only a matter of time before rationality would come back into vogue. Thus entered the European Enlightenment with its broad scientific attitude where analysis and critique were applied more widely than in the highly rational **scholasticism** of the Middle Ages. Enlightenment critics began to think of cabbala as having two faults: (1) it deviated from monotheism, and (2) it encouraged false messianic thinking. The concept that there are many sephiroth makes it seem as though God's unity has been disrupted. And the goal of gathering all the sparks together made a kind of opening for one person who would do this on behalf of others – becoming in effect the world savior. This negative reaction to Jewish mysticism was aggravated when a messiah figure did arise within the tradition in the controversial figure of Shabbetai Tzevi.

Baruch Spinoza

Among the *converso* émigrés from Portugal to Amsterdam was the father of Baruch Spinoza (1632–1677). Spinoza made a serious inquiry about the role of the prophets of the Hebrew scriptures. He demonstrated how scripture could be subject to reason in the way that nature was accessible to analysis. Spinoza's work initiated the historical-critical method of reading scripture. For his historical approach to scripture, Spinoza was shunned by the Jewish community in Amsterdam, and forbidden to attend synagogue. In addition, his works were censored. Nevertheless, Spinoza's radical approach to scripture started a tradition in biblical scholarship that gathered steam for two centuries. Historical-critical methods of reading texts still yield significant results today.

Moses Mendelssohn

In the seventeenth century with the capitalist economic system emerging in Europe, the value of Jewish investment and economic know-how was recognized. Moreover, Jews were being welcomed for their potential cultural contributions. But with this so-called **emancipation** of Jews from their ghettos came social pressure to assimilate into mainstream European society. For example, the French emperor Napoleon Bonaparte (1769–1821) planned for Jews to marry off one-third of their stock to non-Jews. European Jews had mixed reactions to this new exposure to the dominant Christian community. Moses Mendelssohn (1729–1796) was among the first Jewish leaders to embrace emancipation. In line with other Enlightenment thinkers, he mastered several languages (German, Greek, Latin, French, and English), and studied Western philosophy (including John Locke and Gottfried Leibniz). Mendelssohn was convinced that authentic Judaism was not at odds with the scientific spirit of the Enlightenment. Moreover, he was convinced that a Jew could be loyal to tradition while participating in modern society. He translated the Tanakh into German using Hebrew characters, and so helped bring Jews into mainstream European intellectual life by providing an opening to German literacy.

Jews of modern times

Jews received equal status as citizens in Western Europe and the USA starting with the American and French Revolutions. This equality tended to erase the special status of Jews who had lived under their own religious laws for generations. The laws and customs of the secular nation-state in many ways clash with the law prescribed by the Torah. For example, many Jews are called to work on the Sabbath. (Think of nurses, doctors, politicians, and other workers whose jobs require them to work weekends.) In response to these challenges and opportunities, Jews today fall into four main denominations according to how they respond to modernism: Reform, Conservative, Reconstructionist, and Orthodox. Further, a political response to the modern predicament of Jews was a social movement known as Zionism.

Reform Jews

The Reform movement began in Germany, and soon became the dominant Judaic tradition in the USA. Rabbi Isaac Mayer Wise came to the United States from Germany in 1854 with radical ideas for the practice of Reform Judaism. He advocated abandonment of dietary restrictions, along with many ceremonial regulations, including covering the head during synagogue services. The movement is less radical now than when it began, as Reform Jews continued to reinterpret Jewish laws to harmonize with contemporary life. Reform Jews do not see insurmountable contradictions between secular and religious life, and encourage participation in the political and cultural life of the mainstream society in which they find themselves. Principles of the Reform movement include belief that the Torah is culture-bound, written by human beings based on divine inspiration. The first woman Reform rabbi was ordained in 1972 in the United States. Women and men participate equally in rituals.

Conservative Jews

Solomon Schechter founded the Conservative movement in the mid-nineteenth century as a response to the Reform movement, which he considered excessively liberal. The religious observance of Conservative Jews is somewhat middling between Orthodox and

Reform practice. The Torah is considered to be divinely inspired. Beyond that, keeping the dietary regulations of kashrut is essential, along with maintaining high ritual standards on the Sabbath. Rabbis act as interpreters of Jewish law, in consultation with the congregation. Most prayers are said in Hebrew during synagogue services, and women have served as rabbis since 1985. The extent of women's participation in rituals varies by congregation. Conservative Judaism is the main denomination among North American Jews, with over one million members.

Reconstructionist Jews

Rabbi Mordecai M. Kaplan founded the Reconstructionist movement in 1935 with the idea that God is the source of morality innate to humanity, and not a supernatural being. Thus they emphasize individual responsibility as the key to performance of the Jewish mitzvoth. Reconstructionist Jews believe that the Torah was not divinely revealed, but stands as a cultural creation of the Jewish people. They encourage creative interpretations of Jewish rituals and laws. Accordingly they created the bat mitzvah ceremony for girls, and consider women and men as equal participants in religious rituals. Reconstructionist Judaism is the most recent denomination to develop among Jews, and has the fewest adherents among the four denominations.

Orthodox Jews

Orthodox Jews practice Judaism in the most traditional manner among Jews. The term "Orthodox" was coined in 1795 to distinguish this conservative approach to Jewish life from more liberal practices that were emerging in response to emancipation. Orthodox Judaism does not have a single founder, and its many sects differ in their approach to modernity. In common, Orthodox Jews believe in the literal observance of Jewish law as defined in Torah and interpreted in the Talmud. There are no women rabbis, and women continue to participate in rituals largely according to the ways of past generations. Ḥasidic Jews are among the ultra-Orthodox. Their manner of dress is conservative (men in long black coats; women with long sleeves and skirts; both with heads covered), while their spirituality includes dancing, singing, and devotion to a tsaddik.

Zionists

Zionism is not a religious denomination of Judaism. Rather it is a worldwide political movement dedicated to assuring the existence of a Jewish homeland. Theodor Herzl (1860–1904) founded the Zionist movement with the idea that Jews of the diaspora should once again establish themselves in the land to which the patriarch Abraham traditionally is said to have come. This was the land of ancient Palestine where Solomon built the first temple. The Jewish homeland is known as Zion. In 1917 the British government issued the Balfour Declaration that declared its support for the existence of a Jewish homeland in Palestine. Momentum was given to the Zionist movement in the wake of the tragedy of the **Sho'ah**, or Nazi Holocaust, in which an estimated six million Ashkenazi Jews were systematically killed under the genocidal policy of Germany's Third Reich. The fourteenth of May 1948 marked the end of British rule over Palestine, at which time the region was divided, giving one part for a restoration of the ancient Jewish homeland. Jordan and Egypt obtained portions that were not dedicated to the newly established *Medinat Yisra'el*, or State of Israel.

PART 2
JUDAIC TEXTURE

FOUNDATIONAL TEXTURE

The Tanakh (TNKH)

The sacred scripture of Jewish tradition is the **Tanakh**. Tanakh is an acronym comprising the vowel "a" added to the first Hebrew letter of each of three collections of early texts, namely T-N-KH. These core collections are the Five Books of Moses (Torah), the Prophets (Nevi'im), and the Writings (Ketuvim).

The Torah

The Hebrew word *torah* means "guidance" with the connotation of "divine instruction." The Torah is the very core, and most holy of all portions of the Tanakh. Tradition says that the Torah is the law that God gave to Moses on Mount Sinai. This law was transmitted in two streams – one written Torah and one oral. Before any part of Mosaic law was written down, Moses taught the tradition to his brother Aaron, his sons, and the tribal elders. Starting in the fourth century BCE portions of this orally carried law were written down. The written Torah has five sections, also called books: (1) Genesis, including the story of the creation of the world, and accounts of the patriarchs and matriarchs; (2) Exodus, relating the story of Moses; (3) Leviticus, presenting the story of the Israelites living in the desert after leaving Egypt; (4) Numbers, including legal materials, and rituals; (5) Deuteronomy, containing material on the covenant between the Lord and Israel.

According to the "documentary hypothesis" of biblical scholars, material in these books came from four different sources, which they call J, E, P, and D. The book of Deuteronomy is the D source, which stands on its own. The other books of the Torah contain mixtures of J, E, and P. J is from the southern kingdom of Judah, and is probably the earliest, dating from around the tenth century BCE. E is from the northern kingdom of Israel. P is a source in which priests combined elements of the earlier J and P for their own purposes. Both Sadducees and Pharisees followed the written laws of Moses. But the priests (Sadducees) did not recognize an oral Torah.

The Nevi'im

The Nevi'im portion of the Tanakh contains material from former and later prophets. These texts date from about 200 BCE. There are twenty-two books altogether, each carrying the name of a prophet. The book covers the time frame from the twelfth century BCE to the sixth century BCE. It begins with the story of Joshua who does what Moses was unable to do – lead the people directly into their Promised Land. It covers the Babylonian exile and the return. Like the Torah, the Nevi'im traditionally has been considered as divinely inspired.

The Ketuvim

Ketuvim is the Hebrew word for writings. This material traditionally was not counted among works that were divinely inspired. They were grounded in human knowledge and experience. Some of this material reflects Greek (Hellenic), Persian, and Egyptian influences that impacted on the people of Israel. Ketuvim was the last section of the scripture to come into the Hebrew canon.

SUPPORTIVE TEXTURE

The Talmuds

Once the Torah, Nevi'im, and Ketuvim were approved and set into an official Hebrew version they were closed. The Tanakh underwent no further editing after 90 CE when the scriptural canon was fixed. With this monumental task of selection and redaction accomplished, Jewish scholars were free to turn their attention to other literary works from their Hebrew heritage. By this time the role of the Sadducee priests was obsolete, and the approach of the Pharisees gave a new direction to tradition.

The Mishnah

The rabbis began a long tradition of commenting on the Tanakh. The rabbis in Babylon (Babylonia), and Jabneh (Palestine) produced two monumental commentaries known as the Babylonian Talmud and the Palestinian Talmud – named according to the lands where the rabbis lived while working on them. Each Talmud comprises an early layer called the **Mishnah**, which is common to both the Babylonian and Palestinian versions. The Mishnah is a collection of discussions about Jewish law by rabbis known by the **Aramaic** term *tannaim* (teacher). The Mishnah is the written form of the Israelite oral traditions that had accumulated for some 1,000 years, traditionally thought to be from the time of Moses and Aaron. It is composed in Hebrew, and includes both **halachah** (Jewish legal material) and **aggadah** (Jewish stories).

The Gemara'

Two compendia known collectively as the **Gemara**' are legal and ethical commentaries on the Mishnah. Rabbis in Palestine and Babylonia wrote the interpretations, opinions, and judgments. These teachers are known by the Aramaic term *amoraim* (explainers). The Mishnah

BOX 4.2 INTERPRETATIONS: BIBLICAL CRITICISM

A person cannot be utopian (*utopia*=no place) in reading a text: a reader has to stand somewhere. Over time, three main approaches in biblical **hermeneutics** developed on the basis of where readers have chosen to stand: (1) The historical-critical method situates one in the historical background of the text. (2) The literary-critical method situates one in the text itself. (3) The deconstructionist method situates the reader in himself or herself.

Historical-critical hermeneutics. The historical-critical method of biblical hermeneutics dates from the seventeenth century when scholars such as the Jewish thinker Baruch Spinoza in northern Europe began to question the divine absolute authority of biblical texts. Questions asked by those following the historical-critical method include: When was the text written? By whom was it written? What layers of text are combined into this scripture, and from what historical time and circumstances did they arise? Who was the audience, and what was the author trying to convey to that audience? What was the cultural sense of words used in the text in its original context?

An important discovery made by scholars working according to the historical-critical method was that the Torah (Pentateuch, or first five books of the Hebrew Bible) comprised texts from four oral sources, which they called J, E, D, and P. By analyzing scripture according to such linguistic and historical methods, scholars felt they were doing "objective" research that was independent of personal belief.

Literary-critical hermeneutics. A literary critic treats the scriptures as a purposeful whole. This method of criticism deals with all available versions of a text. It also looks to establish the coherence of various books of the canon from a theological and literary point of view. Literary criticism involves "intrinsic" analysis as opposed to "extrinsic" analysis. In other words, the research is largely confined to the texts, without appeal to outside data such as archeological evidence. Literary critics approach texts as works of literary art, and try to understand their meaning and implications for our times. For example, using literary criticism, the biblical story of Adam and Eve might be analyzed in terms of the relationship among the characters. Such analysis could yield a new perspective on the past and future role of women in the Judeo-Christian tradition as modeled by Eve.

Deconstructionist hermeneutics. Deconstruction involves a strategy of reading a text that is hypersensitive to what has been erased, silenced, or omitted from the material. Thus it "may well produce the erased Bible" (Carroll, in Barton 1998: 62). One thing that typically has been omitted from analysis of texts is the reader himself or herself! Deconstructionists scoff at the notion of an "objective" reading of a text that historical-critical biblical scholars "pretend" to have. They say that the neutrality claimed by scholars in their research is a pretense and falsehood. Hence, they aim to make the reader's relationship to the text transparent by attempting to disclose their own biases and ambitions in dealing with the text. From a deconstructionist point of view (which – necessarily – is not a stable point of view because the reader's perspective is always changing) there is no unique meaning, truth, or even text that can be discovered once and for all.

and one set of commentaries became the Palestinian Talmud, while the Mishnah and the other Gemara' collection formed the Babylonian Talmud. All together the talmudic body of law and narrative (i.e., the Mishnah and Gemara' in two collections) was accumulated between 200 BCE and 500 CE. Nowadays the term *Talmud* refers mainly to the Babylonian Talmud.

The Midrash

One body of Jewish literature that aims to discover non-literal meanings of scripture is referred to collectively as **midrash**. A midrash is a story *about* a story in scripture. It is a literary form based on sacred texts that fills in a gap between two words. A midrash makes material in the Tanakh more applicable to a person's life. Sometimes a midrash can change the general understanding of a biblical story – even to the point of altering it for generations down the line. For example, many people familiar with the story of Adam and Eve (Ḥavah) in the Garden of Eden (Genesis 3) will say that Ḥavah ate an apple, but in the scripture the fruit is not named. In the whole story only a fig is mentioned. Jewish tradition suggests that the fruit was either a fig or an etrog (citron, *citrus medica*), but the idea of the apple came from a midrash.

CROSS-OVER TEXTURE

A modern view of Ḥavah

In the Judeo-Christian tradition many people have thought that the woman was cursed. But according to the scripture the Lord cursed the serpent, not Adam or Ḥavah (Genesis 3:14). Therefore, the woman was neither disobedient nor cursed. God wept for the inevitable suffering that comes with birth and death – the toil of producing food, and the hardships of childbearing. But the Lord supported their venture by providing the couple with "vestments of honor and glory – not coverings of shame!" (Halevi 1997: 245). And from that ancient vestment eventually came the yarmulke (skullcap worn by male Jews) *and* the headscarf for women, says Shira Halevi in *The Life Story of Adam and Havah*. A traditional interpretation of the woman's head covering is one of nine curses. Along with various so-called afflictions, such as childbirth, "her head is covered like a mourner" (*Pirke de Rabbi Eliezer*, ch. XIV, cited in Halevi 1997: 214). Yet there is reason to believe that the woman's headscarf is a sacred vestment.

> *Yarmulka* is a Yiddish abbreviation of *yare me-Elohim*, "stand in awe of God." It's a symbol of respect and devotion to God. . . . Whether you cover your head with a yarmulke, a turban, or a scarf, it means the same thing. It means you affirm your allegiance to God and the role you have as one of His chosen, *ahad b'nei Israel* – one of the children of Israel.
>
> (Halevi 1997: 216–217)

Shira Halevi's interpretation of the story of Adam and Ḥavah casts a favorable light on the woman. Her efforts to get at the meaning of the woman taking the fruit of the tree and offering some to her husband yielded a new understanding of the text. Thus in light of a modern woman's interpretation it becomes more clear why, before leaving the Garden of Eden, Adam looked at his wife and proclaimed her name not as death, but as Ḥavah – Life!

Yiddish *teḥinnott*

Teḥinnott are prayers in Hebrew used for private devotion. During the seventeenth through the early nineteenth centuries in Central and Eastern Europe, special *teḥinnott* [*tkhines*] were composed in Yiddish (interwoven with Hebrew scriptural quotes) so that a woman could sanctify her domestic life. Because most women could not read Hebrew, these prayers allowed them to express pious emotions, participate in the religious rhythms of domestic duties, and sometimes glimpse the mystical side of life. A Jewish man's rhythm of life revolved around daily prayer, recited in Hebrew, ideally with a congregation in the synagogue. An expanded version of their prayers was recited on Sabbath days and holidays. Some women recited the Hebrew liturgy while at home, and attended the synagogue on Sabbath days and holidays. Yet a Jewish woman's main religious duties centered on the home. Their supplications covered matters of life, sustenance, and death. In contrast to the Hebrew daily prayers of the men, women recited prayers from Yiddish *teḥinnott* at any time needed, and they were applicable in many different places, and for diverse occasions. Some prayers were for the synagogue, and others for the home. Still other supplications were intended for recitation in the cemetery, or in the bedroom. Women had prayers appealing to the Lord for: overcoming infertility, having a healthy pregnancy, enduring the condition of widowhood, allowing a child to pass through the dangers of illness, protecting one's husband in his travels, and so forth.

PART 3 JUDAIC PERFORMANCE

JEWISH RITUAL LIFE

Jewish tradition established ritual cycles to promote a well-ordered life led in fulfillment of the divine commandments. Jewish rites include individual prayers, family gatherings, communal services, holiday celebrations, and participation in life cycle rites. Home and synagogue provide the two main sacred spaces in which the mitzvoth are observed. Traditionally, women's religious duties were concentrated in the home, while men's duties branched out from the home to the synagogue. Women did not attend the synagogue if doing so required them to neglect domestic duties; and they were exempt from performing mitzvoth that have prescribed times, such as the daily prayers. On the other hand, the women were responsible for preparing food according to the laws of kashrut, observing the Sabbath, and participating in holiday celebrations. In the absence of a male over the age of 13, women fulfilled other observances connected to home and family, including: blessing children on the Sabbath day, arranging for a teenager's coming-of-age ceremony, or an infant's circumcision, and installing the parchment mezuzah scroll by the front door of the house.

Blessings

> Rabbi Yohanan said: "Would that man would pray all day." . . . This thought is further emphasized by the following statement in the *Ethics of the Fathers*: "When you pray, do not make your prayers a set routine, but offer them as a plea for mercy and grace before God."
>
> (Klein 1979: 12)

Judaic tradition is designed to promote a life in which the Lord is always remembered. Thus, in addition to the vast ritual life prescribed by tradition, a Jew knows blessings for many particular occasions, including: before and after eating or drinking anything, upon drying one's hands washed in the prescribed manner, when experiencing something new, and so forth. There are special blessings for experiences through each of the senses. For example, upon seeing a rainbow, one is to say, "who remembers the covenant, if faithful to His covenant, and keeps His promise." Upon smelling fruit, one is to say, "who gives a goodly scent to fruit" (Klein 1979: 47–48). And different blessings are said for each of these: fruit from trees, things that grow in or near the earth, foods that are not the product of the soil, pastry, bread, vegetables eaten both raw and cooked, and so forth.

Daily prayers

There are three daily prayer services for Jewish males: in the morning, afternoon, and evening. The morning prayer is conducted before a person goes about the daily work, sometime within about four hours after sunrise. The afternoon prayer is done as a break in the middle of a day of meaningful activity, sometime between 12:30 p.m. and sunset. This prayer recalls the daily temple sacrifice. The evening prayer is offered after completing the day's tasks. A particular mode of dress is suitable for both praying in one's home and in the synagogue. To promote a contemplative mood, the environment should be clean and free from objectionable odors or objects. Regularity of place and time also helps establish the proper psychological conditions for depth of prayer. It is appropriate to face towards the site of the temple in Jerusalem during prayer. A **minyan** is required for a public prayer service, or for any public reading of the Torah. Traditionally a minyan consisted of ten Jewish male adults. However, since a ruling in 1973 by the Rabbinical Assembly Committee on Law and Standards, women may now count as part of the minyan if the presiding rabbi is agreeable.

The Sabbath day (Shabbat)

The Sabbath is the Jewish form of weekly prayer. It occurs from sunset every Friday until sunset on Saturday. On the Sabbath no work is to be done. Strictly speaking one should not even turn on a light switch, or ride in a car, and so forth. Even pockets should be emptied before the Sabbath so that one is not carrying inappropriate articles on the holy day. To deepen one's appreciation for the Sabbath, each person should have some involvement in preparing for the celebration.

> The sage Shammai began his preparations on the first day of the week. If he saw a choice article of food, he immediately set it aside for the Sabbath. If, subsequently, he found one that was even finer, he set the latter aside for the Sabbath and used the other one beforehand.
>
> (Klein 1979: 55)

The Sabbath is the most sacred day of the week for Jews. Thus a woman had supplications that covered all duties surrounding the Sabbath day preparations, including baking braided bread (challah), baking noodle kugel pudding, and lighting candles to initiate the Sabbath meal. Baking challah is a mitzvah with specific ritual requirements, many of which have symbolic value. (For example, the dough must be mixed with forty-three eggs, just as the word "challah" adds up to forty-three according to Hebrew numerology.) A prayer from a collection of Yiddish *teḥinnott* called *The Three Gates* for offering Sabbath bread is as follows:

> May my *hallah* be accepted as the sacrifice on the altar was accepted. May my *mitsvah* be accepted just as if I had performed it properly. In ancient times, the High Priest came and caused the sins to be forgiven; so also may my sins be forgiven with this. May I be like a newborn child. May I be able to honor my dear Sabbaths and holidays. May God grant that I and my husband and my children be able to nourish ourselves. Thus may my *mitzvah* of *hallah* be accepted.
>
> (Weissler 1998: 33)

The woman's prayer mildly likens her act of fulfilling the commandment of making bread to making a sacrifice on the altar at the temple in Jerusalem. Reciting such prayers in Yiddish helped Jewish women turn their domestic chores into sacred duties. Holding the Sabbath as a day of rest is a challenge in secular societies due to economic pressures to work, and cultural tendencies to engage in non-religious activities. Yet dedicating the Sabbath to prayer is held as an ideal.

Pilgrim festivals

The major Jewish festivals are categorized into (1) Pilgrim festivals, and (2) Days of Awe. On festival days candles are lit, and generally no work should be done. In contrast to the Sabbath restriction, however, the preparation and serving of food is permitted, and the work restriction is not necessarily applied to every single day of the longer festivals. Festivals are spent with portions in prayer and study, and portions in feasting and rejoicing. But even in joy, one's social responsibilities must be remembered. The festivals of Pesach (Passover), Shavu'ot (Pentecost), and Sukkot (Booths) are key ceremonial occasions today in Judaism that survived from the days of the temple. They are called Pilgrim festivals because in ancient times Jews made pilgrimages to Jerusalem to celebrate them. Each Pilgrim festival was originally an agricultural ritual. Jews enhanced the religious meaning of these rituals by associating them with hierophanic events from the Hebrew scriptures and Jewish history.

Pesach (Passover)

The Pesach (Passover) festival elaborates on the biblical phrase: "I am the Lord your God, who brought thee out of the land of Egypt" (Numbers 15:41). There are eight days of Pesach, the first of which occurs on the Sabbath. This day begins the cycle of Jewish festivals according to a lunar calendar sometime in April to May. The festival commemorates the Lord's liberation of the Hebrews from bondage in Egypt around 1200 BCE (according to some estimates). Pesach represents a **revalorization** of the spring festival practiced by people in ancient Palestine. Some prayers recited on Pesach are directly about nature, including a prayer for dew, and descriptions of springtime from King Solomon's "Song of Songs." These poetic sentiments about nature's rebirth after winter are deepened by

BOX 4.3 A SPIRITUAL PATH: THE LIFE CYCLE IN JUDAIC TRADITION

Upon being born. The Talmud specifies that on the birth of a son, the father should say a blessing. Some couples now utter blessings, including some from weddings to show that a marriage is fulfilled in having a daughter. Jewish male infants undergo an ancient ritual known as the covenant of circumcision (brit milah) to observe the biblical commandment given to Abraham: "Throughout the generations, every male among you shall be circumcised at the age of eight days" (Genesis 17:12).

Upon becoming a son or daughter of the commandment. The bar mitzvah is a rite of passage in which a 13-year-old boy becomes an adult member of the Jewish community. Typically on the Sabbath day the initiate reads from the Torah scroll in the synagogue, and delivers a discourse. After he becomes a bar mitzvah, the young man wears the phylacteries (tefillin), and prayer shawl (tallith) for weekday prayers. The tefillin are two small boxes containing Torah passages, which are attached to the body with long leather straps. The Torah says one should keep the Lord's name in one's mind, and in one's heart. Thus one box is placed on the forehead, and the other on the left arm opposite the heart. (When this is secured with the leather straps, it spells the divine name.) The prayer shawl is a rectangular wool cloth with fringes that is wrapped around the head and draped over the shoulders. Nowadays non-Orthodox Jewish women sometimes wear the tallith.

Upon marrying. Upon marrying, both bride and groom take vows according to the Torah. Because the Lord took seven days to create the world, seven glasses of wine are consumed, seven blessings are read, and a traditional bride circumambulates her husband seven times. The couple stands beneath a canopy, and the groom (sometimes nowadays with the bride) breaks a glass to symbolize the second temple's destruction. The shards are often embedded in a piece of art. The groom places a gold ring on the index finger of the bride's right hand to be close to her heart – as a blood vessel links that finger to the heart. Modern couples often exchange rings, and wear them on the fourth finger of the left hand. Marriage in Judaism involves marriage contract (*ketubah*).

Upon dying. After a person is buried, relatives of the deceased "sit *shiva*" (shiva means "seven"). One must sit shiva for seven persons: mother, father, sister, brother, son, daughter, and spouse. Sitting shiva lasts for seven days including the Sabbath (though one never mourns on the Sabbath). While mourning, a person must not wear leather shoes, cut or shave his or her hair, bathe, wear cosmetics, engage in conjugal relations, or put on fresh clothing. During the week of shiva, friends and family "make a shiva call." Prayers for the departed are recited at home, and in the synagogue.

associations with a hierophanic event that meant new life for the children of Israel: the Exodus from Egypt.

Pesach opens with a **Seder** meal partaken at home. A book called the *Haggadah* provides detailed guidance for the celebration. Prayers, songs, stories, and the symbolism of the Seder meal amount to a ritual teaching about the escape from enslavement under a Egyptian pharaoh. By extension, the Seder becomes a teaching about the value of freedom, the need to affirm it, and the merit of rebellion against tyranny. Every Jew is asked to identify with those who were delivered from slavery in Egypt. Beyond that, "[a] Jew does not feel free himself if any one else is denied liberty" (Karp [1962] 1981: 239).

Shavu'ot (Pentecost)

The word *shavu'ot* means a "week of weeks," as the Greek term *pentecost* refers to fiftieth. This indicates that the festival occurs once seven weeks have passed after the beginning of spring. Shavu'ot is a harvest

BOX 4.4 SYMBOLS: THE PESACH SEDER

The focus of Pesach is the Seder, which is a highly symbolic meal. The Seder table is set with various items including cups of wine, unleavened bread (matzo), and a Seder plate. Here are some of the many symbolic meanings given to these items found on the table during the Pesach Seder every year in a traditional Jewish home.

Elijah's Cup. Four cups of wine are placed on the table, with a fifth cup of wine for Elijah. The door is kept open during the prayer recited while pouring wine into Elijah's Cup. Even in times of historical danger for Jews, the door was opened to indicate a fearlessness that accompanies faith in a final redemption to be initiated by Elijah's return to the world.

Plate 4.3 "Passover feast." Jews explain the Passover ritual with these words from the Hebrew Bible (Exodus 12:27): "It is the sacrifice of the LORD's passover, for that He passed over the houses of the children of Israel in Egypt, when He smote the Egyptians, and delivered our houses." The angel of death passed over houses whose side posts and lintels were smeared with the blood of the sacrificial lamb. The focus of Pesach is the Seder, a highly symbolic meal. The Seder table is set with various items including cups of wine, unleavened bread (matzo) and a Seder plate.

Miriam's Cup. Some modern liberal Jews place another vessel called on the table – Miriam's Cup. This sixth cup is filled with water in honor of Miriam, who helped save her brother Moses' life when he was an infant. Miriam was an Israelite leader associated with a well whose miraculous waters sustained the Israelites in the desert after the Exodus.

Unleavened bread. The bread is unleavened in remembrance of the hasty escape from Egypt made by the children of Israel who had no time to let the yeast work in the dough. It is also a reminder to abandon one's "swelling" pride. Three pieces of matzo are used. Two replace the braided bread (challah) used on Sabbath to represent the double share of **manna** that fell in the wilderness for the children of Israel to cover for the day at hand as well as the following day, which was the Sabbath (Exodus 16:22). The third reminds Jews of the poverty they must work to assuage. "The breaking of the matsah represents the bread of affliction – i.e., of the poor man who eats crumbs rather than whole loaves" (Klein 1979: 124).

Seder plate. These items are placed around the Seder plate in the following configuration: a shankbone (top right), a roasted or hardboiled egg (top left), bitter herbs such as horseradish (center), haroset, composed of finely chopped apples, raisins, almonds, and spices mixed with wine (lower right), and a green vegetable, usually celery or parsley (lower left). They are set in order of use, and carry the following meanings:

- The shankbone represents the ritual of sacrifice conducted by the patriarch Abraham and his descendants on special altars throughout Canaan, and subsequently at the temple in Jerusalem.
- A roasted or hardboiled egg reminds Jews of sacrifices at the temple, as well as the renewal of

life in springtime, and the metaphoric rebirth of the Israelites after the Exodus.

- Bitter herbs (such as horseradish) are reminiscent of the bitterness of bondage in Egypt.
- The haroset (made of finely chopped apples, raisins, almonds, and spices mixed with wine) resembles the mortar used by Hebrew slaves in Egypt in their labor. Its sweet taste offsets the herbs' bitterness to symbolize the Lord's loving kindness in leading the children of Israel out of bondage.
- The green vegetable (usually celery or parsley) represents the renewal of life in springtime. It is dipped into salt water, which reminds Jews of the tears shed by the Israelites while slaves in Egypt.

Some modern liberal Jews add a sixth item to the Seder plate – an orange. Because an orange is an unusual item, it is placed among the other foods to symbolize people who have been marginalized from the Jewish community, namely women and homosexuals.

festival. In ancient times harvesting involved gathering wheat, along with the first fruits from the trees. The agricultural harvest is symbolized by the display of green foliage and flowers in the synagogue. This natural symbolism is enhanced with a meaning that is specific to Jewish culture. It relates to the biblical story of the Lord's revelation of the Law to Moses when he ascended the mountain after leading his people out of bondage in Egypt. Pesach had marked the beginning of spring and the Exodus from Egypt. And after seven times seven days, the children of Israel were able to symbolically harvest their first fruits – the commandments from the Lord on how to lead their new lives.

Sukkot (booths)

Sukkot lasts for seven days, the first two of which are treated as full holidays. The Hebrew scripture presents the Lord's commandment "to observe the festival of the Lord [to last] seven days" after gathering the "yield of your land" (Leviticus 23:29). Hence Jews build temporary booths in which they take their meals for one week. Traditionally these were made of olive, myrtle, and palm branches. These days, small huts can be made of bamboo whose greenery serves as roofing. The huts remind Jews of the Hebrews who lived in booths in the desert after the Lord delivered them from bondage in Egypt. Traditional interpretations on the nature of the original "booths" differ. Some say the Hebrews constructed shelters in the desert, while others take the biblical story to mean that the Lord surrounded the children of Israel with "clouds of glory" as protection (Klein 1979: 157). The Pilgrim festival of Sukkot inspired Thanksgiving Day, which is celebrated as a secular holiday by people in the United States of America.

Days of Awe

The Days of Awe include two High Holy Days of the Jewish calendar as well as the ten days in between: Rosh Hoshanah, the Ten Days of Penitence, and Yom Kippur.

Rosh Hoshanah

Rosh Hoshanah signals the beginning of time. Thus it is called the Jewish New Year. It is now observed for two days as a time of self-examination. The color white is used in the synagogue to symbolize moral purification. A shofar (ram's horn) is blown on the first day (except if it falls on a Sabbath day, which is a day only of joy) to call the children of Israel to repent for their misdeeds of the past year. Altogether, 100 blasts of the shofar sound to warn the congregation: "Awake, you sleepers, and ponder your deeds; remember your Creator, forsake your evil ways, and return to God!" Some Orthodox Jewish communities symbolically throw their sins into a body of water. Other symbolism includes bread and apple dipped in honey for a good, sweet year to come, and round loaves of braided bread for a beneficent year ahead.

Ten Days of Penitence

An image that predominates through the High Holidays is that of "three ledgers." On Rosh Hoshanah three ledger books are opened in heaven. One contains names of those who are thoroughly non-virtuous. In another is written the names of those who are thoroughly virtuous. A third lists those who are in between. It is said that on Yom Kippur the names of virtuous people will be inscribed in the Book of Life. Thus, people in the intermediate category have the time between Rosh Hoshanah and Yom Kippur to repent, and join the ranks of the virtuous. Jews should always strive to practice loving kindness and other virtuous deeds. Yet the effort may feel most compelling during the Ten Days of Penitence. This is because only those whose names are included in the Book of Life are fated to live through the year ahead.

Yom Kippur

Yom Kippur is the Day of Atonement. It is the holiest day of the Jewish ritual year. Jews pass this day largely at the synagogue where the atmosphere is solemn and prayerful. A special light is burned throughout the day in memory of departed relatives. Neither leather shoes nor perfumes are worn. Jews fast from its commencement at sunset, until after the sun descends the following day. For twenty-five hours, men (age 13+) and women (age 12+) abstain from all eating and drinking. This is in response to a mitzvah that says "make atonement before the Lord," and "afflict your soul" (Leviticus 16:29–31, 23:27–32; Numbers 29:7). A person's atonement with the Lord is possible on this day, but transgressions against another human being cannot be forgiven unless one asks forgiveness of the person who was wronged. Thus during the Ten Days of Penitence, Jews had sought to reconcile themselves with anyone they may have hurt during the year. Now on the Day of Atonement they recite several times a communal confession of sins.

A LIVING TRADITION

Religion is often transformed through struggle. In the case of Judaic tradition, historically the rabbis struggled to deal with many issues not elaborated by the Torah. Over the past six-plus decades, Jews have debated the means of applying Jewish law to contemporary life, theologically responded to the catastrophe of the Sho'ah, and dedicated themselves to the endurance of the Medinat Yisra'el. Jews working for women's rights call for equal participation in time-bound mitzvoth along with men, and training in Jewish law to qualify them for leadership positions in the community. They consider that in our times family obligations need not prevent women from participating regularly in the prayer life of the synagogue. The traditional Jewish emphasis on family life is also

Plate 4.4 "Kol Nidre." On the eve of Yom Kippur Jews recite a declaration that removes all vows, obligations, and promises taken either unwittingly or under duress. The opening words (shown here) of the declaration in Hebrew are *Kol Nidre*, meaning All Vows. The rite of Kol Nidre annulled forced conversions of Jews to Christianity in Europe during the Middle Ages.

coming under scrutiny, since it gives no adequate role to single women. Women who choose to marry late – or not at all – seek a suitable place in Jewish ritual life with the opportunity to fulfill mitzvoth geared largely toward men, and then toward women who are married.

An organization of young Jewish women called Ezrat Nashim (Helping Women) presented a manifesto at the 1972 Rabbinical Assembly convention that declared the equality of Jewish women. Their demands paved the way for new avenues of worship for women in the Jewish community. Now women educated in Jewish law are seen increasingly as equal to men in their capacity to serve as rabbis. Rabbi Judith Nauptman was a member of Ezrat Nashim, and became the first woman ever to receive a Ph.D. in Talmudic studies. Rabbi Hauptman now works within Conservative Judaism on behalf of all underrepresented persons in Jewish society. For Hauptman, Judaism is a living tradition in which the struggle to "reread the rabbis" must always be waged. The social progress made by rabbis in times past is legitimate and should be furthered.

> That the rabbis find it necessary, in most tractates, to deal with the question of whom the law obligates means that they thought in terms other than those found in the Bible. They must have been interested in including, at least some of the time, groups that were not included in the Bible, such as women, or even groups not mentioned at all, such as the physically handicapped.
>
> (Hauptman 1998: 238)

Rabbi Hauptman has struggled for egalitarian transformation within a tradition whose very name "Israel" means "struggle" in honor of the patriarch Jacob who was made great through his struggle with God.

KEY POINTS

- It is misleading to view any religion as a single, monolithic entity because traditions evolve over time depending upon many circumstances. Therefore Judaism is best thought of as a religious system of Judaisms.
- Abraham is the founding patriarch of both the Judaic and Islamic traditions. Jews trace their religion through the descendants of Isaac whose mother was the Hebrew Sarah, while Muslims trace their religion through the descendants of Ishmael whose mother was the Egyptian Ḥājar.
- Moses received a set of mitzvoth from the Lord. Although ten mitzvoth (the famous Ten Commandments) are often associated with the Lord's message, rabbis identified 613 mitzvoth in the Torah.
- The age of prophecy is thought by Jews to have ended around the time of the Babylonian exile in the sixth century BCE. Stories of the prophets are contained in the portion of the Tanakh called Nevi'im (Prophets).
- The religion of the people of Israel that centered on temple worship was forced to evolve due to historical circumstances of the destruction of Solomon's temple in 587 BCE and Herod's temple in 70 CE. The result was the development of new forms of worship centered on the home and the synagogue.
- The Middle Ages in Europe gave birth to scholastic philosophy as well as to a form of mysticism known as cabbala. Jewish philosophy evolved with the onset of the European Enlightenment, while mysticism spread in the tradition of Ḥasidism.
- The 1700s to 1900s brought the heavy challenges of emancipation and persecution. Jews faced the challenges of assimilation and modern life as they interfaced with mainstream European and American society. European Jews faced the recurring challenge of persecution with the massive slaughter of the Sho'ah.
- Jewish ritual life hearkens back to ancient customs that were revalorized in light of traditional stories about the people of Israel and their relation to the Lord.

STUDY QUESTIONS

1 Who are the patriarchs and matriarchs of the people of Israel? What are their stories and contributions to the Hebrew tradition?

2 Who are the three types of leaders in ancient Israelite tradition? What were their functions?
3 List the three temples that were built in Jerusalem. Give the dates and circumstances of their construction and discontinuance of use.
4 Name some historical and cultural facts about the northern kingdom of Israel and the southern kingdom of Judah. How do their histories differ? What is common to their histories?
5 What is the relationship between Pharisees of the Hellenistic era and the later rabbinical tradition in Judaism?
6 What was the plight of Jews during the Middle Ages in Europe? How did they respond?
7 Name three major Jewish mystics, and outline their views on life.
8 Name and define the various key texts of Judaism: Tanakh (Torah, Nevi'im, Ketuvim), Talmud (Mishnah, Gemara'), Midrash. What is the difference between halachah and aggadah?
9 Name the major components of Jewish ritual life.

GLOSSARY

Abram (=Abraham) Patriarch of Jews, Christians, and Muslims. The Lord renamed him "Abraham" upon giving the command to circumcise all males of the covenant.

Adonai (Hebrew) Term for "Lord" spoken out loud in places where YHVH appears in the Hebrew Bible.

aggadah (pl. aggadot) Narrative. A Jewish legend, parable, joke, sermon, historical tale, or other narrative. Helps interpret biblical material, often by suggesting why something is or how it happened to become so.

Aramaic Ancient Semitic family of languages. Widely used by Jews and non-Jews in Palestine (mixed with Greek words) and Babylon (mixed with Persian words). Language of the Talmud.

Ark A chest made of acacia wood overlaid with gold that was housed in a special shrine in Solomon's temple in Jerusalem (ca. 1000 BCE), but which was lost when that temple was destroyed by the Babylonians in 587 BCE.

Ashkenazim (pl.) Diaspora Jews who lived in Germany and France, and their descendants. Many migrated to Eastern Europe or America. They speak Yiddish, a Germanic language, mixed with Semitic words.

ba'alim (sing. ba'al) Canaanite gods, the worship of whom was forbidden by Mosaic law.

cabbala (kabbala) Jewish mystical tradition.

conversos Jews forcefully converted to Roman Catholic Christianity in Spain and Portugal mainly during the 1400s.

diaspora Dispersion. Used with reference to Jews forced into exile following the destruction of the Jerusalem temple in 70 CE, and more broadly to Jews living outside the land of Israel.

'el A common word used in the Torah with reference to the Israelite God; general Semitic term for a god. The Hebrew Bible speaks of *'el shaddai*, *'el roi*, *'el olam* and *'el bethel* with reference to a mountain, seeing, eternity, and a house of a god.

emancipation The acquisition of equal legal status for Jews in eighteenth-century Europe, starting with US and French citizenship following the American and French Revolutions.

Exodus Exit. Name of the Torah scroll that tells of the Israelite escape from bondage in Egypt (ca. thirteenth century BCE or later).

Gemara' Two collections of commentary on the Mishnah. When combined with the Mishnah they form the Palestinian Talmud and the Babylonian Talmud.

halachah Legal material from the Talmud, Midrash, and later rabbinical writings; the sum total of religious law that defines the Jewish way of life.

Ha-Shem Name for the Lord used in the Tanakh.

Hebrew Members of early Jewish tradition; Semitic language in which Jewish scriptures are written.

Hellenistic era Three centuries from the time of Alexander the Great to the end of the Roman Republic (336–31 BCE) covering lands influenced by Alexander's conquest where culture mixed Hellenic (Greek) and West Asian (e.g., Persian) traditions.

hermeneutics The discipline of interpretation, often of scripture.

Israel Name used collectively for Jews as a people; name of modern nation-state established in May 1948; name of the northern kingdom taken from the Hebrews by the Assyrians in 722 BCE.

Israelites (Hebrew: *benei Yisra'el* = children of Israel) People of Jewish tradition named after the patriarch Jacob who was called Israel.

Jew (=Judean) Term for Jewish people based on the name of the southern kingdom of Judah, whose capital Jerusalem was destroyed by the Babylonians in 586 BCE.

malakhey elohim Angels; messengers of God.

manna A sweet, flaky food that the Israelites believed was provided by the Lord to sustain them in the desert after leaving Egypt.

messiah (Hebrew: *mesiach*) An anointed one from the line of David, the ancient Israelite king. Christians accept Jesus as the Messiah.

midrash A story *about* a story in the Hebrew Bible. A literary form filling a gap between two words – different from a commentary, which elaborates on one word or point.

minyan Ten adult Jews needed for worship. Women are included in Reform, Reconstructionist, and Conservative, but not in Orthodox Jewish sects.

Mishnah A compilation of Jewish instruction written in Hebrew from oral tradition that forms the early layer of the two Talmuds.

mitzvoth (sing. mitzvah) Commandments: 613 religious duties to be observed by Jews.

rabbi Teacher. A scholar of Jewish scripture.

revalorization The attribution of new meaning or value to a religious symbol.

Sabbath (Hebrew: *shabbat*) The last day of creation according to the Torah, celebrated weekly by Jews from before sundown Friday to after sundown Saturday.

scholasticism A movement among medieval theologians of the Abrahamic traditions who aimed to resolve apparent contradictions between faith and reason.

Seder Ritual meal taken on the first night or two of Pesach (Passover), following steps prescribed in the *Haggadah*.

Sephardim Diaspora Jews who lived in Spain, Portugal, or Islamic Mediterranean lands, and their descendants. Many migrated to North Africa or the Middle East. They speak Ladino, a language akin to medieval Spanish.

sephiroth Ten emanations of divine light contemplated by Jewish mystics in the cabbala tradition. They comprise the Tree of Life.

Sho'ah The Holocaust during which an estimated six million Ashkenazi Jews were systematically harassed or put to death under policies of genocide instituted by the German Nazi Third Reich between 1933 and 1945.

Talmud Commentary on the Tanakh (one from Palestine, one from Babylon) comprising collections called the Mishnah and the Gemara'.

Tanakh Name for the Hebrew Bible (Christian Old Testament) made from the first letters of Torah, Nevi'im, and Ketuvim.

tsaddik (m.; f. tsaddeket) "Pious one." A learned, saintly person among Ḥasidic Jews, usually addressed as "rebbe."

YHVH Tetragrammaton of the Lord's name. Jews do not speak this aloud, but substitute "Adonai" (Lord) in its place.

KEY READING

Barton, John (ed.) (1998) *The Cambridge Companion to Biblical Interpretation*, Cambridge: Cambridge University Press.

Brettler, Marc Zvi (2005) *How to Read the Bible*, Philadelphia, PA: The Jewish Publication Society.

Glatzer, Nahum N. (ed.) (1982) *The Judaic Tradition*, New York: Behrman House Publishers.

Hauptman, Judith (1998) *Rereading the Rabbis: A Woman's Voice*, Boulder, CO: Westview Press.
Idel, Moshe (1988) *Kabbalah: New Perspectives*, New Haven, CT, and London: Yale University Press.
Jacobs, Louis (1995) *The Jewish Religion: A Companion*, Oxford: Oxford University Press.
Koulton, Elizabeth (1976) *The Jewish Woman: New Perspectives*, New York: Schocken Books.
Pasachoff, N. and Littman, R. J. (2005) *A Concise History of the Jewish People*, New York: Rowman & Littlefield.

CHAPTER 5

Christian tradition

TIMELINE

	BCE	
	ca. 20–19 BCE	Herod the Great enlarges Jerusalem temple
Jesus of Nazareth	ca. 4 BCE–ca. 30 CE	
	CE	
	ca. 50–150	New Testament written
Paul and Peter martyred	ca. 64	
Perpetua martyred	d. 203	
	313	Edict of Milan
	325	Council of Nicea (first)
Emperor Constantine	d. 337	
Antony of Egypt	ca. 251–356	
	ca. 400	*Confessions* of Augustine
Benedict of Nursia	480–543	
Emperor Justinian	r. 527–565	
	730	Emperor Leo III issues edict to destroy icons
Charlemagne crowned as Holy Roman Emperor	800	
	910	Cluny monastery founded
	1054	Roman Catholic and Orthodox Churches split
	1096	Crusades begin, and continue for 250 years
Francis of Assisi	ca. 1181–1226	
Thomas Aquinas	1225–1274	
Martin Luther	1483–1546	
Ignatius Loyola	1491–1556	
John Calvin	1509–1564	
John Wesley	1703–1791	
	1 January 1901	First Pentecostalist glossolalia experience recorded in the USA
Dorothy Day	1897–1980	
Desmond Tutu	b. 1931	
	1945	*Nag Hammadi* texts discovered

The Christian traditions have their roots in Jewish Palestine of the first century CE. The founder, known as Jesus of Nazareth, came to be called Christ (the Anointed One). Jesus was born as a subject of the Roman Empire under Caesar Augustus (reigned 31 BCE–14 CE) who succeeded his great uncle Julius Caesar. For more than three decades King Herod the Great ruled Jewish Palestine for the Romans, which included both Judea and Galilee. Before his death in around 4 BCE, Herod transferred power to his sons who were princes under Caesar Augustus. When Jesus was aged 18 or so, rule of the empire fell to Augustus' stepson Tiberius (r. 14–27 CE). More than two-thirds of Christian history transpired in the context of the Roman Empire – first as a united empire, then as an expanded and divided twofold empire with eastern and western segments that modulated through fits and starts into the Byzantine and the Holy Roman Empires.

In the course of its complex history, the Christian religion split into three main groups (Orthodox, Roman Catholic, and Protestant) – as well as many subgroups. Three events in Jesus' life form the theological underpinnings of the Christian traditions: (1) the birth of Jesus, which represents the moment of **incarnation**, when God sent his son into the world, (2) the **crucifixion** of Jesus **Christ**, whose death atoned for the sins of humankind, and (3) the **resurrection** of Jesus, which demonstrated the possibility of eternal life for all who have faith in Him. These three events have been interpreted variously in different theological contexts. Their meaning is being debated still.

PART 1 CHRISTIAN PLAYERS

THE ULTIMATE PRINCIPLE

God the Father

In Christianity the ultimate principle involves a trinity: Father–Son–Holy Spirit. This **Holy Trinity** is considered a mystery in which three is one, and one is three. Christians consider God the Father to be the creator God of the Hebrew Bible. Thus they preserved the Jewish Tanakh as their **Old Testament**. Like the God of the Hebrew Bible, the Christian God is the all-powerful, all-knowing creator of the world. Yet Christians believe that God also has a Son who served as the Messiah. This Christ is Jesus of Nazareth.

IMAGINAL PLAYERS

Christ: transfigured and resurrected

According to the **New Testament** narratives, Jesus appeared in the imaginal realm with a body streaming with light. Once, while Jesus was still "alive," he was praying with three disciples on a mountain. His appearance changed to a radiant body of light, and Moses and Elijah joined him. Jesus said that this event, called the transfiguration, was a precursor to his status after death. Later, after being buried, Jesus rose from the dead and appeared to numerous disciples in a resurrection body. This body could eat and act like a real person. Yet it appeared and disappeared at will. For centuries theologians have speculated on the nature of Jesus' transfiguration and the resurrection.

The Holy Spirit

The Holy Spirit is associated with breath and inspiration. It is often symbolized as a dove streaming with light. Jesus was conceived by the Holy Spirit, and also conveyed the power of the Holy Spirit through his breath after being buried and rising from the dead. On one occasion, several disciples were together behind locked doors when the resurrected Jesus came and stood among them. He bid them peace, and showed them his hands and side – both of which had wounds from having been crucified. He bid peace upon them for a second time. "And with that he breathed on them and said, 'Receive the Holy Spirit. If you forgive anyone his sins, they are forgiven; if you do not forgive them, they are not forgiven'" (John 20:22–23). This forgiveness of sins in the name of the Holy Spirit became the basis for the Christian ritual of confessing sins, which are forgiven through the power of the Holy Spirit.

Angels

During the Middle Ages in Europe, Thomas Aquinas (1225–1274) applied his methods of scholastic reasoning to the subject of angels, wondering whether they occupied and moved through physical space. This type of inquiry was lampooned during the Enlightenment, since the question attributed to medieval scholars was put as, "How many angels can dance on the head of a pin?" Nonetheless, angels have played major roles in the Christian religious drama. Angels referenced in the New Testament function just as they do in the Judaic tradition, as the Lord's messengers. The figures of Gabriel and Michael carried over from the Judaic traditions, and new stories about them were added in the Christian context. Christians influenced by gnosticism added a dualistic flavor to their understanding of angels. Gnostic texts from the early centuries CE speak of a cosmic battle between good and evil. For Christians this battle takes place among the angels, and in the human struggle to lead a moral life. Satan, the fallen angel, took on great importance for Christians as an embodiment of evil. As Satan tempted Jesus in the desert, so he was thought liable to tempt any Christian, at any time.

Gabriel the messenger

The New Testament tells of two hierophanic events that pertain to the conceptions of Jesus and John, his cousin who was six months older. First Gabriel appeared to Zechariah to inform him that his wife Elizabeth had conceived. Zechariah was doubtful due to his advanced age, so Gabriel struck him dumb for the duration of the pregnancy. Gabriel then appeared to a young Hebrew woman named Mary to tell her that she would bear a son conceived by the Holy Spirit. The angel Gabriel appeared to Mary and uttered, SHALOM! (Peace! Hail!). Gabriel's word is preserved in Latin as AVE! (Hail!). Over the following 1,600 years, Gabriel's message was crafted into a prayer to Mary that is still recited today called the "Hail Mary." It begins: "Hail, Mary, full of grace! The Lord is with you. You are blessed among women, and blessed is the fruit of your womb, Jesus."

Michael the archangel

Christian tradition holds that Michael will weigh the souls of the dead during the Last Judgment when the world ends. In the meantime, Michael is available to guide Christians in their activities. The martyr Joan of Arc (1412–1431) is among the most famous Christians to whom Michael the archangel appeared. During her trial on 17 March 1431 Joan testified,

> "He was in the form of a true and honest man [*prud'homme*]. . . . As for the angels, I saw them with my own eyes. . . . I believe as firmly the doings and sayings of St. Michael who appeared to me as I believe that our Lord Jesus Christ suffered death and passion for us."
>
> (Pernoud 1966: 172)

Satan the tempter

Not every angel is beneficent. Satan had been an archangel. But he disobeyed God, and was cast down to hell from heaven. Satan is the deviant angel who tried to distract Jesus from his religious mission. And though Christians, following St. Augustine's teachings, believe that evil is the privation of good and does not exist in its own right, the figure of Satan is prominent in the New Testament *Book of Revelation*. There is written a prediction that Satan's army will be defeated by the forces of good at the time of the **apocalypse**.

Saintly figures

Mary mother of Jesus was a historical person. Yet she also appeared in visions to people throughout Christian history such as Bernard of Clairvaux, Dominic, Catherine of Siena, Ignatius Loyola, Teresa of Avila, and Bernadette at Lourdes. Biographical accounts of Christians through the years have told of the appearance of various saints in hierophanic visions. In fact, Joan of Arc testified that two women saints communicated with her – Catherine and Margaret.

EXCEPTIONAL PLAYERS

Mary

Three elements of the sacred story about Mary (fl. ca. 4 BCE) – the mother of Jesus – make her a marginal person who transcends the limits of ordinary history: (1) the Virgin Birth, (2) the Immaculate Conception, and (3) the Assumption. Not all Christians accept these miraculous claims about Mary, but they have great meaning for many who revere her, and call her Mary and Mother of God. The **gospels** of Matthew and Luke claim that Mary conceived Jesus as a virgin through the Holy Spirit. Mary has been called the Mother of God by some Christians, due to their belief in Jesus as the Son of God. Her elevated status called into question how someone with sin could have been the human agent to bring Jesus as God into the world. Thus some theologians posited that Mary was conceived as any other person, but was born without sin. Discussion of whether Mary herself was without sin became a burning question in the history of Christian theology – with mixed results. Those who accept the idea that Mary was born without sin call the phenomenon of Mary's exceptional purity the Immaculate Conception. Along with the idea of Mary's purity came the notion that at death God took her – body and soul – into heaven. This spectacular event is called the Assumption.

Jesus of Nazareth

History versus sacred story

The life of Jesus of Nazareth (c. 4 BCE–c. 30 CE) is known almost exclusively through four texts that cover about three years of his life. Yet the dates of Jesus' birth and death can be fairly well pinpointed on the basis of comments written in the first and second centuries CE by Josephus, Tacitus, Suetonius, and Pliny the Younger. Of the four Christian accounts of Jesus' life, only those attributed to Matthew and Luke relate a birth story – and their accounts contradict each other. This fact suggests that the gospel stories were shaped to impress different audiences. Matthew's gospel indicates that Mary and Joseph were from Bethlehem. According to his version three magi (Mazdean priests from Persia) traveled in search of the auspicious child. They took their cue from the placement of a particular star, and located Jesus (who would have been about 2 years old) in his parents' house in Bethlehem. On the other hand, Luke's narrative situates the home of Mary and Joseph in Nazareth. His version says that the family traveled south to Bethlehem to comply with a Roman order to be counted in the census. Regardless of whether Jesus was born in Bethlehem or Nazareth, historical research suggests that Jesus was raised in Nazareth, a hill town in Galilee (a fertile area north of Judea) with about 2,000 people, most of whom were Jewish.

Archeologists today are working on the remains of the ancient city of Sepphoris, located 3.7 miles northwest of En Nasira, a village thought to be the Nazareth of Jesus' day. It had been destroyed around the time of Jesus' birth, but was soon rebuilt by Herod Antipas who used it as his capital until 26 CE. Sepphoris had a diverse population with people and goods from all over the Roman Empire. Thus, if Jesus and his father lived in Nazareth, they probably made a decent living by working in this multicultural capital of Galilee. And though Jesus may have been a Palestinian peasant, he would have been more culturally astute than many Christian theologians of past decades assumed. Jesus probably had basic knowledge of Greek, could read the Hebrew scriptures, and spoke Aramaic in daily life. In an attempt to discern which events reported in the New Testament are historically true, biblical scholars developed criteria for assessing the likelihood that something actually happened.

The popular image of Jesus is that he was a carpenter who followed in Joseph's footsteps. Yet the image of an unsophisticated hewer of wood possibly conveyed by the gospels may not project an accurate portrait of Jesus. Knowing more details about the cultural circumstances in which Jesus lived enriches our understanding of what his life was like. For example, the Greek word for carpenter – *tekton* – found in the Christian scriptures refers to a person who had mastered many woodworking techniques using a variety of tools. So cultural historians suggest that Jesus and Joseph not only framed houses (which used little wood), but also made doors, window lattices, furniture, plows, and yokes. Beyond a cultural analysis of words such as *tekton*, archeological research provides rich details about the lives of people whose stories are sparsely recorded in the written texts.

Many details of Jesus' life are uncertain. Aside from a gospel report that Jesus impressed his teachers with a deep grasp of scripture at age 12 or so, his life before age 30 is a blank slate. For example, nowhere in the Christian scriptures is Jesus' marital status mentioned. There is no evidence one way or another of Jesus having a wife or becoming a father. Some people believe that the lack of mention means that we can simply assume that Jesus did what would have been typical of a Jewish

BOX 5.1 INTERPRETATIONS: THE SEARCH FOR THE HISTORICAL JESUS

Does a search for the historical reality of the New Testament damage a reading of the scripture as a sacred text? Theologians have struggled with this question since the mid-1700s. In searching for the historical Jesus, biblical scholars developed criteria to assess the historical strength of textual claims about Jesus. Every time a textual claim matches a criterion, its historical plausibility increases in their view. Here are some key criteria reworked from several sources (Meier 1991: 168–84; McArthur 1969: 139–44; Powell 1998: 31–50; Ehrman 2004: 217–23).

Proximity to the original event. A text becomes increasingly plausible the closer its author stands in time and location to the occurrence itself. When an event approaches the status of an eyewitness account and has less time to be forgotten, it has more chance of being accurate. Of course, an eyewitness might *lie* or be *mistaken* about what he or she saw. Thus, it is helpful to have more than one witness, who have no chance to confer with each other.

Independent attestation. If multiple sources present an event as historically true *and* the sources have not been influenced by each other, *then* the claims are independently attested. The two key factors embedded in this criterion are *numerous* and *independent.* A claim made by only one source *may be true.* However, as the number of independent sources attesting to something increases, the stronger the historical evidence grows. Of course, claims made by independent sources may not agree with each other, in which case other criteria must be applied to see how much truth value a claim has.

Non-contradiction among independent sources. The greater the number of sources that independently attest to an event, the more likely the evidence they give is correct. However, a historian could be misled into thinking that because independent sources came up with the same idea, the testimony is correct. All the sources could be equally mistaken. Also, multiple sources that are independently attested might contradict each other. If they do, a historian needs to apply other criteria to decide which version of a story is more likely to be correct.

Internal consistency of a single source. A text or report is judged to be more historically reliable if various pieces of data within it do not contradict each other. However, there are cases where contradictory versions of events presented in a single text might actually render the source *more* historically plausible, because an inconsistent text works against the self-interest of an author.

Contraindication of self-interest. Evidence that goes against the self-interest of the person who gave it is historically persuasive. Generally, an eyewitness or author would not make up stories that go against their self-interest. Thus, if a text presents data that contraindicates the self-interest of its author, that data is more historically plausible than evidence that supports the ambitions of its source. Some people have called this the criterion of "embarrassment."

Unbiased sources. Eyewitnesses or authors who are not prejudiced about an event are more likely to present data that is historically complete and accurate. The greater the lack of bias in the perspective of the source, the greater the chance that the event has been described objectively. For example, a polemical writing whose author wishes to persuade readers of a particular (polemical or one-sided) position is unlikely to present evidence that bolsters the opponent's viewpoint. Historical data might also be presented in a polemical, one-sided manner by a biased source.

male of his day and age: marry and have a family. Yet, from the start, Christians presented Jesus as celibate and unmarried with no heirs. A search for the "historical Jesus" is complicated by the fact that the gospels are sacred stories where (as in all sacred stories) historical details tend to be mixed with reports of events that may carry symbolic rather than literal meaning. In spite of the lack of historical detail about Jesus's life, students of religions must appreciate the fact that the story *as presented in the four gospels* is the basis upon which Christians through the ages have formed their understanding and their faith.

Plate 5.1 "The Four Evangelists." Here in an Egyptian painting (ca. 1175–1200) stand the "authors" of the four gospels of the Christian New Testament. Elsewhere in Christian art these four evangelists are represented as the "living creatures" spoken of in the New Testament (*Revelation* 4: 7) that will appear at the Throne of God when the world ends: Matthew is the human/angel, Mark is the lion, Luke is the ox and John is the eagle.

Baptism and encounter with Satan

The four gospels focus on what was probably a three-year period starting when Jesus was around age 30. At that time Jesus went to the Jordan River to be baptized by John "the Baptist." Jesus' cousin was so-called because John was a powerful teacher who performed the purification ritual of immersion to prepare people for the Kingdom of God – which he said was coming soon.

Luke's gospel (Luke 4:1–13) says that Jesus was "full of the Holy Spirit" after John baptized him – and the Holy Spirit prompted him to go off alone into the desert. So Jesus left the Jordan River, and spent forty days in solitude, privation, and contemplation. "He ate nothing during those days, and at the end of them he was hungry." During the fast, Jesus encountered the devil Satan who tried to pull him away from the spiritual life in a monumental struggle. Satan presented Jesus with three offers – all of which Jesus refused:

- The devil wanted Jesus to perform a miracle: "Tell this stone to become bread!" Jesus fired back, "Man does not live by bread alone!" and refused.
- Jesus found himself transported to a high place and saw "in an instant" vast regions of the world. There Satan enticed Jesus: "If you worship me, it will be all yours!" Jesus retorted with a line from the Hebrew Bible (Deuteronomy 6:13): "It is written: 'Worship the Lord your God and serve him only.'"
- Leading him to the place, Satan demanded that Jesus throw himself off the highest point of Herod's temple in Jerusalem. He said that surely angels would guard Jesus so that even his foot would not so much as strike a stone! Jesus retorted with a verse from the Hebrew Bible (12 Deuteronomy 6:16): "Do not put the Lord your God to the test!"

Jesus prevailed, and Satan departed. Then Jesus left the desert and ate food. He went home to Galilee, and began his ministry.

Ministry and miracles

In Galilee, Jesus preached for probably a little over two years – after which he entered Jerusalem to confront the circumstances of his death on the cross. Jesus' baptismal initiation and triumph over Satan opened what might be called a prophetic mission, although Christians believe that Jesus was the Son of God and not merely a prophet. Yet, Jesus referred to himself indirectly as a prophet like Isaiah.

Jesus earned a reputation in Galilee – but was treated with scorn in the synagogue of his own town of Nazareth where he may have received his religious education. On the Sabbath day Jesus read words of the prophet Isaiah from a scroll of the Hebrew scriptures (Isaiah 61:1):

> *Ruach Adonai YHVH alai y'an Mashach YHVH.*
> (The spirit of the Lord GOD is upon me, because the LORD has anointed me.)

Jesus went on to say: "Today this scripture is fulfilled in your hearing. . . . No prophet is accepted in his home town." Luke's gospel reports that this made the congregation furious. "They got up, drove him out of the town, and took him to the brow of the hill on which the town was built, in order to throw him down the cliff" (Luke 4:29). Jesus walked away from the commotion and left Nazareth for Capernaum. There again he went to the synagogue on the Sabbath, the day of rest. Someone screamed at him, "What do you want with us, Jesus of Nazareth? Have you come to destroy us?" Jesus shouted back, "Be quiet!" and cast a demon out of him.

John the Baptist was beheaded by the order of Herod Antipas. At the king's birthday party, his stepdaughter Salome received on a platter the Baptist's head, which she personally had requested. After hearing the news of John's decapitation, Jesus repaired by boat to a solitary place. He was met by a crowd on shore, and healed who was ill among them. Then as the hour was getting late Jesus assured his disciples that they would all have something to eat. With five loaves of bread and two fish, Jesus fed the whole crowd, with more left over. He contemplated heaven, took the loaves in his hands and broke them. As for the fish, there was enough for all (Matthew 14:13–21). When the time came to leave, Jesus had his disciples go in the boat. He went by himself to pray on the mountain. During the fourth watch of the night, Jesus looked out over the water and began walking toward the boat. His disciples became afraid, thinking they were seeing a ghost. But, as in other such circumstances, Jesus reassured them that it was he. After that Jesus left Galilee forever. He gradually made his way down to Jerusalem, preaching from village to village as he went.

Jews from far-flung areas of the Roman Empire traveled to Jerusalem for the Passover feast that was celebrated at Herod's temple. People needed to convert their currencies to purchase animals for ritual sacrifice at the temple, so they would stop at the money changers' tables. Tradition says that when Jesus arrived at Herod's temple he was outraged at the commercialism, and knocked over those tables. Herod's temple was an extravagant, new temple – only about fifty years old. The king built it to replace Zerubbabel's temple, the modest structure that had served the Jews as a house of worship for 500 years, since the Babylonian exile. Jesus' act of defiance on the temple grounds caught the attention of the Roman authorities who were wary of having large crowds of Jews present for the holidays. Jewish religious authorities would have been disturbed as well. They did not want to stir up the wrath of the Roman officials against them. Jesus had also been so bold as to predict the fall of Jerusalem – as had Prophet Jeremiah immediately before the Babylonian invasion in 586 BCE. Jeremiah, however, lived to see his prediction come true. Jesus did not. He was killed. Just a few days of his presence in Jerusalem were enough to get Jesus arrested, due to the high pitch of political tension. Jesus was apprehended during a meal taken with his twelve closest disciples. The meal came to be known as the Lord's Supper or Last Supper.

According to Christian tradition, at the Last Supper Jesus declared that he was serving his body and blood as the bread and wine of the Passover feast. This event became the hierophanic prototype for the Christian celebration of the Mass – and thus arguably the most famous meal in the history of Western civilization. Among the twelve disciples present was one by the name of Judas Iscariot, who is said to have betrayed Jesus. Jesus seemed to know that this would happen. He announced, "One of you will betray me," but continued with the meal. Not long after, Judas Iscariot identified Jesus for the Roman soldiers, who turned him over to Pontius Pilate, procurator of Judea. After a brief questioning, Pilate sentenced Jesus to death by crucifixion.

Crucifixion

Crucifixion was not a Jewish form of punishment, but thousands of Jews had been condemned to death by crucifixion in Jesus' day. Death by hanging on a cross was the common method of execution in the Roman Empire up until the time of Constantine, the Roman emperor who stopped the persecution of Christians. It was a degrading form of punishment. Roman officials typically chose a main road into a city for the scene of execution where the publicity would act as a deterrent to crime. Crucifixion was meant to be a warning. Yet, many people would cast their eyes in a different direction as they passed criminals hanging on their crosses. Crucifixion is a torturous death because the hanging brings a slow, painful demise that ends in suffocation. In the case of Jesus, the place of crucifixion was a hill called Golgotha, "the skull."

According to the New Testament, Jesus was taken down from the cross. Christians presume that because he was dead on the cross the soldiers did not break the bones of his legs, as they would have done to the other men who were crucified at the same time. Tradition says that before removing Jesus from his cross one soldier pierced his side with a spear, whereupon blood and water flowed out. John's gospel says that these events fulfilled predictions in the Hebrew scriptures (Exodus 12:46, Numbers 9:12, Psalm 34:20, and Zechariah 12:10). Near the place where Jesus was crucified was a garden with a new tomb. A wealthy man named Joseph of Arimathea, who "was a disciple of Jesus, but secretly because he feared the Jews" (John 19:38) asked Pilate for Jesus' body, and with Pilate's permission took it away. Joseph and Nicodemus had strips of linen and a mixture of about seventy-five pounds of myrrh and aloes. Then, in accordance with Jewish customs, they prepared Jesus' body for burial (John 19:39–40).

Resurrection

The death and burial of Jesus do not mark the end of the Christian sacred story. After three days, Jesus rose up. The intent was to keep the body in the tomb until after the Sabbath, when work could be done again. After the Sabbath day, three of Jesus' disciples – three women – came to the tomb and found that the stone that had blocked the entrance had been moved. There was no corpse inside the tomb. This event is called Christ's resurrection. Luke tells of this hierophanic event:

> On the first day of the week, very early in the morning, the women took the spices they had prepared and went to the tomb. They found the stone rolled away from the tomb, but when they entered, they did not find the body of the Lord Jesus. While they were wondering about this, suddenly two men in clothes that gleamed like lightning stood beside them. In their fright the women bowed down with their faces to the ground, but the men said to them, "Why do you look for the living among the dead? He is not here; he has risen!" . . .
>
> When they came back from the tomb, they told all these things to the Eleven and to all the others. It was Mary Magdalene, Joanna, Mary the mother of James, and the others with them who told this to the **apostles**. But they did not believe the women, because their words seemed to them like nonsense. Peter, however, got up and ran to the tomb. Bending over, he saw the strips of linen lying by themselves, and he went away, wondering to himself what had happened.
>
> (Luke 24:1–6, 9–12)

Luke (ch. 24) relates two more incidents where Jesus appeared to people after his death and before he was taken up into heaven. Some theologians believe that Jesus actually rose from the dead, while others think this could be a symbolic story. In either case, Christians generally believe that the New Testament story indicates that others too will be resurrected on the Day of Judgment.

HISTORICAL PLAYERS

Early followers of Jesus

Women followers

More is said about men than about women followers of Jesus – and no female is called a **disciple** in the gospels. However, several women are named in the New Testament, and two became prominent in the Christian tradition: Mary the mother of Jesus, and Mary of Magdala on the Sea of Galilee who is named a dozen times in the gospels. The two women are complementary figures who are at times portrayed as opposites: the sinless virgin and the penitent sinner. Mary the mother of Jesus maintained a presence in her son's life from start to finish in all the years he is tracked by the gospel authors (which are not many), and Mary Magdalene occupies a privileged position in the history of Christianity as the first person to witness the resurrected Christ. Jesus himself in the midst of the hierophany by the empty tomb bids her two things: to refrain from touching him, and to tell others about the appearance of his resurrected body. Other women mentioned by name in the gospels include two sisters Martha and Mary, and Salome. A few more are named in other New Testament texts (such as the letters), and incidents involving unnamed women are scattered throughout the scriptures. Many wives of Jesus' close disciples and brothers were also followers. Overall, it is safe to assume that a number of women were interested in Jesus.

Simon (Peter)

Simon (Peter) and Jesus had a very close relationship. He was somewhat older than Jesus, and the two may have known each other as children. Peter and his brother Andrew worked as fishermen in Galilee, and became Jesus' first two disciples. When approached by Jesus to join him, Peter immediately responded to the call. His faith in Jesus was tried three times: (1) One day Jesus was standing on the water offshore and Peter began to approach him; he suddenly fell when his faith waned. (2) Peter was among the disciples who fell asleep in the Garden at Gethsemane, when Jesus asked them to stay up with him (Matthew 26). (3) Jesus predicted that Peter would deny three times that he knew Jesus after Jesus' trial. Peter objected, but what Jesus predicted came to pass. Although Peter seems to have wavered, it was he who declared his belief that Jesus was "the Messiah, Son of the living God" when Jesus asked, "Who do you say that I am?"

Jesus eventually transmitted the Christian spiritual lineage through Peter. As a symbolic indication that he would provide a rock-like foundation for the Church, Jesus called him Cephas (Peter), meaning rock. Peter founded a church in Antioch, which still exists today as the Antiochian Orthodox Church. Peter later served as the Bishop of Rome for twenty-five years, thus becoming (in effect) the first pope. Every Bishop of Rome thereafter was counted as a successor of Saint Peter the Apostle. The church in which popes normally celebrate the Mass in Rome is called Saint Peter's Basilica because Peter's tomb is there. Peter became a martyr for Christ. His punishment was death by crucifixion. Although there is no historical consensus on the point, tradition holds that Peter was placed upside-down on the cross. It is said that he felt unworthy to be hanged as Jesus was hanged.

The Twelve Apostles

Jesus appointed twelve of his disciples to be apostles "that they might be with him and that he might send them out to preach and to have authority to drive out demons" (Mark 3:14–15). These are called The Twelve: Bartholomew, Thaddeus, and James of Alphaeus about whom basically nothing is known; Thomas, whose name means "twin"; Matthew, a tax collector/customs official; Andrew and Philip, who may have been John the Baptist's disciples; Simon the Zealot, a strict observer of Jewish law; Judas Iscariot, who betrayed Jesus; James and John, brothers that Jesus called the Sons of Thunder; and Simon Peter, possible author of the gospel written down by his disciple Mark. After Judas betrayed Jesus, he committed suicide. The original group that Jesus named as his apostles was then called The Eleven. James was the first Christian martyr. He became head of the early Christian community in Jerusalem, and was eventually stoned to death.

Apostle Paul of Tarsus

Most Jews of the diaspora did not believe that Jesus was the Messiah (Christ). Rabbis were under pressure to preserve their tradition following the destruction of Jerusalem in 70 CE, and were not in a position to tolerate the views of a fringe element that believed the Messiah had come. To consolidate their position in the new environment, they excluded Christians from synagogue life. Rejection from the synagogue prompted some new Christians to allow gentiles (non-Jews) to participate in the rituals of the new faith. A liberal apostle who changed his name from Saul to Paul (d. ca. 62 CE) endorsed this missionary policy. But he only became an apostle after having a hierophanic experience of the risen Christ. Before becoming a Christian, Saul was on his way to Damascus, Syria, to find any followers of Jesus who might be there. He had received authority to take them as prisoners to Jerusalem. Saul had never met Jesus, but fervently opposed the existence of this deviant group of Jews. While on the road to Damascus, Saul was thrown flat on to the ground by some sudden, invisible force. The men traveling with Saul did not see anyone, but stood speechless as they saw him faltering. Saul got himself up, but could not see. They led him by hand into Damascus. Saul remained blind for three days, during which time he ate and drank nothing.

Following the incident Saul had a change of heart, and became an avid missionary. Paul (Saul) believed that the Christian message would bring salvation to Jews and gentiles alike. But he had to argue with Jesus' conservative brother James and others over how to apply the mitzvoth. The early Christians fiercely deliberated over such questions as: Should gentiles be circumcised as a sign of their covenant with God? Should pagan converts eat according to the strict Jewish dietary laws? To what extent should converts abandon their pagan customs and beliefs? Paul established the Greek Orthodox Church by founding Christian communities in the Greek cities of Corinth, Thessalonica, and Philippi that

BOX 5.2 CULTURE CONTRAST: RIVALS TO EARLY CHRISTIANITY – RELIGION IN THE ROMAN EMPIRE

Manichaeism. The cult of the Persian prophet Mani (b. 216 CE) practiced asceticism in order to release particles of light that Satan stole from the world of light and imprisoned in man. A sign of liberation that comes at the moment of gnosis (knowledge) is that light fills the person.

The cult of Eleusis. Initiation into the mystery cult of Eleusis created a spiritual bond among initiates who were to abide together in the afterlife. The main ritual symbol of the cult was a stalk of sacred grain, displayed at the hierophanic moment of the sacred ritual.

The cult of Dionysus. The mystery cult of Dionysus involved a hierophanic experience of the grape when wine was imbibed. Dionysus was a god who died and was resurrected, and the performance of his rituals purified the community. Dionysus was the patron of theater.

The cult of Isis. Isis was the Egyptian wife of the perennial pharaoh Osiris. She had the reputation of answering prayers swiftly. Isis means throne, and she was represented seated on a throne suckling her son Horus.

The cult of Mithras. Soldiers of the Roman army worshiped Mithras. The priest of the cult of Mithras sacrificed a sacred bull to release creative powers into the world. Mithras was a Zoroastrian deity whose birthday was celebrated on 25 December.

The cult of Orpheus. Orpheus was a deity whose music made beasts and even rocks and trees respond. He musically charmed Hades into letting his wife leave the underworld. But he made the mistake of looking back after promising not to, and she slipped down again. Members of the cult made use of sacramental wine, and believed in reincarnation.

were open to both Jews and non-Jews. Corinth was a Greco-Roman city whose majority worshiped at Apollo's temple, so he had to adjust the Jewish message to suit a pagan mentality. Paul focused on the resurrection of the crucified savior God. Paul also went to other places including Antioch, the capital of Roman Syria that had a community of about 40,000 Jews.

Christian martyrs

In the early Christian centuries the followers of Jesus aroused suspicion where they lived in the Roman Empire by acting antisocially – gathering before daybreak, singing hymns, and sharing private meals. In the Roman Empire people were obliged to sacrifice to the gods on important festival days, including the emperor's birthday. These early Christians appeared seditious because they would not buy offerings for the gods, or join in the festivities. Rejection of the Roman gods threatened the public good, because in the Roman view the gods must be pleased.

At first, Christians counted legally as Jews. This was to their advantage because Jews were exempt from the Roman civil festivities, as their long-standing ancient tradition of not worshiping other gods was respected. Pliny the Younger (ca. 110 CE), the new governor of a Roman province, wrote a letter to Emperor Trajan asking for guidance after receiving complaints about the Christians under his jurisdiction. He noted that the followers of Christ appeared to be a group distinct from the Jews. Thus once it dawned on officials that Christians no longer followed the ancient Hebrew religion, they were expected to participate in Roman civil religion. Following Pliny's inquiry the Roman government developed a policy of execution. Christians would be asked twice whether they would sacrifice to the Roman gods. If they maintained defiance, they could be put to death.

Many Christians were willing to die for their faith. Perpetua (d. 203) was one such martyr. She insisted on being killed, and gave birth just before marching to her death in the Roman amphitheater. When beasts mauled her, Perpetua acted as if she were going to heaven. Tens of thousands of people witnessed this type of public death in the amphitheater. Consequently the martyrs' stories began to circulate, and Christians earned a reputation for heroism. In the half century following Perpetua's martyrdom, Christianity grew markedly. The Romans felt threatened because the new faith undermined their relationship with the gods. Thus people were required to show tickets proving they had performed the civic sacrifices. Moreover, the Persians threatened their border regions. With the Roman Empire in crisis, there was a crackdown. Christians were methodically rounded up, and a person could be arrested merely for identifying as a Christian. Ironically, this cult of martyrs actually strengthened the Church. For their part, Christians were tightening their organization and building an administration.

Christian emperors

Constantine

Constantine (272/3–337 CE) was a worshiper of the sun god Apollo. As a Roman general he even persecuted Christians, although his mother Helena was Christian. But the history of Christianity took a sharp turn for the better in the year 312 CE when Constantine was struck by a vision of a cross upon the blazing sun, and the words, "By this sign you will conquer." Inspired by the hierophany, the general ordered his soldiers to paint the sign of the cross on their shields. After their phenomenal success, the cross became a symbol of triumph. The following year Constantine issued the Edict of Milan which allowed Christians to practice their religion openly without threat of persecution. The emperor secured the position of Christianity as a major player in world history by using his political power to do four main things: (1) give economic and political support to create a religious institution, (2) establish a Christian cultural identity, (3) establish an official Church dogma, and (4) root out opposition.

- ***The Christian Church received state sanction and support.*** Constantine instituted legal reforms that included land grants for the Church, and used public funds to copy bibles and build churches. This created an economic boom that enabled the Christian Church to grow into a powerful institution.
- ***The Christian cultural identity matured.*** Constantine fostered an international Christian identity by standardizing certain elements of ritual

and doctrine: (1) He issued the Edict of Milan that fixed the date of Easter, and proclaimed the day of the sun as a public holiday. (2) He authorized his mother Helena to build churches in Palestine on sites where hierophanic events related to Christ's life were believed to have occurred. (3) He created a fifth major center of Christian life by establishing his imperial headquarters at Byzantium (later called Constantinople, and more recently Istanbul) – a city that rivaled Alexandria, Antioch, Carthage, and even Jerusalem.

- ***The divinity of Jesus was officially proclaimed.*** Constantine wanted a unified religious institution to undergird a unified empire. To resolve problematic questions he convened the first **Council of Nicea** at Nicea in Asia Minor (Turkey). At the council over two hundred (225 or 318) Christian bishops established the doctrine of the divinity of Jesus. The bishops concurred that Jesus was truly the Son of God. They used the term *homoousia* to describe a consubstantial Father–Son relationship, which meant that the Son was considered to be of the same substance as the Father. Thus Jesus was officially recognized as an equal component in a Trinity of Father, Son, and Holy Spirit. These official new beliefs became the basis for the Christian Nicene Creed.
- ***Heresy was uprooted.*** The Nicene Creed provided the Church and empire with a standard test of faith through which heretics could be identified. In his quest for unity, Constantine persecuted people whose views lay outside the newly established parameters of the Christian mainstream – including gnostics, and anyone who did not accept the Old Testament.

Among the bishops who participated in the Council of Nicea, all but two accepted the Nicene Creed. They were branded as heretics and banished along with a theologian named Arius (ca. 250–336). The Council condemned Arius' theology as heretical because it made Jesus merely a divine creature, neither truly God nor truly man. The official position of the Church declared that God the Father and God the Son are one. Arius denied the true divinity of Christ, saying that Jesus cannot be the same as God. Arius believed that God created the world from nothing and begot a Son. He granted that the Son was the first creature, and a dignified creature. But Arius did not believe that Christ the Son of God was eternal or equal with God the Father. He thought that the Son of God had to be subordinate, and was not God by nature. Officials of the Church thought that Arius set up a demigod beside God, and rejected his views as contradicting the new Nicene Creed.

Arius was probably a Libyan who had great success as a preacher. People revered him for his asceticism. He wrote little, but embedded what the Church came to think was a heretical doctrine in popular songs about the person of Christ. The melodies were based on popular drinking and theatrical songs, and the public received them with enthusiasm. To counteract the popularity of hymns based on folk tunes, Ambrose, Bishop of Milan, introduced such singing into his services. Thus, congregational singing entered the mainstream church. Arius was exiled, but was allowed to return three years later. He died shortly thereafter. All heretical materials related to the Arian liturgy were destroyed. Hence, little is known about them today.

Justinian

Justinian (r. 527–565) was a Byzantine emperor. Although of peasant stock, he adopted the semi-divine status as did Roman emperors of the old days. From Constantinople, he ruled the Byzantine Empire in its early stages when political and cultural influence from Rome was still great, and Latin was the language of culture. Western Europe was on the brink of what historians sometimes call the Dark Ages (550–1000) because it was still being pounded by barbarian tribes after the sack of Rome in 410. Emperor Justinian sought to extend Christianity into Central and Northern Europe, and to reassert Roman control over the western portion of the old Roman Empire. He managed to extend his (early Byzantine) empire to its farthest reaches from southern Spain, across North Africa through Egypt and north through the holy land of Palestine.

Justinian's ambitions were never realized. It proved impossible for his successors to patch together the eastern and western parts of the old Roman Empire. Within a century of Justinian's death, large portions of the (more mature) Byzantine Empire fell into Muslim hands. By the year 750 the old Roman Empire was reduced to sections of Asia Minor (Turkey), the Balkans, and portions of southern Italy. In the absence of Roman power, this Byzantine Empire gave up Latin and reverted to Greek as its liturgical language. The Hagia Sophia, a great church built by Justinian in Constantinople, was transformed into an Islamic mosque and later into a museum. And Justinian's *Corpus of Civil Law*, which standardized laws across the Roman Empire, persists as the legal foundation for most countries in Western Europe to the present day.

Charlemagne (?742–814)

Western Europe was filled with disruption while Justinian and others tried to rule from Byzantium. The Muslim advance into France was halted in the Battle of Tours in 732 by Charlemagne's grandfather Charles Martel – exactly one century after the death of Prophet Muḥammad in Arabia. But sixty-eight years later Christianity in the West began a monumental climb to power beginning with Charlemagne (742–814). The new Pope Leo III (795–816) put a crown on Charlemagne's head on Christmas Day in the year 800 CE, effectively transforming him from king of the Franks into the first Holy Roman Emperor. This further deepened the split between the eastern and western Christians of the old Roman Empire.

With Charlemagne on the throne, three regional powers came into play. Contact among them stimulated a cross-fertilization of cultures. In fact, Western Europe is deeply indebted to the sophisticated civilizations that the Byzantines and Muslims spawned (with the help of Persian, Egyptian, and Indian cultures).

- ***The Byzantine Empire.*** This was the surviving eastern portion of the old Roman Empire. These eastern Christians rejected Latin and shifted to the older classic Greek as their liturgical language.
- ***The House of Islam.*** Islamic rule pervaded large portions of the Persian Empire, Syria, Palestine, and Egypt, North Africa, and parts of Spain. Muslims used Arabic as their religious language to recite the Qur'ān.
- ***The Holy Roman Empire.*** This was a reconstruction of the old western portion of the Roman Empire, which was cobbled together from the barbarian tribes in Northern Europe and the Mediterranean areas of Southern Europe. It revived Latin as the Church language.

There was one universal (i.e., Catholic) Christian Church for a little over a thousand years after Jesus was crucified in Jerusalem. The Christian community had risen from obscurity and prominence. It had been unified in dogma, law, and ritual for the sake of skillful rule under Constantine, Justinian, and Charlemagne. But that homogeneous agreement came to an end in 1054 with a schism between East and West that has hardly been healed even to this day. For two and a half centuries, during the Crusades, the Roman Catholic and Byzantine Orthodox Churches had their ups and downs as Europeans passed through parts of the Byzantine Empire on their way to and from Jerusalem. After the Crusades there was little communication for 600 years between the Eastern Orthodox Churches and the Roman Catholic Church until 1950.

Christian religious specialists

Deacons, presbyters, bishops, and popes

In the second and third centuries the Christian Church grew into a formal institution that gradually became more and more powerful. Three categories of ministry evolved: deacon, presbyter, and bishop. Bishops were elder presbyters, and popes were drawn from among them – after 1054 when the Bishop of Rome broke from the Bishops of the Byzantine Empire. Bishops headed established Christian churches, while deacons served them and interfaced with the community. Once the Lord's Supper was understood as a sacrifice to God, church authorities believed that religious specialists should perform the ritual imitation of Jesus' last meal. Thus only bishops presided at the early celebrations of the **Eucharist**. As the number of churches grew, the presbyter-elders (bishops) bestowed authority upon other presbyters to perform the sacrificial ritual that offered bread and wine as the body and blood of Christ. This formalization of the Lord's Supper squeezed out women's participation in the institutional affairs of the Church, as only the ministerial office of deacon was considered suitable for women – and that, only for widows. These widowed deaconesses mostly engaged in baptizing other women. Eventually they were removed from this function as well. Once the Christian sacraments were formalized, bishops and presbyters took over the functions of priests, while laypersons of both sexes could function as deacons. And while women could eventually enter into monastic life, such nuns never obtained permission to become priests in the Roman Catholic Church, and the issue remains alive even to this day.

Hermits

Some rare individuals who felt a great calling decided that living alone in the desert was the way to imitate the life of Christ. One such person was Antony of Egypt (ca. 251–356) whose strict program of fasting and praying brought on many intensive visions. A century or so after he died, Mary of Egypt, a prostitute from Alexandria, voyaged with a group of Libyan and Egyptian men to Jerusalem. There at Golgotha, the site of Jesus' crucifixion, Mary had a hierophanic experience. She repented and became a Christian hermit. Legend says that Mary bought three loaves of bread, crossed the Jordan River, and went into the desert, where she lived for forty-seven years until her death.

Monks, nuns, and friars

Not every dedicated Christian was cut out for the harsh life of isolation first exemplified by Antony. And not every dedicated Christian wanted to remain as a layperson or join the formal institution of the Church as a priest. Thus in the few centuries after Christianity was legalized in the Roman Empire, three men came up with rules of community life that shaped the practice of Christian monasticism: Pachomius in Egypt (d. 346), Basil of Caesarea (in Cappadocia, i.e., in modern-day Turkey) (d. 379), and Benedict of Nursia (Italy) (d. ca. 550). This began the Christian monastic movement that continues in the Eastern Orthodox and Roman Catholic Churches today. Eastern monastics use the *Rule of Basil*, while Roman Catholics use the *Rule of Benedict*.

Western Europe prospered between 1000 and 1300. Its population doubled as people lived longer, cities grew, and the economy boomed. As Europe grew more prosperous, monasteries became large-scale landowning institutions. Both men and women had access to monastic educations where they typically observed vows of poverty, obedience, and chastity under the *Rule of Benedict*. However, along with the increased wealth and membership, the overall quality of spiritual dedication found among monastics seemed to decline.

- *Cluniacs.* The French monastery at Cluny (founded in 910 in Burgundy) became a center where monasticism was to be reformed. Cluny was the largest among the monasteries of the time (covering twenty-five acres), and was a powerful seat of Christian culture that became a key pilgrimage site with its relics, and new style of choral music that had a system of chord progressions, intervals, and musical notation. The Cluniac monks earned a reputation for strictly holding to the *Rule of Benedict*, and those who came to Cluny were drawn by its reputation for a purer monastic life. Cluny was the next most important Christian center after Rome in the West, and four popes were drawn from monks educated there. But in time the Cluniac monasteries succumbed to the same problems as their predecessors. Landed wealth and indiscriminate growth in numbers undermined the intensive spiritual quality of its early days.
- *Cistercians.* Bernard of Clairvaux (1090–1153) revived the Cistercian monastic order at Citeaux, France. The Cistercians claimed that the Cluniacs ignored Benedict's emphasis on physical work because they spent so much time in their lengthy liturgical services. Bernard himself was extreme in the practice of penance, and helped the Cistercians earn a reputation for practicing a purer monastic life than the Cluniacs. The financial dealings of the Cistercian monasteries were much stricter than at Cluny, and Bernard did not accept oblates along with their subsidies. Bernard's monks were not allowed even to touch money. He was interested in reform among clergy as well as among laypersons. He was active in Church politics and rallied people to join in the second Crusade. Yet, Bernard was a proponent of non-violence. His attitude toward the Eastern Church was of reconciliation, and he defended Jews of the Rhineland, some five thousand of whom were massacred by participants of the First Crusade on their way to Jerusalem.

- *Nuns.* During the Middle Ages in Europe, married women lived under their husbands' authority, while unmarried women were legally independent. Women had a fair amount of autonomy to participate in professional life. If a woman went into a nunnery, she could advance her social standing, but not to the point of becoming a presbyter (priest) or bishop – hence, never a pope. Yet, it was possible for a woman to become well educated and contribute to the body of knowledge and art. Hildegard of Bingen (1098–1179) was among the most accomplished of such women. Her parents placed her under the direction of a nun from the age of 8. She became abbess of a community of religious women who lived under the *Rule of Benedict.* Hildegard was a woman of many talents. In sophisticated Latin she wrote medical works, poetry, music, and accounts of her many hierophanic visions.
- ***Franciscans.*** Francis of Assisi (ca. 1181–1226) brought Christianity closer to the people and to nature. Francis was known for his ability to commune with the birds. He made use of informal hymns known as lauds (*laudi spirituali*) as opposed to the contrapuntal music sung in the cathedrals. Lauds were based on music familiar to the people from daily life, and they were easy to sing. The followers of Francis did not stay in the monasteries. The Franciscans were friars, not monks. Such a life outside of the monastic setting offered a new and exciting option for leading a religious life. The movement evolved into three branches during Francis' lifetime. Franciscan orders grew up for men, women, and laypersons. Laypersons now felt they could travel the path to knowing and loving God without having to lead a celibate life and give up all possessions. As the celibate Franciscans traveled through the countryside, they would hear the confessions of laypeople and actually challenge them to think about how to lead more spiritual lives. They also worked among the people, contributing in whatever way they could. Francis was especially tender toward the poor. To inspire love of Christ in people, Francis introduced the crèche – the use of which is still very popular at Christmas time. Giotto de Bondone (1267–1337) captured the humanity and tenderness of Francis in his paintings of the saint's life story. Giotto moved away from biblical themes, and promoted the concept of a holy person among the people. Moreover, as Francis brought "baby" Jesus to the people by building the first crèche, Giotto painted the story of Jesus' infancy.

Critics of the Roman Catholic Church (1300–1600)

Johannes Gutenberg invented the printing press and published the first Bible in Germany on 30 September 1452. What had taken the Church a millennium to produce in the way of books was matched in half a century with the advent of the printing press. The new technology paved the way for an expansion of religious thinking – because for the first time in the Western world people had access to texts outside of those rare, costly, and politically managed religious texts coming out of the monasteries. Thinking sprung loose from the heavy authority of the Roman Catholic Church, which had been the primary source of knowledge about the universe. The revolution involved Copernicus who posited the existence of our "solar system" observing that the sun, not the earth, was at the center, and Galileo who found empirical proof of what Copernicus had recognized. In the sphere of religion, Galileo was under pressure to recant – but things had already passed a point of no return.

Criticism from within the Roman Catholic Church started picking up steam through the critical inquiries of religious men scattered all over Europe. Desiderius Erasmus (1466–1536) in Amsterdam wrote a wry critique of Roman Catholics from popes and monks down to the common people – but he stayed with the Roman Catholic Church. By contrast, on 3 January 1521 Pope Leo X excommunicated Martin Luther (1483–1546). That act made Luther into the first Protestant. But Luther in Germany did not operate in a vacuum. The Frenchman John Calvin (1509–64) soon followed Luther, setting up a Protestant community in Geneva, Switzerland. This was something the Swiss Huldrych Zwingli (1484–1531) had begun to do. And paving the way for all these critics of the Church were two men who lived about a century earlier: John Wycliffe (1326–84) in England, and Jan Hus (1372–1415) in Bohemia (Czechoslovakia). This was an exciting and trying time in Europe, where people even within families were pitted against one another over questions of the sacraments and the authority of the Church. It was a bloody time.

Martin Luther

Martin Luther (1483–1546) came from a family of small landholders in Germany. He studied law, but had a conversion experience that impelled him to enter a monastery at the age of 21. A few years later (in 1507) he was ordained as a priest, and the next year enrolled in the University of Wittenberg. Two years after that, Luther was sent to Rome and there was shocked at the contrast between the life of monks, ordinary priests, and high church officials. Upon his return, Luther completed his doctoral degree and became the district vicar as well as a professor at a new university in Wittenberg. Despite his rigorous intellectual background, Luther became disenchanted with the

BOX 5.3 A SPIRITUAL PATH: THE CHRISTIAN SACRAMENTS

Over time Christians developed several ritual **sacraments** to open people to the blessings of the Holy Spirit. The sacrament of marriage was created during the Middle Ages, and new theories about what actually happens during Holy Communion were formulated during the Protestant Reformation. The Roman Catholic and Eastern Orthodox Churches recognize seven sacraments (whose names may vary), while Protestants generally consider baptism and the Lord's Supper (i.e., Holy Communion) as the only true sacraments because Jesus himself practiced them.

The seven sacraments. (1) *Baptism.* Undergoing Baptism is a prerequisite for all the other sacraments. People are baptized once, and become Christians through this ritual. (2) *Confirmation or Chrismation.* A Christian affirms his or her faith at the age of reason through this one time ritual. (3) *Matrimony.* This is the sacred union of two bodies with one soul, and is an optional sacrament. (4) *Holy Orders.* A Christian becomes a member of the clergy through this optional sacrament. (5) *Extreme Unction or Holy Unction.* This is an optional blessing administered with oil when a person is ill. (6) *Penance-Reconciliation.* This involves confession of one's sins to a priest and requires a firm purpose to amend one's life. (7) *Holy Communion or the Eucharist.* Christians are allowed to ritually celebrate Jesus's last supper if they have received the sacrament of Baptism.

Baptism. A parting message from the resurrected Jesus to his disciples was to "go and make disciples of all nations, baptizing them in the name of the Father and of the Son and of the Holy Spirit" (Matthew 28:19). Through baptism a person becomes Christian. Symbolism of the rite can include: (1) *Water purification.* Immersion or sprinkling with water symbolizes cleansing. (2) *A new name.* A new status as member of the Christian Church is indicated by a name the initiate will use. (3) *Pure white clothing.* Donning pure white clothing symbolizes the inner purification from sins. (4) *Sign of the cross.* The sign of the cross made over the initiate is a seal that confers the new status. (5) *Milk and honey.* Pure food indicates fitness for a new life in Christ.

Lord's Supper (Eucharist). During the final meal that Jesus shared with his twelve disciples he said: "I tell you the truth, I will not drink again of the fruit of the vine until that day when I drink it anew in the kingdom of God" (Mark 14:25). These words uttered just before Jesus was taken into custody hinted that the meal was linked to a spiritual reality. After their teacher's death on the cross and his subsequent resurrection, Christians began to ritually recreate this last supper with bread and wine that took on the meaning (and some say reality) of Christ's body and blood.

classical philosophy of Aristotle that still dominated the scholastic curriculum of the university along with the systematic theology of Thomas Aquinas.

Luther grew impatient with the elaborate church ritual and what he perceived to be corrupt economic policies including selling **indulgences**. This not only diverted valuable local funds to Rome, but also supposed that a person could use good works in a kind of transaction with God. Luther eventually formulated objections to any kind of mediation between man and God. He said priests had no authority to mediate, and the seven sacraments had no power to mediate. (Luther rejected all sacraments except baptism and communion, on the grounds that they did not have biblical support. And even those two were only important because they might deepen a person's faith, not because they effected a transaction with God.) Finally, Luther objected to the idea of an intermediate state of purgatory as well.

On 31 October 1517 Luther's radical moment came. A famous story says that he did what was customary for an academic in Wittenberg, Germany: he posted a list of ideas upon the massive door of All Saints Church. Little did Luther know that this list of ninety-five Theses was to set off a full-scale revolt against the Roman Catholic Church. At first, the authorities tried to reconcile Luther with the Church, but Luther refused to recant his views. Two years later, in 1521, he was excommunicated, and people were forbidden to read his writings. Luther spent the next ten years in hiding, when he supervised a German translation of the entire Bible (translating the New Testament himself).

Through close reading of the Bible, Luther came to consider many of the Roman Catholic Church's practices unbiblical, and therefore anti-Christian. A deep theological disagreement developed with regard to the meaning of the ritual that celebrated the Eucharist (Lord's Supper). Luther rejected the Roman Catholic interpretation of the Eucharist as a **transubstantiation** of the bread and wine into the body and blood of Christ, where the internal quality of the substances actually changed. Instead he taught that the bread and wine embodied Christ's "real presence" in a sacramental union – but he did not accept the notion that the substances themselves were transformed. Gradually, Luther developed a full-fledged theology – summarized in four key phrases:

- ***Faith alone.*** Faith alone will bring a person salvation.
- ***Scripture alone.*** The Bible alone is the source of true doctrine, and believers through the Holy Spirit can understand.
- ***Christ alone.*** A change in one's soul comes through a direct, personal relationship with Christ, and through Christ with God.
- ***Grace alone.*** Only God's grace can save a person, not a priest. Luther used the phrase "universal priesthood of all true believers" to indicate that each person stands directly before God with no intermediary.

John Calvin

John Calvin (1509–1564) was a Frenchman who studied the Hebrew language and classics at the University of Paris. At age 24 Calvin had a sudden conversion experience that impelled him to become involved with the Reformation. He wrote an exposition of Protestant ideas that became the foundation of Presbyterian faith, starting with *The Institutes of the Christian Religion* in Latin (later translated into French). The following year in 1534, he broke with the Roman Catholic Church, and a year later he fled to Geneva, Switzerland. Calvin diverged from Roman Catholic theology on three main points: (1) he rejected the authority of the pope; (2) he scaled down the church institution to government by a board of presbyters by eliminating the office of bishop; and (3) he believed in justification by faith alone. Calvin also preached predestination. For Calvin, the Bible was the exclusive source of the law. It must be interpreted.

Calvin, like Luther, accepted only two sacraments as having a biblical basis: baptism and communion. These he simplified further, and claimed that such rituals were less important than preaching God's word. Calvin rejected Luther's teaching on the "sacramental union" of Christ during the Lord's Supper. Instead, he followed Huldrych Zwingli's view, which contends that the celebration of the Lord's Supper is a memorial: the ritual celebration recalls the event of the Lord's Supper as Jesus asked his followers to do; but it does not in any way bring Christ to the altar. According to Calvin, Christ is in heaven and in the heart of faithful Christians at the time of the celebration. Presbyterian theology derived from John Calvin revolves around these main points:

- ***Sovereignty of God.*** Whatever happens in human history is due to the will of God. Everything God wills is just, and God's will is inevitable.
- ***Original sin.*** All humans have original sin. Everyone is rightfully condemned in the sight of God. The nature of human beings is defiled. Humans rebel against God. God allows this so that God's mercy in salvation may be shown. Knowledge of God is thus obscured. One must not blame Adam for one's depravity. The work of Christ on believers opens up the possibility of God receiving us into his favor as if we were righteous.
- ***Predestination.*** Not all people are on an equal status. Not all human beings are lost. God elects who attains salvation. Our duty is self-discipline as we live under God's watch. Those who are "elect" lead a righteous life and have a predilection to true religion.
- ***God's dual church.*** God's church has visible and invisible aspects. The visible church comprises believers. The invisible church is God's elect on heaven and earth.

Calvin's contribution may be called democratization of the faith. Calvin emphasized equality before God. God's "elect" might be from any social class. Moreover, people must become literate so that they can read the Holy Scriptures and understand the principles of their faith. Beyond knowledge, Calvin spoke of specific virtues that all Christians should cultivate, namely thrift, industry, sobriety, and responsibility. The ethics promoted by Calvin emphasized a type of self-denial, hard work, and individual responsibility. The Christian Protestant denominations known as Reformed, Presbyterian, and Congregationalist Churches derive from John Calvin. In turn, John Knox in Scotland and the Puritan revolution carried John Calvin's legacy forward.

Plate 5.2 "Martin Luther and John Calvin." Martin Luther (*above*) and John Calvin (*below*) are household names among Protestant Christians. From their efforts during the Protestant Reformation, a whole new way of relating to the Holy Scriptures emerged. They emphasized that people should become educated and read the Bible themselves, instead of relying on the authority of the Roman Catholic Church to interpret it for them.

Proponents and prisoners of the Catholic Counter-reformation

In the midst of the crisis of the Protestant Reformation the Roman Catholic Church affirmed its doctrines at the Council of Trent (meeting between 1545 and 1563). This began what is known as the Catholic Reformation or the Counter-reformation. A reading list of books forbidden to Catholics was issued. As a complement to the strict emphasis on dogma and tight control of the Vatican, a mystical movement developed in the course of reforming the Roman Catholic tradition. Some reformers founded religious orders as a way of reaffirming the beauty and integrity of their faith, which had been under severe attack. Mystical experience in some ways transcended the details of dogma, even though practices involving such experience had to be approved by the Roman Catholic authorities. Monks and nuns were under tight scrutiny, and had to proceed with the blessings of Roman papal authority. A number of people later called saints by the Roman Catholic Church spent time in prison, or were kept under careful surveillance in the 1500s, including the founder of the Jesuit order, Ignatius of Loyola (1491–1556), and two friends of the Carmelite order, Teresa of Avila (1515–1582) and John of the Cross (1542–1591). Starting in the fifteenth century, the Portuguese and Spanish began a period of colonization whereby missionaries (who were explorers and businessmen) brought Roman Catholicism to South and Central America, as well as to the Far East.

More Protestant Christians

As the number of Roman Catholic organizations grew with the rise of various lay and monastic orders, so did the number of Protestant groups. But while any new developments in the Roman Catholic Church only survived with explicit authority from the pope, Protestants had no such institutional restrictions. Over time, new Protestant groups branched off from the teachings of Martin Luther and John Calvin. Besides that, when King Henry VIII (r. 1509–1547) rejected the pope's authority in 1534 he effectively created the Anglican Church. In turn, from Henry's Church of England came an influential minister named John Wesley (1703–1791) who became a founding member of a Bible group known as the Methodists. Wesley was influenced by the thought of Jan Hus, who emphasized God's love and forgiveness, but who was burned at the stake for heresy. Wesley spent a couple years in the American colonies prior to his decisive spiritual experience of salvation. Upon his return to England, Wesley had a hierophanic experience of salvation through faith. He wrote up *Rules* as Methodist guidelines, and recast the core documents of the Anglican Church. In addition, and though Wesley did not formally break from the Anglican Church, his followers separated and started the Methodist denomination. North America proved to be a place where religion based on Wesley's teachings flourished.

The great hotbed of Protestant activity was Northern Europe, although a group of Anti-Trinitarians grew up in Eastern Europe. (The burning of Jan Hus did not help the cause of the reformation in Eastern Europe.) The Eastern Orthodox Churches were not involved in this Protestant religious battle that occurred exclusively as a critique and rejection of Roman Catholicism. With the settlement of North America new Protestant groups emerged, and continue to emerge today. The points of distinction among Protestant groups stem largely from differences in doctrinal interpretations. Within the larger categories, however, differences in practice seem to distinguish one from another. Some groups splinter off but remain directly within the same lineage, while others are more loosely influenced by an earlier group.

- ***Lutherans.*** Emerging from the core teachings of Martin Luther came Protestant churches in Germany, Sweden, Denmark, Finland, and Norway. These merged to form the Lutheran Council in the United States of America.
- ***Calvinists, or Reformed Christians.*** Emerging from the core teachings of John Calvin came what is known as the Reformed Church, with its various branches. These include Presbyterians, Congregationalists, and Baptists (divided basically into General, Seventh-day, and Particular).
- ***Anglicans.*** Emerging from the Church of England came the Methodist Church founded by John Wesley, which is divided into Episcopalians and Anti-Episcopal Methodists. From Episcopal Methodism emerged the United Methodist

Church in the United States of America. A widespread form of spirituality known as Pentecostalism sprung from the United Methodist Church.

- ***Anabaptists.*** Outsiders called this group of Christians "rebaptizers" (from a Greek term) because they rejected the efficacy of infant baptism. They arose in the sixteenth century, and were marginalized by both Roman Catholic and Protestant authorities for their strict adherence to the ways of the early Christians. In this, they may refuse to do the following: bear arms; take oaths; participate in public schooling; use modern technology; wear fashionable clothes. Included are: Amish, Mennonites, and Hutterites.
- ***Anti-Trinitarians.*** Christians influenced by sixteenth- and seventeenth-century liberal Christian movements in Poland and Transylvania who reject belief in the Holy Trinity, hence the divinity of Jesus. This turned into a modern movement in Europe and North America, which became the Unitarian Universalist Association in 1961.

Pentecostalists

The Pentecostal movement began in the United States of America in Topeka, Kansas. It is grounded in John Wesley's belief that a person can become perfected in love by God's grace. A Methodist minister named Charles F. Parham (1873–1929) one day asked his Bible students to research the figure of the Holy Spirit as presented in the New Testament. From their findings, he became convinced that baptism by the Holy Spirit involved glossolalia, the spontaneous speaking of uninterpretable sounds, or an unknown language. He led his congregation in prayer, and eventually they were all baptized by the Holy Spirit as evidenced by experiences of glossolalia.

The name "Pentecostalist" comes from a description in the New Testament *Acts of the Apostles* of a hierophanic event that occurred fifty days (seven weeks inclusive) after the resurrection of Jesus, which is called Easter. The apostles and women followers of Jesus were gathered to celebrate the Jewish feast of Shavuot, marking the day the Torah was given to Moses on Mount Sinai.

> When the day of **Pentecost** came, they were all together in one place. Suddenly a sound like the blowing of a violent wind came from heaven and filled the whole house where they were sitting. They saw what seemed to be tongues of fire that separated and came to rest on each of them. All of them were filled with the Holy Spirit and began to speak other tongues as the Spirit enabled them.
>
> (Acts of the Apostles 2:1–4)

The feast of Pentecost is celebrated in various ways among Christians to this day. Glossolalia is emphasized among Pentecostalists, but Quakers and others also remain open to the experience of speaking in tongues. For example, members of the Orthodox Church regard speaking in tongues as a private, personal gift of the Holy Spirit that is a minor form of prayer.

A Christian existentialist

Søren Kierkegaard (1813–1855) is called a Christian existentialist philosopher because he wanted to read between the lines of the foundation texts to get for himself, in his gut, the existential value of the stories. He examined what he called the paradox of the faith of Abraham who was asked by God to sacrifice his son. He criticized Christian preachers in Denmark for taking the Old Testament story of Abraham too lightly. He also spoke about Mary, who had to endure the pregnancy with Jesus with no one understanding her. In Kierkegaard's view people of his time cheapened Christianity when they spoke of it without considering the fear and trembling embedded in the paradox of faith. His Christian existentialism carries the sense of a religion of resistance, as a critique of theologians and preachers who represented the status quo in the mid-1800s in Denmark.

Kierkegaard posed new questions about what he called the paradox of faith: Why did Abraham not doubt? Why did he not take the knife and plunge it into his own breast? Why did he not beg to be relieved of his duty to God? The fact that Abraham did not doubt, or kill himself, or ask for relief signaled for Kierkegaard that Abraham had faith. This was a paradox of faith – because as Abraham was going through the act of getting ready to kill his beloved son, he had no assurances that he could keep him. Yet he had faith that God would not ask this of him. Kierkegaard said this faith was absurd. Yet that absurd paradox was the crux of faith. Abraham "took the knife to slay his son" when an angel "called to him from heaven" and said, "[D]o nothing to him." Abraham then saw "behind him a ram caught in the thicket" (Genesis 22: 10–13). Abraham understood this was God's doing. He could sacrifice the ram, and save his son. Mary mother of Jesus also lived the paradox of faith. Kierkegaard noted that though every girl asks why she is not favored like Mary, they fail to realize the fear and trembling a person of faith endures.

> No doubt the angel was a ministering spirit, but he was not an obliging one who went round to all the other young girls in Israel and said: "Do not despise Mary, something out of the ordinary is happening to her." The angel came only to Mary, and no one could understand her.
>
> (Kierkegaard 1985: 93)

Modern activists

Christianity has a modern strain that may be thought of as a religion of resistance. Rather than support the status quo, certain Christians push for a return to the principles of social equality and justice that they see as central to the true practice of their religion.

Dorothy Day (1897–1980)

Dorothy Day was born in Brooklyn, New York. In the early part of her adult life, Day's views of society were shaped by a socialist ideology. She left college after two years and worked as a journalist for several socialist publications, but after seeing Communism in action its appeal wore off because of the materialism and violence she saw in it. Gradually, Day was drawn to Roman Catholicism, which impressed her as the church of immigrants and the poor. In 1932 Day and her friend Peter Maurin started a publication called *The Catholic Worker* with articles based on Catholic social teaching. Paulist Press printed what started as an eight-page pamphlet which Day sold for a penny per copy so that anyone could afford it.

Day's commitment to the Catholic teaching of helping the poor soon extended beyond the printed page. Four years after the first issue of *The Catholic Worker* newspaper, she and Maurin had established over thirty Catholic Worker houses across the country. The two experimented with agricultural communes as well. But at the foundation of their charitable work was the conviction that the epitome of Jesus' message was found in the words, "I was a stranger and you took me in." They felt that, ideally, every Christian should maintain a "Christ room," and every church should have a hospitality house where those without sufficient means could come to stay. Some say that Dorothy Day anticipated a branch of Christian social thought known as **liberation theology**. Yet her orientation was not embedded in the materialism of history, and she was a thoroughgoing pacifist. The Catholic Worker Movement endured a crisis in the midst of World War II: many members left to fight in the war, while others criticized Day's commitment to non-violence. Through it all, Day held firm and *The Catholic Worker* is available today for a penny per copy.

Archbishop Desmond Mpilo Tutu (b. 1931)

Liberation theology has its roots among Christian missionaries who spoke out in defense of indigenous peoples. It took shape in the late 1960s with the aim of bringing liberation to the people through active social involvement. Various liberation theologies developed as an outgrowth of Christian social thought dedicated to people across the globe struggling against poverty, racism, and classism. Christian theologians in developing countries began to give a systematic response to oppression from colonialism, militarism, and the overbearing pressure of Western culture on indigenous perspectives. In North America, Christian liberation theology reacted to prejudice regarding race, class, and gender. It was shaped initially by the civil rights movement and responded to inequities in relation to indigenous peoples as well. Initially, liberation theology had strong proponents within the Roman Catholic

Church, but has been curtailed by negative reactions from the Vatican in Rome. Pope John Paul II and Pope Benedict XVI (formerly Cardinal Ratzinger, head of the Sacred Congregation for the Doctrine of the Faith) criticized liberation theology for tending toward materialism in its sympathy for Marxism. In their view the understanding of Jesus of Nazareth as a revolutionary and liberator of the oppressed did not accord with Christian doctrine – especially if violence was involved. Protestant Christians subsequently had a strong hand in developing liberation theology.

Liberation theology is not a homogeneous movement. Yet Christian liberation theologians generally hold these convictions in common: (1) The goal of salvation involves working for peace and justice in this world. (2) Because oppression tends to be a systemic problem embedded in social structures, religious practice must involve social reform. (3) Christians have a moral responsibility to work within history, as God incarnated in Jesus to demonstrate His will.

Archbishop Desmond Mpilo Tutu is a Christian activist theologian from South Africa whose work demonstrates the three convictions of liberation theology. He worked for equal civil rights for all people alike, regardless of race, along with a common system of education for South Africans without discrimination. He declared that apartheid was un-Christian and began to formulate non-violent means of ending racial segregation in South Africa. Tutu was awarded the Nobel Peace Prize in 1984 for his work to abolish apartheid in South Africa. After officially sanctioned segregation was defeated, he became the first black Anglican archbishop in South Africa. Putting his Christian ethics into practice he acted as chairperson of the Truth and Reconciliation Commission after the fall of apartheid. The Commission held a series of hearings in which both victims and perpetrators of race-based crimes in South Africa could speak of their experience. Those who inflicted violence on others had a chance to repent their deeds, while those who had been victimized were encouraged to practice forgiveness.

PART 2
CHRISTIAN TEXTURE

FOUNDATIONAL TEXTURE

Old Testament

The Christian canon includes the Old Testament and New Testament. The Old Testament contains the three core texts that also comprise the Tanakh (Hebrew Bible): Torah (Pentateuch), Nevi'im (Prophets), and Ketuvim (Writings) – with a slightly modified order of some sections. Christians originally adopted the Septuagint, which was the Tanakh in a Greek translation begun by Jews in Alexandria, Egypt, in the third century BCE. And though Jewish scholars abandoned the Septuagint when they canonized their Hebrew scriptures, Christians continued to use the translation for about 1,500 years – until the Protestant Reformation in Europe. During the European Enlightenment people such as Martin Luther became interested in going back to the Hebrew text of the Bible and discontinued use of that early Greek translation. The books of the Old Testament are known by their Greek names, beginning with the Torah's Genesis, Exodus, and so on. Christians consider that these Jewish sacred texts set the stage for the advent of Jesus, the Messiah. Christians emphasize passages of the Tanakh that are most relevant to the figure of Jesus. These include: (1) discussions of King David's lineage from which the Messiah comes, and (2) predictions about the Messiah uttered by the prophets.

New Testament

By 150 CE Christians had the material for their New Testament that they added to the Septuagint. This new writing was significantly different from the writing Jews were doing during the same period, but both were intent on preserving their teachings in 70 CE after Jerusalem was destroyed and they were forced into dispersion without a temple. Although Jesus probably taught in Aramaic, the New Testament was originally composed in Greek, which made it accessible to greater numbers of people in the Roman Empire. The New Testament comprises twenty-seven documents

Plate 5.3 "Judith slaying Holofernes." Characters from the Hebrew Bible fascinated Christian painters. Here the Israelite widow Judith decapitates Holofernes, an Assyrian general (*Book of Judith*, ch. 13). The foremost Italian female artist of her day Artemisia Gentileschi (1593–ca. 1653) may have executed this work while involved in the seven-month trial of Agostino Tassi, her rapist. The 19-year-old painter was tortured with thumbscrews to elicit confessions that would prove her innocence. In contrast to the otherworldly perspective adopted by Byzantine Christian icon painters, European Renaissance/Baroque artists portrayed biblical themes with realism. This emotional work seems to be rooted in sacred history, social protest, and personal anguish all at once.

including letters, narrative accounts about Jesus, a history of the early Christian community, and a revelation about the end of time. These were composed between 50 and 150 CE.

Letters

The New Testament contains twenty-one **epistles** from the followers of Jesus to members of the early Christian community: fourteen ascribed to Paul, two to Simon Peter, three to John, author of the fourth gospel, one to Jesus' brother James, and one to Jesus' brother Jude.

Gospels

Authors who call themselves Mark, Matthew, Luke, and John wrote the four officially recognized New Testament gospels. Biblical scholars call the first three gospels "synoptic" because they "see together" (i.e., much of their material overlaps). Common material of the **Synoptic Gospels** is presumably drawn from a lost source that biblical scholars call **Q**. John's work is often called the Fourth Gospel. The traditional order in which these writings appear in the New Testament is Matthew, Mark, Luke, and John. Yet scholars generally consider that Mark was written first, followed by Matthew, Luke, and John. The Synoptic Gospels were completed between about 60 and 80 CE, and the work attributed to John came approximately ten years later.

- ***Mark.*** Mark's text is the shortest gospel with 661 verses that review the bare bones of Jesus' life story. These are based on the memory of the apostle Simon Peter. (Mark may have been Peter's interpreter in Rome.) Mark's narrative begins with the baptism of Jesus by John, and ends with the resurrection of Jesus. The main focus of Mark's writing is the end of time predicted by Jesus the Messiah. This gospel was probably written in the 60s. Mark apparently wants to convey the importance of Jesus's suffering and death, rather than his miracle working.
- ***Matthew.*** Matthew's gospel is the first book of the New Testament. It echoes Old Testament themes and presents Jesus as coming from the house of David. It seems to have been written for a Jewish audience to persuade Jewish followers of Jesus not to abandon their new faith. Matthew casts Jesus as the new Moses: Moses goes out of Egypt because of the pharaoh's order to kill first-born sons, while Jesus is taken to Egypt because of the king's order to kill first-born sons; Moses brought the law and Jesus extends the law brought by Moses. The Gospel of Matthew is famous for the Sermon on the Mount, which gives Jesus' teaching on non-violence. It may have been written any time between 65 and 100 CE.

- ***Luke.*** Luke's gospel seems to be geared toward a gentile audience. He emphasizes the miraculous birth of Jesus to a virgin, and Jesus as the resurrected Son of God. Luke traces the genealogy of Jesus to the first man, Adam – who belongs to all human beings. Luke may have been the only non-Jewish writer among the four gospel writers. People think he was a physician because of the images he uses. Beyond that, Luke presents the most information about Jesus and his relationship to women. His account echoes Matthew's Sermon on the Mount – but Luke locates it on a level place, not a mount. This text may have been written as early as 64 CE (along with *Acts of the Apostles*) because *Acts* speaks of the author's travels and stay in prison with the apostle Paul.
- ***John.*** John's gospel contains the shortest verse in the New Testament: "Jesus wept" (John 11:35). The author records Jesus' relationship with John the Baptist, his career in Judea and Galilee, and his death and resurrection. The text takes a different approach from that of the Synoptic Gospels. It includes more symbolism, and arranges events according to the message they convey, rather than chronologically. The characteristic contribution of John's gospel is the labeling of Jesus Christ as the incarnate Word (Latin: *Logos*). *Logos* is the light, and this characterization of Jesus makes the fourth gospel mystically oriented, and possibly influenced by gnosticism. By the time this latest gospel was written, Jesus' crucifixion took on a very positive meaning.

Acts of the Apostles

Acts of the Apostles, the fifth book of the New Testament, is basically a continuation of the Gospel of Luke, and appears to be by the same author. Luke was a talented historical writer attuned to Mediterranean culture and beliefs.

Luke's *Acts* is a history of the early Christian community from the time of Jesus' resurrection to Paul's return to Rome just before he was martyred. It is virtually the sole source of information about Christianity between 30 and 64 CE. The narrative is based on information given by the apostle Paul.

Apocalypse of John

The *Apocalypse of John* or Book of Revelation (written around 95 CE) unveils cryptic details about a final cosmic battle between good and evil at Armageddon. It predicts that Satan's evil army will be defeated, and peace will be restored in the coming of the Kingdom of God, which brings a new heaven and earth. The text describes two hierophanic visions that came to the author while he was exiled on a small island in the Aegean Sea called Patmos. (Some say the author may be Jesus' disciple John, author of the fourth gospel, but most scholars do not agree.) The place is the site of several monasteries and attracts numerous pilgrims to this day. The first vision involves an appearance of someone looking like "a son of man" dressed in a long gown with a golden sash around his chest.

> His head and hair were white like wool, as white as snow, and his eyes were like blazing fire. His feet were like bronze glowing in a furnace, and his voice was like the sound of rushing waters.
>
> (Revelation 1:14)

The second vision occurs behind a door that was opened in heaven. A voice like a trumpet bid John to enter, and he did so because he was "in the Spirit." There he saw someone seated on a throne, with twenty-four other thrones around. The descriptions are magnificent, with talk of rainbows, jewels, a sea of glass, flashes of lightning, and more. Moreover, it is filled with references to mythic creatures such as a dragon, a beast from the sea with ten horns and seven heads, and many angels. There is a heavy dose of numerology with the numbers 3, 7, 12, and their multiples, such as 144,000.

Through the history of Christianity, theologians have responded to the Book of Revelation with ambivalence because it is difficult to interpret. It was accepted (reluctantly by some) as part of the Christian sacred canon, but is not read as part of the liturgy of Orthodox Christians. This text is the main source for Christian apocalypticism, which is emphasized by **Evangelical Christians** in the United States of America. Their **millenarianism** is based on chapter 20, in which the author reports a vision of the End Times. It begins:

> I saw an angel coming down out of heaven, having the key of the abyss and a great chain in his hand. He seized the dragon, the old serpent which is the devil and Satan who deceives the whole inhabited earth, and bound him for a thousand years.
>
> (Revelation 20:1–2)

The author, who is called John of Patmos, knew some of the apocalyptic material from the biblical books of Daniel and Ezekiel – two Hebrew prophets who probably pre-dated him by over six centuries.

SUPPORTIVE TEXTURE

Confessions by Saint Augustine (354–430)

Aurelius Augustinus was an early Christian theologian born in Thagatse, an Algerian North African community of a few thousand people who were Roman citizens. This prospering town was one of the little Romes scattered along the Mediterranean, and Augustine was part of a group of young men from there who went abroad to study. In time, these students were transformed into a cadre of Christian bishops, and exerted a definite impact on the direction of the church in North Africa. His work represents a transitional point between the classical period and the Middle Ages in the history of Christianity. Augustine is famous for writing the first autobiography in the Western literary tradition, *The Confessions.* Augustine defined Christian beliefs as distinct from rival views circulating in the Roman Empire – particularly Manichaeism, which he studied seriously for nine years. He dealt with the problem of evil, since it had a confounding role in the Manichean tradition as an opponent of the good. Augustine determined that evil was simply the privation of good, and had no existential reality of its own. This struck to the heart of Mani's doctrine, which taught that evil, the darkness, was an existential force with its own reality. Augustine, by contrast, underscored the total beneficence and power of God in realizing that only where someone fails to exercise God's goodness does sin prevail.

Ritual validations of the mystery of bread and wine

At the Lord's Supper in Jerusalem before his death, Jesus declared a set of powerful words that became the basis for the key moment of the Christian ritual service. This took place outside of Jerusalem with his disciples immediately prior to his arrest by the Roman authorities. Jesus chose just two of the several traditional foods used at the Seder meal: the unleavened bread and wine. In doing this he gave new meaning and specific ritual power to the symbolism of the original Passover meal. At the Lord's Supper shared with his disciples Jesus identified bread with his body and wine with his blood.

> While they were eating, Jesus took bread, gave thanks and broke it, and gave it to his disciples, saying, "Take it; this is my body." Then he took the cup, gave thanks and offered it to them, and they all drank from it. "This is my blood of the covenant, which is poured out for many," he said to them.
>
> (Mark 14:22–24)

Jesus had used these words before he instituted the ritual meal. Once while teaching in the synagogue in Capernaum, he made a powerful statement about the meaning of bread and wine, calling himself the living bread that came down from heaven. The bread was his flesh; the wine was his blood. This brought a symbolic death and rebirth in him, for he told them: "Whoever eats my flesh and drinks my blood remains in me, and I in him" (John 6:56).

> Jesus said to them, "I tell you the truth, unless you eat the flesh of the Son of Man and drink his blood, you have no life in you. Whoever eats my flesh and drinks my blood has eternal life, and I will raise him up at the last day. For my flesh is real food and my blood is real drink.
>
> (John 6:53–55)

At that time some disciples actually deserted Jesus after they heard him declare this amazing, unusual thing. "On hearing it, many of his disciples said, 'This is a hard teaching. Who can accept it?'" (John 6:60). Jesus asked if it offended them, and knew that not everyone would believe him. Jesus had said in speaking of his body and blood as bread and wine in the synagogue at Capernaum, "The words I have spoken to you are spirit and they are life" (John 6:63). When he broke the bread, Jesus also said, "This is my body given for you; do this in remembrance of me" (Luke 22:19). The Eucharist was counted as a mystery. But what kinds of words were these? And what did it mean to do something in remembrance of Jesus?

Christians puzzled over the words, "Do this in remembrance of me." And over time they came up with a spectrum of interpretations of these foundational words of the New Testament. All Christians do something to recollect the final meal Jesus had with his disciples. But their interpretations provide different theological validations of it. Roman Catholics believe in the doctrine of transubstantiation, which says that the bread and wine used in the Eucharist are actually transformed in substance into the body and blood of Christ. In the Orthodox Church, the Eucharist remained a mystery with the older view that the bread and wine were truly Christ's body and blood – without any explanation of how this was so or specific idea whether or not the substances were transformed. Out of the Roman Catholic view eventually came rejection of the doctrine of transubstantiation by Protestants such as Martin Luther who spoke instead of the "true presence" of Christ. John Calvin accepted neither the doctrine of transubstantiation of the Roman Catholics, nor the true presence of the Lutherans. Instead, Calvin coined the term "consubstantiation," considering the ritual re-creation of the Lord's Supper to be a remembrance. To this day, Christians have various ways of giving valid meaning to the mystery stemming from the powerful words of Jesus about the identification of the bread with his body and the wine with his blood.

In any case, Jesus bid his disciples to repeat the ritual consumption of bread and wine often, and Paul wrote a letter to the community in Corinth reminding the early Christians of how the Eucharist was supposed to be done: "Everyone should eat in a worthy manner, examining himself before eating the bread and drinking from the cup" (1 Corinthians 11:28).

CROSS-OVER TEXTURE

The *Nag Hammadi* Texts

The early Christian community was held together through sharing a rich body of literature that was circulated among its members by 400 CE. Beyond what was set into the New Testament by 150 CE, Christians had additional letters, gospels (lives of Jesus), acts (lives of early followers), and apocalypses (revelations) about the return of Jesus from heaven. In addition, Christian writings included rules of community life, guidelines for the rites of baptism and Eucharist, defense writings with useful arguments for Christians faced with persecution, stories about martyrs, teachings against false teachers, and commentaries on the Old and New Testaments (Ehrman 2005: 24–29). Among these writings are gospels allegedly by Mary Magdalene, a disciple named Philip, and Jesus' brother Judas Thomas. These are marginal materials that were never admitted into the Christian canon. The gospels attributed to Judas Thomas, Mary, and Philip were discovered in 1945, buried near a river in Upper Egypt at the village of Nag Hammadi.

The Gospel of Thomas

The Gospel of Thomas is a collection of 114 of Jesus' sayings. It is attributed to Didymos Judas Thomas – translated as "Judas the Twin" because *didymos* in Greek and *thomas* in Aramaic both mean "twin." Tradition in the Syrian Christian church says that Judas Thomas was Jesus' brother who founded the church at Edessa, among others. (Later Syrian tradition says that Twin Judas also traveled to India.) It is likely that the proverbs, parables, rules, and prophecies attributed to Jesus were circulated first in Aramaic, the everyday language Jesus used.

In its oldest form *The Gospel of Thomas* seems to have emphasized *gnōsis* (wisdom) rather than **eschatology.** In other words, Jesus guided people to look for the Kingdom of the Father inwardly in the knowledge of oneself – not somewhere up in the sky.

> Jesus said, "If those who lead you say to you, 'See, the kingdom is in the sky,' then the birds of the sky will precede you. If they say to you, 'It is in the sea,'

then the fish will precede you. Rather, the kingdom is inside of you, and it is outside of you. When you come to know yourselves, then you will become known, and you will realize that it is you who are the sons of the living father. But if you will not know yourselves, you dwell in poverty and it is you who are that poverty."

The Gospel of Thomas – verse 3 (Robinson 1996: 126)

The Gospel of Thomas takes a gnostic perspective, understanding that each person originally dwelled in the Kingdom of Light. All persons are fundamentally of divine substance, but their light became entrapped in the prison of the material body. They are in spiritual sleep and need to be awakened. In the Christian gnostic view, Jesus is a savior who comes to remind people of their origins in light, and to release them from the prison of their bodies. Through asceticism the spirit gains release from the body. But the body is considered negative, and physical death marks a kind of salvation because the spirit of light is released from the material world.

The Gospel of Mary

The Gospel of Mary was originally written in Greek in the second century. It contains a dialogue between Jesus after he rose from the dead, and his disciples. Jesus told the disciples to go out and preach; but they wept and grieved after he had departed, knowing they could be killed for doing so. Mary Magdalene comforted them, saying that Jesus' grace would protect them. Then Peter asked Mary to speak about things she might know that he never heard: "Sister, we know that the Savior loved you more than the rest of women. Tell us the words of the Savoir which you remember – which you know (but) we do not, nor have we heard them" (Robinson 1997: 525). Mary responded by talking about a vision she had of the Lord. Mary reported that when he appeared, the Savior said, "Blessed are you, that you did not waver at the sight of me. For where the mind is, there is the treasure." Then Mary asked the Lord whether visions are perceived through the soul or the spirit. The Lord answered that one sees a vision with neither the soul, nor the spirit – but with "the mind which [is] between the two" (Robinson 1997: 525–526).

After Mary recounted details of her vision of Jesus in the imaginal realm, Andrew said, "I at least do not believe that the Savior said this. For certainly these teachings are strange ideas." Then Peter also proclaimed frustration and doubt, saying: "Did he really speak with a woman without our knowledge (and) not openly? Are we to turn about and all listen to her? Did he prefer her to us?" Mary wept at this, saying: "My brother Peter, what do you think? Do you think that I thought this up myself in my heart, or that I am lying about the Savior?" (Robinson 1997: 526). Then Levi defended Mary and exhorted them all to do as Jesus had asked in his appearance to them all before Mary had spoken of her vision.

Women's rights and the *Woman's Bible*

Elizabeth Cady Stanton (1815–1902) and Susan B. Anthony (1820–1906) were two colleagues who led the charge for women's right to vote in the United States of America. A half century after beginning their campaign for a woman's right to vote Stanton made her contribution to religious studies with the publication of the *Woman's Bible*. The text provides an English translation and commentary on all passages related to women in the Old Testament and New Testament. The work was done under Stanton's watch by an international committee, including twenty women from the United States of America, and one each from Finland, England, Austria, Scotland, and France. Some critics remarked on the women commentators' sense of humor, while others praised its efforts to dignify women. The *Woman's Bible* represents a crossover text in the sense that it was motivated by the social conscience of women who opposed the status quo, and were fighting for a voice in the culture dominated by white Christian males.

Had Stanton known about the *Nag Hammadi* texts, she surely would have appreciated *The Gospel of Mary* in which Mary defended herself against Andrew and Peter who disbelieved her words. As it was, Stanton and her colleagues used passages from the Old and New Testaments on women's equality to critique the treatment of women in their society at the close of the nineteenth century. For example, Stanton uses Jesus' egalitarian teachings on marriage (Mark 10:2–9) to condemn divorce laws in England and the United States of America (Stanton 1974: 129–130). On the other hand, the commentators highlight passages that indicate mistreatment or deprecation of women in biblical culture. They flag such passages to raise awareness about the pernicious influence of biblical misogyny on the culture of their own day. Normally in their commentary, Jesus himself appears beyond reproach, while his disciples and male figures of the Old Testament are found lacking in respect for women. About the woman from Canaan who begged Jesus in his mercy to cure her daughter, Stanton wrote (with reference to) Matthew 15:21–28:

> The woman of Canaan proved herself quite equal in argument with Jesus; and though by her persistency she tried the patience of the disciples, she made her points with Jesus with remarkable clearness. His patience with women was a sore trial to the disciples, who were always disposed to nip their appeals in the bud.
>
> (Stanton 1974: 121)

Stanton's interest in biblical criticism was based in social activism. She found Jesus to be an advocate of women's rights; and in her fight against a double standard in US divorce law, Stanton makes reference to Mark 10:11 where Jesus argues to protect women from unwarranted divorce (see Stanton: 130). Her work engages the issue of women's rights on many fronts. For example, the *Woman's Bible* responds to the questions: "Have the teachings of the Bible advanced or retarded the emancipation of women?" "Have they dignified or degraded the Mothers of the Race?" By bringing these questions into public discussion, Elizabeth Cady Stanton and her colleagues opened up what they saw as a brighter future for both women and men in their society. Stanton was convinced that people of both sexes "rise or fall together."

PART 3 CHRISTIAN PERFORMANCE

THE HISTORY OF ICONS

The iconoclastic controversy

Icon painting is a key aspect of religious "performance" in Orthodox Christianity. But the artistic tradition survived only after centuries of hard-fought cultural battles. If history had taken a different turn, icons would now be extinct as an art form. On the other hand, some other historical twists might have allowed icons to pervade the entire Christian world. The contact between Christians and Muslims, especially in the Byzantine Empire, provoked a Christian discussion of the positive or negative value of depicting sacred persons. Soon after Islam penetrated the Christian world, Byzantine Emperor Leo III (r. 717–741) began his attack on Christian sacred art. He argued that the use of icons was a major obstacle in the conversion of Jews and Muslims to Christianity. In a decree of 730 he ordered icons to be destroyed, starting with the statue of Christ above his palace entrance. The **iconoclastic controversy** occupied the Christian world (especially Byzantium) for over a century. Saints were martyred, Orthodox bishops were exiled, and faithful laypersons were put to death. But in 843 a council held in Constantinople officially re-established the veneration of icons.

The verdict coming from the Christian cultural controversy over the use of images in the ninth century was decided in favor of using icons. The form of sacred art that represented divine persons was officially preserved. Yet Christians developed their art in very different ways – especially after the schism between the eastern and western Roman empires in 1054. The Western Church in the thirteenth century devoted itself wholeheartedly to the three-dimensional graven images, while the Eastern Church never developed sculpted images and poured its artistic talent into the creation of icons. The crucifix and graven (sculpted) images are still not used in the Eastern Orthodox Church.

Christian art: flat or round?

The production of an icon requires the work of several artists. Generally the paintings are anonymous creations, and are considered as collective works of the Orthodox Church. The foundation of every icon is a hierophanic vision, and no icon is produced without prayer. Without the hierophany, the icon is just a board. The original hierophanic vision is brought into concrete form through special techniques that have their origins in the creation of Egyptian sarcophagi. In fact images in the catacombs, icons, and the Egyptian funeral masks are similar in the respect that they are not naturalistic portraits. They all portray the person as suits a spiritual realm of existence – even though the meaning of the figures takes on a specifically Christian value in the catacombs and the icons.

European religious art reached a high point of symbolic value in the Gothic cathedrals. Roman Catholic sculptors – like icon painters of the Byzantine world – were required to follow a strict iconic code.

> The art of the Middle Ages is first and foremost a sacred writing of which every artist must learn the characters. He must know that the circular nimbus placed vertically behind the head serves to express sanctity, while the nimbus impressed with a cross is the sign of divinity which he will always use in portraying any of the three Persons of the Trinity. He will learn that the aureole (*i.e.*, light which emanates from the whole figure and surrounds the body as a nimbus) expresses eternal bliss, and belongs to the three Persons of the Trinity, to the Virgin, and to the souls of the Blessed. He must know that representations of God the Father, God the Son, the angels and the apostles should have bare feet, while there would be real impropriety in representing the Virgin and the saints with bare feet. In such matters a mistake would have ranked almost as heresy.
>
> (Male 1958: 1–2)

If the cultural rift between the Eastern Orthodox Church and the Roman Catholic Church was carved along with the statues of the cathedrals, it reached a point of no return when, during the Renaissance in Europe, canvas replaced the board of the Byzantine icon. The new European sense of three dimensions and realistic perspective replaced the conservative Orthodox two-dimensional portrait. This move to 3-D opened up the scientific mind that observed things as they are in this world. But from the Orthodox point of view, it clapped shutters on all windows to the realm of hierophany. What was this icon so prized by the Orthodox Church? And why would faithful members of the Eastern Christian Churches feel so strongly about keeping their tradition of icon painting?

The first icons

The liturgical tradition of the Orthodox Church suggests that icons date back to Jesus himself. On 16 August each year the Holy Face is honored on the basis of the following story:

> Prince Abgar V. Ukhama of a small country between the Tigris and Euphrates rivers was a leper. He sent a painter named Hannan from the capital city of Edessa (Orfu, Rogais) to Palestine to ask Jesus to come to heal him, or paint a picture to bring back. When Hannan found Jesus teaching a large crowd, he decided to recreate an image of Jesus to take to Abgar. He could not paint the face, however, because Jesus' face emitted so much light it was always changing. Jesus noticed what Hannan was trying to do, and so washed his face. Jesus then dried his face with a linen hand cloth – and the impression of his face was fixed on the cloth. This, he gave to Hannan to take back. Jesus also sent a letter promising that when his own mission was done, one of his disciples would come. The portrait healed Abgar, except for a few marks on his face. These were removed when the apostle Thaddeus came to Edessa. After that, Abgar became a follower of Christ.
>
> (Ouspensky 1978: 60)

However far-fetched the story of Jesus' linen cloth may seem, a chronicle of the city of Edessa notes that a Christian church was destroyed in a flood in the year 201, at which time it was already ancient. And some time between 170 and 214 the kingdom of Edessa became the first Christian state under the rule of Abgar IX. Regardless of the historicity of the creation of the

Holy Face, the Orthodox tradition of icon painting based on Christ's holy face was established. Beyond that, the subject matter of icons was extended to include the mother of God, angels, saints, and holy people.

Orthodox icon painters believe that Luke, author of the third Christian gospel, created the first icons of Mary mother of Jesus some time shortly after the Pentecost, when tongues of fire of the Holy Spirit descended upon the group of apostles and women followers of Jesus on the fiftieth day after Easter when Jesus rose from the tomb. Luke made three icons of Mary – two of the Madonna and Child, and one of Mary alone. The tradition presumes that these and other paintings by Luke were copied over and over down through the ages. One Orthodox text states that Mary herself approved the first icon and conferred her grace upon it. Historical references to these have been made, but no copies survive to this day (Ouspensky 1978: 46).

BYZANTINE SACRED ART

Icons as symbols

The creation of sacred art is not a matter of aesthetics. Icons are not mere cultural artifacts. The icon painted on the board is a religious symbol that points to the spiritual world. It is not an idol; it is like a window. Moreover, people who understood this were martyred for their convictions during the period of iconoclastic controversy. Supporters of icon use felt that destroying an icon was like blocking up a window, and thus preventing light from entering our dark world. They felt the tragedy of blocked access to spiritual light. For example, a faithful person can gain a spiritual sense of the biblical event known as the transfiguration of Christ.

The transfiguration of Christ

One day, Jesus took Peter and the two brothers James and John up to Mount Tabor to pray. There they had a hierophanic experience that foreshadowed Jesus' resurrection from the dead. As Jesus was praying, his face changed radically (Luke 9:29). "There he was transfigured before them. His face shone like the sun, and his clothes became as white as the light. Just then there appeared before them Moses and Elijah, talking with Jesus" (Matthew 17:2–3). The three imaginal figures appeared in a cloud. The three disciples fell flat on their faces upon hearing a voice boom from the cloud, "This is my Son, whom I love; with him I am well pleased. Listen to him!" (Matthew 17:5). Then Jesus, back to himself, touched them. He told them to get up, not to be afraid, but to keep quiet about the event until after his resurrection from the dead. As they came down from Mount Tabor, the three men began puzzling over "what 'rising from the dead' meant" (Mark 9:10).

The sun as an iconic visual image

The Syrian monk John of Damascus (ca. 676–749) noted that the light of the sun is just a verbal image used to speak of the divine light of Christ's transfiguration because the sun can never compare to the divine light. Thus, while icons often depict persons or events in sacred texts, they do not merely illustrate the poetic imagery. How, then, can an artist show in an icon something resembling the light of Jesus' face that shines brighter than the sun? Icon painters draw a halo to indicate such hierophanic manifestations. The light shining from a saint's face, head, and upper body is represented by the symbol of a luminous sphere. That is not what the actual spiritual illumination looks like, but it is an indication of the phenomenon.

> The halo is not an allegory, but the symbolical expression of an authentic and concrete reality. It is an indispensable part of the icon – indispensable yet insufficient. . . . It is only an iconographic device, an outward expression of holiness, a witness of the light.
>
> (Ouspensky 1978: 205)

How to portray a hierophany

There are four kinds of icons, depending on the hierophanic experience in which they originate: (1) biblical icons, based on the revealed Word of God in the Bible; (2) portrait icons, based on the icon painter's direct spiritual experiences and memories of them; (3) Holy Tradition icons, based on the record of another person's spiritual experience; and (4) revealed icons, based on an icon painter's own spiritual experience from vision or dream.

Orthodox artists use three terms to define the nature of persons depicted on the icon: face, mask, and countenance.

Face

A sketch portrays the face that represents Christ, the Virgin Mary, a saint, or a holy person. This portrait reflects only one of many possible ways of sketching the features of the person.

> [A] *face* is the perceptual raw material upon which the portrait-artist is now working. . . . By *face* . . . we mean that which we see in ordinary daylight consciousness, that which we see as the recognizable appearance of the real world; and we can speak – doing no violence to ordinary language – of all natural things and creations with whom we are in conscious relation as having a face: as, for example, we speak of the face of nature. Face, we may thus say, is nearly synonymous with the word *appearance* – meaning, however, *appearance to daylight consciousness.*
>
> (Florensky 1996: 50–51)

Mask

If an icon face is painted on the basis of no hierophanic experience then the figure is simply a mask. The person who has a direct hierophanic experience paints a "first appeared" subject. Subsequent artists try to capture the spiritual sense of the icon they copy. If the artist has no visible sense of illumination, the figure is a mask, and the painting is an object of profane art rather than a window to the world of light to which the figure belongs. Icon painters say the masks are like a larva – what is left after death, empty and without substance.

> The first meaning of mask may be seen in the old word "larve" (related to modern *larva*), making that which resembles a face, being both presented and accepted as a face but which is empty inside; that is it has physical materiality but no metaphysical substance.
>
> (Florensky 1996: 53)

Countenance

The opposite of a mask is a countenance. The countenance that appears on the face of an icon partakes of spiritual illumination.

> We are beholding a countenance, then whenever we have before us a face that has fully realized within itself its likeness to God. . . . [T]hose among us who have transfigured their faces into countenances proclaim – without a word and solely by their appearance to us – the mysteries of the invisible world.
>
> (Florensky 1996: 52)

The face becomes a countenance when everything caused by things external to the spiritual essence of the divine is swept away by a strong energy. The face conveys a spiritual structure that is different from the worldly face. And it may seem odd, but sometimes this countenance is ugly by worldly standards!

Iconographic technique

- ***Preparing the board.*** Preparation of the Egyptian mask and inner surface of the sarcophagus resembles techniques of preparing the icon board and painting the figures. The front surface of a dry board is pressed to make an upraised margin frame. Then linen cloth is glued on and many layers of gesso are applied over a period of three to four days. Finally, the surface is polished.
- ***Engraving.*** Using charcoal or pencil the icon artist draws the pattern of an iconic image that is specific to the canon. Then the pattern is cut in with a sharp instrument down to every fold in the garments.
- ***Coloring.*** There are two kinds of icon colorists. The colors and the way they are applied have to be in line with the tradition. Some paint the clothes and background, including things of the natural and man-made environment. Their work represents the outward life that manifests in the world. Others paint the face, hands, and any uncovered parts of the body. Their work points to the inner life that manifests spiritual principles. The face representing the countenance is painted last.

BOX 5.4 SYMBOLS: WAS JESUS UGLY?

Plate 5.4 "A Russian icon of Jesus." A century or so after Jesus died, Christians began to argue about whether Jesus was ugly or not. A verse in the Hebrew Bible was taken to mean that the Messiah would have no outward beauty to distract a person from the true grandeur of the Lord. The tradition of icon painting called for the sense organs of holy people in portraits to look "ugly." This was to symbolize the spiritual attitude of turning away from attachment to sense objects. What do you notice in this Russian icon?

Christian writings from the second century seem to disagree as to whether Jesus was ugly or beautiful (see Ouspensky 1978: 69). St. Justin Martyr, Clement of Alexandria, Tertullian, St. Cyril of Alexandria and St. Irenaeus said that Jesus was ugly because Isaiah said,

> Who has believed our message and to whom has the arm of the LORD been revealed? He grew up before him like a tender shoot, and like a root out of dry ground. He had no beauty or majesty to attract us to him, nothing in his appearance that we should desire him.
>
> (Isaiah 53:1–3)

On the other hand, Gregory of Nyssa, Ambrose of Milan, John Chrysostom, Jerome, and Origen thought Christ had a very beautiful physical aspect because Psalms 45:2 says: "You are the most excellent of men and your lips have been anointed with grace, since God has blessed you forever." Finally, with his knack for resolving conflict, John of Damascus stated that Christ's radiance transcends the usual concept of beauty or ugliness.

Icons portray many facial and bodily features that might be considered ugly by the standards of an ancient Greek sculpture, for example. Ears sometimes look deformed, dark circles appear under the eyes, and noses are often extremely thin. But there is a reason for these strange looks. The symbolism indicates that persons with such features have turned away from what the senses would bring them in this world. They may be deaf to the things of this world. They are focused on the spiritual world beyond. For icon painters, the figures relate to spiritual beauty, which has only a tenuous connection with the material form of worldly things.

> The unnatural details of appearance which we see in the icon – in particular the sense organs: the eyes without brilliance, the ears which are sometimes strangely shaped – are represented in a non-naturalistic manner not because the iconographer was unable to do otherwise, but because their natural state was not what he wanted to represent. The icon's role is not to bring us closer to what we see in nature, but to show us a body which perceives what usually escapes man's perception, *i.e.*, the perception of the spiritual world.
>
> (Ouspensky 1978: 208)

- ***Applying the finishing touches.*** One person is a specialist in the application of gold leaf. Gold leaf is distinct from paint. It depicts the supernatural light. It is not a color and not of the same substance as paint. Gold leaf shines and highlights the invisible realm. Paint and gold are like a magnet and its force field. The pigments correspond to the magnet. But how can the force field be depicted? This is with the gold leaf. After the gold leaf is applied, another artist applies the finish and polishes the icon's surface. But the piece of art is not an icon until the Church recognizes it as such. Someone under a bishop's authority examines the icon to see whether or not it is truth-telling. If it conforms to the sacred art canon the icon warden writes the name of the subject portrayed in the icon on the board or on a metal plate attached to it.

Degeneration of art

Qualifications of the artist

The icon painter should live a very religious life to be able to see the spiritual countenance of the face being painted. Most painters make copies of older icons whose faces were drawn by saintly persons themselves. Those saintly persons were able to see beyond the material outlines of the face and grasp the outlines of the spiritual energy. That is why the faces they paint do not simply resemble the material person in ordinary life. An icon painter who copies an icon created by a saintly person must be able to gather some of the spiritual meaning – and to have an experience of the countenance of the face while painting it.

How does the tradition get any new icons? Sometimes a person has a new vision. The old forms may be modified according to the new vision. There could be a first vision that is not totally clear. Later on, someone may have a clearer experience of it, and modify the icon. If an icon painter has only a weak ability to perceive the spiritual world the icon figure will reflect a lack of countenance. If something unnecessary is painted out of the artist's personal mundane conception, it is like mud on the icon. It will have superfluous imagery or misshapen lines that do not correspond to the spiritual world.

Degeneration of portrayals

If too many painters lack the spiritual capacity to perceive hierophany, then the icons of the historical period degenerate. The icons begin to reflect mere allegorical images that do not have a direct connection with the spiritual world. The visual subjects are created either out of naturalistic impressions (how things look in the natural world), rational constructions based on some complex theology with conventional images, or even filling in historical details that have nothing directly to do with any hierophany.

The folds in the clothing on the icon figures changed according to the period of history, but in all cases they are meant to represent the spiritual life of the subject. When the folds begin to express sensuality, it is a sign of the degeneration of spiritual capacity. Clothes are part of the visual symbolism of the icon. They give an idea of the culture's spiritual style, and it may reflect a degeneration of spiritual values if the folds of a certain time convey sensuality and pull one into this world.

> We can call their clothes the covering woven by their acts of spiritual discipline. . . . [T]he clothes are like an amplifier of the body, making louder and more direct the words the body is saying as witness to its own inner idea.
>
> (Florensky 1996: 118)

Experiencing the icon

A sign of degeneration of art is the lack of hierophanic experience by people using the sacred art. Properly viewing an icon is not just a psychological experience. "Now, an icon reaches its goal when it leads our consciousness out into the spiritual realm where we behold mysterious and supernatural visions" (Florensky 1996: 66). One may look at the icon with a steady gaze or a quick intuitive glance. But if the icon is just naturalistic, it will not convey the spiritual countenance of the face painted there. If pictures pretending to be sacred art only portray people who have worldly beauty, it may be an indication that the art and culture have degenerated.

KEY POINTS

- Jesus of Nazareth, the founder of Christianity, was born around 4 BCE in Jewish Palestine about fifteen years after King Herod enlarged the Zerubbabel's temple. Christianity takes its name from a word used to describe Jesus. Christ is Greek for the Hebrew word *Mesiach*, meaning Anointed One.
- After the Romans destroyed the Jerusalem temple in 70 CE, early Christians along with Jews relocated to major cities of the Mediterranean region. Soon after, Roman officials considered Christians as religiously separate from Jews, and persecuted them until Constantine came to power in the fourth century.
- Several options for religious life opened up for Christians as the tradition developed, including those who served the institution of the Church, hermits, monastics, and friars. Women occupied a fairly strong place in Christianity until the rise of universities during the Middle Ages.
- A major Church schism in 1054 created: (1) the Byzantine Orthodox Churches headed by bishops who used Greek as the liturgical language, and (2) the Roman Catholic Church that used Latin as the liturgical language, and was headed by the pope.
- By the fifteenth century Roman Catholics such as Martin Luther and John Calvin called for reform in their Western Church. This fostered the Protestant Reformation, and a Catholic Counter-reformation.
- Protestant denominations multiplied, and continue to branch out in search of authentic ways of living a Christlike life. Certain Roman Catholics and Protestants oriented themselves to social welfare, and developed liberation theology.
- A critical question in the history of Christian art was whether or not to visually represent saintly people, and whether or not to make statues as opposed to flat icons.

STUDY QUESTIONS

1. What events of Jesus' life and teaching made him into a successful religious leader?
2. What factors contributed to Christianity becoming a separate religion from Judaism?
3. What turning points in the history of Christianity occurred in the fourth, eleventh, and sixteenth centuries?
4. What new ideas prompted the separation of Protestant Christians from the Roman Catholic Church? What new ideas does the *Woman's Bible* bring up?
5. What options for religious practice opened up for Christians from the time of Jesus through the Middle Ages? Were the roles of men and women the same?
6. What ideas never made it into the official Christian canon? (Think about the Nag Hammadi Library, as well as heretics such as Bishop Arius.)
7. What are the main ideas behind icon painting? Why is this form of art so important to the Christian Orthodox Churches?

GLOSSARY

apocalypse (Greek: *apokalypsis* = unveiling) A revelation that professes to reveal the future. The New Testament's *Apocalypse of John* predicts a cataclysmic struggle between good and evil at Armageddon bringing the end of the world.

apostle (Greek: *apostolos* = messenger) A handful of disciples appointed by Jesus of Nazareth to heal and spread his message, plus other prominent early Christians such as those who witnessed Jesus' resurrection, Paul, and early missionaries.

Christ (Greek: *christos* = anointed one) Christian term meaning Messiah. From the early days of Christianity used to qualify the name of Jesus: Jesus Christ.

Council of Nicea (I) A Christian council held in Nicea (Turkey) in 325 CE that affirmed the Incarnation, composed the Nicene Creed, and condemned Arius as a heretic for denying the divinity of Jesus.

crucifixion Death by hanging on a cross, used as a form of capital punishment in the Roman Empire. Christians invested great meaning in the death of Jesus on the cross as atoning for the sins of humankind.

disciple In a general sense, a follower of Jesus of Nazareth, past or present. In a narrow sense, only Jesus' closest male followers are called disciples in the Christian scriptures.

epistle (Greek = letter) Twenty-one letters in Greek attributed to Jesus' apostles written to Christian communities threatened by loss of faith and organizational difficulties. The earliest New Testament writings.

eschatology (Greek: *eschatos* = last) Refers in general to the "last things" or the final condition of humanity and the cosmos.

Eucharist (Greek: *eucharistia* = thanksgiving) [*yoo*'kah'rist] The central ritual of Christian worship, based on the last meal shared by Jesus with his disciples prior to the crucifixion. Also known as Holy Communion, or the Lord's Supper.

Evangelical Christians Protestant Christians whose spirituality centers on experience of personal conversion and salvation through Jesus Christ, with an emphasis on millenarian expectations.

gospel (translated from Greek: *euaggelion* = good news) A New Testament narrative of the life of Jesus. Those written under the names Mark, Matthew, Luke, and John are officially part of the Christian scriptures.

Holy Trinity Christian mystery of three divine persons in one: God the Father, Jesus Christ the Son, and the Holy Spirit.

icon (Greek = image, portrait) A two-dimensional visual representation of a saintly figure which introduces the viewer to that figure in the imaginal realm. Used in Orthodox Christianity.

iconoclastic controversy Arguments over whether or not icons should be used. The debate first occupied the Christian world (especially Byzantium) for over a century starting in 730 CE.

incarnation (Latin = made flesh) A physical body through which an immaterial body of another being comes into this world. Most Christians consider Jesus to be an Incarnation of God (God born into the flesh), and thus call Jesus the Son of God.

indulgences Certificates representing acts of penance sold through the Roman Catholic Church. Martin Luther criticized them for representing transactions with God, and diverting funds to Rome.

liberation theology A branch of Christian theology that promotes the social values of peace, justice, and equality. It emerged in Latin America in the 1960s, and spread worldwide.

millenarianism, millennialism Christian belief in the future millennium during which Christ will come again to reign over a new world (for 1,000 years), based on Revelation 20.

New Testament The portion of Christian scripture that complements the Old Testament. It contains twenty-one epistles, four gospels, a history of the early church, and a prophecy about the end of the world.

Old Testament The portion of Christian scripture that was adopted from Judaism, basically equivalent to the Hebrew Tanakh.

Pentecost A Christian holiday fifty days after Easter that commemorates the experience of glossolalia by a group of Christians in which they began speaking in tongues.

Q (German: *Quelle* = source) Name given by German biblical scholars to a hypothetical *quelle* (source) from which Synoptic Gospel authors drew their material.

resurrection Rising up after death. In Christianity the term for Jesus rising up on the third day after dying on the cross and being placed in a tomb. Easter celebrates this event.

sacrament A ritual that mediates divine grace (normally from the Holy Spirit). Typically it recalls a hierophany. Roman Catholic and Orthodox Christians recognize seven sacraments, while many Protestant Christians recognize two.

Synoptic Gospels The Greek term *synoptic* (*optics* = seen and *syn* = together) describes the Christian gospels of Matthew, Mark, and Luke because they contain much common material.

transubstantiation Actual transformation of the inner essence of the bread and wine of the Eucharist into the body and blood of Jesus Christ. Belief held by Roman Catholics since the Council of Trent (1545–1563), but rejected by other Christians.

KEY READING

Dillenberger, John and Welch, Claude (1954) *Protestant Christianity Interpreted through its Development*, New York: Charles Scribner's Sons.

Florensky, P. (1996) *Iconostasis*, trans. D. Sheehan and O. Andrejev, Crestwood, NY: St. Vladimir's Seminary Press.

Fosdick, Harry Emerson (ed.) (1952) *Great Voices of the Reformation*, New York: Random House.

Leclercq, J. ([1957] 1985) *The Love of Learning and the Desire for God: A Study of Monastic Culture*, trans. C. Misrahi, New York: Fordham University Press.

Meier, John P. (1991, 1994, 2001) *A Marginal Jew: Rethinking the Historical Jesus*, 3 vols to date, New York: Doubleday.

Pelikan, Jaroslav (1999) *Jesus through the Centuries: His Place in the History of Culture*, New Haven, CT: Yale University Press.

Robinson, J. M. (ed.) (1996) *The Nag Hammadi Library in English* (4th edn), trans. and intro. by members of the Coptic Gnostic Library Project, Leiden: E. J. Brill.

Schüssler Fioranza, Elizabeth ([1983] 1994) *In Memory of Her: A Feminist Reconstruction of Christian Origins*, New York: Crossroad.

Walker, Williston, Norris, Richard A., Lotz, David W., and Handy, Robert T. (1985) *A History of the Christian Church* (4th edn), New York: Scribner; Edinburgh: T. & T. Clark.

Zernov, Nicholas (1961) *Eastern Christendom: A Study of the Origin and Development of the Eastern Orthodox Church*, New York: Putnam.

CHAPTER 6

Islamic tradition

TIMELINE

	CE	
Muḥammad ibn 'Abd Allāh born (Prophet of Islam)	ca. 570	
Muḥammad migrates to Yathrib	622	Islamic calendar dates from the hijra; year 1 AH
Muḥammad passes away	632	
	632–661	Rightly Guided Caliphs rule
	661–750	Umayyad caliphs rule
	771	Invasion of Spain
	750–1258	'Abbāsid caliphs rule
al-Kindi	803–873	
Rābi'a al-'Adawiya	d. 801	
	810–870	Bukhārī compiles ḥadīth
Ibn Sina (Avicenna)	980–1037	
	1055–1220	Seljuk Turks ally with Sunnīs; Sunnī Islam becomes the international form
al-Ghazālī	1058–1111	
	1099	Christians take Jerusalem from Seljuk Turks
Ibn Rushd (Averroës)	1126–1198	
al-Suhrawardī	1154–1191	
Ibn al-'Arabī	1165–1240	
	1187	Salāḥ ud-Dīn retakes Jerusalem
	1380–1918	Ottoman Empire
	1526–1857	Mughal Dynasty in India
Mullā Ṣadrā	1571–1640	
Hamzah Fansuri, Malay poet	ca. 1600	
Muḥammad Iqbāl	1877–1938	
	1919–1984	Muslim countries gain independence from European colonial rule
Malcolm X	1925–1965	
	1979	Iranian Cultural Revolution
	1980	Halveti-Jerrahi Turkish Ṣūfī lineage to America

In the sixth century CE, Abyssinia (Ethiopia) was a Christian country, and Jews were living in South Arabia and Yemen. Yet no Abrahamic religion had developed among the Bedouin tribes of the Arabian Desert near Mecca. The Abyssinians wanted to convert the Meccan polytheists to their Christian faith, but failed when the army contracted smallpox and retreated from a military advance on Mecca. This happened in the year of Muḥammad ibn 'Abd Allāh's (**pbuh, as**) birth. But it would not be long before all Arabia would hear God's word and adopt Islam as their religion. Muḥammad identified with the ḥanīfs, monotheists who traced back to Abraham's son Ishmael and his Egyptian mother Ḥājar. Yet no religious cult had been passed down from Ishmael, as it had from the Hebrew line of Abraham's second son Isaac. Instead, the inspiration was given to Muḥammad to bring to the **Arab** people – and to the world. In 610 CE the first message from Allāh came to Muḥammad through the Angel Gabriel, and, after a rough start, the Muslim community was established in 622. Thus, having made God's will known to the Arab people, Muḥammad became not only a prophet of God (*nabī*), but also a messenger of God (*rasūl*).

For ages, in times of economic hardship the Bedouin tribes of the Arabian Desert migrated north to the Fertile Crescent and the Nile. Ancient migrations of a Semitic people traveling northward occurred around 3500 BCE. The typical pattern for migration was that a core group would travel north, and a much larger group would follow. Abraham's family had done this, and the first **Muslim** community founded by Muḥammad was to seek its fortune along the same route. The Islamic expansion beyond Arabia in the seventh century CE brought a cultural transition from Bedouin tribal customs to a sophisticated and powerful urban life. Their inheritance from the Persian and Byzantine empires caused both problems and progress for the new Islamic faith in the century following the death of Prophet Muḥammad.

PART 1
ISLAMIC PLAYERS

THE ULTIMATE PRINCIPLE

Allāh, the one God

The basic name for God in Arabic is **Allāh**, derived from the noun al-ilah or "the God." The word Allāh was not new to the Arabs when Muḥammad received the **Qur'ān**. Yet this Muslim holy scripture placed the God (Allāh) above the Arabian deities, and eliminated all consideration of them. Allāh is credited with performing every act that Arabs had associated with their lesser deities, such as sending rain. Nature is Allāh's creation, and nothing in the universe evades the scope of divine awareness. Allāh is the omniscient creator of the universe, and has no partner. In the whole universe only Allāh is divine.

Muslims describe the divine with ninety-nine names. The first is Allāh, the God. According to one mystical commentary, the word Allāh itself summarizes a person's entire existence from the cradle to the grave. A or alif is the first letter of the Arabic alphabet. It is the "ah" sound. This represents descent into this world, which takes two main forms: the descent of the Angel Gabriel (Jibrīl) to reveal Allāh's message to the prophets, and birth into this world. Ah is the first sound made by a baby. The last letter of the word Allāh is the "h" sound, which is the sound of a person's dying breath. Thus, Allāh encompasses all birth and death. Other names include:

- ar-Rahmān, the Most Compassionate
- ar-Rahīm, the Merciful
- as-Salām, the All-Peaceful
- al-Ghaffār, the Forgiver
- al-Latīf, the Gentle, knower of subtleties
- ash-Shakūr, the Grateful
- al-Mujīb, the Responsive
- al-Hamīd, the Praiseworthy
- al-Mumīt, the Cause of Death
- an-Nūr, the Light
- as-Sabūr, the Patient One

IMAGINAL PLAYERS

Allāh's angels

Muslim mystic cosmology posits a three-tiered hierarchy of creation: (1) corporeal things, (2) imaginal phenomena (***barzakh***), and (3) pure spirit. Corporeal things are dense, dark, and physical, while pure spirit is associated with intensive light and has no form. Allāh created the angels from light to bridge the gap between pure spirit and the physical realm. Angels have neither sin nor ideas of their own. They do not intercede between human beings and Allāh. Rather, they protect people and do as Allāh commands. They carry messages from Allāh, and keep a record of people's deeds. All human beings at birth are assigned two angels (one to sit upon each shoulder) who record their positive and negative deeds and report back to Allāh on the Day of Judgment.

Angel Gabriel bridged the gap between pure spirit and our corporeal world when he brought Allāh's message to Prophet Muḥammad over a period of twenty-three years to make up the Qur'ān. The message came in the form of inspirations. Among the angels, one does not fit the general pattern of God's messenger. This is Satan. At the time of creation, Allāh told the angels to bow down to Adam, the first man. Every angel except Satan obeyed Allāh's wish, so he descended from heaven to hell. Satan claimed he did not listen because he wanted to bow before no one but Allāh. Muslims believe that the disobedient Satan tempts human beings to disobey Allāh's will, as he tempted Abraham not to sacrifice his son (see page 158).

Khiḍr

The Qur'ān records an occasion when a youthful figure known as Khiḍr, the green one, acted as a spiritual guide for Moses. Khiḍr appeared to Moses and began to do a series of puzzling acts. He insisted that Moses be patient and not question his acts when he made a hole in a boat to drown some people, slew a young man, and rebuilt a wall in a village whose people refused them hospitality. Khiḍr told Moses, "Behold, thou wilt never be able to have patience with me – for how could thou be patient about something that thou canst not comprehend within the compass of [thy] experience?" (Qur'ān 18:67–68). Moses got impatient; but in the end Khiḍr explained the higher purpose of all he had done. Muslim mystics say Khiḍr guides people who are lost in a spiritual wilderness. His style of guidance may seem to us quite strange at first; but often in the history of religions this is the case with spiritual guides. The medieval mystic philosopher Ibn al-'Arabī said that those who possess the knowledge of Khiḍr know the real nature of God's work, because it "synthesizes the corporeal and spiritual aspects of reality" (Bashier 2004: 61).

Bedouin godlings

Prior to their acceptance of Islam, the Bedouin tribespeople of Muḥammad's day revered the spirits of trees, caves, stones, wells, and springs. The Ka'ba was used as a shrine for many deities, including Hubal, meaning "vapor, spirit" in Aramaic. The Bedouin also venerated three goddesses: (1) al-Manāt, the goddess of fate; (2) Lāt, the protectress of a sacred precinct where no tree could be cut down, no animal killed; and (3) al-'Uzza, who was Venus, the morning star. These figures are actually named in the Qur'ān (53:19 ff.) as the daughters of Allāh who prayed to the divine on behalf of the people. In the early days of Islam, the presence of these three familiar figures in the Prophet's message seemed to make the Quraysh tribe more receptive to the new faith.

Muḥammad was disturbed by the Qur'ānic verses on the three goddesses, so he prayed over it. In response, the Angel Gabriel appeared and made clear that al-Manāt, Lāt, and al-'Uzza should not be worshiped. In fact, eight years after establishing Islam Muḥammad sent one of his faithful to destroy the sanctuary of al-'Uzza who was the object of a cult east of Mecca. She had been a deity to whom members of the Quraysh offered human sacrifice. Muslims worshiped none of these deities – but they do believe in the existence of jinn, which are spirits that Allāh created from smokeless fire. A pre-Islamic custom was to call upon the jinn. Religious specialists known as *kahins* would enter a shamanic trance as they became possessed by these beings.

EXCEPTIONAL PLAYERS

Al-Mahdī

Al-Mahdī is a holy figure descended from Prophet Muḥammad who will appear at the end of time. Both **Sunnī** and **Shī'ī** Muslims expect that this "guided one" will usher in a new age, and help the faithful before the Day of Judgment. There is not total agreement on all details of his return, however. Some say that al-Mahdī will become known unexpectedly at the age of 40, and will be active for seven years. According to some **ḥadīth**, he will be tall, of fair complexion with facial features like Prophet Muḥammad's, and speak with a stutter. He will be victorious in a great battle, and open the way for Islam to spread throughout the world. **Imām** Mahdī will prepare the way for the return of Jesus, who will appear in a Second Coming on earth during al-Mahdī's lifetime. Muslims have great expectations for the arrival of Imām Mahdī at a time when justice must be restored. Although Muslims do not call Jesus the Son of God, they view him as Allāh's Prophet with a messianic role to play on the Day of Judgment.

Most Shī'ī Muslims today are called Twelvers since they believe in a lineage of twelve imāms. Al-Mahdī is the Twelfth Imām, a spiritual leader named Muḥammad al Muntazar who lived in the ninth century. After his birth, the child's father, the Eleventh Imām, hid him. He appeared at age 6 to claim succession in 'Alī ibn Abī Ṭālib's lineage, and hid again. At auspicious moments this Twelfth Imām communicated to devotees through spiritual leaders called Babs or Gates. Twelver Shī'a believe that Muḥammad al Muntazar did not die, but went into a great occultation. He is hidden, but some of the faithful see him in visions.

Allāh's prophets

The Qur'ān announced that in different times and places 124,000 prophets have already brought Allāh's word to humankind. Of these, twenty-five are specifically named, and three of the best known are Abraham, Jesus, and Muḥammad.

Abraham

The prophet Adam was the first to believe in one God, and Abraham restored the original belief. Through Abraham's two sons came Judaism, Christianity, and Islam. Sarah, his Hebrew wife, was not expecting to bear a child, and presented Abraham with Ḥājar, her Egyptian maid, to conceive a son. According to custom, if a wife did not produce a son, the husband could have another woman produce a male heir. Indeed, Ḥājar gave birth to Ishmael. But later Sarah conceived and gave birth to Isaac. She then asked Abraham to send Ḥājar and Ishmael away, so he took them to Arabia. Abraham's descendants continued in two lineages that intersected when: (1) Isaac's first son Esau married into his cousin Ishmael's line, and (2) Moses married a woman whose father Jethro was a ḥanīf who believed in one God.

Jesus

No prophet is more than human, including Jesus (believed by Christians, but not Muslims, to be an integral part of a divine trinity). Jesus came from the womb of the virgin Maryam (Mary), and will reappear before the Day of Judgment. He did not die upon the cross. His body was taken up directly into heaven. There was no redemption through the death of Jesus, since for Muslims there is no original sin requiring redemption.

Muḥammad

Muḥammad is the last in line of 124,000 prophets of God. Therefore, he is called the Seal of the Prophets. Although Muslims consider all prophets to be essentially the same, they place Muḥammad at the focal point of Islam. This place of prominence is based on the belief that the Qur'ān revealed through Prophet Muḥammad is an accurate, complete, and uncorrupted divine message sent through him for all the world's people.

Prophet Muḥammad (571–632)

Early life

Muḥammad was born to the elite Banu Hashim family of the Arabian Quraysh clan. He was named Aḥmad or

Muḥammad, which are two variants of "highly praised." Shortly after birth, the child was sent to live with a Bedouin tribe in the Arabian Desert. The Quraysh of Mecca were not many generations removed from the desert; so they kept the custom of having their infants suckled by Bedouin women for a couple of years. This arrangement was mutually beneficial as Bedouin women received income and protection for their families, while Meccan children absorbed the authentic Arab virtues of hospitality and so forth.

Muḥammad returned to his mother in Mecca at the age of 5, but the following year she passed away, and he moved in with his father's father. At that time Muḥammad got his first look at the **Ka'ba**, the Arabian place of pilgrimage that became so important to him later on. But the grandfather who took Muḥammad around the sacred site passed away two years later. After that, the child was taken to live with his paternal uncle Abu Ṭālib, who remained a key figure in his life for many years thereafter.

The traditional sacred biography of Muḥammad indicates that this future apostle of God was an unusual child. Muḥammad had eyes that naturally appeared as though treated with salve. Halima, the woman who suckled Aḥmad, observed that her home was blessed during the time he stayed with her family. When he was 4 years old, two angels laid him on the ground, removed a black drop from his heart, and washed his inner parts with melted snow from a golden vessel. At the age of 12, when Aḥmad went with his uncle to Syria with a trading caravan, a Christian monk noticed that a cloud sheltered him, and trees lowered their branches to provide shade. The monk found a bodily sign between the boy's shoulders that indicated a seal of prophetic office.

Marriage to Khadījah bint Khuwaylid

Muḥammad was 25 years old when he was offered employment with a caravan sponsored by a Qurayshi businesswoman named Khadījah (c. 554–619) who was twice widowed and fifteen years his senior. Khadījah was impressed by Muḥammad's gentle disposition and anointed appearance. Her sense that he was an unusual person was confirmed when she once saw two angels shading him on a return trip to Mecca. Khadījah offered her hand in marriage, and he accepted. Later, after the trauma of Muḥammad's first revelation, she encouraged him and had faith that what had happened was authentic and beneficent.

While Khadījah was alive, she was Muḥammad's only wife. Khadījah bore several children in the course of their loving, stable, and fortunate union. Their daughter Fāṭima was the only one among their children who survived him. She married Muḥammad's cousin 'Alī, and together they had two sons. Their first-born was al-Ḥasan ibn 'Alī who resembled his grandfather from head to chest in well-articulated facial features and noble countenance. Then came al-Ḥusayn ibn 'Alī who took after Muḥammad from chest to feet with brave bearing and a generous spirit.

Muḥammad had been married to Khadījah for fifteen years when dramatic events turned his life single-pointedly toward religion. At the age of 40 the future apostle of God was a well-trusted and respected member of the community. He loved solitude and repaired to a rocky cave each year during the month of Ramaḍān for prayer. As a ḥanīf he would have prayed to the God of Abraham, the God of his forefathers.

"Iqra!" ("Recite!")

In the year 610 CE Muḥammad went to a cave on Mount Ḥirā on the outskirts of Mecca for his meditation retreat, as he did each year. One night, sometime in the last third of the month of Ramaḍān as he slept, someone began choking him. The "person" was the Angel Gabriel, who pressed down upon Muḥammad with so much force that he could hardly bear it. The angel insisted, "Iqra!" ("Recite!") . . . and released him. Muḥammad said he did not know how to read. Then he started choking again, and heard for a second time the command, "Iqra!" He replied as before. A third time the angel pressed upon the Prophet of Islam, released him, and insisted, "Iqra! Bismi Rabbika!" ("Recite in the name of thy Sustainer!")

Muḥammad, shaken to the core, made his way down Mount Ḥirā to Khadījah. He begged her, "Cover me! Cover me!" When his heart stopped pounding with fear, the Prophet – for now he could be called a prophet – told her about the angel, and confessed his fear that something might happen to him. Khadījah reassured her husband, saying Allāh would not disgrace him. She advised him according to traditional Bedouin ethics to help poor and needy people, and to always be generous to guests.

The Message

After the second encounter with the Angel Gabriel, the inspirations continued regularly for about two decades until Muḥammad died in 632 CE. The basic practices of prayer were revealed, and Khadījah and 'Alī (the Prophet's cousin) became the first Muslim converts. Three years after the initial inspiration the **companions** of the Prophet numbered forty. These early followers were members of his Quraysh clan. Among them were some highly respected members of Arabian society, namely Abu Bakr and 'Umar ibn al-Khattāb. Later, these became the first two caliphs of Islam. The Quraysh were not threatened at first, although Muḥammad appealed to the young clansmen, and began to speak out against their elders who were pagan non-believers. In these early days he targeted two aspects of Meccan society: the worship of many gods and social inequalities. As the Qur'ānic message intensified, the Meccan elite felt increasingly threatened by the Prophet's work, and tried to end the religious reform movement – even boycotting him and his clan for months.

In this changing environment where houses of Meccans were sometimes divided between young followers of Islam and traditional elders, Muḥammad drew emotional strength from Khadījah. In addition, Muḥammad was protected by the influence of Abu Ṭālib. One can imagine how devastated Muḥammad became when in a single year both Khadījah and Abu Ṭālib passed away in 619. That period was the darkest in the Prophet's life – and certainly after the death of his uncle, Muḥammad's life and new religion were both in danger. After a monogamous life with Khadījah who passed away in Mecca before the hijra, Muḥammad remarried a number of times, including at least eight widowed women. Aside from 'Ā'isha bint Abī Bakr (who was a special case, being only 9 years old at the time of betrothal), the Prophet's wives ranged from 17 to 50, averaging around 30 years of age. Several of the Prophet's marriages cemented political alliances, while others were undertaken to offer protection to widows. With regard to the care the Prophet bestowed upon his wives, this opinion can be considered:

> Although the political nature of the Prophet's marriages is clear enough it is evident that feelings played their part both in the relationships Mohammad had with his wives, and between the wives themselves. In all material and mundane matters it was quite possible for Mohammad to treat them all with equality, but by common consent A'isha was his most beloved wife, although she never threatened the special place of Khadija, as Mohammed himself once told her.
>
> (Roberts 1982: 180)

The Prophet had two sons (one by Khadījah), but left no male heir since they predeceased him. Because the practice of polygyny is far removed from the cultural norms of Western society, it is easy to misunderstand Prophet Muḥammad's actions. However, in context, these alliances do not appear negative.

Hijra

Facing the prospect of increased hostilities, the Prophet sent some companions to seek protection in Abyssinia, which was ruled by a Christian king. The Prophet himself was invited by new Muslim converts to Yathrib, a city some 250 miles through the desert to the north of Mecca. Thus in the year 622 CE Muḥammad moved from Mecca to Yathrib. This momentous event in the history of Islam is known as the **hijra** or immigration. To elude his pursuers Muḥammad hid in a cave. There a miracle of nature occurred as a sign that Allāh was protecting him. Although those in pursuit arrived at the cave while Muḥammad was inside, they thought it was empty because an elaborate spider's web graced the entrance. Thinking this would have been disturbed had anyone entered the cave, the men left the scene. Muḥammad remained safely inside.

Soon after Muḥammad arrived in Yathrib it was renamed Madīna, the "City." He was inspired to construct the first Islamic mosque, and instituted the ritual call to prayer. After the hijra, the Prophet led the Muslim community for a full decade from 622 to 632 CE. His activity involved the practical problem-solving of daily life, as well as a series of battles and political negotiations. During this time the number of believers grew from a relatively small core to the entire population of Madīna. Muḥammad drew up a constitution at Madīna to regulate the relationship within the community, and between Muslims and non-believers.

In spite of his generally quiet character, the Prophet was pressed into administrating and defending the fledgling Muslim community that grew up once he made the move to Yathrib. Muḥammad's double role as spiritual and military leader corresponds to the dual significance of Islamic **jihād**, which refers to both inner and outer struggle. Inwardly a Muslim engages in jihād against forgetfulness of the unity of Allāh. Outwardly a Muslim struggles against forces that threaten or harm Islam in society. The Prophet said that the inner jihād is the more difficult of the two struggles, although both were essential. The armed conflicts in which the Prophet and his companions engaged were expressions of the outer jihād. But they were to maintain impeccable moral standards according to God's will as presented in the Qur'ān. The tradition of jihād continues to this day in Islam, but there is no central Muslim authority that interprets what specifically constitutes a threat to Islam. A study of Muslim history reveals a spectrum of reactions to threat. Even among Muḥammad's immediate successors a range of attitudes is evident. It seems that 'Alī (who married the Prophet's daughter) was more inclined than some others to let Allāh punish transgressions rather than take retribution into his own hands.

Plate 6.1 "Prophet Muḥammad's Night Journey." The Qur'ān (17.1) speaks of a night journey (*al-Isra'*) in which the Prophet was transported from a "sacred place of worship" (*al-masjid al-haram*) to a "further place of worship" (*al-masjid al aqsa*). A tradition based on the qur'ānic verse says that Muḥammad was transported on a winged creature (*burāq*) from the Ka'ba in Mecca to Jerusalem – from where he ascended through seven levels of heaven to the Throne of God. On the heavenly ascent (*al-mi'rāj*) he met Adam, Abraham, Moses, Jesus, and other prophets. Muslims debate whether the Night Journey was physical or spiritual. In this picture you see the Ka'ba, the burāq and angels – but not much of Muḥammad. Traditional Islamic art does not represent Muḥammad's face after he became a prophet of God.

Final days

The resanctification of the Ka'ba was among the last of Prophet Muḥammad's acts. Ten years after the migration to Madīna, the Prophet made his first and only pilgrimage to Mecca. There he delivered what became known as the "farewell speech" on the plain of 'Arafāt. On a Friday afternoon, in the midst of a huge gathering on the Mount of Mercy, Muḥammad gave his final ethical advice on the treatment of women, sharing of goods, and so forth. It contained the final legal matter ever revealed through the Prophet, including these words of peacemaking. In this inspiration all Muslims are enjoined to put away hatred even for those who appear to be their enemies:

> O you who have attained to faith! Be true to your covenants! . . . And never let your hatred of people who would bar you from the Inviolable House of Worship lead you into the sin of aggression: but rather help one another in furthering virtue and God-consciousness, and do not help one another in furthering evil and enmity; and remain conscious of God: for behold, God is severe in retribution! . . . Today, all the good things of life have been made lawful to you.
>
> (Qur'ān 5:1, 2, 5; Asad 1980)

The Prophet died from fever eighty-one or eighty-two days after the gathering on the Mount of Mercy. He was at Madīna in his home next to the mosque. Muḥammad died with his head in 'Ā'isha's lap. In the years following this event, 'Ā'isha contributed significantly to the body of knowledge about the Prophet's life. For example, she related from firsthand experience how her husband appeared after an inspiration: even on a cold day, he would have perspiration on his brow. Physical pain accompanied these hierophanic experiences. Sometimes the Apostle of God fell to the ground as the force of an inspiration pressed upon him. If he was riding a camel when an inspiration came, the camel's legs would slip sideways beneath the beast under the pressure of the event. But henceforth, from the year 632 Muslims would have to make their way without the Prophet's leadership. They were to rely upon the message delivered through him – the Qur'ān.

Despite the companions' loss of their leader, Islam survived. Muḥammad had established the foundation of a full-fledged monotheistic religion, and planted the seeds of an Islamic social order. Yet it is said that Muḥammad maintained his humility throughout the twenty-three years during which he served as Allāh's apostle. He milked goats, mended his own clothes, and carried his grandsons al-Ḥasan and al-Ḥusayn around on his back. Muḥammad's personal conduct and advice set the standard for Muslim behavior. From general values down to fine details such as how to cut one's nails, the Muslim community looked to their beloved prophet as a role model.

HISTORICAL PLAYERS

The Rightly Guided Caliphs (632–661)

After the Prophet of Islam passed away, four leaders who were given the title caliph (Arabic: *khalīfa* = deputy) emerged, and became known as the **Rightly Guided Ones**: Abu Bakr, 'Umar, 'Uthmān, and 'Alī.

Abu Bakr (580–634)

The first caliph of Islam was Abu Bakr, who had been Muḥammad's chief military advisor. He had traveled with the Prophet to Yathrib, and gave his daughter 'Ā'isha to Muḥammad as a wife. After Muḥammad passed away Abu Bakr ruled the Arab tribes for just over a year (632–634). Under the force of his personality and authority he managed to bring the Arab tribes back into the fold when it seemed as though the Muslim confederation would fall apart. He gained control over central Arabia, and following Muḥammad's intentions he directed the Muslim army into Damascus, Syria.

'Umar ibn al-Khattāb (d. 644)

'Umar shored up the military efforts of Abu Bakr by leading a siege on Damascus in 635. After that, practically every year over the course of a decade (634–644) this second caliph moved the Muslim army into Palestine, North Africa (including Egypt), Persia, Iraq, and Asia Minor (Turkey). In Jerusalem, 'Umar built a simple mosque at the site where the first temple had stood, out of respect for the prophet Solomon, and to sanctify the spot where Prophet Muḥammad mystically rose to heaven on his Night Journey. He also forbade any non-Muslim from inhabiting Arabia, the Islamic homeland. At the end of Caliph 'Umar's reign Muslims began dating their lunar calendar starting with the year of the hijra. A Persian slave killed him with a poisoned dagger.

'Uthmān ibn Affān (d. 655)

The early Muslim caliphs followed one another in close succession. 'Uthmān was married, in turn, to two of Muḥammad's daughters. This third caliph ruled the nascent Muslim empire from 644 to 656. He maintained a strong centralized administration, and to help homogenize the Islamic territory 'Uthmān had the Qur'ān standardized to eliminate all controversy. A group of soldiers who had served in Egypt stormed 'Uthmān's house in Madīna, and assassinated him. They became disaffected over his appointment of certain people to high positions.

'Alī ibn Abī Ṭālib (600–661 CE)

'Alī was the Prophet's cousin and son-in-law. He and Fāṭima, the Prophet's daughter, had two sons, al-Ḥasan and al-Ḥusayn. 'Alī is traditionally portrayed as embodying a deep spirituality, and stands as a Muslim

Plate 6.2 "The mosque of 'Umar, or the ancient site of Herod's temple." When the city of Jerusalem fell to 'Umar in 638 CE, the Muslim caliph entered the precincts on foot wearing a simple tunic made of camel hair – such was his reverence for the Holy City. Caliph 'Umar regretted the terrible neglect by Romans and Christians of the site where the second temple had been destroyed. Tradition says he began clearing the area of refuse with his bare hands. Then he built a wooden mosque over the ancient rock altar where Abraham took his son for sacrifice, and Muḥammad ascended to heaven. This original structure was big enough for 3,000 people. In 691 CE, Caliph Abd al-Malik replaced it with the Dome of the Rock. Today Jews pray at the Wailing Wall, the retaining wall on the western side of what was once Herod's temple.

role model. For example, it is said that 'Alī gave most of what he earned each day to the poor. 'Alī became the fourth successor to Prophet Muḥammad. However, his political reign was brief and tragic.

Sunnī and Shī'ī Muslims

The activities of the Rightly Guided Ones rapidly launched the qur'ānic message outside of Arabia, but disagreements emerged over who was the Prophet's legitimate successor. These early divergent views created a political split in Islam. Over several centuries, this disagreement over leadership led to the development of sectarian identities known as Sunnī and Shī'a respectively. Sunnī Muslims remember the first four successors as very pious and legitimate. They are convinced that the Muslim community should choose Muḥammad's successors – who may or may not be relatives of the Prophet Muḥammad.

One contingent of companions thought that the true succession to the Prophet should continue through Muḥammad's family line. They claimed that 'Alī should have been the first caliph – whereas he finally became the fourth. These Shī'a Muslims or "partisans" believed that the Prophet transmitted charismatic authority and knowledge to 'Alī, which continued in a transmission through 'Alī's family. The partisans of 'Alī disagreed as to whether the transmission could run laterally from one of 'Alī's sons to another, and could not build consensus. In spite of their divergent views, all Shīʿa today agree that: (1) ʿAlī was the rightful successor to the Prophet, (2) ʿAlī transmitted the line of designation (*nass*) to one of his sons, and (3) the Muslim line of designation ran through one imām after another. The Ismaʿīlīs hold that this line has continued in an unbroken succession to this day.

Umayyad caliphs (661–750)

The Umayyad caliphs were the first military leaders after the Rightly Guided Caliphs. Ruling from 661 to 750, their political success transformed Islam into a widespread and culturally forceful empire. In the eyes of Shīʿī Muslims, shifting the seat of power from Mecca to Damascus under the Umayyads represented a degeneration of religious values spurred by the ambition of Arabian nobles who misused Islam for their own gain. The Umayyad line was drawn from the Quraysh tribe, but not from the Prophet's clan. Moreover, the first and second caliphs of this Umayyad line violated the claims to succession of members of the Prophet's family. Mu'āwiyah, the first Umayyad caliph, took charge of all Muslim lands after the Prophet's cousin ʿAlī, the fourth caliph, was assassinated in 661 CE. ʿAlī's first son al-Ḥasan passed his claim to the caliphate on to his brother al-Ḥusayn. In turn, Mu'āwiyah's son fiercely defended the Umayyads' right to rule and keep intact the Islamic state established by his father. To this end, the Umayyad army aborted the succession of al-Ḥusayn who was beheaded at the battle of Karbalā' in Iraq.

Prophet Muḥammad's grandson al-Ḥusayn is respected by both Sunnī and Shīʿī Muslims. The Shīʿa recall al-Ḥusayn's martyrdom with deep anguish on the tenth day of Muharram in the first month of the Islamic lunar calendar, known as the Day of 'Ashura'. Shīʿī Muslims believe that ʿAlī's lineage continued through a number of generations of imāms. Although they do not agree on the exact number of imāms, all Shīʿa believe in the legitimacy of ʿAlī, husband of the Prophet's daughter Fāṭima. The Shīʿa also consider that the guidance of imāms is a necessary part of the divine plan. Therefore, their ḥadīth include reports from the imāms.

The Umayyad court centered at Damascus found itself in a position of enormous wealth and political power, and the caliphate abandoned the simple ethical standards of the Rightly Guided Ones. But it is a fact of history that a golden age of Islamic culture was founded under their leadership. The Qur'ān became the vortex of energy around which a new Arabic literature, art, and architecture spun out. But with a huge empire to rule, the logistics of administration were overwhelming. In response to such challenges a power struggle ensued, and a rival caliphate emerged.

ʿAbbāsid and later caliphs

In 750 the Umayyad caliphate fell to a new dynasty, the ʿAbbāsids. The ʿAbbāsids claimed to be rightful heirs to the Islamic territory, due to their descent from one of Prophet Muḥammad's uncles. The ʿAbbāsids further justified their rule on moral grounds by objecting to Umayyad extravagance. They sought to create a more religiously conservative state without compromising Prophet Muḥammad's initiative as military leader. The ʿAbbāsids moved the seat of Islamic political power from Damascus, Syria to Baghdad – a new capital in Iraq. The ʿAbbāsid caliphate ruled from Baghdad for 508 years, from 750 to 1258.

One Islamic empire followed another. The Muslim world covered vast stretches of territory including portions of what are now Spain, Egypt, Western and Central Asia, South Asia, and Russia:

1. The one surviving member of the old Umayyad ruling family established an Umayyad emirate, based in Córdoba (in today's Spain) that lasted from 756 to 929. Then, from 939 to 1021 an Umayyad caliphate re-emerged to turn the city into a luxurious cultural center where intellectual life flourished. Córdoba became a model city with street lamps, libraries, and hospitals.
2. Fāṭimid imāms (descended from the Prophet's daughter Fāṭima bint Muḥammad) established a Shīʿī seat of government in Egypt from 909 until 1171.
3. Seljuk Turks from Central Asia converted to Sunnī Islam and established a series of dynasties in the twelfth and thirteenth centuries in Persia, Iraq, and Syria. The powerful Sunnī leader Salāḥ ud-Dīn ended the Fāṭimid dynasty in Egypt (1171), and recaptured Jerusalem from the Christians (1187).

4 From the thirteenth to fifteenth centuries Mongol armies ruled Muslim populations in Iraq, Persia, Afghanistan, and parts of southern Russia.
5 In the wake of Mongol power, four Muslim empires arose to carry Islam into modern times: Uzbeks in Central Asia, Safavids in Persia, Mughals in India, and Ottomans in Asia Minor.

The Qur'ān affirms that there is no compulsion in Islam. This means that although Muslims are to profess their faith, they are forbidden to force any person to convert to Islam. Thus, Islamic rulers allowed People of the Book to practice their faith in Muslim society. These were people who had a revealed scripture – typically Jews, Christians, and Zoroastrians. Members of these religious had to pay extra taxes, bear no arms, and refrain from proselytizing their faiths. In return, a contract (*dhimmah*) of protection required the Muslim government to provide services to these non-Muslim **dhimmīs**, and protect them from harm.

Muslim theologians

In the first Islamic centuries vast amounts of new territory had to be managed. As Muslims contacted and overtook the sophisticated cultures of the Sassanid and Byzantine empires, new applications of Qur'ānic principles were needed. Thus the **'ulamā** (scholars) became increasingly relevant to the managing of Islamic territories. In 832 the 'Abbāsid caliph established the House of Wisdom in Baghdad where scholars translated fundamental philosophical and scientific texts from Greek, Iranian, and Indian languages into Arabic. Such research spurred the development of dialectical theology (*kalām*). This style of theological training allowed Muslims to engage in high-level discussions among themselves and with non-Muslim scholars in the world newly contacted by the Arabs. Islamic theologians established reason as a key element in religious discourse, and some introduced the idea of allegorical explanations for religious claims that were inaccessible to reason. Five main schools of Islamic theology evolved – four among Sunnī Muslims, plus the Twelver Shī'ī school. These remain relevant today throughout the Muslim world.

Muslim philosophers

By the third Islamic century (822–922 CE) Muslim philosophy emerged in contrast to the dialectical theology. While Islamic theologians sought to broaden the application of Qur'ānic principles, Islamic philosophers encouraged the study of Greek, Persian, and Indian science, mathematics, music, and literature. For example, al-Kindi (803–873), who tutored the caliph's son in the 'Abbāsid court in Baghdad, researched medicine, mathematics, geography, astronomy, physics, and music. He developed a vocabulary for Arab philosophy, and studied Indian mathematics. Abī Bakr Muḥammad ibn Zakariyyā al-Rāzī (864–925) was an early Iranian thinker who wrote on the ethics of non-violence, and advocated the study of philosophy because it imitated a quality of Allāh as the knowledgable one. One of al-Rāzī's practical scientific experiments involved recommending the site for a hospital where pieces of raw meat showed the least putrefaction.

Interest in Islamic philosophy began to wane after two centuries. This was due in part to a scathing attack by Abū Ḥāmid Muḥammad al-Ghazālī (1058–1111) who argued that philosophy was dangerous in the hands of unqualified students, and fiercely opposed what he considered to be the subversive work of Islamic philosophers. To counteract the declining fortunes of Islamic philosophy, Ibn Rushd (1126–1198) wrote a rebuttal to al-Ghazālī's attack on philosophy. This Spanish-Arab (known to Europeans as Averroës) made translations of Aristotle's works and commentaries into Latin from Arabic and Hebrew. These texts were well received among the European scholastic philosophers. However, despite the success of what came to be known as Averroism in Europe, interest in Aristotle continued to decline in the Islamic world.

Despite the animosity between Christians and Muslims over the Holy Land in the period of the Crusades, the traffic of Europeans to and from Jerusalem stimulated trade and the exchange of ideas – as well as fleas that brought the plague to Europe. In 1055 the Seljuks, a Turkic people of Central Asia recently converted to Islam, took over Baghdad in Iraq. The Seljuks threatened the Christian world by conquering Persia, Palestine, Syria, and much of Asia Minor. Due to their proximity, the Byzantine Christians were the most immediately threatened. However,

BOX 6.1 INTERPRETATIONS: THE QUR'ĀN AND ISLAMIC COSMOLOGY

Three Muslim thinkers developed the notion of the imaginal world (Arabic: *'alam al-khayāl*) to help interpret events in the Qur'ān, such as the Prophet's Night Journey. Shihāb al-Dīn Yaḥyā al-Suhrawardī, Ibn al-'Arabī, and Mullā Ṣadrā were fascinated by mystical cosmology, and the possibility of becoming conscious of the imaginal realm of reality. This world is included in Ṣūfī mystical cosmology as the intermediate arena with many levels that stands between the ordinary human world and the world of the Pure Spirit.

Zoroastrian influences. The Persian al-Suhrawardī (1154–1191) was the first Islamic thinker to explore the cosmology of the imaginal world. He drew heavily from the Zoroastrian tradition, and spoke of angelic beings from different levels of the imaginal world. In *The Chant of Gabriel's Wing*, he presents a conversation between a person on the spiritual path and the Angel Gabriel. The seeker had broken away from the bonds of sensual pleasure, and entered the desert. There he saw ten old men of mesmerizing glory.

> I asked from which direction have you, the exalted ones come. The old man who was at the corner replied that they are a group of incorporeals who have come from "the nowhere but prosperous land" (*nakuja abad*). I did not understand that, so I asked to which region that city belongs? He said "It belongs to the domain where the index finger cannot point to." So I came to know that the old master knows [the secrets].
>
> (al-Suhrawardī: Razvi 1997: 87)

Al-Suhrawardī developed a theory of mystic colors and lights that appear in connection with perceptions of the imaginal world. There are fifteen steps characterized by different experiences of light. After a vision called "the idea of the light of God" the seeker may obtain knowledge through the use of a special creative light. A seeker must be purified and prepared for this journey, since it ends with a violent experience of light that could tear apart the body limb from limb.

The unity of existence. The Spanish-born Ibn al-'Arabī (1165–1240) developed the concept of the "unity of existence." God emanated creation so that God would not be alone in the universe; and all creation longs to return to God. Created things both find and are found by the Creator. This finding occurs through the deep exploration of the world, including experience of the *barzakhi* imaginal realm. He developed the Islamic cosmological notion of the imaginal realm by elaborating on the term *barzakh*, the intermediate barrier between two things. According to Ibn al-'Arabī things perceived in the imaginal realm are analogous to things seen in a mirror: they are not the mirror; nor are they the material object whose reflection appears in the mirror. This imaginal realm is as much part of our universe as the realm in which events of ordinary life take place. But to realize its existence, a person must use the spiritual faculty of creative imagination. One who perceives it appreciates the unity of God's creation, and finds the linkage between the sensory and transcendent realms of existence. Angels (such as Gabriel who delivered the Qur'ān to Muḥammad) descend from this *barzakhi* realm to bring inspiration and bridge the gap between God who transcends the senses, and humans who normally only perceive gross sensory forms. In the imaginal realm things exist in time and space, but they do not always play by the rules of the ordinary sensory realm. Ibn al-'Arabī says this about his own experience of the peculiar nature of *barzakhi* space.

> I saw a tremendous place of witnessing, in sensory form – not in intelligible form – a form of the Real, not a meaning. In this self-disclosure there became manifest to me the manner in which the small expands in order for the large to enter into it, while it remains small

and the large remains large, like the camel,
which passes through the eye of a needle.
(Bashier 2004: 79)

The objective reality of the imaginal world. The Persian Mullā Ṣadrā (1571–1640) further developed the concept of the imaginal realm in Islamic thought, stating that it has an objective reality independent of human beings. Forms in the imaginal realm are not material; yet they display all the other physical properties of forms, such as shape, color, and odor. Human beings can enter into the imaginal world at the time of death, and seers can experience them during life. Within the realm, a person has a kind of subtle body. The issue of prophecy may be understood in connection with the imaginal world, which links the corporeal with the world of higher ideas.

Christians in the more distant Holy Roman Empire also felt threatened because the Seljuk Turks made travel to the Holy Land hazardous. Western Europeans liked to go on pilgrimage to Rome in Italy, and then move on to Santiago de Compostela in Spain, and wind up in Jerusalem. Earlier Muslim rulers in Jerusalem had not created a problem for Christian pilgrims.

Initially the Christians of East and West thought they could bond together to effectively resist the Seljuk Muslims. But this did not happen. The delicate relationship between the Holy Roman and Byzantine empires was aggravated when – in advance of the formal First Crusade – 75,000 low-level knights and peasants including hungry women and children (already down from 100,000 through fighting) from Western Europe passed through Constantinople on their way to recapture Jerusalem from the Seljuks. At one point the Byzantine Orthodox Christians and Muslims even fought together against the Roman Catholics in Jerusalem. For about 250 years the Western Europeans engaged in Crusades to the Holy Land, with initial success, the First Crusade starting out from France in 1096 and wresting control of Jerusalem in 1099. None of the numerous subsequent Crusades produced favorable religious results, and some (including a Children's Crusade) were disasters. Finally, the Kurdish Muslim leader Salāḥ ud-Dīn captured the Kingdom of Jerusalem, thereby ending Crusader rule.

Muslim mystics

In the early days of Islam, mysticism was infused naturally and thoroughly into the spirituality of the Prophet and his companions. However, the inner and outer aspects of religious life that were united in the original Muslim community began a gradual process of independent development after Muḥammad passed away. Under his leadership, contemplative life was fully integrated with all other aspects of life including belief, ritual, and politics. Under the Rightly Guided Ones – and even in the early days of the Umayyad caliphate – law, theology, and asceticism were more or less undifferentiated as the full spectrum of Muslim spiritual life from outer religious law to inner spiritual promptings fell under a unified **sharī'a**. However, by the second Islamic century (eighth century CE) some Muslims resisted the trend of the 'ulamā toward theological argumentations, philosophical speculations, and legalistic applications. These practitioners – who became known as **Ṣūfīs** – wished to explore the meaning of the Qur'ān in relation to the Creator and creation. To Ṣūfīs this meant applying themselves to the personal religious experience of Allāh and attending to social work. They sought to keep Islamic spiritual life free from the materialism and social corruption they felt was endangering Islam in the environment of its new-found prosperity.

Rābi'a al-'Adawiya (713/14–801)

Great Ṣūfī teachers include both women and men. Prophet Muḥammad's daughter Fāṭima is considered by some Ṣūfīs to be the first of their spiritual leaders. After that Rābi'a al-'Adawiya is the first woman Ṣūfī known to Islamic history. She was born in Basra, Iraq in the second Muslim century. Her life spanned the Umayyad–'Abbāsid transformation of Islam, and she was probably the first woman saint to be born as a

BOX 6.2 CULTURE CONTRAST: ARISTOTLE AND THE MEDIEVAL SCHOLASTIC PHILOSOPHERS

The works of Aristotle had been reintroduced to Europe through Arabic and Hebrew translations and commentaries by the year 1200. This classical Greek material (translated into Latin) was the "new learning" that came into the medieval Christian universities at Bologna, Paris, and Oxford from intellectual centers in Córdoba and Baghdad. Previously, Aristotle's thought was available in Europe only through Latin translations of his works on logic by the Roman Catholic writer Boethius (480–524).

Muslim, Jewish, and Christian theologians of the Middle Ages worked to reconcile the fruits of human reason with their holy scriptures, which they believed were divine revelations. They used allegory to interpret passages that were not susceptible to reason, and applied Aristotelian logic to overcome scriptural contradictions. Among the scholastic philosophers committed to reconciling revelation and reason were three of the most illustrious thinkers in the history of ideas: Ibn Sīnā (a Muslim), Maimonides (a Jew), and Aquinas (a Christian).

Ibn Sīnā. Ibn Sīnā (Avicenna) (980–1037) was born near Bukhara, Persia. He had wide-ranging interests in philosophy, geometry, jurisprudence, logic, medicine – and even Indian mathematics. His *Book of Healing* (mostly translated into Latin by 1150) presented a cosmology that allowed Christian thinkers to apply Aristotle to a religious context. Although a rationalist, he thought miracles were possible in the context of natural law as mind over matter, and wrote several Neoplatonic allegories that impacted upon Ṣūfī thought. Ibn Sīnā may be considered the first scholastic philosopher.

Maimonides. Moses Maimonides (1135/8–1204) was born in Córdoba, Spain. He was the first Jewish thinker to incorporate Aristotle's work into the philosophical thought of Judaism, and his influence spread throughout the European Renaissance among Jews and non-Jews. He wrote *Guide of the Perplexed* (composed in Arabic, then translated into Hebrew and Latin) examining the relationship of philosophy to scripture for deep thinkers who were perplexed about the role of reason in faith.

Aquinas. Thomas Aquinas (1225–1274) was born in Roccasecca, Italy. He wrote thirteen commentaries on Aristotle, and a summary of theology (*Summa theologiae*) that applied Aristotle's thought in a comprehensive analysis of Christian sacred doctrine. He had particular interest in two doctrines that distinguished Christianity from Judaism and Islam: the trinity of three persons in one God, and the mystery of the incarnation of God in Jesus Christ. In formulating his views Aquinas was influenced by the work of Ibn Sīnā and Maimonides.

Muslim. Rābi'a considered attraction to material things, other beings, or pain and pleasure as distractions from the divine. And though even saints in Islam tended to marry, she declined several proposals – including one from her friend the eminent Ṣūfī, al-Ḥasan of Basra. Rābi'a claimed she had no hand to give in marriage because her life was in Allāh, and she had ceased to exist in herself. She believed that the highest love involved perfect attention to Allāh while fearing or seeking nothing.

> O God, if I worship Thee for fear of Hell, burn me in Hell, and if I worship Thee in hopes of Paradise, exclude me from Paradise; but if I worship Thee for Thy own sake, grudge me not Thy everlasting beauty.
>
> (Rābi'a: 'Aṭṭār 1966: 51)

Rābi'a counseled her many disciples to associate only with trustworthy people according to the Qur'ānic verse: "O you who have attained to faith! Turn unto

God in sincere repentance" (Qur'ān 66:8). Accordingly, she made continuous efforts to work on her inner faults, confident that this would lead to a reduction of outer transgressions. Keeping her sins in full awareness, she wept constantly while in prayer. Although Rābi'a was sometimes weakened from the life of poverty, she lived to a ripe age.

Many stories grew up about Rābi'a's mystic powers. It was said that light emanated from her fingertips (which glowed in the dark), and she could fly on a carpet. A famous story speaks of a miracle that happened at the time of her death. Although Rābi'a was clothed in a simple shroud and woolen scarf, she appeared in a dream dressed in gilded and embroidered green silk. She explained:

> They were taken from me and I was clothed with what you see upon me and what I wore as a shroud was folded up and sealed and carried up to the angels, so that my garments might be complete on the Day of Resurrection.
>
> (Rābi'a: Smith 1977: 44)

Abū Ḥāmid Muḥammad al-Ghazālī (1058–1111)

Al-Ghazālī's thought represents an integration of outer ritual and inner spirituality. Prior to al-Ghazālī's declaration of the moral dangers of philosophy, he himself had done philosophical and other rigorous intellectual work. He had achieved recognition early in life for his written work, and was an eminent professor in Baghdad. Al-Ghazālī's studies somehow threw him into a crisis, however. One day while lecturing, he was suddenly struck dumb. He remained unable to speak for half a year, and realized the need to penetrate into the deeper meaning of what he had been teaching. Thus for a decade al-Ghazālī practiced asceticism and studied with Ṣūfī masters. On one hand he understood that mystical religious practice enabled a person to realize the orthodox teachings of Islam. On the other hand, he advocated restoring mainstream values to Ṣūfīsm. Thus, al-Ghazālī helped to reintegrate Ṣūfīsm into Muslim life.

Ṣūfīsm is not a separate Islamic sect, and has adherents among both Sunnī and Shī'a Muslims. Typically Ṣūfīsm was a profound aspect of a mystic's personal religious identity – but many became famous for their specific contributions to philosophy, theology, music, science, and other fields of knowledge. Only in the fourteenth century were the first Ṣūfī orders established on the basis of lineages that traced back to the early teachers.

Hamzah Fansuri (ca. 1600)

People of the Malay-Indonesian archipelago cultivated a deeply Muslim identity between the sixteenth and seventeenth centuries. The blossoming of a new indigenous literature was a powerful factor that generated this religious transformation. Aceh became a center of Islamic culture as 'ulamā came in from Mecca, Yemen, and Gujarat. This influx of Islamic thought spurred Malay Muslims to write in the areas of theology and metaphysics. They leaned toward Ṣūfīsm, and were deeply impacted by Muḥyi al-Dīn Ibn al-'Arabī's teachings on the unity of existence – which says that the divine essence is like a hidden treasure within creation.

Hamzah Fansuri was among the most illustrious Malay writers of this period, and his works of poetry and prose shaped subsequent Malay literature. His poetry is infused with Qur'ānic themes and Arabic quotations, with heavy Persian influence. Here is a mystical verse in the original Malay with an English translation. It tells of Prophet Muḥammad's behavior from a paradoxical Ṣūfī perspective.

> Rasūl Allāh itulah yang tiada berlawan
> Meninggalkan ta'am sungguhun makan
> 'Uzlat dan tunggal di dalam kawan
> Olehnya duduk waqtu berjalan.
>
> God's Messenger, the incomparable one
> Went without food while yet partaking of it
> He practised retreat and seclusion while
> among his companions
> Just as he was seated while walking.
>
> (Hamzah Fansuri: Drewes and Brakel 1986: 67)

Hamzah Fansuri wrote of his own spiritual experience, and felt that the purpose of a human being is to recapture the hidden treasure to which the Qur'ān leads. Yet he warns the mystic not to neglect the earlier levels of religious practice for the later ones. His calls

BOX 6.3 A SPIRITUAL PATH: THE ṢŪFĪ PATH OF SEVEN VALLEYS

The Conference of the Birds is a Persian Ṣūfī poem in which Farid ud-Din 'Aṭṭār (1145?–1220) describes seven stages leading to the divine in one's heart. 'Aṭṭār's allegory embodies the paradox of a path with no destination. A flock of birds set out to find a divine bird called the Simurgh, but in the end realize that the word "simurgh" means thirty (*si*) birds (*murgh*). After traversing these seven valleys they figured out that there was really nowhere to go.

Valley of the Quest. This valley represents the first step in a pilgrim's search for greater meaning in life. One may feel very alone in this quest and grieve for years, never knowing after how long – if ever – this stage will end. Great patience is required, and one may even come upon new misfortunes. 'Aṭṭār advises that a seeker must not become downhearted even if he or she searches for 100,000 years. Traversing through this valley expands the seeker's heart.

Valley of Love. In the second valley, the pilgrim finds a trace of the traceless, catching a hint of the fragrance of the invisible world. One experiences ecstasy where the sun shines so brightly that the intellect flees, the heart is burnt, and the spirit is cleansed. One finds no remedy for this love. One risks all to enter here, and feels the pain of absence from the Beloved.

Valley of Insight into Mystery. The third valley is like an uncharted sea, through which each pilgrim takes a different route. 'Aṭṭār advises the seeker to stay awake so as not to drown. Knowledge comes of the hidden essence of things, and doubt gives way to certitude. On this stage of the spiritual path one's inner eyes open, and the seeker converses privately with the Beloved.

Valley of Detachment. The experience of deep serenity emerges during this fourth stage of the spiritual path, and new insight dawns. The world appears as a vast passing dream wherein the whole is contained in the smallest part. The seeker feels as though heaven and earth can be seen in a single grain of sand.

Valley of Unity. On the fifth stage of the path, the pilgrim perceives pure unity. Things in the world appear transient like a wax toy. Crossing the fifth valley involves realization of non-duality where self and other are indistinguishable. There is no plurality here.

Valley of Bewilderment. The pilgrim experiences bewilderment, grief, and discontent. Everything is a new, momentary creation. The perception of unity fades and what seemed like certain knowledge diminishes. In this sixth valley the seeker even doubts doubt itself. One's heart feels both full and empty of love.

Valley of Poverty. Crossing this seventh and final valley, the pilgrim feels as if lame and deaf – unable to move or speak. The seeker gains the insight that though things in the world may outwardly appear to be separate, they have the same essence. 'Aṭṭār uses the metaphor of ash that comes from twigs and incense. One feels like a drop in an ocean with no shores.

Return! In the end, thirty birds survived the trip across the seven valleys. Upon arriving at their destination, they thought they had found nothing special after all. They could not find the divine Simurgh. The birds began to feel hopeless. . . . But 'Aṭṭār says love gave them courage. Suddenly the veils blocking their perception drew back, and the seekers experienced the inner light of light. The thirty birds saw that they were none other than simurgh – "thirty birds." They became silent, realizing that the Divine had been with them all the time.

to seek God are balanced with admonitions for all Muslims to maintain the standard ritual Islamic practices – including both obligatory and recommended acts of sharī'a. By penetrating the innermost aspects of one's being, a person's life is fulfilled. In line with Ibn al-'Arabī's thought, Hamzah feels that God calls people to God – and one's longing for God is the expression of God's call.

Postcolonial activists

Muḥammad Iqbāl (1877–1938)

Modern science, political thought, and Western culture inspired vigorous reactions from various quarters of the Muslim world. This became especially true after the demise of nineteenth-century European colonialism and the exit of Western political (imperialist) forces from fundamentally Muslim countries. For example, the creation of Pakistan following the downfall of British rule in India challenged Muslims to define themselves *vis-à-vis* the West. As president of the Muslim League (in 1930) Muḥammad Iqbāl spoke in favor of creating a state in northwest India for Indians of Muslim heritage. This concept was radicalized in the creation of the Islamic Republic of Pakistan from formerly Indian territory in 1947. Thereafter Iqbāl became a key figure in Pakistan's efforts to mold its religious identity by blending positive aspects of modernity into an authentic, creative, and dynamic Islamic framework. This manner of dealing with modernity and Western canons of knowledge became known in the 1970s as the Islamization of Knowledge.

Muḥammad Iqbāl was born on what is now the Pakistani side of the India–Pakistan border. Beyond his studies in Lahore, India, Iqbāl was inspired by a Western education in England (where he was knighted), and in Germany (where he was influenced by Goethe's thought). But Iqbāl became disaffected with what he saw as the moral and cultural damage caused by Western industrialization and colonialism. He believed that Islam, as expressed in the Qur'ān and **Sunnah** (tradition), should absorb modern advances in science and the academic disciplines – but re-create them with an infusion of Muslim values. His *Reconstruction of Religious Thought in Islam* was a groundbreaking work that attracted the interest of members of two groups of scholars that were somewhat isolated from each other at the time (as they can be, even today) – those with traditional Islamic training and those with Western-style university educations. Today, Muḥammad Iqbāl is Pakistan's national poet, and the day of his death (21 April) is a national holiday. And though his immediate focus was on India, he looked forward to a much broader Islamic political and spiritual renaissance. He stands as an early liberal Muslim who felt that "[e]quipped with penetrative thought and fresh experience" the Muslim world "should courageously proceed to the work of reconstruction before them" (Iqbāl 1962: 179).

Ruḥallāh Khumayni (1902–89)

Ruḥallāh Khumayni was from a line of Iranian 'ulamā. He turned from scholarship to political philosophy in 1963. He took power in the midst of a mass movement in which religious and secular Iranians revolted against the monarchical rule of Mohammad Reza Pahlavi in 1979. Under Khumayni's leadership the Islamic Republic of Iran adopted a constitution on 24 October 1979 that provided for a presidential election through a national direct vote every four years, as well as the public election of a National Assembly. Khumayni adopted the authoritative (and controversial) title Imām, and became the Supreme Leader of the nation. As a Shī'ī imām he retained ultimate control over both the National Assembly and the president. According to Shī'ī jurisprudence, application of sharī'a relies on an ongoing process of legal interpretation based on the reasoning of a qualified spiritual leader. (This is unacceptable to Sunnīs who emphasize community consensus and reasoning by analogy.)

During the Iranian Cultural Revolution, some of Ayatollah Khumayni's reforms met with criticism from other revivalist religious leaders. After allowing women to appear in the media, he responded to the displeasure of more conservative religious leaders, saying:

> I feel it necessary to express my despair about your understanding of the [Shī'ī] traditions. . . . The way you interpret the traditions, the new civilization should be destroyed and the people should live in shackles or live forever in the desert.
>
> (Ayatollah Khumayni: Kurzman 1998: 25)

North American Muslims

Malcolm X (1925–1965)

Malcolm Little was a black American born into a Christian family. He spent about half a decade (1946–1952) in prison after being convicted of drug dealing and burglary. While confined, Malcolm joined a movement called the Nation of Islam, which had been started in the early 1930s. Malcolm changed his last name from "Little" to "X" to symbolically cut ties to white oppressors by eliminating his slave name. He became a minister of the Nation of Islam under the strict direction of another black American named Elijah Muḥammad. In 1963 Malcolm X was suspended from the Nation of Islam. The following year he started a movement called Muslim Mosque, Incorporated. In April 1964 he went on a pilgrimage to Mecca, and a couple of months later started the Organization of Afro-American Unity.

Plate 6.3 "Shī'ī men pray in Iraq." Baghdad first became the seat of Islamic rule in 750 CE. Here are Muslims in 2006 attending the Friday noon prayer in traditional dress. A group of the faithful awaits an appearance of Shī'ī cleric Muqtada al-Sadr at a mosque in Fallujah, Iraq. This picture was taken during the US-led occupation of Iraq, three years after the fall of Saddam Hussein. Can you explain the difference between the prayer postures of the two men in the back row, as opposed to the posture of those standing in front of them? (See *Plate 6.4*, "Muslim prayer postures.")

Malcolm X's spiritual life was transformed during the **ḥajj** in Mecca. He was profoundly moved by the ritual in which Muslims of all races, social classes, and cultural backgrounds worshiped together. Malcolm X took to heart the Qur'ānic message of human equality. He remained politically active, urging African-Americans to focus on their human rights, and to take their case before the United Nations. After the ḥajj, Malcolm X changed his name to El-Hajj Malik al-Shabazz. This represented a commitment to traditional Islam. Malcolm X died in 1965, apparently at the hands of assassins from the Nation of Islam. The circumstances of his death remain controversial. Today El-Hajj Malik al-Shabazz is respected in the Muslim world, and particularly inspires African-Americans.

Shaykha Fariha al-Jerrahi (b. 1947)

Shaykha Fariha al-Jerrahi was born to Roman Catholic parents in Texas. At the age of 29, she converted to Islam after meeting the Turkish master Shaykh Muzaffar Ozak who brought the Halveti-Jerrahi Ṣūfī lineage to America in 1980. One branch of this Ṣūfī order passed to the American teacher Lex Hixon (Shaykh Nur), and then in 1995 to Shaykha Fariha al-Jerrahi. Although their lineage connects itself back to the first woman Ṣūfī, Rābi'a, she is the first woman leader in the order in three centuries. Shaykha Fariha emphasizes the spiritual practice of dhikr, which involves recitation of God's ninety-nine beautiful names. According to Ibn al-'Arabī, human beings can glimpse the divine essence of created things through such meditation on God's names.

Shaykha Fariha al-Jerrahi teaches her students to take note of their particular experiences from moment to moment to deepen their appreciation of God's creation. The ninety-nine beautiful names hint at as many aspects of reality. Thus, the spiritual practice involves matching aspects of daily experience with the appropriate Name of God. For example, when seekers are called upon to be patient, recitation of the Name as-Sabur, the Patient One, would be appropriate. Meditating on the divine quality of patience is supposed to help Ṣūfīs cultivate this virtue. Then again, if something of subtle beauty attracts their attention, the seekers recite (aloud or in silence) the corresponding Name al-Latif, the Subtle One. Other examples of the correspondence between experience and a beautiful Name include: ash-Shakur, which relates to being grateful; an-Nur, which relates to being enveloped in light; and so forth.

PART 2
ISLAMIC TEXTURE

FOUNDATIONAL TEXTURE

Qur'ān: The Recital

The Muslim sacred scripture is called the Qur'ān or Recital. This is because Prophet Muḥammad recited what he heard from Gabriel, the angel who brought messages from Allāh. The Qur'ān has 144 chapters known as **sūras** that range in length from 286 down to 6 verses (Qur'ān 2 and 114). In general, the most lengthy sūras are placed first, with the shortest at the end of the recital. The inspirations that came to the Prophet in Mecca tend to be short and treat doctrinal subjects, such as divine unity, the Day of Judgment, and social ethics. After the migration to Madīna in 622 the Prophet generally received longer inspirations that dealt with practical political and community matters, along with references to the Jewish and Christian scriptures.

Oral tradition

The Arab Bedouin culture had been an oral culture that measured intelligence by versatility with words and poetic skill. When the Qur'ān was delivered to this desert people who were refined in the use of the spoken word, the faithful recognized it as an astounding oral composition. Prophet Muḥammad obeyed the instruction, "Iqra!" (Recite!) He taught the pronunciation and rhythm of the wahy (revelation). In turn, faithful companions made a concerted effort to preserve the sounds of the recital intact, and to this day Muslims make efforts to keep the sound unaltered.

When angels speak

When the Angel Gabriel first appeared to Muḥammad on Mount Ḥirā, the soon-to-be Prophet felt himself being pressed. After being pressed three times he was overwhelmed and heard words commanding him to recite in the name of the Lord:

> Read in the name of thy Sustainer, who has created –
> created man out of a germ-cell!
> Read – for thy Sustainer is the Most Bountiful One
> who has taught [man] the use of the pen –
> taught man what he did not know!
> (Qur'ān 96:1–5: Asad 1980)

After a silence of six to thirty-six months, Gabriel delivered a second revelation to the Prophet. It began with these words:

> O thou [in thy solitude] enfolded!
> Arise and warn!
> And thy Sustainer's greatness glorify!
> And thine inner self purify!
> And all defilement shun!
> And do not through giving seek thyself to gain,
> but unto thy Sustainer turn in patience.
> (Qur'ān 74:1–7: Asad 1980)

The Angel Gabriel spoke to the Prophet on behalf of Allāh. But listening to an angel is not easy. Sometimes the revelation sounded with the clang of a bell. In those cases the words branded themselves on the Prophet's heart. But when Gabriel spoke with Muḥammad as one person speaks to another the communication was harder to grasp. Around a quarter of the sūras start with letters that have never been deciphered. Fourteen of the twenty-eight Arabic letters appear in this way. The so-called disjointed letters are simply pronounced individually with no known meaning – for example, the twenty-eighth sūra begins: *Ta. Sin. Mim.*

Sometimes the divine messages connect with "circumstances at the time of revelation" (*asbal al-nuzul*). Once, when the Prophet was speaking with a group of influential Meccan chiefs about the truth of revelation, a blind man who was a faithful Muslim approached. When the blind man asked the Prophet to recite some Qur'ānic verses, Muḥammad frowned and turned away. Just then a revelation burst forth.

> He frowned and turned away because the blind man approached him! Yet for all thou didst know [O Muḥammad] he might perhaps have grown in purity, or have been reminded [of the truth], and helped by this reminder.
>
> (Qur'ān 80:1–4: Asad 1980)

This revelation contains a great lesson for humankind. Never disregard a faithful person, no matter how humble. Afterwards on seeing the blind man Muḥammad would say, "Welcome unto him on whose account my Sustainer has rebuked me!" (Asad 1980: 930, n. 1).

The penned recital

The Qur'ān praises writing, and calls itself "a discourse sublime upon an imperishable tablet" (Qur'ān 85:21–22). Thus, traditional Muslims believe that the Qur'ān reflects a divine template known as the Umm al-Kitāb, "Mother of Books." Although Muḥammad recommended that the faithful recite qur'ānic verses by heart, he was interested in the written record. When the Prophet received some verses, he dictated them to one of his scribe companions. Muslims consider it impossible and inappropriate to translate the recital. Therefore, when the Arabic words of the Qur'ān are rendered into other languages, the texts are called "interpretations," not "translations."

Muslim tradition claims that the Prophet's companions wrote verses on bones, bark, leaves, and parchment scraps. In the decade after the Prophet's death in 632 CE several attempts were made to preserve the entire inspiration. Abu Bakr, the first caliph, asked Muḥammad's head scribe to make a copy of the Qur'ān. He continued his work under 'Umar, the second caliph, by gathering information from copies of verses owned by individuals. Uthmān, the third caliph, standardized the Qur'ān. He consulted Muslims who knew the verses by heart, and checked his version against the original copy. Scholars currently argue as to whether any pieces of these early manuscripts survive.

The Qur'ān was the first book of prose in the Arabic language. The very message of the Qur'ān promoted the transformation of oral Bedouin culture by calling itself a "divine writ" bestowed "from on high" (Qur'ān 39:1). The Arabs believed they had received a gift from God, and used the Qur'ān as a cultural template for Arabic literature as well as sacred ritual speech and calligraphy. This Muslim fascination with the beauty of the word inspired an Arabic science of grammar early on. Great artistic attention was paid to writing the verses of inspiration.

Six Articles of Faith

Six Articles of Faith ground Muslim teachings. They are derived from the Qur'ān – the foundation text of Islam.

The unity of Allāh (tawḥīd)

Tawḥīd, belief in the one and only God, is the first article of faith in Islam. Two major offenses in Islam are **shirk** (polytheism) and **kufr** (disbelief) because they disregard this absolute unity of God. Any thought, word, or deed that detracts from remembrance of Allāh is a grave sin falling into one of these two categories. For example, idolizing money is shirk, and ungratefulness is kufr.

Allāh's angels

The sanctity of the Qur'ān depends upon a belief in Allāh's angels, for it was an angel who delivered Allāh's message to Prophet Muḥammad. But Muḥammad was not the only person to hear from an angel. An angel appeared to Ḥājar while she and Ishmael (her son with Abraham) were thirsty and alone in the desert. An angel also appeared to Maryam (mother of Jesus) to tell her she would have a son. Two angels are assigned to each person created on this earth. One sits on each shoulder recording the good and bad deeds done in life, for a report to be given on the Day of Judgment.

Allāh's books

The Qur'ān manifests a divine archetype. But it is not the first book to do so. The Torah, Injīl (Gospel of the Christians) and many books not named specifically in the Qur'ān had already been sent to various peoples of the world based on the Umm al-Kitab. Muslims believe that all these books represented Allāh's authentic message, except that the earlier books were corrupted in the course of human history. On the other hand, Muslims have faith that the Qur'ān remains completely valid, uncorrupted, and stands as the final inspiration of Allāh's word in the present age of humankind.

Allāh's prophets

The existence of Allāh's books depends upon both angels and prophets. There would be no Qur'ān without a prophet. Among the twenty-five prophets named specifically in the Qur'ān, not all have been identified. Adam, Noah, Abraham (Ibrāhīm), Ishmael (Ismā'īl), Isaac, Jacob, Joseph, Job, Jethro, Moses, Aaron, David, Solomon, Elijah, Elisha, and Jonah are known to Jews and Christians – while John the Baptist and Jesus are figures from the Christian New Testament. All 124,000 prophets (named and unnamed) brought Allāh's message and are equal to one another. Yet, Muḥammad is called the Seal of the Prophets. He is the final apostle of Allāh because he received the last inspiration of this age.

The Day of Judgment

This is the last event in the cosmos. On that appointed day everything will be annihilated. Signs indicating the coming of the world's end include the degeneration of society through intensive warfare, and natural disasters. On the Day of Judgment every human being will be restored to life and presented before Allāh, feeling as though just the time it takes to snap one's fingers has passed. The reward of heaven or the punishment of hell is assigned according to how people performed their duties to Allāh.

Divine will

Everything happens according to the will of Allāh, including human destiny. The doctrine of predestination implied by this article of faith must not be confused with the philosophical position of fatalism. Human beings are different from animals because they have the capacity to know right from wrong, and the free will to act upon their knowledge. If predestination meant fatalism, human beings would not be responsible for anything. On the contrary, Allāh sent his Books to help human beings live a life in accordance with the divine will. Muslims have a responsibility to follow the Qur'ān's guidance to the best of their ability.

SUPPORTIVE TEXTURE

Ḥadīth

The Prophet received dictations from the Angel Gabriel over a period of twenty-three years. Not everything that Muḥammad experienced was in the category of inspiration, however. After he became the Apostle of God, people paid attention to everything Muḥammad said and did, even when he was not in the midst of a dictation. Soon after the Prophet's death, the project of recording what he taught and did began. In general, material about Prophet Muḥammad's life is known as Sunnah. This includes legal perspectives, orders, matters of worship, sayings, habits, and so on. As part of the total record of what the Prophet did and said, the ḥadīth are reports that relate Muḥammad's specific words in a narrative context, or accounts of his actions. Two famous collections are by Muslim ibn al-Ḥajjāj al-Nīsābūrī, and Muḥammad bin Ismā'īl al-Bukhārī.

'Ā'isha's reports

Among the most trusted ḥadīth are those recalled by Muḥammad's wife 'Ā'isha. She was one of three wives who memorized the Qur'ān, and the Prophet is said to have compared her in spiritual perfection to Mary, mother of Jesus. About one-third of all ḥadīth were reported by the Prophet's wife 'Ā'isha. She was in an unusual position to contribute to the flowering of Islam, because she was with Muḥammad for ten years, possessed a phenomenal memory, and survived for nearly five more decades after his death. Based on intimate knowledge of Muḥammad's life, 'Ā'isha passed down her recollections to help shape Muslim tradition. For example, she was with the Prophet when he passed away. The following is one of her reports (ḥadīth):

> She said: I saw the Prophet when he was dying. He had a drinking cup containing water, and he would put his hand into the cup, then wipe his

face, then say, "O God, help me to bear the evils of death," or "the pangs of death."

(Robson 1965: 327)

Based on this observation, 'Ā'isha made this comment:

'A'isha said, "I do not envy anyone an easy death after having seen the severity of the death of God's messenger."

(Robson 1965: 326–327)

The meaning of a difficult death becomes clearer through a study of other reports. For example:

Anas reported God's messenger as saying, "When God has a good purpose towards His servant He gives him punishment beforehand in this world, but when He has an evil purpose towards His servant He refrains from dealing with his sin till He takes from him full payment for it on the day of resurrection." Tirmidhi transmitted it.

(Robson 1965: 327)

The Ḥadīth of the Angel Gabriel

There is a magnificent ḥadīth recalled by 'Umar, the man who became the second Rightly Guided One. It reports a hierophanic event in which the Angel Gabriel came in the form of a man while the Prophet was with some of the companions in Madīna. The Arabic custom was to kneel, so Muḥammad was kneeling. In the midst of the conversations a man came and sat knee to knee in front of Muḥammad – placing his hands upon the Prophet's thighs. This event was unusual for several reasons: (1) The man was a stranger, and no one knew from where he had come or when he had arrived. (2) The man was not sullied as if by recent travel. (3) The man acted in a very intimate way with the Prophet, as only a brother or close friend might do. (3) The man addressed the Prophet by name and spoke without introducing himself. Here is the ḥadīth:

'Umar ibn al-Khattab said: One day when we were with God's messenger, a man with very white clothing and very black hair came up to us. No mark of travel was visible on him, and none of us recognized him. Sitting down before the Prophet, leaning his knees against his, and placing his hands on his thighs, he said, "Tell me, Muḥammad, about submission."

He replied, "Submission means that you should bear witness that there is no god but God and that Muḥammad is God's messenger, that you should perform the ritual prayer, pay the alms tax, fast during Ramadan, and make the pilgrimage to the House if you are able to go there."

The man said, "You have spoken the truth." We were surprised at his questioning him and then declaring that he had spoken the truth. . . .

Then the man went away. After I had waited for a long time, the Prophet said to me, "Do you know who the questioner was, 'Umar?" I replied, "God and His messenger know best." He said, "He was Gabriel. He came to teach you your religion."

(*Mishkāt al-masabih*: Murata and Chittick 1994: xxv–xxvi)

The ḥadīth about the Angel Gabriel contains all the Prophet's teachings in a nutshell. From the earliest days of the Islamic tradition, such ḥadīth have been considered indispensable for the development of sharī'a – although not every detail of ḥadīth is directly relevant to Islamic law. (For example, descriptions of the Prophet's physical features would not be used in the creation of sharī'a.) The body of tradition (Sunnah) about the Prophet and the authentic collections (ḥadīth) of his sayings complement each other. Both have been central to the development of Islamic sharī'a. The texts helped Muslims learn to apply Qur'ānic teachings to both personal conduct and government policy.

Sharī'a

Sharī'a is an Arabic word for road, or way to water. In the context of Islam, sharī'a means religious law. Islamic law specifies behavior that is required to please Allāh and travel the straight path in daily life. Personal actions are categorized into five types – listed here with examples:

1 Obligatory. A Muslim is obliged to pray five times each day.

2 Recommended. Extra prayers and extra fasting are meritorious.
3 Neutral. Driving a car is neither meritorious nor non-meritorious.
4 Reprehensible. Smoking is considered non-virtuous.
5 Forbidden. Drinking, gambling, eating pork, and committing adultery are among the worst acts for a Muslim.

In modern times some Muslim countries have official positions on matters of Islamic law. Yet in the modern Muslim world there is no central authority that interprets the sharī'a. Rather there are different schools of law that inform decisions from one country to another. From the early days of Islam until today, a qualified scholar could pronounce a legal decision (*fatwā*) as a point of guidance for others interpreting the law. Any *fatwā* should be issued only on the basis of the Qur'ān or ḥadīth by someone free from motives of self-interest.

Postcolonial sharī'a

The Islamic Iranian constitution adopted after the Cultural Revolution in 1979 acknowledged the contributions of women in helping to overthrow the monarchy. It formally allowed all members of the community – men and women – to participate in political decision-making. Yet in the attempt to promote Islamic social values, Imām Khumayni authorized laws whereby women must cover their hair with a headscarf that is not of a bright color, and wear long, loose-fitting clothes. Various other cultural decisions were mandated in the Islamic Republic of Iran: drinking alcohol was strictly prohibited and penalized by flogging, jail, or fines; the mass media were adjusted to serve Islamic culture while censoring immoral programming; judges were required to be schooled in Islamic principles; and the clergy was to maintain a position of continuous leadership and oversight.

Article 13 of the Iranian constitution recognizes Zoroastrian, Jewish, and Christian Iranians as religious minorities. "Within the limits of the law" these dhimmīs are officially free to practice their rituals and ceremonies, and act in accordance with their own rulings on personal affairs and religious education. And though people of other faiths are not officially recognized in the Islamic Republic of Iran, Article 14 requires that all non-Muslims be treated well as long as they are not counted as threats to Islam:

> In accordance with the sacred verse, "*God does not forbid you to deal kindly and justly with those who have not fought against you because of your religion and who have not expelled you from your homes*" [Qur'ān 60:8], the government of the Islamic Republic of Iran and all Muslims are duty-bound to treat all non-Muslims in conformity with ethical norms and the principles of Islamic justice and equity, and to respect their human rights. This principle applies to all who refrain from engaging in conspiracy or activity against Islam and the Islamic Republic of Iran.
>
> (*Iran-Constitution.* Available online)

Establishment of the Islamic Cultural Revolution cost thousands of lives in the 1980s as political prisoners were executed in the name of religious reform. The Islamic culture established during the Revolution remains in place to this day.

Cultural challenges to sharī'a

Already in the first century after Prophet Muḥammad passed away, Muslims were asking how qur'ānic principles should be applied as Islam expanded out of Arabia. In the postcolonial era a major challenge to Islamic sharī'a again presses upon the Muslim world. Key questions include: What kind of government best supports the practice of Islamic religion? What constitutes a Muslim identity? What is the role of the traditional 'ulamā? What is the value of Western or modern culture? In the midst of an intensive self-critique, Muslims tend to adopt one of these three orientations: customary, revivalist, or liberal (Kurzman 1998: 5–6).

- ***Customary Islam.*** A great number of the world's Muslims fall into this category. Their practice of Islam is mixed with many customs taken from the culture in which they live. Since customs vary from country to country, these Muslims would have different customary practices of daily life depending on whether they live in Turkey, Africa, Indonesia, Pakistan, the United States, and so forth. Such Muslims may feel comfortable with non-Islamic holidays, drumming, belief in spirits, or other local practices when such cultural traditions have been integrated into the lives of their families for generations.

- ***Revivalist Islam.*** Revivalists feel that customary Muslims are too complacent in the face of cultural challenges to the Islamic way of life. They advocate eliminating many elements of local cultures, and stress the use of Arabic in religious contexts. They strictly adhere to details of the sharīʾa according to official interpretations. In the eighteenth century Muḥammad ibn ʿAbd al-Wahhab led a revivalist movement aimed at clearing away un-Islamic practices in Arabia. An Iranian term that translates as "westoxication" captures the revivalist attitude toward poisonous Western cultural elements perceived as infiltrating Muslim life. Yet a range of views exists among revivalist Muslims. Revivalist Islam is also called Islamism, Wahhabism, **Salafism**, or fundamentalism.
- ***Liberal Islam.*** Liberal Islam developed in the eighteenth century from the revivalist movement. Shah Wali-Allāh (1703–1762), an Indian-born Muslim, agreed that certain un-Islamic traditions should be eliminated from Muslim life. But he thought that the original sources of Qur'ān (the divine revelation) and Sunnah (divinely inspired practice of the Prophet Muḥammad) allowed some flexibility in adjusting to different cultures. Today three basic approaches to the application of Islamic law are found among liberal Muslims: liberal, silent, and interpreted (Kurzman 1998: 14–18)
  1. *Liberal sharīʾa* says the Qur'ān prefigures and establishes freedom of scientific and political thought. All legal applications should be justified in relation to orthodox Islamic sources that serve as their prototype.
  2. *Silent sharīʾa* says the Qur'ān provides only general principles, and whatever is not mentioned in orthodox sources is permitted. Its silence indicates that people are supposed to adapt to changing historical circumstances, and to work out political details at their own discretion.
  3. *Interpreted sharīʾa* says the Qur'ān is subject to many types of interpretation, and God sanctions differences of opinion. Although human beings can make mistakes in their application of Qur'ānic principles, differing opinions promote creative thinking which is beneficial to humankind. More recently, women and men following this direction are calling themselves "progressive" Muslims.

CROSS-OVER TEXTURE

Islam and women

The application of Islamic law with respect to women is a subject that merits much discussion, because it often strikes non-Muslims as unjust. In Prophet Muḥammad's community, men were taught to respect women. Moreover, Islam improved the condition of women in Arabia by giving such rights as inheritance, property, and input into the marriage contract. Yet from an outsider perspective Muslim women may appear to be oppressed. Partly this perception reflects social realities – as over the centuries women in Islam have suffered the misfortunes of women in numerous times and places across the globe. But cultural conditioning aggravates the outsider view that Muslim women are oppressed. Contrary to the modern mode of dress, many Muslim women (whether forced or voluntarily) wear clothing in public that covers all but their faces, hands, and feet – sometimes even more. Yet from an insider point of view, the traditional manner of dress (called ḥijāb in Arabic; purdah in South Asia) follows the custom that women in Prophet Muḥammad's family observed. As such it is a noble, archetypal form of dress. Even in times when the traditional mode of dress is not observed among Muslim women, a woman in her later years may adopt it again. Moreover, since the 1970s there has been a revival of interest in veiling among women for the sake of reinforcing their Muslim identity.

Contrary to the tradition of monogamy prevalent in the Western world, a Muslim man can be married to as many as four women (provided they are treated equally), while a Muslim woman is allowed to have only one husband. From an outsider point of view perhaps this legal ruling seems unfair – and by an absolute measure it may well be. Yet polygyny may be viewed from the inside as both practical and compassionate under socio-economic circumstances where women outnumber men after wars, or widows are disadvantaged. As always, a student of the world's religions should make an effort to distinguish between realities, and perceptions that are skewed due to an outsider's cultural ignorance. And while measuring the extent to which Muslim women need support, it would be helpful to measure the extent to which people of all religions are socially oppressed.

Women's sharī'a

The public face of Islam in the West does not present a holistic portrait of the experience of the Muslim religion. Laila Ahmed, a contemporary Egyptian writer, distinguishes between "women's Islam" and "men's Islam" in her autobiography. After years of speaking with people from the Muslim world, Ahmed concluded that the Islam of the folk, family, and women is not the Islam of the official clerics. The Islam practiced by women in the home is based on "a broad ethos and ethical code and as a way of understanding and reflecting on the meaning of one's life and of human life more generally" (Ahmed 1999: 125). Moral values and the cooperative social attitudes of this women's Islam stretch back generations – and were passed down by the women through the family. As a scholar of women's studies, Ahmed notes the discrepancy between women's Islam and official Islam pronounced by many male clerics.

> Aurally what remains when you listen to the Quran over a lifetime are its most recurring themes, ideas, words, and permeating spirit, reappearing now in this passage, now in that: mercy, justice, peace, compassion, humanity, fairness, kindness, truthfulness, charity, mercy, justice. And yet it is exactly these recurring themes and this permeating spirit that are for the most part left out of the medieval texts or smothered and buried under a welter of obscure and abstruse "learning." One would scarcely believe, reading or hearing the laws these texts have yielded, particularly when it comes to women, that the words "justice," "fairness," "compassion," "truth," ever even occur in the Quran.
>
> (Ahmed 1999: 126)

Women's Islam permeated household life. Grandmothers passed down prayers and stories from the Qur'ān to their granddaughters. But they generally did not attend mosques for Friday prayers due to family obligations, and a sense that "'there is no priesthood in Islam' – meaning that there is no intermediary or interpreter, and no need for an intermediary or interpreter between God and each individual Muslim and how that Muslim understands his or her religion" (Ahmed 1999: 125). Survival of this "women's Islam" is of concern to Laila Ahmed.

> We seem to be living through an era of the progressive, seemingly inexorable erasure of the oral and ethical traditions of lived Islam, and simultaneously, of the ever-greater dissemination of written Islam, textual, "men's" Islam (an Islam essentially not of the Book but of the Texts, the medieval texts) as *the* authoritative Islam.
>
> (Ahmed 1999: 128)

Laila Ahmed's observations about the overriding influence of the written over the oral tradition of Islam could be applied to "women's religions" the world over – where folk values are passed along orally by the women in the context of family life.

PART 3
ISLAMIC PERFORMANCE

MECCA: THE HOLY CITY

Although it sits isolated in the midst of desert, one could argue that Mecca is the most powerful place on our planet. One-fifth of our world population holds dear the aspiration to make a spiritual journey there – at least once. Mecca, ringed by mountains, is situated along the trade route in a fertile area known as al-Hejaz. This fertile strip served as an oasis for camel caravans with its dates, apricots, almonds, citrus fruits, apples, bananas, and grains. In pre-Muslim days a period of four months a year was devoted to trade, so the Bedouin kept the custom of holding a concurrent four-month truce. During this peaceful time, traders stopped at the Ka'ba to make offerings to the idols to gain some benefit. Sacrifices of camel and sheep were made, and a secondary industry grew up around this religious activity in Mecca, consisting of inns and religious specialists.

For millennia Mecca has housed the sacred Ka'ba shrine – the focal point of deep religious attention. The Ka'ba is symbolically an axis mundi that represents the center of the world. *Ka'ba* means cube. The cube of six sides (including top and bottom) symbolizes the all-pervasiveness of Allāh who represents all directions, but has no direction. A sacred Black Stone is embedded in the southeast corner within a silver frame. The other three corners each represent an area of the Muslim world: Syria to the northwest, Yemen to the southwest, and Iraq to the northeast. The Ka'ba marks the direction (*qiblah*) toward which all Muslims face when performing daily prayers. The shrine thus becomes the hub of a worldwide wheel toward which all bowed heads point. People of all nations become a united "house of Islam" (*dār al-Islām*) under Allāh's sky and on Allāh's earth.

The Ka'ba was a place of pilgrimage during Muḥammad's lifetime. But prior to the establishment of Islam in Mecca, the cubic structure housed over three hundred idols, one for each day of the year. The Prophet's culminating act was to free the Ka'ba of idols and rededicate the shrine to the one God. Since then, the Ka'ba has remained an empty cubic structure. At that time, Muḥammad declared that in the region of the Ka'ba certain acts should always be prohibited. To this day there is no fighting, no killing, no hunting, and no uprooting of plants in the holy city of Mecca.

Prophet Muḥammad made only one pilgrimage to Mecca, but he enjoined all Muslims to continue the tradition of making the ḥajj. Thus, pilgrimage became one of **Five Pillars of Islam.** The Muslim creed, prayer, fasting, and donations for social welfare are all deeply embedded in the holy visitations to Mecca. Thus, it is easy to distill the essence of Muslim life by exploring the holy city of Mecca – the place from which every Muslim draws inspiration in the practice of living according to Allāh's will.

THE FIVE PILLARS OF ISLAM

Shahāda: proclaiming the creed of Islam

"La ilaha illa Muḥammad rasūl Allāh." (There is no God but God. Muḥammad is Allāh's prophet.) This is the **Shahāda**. The points of faith embedded in this creed of Islam are:

- God is one.
- God alone is worshiped.
- Muḥammad is God's messenger.
- As the Seal of the Prophets there is no prophet after Muḥammad.

The shahāda is recited seventeen times each day in the course of obligatory prayers, and is proclaimed in rites of passage such as birth and death. A person converts to Islam by understanding the shahāda and confessing it to Allāh. The confession of faith is the first Pillar of Islam. In order to establish monotheism, the Prophet cleared the Ka'ba of idols and forbade cultic practices that conflicted with this creed of divine unity. Muḥammad converted the Ka'ba into a Muslim shrine based on the Qur'ānic message that left no room for worship of anything but Allāh.

Prayer

Prayer (Arabic: *ṣalāt*) is the second Pillar of Islam. Muslim prayer occurs in terms of three cycles of time: continuous prayer, prayer five times per day, communal prayer in a mosque once per week.

Continuous prayer

The Angel Gabriel admonished the Prophet to remember Allāh. Thus dhikr became central to Islamic prayer. Ṣūfīs emphasize continuous dhikr in their prayer life. This can be done by placing the divine beautiful names within the heart, or hearing the subtle sound of animals, plants, and minerals, for example.

BOX 6.4 SYMBOLS: SYMBOLS OF THE ḤAJJ

The Muslim pilgrimage to Mecca is symbolically rich. The Ka'ba shrine with its Black Stone and the water of the Zamzam well gain religious meaning in association with hierophanic events.

Black Stone. The Ka'ba is now a cube-like structure, 39.5 feet high, with a Black Stone built into its southeastern edge. In pre-Islamic days, descendants of both Ishmael and Isaac had journeyed to the sacred site. But in Muḥammad's day it was a shrine filled with numerous idols held sacred by the Bedouin polytheists. Muslim tradition holds that Adam, the first man, built the Ka'ba according to a celestial archetype. After the Flood, Abraham and Ishmael rebuilt it with a remarkable Black Stone (perhaps a meteorite) sent from the sky to Ishmael by the Angel Gabriel. Their concept was consistent with the ancient Semitic custom of using stones to establish sacred sites.

Zamzam. On the ḥajj, pilgrims drink sacred water from the Zamzam well. Reverence for sacred water is an old religious sentiment among the Bedouin. And beyond its deep cultural attraction, this object is associated with the activity of an angel. After Sarah gave birth to Isaac, Abraham led Ishmael and his mother into Arabia. Sometime after he left, Ḥājar and Ishmael ran out of water. While Ishmael lay on the ground, Ḥājar stood on a high knoll looking for help, to no avail. In desperation, she found another high place, again to no avail. Ḥājar had gone seven times between the two points – now called Sara and Marwa – when Ishmael cried. Allāh responded by sending an angel to tell Ḥājar that a great nation would stem from her son. Then her eyes caught sight of a beautiful spring where Ishmael had pressed his heel. Later, this sacred spring was made into the Zamzam well.

Revalorization of symbols. Stones and springs have captured the Arab imagination for millennia. Beyond that, the ceremonial standing, hurrying, and stoning prescribed for pilgrims during specific periods of the ḥajj hearken back to ancient rituals. Yet, the meaning of these sacred objects and timeless actions has been revalorized (given new symbolic value) in the Muslim rite of the ḥajj. They are associated with events in the life of Abraham, and with Muḥammad's acts. The fact that the ḥajj becomes tied into sacred history separates the ḥajj from pre-Muslim seasonal cycles. The Islamic calendar goes according to the lunar year, which is about eleven days shorter than the solar year used in Western countries. A new month begins with every new moon; and so the months migrate backward annually by eleven days. Thus ḥajj season (as well as the fasting month of Ramaḍān, and other sacred times) are not tied into any pre-Muslim pagan agricultural time frame. Muslim ritual events move gradually through all the seasons every thirty-three years or so. This means a 100-year-old Muslim will experience the time of ḥajj in the same season as it was in his or her birth year only three times.

> You say you hear certain words, but not from the organ of speech, or through the organ of sound. Speech and Sound belong to this world: what you hear belongs to Malakut [angelic realm].
>
> A pilgrim may hear the "sound" in his body, nay, in the minerals, plants, and animals.
>
> (Shaikh Sharfuddin Maneri: Maneri 1974: 28)

Daily prayers

Muslims pray five times per day facing the Ka'ba in Mecca. A muezzin calls people to perform ṣalāt. The prayers are done according to where the sun is in the sky.

- Morning prayer – after dawn, before sunrise.
- Noon prayer – after the sun passes the zenith, until midway to sunset.

Plate 6.4 "Muslim prayer postures." Postures 1 to 7 constitute the first prayer unit (*rak'ah*). After performing 2 to 4 prayer units, the session concludes with postures 8 to 10. Prerequisites for offering prayers are: (1) One must be a Muslim. (2) One's clothes and body must be free from impurities. (3) One's place of prayer must be clean. (4) One must face the Ka'ba (in Mecca, Arabia). (5) One must form a sincere intention to pray the type of prayer to be done. (6) One must observe the correct time and prescription for the specific prayer. (7) One must have ritually washed the hands, mouth, nostrils, face, arms up to elbows, head, and feet. (8) One must have taken a bath after being in a state of great impurity.

- Afternoon prayer – after the noon prayer, but before sunset.
- Evening prayer – between sunset and disappearance of light.
- Night prayer – after dark, before dawn, preferably before midnight.

Muslim tradition prescribes very precisely the method of prayer, including preparations, postures, attitudes, and words for recitation.

Friday noon prayer

Muslims meet together for communal prayer in a mosque once per week on Friday for the noon qiblah prayer. Each mosque has a niche or mark set into the wall to indicate the exact qiblah or direction of Mecca. Thus worshipers orient themselves to face the Ka'ba when performing ṣalāt. In prayer Muslims make a kind of giant wheel with Mecca at the center.

Social welfare tax

Wealth departs from a society whose members lose cognizance of the divine. On the other hand, wealth properly dedicated to the benefit of others is the basis of a prosperous society. The third Pillar of Islam, the social welfare tax (Arabic: *zakāt*), encourages the proper use and distribution of wealth. (Qur'ān 9:60). Only adults have the obligation to pay zakāt, and only then if a certain minimum level of worth has been achieved (calculated as the current value of 85 grams of pure gold). Specifically, zakāt requires that 2.5 percent or one-fortieth of a Muslim's total economic worth be dedicated for social benefit each year.

Zakāt targets social ills, which were always of primary concern to Prophet Muḥammad. Providing for the Grand Mosque at Mecca or any mosque is considered proper use of wealth because it supports the cause of Allāh. Supporting the cause of Allāh also includes donations that encourage people whose hearts are attracted toward Islam. Such giving can involve freeing captives who turn to the faith, helping new converts to Islam financially, and sustaining Muslim missionaries. A further interpretation of zakāt for the cause of Allāh is paying people engaged in jihād, struggle, and providing them with arms. Beyond that, zakāt should be given to deserving people in these categories: the poor (who beg and who do not beg), travelers, people who suffer from debt, and those who collect and distribute zakāt.

One meaning of the word zakāt is purification. Thus, one's wealth is purified through appropriate giving. Zakāt should be performed without expectation of repayment, reputation, or reward of any sort. Anonymous annual giving became a customary means of discouraging self-interest. The principle behind zakāt is that Allāh created all things, and human beings merely hold them in trust. Properly speaking, human beings do not own their wealth. Wealth that comes to a person is bestowed because wealth has been respected as Allāh's gift in the past. To gain wealth, a Muslim must give to charity. Muḥammad said that even those who have no wealth should encourage others to do good, and restrain themselves from wrongdoing as a form of charity.

Fasting during Ramaḍān

Fasting (Arabic: *ṣawm*) from dawn to dusk in the month of Ramaḍān is the fourth Pillar of Islam; ṣawm begins at the start of the first day of the ninth month of the lunar calendar. Traditionally, dawn was counted as the moment one could distinguish a black thread from a white thread, and dusk was counted as the moment one could no longer distinguish between the two threads. Participants in the Ramaḍān fast should allow nothing to pass their lips into the mouth during these light hours. They refrain from eating, drinking (including water), smoking, and unnecessary talking. After dusk, a big meal is usually consumed quietly with family and friends. Sick people, pregnant or menstruating women, and generally those who are younger than 12 years old do not fast.

Not eating during the light hours of the days of Ramaḍān helps the faithful understand the plight of poor people. Fasting also eliminates distractions, and thus allows Muslims to recite and contemplate the Qur'ān more intently than usual. During Ramaḍān, about one-thirtieth portion of the Qur'ān is read each day so that the entire recital is covered during the fast. At the end of Ramaḍān, the final day of fasting is broken with the holiday called 'Īd al-Fiṭr, the festival of fast-breaking and sharing food. 'Īd al-Fiṭr is one of two major Muslim holidays. The second is 'Id al-Aḍḥa. This comes during the ḥajj – the fifth Pillar of Islam.

Ḥajj: Pilgrimage to Mecca

Mecca from ages past was a business center that welcomed international caravans. It still is. Ideally, at least once in a lifetime every Muslim should make a pilgrimage to Mecca. The official days scheduled for the ḥajj are the eighth through tenth days of the month of Dhū'l-Ḥijja.

The first day

- ***Crossing the mīqāt.*** The preparation ritual begins when Muslim pilgrims come to the boundary (mīqāt) of Mecca, which is specially marked several miles outside the city in four directions toward Madīna, Syria, Iraq, and Yemen. To cross the mīqāt, aspiring pilgrims must declare a sincere intention to make the ḥajj, change into appropriate attire, and begin to restrain their behavior in specific ways. This is called entering the state of iḥrām.
- ***Circumambulating the Ka'ba.*** After crossing into the sacred territory of Mecca, go to the Grand Mosque and walk seven times counter-clockwise around the Ka'ba.
- ***Contemplating Abraham's footprints.*** A hexagonal shrine known as Abraham's Place stands in front of the Ka'ba, near the Black Stone. According to Muslim sacred history, Abraham found the Black Stone through the inspiration of the Angel Gabriel, and stood in prayer at that spot after rebuilding the Ka'ba with Ishmael. Pilgrims can see a rock face with footprints etched by Abraham's feet.
- ***Remembering Ḥājar's search.*** Recollection of the sacred past continues with attention to Ḥājar's story. Pilgrims move quickly between two hills, searching for help as Ḥājar had done when she and Ishmael were suffering from dehydration. The hills, called Safa and Marwah, are located 200 yards and 150 yards from the Ka'ba. Pilgrims may go to the Zamzam well and drink some of holy water, which first sprang up beneath the child Ishmael's heel in answer to Ḥājar's prayers.

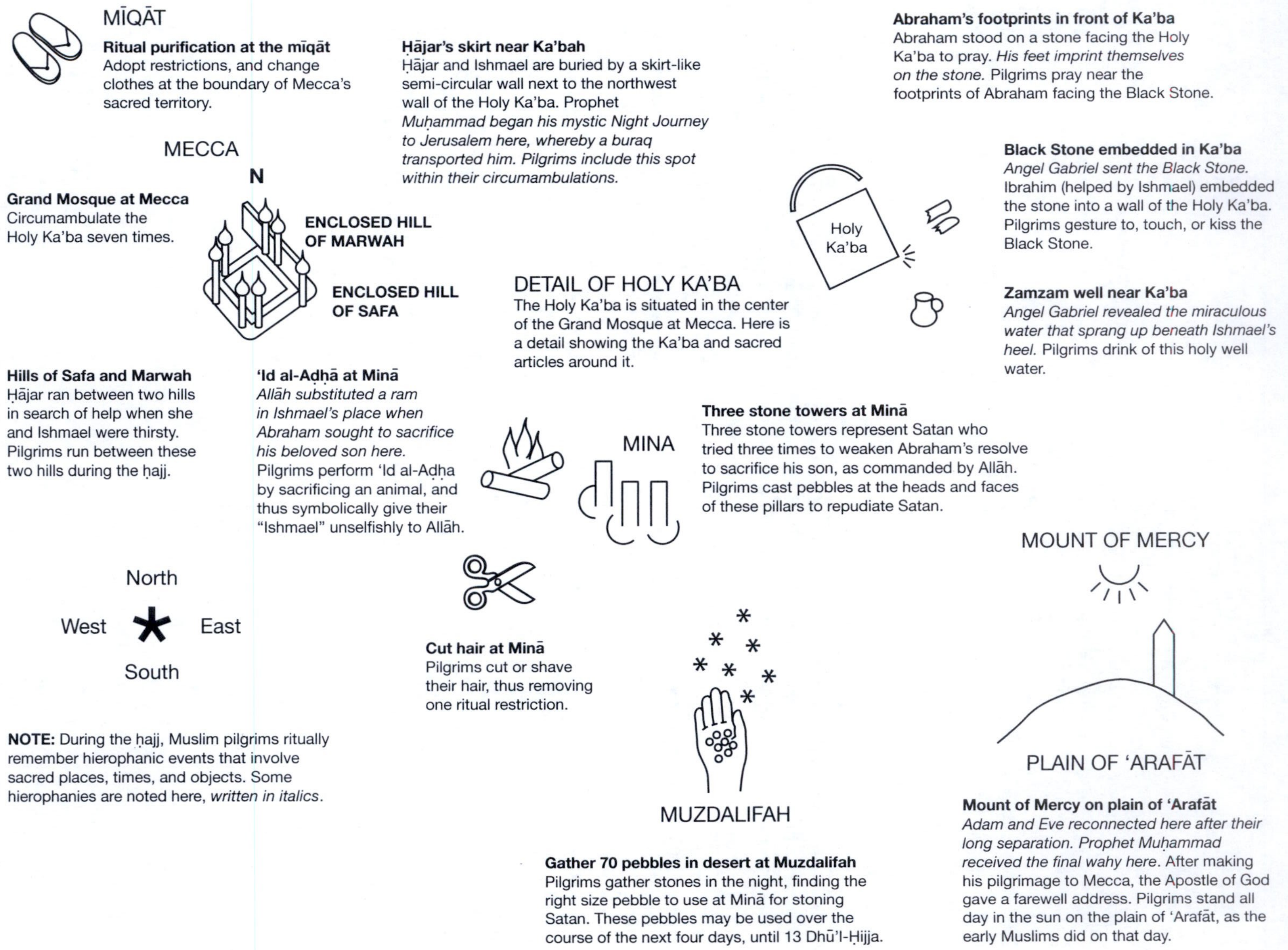
MĪQĀT
Ritual purification at the mīqāt
Adopt restrictions, and change clothes at the boundary of Mecca's sacred territory.
MECCA
N
Grand Mosque at Mecca
Circumambulate the Holy Ka'ba seven times.
ENCLOSED HILL OF MARWAH
ENCLOSED HILL OF SAFA
Hills of Safa and Marwah
Ḥājar ran between two hills in search of help when she and Ishmael were thirsty. Pilgrims run between these two hills during the ḥajj.
Ḥājar's skirt near Ka'bah
Ḥājar and Ishmael are buried by a skirt-like semi-circular wall next to the northwest wall of the Holy Ka'ba. Prophet *Muḥammad began his mystic Night Journey to Jerusalem here, whereby a buraq transported him. Pilgrims include this spot within their circumambulations.*
'Id al-Aḍḥā at Minā
Allāh substituted a ram in Ishmael's place when Abraham sought to sacrifice his beloved son here. Pilgrims perform 'Id al-Aḍḥa by sacrificing an animal, and thus symbolically give their "Ishmael" unselfishly to Allāh.
DETAIL OF HOLY KA'BA
The Holy Ka'ba is situated in the center of the Grand Mosque at Mecca. Here is a detail showing the Ka'ba and sacred articles around it.
Holy Ka'ba
Abraham's footprints in front of Ka'ba
Abraham stood on a stone facing the Holy Ka'ba to pray. *His feet imprint themselves on the stone.* Pilgrims pray near the footprints of Abraham facing the Black Stone.
Black Stone embedded in Ka'ba
Angel Gabriel sent the Black Stone. Ibrahim (helped by Ishmael) embedded the stone into a wall of the Holy Ka'ba. Pilgrims gesture to, touch, or kiss the Black Stone.
Zamzam well near Ka'ba
Angel Gabriel revealed the miraculous water that sprang up beneath Ishmael's heel. Pilgrims drink of this holy well water.
MINA
Three stone towers at Minā
Three stone towers represent Satan who tried three times to weaken Abraham's resolve to sacrifice his son, as commanded by Allāh. Pilgrims cast pebbles at the heads and faces of these pillars to repudiate Satan.
North
West
East
South
Cut hair at Minā
Pilgrims cut or shave their hair, thus removing one ritual restriction.
MOUNT OF MERCY
PLAIN OF 'ARAFĀT
MUZDALIFAH
NOTE: During the ḥajj, Muslim pilgrims ritually remember hierophanic events that involve sacred places, times, and objects. Some hierophanies are noted here, *written in italics*.
Gather 70 pebbles in desert at Muzdalifah
Pilgrims gather stones in the night, finding the right size pebble to use at Minā for stoning Satan. These pebbles may be used over the course of the next four days, until 13 Dhū'l-Ḥijja.
Mount of Mercy on plain of 'Arafāt
Adam and Eve reconnected here after their long separation. Prophet Muḥammad received the final wahy here. After making his pilgrimage to Mecca, the Apostle of God gave a farewell address. Pilgrims stand all day in the sun on the plain of 'Arafāt, as the early Muslims did on that day.

Figure 6.1 Hierophany and the Ḥajj

(Sometimes this remembrance of Ḥājar is done on the last day of the ḥajj.)

- ***Praying at the Minā encampment.*** Leaving the Grand Mosque, pilgrims begin the greater ḥajj by setting off for 'Arafāt (via Minā) as Muḥammad had done after his pilgrimage to the Ka'ba in 632 CE. Minā is a desert town some three miles east of Mecca. There the faithful perform ṣalāt, moving through an entire day's prayer cycle: noon, afternoon, evening, night, and morning.

The second day

- ***Standing at the Mount of Mercy.*** After the morning prayer at Minā, pilgrims proceed to the Mount of Mercy on the plain of 'Arafāt – a desert location some thirteen miles through the mountain passes east of Mecca. This is where Prophet Muḥammad delivered his final speech *en route* to Madīna, upon returning with crowds of the faithful from his Meccan pilgrimage. This moving speech culminated in the final Qur'ānic inspiration that was destined to come through the Prophet. Muḥammad passed away unexpectedly eleven and a half weeks later. At that time, in 632 CE, thousands of Muslims stood in the heat listening to their Arabian Prophet of Islam. Since then pilgrims have stood under the blazing sun praying to Allāh in memory of that holy day. Beginning with the noon prayer, the repentant pilgrims ask Allāh's forgiveness for their sins, and spend as much time as possible reading the Qur'ān. Once the afternoon prayer is completed, pilgrims may rest in tents until the evening prayer. Then, making haste, they all pour out of 'Arafāt before dark. No one stays on the plain of 'Arafāt for the night.
- ***Gathering stones in the desert night.*** Pilgrims make haste to Muzdalifah, midway between 'Arafāt and Minā, in what amounts to a stampede. According to an ancient custom, they must hurry. Thousands of the faithful then pass the night in the middle of the desert. By the light of the moon and stars, they recite prayers and gather seventy (or at least forty-nine) pebbles from the nearby hills in the moon and starlight. Each smooth, pistachio-sized pebble will be used as a kind of projectile in the stoning of Satan in the day or days ahead.

The third day

- ***Repudiating Satan.*** Before sunrise on the third day of the ḥajj, pilgrims return to Minā. There they approach three ancient stone pillars that represent idols, and throw the pebbles gathered the previous night to strike the head and face of the pillars. Sacred tradition says that three times at this very place, Satan whispered to Abraham not to sacrifice his son Ishmael, and three times Abraham repudiated Satan determined to follow God's will. Abraham stoned Satan; and in the patriarch's memory the pilgrims stone Satan, determined to resist for themselves the ongoing threat of disobedience to God's will.
- ***Remembering Abraham's sacrifice.*** After the symbolic stoning of Satan, the pilgrims make a symbolic sacrifice known as 'Id al-Aḍḥa. Ishmael represents to each Muslim something difficult to offer in worship of God. If affordable, an animal is sacrificed by the pilgrim or on behalf of the pilgrim. This could be a goat, sheep, bull, or camel in memory of the hierophanic event in which Allāh miraculously provided a ram in place of Ishmael. They also form an inner resolve to sacrifice attachment to money, social status, or anything that makes a person an idolater.

  After 'Id al-Aḍḥa, the restrictions of iḥrām (not cutting hair, wearing the iḥrām garments, and so forth) are lifted except for abstaining from conjugal relations. Thus, men shave their heads, or crop the hair equally all around, while women cut off at least one lock of hair. The ḥajj is basically completed with this act on the tenth day of Dhū'l-Ḥijja, the final month of the Muslim calendar.
- ***Circumambulating the Ka'ba.*** Pilgrims again circumambulate the Ka'ba, and touch or gesture toward the Black Stone. If they have not already done so, the pilgrims "run" between Safa and Marwah, and drink from the Zamzam well. While the faithful were away from Mecca the inside of the Ka'ba was cleaned in a symbolic gesture of rejecting idols, and a new black silk, gold-embroidered covering was draped on the outside

of the shrine. After the final circuit around the Ka'ba, the pilgrims leave the Grand Mosque and iḥrām restrictions are completely lifted. The ḥajj is technically complete. They are now *Ḥajjis.*

Pilgrims are encouraged to return to Minā for two or three more days (at the most), and then return to Mecca immediately prior to leaving for home. Often the faithful make a visit to Madīna to see Prophet Muḥammad's grave at the mosque he first constructed on divine inspiration after the hijra in 622 CE.

Allāh's will

The social consciousness of Islam is reflected in its five ritual pillars. Every Muslim is equal in Allāh's view, and no reward should be expected from anyone other than Allāh. This basic premise is established in the first pillar, the shahāda: There is no God but Allāh (The God), and Muḥammad is his Prophet. Ṣalāt is the second pillar, which deepens a Muslim's conviction about the unity of Allāh in remembrance of Allāh. Consideration of the needy is given through annual tithing according to the guidelines of zakāt, the third pillar; ṣawm brings humility in the face of the divine and humankind with special attention to the hungry as Muslims fast during the month of Ramaḍān as the fourth pillar. Finally ḥajj, the fifth pillar, allows practice of the other four pillars to deepen. All markers of discriminative social identity (aside from gender) are stripped from a Muslim who makes the pilgrimage to Mecca. In Mecca, Muslims present their souls to Allāh while maintaining social equality – as it will be on the Day of Judgment.

KEY POINTS

- Islam is a monotheistic tradition, focused on the worship of Allāh who delivered his message to all the Peoples of the Book, the last of whom were given the Arabic Qur'ān.
- The Muslim community was established in 622 CE (1 AH) with the hijra or migration of Muḥammad and his companions from Mecca to Yathrib (Madīna).
- Islam spread through Arabia in Muḥammad's lifetime, and within a century after his passing away, Muslim rule was established to the north, east, and west from Spain to Persia under the four Rightly Guided Ones and the Umayyads.
- The sharī'a or Islamic law is founded on the Qur'ān and ḥadīth. In addition, Sunnī Muslims emphasize consensus of the community and reasoning by analogy, while Shī'ī Muslims rely upon divine guidance revealed through their imāms, and the reasoning of learned scholars.
- The concept of the imaginal realm became a standard part of Ṣūfī cosmology after the writings of Suhrawardī, and Ibn al-'Arabī in the twelfth century – and was further elaborated by Mullā Ṣadrā four centuries later.
- There are variations in the practice of Islam across the Muslim world based in an oral heritage that has more to do with a way of living than with the teachings of religious scholars. Contemporary Muslims disagree about the extent to which non-Islamic cultural influences should impact upon their daily lives.
- Mecca, Madīna, and Jerusalem are sacred cities for Muslims – each with an important shrine: (1) Mecca has the Ka'ba where pilgrims perform the ḥajj; (2) Madīna has the first mosque and tomb of the Prophet; and (3) Jerusalem has the stone within the Dome of the Rock visited by the Prophet on his mystic Night Journey.
- The Six Articles of Faith and Five Pillars of Islam comprise the central Muslim beliefs and practices, which are sanctioned in the Qur'ān.

STUDY QUESTIONS

1. Name some prophets in the Muslim tradition, and state why they are so important to Islam. What is special about Prophet Muḥammad?
2. What happened in the 100 years after Prophet Muḥammad passed away? How did the Islamic tradition change? In what ways did it stay the same?
3. Who are Ṣūfīs, and what are some of their major concerns as opposed to Muslim philosophers or theologians?
4. What have been some Muslim concerns after European colonialism? What have been some

Muslim responses to religious life in the post-colonial period?

5 What are the Qur'ān and ḥadīth? Why are they important to Muslims?
6 What are the Six Articles of Faith in Islam, and how do they work to reinforce each other?
7 Describe the Muslim pilgrimage to Mecca (the ḥajj). Pay attention to some of the symbolism involved in this Pillar of Islam.

GLOSSARY

Allāh (Arabic from *al-ilah*, the deity) Primary name for God in Islam.

Arab Nomadic Bedouin tribes of Arabia and their descendants; people whose language is a dialect based on Arabic; people who use Arabic as a ritual language, i.e., Muslims.

barzakh (Arabic) A (hidden) barrier between two things. Describes the imaginal realm in Islamic cosmology where angels abide.

companions Early Muslims who saw or heard Muḥammad speak at least once.

dhimmī (Arabic) Protected people. People of the Book (typically Jews, Christians, and Zoroastrians) who may practice their faith in a Muslim country under certain restrictions.

Five Pillars of Islam Five key rituals performed by Muslims: proclaiming the creed, prayer, social welfare tax, fasting, and pilgrimage.

ḥadīth (Arabic = narrative) Traditional report that relates Prophet Muḥammad's words, deeds, or silent approval under various circumstances. Narrative presentation of Sunnah.

ḥajj (Arabic) Muslim pilgrimage to Mecca, Minā, 'Arafāt, and Muzdalifah. One of the Five Pillars of Islam.

hijra (Arabic) Migration. Muḥammad's migration from Mecca to Yathrib (Madīna) on Friday, 16 July 622 CE. This marks the formation of the Muslim community, and the start of the Islamic calendar as year 1 AH (*Anno Hegirae*).

iḥrām (Arabic = making forbidden or sacred) A state of ritual purity adopted by Muslim pilgrims before entering Mecca and circling the Ka'ba.

imām (Arabic) Leader. Honorific title for a Muslim who leads the daily prayers. Refers to divinely sanctioned spiritual-political leaders in Shī'ī Islam.

jihād (Arabic *jahada* = "he made an effort") Struggle. The inner (personal) and outer (political) effort to overcome threats to the practice of Islam. Both are of equal importance, but the inner jihād is more difficult.

Ka'ba (Arabic = cube) Cube-shaped shrine in Mecca, Arabia that is the focal point of Muslim pilgrimage and daily prayer.

kufr (Arabic) Disbelief; denial of God. A major offense in Islam because it shows ungratefulness to Allāh.

Muslim One who "surrenders" (to Allāh's will). A person of the Islamic faith. Words "Muslim" and "Islam" stem from the Arabic root *salam*, meaning peace, surrender.

pbuh Letters standing for "peace be upon him" that Muslims write after the name of a prophet. In Arabic, "alaihi as-salam" abbreviated "as" instead of pbuh.

Qur'ān (Arabic) Recital. The Muslim holy scripture.

Salafism (Salafiyyahs in Arabic = predecessors) General term for the Islamic fundamentalist movement that includes Muslims who strive to return to the disciplined ways of their predecessors in the early days of Islam.

shahāda (Arabic) Muslim creed: "There is no God but God; Muḥammad is his Prophet." One of the Five Pillars of Islam.

sharī'a (Arabic) Body of sacred law in Islam.

Shī'a (Arabic) Branch of Islam concentrated in Iran, Iraq, Lebanon, Bahrain, parts of Afghanistan, and Pakistan (adjective: Shī'ī) (about one-fifth of Muslims are Shī'a).

shirk (Arabic) Polytheism, or associating someone or something with God's power. A major offense in Islam because it disregards Allāh's unity.

Ṣūfī Muslim mystic.

Sunnah (Arabic) Tradition, or path. The body of Muslim tradition about Prophet Muḥammad including legal perspectives, orders, matters of worship, sayings, habits, and so on.

Sunnī (Arabic) Branch of Islam whose members refer to themselves as people of the tradition (Sunnah) and community (about four-fifths of Muslims are Sunnī).

sūra (Arabic) Chapter of the Qur'ān. There are 114 altogether.

tawḥīd (Arabic) Belief in the unity of God.

'ulamā (Arabic, plural of *'alīm* = one with knowledge) Scholars involved in research on any of the Islamic sciences based in the Qur'ān, Sunnah, and sharī'a, such as jurisprudence or theology.

KEY READING

Chittick W. C. (1989) *The Sufi Path of Knowledge: Ibn al-'Arabi's Metaphysics of Imagination*, New York: State University of New York Press.

Denny, F. M. (2006) *An Introduction to Islam*, 3rd edn, Upper Saddle River, NJ: Prentice Hall.

Helminski, C. A. (2003) *Women of Sufism: A Hidden Treasure – Writings and Stories of Mystic Poets, Scholars, and Saints*, Boston/London: Shambhala.

Hitti, P. K. (1970) *Islam: A Way of Life*, South Bend, IN: Regnery/Gateway.

Hodgson, M. G. S. (1974) *The Venture of Islam*, 3 vols, Chicago, IL: University of Chicago Press.

Lings, M. (1983) *Muḥammad: His Life Based on the Earliest Sources*, London: George Allen & Unwin, and Islamic Text Society.

Murata, S. and Chittick, W. C. (1994) *The Vision of Islam*, New York: Paragon House.

Qur'ān (1980) *The Message of the Qur'ān*, trans. M. Asad, Gibraltar: Dar al-Andalus. Quotes from the Qur'ān used in this book are from Asad's book. Other renderings of the Qur'ān in English include: *The Koran Interpreted* (1955), trans. A. J. Arberry, New York: Macmillan; *The Meaning of the Glorious Koran*, trans. and explained by M. M. Pickthall, New York: Mentor Books; and *The Meaning of the Glorious Qur'ān*, 2 vols (1934), text, translation, and commentary by A. Y. Ali, Beirut, Lebanon: Dar al-Kitab al-Masri.

Rahman, F. (1979) *Islam*, Chicago, IL: University of Chicago Press.

—— (1980) *Major Themes of the Qur'ān*, Minneapolis, MN: Bibliotheca Islamica.

Schimmel, A. (1975) *Mystical Dimensions of Islam*, Chapel Hill: University of North Carolina Press.

Trimingham, J. S. (1971) *The Sufi Orders in Islam*, London: Oxford University Press.

CHAPTER 7

Bahá'í tradition

TIMELINE

	CE	
	874	Disappearance of Twelfth Imám* of the Shí'í Muslims
Táhirih	1817–1852	
Bahá'u'lláh	1817–1892	
The Báb	1819–1850	
	22 May 1844	The Báb's declaration that he was the Gate
Birth of 'Abdu'l-Bahá	23 May 1844	The Báb's declaration commemorated
'Abdu'l-Bahá	1844–1921	
	21 April 1863	Bahá'u'lláh's first public declaration that he was "Him Whom God shall make manifest."
Shoghi Effendi	1897–1957	
Louis G. Gregory	1874–1951	
Ruhiyyih Khánum	1910–2000	
	1912	'Abdu'l-Bahá in America
	June 1993	Bahá'ís introduce an equal rights amendment at UN Conference on Human Rights – Vienna, Austria

* This chapter uses the Bahá'í transliteration style, even with Islámic terms.

A new religious tradition known as the Bahá'í Faith surfaced in Iran about 150 years ago. This was after Persian culture had become deeply Islámicized through over 1,000 years of Muslim rule. The Bahá'í community emerged in response to two figures who came to be known as the *Báb* (**Gate**), and Bahá'u'lláh (**Glory of God**). During the Báb's ministry (1844–1850) he provided new laws for what became a distinctive religious community known as the Bábís. He was viewed as a gate that opened the way for "Him Whom God shall make manifest." Among the Bábís was a person who declared himself to be the **Manifestation** predicted by the Báb. He was titled Bahá'u'lláh, and those who believed in his prophetic work became known as Bahá'ís. Leadership of the Bahá'í community passed to 'Abdu'l-Bahá (Bahá'u'lláh's son), and then to Shoghi Effendi ('Abdu'l-Bahá's grandson).

The style of succession was rather unique in the history of religions, as it was passed from person to person in writing, through wills rather than orally or by traditional custom.

The early Bahá'í community was steeped in Persian influences, especially Shí'í Islám. Gradually it became more global in outlook. Bahá'ís believe that their message is essentially the same as that presented by all God's prophets, but they feel its focus is uniquely suited to modern times. Bahá'ís promote lay participation (with no clergy), interracial marriages, and gender equality. There are some five million Bahá'ís spread throughout the world today. They study scriptures of the world religions for inspiration, while following the teachings of the Báb, Bahá'u'lláh, and 'Abdu'l-Bahá for specific guidance.

PART 1 BAHÁ'Í PLAYERS

THE ULTIMATE PRINCIPLE

God

Bahá'ís speak about a unique, omnipotent, and omniscient God who created the world. God is too great and subtle to be comprehended fully by any creature. Yet human beings can progress through stages of spiritual development and open their hearts to the transcendent beauty of this Beloved One. The creation has many signs that human beings can contemplate to arrive at a primal knowledge of God's attributes. These attributes include all-powerful, all-loving, and infinitely just. Human beings come to know God through contemplating hints of the divine attributes in themselves and various aspects of the world. God sends messengers who teach people by words and by example how human beings can manifest divine attributes such as trustworthiness, mercy, and so forth.

IMAGINAL PLAYERS

Manifestations

According to Bahá'í teachings, there are two worlds: a spiritual world and a physical world. In this context, only three levels of being are relevant to Bahá'í spirituality: God, Manifestations, and human beings. (Bahá'ís regard angels, demons, heaven, and hell as symbolizing the stages of human development: pure conduct is angelic, and coming close to God is heavenly.) God sends Manifestations from the spiritual world into the physical world. They have a pre-existence in the spiritual world, unlike ordinary human beings who come into existence at the moment of conception. Manifestations are an intermediate type of being between God and human beings. They receive divine revelations, and also know the realities of human life. All Manifestations have the same nature, and thus all are equal to each other from a metaphysical point of view. They exhibit all the attributes of God, so that God can be approached through them – but they should hot be identified with the essence of divinity. Bahá'u'lláh, founder of the Bahá'í Faith, named Zarathushtra, Abraham, Moses, Jesus, Muḥammad, the Báb, and himself as Manifestations. After him, Buddha and Kṛṣṇa were added to the list. Bahá'ís feel that the names of many Manifestations of God have been lost to history.

EXCEPTIONAL PLAYERS

The Báb (Siyyid 'Alí Muḥammad)

Siyyid 'Alí Muḥammad (1819–1850) was born in Shiraz, Iran and was a distant relative in Prophet Muḥammad's family line. He was orphaned, and raised by his mother's brother. He belonged to a Shí'í Muslim spiritual community that anticipated the imminent coming of the Mahdí (Messiah), whom they called the Qá'im ("One who shall arise"). The Mahdí was an historical figure in Prophet Muḥammad's lineage, counted as the twelfth leader of Shí'í Muslims. This Twelfth Imám disappeared as a child when his father died in 874 CE, but had mystically maintained contact with Muslims through various people known as "gates." At one point, people lost their spiritual connection with the Twelfth Imám. But from time to time someone claimed to be a new Báb that gave access to the Mahdí. On 22 May 1844 Siyyid 'Alí Muḥammad, at the age of 25, declared that he was the Qá'im. Later on he wrote that as a Báb he was making way for "Him Whom God shall make manifest."

On 9 July 1850 the Báb was executed by firing squad for heresy against Islam. Bahá'ís commemorate his martyrdom every year.

BOX 7.1 SYMBOLS: BAHÁ'Í SYMBOLISM

The ring stone symbol. The ring stone symbol used on Bahá'í rings is a form of the **Greatest Name** designed by 'Abdu'l-Bahá. The Greatest Name is the Name of God: Bahá (Glory, Splendor, Light). Two invocations are used as variants of this Greatest Name: (1) Yá Bahá'u'lláh (O Glory of Glories), and (2) Yá Bahá'u'l-Abhá (O Glory of the All-Glorious). Wearing the ring stone symbol is not obligatory, but when worn it is placed on the right hand. The three horizontal strokes represent (from the top down) the world of God, the world of the Manifestation, and the world of humanity (i.e., the Creation). The vertical stroke is again the world of the Manifestation, which joins the creator God and Creation. The shape of the stars represents the human body with its head, two arms, and legs. The two particular stars stand for the two Manifestations for this time: the Báb and Bahá'u'lláh. The letters of the symbol are "b" and "h" – "b" for Bahá, and "h" for the name "Báb."

The number 9. Each letter of the alphabet in the Hebrew and Arabic languages is associated with a number. Letters instead of numeric figures could be used when writing in these Semitic languages, and every word can represent a numerical value as well as a literal meaning. The original Bahá'í scriptures make use of the Arabic alphabet, and symbolism of the number nine was incorporated into Bahá'í art, ritual, and architecture.

The number nine is used in the Bahá'í Faith as a symbol of completeness because it is the highest single digit number: (1) The numerical value of the word "Bahá" is nine; (2) a nine-pointed star has been used for about a century as a symbol of the Bahá'í Faith; (3) all Bahá'í houses of worship have nine sides; (4) the Bahá'ís have nine holy days; and (5) Bahá'u'lláh (then called Bahá) had the hierophanic experience hinting at his future mission in the Black Pit prison nine years after the Báb told people to watch for the advent of "Him Whom God shall make manifest."

Plate 7.1 "The Bahá'í ring stone symbol."

Bahá'u'lláh (Mirzá Husayn 'Alí Nurí) (1817–1892)

Mirzá Husayn 'Alí Nurí was born to a noble family in Tehran, Iran on 12 November 1817. He encountered the Bábís shortly after Siyyid 'Alí Muḥammad declared himself to be the gate to "Him Whom God shall make manifest." In retaliation for the Báb's execution, three Bábís tried to assassinate the Qájár ruler. In response, Mirzá Husayn 'Alí Nurí (then called Bahá, and later Bahá'u'lláh) was imprisoned for four months due to his prominent position among the Bábís. In the *Epistle to the Son of the Wolf* Bahá'u'lláh wrote of the hierophanic experience that occurred while he lay in the dungeon.

> During the days I lay in the prison of Tihran (Tehran), though the galling weight of the chains and the stench-filled air allowed Me but little sleep, still in those infrequent moments of slumber I felt as if something flowed from the crown of My head over My breast, even as a mighty torrent that precipitateth itself upon the earth from the summit of a lofty mountain. Every limb of My body would, as a result, be set afire. At such moments My tongue recited what no man could bear to hear.
>
> (Bahá'u'lláh 1979: 22)

This event in the Black Pit marks the beginning of Bahá receiving revelations from God. Yet it would be ten years until Bahá openly declared that vocation.

After imprisonment in Iran, both he and his half-brother were sent into exile. After that the Bábís split into two groups – one backing each brother. The itinerary of Bahá'u'lláh's exile occurred in three stages: (1) Exile in Iraq (1853–1863); (2) Exile in Turkey (1863–1868); (3) Exile in Palestine (1868–1877).

After Bahá'u'lláh was released from the confines of the prison city of 'Akká (Acre), he continued to live in Palestine under house arrest until his death fifteen years later. He arranged to purchase an abandoned mansion, into which some members of his family moved. Other family members remained in 'Akká in rented quarters. (About a half-century later his great-grandson, Shoghi Effendi, designed the beautiful gardens that can be seen there today.) Bahá'u'lláh received a steady stream of visitors – Bahá'ís and others – until he passed away (ascended) on 29 May 1892 while in Bahjí (in present-day Israel).

Bahá'u'lláh appointed several close disciples as **Hands of the Cause of God**. These were dedicated Bahá'ís who were chosen to help spread Bahá'u'lláh's message. Bahá'u'lláh sent the Hands to take the Bahá'í teachings to various places throughout the Ottoman Empire (Iraq, Turkey, Lebanon, Syria, and Palestine) and beyond to Central Asia, Egypt, Sudan, India, Burma, and Indonesia. This work would be carried on for the next three decades by his eldest son 'Abbás Effendi (who later called himself 'Abdu'l-Bahá). It took about a decade before the Bahá'í community stood fully behind 'Abdu'l-Bahá because not everyone in the family supported the Bahá'í **Covenant** that after Bahá'u'lláh passed away, the divine guidance continued working through 'Abdu'l-Bahá. Ultimately Bahá'u'lláh's

Plate 7.2 "Photograph of 'Abdu'l-Bahá." Representations of Bahá'u'lláh, the Bahá'í founder ("Him Whom God shall make manifest") are not publicly distributed, and are only shown to pilgrims in Haifa, Israel. Here is a photograph of Bahá'u'lláh's son and successor.

BOX 7.2 A SPIRITUAL PATH: THE FOUR VALLEYS

While exiled in Baghdad, Bahá'u'lláh wrote a letter to a Muslim shaykh who was living in the Kurdish city of Karkuk. He described the process of coming to see the Unseen according to four similar Arabic words that describe aspects of God: (1) Intended One (*maqṣúd*); (2) Praiseworthy One (*maḥmúd*), (3) Attracting One (*majdhúb*), and (4) Beloved One (*maḥbúb*).

Intended One. The seeker in the first valley begins with a motivation to search for the Intended One (*maqṣúd*). The spiritual journey is still "in the realm of conflict, yet it endeth in attainment to the throne of splendor" (Bahá'u'lláh 1975: 50). The key to the early phase of seeking the divine is to find God's signs everywhere – all around *and* inside oneself. Bahá'u'lláh quotes the Qur'án to emphasize that "there is no God save Him."

> Hereafter We will show them Our signs in the regions *of the earth,* and in themselves, until it become manifest unto them that it is the truth (41:53).
>
> (Bahá'u'lláh 1975: 51)

Praiseworthy One. In the second valley, knowledge of the truth of God's signs is attained. Impressed by the presence of God's signs in so many places, the seeker finds a place to dwell with the Praiseworthy One (*maḥmúd*). Bahá'u'lláh quotes a qur'ánic verse from a súra called "The Cave," suggesting that a great truth lies hidden in it.

> And thou mightest have seen the sun when it arose, pass on the right of their cave, and when it set, leave them on the left, while they were in its spacious chamber. This is one of the signs of God (18: 6).
>
> (Bahá'u'lláh 1975: 53)

This is the stage of primal reason. No ordinary reasoning can bring comprehension of universal truth. Here the seeker undergoes many trials, as if being lifted up to heaven and cast down to the depths. Yet the trials end with the bestowal of knowledge. Speaking of this knowledge Bahá'u'lláh quotes Prophet Muḥammad: "Knowledge is a light which God casteth into the heart of whomsoever He willeth" (Bahá'u'lláh 1975: 54).

Attracting One. In the third valley, the seeker becomes a lover and dwells "within the precincts of the Attracting One (*majdhúb*)." This stage of the spiritual path cannot be described in ordinary words. It involves a tremendous force of attraction in which the Beloved's inner reality is experienced. Here the seeker "cannot tell one limb from another, one part from another. To them . . . going away is returning" (Bahá'u'lláh 1975: 55). Bahá'u'lláh quotes the Persian poet Rumi to explain further how the signs of God are present in this stage of the search for the Unseen: "The lover's teacher is the Loved One's beauty, His face their lesson and their only book."

Beloved One. In the fourth valley, the seeker's heart opens up and is struck by the beauty of the Beloved One (*maḥbúb*). During this phase of the spiritual journey the mystic knower goes through the blackest night – and the secret of divine guidance is revealed. Love is the light in this blackest night. But love only dwells in a heart that is fearful of nothing but God. Worldly fear departs. The secret is so profound that if the seeker "were to reveal but its faintest trace they would nail him to the cross" (Bahá'u'lláh 1975: 58).

following grew into a worldwide movement. The group that backed his half-brother dwindled, although some of these Bábí-Azalís live in Iran today.

'Abdu'l-Bahá ('Abbás Effendi) (1844–1921)

'Abbás Effendi was born in Tehran on 23 May 1844 – just hours after Siyyid Alí Muḥammad in Shiraz declared that he was the Báb. As a child, 'Abbás stayed close to Bahá'u'lláh. It is said that he recognized his father's spiritual prominence even before it was openly discussed. Shoghi Effendi later wrote of the child:

> Against Him, in his early childhood, whilst His Father lay a prisoner in that dungeon, had been directed the malice of the mob of street urchins who pelted Him with stones, vilified Him and overwhelmed Him with ridicule. . . . He felt himself to have grown old though still a child of tender years.
>
> (Adamson and Hainsworth 1998: 80)

'Abbás Effendi married Munírih Khánum, who is said to have been conceived through the Báb's blessing. After Bahá'u'lláh passed away on 29 May 1892, 'Abbás chose the name 'Abdu'l-Bahá (Servant of Bahá). In his will, Bahá'u'lláh named 'Abbás as his successor. This carried with it the authority to interpret his teachings. Yet the level of authority that 'Abdu'l-Bahá seemed to be taking did not please his half-brother, who attempted to have him killed on several occasions. Other family members became embroiled, and did not uphold the terms of Bahá'u'lláh's will, which gave authority to 'Abdu'l-Bahá. By the time he died, 'Abdu'l-Bahá had declared all family members as having broken his father's Covenant, except his four daughters and their husbands, his sister, and his wife.

'Abdu'l-Bahá was imprisoned for seven years in Palestine at 'Akká as his father had been, due to oppressive policies of the Ottoman government. He was released in 1908 when the Young Turk Revolution forced the Ottoman ruler to restore the constitution after it had been suspended for over three decades. After leaving Palestine, 'Abdu'l-Bahá traveled to Egypt, and to Europe. In 1912 he sailed to North America, and visited Canada and the USA. In turn, converts from the USA took the Bahá'í teachings to Europe, Hawaii, Mexico, Japan, Brazil, and Australia, and though 'Abdu'l-Bahá was not permitted to return to Iran, he directed social reforms from afar. His letters directed Iranian Bahá'ís to provide equal early education for girls and boys, and to work toward the emancipation of women. 'Abdu'l-Bahá was knighted by the British government in 1920 for helping starving people in Palestine during the First World War. He had directed Bahá'ís to plant and store grain well before the war began. The grain was then distributed when famine hit.

HISTORICAL PLAYERS

Qurratu'l-Ayn (Táhirih)

An Iranian woman named Fátimih Umm-Salamih (1817–1852) was martyred in Tehran in 1852. She was choked with her veil for being a Bábí. Her influence in educating women was threatening to the established orthodoxy. This occurred four years after Elizabeth Cady Stanton and others in the United States held the First Women's Rights Convention at Seneca Falls, New York. While women in the West were looking for the right to vote, she was promoting the message of gender equality in the Bábí movement. Bahá'u'lláh gave her the name Táhirih, Pure One, and others called her by the surname Qurratu'l-Ayn, Solace of the Eyes. 'Abdu'l-Bahá wrote this about her:

> Among the women of our time is Táhirih, the daughter of a Muslim priest. At the time of the appearance of the Báb, she showed such tremendous courage and power, that all who heard her were astonished. She threw aside her veil, despite the immemorial custom of the Persians; and, although it was considered impolite to speak with men, this heroic woman carried on conversations with the most learned men, and in every meeting she vanquished them. When imprisoned she said: "You can kill me as soon as you like, but you cannot stop the emancipation of women!"
>
> (Root 2000: 71)

Táhirih had become the first female disciple of the Báb. And though she only met the Báb in a dream, he named her a Letter of the Living, a designation given to his first eighteen disciples. It is said that Táhirih's poetry is recited and sung in Iran today – but only when references to her Bábí faith are obscured.

Shoghi Effendi Rabbani (1897–1957)

Shoghi Effendi Rabbani was born in 1897 to 'Abdu'l-Bahá's eldest daughter, in the Palestinian prison city of 'Akká. Through his efforts the teachings of his grandfather and great-grandfather continued to spread. He was educated at Oxford University in England, and was a talented organizer. Under Shoghi Effendi's guidance, the Bahá'í Faith took root in twenty-two countries. Bahá'ís hold the writings of Shoghi Effendi as authoritative, but they do not consider him to have been more than an ordinary human being. One of his main accomplishments is the establishment of a Bahá'í center at Haifa (then in British-administered Palestine). Specifically he: (1) established the Bahá'í World Center as the administrative headquarters of the Bahá'í community; (2) bought holy places related to Bahá'í history, such as the graves of Báb, Bahá'u'lláh, and

BOX 7.3 INTERPRETATIONS: PROGRESSIVE REVELATION

The Bahá'í community relies on the principle of **progressive revelation** to explain the nature of its teachings. There are four main assumptions embedded in this principle:

1 God guides human beings through the revelations of messengers.
2 God's messengers teach according to the needs of their historical situation.
3 Religious truth is relative, not absolute.
4 No revelation is ever final.

Bahá'ís believe that God sends Manifestations at different points in history to give guidance to humanity in accordance with the times. The Bahá'í revelation that came through Bahá'u'lláh is not considered to invalidate earlier revelations because they all stem from the same universal principles. Each revelation provides an underpinning for the next. Thus Bahá'ís respect founders of the world religions, and draw inspiration from their teachings. Moreover, they fully expect that another Manifestation of God will follow Bahá'u'lláh after about 1,000 years. Shoghi Effendi emphasized the point that none of God's revelations is final.

> It should also be borne in mind that, as great as is the power manifested by this Revelation [of Bahá'u'lláh's] and however vast the range of the Dispensation its Author has inaugurated, it emphatically repudiates the claim to be regarded as the final revelation of God's will and purpose for mankind. To hold such a conception of its character and functions would be tantamount to a betrayal of its cause and a denial of its truth. It must necessarily conflict with the fundamental principle which constitutes the bedrock of Bahá'í belief, the principle that religious truth is not absolute but relative, that Divine Revelation is orderly, continuous and progressive and not spasmodic or final.
>
> (Quoted in Adamson and Hainsworth 1998: 343)

Sometimes in the Bahá'í literature, Manifestations are called Prophets of God. In this case, the term "prophet" should be understood as a "universal" prophet, as opposed to a "minor" prophet. Bahá'ís say that at times ordinary people have served the Divine Will as minor prophets to fulfill particular religious functions. Examples include the Hebrew prophets Isaiah and Jeremiah who did not provide the full corpus of God's message. By contrast, the comprehensive function of a universal messenger of God is always to bring the law and found a new cycle of sacred history. Bahá'u'lláh said his dispensation would last at least 1,000 years – after which another Manifestation would arrive.

'Abdu'l-Bahá, and sites associated with Bahá'u'lláh's life; (3) constructed the International Archives building, and arranged for a structure to be built over the grave of the Báb. (Some thirty-five years after his passing, construction began on nineteen terraced gardens that now go up Mount Carmel from base to top.)

Shoghi Effendi died unexpectedly of the Asian flu while on a visit to England. He had no children, and did not appoint a successor. He had been designated by 'Abdu'l-Bahá as the first Guardian of the Faith. Thereafter, a succession of male Guardians was to come from Bahá'u'lláh's lineage. But when he died in 1957 there was no eligible male because (like his grandfather) Shoghi Effendi found it necessary to remove numerous family members from the Bahá'í Covenant for the sake of unity. In the absence of an heir, the Hands of the Cause of God took over stewardship of the faith. They arranged for the completion of Shoghi Effendi's goals for the Ten Year Crusade; oversaw the establishment of a number of National Spiritual Assemblies; and arranged for the election of the **Universal House of Justice** in accordance with instructions found in Bahá'u'lláh's writings. Thereafter every five years, a similar election has been held to elect a ruling body of nine men to the Universal House of Justice.

Ruhiyyih Khánum (Mary Maxwell) (1910–2000)

Mary Maxwell was married to Shoghi Effendi, the Guardian of the Faith. She was a writer and poet. He married at the age of 41 – choosing the daughter of two devoted Canadian Bahá'í converts. The marriage was a surprising testimony to the Bahá'í principle of the unity of humanity, as East met West. Mary wrote this account of their wedding:

> By the time the afternoon came, I went over and the beloved Guardian came out and got into his car. I got in beside him, and the heavens fell in Haifa, because no one had wind of this. They were all simply astonished at the Guardian, since going off in an automobile with a Western Bahá'í woman was simply unheard of. . . . We went over to the Shrine of Bahá'u'lláh [at 'Akká] and prayed, and this ring that I wear was Shoghi Effendi's Bahá'í ring. . . . We just had prayers in the Shrine, and he put the ring on my finger. That was all. Silently.
>
> (Quoted in Miller 1974: 296)

Shoghi Effendi chose the name Ruhiyyih Khánum (Lady Spiritual) for Mary Maxwell, and after many years designated her a Hand of the Cause of God. Following the Guardian's unexpected death in 1957, Ruhiyyih was involved in keeping the Bahá'í community organized until membership of the Universal House of Justice was established. Then she traveled to impoverished areas of the world to do Bahá'í missionary service, and worked continually on behalf of the Bahá'í community. Upon her death in 2000, Ruhiyyih was buried in Haifa, Israel.

Louis G. Gregory (1874–1951)

The American-born Louis G. Gregory was raised in Charleston, South Carolina. His father was a freed slave, who passed away when the boy was 5 years old. Suffering racial discrimination in the South, Gregory was moved to work for social change. After earning a law degree at Howard University in Washington, DC, he gained employment at the US Treasury Department. He encountered the Bahá'í teachings in 1908, and appreciated the community's emphasis on racial harmony. Increasingly, Gregory realized that political equality for the races would only be realized after people experienced some change in moral consciousness. 'Abdu'l-Bahá encouraged Gregory to marry Louisa Matthew, one of his English disciples. This was a socially radical suggestion, as Louisa was a white woman.

In the Bahá'í view, intermarriage among the races is a key to bringing harmony among peoples of the world. However, at the beginning of the twentieth century in the United States interracial couples were rare. The couple moved to Maine, which was one of the few states where their marriage was legally recognized. Gregory traveled around the United States mostly without his wife, as he risked the dangers of holding interracial meetings in the southern United States. Despite the pressures of racial discrimination, Gregory's commitment to laughter as a spiritual tool, and the moral support of the growing Bahá'í community provided solace. Gregory became the first African American to serve as a member of the Bahá'í National

Spiritual Assembly of the United States and Canada. When he passed away, Shoghi Effendi (who had succeeded 'Abdu'l-Bahá three decades earlier) sent a cable in which he designated Louis G. Gregory, posthumously, as a Hand of the Cause of God. The cable read, in part: "Deserves rank first Hand of the Cause of his race. Rising generation African continent will glory in his memory and emulate his example" (Adamson and Hainsworth 1998: 209).

PART 2
BAHÁ'Í TEXTURE

FOUNDATIONAL TEXTURE

The Bahá'í Faith does not have a definite canon in the sense that many works have not yet been gathered, edited, or made publicly available. However, the basic scripture is formed of writings by the Báb Bahá'u'lláh, and 'Abdu'l-Bahá. Since the Báb and Bahá'u'lláh are considered to be Manifestations of God, Bahá'ís think of their work as God's revelation. 'Abdu'l-Bahá's writings are regarded as infallible, though not revealed (because he was not a Manifestation). Only a small portion of the Bábí-Bahá'í writings has been translated from Persian or Arabic into any Western language, but Bahá'ís are active in making the teaching accessible.

The *Bayán*

The Báb wrote numerous manuscripts in Persian and Arabic, many of which were confiscated in the course of religious persecution. His writing included qur'ánic-style verses, prayers, and commentaries. The Báb called most of his later writings *Bayán* (Utterance, Exposition). He wrote an Arabic *Bayán* and a Persian *Bayán* – and it is these works that are mostly read by the Bahá'í community. Bahá'ís are particularly interested in the Báb's discussion of the "world to come," as ushered in by "Him Whom God shall make manifest." In calling himself the Qá'im, the Báb aroused expectations for the end of time. Both Shí'í Muslims and Bábís expected the second coming of Jesus to follow the arrival of the Qá'im at the time of the Last Judgment at the end of the world. Yet Bahá'ís do not expect the world to literally end at the time of the Last Judgment. Bahá'ís interpret Judgment Day *as a spiritual event that occurred with the advent of Bahá'u'lláh.*

Basic teachings

Bahá'u'lláh wrote some 15,000 Tablets, including letters, prayers and commentaries. Moreover, Bahá'u'lláh's *Kitáb-i-Aqdas* (Most Holy Book) is the book of laws that serves as a charter of the new Bahá'í world order. Bahá'u'lláh's writings form the core of Bahá'í scripture, and emphasize the unity of God, the divine message, and humanity.

One God

Bahá'í teachings are strictly monotheistic. They state that there is one – and only one – God who created the world. Bahá'ís believe that this unique God has been the object of worship in many forms throughout human history, despite the fact that cultural descriptions and religious rituals have differed. Variations in the human concept of God are due to the fact that the totality of God can neither be grasped by the human intellect, nor expressed through human creativity. Because human beings have the same basic capacities that reflect God's nature, Bahá'í believe that the existence of God can be appreciated.

One divine message

In principle, Bahá'í accept the basic teachings of all the monotheistic religions. They believe that there has been only one religion for all humankind: it came from God through numerous prophets, and was sent in accordance with the needs of the times. According to the writings of Bahá'u'lláh, a new form of the eternal message will be presented upon the arrival of the next Manifestation of God.

One humanity

Bahá'ís view the human race as an organic unit that evolves over time. The Bahá'í community is supposed to provide a model for the future mature state of humanity. A key conviction that all humanity will eventually grow to accept is that people of any gender, race, and social class are equals. Social welfare programs are thus an integral part of Bahá'í ethics. Bahá'ís work in poverty-stricken areas around the globe to provide health care and education – and promote economic development. They promote the principle of one humanity by encouraging marriages across social and ethnic boundaries. At the same time, Bahá'ís try to remain sensitive to cultural differences, and to find unity in diversity.

The Most Great Peace

Instead of time coming to an end on the occasion of a Last Judgment, Bahá'ís believe in an age of The Most Great Peace. This Most Great Peace will evolve in this millennium as humankind matures. Bahá'ís view their community as a kind of embryo that is the seed of future humanity. They believe that through an evolutionary process the distinctiveness of their lives will become increasingly evident. The marks of a Bahá'í lifestyle will become clearer over the coming generations as the community follows the guidance of God's laws meant for this age. They strive to model a life based on non-violent values to contribute to the social good. For example, at the United Nations World Conference on Human Rights in Vienna, Austria (June 1993) the Bahá'í International Community called upon the world community to acknowledge the widespread occurrence of domestic violence:

> Domestic violence is a fact of life for many women throughout the world, regardless of race, class, or educational background. In many societies traditional beliefs that women are a burden make them easy targets of anger. In other situations, men's frustration is vented on women and children when economies shrink and collapse. In all parts of the world, violence against women persists because it goes unpunished.
>
> (BIC Document #93–0611)

Rather than use political agitation, Bahá'ís strive to work within legitimate governmental channels. On principle they are non-partisan and observe the laws of the lands in which they live. Through this type of social action they believe that people will eventually realize the benefits of the consultative process. Bahá'ís believe that a Lesser Peace will come once governments collectively decide that wars are not an effective means of solving political disputes. Once the nations of the world resolve to stop war, the way is opened for a Most Great Peace.

SUPPORTIVE TEXTURE

Authoritative works

Shoghi Effendi translated many important works by Bahá'u'lláh from Arabic and Persian into English, and wrote around 36,000 letters, and one book called *God Passes By*. The words of Shoghi Effendi are authoritative and binding in the Bahá'í community, but they are not counted as sacred works. They are interpretations. A key theme that recurs in Shoghi Effendi's writings is how to live a life free of prejudice and racism. He was convinced that racism was the most challenging social problem that confronted not only the world at large, but also the Bahá'í community itself. Because of his sense of urgency, all Bahá'ís are continually urged to help each other eliminate racial prejudice in their communities and in their dealings with all human beings generally. As new situations arise within the Bahá'í communities the Universal House of Justice issues timely statements. Examples are: (1) "The Promise of World Peace to the Peoples of the World" from The Universal House of Justice (1985), and (2) "Two Wings of a Bird: The Equality of Women and Men" from the National Spiritual Assembly of the Bahá'ís of the United States (1999).

Inspirational works: world scriptures

A regular feature of Bahá'í meetings is reading aloud from scriptures of world religions. They are thought to provide inspiration; but they are not used per se as guidelines for how to live a Bahá'í life. The foundational sacred writings of Bahá'u'lláh and 'Abdu'l-Bahá take precedence over all other writings in this regard. There is a Center for the Study of Sacred Texts in Haifa, Israel at the Bahá'í World Center.

CROSS-OVER TEXTURE

Healing through science and spirituality

The Bahá'í Faith teaches that both the physical and spiritual dimensions of existence affect human health. Thus Bahá'ís are advised to treat illness and preserve health in a manner that integrates the findings of science with spirituality. Thus both the power of prayer and the use of medicines are accepted as proper religious behavior. Bahá'ís aim to balance science and religion with two key ideas in mind.

Health depends on both spiritual and physical well-being

This means that medical remedies are only considered to be effective for illnesses caused by physical problems. On the other hand, illnesses due to spiritual causes disappear through spiritual means. For example, fear, sorrow, and nervousness are helped more by spiritual treatment. Happiness has a healing effect. Thus it is important to visit people who are ill, and to interact with them through kindness and compassion. No healing is complete or lasting without a spiritual remedy. Bahá'ís consider obedience to God's laws and commandments as the best spiritual remedy.

It is important to preserve one's health

Bahá'ís are advised to preserve their health in order to help others. To maintain health they are enjoined to follow these guidelines: (1) Be clean because physical cleanliness has an effect on the inner person, in the way that sound vibrations not only affect the ear's auditory nerve, but also move the heart. (2) Refrain from the use of tobacco and intoxicants to maintain a keen mind and body strength. (3) Be content. Bahá'ís are advised not to yield to grief, jealousy, anger, and other debilitating emotions.

PART 3
BAHÁ'Í PERFORMANCE

LIFE ACCORDING TO THE BAHÁ'Í CALENDAR

Bahá'ís use a calendar created by the Báb. The Báb inaugurated a new calendar for his community to signal the start of a new era. He abandoned the lunar calendar used by the Shí'í Muslims of Persia in favor of a solar calendar. Yet he kept the ancient Persian New Year, which is astronomically fixed at the spring equinox – ordinarily falling on 21 March. The calendar is based on the number nineteen. There are nineteen years in a cycle; each year has nineteen months; and each month has nineteen days. To make sure that the spring equinox falls on 21 March every year, four extra (intercalary) days are added on ordinary years, with five extra days in a leap year. The Báb inserted these intercalary days at the close of the eighteenth month, before the nineteenth month begins. They readjust the days to correspond with the annual solar cycle.

Bahá'ís set aside no specific weekday for worship because worship is done every day individually, and collectively on the first day of every Bahá'í month for a **Nineteen Day Feast**. The gathering starts off the nineteen days of that month with devotions that are meant to make the days ahead spiritually rewarding. The meetings also have a consultative portion during which community business is discussed.

The worldwide Bahá'í community devotes the intercalary days each year to family gatherings, gift giving, and serving the needy. They then fast during the entire nineteenth month. On this last month of the year from 2 to 20 March they neither eat nor drink from sunrise to sunset. The fast is not necessary for people under 15 or over 70 years of age. Women who are pregnant, nursing, or menstruating refrain from fasting as well. In addition, those who are traveling, ill, or engaged in heavy physical labor need not fast. In this custom of fasting, Bahá'ís are akin to their Muslim brothers and sisters who refrain from eating and drinking during daylight hours in the month of Ramaḍán.

Bahá'ís believe that their calendar is appropriate for the age of global unity and harmony. Other calendars tend to be culture-bound, as they generally associate days, months, and years with figures or events specific to a single religion. The Bahá'í calendar is also culture-bound, because it is linked to a particular divine revelation within a monotheistic worldview. Yet in making the months stand for divine attributes, they are also meant to reflect aspects of human existence that transcend cultures.

KEY POINTS

- Bahá'ís speak of their religion in the collective as the Bahá'í community. Its teachings focus on

BOX 7.4 CULTURE CONTRAST: THREE NEW RELIGIONS

From time to time a distinctive spiritual lineage emerges into human culture that provides the foundation for a new world religion. In the 1800s three new lineages emerged within a span of thirty-two years, in three cultural zones: West Asia, East Asia, and North America. Out of three founders' revelations came the Bahá'í, Tenrikyō, and Mormon traditions. These stand today as worldwide independent religions.

New religions institute rituals that are embedded in their own sacred times and sacred places. Students of religions can learn much about the worldview of a tradition by exploring the symbolism reflected in new calendars and pilgrimage sites.

Three new religions of the 1800s

	Bahá'í	*Tenrikyō*	*Mormon (LDS)*
		Founders	
Birth name	Mírzá Husayn 'Alí-i-Núrí	Nakayama Miki	Joseph Smith
Religious name	Bahá'u'lláh	Kami no Yashiro	Joseph Smith
Date born	12 November 1817	18 April 1798	1805
Date died	29 May 1892	26 January 1887	27 June 1844
Place born/died	Iran/Palestine (present-day Israel)	Japan/Japan	USA/USA
Initial affiliation	Muslim	Buddhist; Shintō	Protestant Christian
Initial hierophany	1852	1838	1820
Religious function	Reintroduce God's eternal message	Prepare for perfect divine kingdom	Present complete Christian truth
Spiritual position	Manifestation of God	Living Shrine of God (Kami)	Prophet of God, Seer, Revelator
Difficulties	Imprisonments	Imprisonments	Assassination
Successor	'Abdu'l-Bahá	Iburi Izō	Brigham Young
		Key features	
Concept of divinity	One creator God	One creator God	One creator God
Sample idea	Unity in diversity; Most Great Peace	Purification through transmigration	Families sealed together for eternity
Scripture	Works by the Báb, Bahá'u'lláh, and 'Abdu'l-Bahá	Two works by Nakayama Miki, and one by Iburi Izō	Bible, Book of Mormon, and John Smith's revelations
		Organization	
Official founding	Emerged from the Bábí Faith as the Bahá'í Faith in 1863	Tenrikyō officially became a Shintō sect in 1888	Officially became Church of Jesus Christ in 1830
Current members*	Five million in 2001	2,350,000 in 1999	Four million in 1984
World headquarters	Haifa, Israel	Tenri City, Japan	Salt Lake City, Utah
Official website	www.bahai.org	www.tenrikyo.or.jp	www.lds.org

* Estimates from www. adherents.com.

Table 7.1 The Bahá'í calendar

Month	*Arabic name*	*Meaning*	*First day*
1st	Bahá	Splendor	21 March
2nd	Jalál	Glory	9 April
3rd	Jamál	Beauty	28 April
4th	Azamat	Grandeur	17 May
5th	Núr	Light	5 June
6th	Rahmat	Mercy	24 June
7th	Kalímát	Words	31 July
8th	Kamál	Perfection	1 August
9th	Asmá	Names	20 August
10th	'Izzat	Might	8 September
11th	Mashíyyat	Will	27 September
12th	'Ilm	Knowledge	16 October
13th	Qudrat	Power	4 November
14th	Qawl	Speech	23 November
15th	Masáil	Questions	12 December
16th	Sharaf	Honor	31 December
17th	Sultán	Sovereignty	19 January
18th	Mulk	Dominion	7 February
	Intercalary days are 26 February through 1 March		
19th	'Alá	Loftiness	2 March

unity, claiming one God, one divine message, and one humanity.

- The Bahá'í community emerged from the Bábí Faith that was led by the Báb (gate). The Bahá'í founder is Bahá'u'lláh, who is believed to be the most recent in a line of God's Manifestations.
- Bahá'í teachings appeared about 160 years ago, and people faithful to the Covenant view them as the updated version of God's eternal message, suitable for the next 1,000 years.
- Bahá'ís believe that the Last Judgment spoken of by Christians, Muslims, and Zoroastrians is a spiritual event that already occurred with Bahá'u'lláh's arrival. They anticipate the Golden Age of the Bahá'í Era, in which The Most Great Peace will be achieved.
- The Bahá'í spiritual lineage was initiated by Bahá'u'lláh, and passed on to his son 'Abdu'l-Bahá, and great-grandson Shoghi Effendi. Thereafter authoritative Bahá'í leadership passed to the elected membership of the Universal House of Justice.
- The Bahá'í community anticipates a Lesser Peace, followed by a Most Great Peace in the coming 1,000 years. The Lesser Peace will come when governments give up war, and the Most Great Peace will come with the end of racism, sexism, and economic exploitation of one human being by another.
- The Bahá'í calendar measures time in the new era following the Báb's declaration about the coming of "Him Whom God shall make manifest." It is based on the solar year, measured in nineteen-year cycles, with nineteen months per year, and nineteen days per month. Names of months and days are the same, and are meant to reflect divine attributes.

STUDY QUESTIONS

1 Describe the role of God's Manifestations in this world.

2 What was the historical relationship between the Bábí Faith and the Bahá'í Faith?

3. Describe the Bahá'í mystical path according to Bahá'u'lláh's teaching on the "four valleys."
4. What is the Bahá'í attitude toward other world religions? (Account for the concept of "progressive revelation" in your answer.)
5. What are the key Bahá'í teachings that relate to unity?
6. What is the Bahá'í understanding of history? What is the role of the Bahá'í community in the course of history?
7. Name five key figures in Bahá'í history and note their contributions.

GLOSSARY

Covenant Bahá'í term for God's assurance of continuing guidance to humanity based on divine guidance that came through Bahá'u'lláh.

Gate (*Báb*) Religious name for the founder of the Bábí Faith (from which came the Bahá'í Faith).

Glory of God Translation of the name of the Bahá'í founder, Bahá'u'lláh.

Greatest Name Term in the Bahá'í Faith for the Name of God, which is "Bahá" (Glory, Splendor, Light).

Hands of the Cause of God People appointed by Bahá'u'lláh, 'Abdu'l-Bahá, and Shoghi Effendi to protect and propagate the Bahá'í message.

Manifestation Bahá'í term for one of God's messengers or universal prophets. Each perfectly reflects God's attributes on earth, but is not God. Bahá'ís consider that Bahá'u'lláh is God's messenger for this age.

Nineteen Day Feast A monthly gathering among all local groups of Bahá'ís, held on or about the first day of each of the nineteen months of the Bahá'í calendar.

progressive revelation Bahá'í belief that God's revelation is never final, and that Manifestations of God revealed God's teachings and laws according to the needs of the times in which they lived.

Universal House of Justice The supreme administrative body of the Bahá'í community, ordained by Bahá'u'lláh. Nine members are elected by the membership of the National Spiritual Assemblies.

KEY READING

'Abdu'l-Bahá ([1930] 1984) *Some Answered Questions*, collected and translated from the Persian by Laura Clifford Barney, Wilmette, IL: Bahá'í Publishing Trust.

Adamson, Hugh C. and Hainsworth, Philip (1998) *Historical Dictionary of the Bahá'í Faith*, Lanham, MD, and London: The Scarecrow Press.

Bahá'u'lláh ([1945] 2003) *The Hidden Words*, translated by Shogi Effendi with the assistance of some English friends, Wilmette, IL: Bahá'í Publishing Trust.

Bowers, Kenneth E. (2004) *God Speaks Again: An Introduction to the Bahá'í Faith*, Wilmette, IL: Bahá'í Publishing Trust.

Hornby, Helen (compiler) (1988) *Lights of Guidance: A Bahá'í Reference File*, New Delhi: Bahá'í Publishing Trust.

Miller, William McElwee (1974) *The Bahá'í Faith: Its History and Teachings*, South Pasadena, CA: William Carey Library.

Momen, Moojan (ed.) (1981) *The Bábí and Bahá'í Religions, 1844–1944: Some Contemporary Western Accounts*, Oxford: George Ronald.

CHAPTER 8

Jain tradition

TIMELINE

	BCE	
	400,000–200,000	Human beings in India
	ca. 2700–1500	Indus Valley Civilization (Harappān people)
Pārśva	b. 800s	
	ca. 500 onward	Flowering of Jain Culture
Mahāvīra Vardhamāna	ca. 599–527 (Śvetāmbara) or d. 510 (Digambara)	
Bhadrabāhu	fl. ca. 350	
	CE	
	ca. 300s	Jain sacred texts written
	ca. 800s	Early Mahāvīra biography
Lonkā Shāh	ca. 1450	
Gurudev Shree Chitrabhanu	b. 1922	

Jains trace their lineage back through twenty-four human beings known as **tīrthaṅkaras** or **Jinas**. Tradition says that these Jinas followed in an infinitely long line of tīrthaṅkaras that already appeared in the course of cosmic history. But of the twenty-four tīrthaṅkaras, only the final two are people known to history: (1) Pārśva who taught in north India around the ninth century BCE, and (2) Vardhamāna (called Mahāvīra or the Jina) who was born into the same area about 250 years later. The written Jain scriptures that exist today are based on Mahāvīra's teachings, along with summaries of Pārśva's ideas.

During the sixth century BCE Vardhamāna Mahāvīra taught mainly in the environs of Magadha and Kośala. A great cultural experiment was taking place in these two Ganges basin territories. Urban life had been slowly shaping up since Pārśva's day as people created cities to begin inventing new lives and identities for themselves. Prominent members of the two upper classes were asking questions that pressed beyond what was known, and taking up new challenges in their religious lives. Certain thoughtful ***brāhmaṇas*** deviated from a spiritual path that was based on sacrifice to wonder about the inner meaning of their ritual acts. And certain adventuresome **kṣatriyas** redirected their warrior's efforts to challenge their inner enemies, namely emotions and attitudes that wrought violence. These progressive priests and nobles courageously abandoned home life. They became ***śramaṇas***, wandering free of possessions in search of the way to end destruction, suffering, and rebirth. Merchants too joined the Gangetic cultural movement – some as renunciates, and some as wealthy patrons of renunciates. Gradually both renunciates and merchants carved out a secure place in Indian society. In this atmosphere, Vardhamāna Mahāvīra gave greater shape to the old Nirgrantha Order as its twenty-fourth Jina, and Gautama Buddha founded the Buddhist religion. Both the Jain and Buddhist traditions cut the association between religion and social class. For them, birth into one of the Āryan social classes did not necessarily reflect a person's level of spiritual maturity. Meanwhile the Vedic *brāhmaṇas* set the groundwork for the Hindu religion, which was to safeguard Āryan values and religious perspectives.

PART 1
JAIN PLAYERS

THE ULTIMATE PRINCIPLE

The life force: *jīva*

Jains do not speak of a Creator God. They believe that the cosmos undergoes endless cycles with neither a beginning nor an end. This eternal cosmos comprises two types of things: (1) living (**jīva**) and (2) non-living (*ajīva*). Anything of the former type is alive because it has a jīva. Thus it is the living soul that accounts for all force, movement, growth, and awareness in the cosmos. This is to say that jīva is the ultimate principle of the universe. The life force runs through all living beings from single-sensed micro-organisms to heavenly godlings. Jains classify beings with jīvas according to the number of sense organs they possess.

The final objective of every living being is to free its jīva from bondage to a material body. Until attaining **mokṣa** (liberation from rebirth in **saṃsāra**), the jīvas of all living beings – from earth bodies to godlings – are saddled with the dust of **karma**. Living beings who thoroughly purify their jīvas leave the physical world behind at the time of death. At that point, the purified jīva detaches from its material body, and ascends straight upward to the apex of saṃsāra. There the jīva dwells for eternity. Living beings who thus attain mokṣa are called **siddhas**. Others may be reborn as any of four types of living beings (jīvas) that inhabit saṃsāra: (1) human beings, (2) beings in the twelve heavens, (3) beings in the seven hells, or (4) animals and plants.

IMAGINAL PLAYERS

Twenty-four tīrthaṅkaras

The objects of Jain worship are living beings with purified jīvas called ***kevalins***. A tīrthankara is a special kind of *kevalin*. All *kevalins* can teach about the path to liberation based on experience; but a tīrthankara is a *kevalin* who newly reintroduces Jain teachings to the world. They demonstrate the means to attain ***kevala-jñāna*** (see page 187). Once they actually attain this unique knowledge, tīrthaṅkaras cease to engage in worldly work. Jain tradition then develops through disciples who take over the physical job of teaching and establishing ***tīrthas*** (communities) for monks, nuns, laymen, and laywomen. Finally, when it is time to pass away, tīrthaṅkaras free their jīvas from material

Table 8.1 Living beings according to Jain cosmology

#	*Sense added**	*Examples of jīvas*
1	Touch	Earth-bodies, fire-bodies, water-bodies, air-bodies, and flora-bodies
2	Taste	Worms, leeches
3	Smell	Lice, ants
4	Sight	Flies, bees
5	Hearing	Animals, human beings, hell beings, heavenly godlings

* The number of senses increases by one as the sense indicated in this column is added.

BOX 8.1 CULTURE CONTRAST: THREE VIEWS OF KARMA

Jains, Buddhists, and Hindus (except Hindu fatalists) agree that someone's acts of body, speech, and mind impact upon that person's experience in current and future lifetimes. They also believe that karma (both positive and negative) binds one to the cycle of rebirth (*saṃsāra*). Yet the traditions differ in their analyses of karma (action). In a very general sense, the three understandings of karma are as follows.

Jain karma. Karma is a kind of dust or subtle matter that attaches itself to the pure energy of the soul (jīva). When an act of thought, word, or deed is performed that has a tinge of violence, karmic dust is attracted to the soul and sticks to it. The accumulation of karma depends upon the *action* performed through body, speech, or mind. To clean the soul of such dust requires restraint from action. Karmic dust must be worn off of the soul to free it from rebirth.

Buddhist karma. Karma is a kind of mental impression, like a code in a person's subtle consciousness. Because Buddhists do not accept the existence of a soul entity (ātman or jīva), they speak more in terms of karma created by a person's *motivation.* To rid oneself of karma one must gain insight into the nature of the world. This insight eliminates the selfish motivation that creates karma. The nature of any accumulated karma depends on a person's acts of body, speech, and mind. But acts without ignorance do not generate karma.

Hindu karma. Karma is related to the performance of certain duties (dharma) related to the social class into which a person is born. Metaphorically speaking, a person's soul (ātman) is "dressed" by the body. People born into each Hindu social class have different clothing (i.e., different quality bodies). The relationship between a person's acts and class duties determines whether the soul will get better clothing in the next life. Better clothing (i.e., being born into a higher social class) is the result of doing acts that were appropriate to a person's social caste and stage of life. The most favorable karma is created when a person does his or her appropriate class duty without hankering selfishly after the results of the actions.

entrapment by burning off all excess karma. They ascend to the highest point in the universe, and abide as immaterial siddhas free of birth and death.

Jain cosmology presents a theory of periodic world evolution and devolution. Six phases of evolution are followed by six phases of devolution, and these are endlessly repeated. During the course of evolution, life becomes increasingly pleasant, and beings become more spiritually inclined as time passes. During the course of devolution, life becomes increasingly unpleasant, and beings become more spiritually degenerate as time passes. Tīrthaṅkaras always appear in the third and fourth phases of both the upward and downward cycles of cosmic history. During these middle (of six) phases, life is fairly balanced between pleasure and pain, and beings are most receptive to religious teachings on how to escape *saṃsāra.* They have enough pain to motivate a search for release from pain, but not so much pain that they become overwhelmed by it. Twenty-four tīrthaṅkaras appear during each evolution and each devolution. Due to their teachings other people can become *kevalins.* Because the cosmos is vast, there is always a tīrthankara somewhere, ready to teach whoever is capable of learning.

Yakṣas and *yakṣīs*

Jains acknowledge the existence of a variety of godlings in this universe, such as *devas, nāgas, gandharvas,* and *yakṣas.* Strictly speaking, Jains would have no reason to worship these beings because none of these godlings is qualified to show the path to liberation from the cycle of rebirths. Yet *yakṣa* and *yakṣī* images are found in nearly every medieval Jain temple, for example. They

Plate 8.1 "The thousand-hooded Pārśvanātha." Pārśva, the twenty-third tīrthaṅkara, stands here with a thousand snakes shading him. The cobra is Pārśva's symbol. Attending him are a *yakṣa* and *yakṣī* (half-human, half-snake) holding *chauri* whisks. The huge painted eyes are typical of Śvetāmbara Jain iconography. The eyes are painted during a consecration ceremony.

are thought of as guardian deities and appear as serpent-like beings whose upper torsos are human.

EXCEPTIONAL PLAYERS

Pārśva (b. 800s BCE)

Pārśva is the first Jain tīrthaṅkara known by historical standards to have lived. He is thought to have been teaching in India 250 years prior to Vardhamāna's renunciation. He lived in the middle Ganges basin, and taught in Vārāṇasī. He lived to the age of 100. Pārśva's followers continued down to the time of the next tīrthaṅkara named by Jain tradition, Vardhamāna. Indeed, Vardhamāna's parents are said to have been followers of Pārśva. Jain tradition counts Pārśva as the twenty-third in line of tīrthaṅkaras who appeared in our current phase of the cosmic cycle. His teaching was centered upon the dharma of the Four Restraints (*cāturyāma-dharma*), according to which disciples were committed to: (1) avoid doing harm, (2) avoid telling untruths, (3) avoid taking what is not given, (4) avoid possessions. It is still an open question as to whether or not Pārśva practiced non-possessing to the extent of giving up clothing.

Vardhamāna Mahāvīra (599–527 BCE)

Śvetāmbara Jains give the dates of Vardhamāna Mahāvīra's life as 599 to 527 BCE, while Digambara Jains hold that he died in 510 BCE. Mahāvīra is thought to have been just slightly older than Gautama Buddha, whose dates are often given as ca. 563 to 483 BCE. (However, some scholars are inclined to shift Mahāvīra's dates to tally with a suggestion that Buddha died as late as 411 to 400 BCE.) The earliest complete, independent biography of Mahāvīra dates from the 800s CE, well over a thousand years after he lived. Over time, Jains of the Śvetāmbara and Digambara schools developed different versions of the life story (with much overlap). There are four main events in the life story of a Jina: birth, renunciation, obtaining omniscience, and liberation. In relating the story here, the letter Ś follows the *italicized* report of an incident that is limited to the Śvetāmbara version.

Birth

Mahāvīra lived in the middle Ganges basin in the territory of Vaiśali. His father was a chief of the Jñātri clan, and his mother, Triśalā, was the sister of a Vaiśali ruler. Thus he was born into the kṣatriya class. Before giving birth a number of auspicious signs appeared to his mother in a dream. *The auspicious signs actually appeared to two women, as the child inhabited two wombs. Mahāvīra was unusual in having a kind of double birth. Devānandā, a brāhmaṇa woman, first conceived him. But a supernatural being transplanted the embryo from her womb to Triśalā's womb, giving Triśalā's embryo to Devānandā in return. Śvetāmbara tradition says this obstetric switch was done because Jinas are always born into kṣatriya families. As Mahāvīra's embryo departed, Devānandā was distressed to see images of the auspicious signs leaving her by mouth* (Ś).

Triśalā enjoyed the blessing of the visions that attended having the embryo in her womb. This should have been a joyful pregnancy, but at one point the baby stopped moving. This stillness perhaps foreshadowed the intense spiritual discipline that Mahāvīra undertook in later years, when he spent extensive periods holding a single posture. Noting his mother's worry, he finally kicked a little for reassurance. *At that point in the womb, he decided he would not become a śramaṇa until his parents passed away, to spare them any future worries* (Ś).

The baby received the name Vardhamāna (he who brings prosperity) because his parents' wealth increased while he was gestating in Triśala's womb. When small, Vardhamāna subdued a snake. He was able to do this because he radiated peace. Nothing more is recorded of the child's early life. *Vardhamāna married and had one daughter. He abided by his determination made in the womb to leave the family in search of liberation only after both his parents passed away* (Ś). At the age of 30 the appearance of some godlings somehow motivated Vardhamāna to take up the life of a renunciate.

Renunciation

In Vardhamāna's day some fifty *śramaṇa* groups wandered around the middle Ganges basin. Mendicant life was surely an intriguing option for noble kṣatriya men such as he. The custom of abandoning the world had already begun to take root in the century or so prior to Mahāvīra's renunciation. Pārśva seems to have been part of that social movement some 250 years before Mahāvīra followed in his footsteps. On the day that the noble Vardhamāna chose to renounce the world he gave away his possessions. Then he walked to the foot of a sacred Aśoka tree, and sat down to meditate. With his hands Vardhamāna pulled out all his hair by the roots. According to an ancient tradition, this spelled his commitment to a life in which pride and possession were both renounced. The question of what the new renunciate wore is disputed between the Digambara and Śvetāmbara Jains. Digambaras say that Vardhamāna removed all his ornaments and clothing, and thereafter walked naked for the rest of his life. Śvetāmbaras say that the godling who placed the Jina in Triśalā 's womb now presented with a divine cloth. *He eventually gave half the cloth out of generosity to a brāhmaṇa, and abandoned the other half after thirteen months, when it got snagged in thorns, and came off* (Ś). Both Jain traditions agree that Mahāvīra traveled around on foot without clothing *after thirteen months* (Ś). Vardhamāna wandered for twelve years. He undertook strict penance. Often for a week at a time, the *śramaṇa* abstained from both food and water. He carried no begging bowl, but cupped his hands to receive food when begging alms. Beyond that Vardhamāna Mahāvīra restrained his speech. He would keep silent for long stretches of time, and generally barely spoke.

Omniscience and liberation

In the thirteenth year after renouncing worldly life, Mahāvīra attained *kevala-jñāna*. This realization comprises knowledge (Sanskrit: *jñāna*) and intuitive sight (Sanskrit: *darśana*). *Kevala* is considered to be unobstructed, complete, and unimpeded realization. In

English the word "omniscience" is used to describe it. A Śvetāmbara scripture, the *Kalpa Sūtra* (v. 121), describes the moment when Vardhamāna became a Jina:

> During the thirteenth year, in the second month of summer . . . on the bank of the river Rigupâlika, not far from an old temple, in the field of the householder Sâmâga, under a Sal tree, when the moon was in conjunction with the asterism Uttaraphalgunî, (the Venerable One) in a squatting position with joined heels, exposing himself to the heat of the sun, after fasting two and a half days without drinking water, being engaged in deep meditation, reached the highest knowledge and intuition, called Kevala, which is infinite, supreme, unobstructed, unimpeded, complete, and full.
>
> (Jacobi 1968a: 263)

After achieving *kevala-jñāna*, Mahāvīra's body emanated the *divyadhvani*, the divine sound typically heard coming from the bodies of Jinas. His body became so pure that it appeared as crystal. He was no longer hungry, thirsty, sleepy, or fearful. He did not age, contract disease, or perspire. In short, his body exhibited no evidence of decay. Jain tradition says that godlings and demi-godlings gathered along with human beings and animals to witness the spectacle. Thereafter, Mahāvīra taught for forty years before his jīva passed from his body to ascend into the realm at the top of the universe. At the age of 72, the Jina became a siddha. This meant he had cut ties to the material world forever. His jīva would never again take rebirth, and thus acquire another body.

HISTORICAL PLAYERS

The eleven *gaṇadharas*

Mahāvīra had eleven *gaṇadharas* (supporters of the order). These were unusually talented disciples who were able to interpret the divine music that emanated from his body after he achieved *kevala-jñāna*. All eleven came from the area of Pāṭaliputra, and took monastic vows the day they became Mahāvīra's disciples. The youngest was 16 years old at the time of taking vows, while five of the oldest were in their early fifties. Following Mahāvīra's example, the *gaṇadharas* gave up all possessions, including clothes. They followed the Jina's example and ate food from their "hand bowls." All eleven eventually became *kevalins*. That is to say, they reached a level of realization equivalent to Mahāvīra's. As *kevalins* these key disciples served as a kind of bridge between the Jina, and their fellow Nirgranthas – people without (sanskrit: *nir*) bonds (Sanskrit: *grantha*). The *gaṇadharas* established the Nirgrantha community according to four paths (*tīrthas*): monks, nuns, laymen, and laywomen. At the time Mahāvīra passed away and became a siddha, only two of his eleven *gaṇadharas* were still alive.

Digambara and Śvetāmbara Jains

The Nirgrantha community grew during the forty years of Mahāvīra's wandering after his enlightenment. A traditional number given in the Jain *Kalpa Sūtra* is 14,000 monks, 36,000 nuns, 159,000 laymen, and 318,000 laywomen (Jaini 1979: 37). The surprising number of women disciples of the Jina is attributed to the fact that men often had more than one wife – and a woman was inclined to take up a position comparable to her husband's position. In spite of the Nirgranthas' initial success, the early Jain community had to cope with hard times. Approximately three centuries after Mahāvīra passed away famine struck the middle Ganges basin. This stress eventually led to the formation of two communities, known today as the **Digambara** and **Śvetāmbara** Jains. The Digambaras explain the origin of their branch in terms of divergences that appeared while the two groups were separated. Digambara tradition reports that the *ācārya* Bhadrabāhu (fl. ca. 350) led members of his community south (into present-day Mysore) to escape the famine. Their descendants returned to Pāṭaliputra after economic life stabilized up north. Meanwhile the Nirgranthas who did not leave the area around Pāṭaliputra canonized their scripture and adopted some new habits. The returnees found what they thought were errors in the newly canonized scripture. They rejected it, and developed their own literature. Moreover, the returnees criticized the Jains who stayed behind for relaxing their discipline. Those who lived through the famine took up the custom of wearing white garments instead of practicing nudity. Nudity was supposed to be a sign of non-attachment to worldly

BOX 8.2 SYMBOLS: SACRED IMAGES IN THE JAIN TRADITION

Jain tradition is split into two main branches – sky-clad and white-clad. They have differing attitudes not only about whether or not monks should own clothing, but also about whether sacred art should be clothed and decorated. Digambara Jains whose monks wear no clothes say that Pārśva himself gave up wearing garments. They believe that the practice of nudity is necessary for achieving mokṣa because it signals inner non-attachment. Thus Digambaras do not adorn or clothe their statues. On the other hand, Śvetāmbara monks and nuns wear white clothes because Pārśva's followers wore clothes, and initially Pārśva himself wore a garment.

The style of worship using images known as pūjā (see page 237) is common among Jain laypersons. Yet some Jains minimize or eliminate the use of statues. In the mid-fifteenth century the Śvetāmbara teacher Lonkā Shāh led a movement that declared the worship of idols (Sanskrit: *mūrti-pūjā*) to be heretical. He was a precursor to Jains who later formed the Sthānakavāsī sect. The name Sthānakavāsī (meaning "dwellers-in-halls") was adopted in contrast to "dwellers-in-temples." Sthānakavāsīs did not totally oppose the use of idols because they realized that Jina images inspired people to emulate the tīrthaṅkaras. Yet they strongly advocate meditation for laypeople in place of elaborate ritual worship. A second protestant Jain sect emerged from the dwellers-in-halls in 1760 when five Sthānakavāsī monks formed the Terāpanthī sect. Terāpanthīs reject both physical *and* mental use of images. Members of the Terāpanthī lay community focus their respect on living mendicants.

Plate 8.2 "The Nandyāvarta." Each of the twenty-four Jain tīrthaṅkaras is associated with a sign (*cihna*). Pictured here is the Nandyāvarta (curvilinear svastika) used by Digambara Jains to signify Aranātha, the eighteenth tīrthaṅkara. During Jain rituals this figure is created from grains of rice. Signs for the tīrthaṅkaras include: animals (elephant, cobra), objects (pot, flower, umbrella), and geometric designs (svastika, nandyāvarta). These insignia along with inscriptions identify the statues of tīrthaṅkaras that otherwise look very similar.

Table 8.2 Jain iconography

	Śvetāmbara	*Digambara*
Eyes	eyes gaze outward; eyes are painted or large eye sockets are inlaid with shiny glass during consecration ceremonies	unmarked eyes half-closed gaze downward toward the nose in meditation
Adornment	images adorned with jewels and golden ornaments. The figures are shown as if wearing loincloths	images have neither adornment nor representation of clothing
Posture	Jinas shown in postures adopted at the time of their release from saṃsāra. 1 Ṛṣabha, Nemi, and Mahāvīra seated in the lotus position (*padmāsana*) 2 Other tīrthaṅkaras standing (*kāyotsarga*)	

Sources: Wiley (2004: 132); Sangave (1997: 136–137); Bhattacharya ([1939] 1974: 20)

goods, and the community of Jains that stemmed from Bhadrabāhu's community continued to practice nudity. Hence they were called Digambara or "sky-clad." The Nirgranthas who wore garments became known as the white-clad or Śvetāmbara. This split between Digambara and Śvetāmbara Jains remains to this day, and each community has its own scriptures. Further down the line two groups splintered off from the Śvetāmbara community: Sthānakavāsīs and Terāpanthīs.

A modern "renunciate"

Sometimes a person feels moved to renounce renunciation itself! This happened to Gurudev Shree Chitrabhanu (b. 1922) who had been a Śvetāmbara monk for twenty-nine years. According to the ancient Nirgrantha custom, he never rode in a vehicle. Rather he walked everywhere barefoot, covering an estimated 30,000 miles. But after a penetrating realization, Gurudev was moved to social action. He founded the Divine Knowledge Society, through which volunteers were coordinated to help the needy afflicted by flood and famine. He then expanded beyond traditional confines of the Jain holy life by traveling outside of his homeland. Visits to Africa, Europe, and America required riding in vehicles, and engaging with people in ways uncustomary for a Jain monk. Through his contact with non-Jains Gurudev realized that many people – young and old, ancient and modern – could appreciate the meaning of Mahāvīra's teachings. Thus he began preparing materials from Jain scriptures that could apply well to the daily lives of students both inside and outside of India. He forfeited his monk's vows, took up the life of a householder, and established the Jain Meditation Center in New York City.

PART 2
JAIN TEXTURE

FOUNDATIONAL TEXTURE

Vardhamāna's *divyadhvani* (divine sound)

Tīrthaṅkaras do not teach anything new, but their presence in the world serves to awaken human beings to a unique (*kevala*) knowledge (*jñāna*) of reality. When a tīrthaṅkara – or any human being – becomes a *kevalin* that person does not speak in any ordinary way. Thus instead of emitting words after attaining the unique knowledge, the *kevalin* Mahāvīra emanated divine sound-waves that might be compared to the beating of a magnificent drum emitting the mantra *AUṀ*. Thus the true Jain foundational material is Vardhamāna's *divyadhvani* (divine sound). Digambaras believe that the *divyadhvani* is unarticulated sound that blends all cosmic vibrations. In their view only an exceptionally gifted disciple (i.e., a *gaṇadhara*) can interpret it. On the other hand Śvetāmbaras believe that Mahāvīra continued to give teachings that could be understood by living beings. They claim that the *divyadhvani* is "divine" (Sanskrit: *divya*) because the *kevalin*'s teachings can be understood by all living beings who are rational and have five senses. In either case the written Jain scriptures are second to *kevala-jñāna*. The real Jain texture is the divine sound. This sound encompasses the vibrations from which all words come and into which all words dissolve.

The *Five Homage Mantra*

The *Five Homage Mantra* is the key Jain prayer. It can be reduced to the sacred syllable AUṀ, which is the foundational *divyadhvani*. This *Mantra* is said to purify the jīva of someone who recites it with Right Faith. Every Jain layperson, monk, and nun repeats this most auspicious *Mantra*, which conveys the essence of liberation from the cycle of rebirth. When recited in Sanskrit, it goes like this:

ṇamo arahaṃtāṇaṃ	(Obeisance to the *arhats*)
ṇamo siddhāṇaṃ	(Obeisance to the siddhas)
ṇamo āyariyāṇaṃ	(Obeisance to the *ācāryas*)
ṇamo uvajjhāyāṇaṃ	(Obeisance to the *upādhyāyas*)
ṇamo loe savva-sāhūṇaṃ	(Obeisance to all [Jain] *sādhus* in the world)

The *Five Homage Mantra* expresses obeisance to *arhats*, siddhas, *ācāryas*, *upādhyāyas*, and *sādhus*. These five represent the possibilities for human salvation from the round of rebirths. *Arhats* are omniscient human beings who became pure by eliminating all their karma. (Jains more regularly use the term *kevalin* to designate such persons.) Siddhas are the disembodied jīvas who have attained mokṣa, and dwell at the apex of the universe. *Ācāryas*, *upādhyāyas*, and *sādhus* (feminine = *sādhvīs*) are the mendicant leaders, teachers, and monks (and nuns) in the Jain community.

Mahāvīra's last sermon

Before leaving his body Mahāvīra gave words of advice to Indrabhūti Gautama who had not yet become a *kevalin*. Attaining *kevala-jñāna* was particularly difficult for the *gaṇadhara* because he was so deeply attached to Mahāvīra. Thus according to the Śvetāmbara *Uttarādhyayana Sūtra* (X:1–4, 28, 32–34), Mahāvīra told him:

Plate 8.3 "Shrine of a perfected being." This is a Jain altarpiece commissioned in 1333 by a Jain merchant. The presence of a perfected being is indicated through the siddha's absence. Digambara Jains depict the transcendence of saṃsāra with an empty silhouette of a standing tīrthaṅkara above a lotus, and between two chauri whisks. Such images are called *siddha-pratima yantras* (magical diagrams of perfected beings).

> As the fallow leaf of the tree falls to the ground, when its days are gone, even so the life of men (will come to its close); Gautama, be careful all the while!
>
> As a dewdrop dangling on the top of a blade of Kusa-grass lasts but a short time, even so the life of men; Gautama, be careful all the while!
>
> As life is so fleet and existence so precarious, wipe off the sins you ever committed; Gautama, be careful all the while!
>
> A rare chance, in the long course of time, is human birth for a living being; hard are the consequences of actions; Gautama, be careful all the while! . . .
>
> Cast aside from you all attachments, as the (leaves of) a lotus let drop off the autumnal water, exempt from every attachment; Gautama, be careful all the while! . . .
>
> Now you have entered the path from which the thorns have been cleared, the great path; walk in the right path; Gautama, be careful all the while!
>
> Do not get into an uneven road like a weak burden-bearer; for you will repent of it afterwards; Gautama, be careful all the while!
>
> You have crossed the great ocean; why do you halt so near the shore? make haste to get on the other side; Gautama, be careful all the while!
>
> (Adapted from Jacobi 1968b: 42–46)

This final teaching that Mahāvīra gave Indrabhūti Gautama has been well loved by Śvetāmbara Jains for centuries.

SUPPORTIVE TEXTURE

The lost scriptures

Two of the eleven *gaṇadharas* were still alive at the time Mahāvīra passed away: Indrabhūti Gautama and

BOX 8.3 INTERPRETATIONS: THREE JAIN PRINCIPLES

The central focus of all Jain religious practice is ahiṃsā as it manifests in thought, word, and deed. In their search for the most thorough means of practicing ahiṃsā, Jains developed the principles of *aparigraha* and *anekānta*.

Ahiṃsā. Non-violence is the keystone of Jain spirituality. Jains scrutinized the spectrum of human conduct to determine how violence (*hiṃsā*) occurs. Recognizing the causes of violence, Jains studied in detail various means of eliminating *hiṃsā*. Jains operate under the assumption that violence is born from the mind. They recognize that speech and physical actions reflect mental violence, which can be gross or subtle. Modern Jains apply their expertise in non-harming in the fields of conflict resolution, medicine, politics, and business.

Aparigraha. *Aparigraha* is usually translated as non-grasping. The mental attitude of wanting to take for oneself leads to acts of violence. Mental possessions include likes, dislikes, hatred, anger, pride, and so forth. Fasting is a key method of reducing greed. Thus both Jain laypeople and mendicants practice fasting regularly. Non-grasping applies to many areas of life from personal to political. It includes not using more than one needs, and limits to holding positions of power.

Anekānta. *Anekānta* is translated as "relative pluralism" or "multiplicity of views. *Anekānta* literally means not (*an*) one (*eka*) side (*anta*). To illustrate this principle Jains tell a story of seven blind persons describing an elephant. Each touched just one part of the great elephant and spoke of the animal only in terms of the specific data acquired. Each description was therefore partial. Keeping in mind the existence of many "parts of the elephant," a Jain tries to look at more than one side of an issue. A Jain practicing *anekānta* does not get stuck in a single perspective without considering alternative views. But this does not mean that such a Jain fails to take a moral stand on issues.

Sudharman. Neither had yet become a *kevalin*. This meant that they were able to teach and administer the spiritual community. Indrabhūti Gautama attained *kevala-jñāna* shortly after Mahāvīra passed away. After that Sudharman took responsibility for handing down teachings preserved by Indrabhūti Gautama as well as those he garnered himself. Sudharman taught the scriptures orally for about twelve years after Mahāvīra passed away. The first generation of Mahāvīra's disciples ended with the death of Sudharman – the last *gaṇadhara* – who was 100 years old at the time. A disciple named Jambū succeeded him and taught for eight years. This explains why most Jain scriptures begin with words spoken by Sudharman to Jambū: "Oh long-lived One! Thus have I heard the following discourse from the Venerable [Mahāvīra]" (Jaini 1979: 46).

At least two centuries passed before Mahāvīra's Jain teachings were committed to writing. Much of the original oral teaching seems to have been lost due to famine and other hardships suffered by Jain communities. Jains generally agree that at one point their scripture comprised teachings that were handed down through the *gaṇadharas*. That texture contained a group of fourteen teachings (called *Pūrvas*) given by Pārśva, the twenty-third tīrthaṅkara. Digambara Jains believe that Bhadrabāhu (who traveled south to escape famine with his disciples) was the last person to have memorized the fourteen *Pūrvas*. Nowadays only descriptions of their contents survive. Eventually two sets of Jain scriptures emerged because the Digambaras did not recognize the validity of the Śvetāmbara scriptures. To this day, each sect uses its own collection of teachings. Digambaras tend to regard their scriptures as metaphorical, considering that the original records of both Pārśva's and Mahāvīra's teachings have been long lost.

A story on spiritual protection

Jains are non-theistic and do not rely upon divine aid. They say that a person becomes happy and purified by his or her own efforts. But there is more to this independence. Jains find protection in a state of mind devoted to non-violence. They are also inspired by contemplating the lives of the five types of holy persons revered in the *Five Homage Mantra.* The following story illustrates the Jain teaching on unprotectedness (*asharana*). It shows that although Jains do not speak of a Creator God, they have a spiritually profound life through blessings that come in response to their efforts at self-purification.

Once, in the days of Mahāvīra, there was a young man who had everything he thought he could ever want – a wonderful family, wealth, and so forth. He also had love. But when a terrible fever came upon him, he felt helpless. He could no longer digest anything, and even the sandalwood paste applied by his wife did not keep him from getting sicker. Then he remembered the words he once, in passing, heard Mahāvīra utter:

> When you are helpless and there is no protection, accept the protection of these four pure elements: *Arihanta* – those who have conquered all inner weaknesses; *Siddha* – the Perfect Souls; *Sahu* – the Saints, whose energy is vibrating in the universe; *Dharma* – the Pure Teaching which comes from the Enlightened Ones. With pure feeling, move toward that. When there is no protection, take the protection of these four.
>
> (Chitrabhanu 1980: 22)

The young man repeated Mahāvīra's words over and over. They provided a kind of mental blessing, and he was able to absorb their energy. He became calm and slept well. In the morning it seemed that the sandalwood paste and various herbal medicines given by the physician had helped. Maybe so, but the young man felt deeply that connecting to the truth of the four pure elements was the ultimate healer. He said:

> I connected to that invisible inner force, which is always there, and ultimately I became in tune with it. My mind which was creating so many turbulent thoughts became calm. In the state of calmness, I merged into that pure state, and I thought, "I take protection of all the Perfect Souls who became pure consciousness. I associate with their vibrations. I take refuge in the Conquerors or inner weaknesses. I join myself with the Saints of the universe wherever they are. And I merge in that Teaching of *Dharma,* that flow which comes from the compassion, love, and deep peace of the Omniscient Ones."
>
> (Chitrabhanu 1980: 23)

CROSS-OVER TEXTURE

Extraordinary perception Jain psychology

Generations of India's yogīs (Hindu and Buddhist as well as Jain) propounded teachings based on their meditative practices. Their descriptions and explanations of certain siddhis (supernormal powers) were refined through a long commentarial tradition.

*Unique knowledge (*kevala-jñāna*)*

Two classes of supernormal ability gained through meditation are described in the Jain texts as clairvoyance (*avadhi-jñāna*) and telepathy (*manaḥparyāya*). These are, however, inferior perceptions that become available prior to the ultimate attainment of *kevala-jñāna. Kevala-jñāna* is full knowledge that comes when all the veils obstructing omniscience are removed. *Kevala-jñāna* is direct perception of reality. This is the final state of mental development posited in Jain psychology.

Clairvoyance

Jains define clairvoyance (*avadhi-jñāna*) as the perception without use of the sense organs of things that have shape, color, and extension. All living beings have some capacity for clairvoyance. But the extent to which things can be seen depends on the type and quantity of karma affecting their jīvas. The most powerful clairvoyance includes penetration into a "countless number of cycles of time, both past and future" (Gopalan 1973: 104). Sometimes clairvoyance increases in scope and duration as time passes; but this does not always happen. Clairvoyance is limited to material objects.

Objects beyond the scope of *avadhi-jñāna* include jīvas, space, and time.

Telepathy

Jains define telepathy (*manaḥparyāya*) as the direct apprehension of another living being's thoughts, which are made of subtle matter. Only humans have the potential to perceive things through telepathy. To develop this capacity a human being must be free from passions, among other things. The extent of time and space that can be penetrated through telepathy depends upon the adept's state of spiritual development. Those who are less developed might know only the thoughts of beings within the range of one to eight past or future lives (Gopalan 1973: 106).

PART 3 JAIN PERFORMANCE

THE RITUAL OF HOLY DEATH: *SAṂLEKHANĀ*

A Jain uses life to prepare for a holy death. The most holy death is called ***saṃlekhanā***, which involves ceasing to eat or drink. The practice of holy death is relatively rare among Jains, yet it is an ideal that expresses the key values of Jain tradition. Having the option of adopting a holy death after leading a holy life prompts Jains to *deeply* consider the ethical implications of *ahiṃsā*. For his or her whole life every Jain aims to minimize violence in thought, word, and deed. Violence (*himsa*) brings the heaviest of all karma to a person's jīva. Thus how paradoxical it seems that for Jains the natural culmination of a holy life of non-violence is a holy death through self-starvation.

Ritual requirements for the holy death

Jain teachings forbid suicide because it involves violence to oneself. But the practice of holy death is not suicide. *Saṃlekhanā* is a ritual of leaving one's body in order to break free from karma and the cycle of rebirth. Jain scriptures name six circumstances in which a person may decide to perform the ritual of holy death (Shah 1998: 200):

1 Unpressured personal decision, as a voluntary act to pass out of the body.
2 Under conditions of pressing hardship, such as being held captive and tortured.
3 Under conditions of famine, when acceptable food cannot be obtained.
4 In the extreme of old age, with physical and mental impairment that disallows religious practice.
5 In case of terminal illness or fatal injury.
6 When natural death is imminent, as predicted through traditional means of prognostication.

There are two main requirements for undertaking *saṃlekhanā*: (1) A person must have enough determination as well as the physical strength to carry it out. (2) The person's family must approve of the decision. The ritual can take place in any peaceful environment, including home, forest, holy place, or monastery. However, sometimes the location many turn out to be an unseemly place, such as a prison.

The experience of *saṃlekhanā*

The process of ritually leaving the body includes taking vows, fasting, praying, and meditating. Before engaging in the ritual of holy death the aspirant should have a joyful mind that is free of all prejudice or ill will toward anyone. To achieve the proper attitude the person recites prayers of confession, asks forgiveness from others, and meditates on auspicious subjects. Then, after obtaining permission from his or her family, the aspirant vows to undertake *saṃlekhanā*. Thereafter, he or she gradually restricts the intake of nutriments – solid food, liquid food, and water in that order. Sometimes people take the full vows of an ascetic before death comes. In any case, no sensual pleasures are sought during the entire process. Here are two accounts of *saṃlekhanā* dating over seven centuries apart.

1 An inscription on a stone in the temple of Pārśvanātha in Karnataka from 1255 CE records the deaths of two illustrious Jain ascetics who took the vow of *saṃlekhanā* together. In part, their epitaph reads:

> They had given up even water. They were endowed with all virtues and character. They

had been spending their time in reading scriptures, meditation, complete silence and contemplation. They had acquired knowledge and made full progress. They were free from falsehood, delusion and desire; they had full control over their mind, body and speech.

(Tukol 1976: 46–47)

2 In 1973 Sudharmasāgara Muni went to a place of Jain pilgrimage to ritually leave his body. On the full moon day of 13 August he accepted the vow of *saṃlekhanā*, and began to take only milk and water. For the most part he maintained silence. On 26 August a cobra over six feet long slithered into the cave where Muniji was meditating. It opened its hood, and remained peacefully next to the ascetic who had spent years in the practice of non-violence. After about an hour Muniji blessed the snake. Addressing it, he said its work was over, and it could depart. Thereafter he gave up drinking milk, and began taking water only every two to three days. On 9 September Muniji had his last drink of water. About 15,000 people gathered to participate in the sacred event of Muniji's passing. Holy death came to Sudharmasāgara Muni at 1.30 p.m. on 24 September. His *saṃlekhanā* had lasted forty-two days.

RITUALS OF A HOLY LIFE: PIOUS ACTION

The ritual of holy death is no substitute for living a virtuous life. No Jain would expect a jīva that is heavily mired in karma to suddenly shed a great mass of impurity through the ritual of holy death. *Saṃlekhanā* is appropriate only for persons who have consistently worked to purify themselves through virtuous action and the practice of austerities over many years. Jains believe that every jīva is intrinsically pure. But that purity is marred by non-virtuous action. Karma attaches itself to the soul whenever a living being opens itself up to karmic vibrations – and that karma cannot be eliminated suddenly by any single gesture, no matter how wonderful. Yet gradually karma can be removed through practice of the **Three Jewels**: Right Thought, Right Faith, and Right Conduct. Only after a life dedicated to these Three Jewels would either a Jain *śramaṇa* or a householder finally be prepared to ritually remove a few remaining traces of karma by undertaking the ritual of holy death.

Jains live by an ethical code based in non-violence. Yet they are realistic in supposing that their souls regularly accumulate karma due to an imperfect observance of ahiṃsā. Thus a key ritual done by both Jain *śramaṇas* and householders is the penitential retreat (*pratikramaṇa*), which is a rite of confession designed to cleanse the jīva. The Sanskrit word *prati-kramaṇa* means "turning back" in the sense of returning the soul to its original state of purity. During the ritual Jains recite prayers in which they: (1) request penance to rid the jīva of karma, (2) ask forgiveness for having harmed any living being by walking or any other movement, and (3) ask forgiveness for committing any of eighteen types of sins, namely "taking life, untruth, stealing, improper sexual relations, hoarding and attachment to material things, anger, pride, deceit, greed, attraction, aversion, discord, accusation, slander, excessive feelings of pleasure and pain, defamation, lying and deception, and misguided beliefs" (Shah 1998: 191). Prayers recited during the penitential retreat also include the *Five Homage Mantra*, praises to the tīrthaṅkaras, and reverential prayers to Jain mendicants of the past, present, and future. The penitential retreat is a daily observance designed to eliminate the particles of karma that have attached themselves to the jīva in the course of everyday activities. "If *pratikramana* is not performed, the soul continues to be obscured by karmic particles and purification may become impossible" (Shah 1998: 186). In addition to daily penance, Jains of all sects participate in an annual rite of confession. For a period of eight to ten days, Jain laypersons take temporary vows that bring them closer to participating in the lifestyle of monks and nuns. People confess their negative actions and make pleas for forgiveness. Finally they extend forgiveness to all living beings, reciting these words from the *Pratikramaṇa Sūtra*:

khāmemi savvajīve savve jīvā khamantu me
metti me savvabhūesu veraṃ majjha na keṇavi

I ask pardon of all living creatures; may all of them pardon me. May I have a friendly relationship with all beings and unfriendly with none.

(Quoted in Jaini 1979: 216)

BOX 8.4 A SPIRITUAL PATH: THE SIX ESSENTIAL DUTIES

Vows for a Jain layperson

Vows guide the spiritual practice of Jain laymen and laywomen. The Sanskrit term for vow is *vrata*, based on the root *vṛ*, meaning to "fence in." This etymology suggests that the *vratas* help people limit their activities. There are four classes of *vratas*: (1) eight basic restraints (*mūlaguṇas*), (2) five restricted vows (*aṇuvratas*), (3) three vows that strengthen the basic restraints (*guṇavratas*), and (4) four vows of spiritual discipline (*śikṣāvratas*). These are supplemented by the non-obligatory vow to undertake the ritual of holy death.

Eight basic restraints (mūlaguṇas). This vow involves refraining from consuming meat, alcohol, honey, and five types of figs. The reason for this eightfold restraint is that each of these foods contains many single-sensed organisms (see Table 8.1).

Five restricted vows (aṇuvratas). See Table 8.3.

Three vows that strengthen the basic restraints (guṇavratas). To decrease the amount of harm caused to living beings, and to help purify one's jīva, a Jain further limits his or her activity. The restraints involve vows in which a person determines to do the following:

1. Limit the location of one's activity to a certain distance in all directions away from where one normally stays, or to an area geographically bound between certain mountains and rivers, for example.
2. Limit certain tasks or use of various items in order to minimize the causing of harm. For example, do not cook at night when more insects tend to fly into the cooking flame, use only filtered water so as not to harm one-sense jīvas, do not eat foods such as potatoes that tend to harbor many microscopic jīvas, and so forth.
3. Refrain from unwholesome activity such as gambling, gossiping, and so forth.

Four vows of spiritual discipline (śikṣāvratas).

1. Meditate for forty-eight minutes quietly on peace. This represents one-thirtieth of the day at each sitting spent in equanimity.
2. Make a further (temporary) restriction on the area in which one remains. This is usually the place of retreat.
3. Fast on four holy days every month, namely the eighth and fourteenth days of the waxing and the waning lunar periods.
4. Perform charity (*dāna*) by making food, place of residence, medicines, and reading materials available to mendicants and other appropriate parties.

The vow to undertake* saṃlekhanā *(not obligatory). This is a supplemental vow taken by few Jains. To pass from this life by gradually restricting one's intake of food and liquids is upheld as an ideal way to cleanse the jīva of all dust of karma that remains at the end of life.

Table 8.3 The five main Jain vows

Vow	*Sanskrit term*	*Explanation**
Non-violence	Ahiṃsā	Avoid harm to any living being that has a jīva
Truthfulness	Satya	Avoid saying anything untruthful, including gossip
Non-stealing	Acaurya	Do not take anything that is not given to one
Celibacy	Brahmācarya	Monks and nuns are celibate; monogamous marriages; no misuse of the senses, etc.
Non-attachment	Aparigraha	Avoid attachment to worldly objects and power

*Jain tradition gives very detailed and comprehensive explanations.

KEY POINTS

- Tīrthaṅkaras appear at regular intervals in the course of a world cycle. They are born as human beings, and deities do not assist them. This stark human independence is a key feature of the Jain tradition.
- Jains are non-theistic, and do not expect divine assistance. Yet they rely on tīrthaṅkaras to guide them on the path to liberation. Tīrthaṅkaras are worthy of respect because they achieve the ultimate goal of liberation by their own efforts.
- Vardhamāna Mahāvīra is the last tīrthaṅkara of the present cosmic half-cycle. The existing Jain canon reflects concerns voiced by people of Mahāvīra's day (sixth century BCE), as well as traditions that appear to be much older.
- Vardhamāna Mahāvīra is said to have been an older contemporary of Gautama Buddha. Both lived in the middle Ganges basin, established fourfold spiritual communities, and had disciples who believed they achieved liberation from *saṃsāra.*
- Jains are divided into two main groups: Digambara (sky-clad) and Śvetāmbara (white-clad). They disagree about the nature of non-attachment, which involves divergent opinions on the importance of wearing clothes.
- Jains aim to purify themselves by eliminating all action that causes the subtle dust of karma to cling to their jīvas. A jīva that is free of karmic dust will ascend straight up to the upper reaches of the universe, and is never again weighted down and mired in the material cycle of birth and death.
- To free their jīvas of all karma, some mentally strong and morally dedicated Jain practitioners practice the ritual of holy death (*saṃlekhanā*), usually in their old age.

STUDY QUESTIONS

1. Which Jain tīrthaṅkaras are known to be historical persons? When and where did they live?
2. What is the relationship between jīva and karma in Jain thought?
3. What is *kevala-jñāna*, and what happens when a person attains it?
4. What cultural conditions were developing in India's Ganges basin during the sixth century BCE?
5. What distinguishes Digambara Jains from Śvetāmbara Jains? Why did the Sthānakavāsī and Terāpanthī sects splinter off from the Śvetāmbaras?
6. Why does one need to consider the meaning of *divyadhvani* to understand the role of scripture in the Jain religion?
7. What is involved in the Jain ritual of holy death (*saṃlekhanā*)?

GLOSSARY

ahiṃsā (Sanskrit) Non-violence. The core value of Jain tradition, which involves minimizing harm to oneself or other beings through acts of body, speech, and mind.

anekānta (Sanskrit) Not one-sided. Non-bias. The ideal perspective in Jain tradition, which involves seeing all sides of an issue or situation.

aparigraha (Sanskrit) Non-grasping. A form of non-violence in Jain tradition that entails not clinging to material things or opinions.

brāhmaṇa (Sanskrit) A member of the priestly class of ancient India, according to Vedic teachings. The caste persists today among Hindus.

Digambara (Sanskrit) The "sky-clad" community of Jains whose monks take a vow of nudity.

divyadhvani (Sanskrit) Literally, divine sound. Sound emitted from a Jain who attains the highest knowledge. Digambaras believe it is inarticulate sound that can only be interpreted by special disciples. Śvetāmbaras believe it is divine because certain non-humans (such as godlings) can understand it.

Jina (Sanskrit) Conqueror, victor. Title given to Jain tīrthaṅkaras because they are victorious over the suffering of *saṃsāra.*

jīva (Sanskrit) Life force or soul. Used by Jains to describe any living being with one to five senses, including earth bodies, human beings, godlings, and so forth.

karma (Sanskrit) Literally, action. Actions of body, speech, and mind that bring effects in line with their causes. Jains, Buddhists, and Hindus have slightly different interpretations on the nature of such action.

kevala-jñāna (Sanskrit) Literally, unique knowledge. The highest realization according to Jain teachings, after which a person becomes a siddha upon dying.

kṣatriya (Sanskrit) A person of the warrior or ruling class in ancient India according to Vedic teachings. Contemporary Hindus still abide by such notions of caste.

mantra (Sanskrit) A set of sacred words whose vibrations have a purifying effect on the person who recites them. For Jains and Hindus the most inclusive sacred word is AUṀ.

mokṣa (Sanskrit) Liberation from the cycle of rebirth. Jains and Hindus aspire to this. Buddhists (and sometimes Jains) call it nirvāṇa.

saṃlekhanā (Sanskrit) Jain ritual of holy death in which consumption of food is gradually curtailed, until nothing is eaten or drunk.

saṃsāra (Sanskrit) The cycle of rebirth. Literally, wandering around.

siddha (Sanskrit) The disembodied jīva (soul) of a Jain who has attained liberation. These beings abide at the apex of the universe.

siddhi (Sanskrit) A supernormal power such as clairvoyance or telepathy that comes as a side-product of meditation. Discussed in Jain, Buddhist, and Hindu texts.

śramaṇa (Sanskrit) Literally, a striver. A renunciate mendicant of India who seeks liberation from saṃsāra.

Śvetāmbara (Sanskrit) The "white-clad" community of Jains, who wear clothes.

Three Jewels In Jain tradition: Right Thought, Right Faith, Right Conduct. All these hearken to the principle of ahiṃsā (non-violence).

tīrtha (Sanskrit) Literally, ford or crossing-place. Metaphorically, a ford that enables one to cross the river of *saṃsāra*. Refers to Jain holy places and the fourfold spiritual community that includes monks, nuns, laymen, and laywomen.

tīrthaṅkara (Sanskrit: *tīrtha* = ford, crossing-place, *kara* from *kṛ* = to make) Human beings born into the world to show living beings how to cross the ford (stream) of *saṃsāra*. They reintroduce the Jain path, and inspire disciples to establish *tīrthas*. Twenty-four appear in each phase of an endless cosmic cycle.

KEY READING

Dundas, Paul (2002) *The Jains* (2nd edn), London and New York: Routledge.

Jacobi, Hermann (trans.) (1968a, b) *Jaina Sutras*, 2 parts, New York: Dover Publications.

Jaini, Padmanabh S. (1979) *The Jaina Path of Purification*, Berkeley and Los Angeles: University of California Press.

Lalwani, K. C. (1975) *Sramana Bhagavan Mahāvīra: Life and Doctrine*, Calcutta: Minerva Associates (Publications).

Sangave, Vilas A. (1997) *Jaina Religion and Community*, compiled and edited by B. Srinivasa Murthy, Long Beach, CA: Long Beach Publications.

Shah, Natubhai (1998) *Jainism: The World of Conquerors*, 2 vols, Brighton and Portland: Sussex Press.

Wiley, Kristi L. (2004) *Historical Dictionary of Jainism*, Lanham, MD: The Scarecrow Press.

CHAPTER 9

Buddhist tradition

TIMELINE

	BCE	
Gautama, the Buddha	ca. 563–483 or d. ca. 411–400	
	Third century	*Jātakas* first written
Aśoka Maurya reigns	200s	
	29–17	Nikāya Buddhist canon written in Pāli language
	First century BCE	Gandhāra art begins
	CE	
	First century	Chinese begin translating Indian Buddhist texts
	Fifth century	Buddhaghosa writes Pāli commentaries
Bodhidharma	fl. 480–520	
Hui-neng (China)	638–713	
	668–935	Silla Dynasty (Korea)
Padmasambhava travels to Tibet	746	
	750–800	Pāla Dynasty (India)
Kūkai (Japan)	774–835	
	809–823	Emperor Saga reigns (Japan)
	845	Persecution of Buddhists (China)
	935–1392	Koryŏ Dynasty (Korea)
Milarepa (Tibet)	1040–1135	
Hōnen (Japan)	1133–1212	
Eisai (Japan)	1141–1215	
Chinul (Korea)	1158–1210	
	1185–1336	Kamakura period (Japan)
Shinran (Japan)	1173–1261	
Dōgen (Japan)	1200–1253	
Nichiren (Japan)	1222–1282	
Tsong-kha-pa (Tibet)	1357–1419	
Hakuin (Japan)	1685–1768	
Bashō (Japan)	1644–1694	
Sulak Sivaraksa (Thailand)	b. 1933	
Tenzin Gyatso (Tibet, India)	b. 1935	

Buddhism is named after a man called Gautama. He was given the title Buddha or Awakened One because he woke up to see reality as it is. Gautama Buddha lived in the sixth century BCE during a culturally fertile time when cash flow, trade, cities, and armies were all growing in north India. Gautama was part of a heterodox *śramaṇa* movement that challenged the authority of the Āryan religious system headed by brāhmaṇa priests. Gautama established orders of monks and nuns. The social forms of Buddhist monastic life eventually spread throughout Asia. Springing from early Buddhism, the tradition split into two major groups, now known as **Nikāya** and **Mahāyāna**.

The Nikāya Buddhist canon was first written in the Pāli language. The Nikāya tradition is called Southern Buddhism because it took root in Sri Lanka, Myanmar, Siam, Kampuchea, and Laos. Mahāyāna Buddhism is based on Indian texts written in Sanskrit that were eventually lost in India, but translated into Chinese and later Tibetan. It is called Northern Buddhism because it spread into Tibet, Central Asia, China, Korea, and Japan. Both Nikāya and Mahāyāna Buddhism heavily influenced Vietnam.

PART 1 BUDDHIST PLAYERS

THE ULTIMATE PRINCIPLE

Universal dharma and Buddha-dharma

Dharma is the transcendent principle of the universe that upholds all existence. Gautama's teachings are called **Buddha-dharma** because they are based in his discovery of the law of the universe. Buddha boiled down the universal dharma to four great facts, usually called the Four Noble Truths. Buddha discovered in the very fabric of the universe the secret of how to transcend the universe.

IMAGINAL PLAYERS

Enlightened beings

The concept of what kinds of beings are in the cosmos differs between Nikāya and Mahāyāna Buddhists. Nikāya Buddhists limit their discussion to (generally) four buddhas of past history, and one future buddha named Maitreya who abides in a place known as **Tuṣita heaven**. Mahāyāna Buddhists completely agree with the Nikāya Buddhists with regard to the five buddhas. However, they also speak of several more enlightened beings who are objects of prayer, including the Buddha of Boundless Light (who is the focus of Pure Land Mahāyāna practice), and several bodhisattvas (who are very popular in Tibetan Buddhism).

Buddha Amitābha (Amitayus)

The Mahāyāna Buddhist theory of the three **buddha bodies** accounts for the appearance of beings in the imaginal realm. A **buddha** or a high-level **bodhisattva** can appear to practitioners in a visionary form known in Sanskrit as the *sambhogakāya*, where *kāya* means body, and bhoga is from the root bhuj, which means to enjoy – as in a meal. (Not all sects of Buddhism acknowledge or emphasize the sambhogakāya. But visionary buddhas and bodhisattvas are important in Northern Buddhism among Pure Land, Shingon, and Tibetan Buddhists.)

Bodhisattva Avalokiteśvara

Avalokiteśvara is the lord (*īsvara*) who gazes down upon (*avalokita*) suffering living beings with compassion. This bodhisattva specializes in freeing people from pain and teaches them compassion. Avalokiteśvara is known as Chen-re-zig in Tibetan, Kwan-yin in Chinese, and Kannon in Japanese. Faithful Tibetan Buddhists consider that Avalokiteśvara appears in the person of the fourteenth Dalai Lama, as well as in the imaginal realm. The Sanskrit mantra associated with this bodhisattva of compassion is: OṂ MAṆI PADME HŪṂ. Pure Land Buddhists of East Asia pray to this visionary bodhisattva for mercy.

Plate 9.1 "OṂ MAṆI PADME HŪṂ." This is the Tibetan mantra of compassion associated with the Bodhisattva Avalokiteśvara. Faithful Tibetan Buddhists consider the Dalai Lama Tenzin Gyatso to be a human manifestation of this Bodhisattva because he continually meditates to generate compassion for all living beings in this world. This stone-carved mantra is found near the Dalai Lama's residence in Dharamsala, India.

Bodhisattva Mañjūśrī

Mañjūśrī is the bodhisattva of wisdom. This bodhisattva is depicted in iconography with a sword in his right hand that symbolizes discriminating wisdom, and a book in his left that symbolizes learning. These items indicate that Mañjūśrī helps dedicated practitioners develop their wisdom. According to the *Lotus Sūtra* (a Mahāyāna text) Mañjūśrī was Gautama Buddha's teacher in a past life. This wisdom bodhisattva also appeared to the Tibetan Buddhist reformer Tsong-kha-pa in the fourteenth century, among other fortunate disciples through the ages. Mañjūśrī's Sanskrit **mantra** is: OṂ ARA PACANA DHĪ.

Bodhisattva Tārā

Tārā is a feminine bodhisattva who shows up in twenty-one colors. Her white form symbolizes health and long life, while her green form symbolizes prosperity in life and spiritual practice. Tārā's outstanding feature is a quick response to the plight of others who appeal to her for help. She frees people from fear and clears obstacles. Tārā's mystic lineage demonstrates the mental nature of the imaginal bodhisattvas: Tārā was created from one of the tears of Avalokiteśvara, the bodhisattva of compassion. In turn, Avalokiteśvara was created from the mind of Amitābha, the Buddha of Boundless Light. And Amitābha was created from the mind of a personification of the primal ground of awareness known as the Ādi Buddha. Tārā's Sanskrit mantra is: OM TĀRE TUTĀRE TURE SVĀHĀ.

Saṃsāra's invisible beings

Buddhist cosmology speaks of many godlings that are not normally seen by human beings. These exist within saṃsāra, which means they are not enlightened and are therefore still subject to rebirth. Buddhists do not worship these godlings, but recognize their existence. There are different imaginal places where godlings live, including: the arena where the proud demi-gods (also called titans) endlessly fight; the Heaven of the Thirty-three (godlings) headed by Indra; the arena of the godling Yama; Tuṣita heaven where Maitreya, the future buddha, abides; and the **Abodes of Brahmā** where (in a realm of pure form) the godling Brahmā manifests the four pure emotions of loving kindness, compassion, sympathetic joy, and equanimity.

Buddhist cosmology also speaks of two types of beings with forms of life that are lower than humans or animals: hungry ghosts who endlessly crave food and drink; and hell beings who suffer tremendously in either hot or cold regions of hell. Humans do not usually see these lower beings, although on occasion they do appear in visions and dreams. Like the godlings of saṃsāra, hungry ghosts and hell beings will be reborn over and over again somewhere in saṃsāra until they become enlightened. Some bodhisattvas visit them or live with them so as to be of help. In addition, some people regularly leave a small portion of each meal as an offering for the hungry ghosts.

EXCEPTIONAL PLAYERS

Supreme buddhas

Gautama, the founder of Indian Buddhism, is counted as the fourth or seventh **supreme buddha**. Maitreya, the future buddha, is expected to descend from Tuṣita heaven into our world when all remnants of Gautama's teaching are forgotten. Maitreya is a messiah figure depicted in artwork seated on a Western-style chair with one leg crossed and the other touching the ground, as if poised to come and help worldlings quickly. Twelve acts characterize the life of every supreme buddha beginning with a descent from Tuṣita heaven, culminating in an awakening, and ending with passing away in the town of Kuśinagara. (Gautama's biographers were aware of this tradition, and made his life story fit the pattern.)

Arhats

An **arhat** is an exceptional person who sees reality as it is. Due to the realization of **non-self**, arhats escape the round of rebirths. Many of Gautama's disciples became arhats. Nikāya Buddhists emphasize the goal of becoming an arhat – which is accomplished in four stages as the person becomes a stream-entrant, once-returner, non-returner, and finally arhat. In the course of this spiritual development ten fetters (mental obstacles) are destroyed. (1) Stream-entrants are never again reborn in saṃsāra's lower realms (as animals, hungry ghosts, or hell beings) because they no longer: believe in **ātman**, an eternal self; consider that rituals eliminate ignorance; and doubt that Buddha-dharma is a proper guide to **nirvāṇa**. (2) Once-returners are reborn into the human realm at most one more time because they have weakened sensual desires and hatred. (3) Non-returners are reborn into the pure form and formless realms of saṃsāra, but never again as human beings because they have destroyed sensual desires and hatred. (4) Arhats are never reborn again after passing away. In their last life they may still experience physical suffering, but it does not cause mental **duḥkha** because they have destroyed subtle desire for the pure form and formless realms, pride, restlessness, and finally ignorance.

Bodhisattvas

A person becomes a bodhisattva the moment he or she generates **bodhicitta**, the profound thought to become enlightened based on great compassion for the suffering of others. Bodhisattvas practice the six perfections after vowing to work for the sake of all sentient beings – including animals, hell beings, one's enemies, and so on. The six perfections are:

- ***Generosity.*** This involves giving material aid, freedom from fear, and helpful advice. Bodhisattvas cultivate a keen sense of generosity toward all sentient beings without exception. They work to ever increase their spirit of giving even for those who may try to harm them.
- ***Morality.*** This involves steps on the Noble Eightfold Path in the category of morality, namely right speech, right action, and right livelihood. Bodhisattvas cultivate loving kindness (giving happiness to others) and compassion (removing the suffering of others) while engaging in these acts.

- *Patience.* This is not a passive withdrawal from the world. It is a courageous practice that gives inner strength and freedom from fear in difficult situations. It involves the forbearance of forgiveness, and enduring hardship.
- *Joyous effort.* This is enthusiasm to persevere in virtuous work. Bodhisattvas adopt a joyful attitude toward religious practice, and never give up. This is opposite to laziness, discouragement, or a sense of inferiority that says: "This will never help." "How could I possibly do this?"
- *Calm abiding.* This is right contemplation on the Noble Eightfold Path. This balanced, flexible, and concentrated mental state (known as **śamatha**) leads to an experience of the pure form and formless realms.
- *Wisdom.* The perfection of wisdom involves seeing the actual nature of phenomena. It is the opposite of ignorance. Bodhisattvas recognize non-self as applied to everything in the universe. This means they see that all phenomena arise depending on causes and conditions, and hence are empty of self-nature. The Sanskrit word for emptiness is **śūnyatā**.

Gautama Buddha (563–483 BCE)

The following story of Gautama's life is in line with a traditional insider perspective. Many elements are symbolic. Other details are taken from Buddhist scriptures that are supposed to relate Gautama's words about his experiences and mental development. It is important to keep in mind that Buddhist tradition finds meaning in these events, although they do not always reflect reality from a strictly historical perspective.

Former lives

On occasion Buddha related ***Jātaka* tales** about his previous lives to inform his audience about their meetings in past lives. The *Jātakas* were put into writing starting in the third century BCE. They resemble Aesop's fables, in which a moral encapsulates a brief tale of talking animals or other adventuresome beings. The *Jātaka* tales are lessons on character development based on the many lives of the bodhisattva Sumedha (including humans and non-humans) up until his eventual birth as Gautama Buddha. They are grouped according to the moral perfections of: generosity, morality, renunciation, wisdom, energy, patience, truthfulness, determination, loving kindness, and equanimity.

The *Jātakas* begin by illustrating the powerful turn of mind called bodhicitta. With this aspiration to become enlightened for the sake of all living beings, Sumedha started on the path to Buddha-hood. It so happened that four innumerable and 100,000 eons ago the ascetic Sumedha left his hermitage in his bark garments and flew through the air (demonstrating a **siddhi**). He noticed a crowd of people, and was told that the path was being cleared for Buddha Dīpaṃkara – one Buddha in a long line of Awakened Ones. Upon hearing the word "buddha," his heart spontaneously became joyful. Sumedha wanted to help clear the path, not to miss this opportunity to practice virtue. In doing so, he maintained awareness of the sound "buddha, buddha, buddha" in his heart. Sumedha had not finished clearing his part of the path by the time Dīpaṃkara arrived. Seeing this, the ascetic prostrated himself, and spread his long hair for Dīpaṃkara to use as a mat. At that moment, face down in the mud, with Buddha trampling his hair, Sumedha generated a profound thought: He resolved to become a supreme buddha like Dīpaṃkara.

Early life

Gautama was born in the town of Kapilāvastu, capital of the Śākyan confederacy in the Himālayan foothills. His father Śuddhodana was a tribal chieftain who married two sisters in cross-cousin marriages: Prajāpati and Māyā. Māyā, the younger sister, gave birth to Gautama, but died when the prince was just a week old. Therefore Aunt Prajāpati raised the boy whom some texts call Siddhartha. According to custom, brāhmaṇa soothsayers were invited to assess the infant's potential. Traditional stories of Buddha's life say they agreed that the child would become a great *dharmacakrin* or turner of the wheel of law. Yet it was unclear to all but one brāhmaṇa whether the child would become a worldly ruler or spiritual teacher. The seer who predicted a religious future for the child kept an eye on him over the years, and became one of Gautama's earliest disciples. But Śuddhodana resisted the notion that his son would abandon his kṣatriya (warrior) status to adopt the life of a wanderer. Hoping that Gautama would never become disillusioned with power and politics, Śuddhodana provided his son with luxurious meals, musical entertainment, and courtesans. At age 16 Gautama married his cousin Yaśodharā, and thus led a householder's life.

Plate 9.2 "Buddha's mother giving birth." As Buddha's mother Māyā Devī conceived, she dreamed of a white elephant who touched her side. The child was born in the Lumbinī Gardens as she was *en route* to her native home. As Māyā Devī stood with her right hand stretched out to hold the branch of a tree, it bent down to assist her. Then the future Buddha was born from her right side. Māyā Devī died seven days later.

The Great Renunciation

Chieftain Śuddhodana remained apprehensive about his son's fate for nearly three decades. Thus, when Gautama wished to leave the palace compounds at Kapilāvastu to see the spring groves in full bloom, Śuddhodana ordered his son's path to be cleared of anything repulsive. It is said that the worldly godlings were jealous of the city's sparkling beauty with its streamers and garlands, so they made four figures appear to Gautama in turn: one old, one diseased, one dead, and yet another who was dead to the world. The old man had bulging veins, loose teeth, wrinkles, scrawny hair, and patchy skin. The sick man was panting and muttering, with his swollen belly heaving and limp arms dangling. The dead man was hard like a piece of wood, being carried to his funeral pyre with weeping relatives in tow. After witnessing these miserable scenes, Gautama was stunned like a lion jabbed with a poisoned dart.

The shock of the old man, sick man, and corpse abated only when Gautama saw a scrawny śramaṇa wandering around begging alms. At this fourth sight Gautama was moved to renounce his life of luxury and join the śramaṇa movement in search of an end to duḥkha. What passed as ordinary features of life in the Ganges Valley gave Gautama an aesthetic shock. Determined to find an end to suffering, the prince stole away from the palace compound into the forest with one companion and his horse late one night – against the wishes of his father. This rejection of his kṣatriya roots is known as the Great Renunciation. Gautama sent his companion Chandaka home with the horse and jewelry; cut his hair to the length of two inches (a style he kept for the rest of his days because his hair did not grow); and dressed himself in rags. For the next six years the former prince led a *śramaṇa's* life of poverty and renunciation.

The Ascetic period

The former Śākyan prince sought spiritual guidance, and studied under two gurūs who taught him how to transcend the sense desire realm, and enter the pure form and formless realms. He was so avid in his spiritual labors that people called him a *mahaśramaṇa*, great striver. Under Āḷāra Kālāma's guidance Gautama passed through the four boundless emotions of the

Brahmā Abodes in the pure form realm, and up to the third level of the realm of no form known as "nothing whatsoever". But that was not enough for Gautama, so he sought Udraka Rāma's guidance and attained the fourth and highest level – neither perception nor non-perception. This was no small accomplishment. Yet, the great striver was not satisfied because he realized that these high spiritual states were still in the realm of saṃsāra. Gautama found that negative attitudes could still manifest once he descended from the pure form and formless realms. (For instance, although unbounded love characterized experience on the first level in the pure form realm, that love could be corrupted by hatred once the meditation was over.) Even reaching the bounds of experience itself at the level of neither perception nor non-perception, the mahaśramaṇa felt no assurance that ties to the cycle of birth and death were cut. Thus, feeling he could learn no more from any teacher, Gautama struck out on his own. At that point he had five disciples who followed him – one of whom was the brāhmaṇa who had predicted his spiritual vocation some three decades earlier.

The Middle Way

Gautama took up a regimen of severe asceticism, thinking it might help him conquer suffering and attain a deathless state. Consuming dirt, herbs, and the soup of one bean a day, he grew emaciated to the point of collapse. Hair fell from his pores; his limbs and hair became discolored; and his spine poked out from the front of his stomach. Then, Gautama dreamed that a woman would offer him food; it would be helpful, and he should accept it. Thus, knocking on death's door, the mahaśramaṇa determined that this extreme practice was opening the way to death, but not to deathless enlightenment. Feeling he could not realize anything more in such a weakened condition, Gautama accepted food when a village girl offered him rice and yogurt. Partaking of this offering reflected a new attitude toward spiritual practice, which involved rejecting the extremes of denial and indulgence. (Buddhists call this the Middle Way.) Then the mahaśramaṇa determined that no matter what happened to him – live or die – he would not budge until he had found a way to conquer duḥkha. With such determination, new things started happening to Gautama as he stayed in what became known as the Immovable Spot.

The enlightenment

Prior to his enlightenment, Gautama experienced a kratophany as he sat under a fig tree near the Nairanjana River determined to escape compulsory rebirth and thus conquer death. Three challenges put to the mahaśramaṇa by a character called Māra, lord of illusion: (1) Māra offered his daughters, but Gautama promptly identified them by name as discontent, delight, and desire. (2) Māra attacked the mahaśramaṇa with his army, but Gautama turned the fiery arrows into flowers by meditating on compassion. (3) Māra tried to snare Gautama with the illusion of self; but the mahaśramaṇa recognized himself to be the actual house builder who constructs the illusion of an independent self.

The night in which Gautama attained enlightenment was divided into three watches:

- ***First watch***: 6 p.m. to 10 p.m. Gautama recalled his own past lives including name, family, diet, pleasures, pains, and death. His inner vision was unobstructed as he opened the divine eye.
- ***Second watch***: 10 p.m. to 2 a.m. The universe appeared as though in a spotless mirror as Gautama's divine eye opened further. He saw the past lives of countless beings, disappearing and reappearing over eons, and generated great compassion. He understood the law of karma and its fruits: harmful deeds produce suffering, while kind deeds produce happiness.
- ***Third watch***: 2 a.m. to 6 a.m. Gautama's divine eye was fully opened, and he awakened by gaining wisdom and ending sorrow. He realized the Four Great Facts, which posit that suffering ends (nirvāṇa) with the cessation of birth, old age, and death. He comprehended the chain of dependent arising devolving from enlightenment to ignorance.

Gautama invented a mindfulness meditation that involved careful attention to his mind–body process. He initiated this meditation from the fourth *dhyāna* of equanimity in the realm of pure form (see Table 9.1). Through it, he deeply understood the **three marks of**

existence: impermanence, suffering, and lack of intrinsic self. Thus Gautama became a buddha. He woke up, and would not be subject to rebirth again. After awakening to the nature of reality, he remained in contemplation for seven weeks. Then, prompted by a godling, the new buddha overcame an initial reluctance to teach, and declared that the path to transcendence was open to all.

BOX: 9.1 SYMBOLS: MĀRA'S CHALLENGES

The character Māra, lord of illusion, functions as a religious symbol in Buddha's biography. In Buddhist cosmology he is situated at the highest level of saṃsāra, acting like a guardian whose job is to incite desire so that beings will remain in the cycle of becoming. Ironically, Māra's appearance seems to inspire Gautama to clarify the terms of his own search for enlightenment. In Buddha's life story Māra appears at critical moments when Gautama is at a turning point:

- Māra asks Gautama to turn back when the prince leaves home to embark on the Great Renunciation.
- Māra appears immediately prior to Gautama's enlightenment, and tries three times to dissuade the mahaśramaṇa from going forward with enlightenment by offering his daughters, attacking with his army, and presenting the illusion of self.
- After Gautama awakens, Māra appears to persuade him to pass away without teaching; but the new Buddha promises to pass away only after the fourfold **saṃgha** of monks, nuns, laymen, and laywomen is fully established.
- Three months before Buddha passes away Māra appears to collect upon Gautama's promise made some forty-five years earlier. At that point, since the saṃgha was fully established and neither Ānanda nor any other disciple requested that their teacher live to his full complement of years, Buddha agrees to pass away after three months.

Past the sense desire realm ruled by Māra are two higher realms of saṃsāra. The three realms of saṃsāra involve a range of experiences for sentient beings – from hot hells to rarified mental states where there is no form whatsoever. The trouble with all these states is that beings are bound to cycle around from one type to another endlessly – unless they attain enlightenment by seeing the true nature of reality (see Box 9.4).

Table 9.1 Realms of saṃsāra

Abstract States	8th dhyāna	Neither perception nor non-perception	No form
	7th dhyāna	Nothing whatsoever	No form
	6th dhyāna	Boundless consciousness	No form
	5th dhyāna	Boundless space	No form
Brahmā Abodes	4th dhyāna	Boundless equanimity	Pure form
	3rd dhyāna	Boundless joy	Pure form
	2nd dhyāna	Boundless compassion	Pure form
	1st dhyāna	Boundless love	Pure form
High	High rebirth	Worldly godlings (Devas)	Sense desire
	High rebirth	Titans	Sense desire
	High rebirth	Humans	Sense desire
Low	Low rebirth	Animals	Sense desire
	Low rebirth	Hungry ghosts	Sense desire
	Low rebirth	Hell beings	Sense desire

Establishing the saṃgha

The Buddhist saṃgha was fourfold, comprising monks, nuns, laymen, and laywomen. But the establishment of a saṃgha for women seemed to cause Gautama some hesitation. After her husband Śuddhodana (Gautama's father) died, Prajāpati came with "five hundred" Śākyan women to see the new Buddha. Gautama was her sister's child, whom she had raised from early infancy. She asked him to found a spiritual community for women – but only after being asked three times did he consent. On the third try, Buddha admitted that nothing inherent in a woman would prevent her from awakening. Thus, having articulated the egalitarian potential of all women, and seeing his aunt's single-mindedness, Buddha established a **bhikṣunī** order. Members of the early saṃgha included members of Gautama's family, other members of the Śākya clan, and people from neighboring clans.

While the new śramaṇa tradition was quite successful, there were detractors – not the least of whom was Devadatta, the jealous cousin who twice tried to kill Buddha. Some laypeople accused Buddha of splitting up families by drawing not only men but also women away from their household lives. Under such lines of attack Buddha and his renunciate saṃgha came up

BOX 9.2 INTERPRETATIONS: ADVICE ON LEARNING

A Buddhist is advised to approach the Buddha-dharma in three stages, by: (1) listening to the teachings, (2) thinking about them, and (3) meditating upon them (Tsong-kha-pa 2000: 55–63).

Listening. A person should be very attentive when listening to religious teachings, so that the meaning can be understood. Listening involves contemplating the benefits that come from hearing the Buddha-dharma. The benefits include understanding how to lead one's life. To help one listen more closely, the person is advised to respect the teacher. A metaphor is used to illustrate three faults of listening that a person should avoid. The person should avoid being like three pots: one that is turned upside-down, one that is dirty inside, and one that has a hole in it. The upside-down pot indicates that one should be receptive to the teachings. The dirty pot suggests that one should have a pure mind (free of arrogance or contempt) while listening. The pot with a hole points out that one should not be forgetful or distracted when hearing religious teachings.

Thinking. It is not enough to just hear the words of Buddha's teachings. After listening, a person should consider the meaning of the texts, asking questions like: What sense do the teachings make? How might contradictions in the teachings be resolved? How could these teachings be applied?

Meditating. After intellectually analyzing the spiritual teachings, a person must meditate on what one has discerned by thinking. This involves "mixing one's mind with dharma" by taking a realization and contemplating it deeply. For example, a teaching on the virtue of patience might be first heard, and then analyzed with questions such as: What are the benefits of patience? What are the ill-effects of anger? Then, for example, once the person has a slight inkling that there might be a benefit to patience, that inkling is held steady in clear awareness so that the insight can deepen.

There are two levels of truth to the Buddha-dharma: ultimate and provisional. Thus most of Buddha's teachings are interpretable – meaning they are not absolutely true from the most profound point of view. Only passages speaking of no sentient beings, no composition, and no production are definitive, because they speak about the ultimate nature of reality. Statements that refer to living beings, self, and humans are provisional. This is because such things are dependently arising and do not exist independently (Tsong-kha-pa 2002: 112–113).

with rules that were at once respectful to society, and conducive to awakening. To avoid scandal and distraction, bhikṣus and bhikṣunīs did not live together during the rainy seasons, and they observed a rule that forbade one man and one women śramaṇa to sit alone together. While some training precepts were to prevent moral collapse among the renunciates, the rule that assured the seniority of every male over every female member of the saṃgha seemed to reinforce a misogynist cultural habit. At the end of her life Prajāpati asked Buddha to drop the extra rules for women – but he did not. Yet at the end of his life Buddha stated that unimportant rules of conduct might be omitted. Apparently, because the **Tathāgata** did not specify which rules were unimportant, the early saṃgha did not amend any. And though some customs observed by members of the saṃgha were modified according to cultural circumstances, the rules that pertain to perpetual lack of a woman's seniority over a man has never been changed.

Initially, the bhikṣus and bhikṣunīs assembled for the duration of the rainy season, and wandered for the rest of each year. They were not to frequent the same houses over and over again, and were to eat what was given to them. This meant a small handful of the food prepared for the family – not anything special for the almsmen and almswomen. They were allowed to eat meat if it was offered, as long as no animal was killed for them and they had not asked for meat or chosen the animal. At times Gautama and some of the renunciates would accept a dinner invitation – which according to their custom should be completed before noon. Devadatta initiated a saṃgha reformist movement, arguing that the rules were too lax. He siphoned off a group of disciples from the **bhikṣu** saṃgha. They began to live by more stringent rules – sleeping under trees instead of in huts, not eating meat, refusing dinner invitations, and so forth. Gautama persisted in his Middle Way approach to spiritual life, and condemned Devadatta's efforts to cause schism in the saṃgha. It is said that Devadatta's followers left him and returned to the main fold. (To this day, causing schism in the saṃgha is considered among the most heinous of non-virtuous acts.) Devadatta's ambitions came to a bitter end with an untimely death, however.

Laypeople supported the renunciate saṃgha through almsgiving as bhikṣus and bhikṣunīs arrived before noon at their doors. Those with more wealth donated land and resources for the establishment of rain retreat residences. The courtesan Amrapālī is well known for her donation of a mango grove to support the fledgling Buddhist community. (She actually became a bhikṣunī later in life.) Her gift allowed Buddha's disciples to reside safely during the rainy season when travel was prohibited, due to the injury to living beings caused by trampling about in the mud. Gradually as the renunciate saṃgha grew, the land and property dedicated for them needed maintenance. King Bimbisāra had donated land that turned into a whole village establishment. Eventually, this accumulation of resources laid the foundations for the Buddhist monastic institution. Monasticism became a hallmark of Buddhist life as it spread from India throughout Asia – and it continues until today.

Buddha's parinirvāṇa *and legacy*

On the full moon day in the month of Vaiśāka (April/May) Gautama attained **parinirvāṇa**. This was exactly eighty years after his birth, and forty-five years after waking up. Buddha left no successor. His son the bhikṣu Rāhula had passed away – as had his mother, Gautama's former wife. Furthermore, his two chief disciples Śāriputra and Maudgalyāyana had also passed away. In any case there was no indication that Gautama intended to appoint a successor. Instead, he instructed the disciples to use the Buddha-dharma as their guide. When the Tathāgata attained parinirvāṇa, his body was cremated and the relics were distributed. These were enshrined in simple stūpas, funeral monuments.

Monks and nuns who were Gautama's disciples did not use images. They were free of all possessions except ten items: three robes (outer garment, undergarment, cloak), a food bowl, a belt, a razor, a needle, a water strainer, a staff, and a toothpick. The earliest surviving images widely used in the Buddhist tradition were **aniconic**, including an empty throne, tree of enlightenment, wheel of the law, and footprints. These symbols represented the fact that Buddha left no trace of his physical self after the parinirvāṇa. As the Buddhist lay form of worship developed, pictorial representations of Buddha's life story became a popular means of decorating the stūpas. The Mahāyānist emphasis on bodhisattvas also inspired figural representations of those beings who purposefully take rebirth in the world to rid others of suffering. Buddha was even given a Greek-looking face by the artists of Gandhāra.

A Buddhist council was called during the first rainy season after Gautama passed away. The arhats gathered to consolidate their knowledge by reviewing oral texts that became the vinaya and sūtra baskets of the Tripiṭaka. But in the years that followed, the Buddhist tradition fragmented. About a century after Buddha's parinirvāṇa, a second Buddhist council was held. In the prosperous city of Vaiśālī participants were polarized into two main camps: (1) a liberal group called the Mahāsāṃghikas, or Great Saṃgha, and (2) over a dozen splinter groups of traditionalists that can be called Nikāya Buddhists. These Nikāya Buddhists spread throughout India and Southeast Asia. Among them, only the Sthaviravāda group survives today as the Theravāda or Way of the Elders school. Meanwhile, the Great Saṃgha group became the basis of the numerous Mahāyāna schools of Central and East Asia. About a century after the initial main break into two camps, King Aśoka called a third Buddhist council. He was the first Buddhist king of India, and wanted to bring doctrinal clarity to the religion. From an outsider perspective, this move may be viewed as an attempt to make Buddhism a status quo religion that would reinforce the political structure of the Mauryan Empire.

HISTORICAL PLAYERS

Aśoka Maurya (third century BCE)

In Gautama's lifetime, Magadha had become the most powerful among sixteen territories in the Ganges Valley. After decades of warring, Magadha absorbed the smaller territories, including Buddha's own native region that had been democratically ruled by the Śākya clan. Buddha's old stomping ground became the center of the first Indian empire shortly after Alexander the Great's arrival and precipitous departure from the Indus Valley. A young, capable, and ambitious man named Candragupta Maurya seized the Magadhan throne and extended the boundaries of this powerful state, forming India's first empire. His grandson Aśoka Maurya (200s BCE) became the first Buddhist king. Aśoka's empire was the largest established in India to that date, extending from Gandhāra in the west to Bihār in the east. Yet, after Aśoka's death the Mauryan Empire atrophied. In the course of Aśoka's first (and only) armed conquest, the king experienced a radical change of heart. While he initially enacted the more aggressive administrative policies of his father and grandfather, the shock of seeing 100,000 people slain in the Kaliṅga war on the eastern seaboard prompted the emperor to adopt a policy of non-violence.

Aśoka had edicts inscribed on boulders at the borders of Mauryan territory that broadcast details of his social, judicial, and administrative policies to assure outsiders of the benevolence of his reign. He aimed to impress upon neighboring regions that his policies were non-aggressive by declaring that Mauryan officials were to administer the empire according to dharma (religious readings). Moreover, he had dharma teachings carved on rocks, pillars, and cave walls to instill morality into people of the empire. Aśoka considered the people's welfare his greatest duty, so he composed the edicts in the common people's language to achieve maximum exposure. In the edicts, Aśoka made broad use of the word dharma or duty, combining it with other words showing his subjects where to focus their morality: for example, giving (*dharma-dāna*), distributing wealth (*dharma-samvibhaga*), kinship (*dharma-sambandha*), moral pleasure (*dharma-rati*). Through these edicts, his subjects were taught to respect the authority of their parents, elders, and teachers. Following the king's example, they were also encouraged to consider the needs of religious ascetics, as well as the poor, infirm, and aged. Aśoka situated massive stone pillars, identified by the royal insignia, along prominent roadways, urban sites, and places of pilgrimage – while cave edicts dedicated their hallowed spaces to monks for use during the rainy season.

In the tenth year of Aśoka's reign, two years after the aggression on Kaliṅga, the king gave up his royal pleasure tours in favor of dharma tours. He began preaching to people of all social stations, distributing gifts to brāhmaṇas and *śramaṇas*, and making pilgrimages. He provided welfare subsidies and built roads lined with rest houses, watering sheds, medicinal herbs, and shade trees. To promote happiness here and in the hereafter, Aśoka instituted a government position for moral supervisors (*dharma-mahāmātra*). The officers were to assure the support of all religious sects within the empire, and promote religious toleration among the people. They were also charged to distribute honors, impose penalties, and supervise public morality, including the humane treatment of animals. The king specifically named animals that had the right to life in his territory including those with two feet, four feet, birds, and aquatic creatures. Rock Edict I states that no living creature should be killed in Pāṭaliputra, his capital. Pillar Edict V tells people that twenty-six years after his coronation, the king made it illegal to kill parrots, wild geese, pigeons, squirrels, and household animals . . . just to name a few! Aśoka's inscriptions probably became indecipherable fairly shortly after his reign, as his empire shrunk and policies were reversed. The edicts were not deciphered again until 1837.

In gestures of goodwill, and perhaps for self-assurance, the king provided medicine to neighboring

BOX 9.3 CULTURE CONTRAST: CROSSING THE SILK ROUTES – CHINA MEETS INDIA

Buddhism crossed the Silk Routes and entered China during the second half of the Han Dynasty (206 BCE–220 CE). The Chinese already had two long-established complementary traditions, Confucianism and Daoism. But there was some degree of psychological readiness among the elite as well as the peasants for a new perspective on life. Peasants were interested in the prospect of help from bodhisattvas, while the elite were curious about the personal charisma and power of Buddhist monks. In spite of this, it took about three centuries for the alien tradition to be accepted into scholarly circles. Texts had to be translated – and ironing out the incompatibilities between Indian and Chinese worldviews required some finesse.

Language. As if it were not enough of a problem fitting Indian thought into Chinese culture, the very project of literally translating concepts from Sanskrit into Chinese posed challenges. Sanskrit uses an alphabet, and has a detailed grammar, while Chinese uses characters without systematic and elaborate grammatical rules. Given this foundation, sophisticated philosophical concepts became even more difficult to render. (Some Indian abstract notions were put into very concrete terms with Chinese cultural nuances – such as "round" for "perfection.")

Perspective. Buddhist thought was very psychological, while Confucian thought was politically minded, and classical Daoist thought was nature-oriented. Yet Confucians became interested in Buddhist ethics, which seemed to reinforce their native values in many respects. On the other hand, Daoists became fascinated by the meditative skills of Buddhist monks. (Chinese culture creatively assimilated features of Buddhism that were culturally compatible.)

Afterlife. The Indian and Chinese goals for the afterlife were at odds. The Indian worldview placed human beings in a nearly endless cycle of past and future rebirths – holding the ultimate value of removing oneself from the compulsory cycle of rebirth. The Chinese worldview placed human beings in a long line of ancestors – awarding high status to those who were powerful and long-lived. From the Chinese point of view ancestors must be kept in the loop of communication, and the prospect of an uncertain rebirth rips the social fabric.

Family values. Indian culture dealt with the discomfort of supporting a population of religious wanderers who rejected family life. The option of renouncing the world had already been deeply inculcated into India's value system before Buddhism made its way to China. By contrast, the Chinese could not easily justify a lifestyle of alms begging and celibacy. Thus in Confucian cultures the Buddhist altar included reminders of the ancestors, and celibate clergy were understood as bringing spiritual rewards to their families.

territories, and preached respect for their traditions. Aśoka's influence is felt to this day not only within India, but also in greater India. He sent emissaries to five Hellenistic empires, including Syria and Macedonia. In addition, in line with his enthusiasm for dharma, he sent his son and daughter to establish a Buddhist lineage for monks and nuns in Sri Lanka. The lineage of monks established by Aśoka's son persists in Sri Lanka to this day, but the line of bhikṣunīs was eliminated centuries ago under the pressure of warfare. Today, women in Sri Lanka take the novice vows and wear white garments to show their commitment to the Buddhist dharma. Sri Lanka remains the country with the longest continuous history of Buddhism in the world.

Bodhidharma (fifth–sixth century CE)

The Chinese received Buddhism in bits and pieces, with no overarching structure, as texts, clergy, and artwork trickled in along with the merchants. The Chinese had three basic approaches to Buddhism: (1) Some tried to copy Indian Buddhism; these did not pan out over the long run. (2) Some arranged the diverse Indian texts hierarchically (for example, Tian-tai and Hua-yan); these were spiritually effective, intellectually challenging, and grew into elaborate institutions, but they had difficulty surviving the persecution of 845 CE. (3) Some developed new religious forms that carried the essence of Buddhism (Chan and Pure Land). These had the most widespread staying power.

Chan is one Buddhist school that focused on what its proponents felt was the essence of Buddha-dharma, namely meditation. Thus it was named as such. Dhyāna, the Sanskrit word for meditation, was transliterated as Chan in China, Sŏn in Korea, Thiên in Vietnam, and Zen in Japan. The meditation school of Buddhism took root and flowered in East Asian soil from Indian seeds. It originated in the spark of an encounter between Śākyamuni Buddha and the Great Kāśyapa during the so-called Flower Sermon, but it never grew up as a separate school on Indian soil.

One day Buddha came to teach on Vulture Peak in north India, but on this particular day he said no word whatsoever. After a long silence, Buddha lifted up a flower. Of all those assembled, only Kāśyapa smiled. At that moment, Kāśyapa's mind and Buddha's mind were not two, but one. Kāśyapa's smile was Buddha's smile. At that moment Kāśyapa received the silent transmission that initiated the meditation lineage. Subsequently, one by one, this lineage was transmitted through history, without words. In turn Kāśyapa provoked the same enlightening realization in Buddha's cousin Ānanda just before the first Buddhist council. From Ānanda the transmission of silent wisdom was passed down all the way to Bodhidharma, who was the twenty-eighth person to awaken as Kāśyapa had awakened when Gautama quietly lifted up a flower.

Bodhidharma was one of the greatest meditators in Buddhist history – though his life story remains largely legendary. He brought the meditation method known as wall-gazing over the Silk Road from India to China in the sixth century CE. When Bodhidharma met the Chinese emperor Wu-di, they had a weird conversation that was adopted as an early **kōan** of the Chan school (paraphrased as follows):

Emperor:	What merit is mine for building many monasteries?
Bodhidharma:	None whatsoever.
Emperor:	What's the heart of Buddha-dharma?
Bodhidharma:	There's not any.
Emperor:	Who stands before me now?
Bodhidharma:	Don't know! (No idea!)

Wu-di, emperor of the Northern Wei Dynasty, commissioned the translation of Buddhist texts from the classical Indian Sanskrit language into Chinese characters. He built a Buddhist temple in the remains of a forest on Songshan, one of China's five holy mountain peaks in Henan province in central China. Buddhist monks involved in this translation project lived at the Shaolin ("new forest" in Mandarin) temple, so named because new trees were planted around the edifice. When Bodhidharma went to see them, he was turned away from Shaolin. He settled in a nearby cave and wall-gazed for nine years – boring a hole in the side of the cave with his unswerving gaze. The Shaolin monks were taken aback, and admitted Bodhidharma to the temple. Finding the Shaolin monks in poor health, unable to protect themselves from bandits and wild animals, Bodhidharma developed a movement meditation for strength, speed, and agility based upon the movement of animals, such as the tiger, cobra, leopard, and dragon. Though Bodhidharma did not create the exercises as a martial art, over time the Shaolin movement meditation developed into a distinctive style within an ancient system of Chinese martial art.

Daoists were the first Chinese sages to take an interest in Bodhidharma's rigorous style of meditation. Indian teachings offered techniques, a lineage, and generations of experience in the development of mental awareness; and many Daoists found that these Buddhist teachings enhanced their own. Because the early Chan practitioners were Daoists, the Indian tradition took on Daoist coloration. Although no formal dhyāna school evolved in India, the lineage that Gautama passed to the Great Kāśyapa flourished in East Asia, and profoundly impacted upon the artistic culture of China. The early Chan Buddho-Daoists recognized Bodhidharma as the twenty-eighth in line from Buddha Śākyamuni, and identified him as the first Chan patriarch. Tradition states that after Bodhidharma, the mind-to-mind transmission was received by Hui-ke (487–593), then Seng-can, and down to Hui-neng, the sixth Chan patriarch. Thereafter, the lineage branched out, and was taken to Japan some six centuries later. The Shaolin monastery where Bodhidharma taught is about two hours by bus from the modern-day city of Zhengzhou. In 1985 it became possible for tourists to visit, and to participate in some daily trainings. Nearby is a cave in which Bodhidharma is said to have meditated.

Hui-neng (638–713 CE)

The *Platform Sūtra*, a Mahāyāna text, tells Hui-neng's story. It is thanks to this text, and one of Hui-neng's able and ambitious disciples, that the sixth patriarch's influence coalesced in the Chan tradition. Hui-neng himself appears to have been quite humble. Having lost his father at a young age, he resorted to gathering wood to sell in the Cantonese markets. One auspicious day, when he was in his teens, Hui-neng by chance heard a monk reading from a Prajñāpāramitā text known as the *Diamond Sūtra*. These penetrating words gave him an aesthetic shock that was a moment of sudden enlightenment: "Allow mind to flow without dwelling on a thing." Hui-neng determined then and there to seek an enlightened teacher. According to the custom of filial piety, he first made provisions for his aged mother. Then, after considerable difficulties, Hui-neng located the fifth Chan patriarch in the mountains of present-day Hupei. Being from southern China and illiterate, Hui-neng was considered a barbarian by the students of his teacher Hung-ren (602–675), who made him do menial work in the monastery.

The fifth patriarch realized the depth of Hui-neng's insight in the course of a poetry contest he set up for disciples at the monastery. The challenge was to write a verse of illumination. Hung-ren publicly praised the verse composed by foremost student Shen-xiu – though it was inadequate:

> The body is the Bodhi tree [enlightenment].
> The mind is like a clear mirror standing.
> Take care to wipe it all the time,
> Allow no grain of dust to cling.
>
> (Shen-xiu: Dumoulin 1979: 44)

Hui-neng heard this verse, which was inscribed on the temple wall, and requested someone to write a contrary thought. While Shen-xiu's verse indicated the perspective of gradual enlightenment, Hui-neng's verse cut through to śūnyatā. He asked someone to write these words, which Hung-ren saw the next morning:

> The Bodhi is not like a tree,
> The clear mirror is nowhere standing.
> Fundamentally not one thing exists;
> Where, then, is a grain of dust to cling?
>
> (Hui-neng: Dumoulin 1979: 44)

The fifth patriarch recognized that his illiterate disciple had realized emptiness. But he erased the poem, and declared publicly that its author lacked enlightenment. Privately, however, Hung-ren passed on to Hui-neng the bowl and robe that had belonged to Bodhidharma. He then insisted that Hui-neng flee to the south with these tokens of initiation, crossing the Yangtze River to escape repercussions from jealous disciples.

Chan Buddhism permeated Chinese culture of the Tang Dynasty. Over time masters of the formidable Chan lineage traced themselves back to Hui-neng the sixth patriarch, and promoted the concept of sudden enlightenment. The atmosphere of Chan during the

Tang period was anti-intellectual, and stories of Hui-neng portrayed him as illiterate. They considered too much learning to be a hindrance to spiritual development, and so the notion that enlightenment need not be based on a gradual course of learning appealed to them. Practitioners in Hui-neng's lineage expected *bodhi* (penetrating awareness) to arise suddenly through personal encounters between a disciple and a master, based on the model of Gautama's Flower Sermon. Any particularly potent exchange between a Chan master and a disciple was later formulated as a gongan or **kōan**. The words and gestures then constituted a public record or case study of the enlightened mind to be contemplated by generations of practitioners thereafter. Hui-neng's life underscores for the Chan tradition the notion that enlightenment strikes all of a sudden, and it can happen anywhere, any time.

Tantric adepts

Tantra is a form of Buddhist practice that originated in India among Hindu and Buddhist yogīs who visualized the body's inner geography with its winds, channels, and centers made of *prāṇa* or subtle energy. The history of tantra is peculiar, because on the one hand it is an esoteric science passed on by oral tradition. On the other hand, because of its expertise at manipulating energy, it developed an elaborate ritualistic aspect. This almost magical quality of tantra attracted the attention of ruling families, who were interested in any protection for themselves and their domains that it might provide. For example, rulers of the Pāla Dynasty favored tantric ritual. The Pālas established a Buddhist empire that encompassed north India between 750 and 800 CE.

Perhaps tantra would have had a more long-standing and illustrious future in India had the Pālas survived, or had another Buddhist dynasty followed after them. However, after the Pālas, India had no more Buddhist rulers. The tradition lost patronage when the Sena rulers came into power. Once it lost royal patronage, tantric Buddhism reverted to a low profile in India, and maintained itself as an esoteric science among the **siddhas**. Meanwhile, tantric forms of Buddhist practice made their way into other parts of Asia. Tantra assumed an entirely new life in Tibet, where it became an integral part of the Tibetan Mahāyāna approach to Buddhism known as Mantrayāna or Vajrayāna.

The Tibetans became fascinated with the tantric approach to spiritual practice, and eventually Tibetan scholars systematically developed tantra into four categories. They wrote detailed commentaries on tantric practice dealing with matters ranging from the external placement of a vase, down to the movement of subtle energy coursing through the body's inner landscape. Beyond the Tibetan interest in tantra, esoteric Buddhism was favored by the Chinese court of the Tang Dynasty. There it was called Chen-yen (Sanskrit: *mantra*). And at the highpoint of the Tang, the newly established Japanese royal household under Emperor Saga (r. 809–823) also became attracted to the elaborate ceremony and magical power of tantric ritual, known in Japan as Shingon.

Kūkai (774–835)

Kūkai (Kōbo-daishi) was the Japanese founder of the tantric Shingon sect in Japan. He was an artist who committed himself to the Buddhist path when he was 24 years old. He had studied the Confucian classics, but in his search for a deeper spiritual experience turned his attention to the Buddha-dharma. Instead of pursuing studies that would suit him for government work, he began a program of austerities, and thereby drummed up magical powers. At age 31 Kūkai went to China, but though he had intended to spend two decades there, he came back after thirty months. He sought the meaning of the *Mahāvairocana Sūtra*, (Discourse on the Great Vairocana).

In China Kūkai's studies combined the best of Indian and Chinese culture: Sanskrit language and the Indian forms of Buddhism as well as Chinese poetry and calligraphy. There he also became immersed in Chen-yen, the esoteric tantric Buddhism adopted from India by the people of the Chinese royal court. He met the Chinese master Hui-guo (746–805), and was made the eighth patriarch of the Chen-yen lineage. Kūkai delved deeply into tantric Buddhism, and seems to have found the meaning of the Mahāvairocana Sūtra that he sought. Kūkai remarked:

> The essence of Esoteric Buddhism is not to be obtained from written words but to be transmitted from mind to mind; the written words are mere lees and dregs; they are bricks and pebbles.
>
> (Kūkai: Hakeda 1972: 43–44)

Shingon is called esoteric Buddhism because a person must be initiated into the practice in order to establish a personal relationship with the buddhas and bodhisattvas. Kūkai was especially connected with the dhyani Buddha Vairocana – the Cosmic Sun Buddha, featured in the sūtra that had so captivated him. He was convinced that the sūtra on the Great Vairocana contained the whole Buddha-dharma, but with a kind of in-built depth not easily attained elsewhere. The tantric form of spiritual practice involves much ritual, including the use of **maṇḍalas** and mantras – and these provided access to the deeper levels of realization than is apparent on the surface. Kūkai especially appreciated the artistic aspects of tantra, and found aesthetic value in religious practice.

Padmasambhava (8th century CE*)*

Padmasambhava is a somewhat mysterious tantric practitioner. He is considered to be the historical founder of the oldest Tibetan Buddhist school, the Nyingma. Yet information about him is infused with mythic, symbolic elements – such as the description of his birth from a lotus (*padma*) flower. He came from the area in northern Pakistan known as Swat, and traveled northward to Tibet from there in 746 CE. Padmasambhava was reputed to have been a magician; this is not surprising because he was an accomplished tantric yogī. He is credited with transmitting a lineage of tantric yoga to Tibet, and wrote commentaries on esoteric works such as the *Tibetan Book of the Dead*. His stay in Tibet caused controversy, and he probably had to escape to save his life. Before leaving, Padmasambhava is said to have buried precious objects and texts. Later, these were on occasion discovered at appropriate times, just when they were needed. Such objects are revered in the Nyingma school, and the strange claims regarding how they were deposited and discovered have been taken with great seriousness in the tradition.

Milarepa (1052–1135)

Milarepa was a tantric master who was born in Tibet, and became one of its most accomplished poets. He practiced tantra within the Kagyu school, and sang songs of enlightenment to villagers, scholars, and whomever he encountered – even demons. He liked to use metaphors to describe points of Buddha's teaching as well as tantric experiences involving energy centers, channels, and winds of the subtle body. Milarepa practiced highest yoga tantra, which did not involve outer rituals. His tantric practice was strictly based on an inner geography. As part of his inner landscape, Milarepa had many encounters with fairy-like beings known as *ḍākiṇīs*, who inspired his yoga practice. His approach to mental transformation was based on a space-like meditation practice known as Mahāmudra:

> A wise man knows how to practice
> The space-like meditation.
> In all he does by day
> He attaches himself to nothing.
> With a liberated spirit,
> He desires nor wealth nor beauty.
>
> One should see that all appearance
> Is like mist and fog;
> Though one has vowed to liberate all living
> beings,
> He should know that all manifestations
> Are like reflections of the moon in water.
>
> (Milarepa: Chang 1962: 102)

Chinul (1158–1210): a Korean reformer

Buddhism was officially brought to Korea in the fourth century CE to provide ritual protection for the ruling clan. Thereafter, the tradition proved to be a convenient aid for political unification of the clans. At the same time as the Tang Dynasty flourished in China, the three Korean kingdoms were merged under the victorious Silla Dynasty (668–935). During the Silla period five Buddhist schools came to the fore, and maintained themselves through subsequent centuries. The Silla Dynasty ended in economic decline, and as in China Sŏn (Chinese: Chan) and Pure Land proved to be the variants of Buddhism with sufficient resilience to survive. After the Unified Silla Dynasty came the Koryŏ Dynasty (935–1392), which maintained Buddhism as the state religion. Over time, corruption crept into the Korean Buddhist saṃgha, as the monastic institutions controlled increasingly more land. The government pressured the monks to stay out of business and politics, proponents of the five schools vied against each other, and generally it became clear that some kind of reform was needed. Right in the middle of the Koryŏ period came an ambitious young man who responded to the needs of the times.

Chinul was sickly as a child. According to a "Buddhist" cultural custom, his father's solution was to dedicate the boy to the monastery should his child survive. Indeed, at age 7 a healthy Chinul went to live among the monks, and became a novice when he was 15. He studied diligently and, when the time came to do so, took the required Sŏn exams. He passed the exams, but he felt they could not possibly measure a person's degree of enlightenment. Success in the exams was thus of limited value, and misleading. More than that, the elaborate lifestyle of the city monks disturbed him.

Chinul and his cohort of young monks were disappointed by the current Sŏn establishments, which were embroiled in wealth and politics. Some of them began to travel in search of a deeper religious experience, and a more modest lifestyle. At the time, Korea had two rival orientations to Buddhist practice: to attain sudden enlightenment through Sŏn, or awaken gradually through study of Buddha's discourses. Chinul traveled throughout Korea, educating himself in both Sŏn and Hua-yan Buddhist perspectives. He never made it to China, but was deeply influenced by the work of Chan master Dahui Zonggao (1089–1163).

Chinul considered the various forms of Buddhism available to him in Korea as complementary. He integrated aspects of them into his main tradition of Sŏn. The foundation for Chinul's reform teachings was based on three awakenings that came in reaction to *The Platform Sūtra*, the *Avatamsaka Sūtra*, and *The Records of Da-hui*. The *Avatamsaka Sūtra* is a key text from the Hua-yan (Korean: Hwa-om) school, while the other two are classic Chan texts. This indicates Chinul's commitment to both study (characteristic of Hua-yan, which classifies Buddha-dharma into five levels), and meditation (characteristic of Chan).

Monks of the sūtra schools would spend decades studying sūtras, thinking that by doing so they gradually came closer to enlightenment. This was in contrast to the Sŏn schools which taught that everyone is already Buddha by virtue of the original mind. Chinul harmonized the two views. Buddha-nature is the original mind within one's own body that can be glimpsed through a sudden awakening, as promoted by Hui-neng. This sudden awakening matures into full awakening through the cultivation of *samādhi* (meditation) and ***prajñā*** (wisdom), as promoted in sūtra schools such as Hua-yan. According to Chinul, a practitioner must gradually reduce habitual patterns of body, speech, and mind because the seeds of these patterns are not destroyed merely through the penetrating initial awakening. Ultimately, however, concepts derived from scripture or anywhere else must be transcended through sudden insight.

Chinul maintained Sŏn as his fundamental Buddhist orientation, and developed the method of **hwadu** practice used by the Chinese master Dahui Zonggao. This involves meditation on kōans through a focus on the critical word or phrase that is its essential point. Chinul established a new monastic center as well as the new school of Korean Sŏn. Both were named Chogye after the mountain on which the sixth patriarch Hui-neng lived in south China. The Chogye Order is the main form of Buddhism practiced in Korea to this day. It involves sudden awakening and gradual practice, stressing the balance between meditation and scriptural study. Along with the cultivation of meditation and wisdom, the Chogye school emphasizes the hwadu.

Thirteenth-century Japanese reformers

Tendai Buddhism (Chinese: Tian-tai) was named after the sacred mountain in southeast China. Tian-tai is a Mahāyāna school that systematized the Buddha-dharma as received into China by the sixth century CE. It gives primary focus to the *Lotus Sūtra*, and takes to heart the three Pure Land sūtras – promoting meditation as well as devotional practice. Tian-tai was popularized in China by Chih-i (538–597) and in Japan by Saichō (767–822). By the thirteenth century in Japan, it had become thoroughly established and seasoned. So comfortable had Tendai become that a number of its most thoughtful monks began to question its relevance.

The thirteenth century was an enormously creative time for the arts and spiritual traditions in Japan. It was a transitional time between the Heian and the Kamakura periods, during which several Buddhist reformers made original contributions to the history of religious ideas. Eisai, Dōgen, Hōnen, Shinran, and Nichiren were all disappointed with the Buddhism of their day – principally Tendai and Shingon. Each rejected the elite monastic lifestyle that had grown up over the generations in Japan since Saichō and Kūkai first established these Buddhist schools in the ninth century. In place of the complex Tendai literature and esoteric Shingon ritual, the forward-looking monks were drawn to the simpler Chinese forms of Buddhism that had evolved on the mainland particularly after the persecution of Buddhism in 845 CE: the Chan and Pure Land schools.

The simplicity sought by the reform-minded Japanese practitioners was achieved in one of two ways: through **jiriki**, self-power, or through **tariki**, other power. The Japanese invented these categories to distinguish between religious practices that rely on one's own efforts, and those that surrender to the compassion of an enlightened being. Zen is characterized as jiriki because it calls for strict personal discipline with consistent effort devoted to meditation. Pure Land is designated as other power, as practitioners rely on the all-pervasive compassion of Amida Buddha.

Eisai (1141–1215)

Eisai was a Tendai monk who traveled to China to see its original home monastery on the Tian-tai mountain. He returned with scriptures, green tea, and a new perspective on religious practice. He brought Chan back from China, and started the Rinzai sect. Eisai found the most receptivity for the meditation school in northern Japan at Kamakura. This was on account of the samurai warriors who heartily accepted meditative discipline to gain focus and fearlessness. Eisai favored use of the kōan, and adopted the spiritual technique of meditating on the public records (Chinese: gongan) of the great Tang masters as a centerpiece of Rinzai training.

Dōgen (1200–1253)

Dōgen was born into a noble Japanese family. He was orphaned at age 7, ordained as a novice Buddhist monk at 13, and traveled to China at the age of 23, where he realized his Buddha-nature. On his return from the mainland, people asked Dōgen what he brought back; he declared: "Empty hands." When asked about realizing the Buddha-dharma, he gave a very Zen response: "Eyes horizontal! Nose vertical!" Dōgen was talking about something that became his signature style of Zen practice: **shikan-taza** . . . just sitting. Shikan-taza represented the highest form of meditation. In advocating simple sitting with total attention and awareness, Dōgen returned to Gautama Buddha's emphasis on mindfulness training: what is heard is just heard; what is felt is just felt.

Dōgen did not compose a systematic study of Zen. He wrote lectures and poetic verses that were brilliant and original interpretations of Gautama Buddha's insights. Dōgen spoke much about Buddha-nature, the inherent enlightened condition of all living beings. Japanese Tendai Buddhists had already taken cognizance of the natural world, claiming that plants, animals, and geographical formations *had* Buddha-nature. Dōgen's original insight was that everything did not *have* – but everything *was* – an expression of Buddha-nature. Dōgen noticed that mountains flowed, and grass was enlightened. This meant that at the most profound level of perception there is no distinction between mind and entities. He then continued to ponder the implications of this non-dualism.

At a young age Dōgen felt a nagging question that he spent years trying to resolve: "If as the sūtras say, our essential nature is enlightened (bodhi), why did all the Buddhas have to strive to awaken?" Finally, he concluded that an enlightened person should continue to practice meditation because **zazen** sitting practice is none other than enlightenment itself. Even after attaining **satori**, one should practice meditation.

Dōgen founded the Sōtō school of Zen Buddhism in Japan, which persists today. In contrast to the methods of the Rinzai Zen sect founded by Eisai, Dōgen did not formally emphasize kōans. In Sōtō training shikan-taza was used as the key to discovering Buddha-nature. In spite of the tremendous discipline required for Zen practice, Dōgen realized that the most difficult practice is none other than the most simple. Dōgen's legacy could well extend beyond the confines of Zen, and form the basis of a modern Buddhist environmentalism. Dōgen teaches us that people are not as separate from nature as they might think. Embroiled in a profound interdependency, nature actually responds to the virtue of human beings. Things of nature – in their own ways – are aware of those who love them. Moreover, things of nature (such as mountains) actually impel living beings to participate in life with them.

Hōnen (1133–1212)

Hōnen was a Tendai monk at the prestigious Mount Hiei. He eventually became disillusioned with the standard Buddhist practice in Japan, and entered a period of seclusion and study. After delving into the Pure Land sūtras, and giving deep consideration to Amida Buddha's forty-eight vows to save all beings, Hōnen became a Pure Land adept and established Jōdo-shū, the Pure Land sect in Japan. He believed that ordinary people should have the opportunity to participate in Buddhist practice despite their lack of sophistication. He taught that rebirth into the Pure Land was the most suitable goal for people of his time. Due to Amida's great compassion, rebirth into the Western Paradise was attainable through simple measures of faith, rather than the complicated approach of elite Tendai priests.

Nichiren (1222–1282)

Nichiren became very interested in Hōnen's Pure Land reforms. He followed suit with a perspective on Pure Land spirituality that proved to be immensely popular inside as well as outside of Japan. Nichiren studied widely both the old and emerging forms of Buddhism in Japan. His Buddhist education started early with Tendai, and later he lived as a Tendai monk on Mount Hiei, the prestigious Tendai center, and studied at Mount Kōya, center of the tantric Shingon sect. Beyond that, Nichiren studied Zen and Pure Land Buddhism. After this, he rejected all their approaches and put total stock in the teaching of the *Lotus Sūtra*, a Mahāyāna text available to them, but, in his view, not sufficiently emphasized. While Pure Land practitioners recited the name of Amida Buddha, Nichiren taught his disciples to revere the *Lotus Sūtra* itself as the heart of Buddha's teaching and to recite: *Namu myoho rengye kyo* (Adoration to the Lotus of the True Law). In his view the *Lotus Sūtra* was the only relevant teaching among those contained in the Buddhist tradition at large. On 23 April 1253 he publicly denounced all forms of Buddhism except Nichirenshū, the one he was propagating based on the *Lotus Sūtra*.

Nichiren's Buddhist teachings have been taken up by the Sōka Gakkai International (SGI) organization, founded in 1930. This "society for the creation of values" is now established in 190 countries with an estimated twelve million members, including the American superstar vocalist-performer Tina Turner. The SGI separated from an older organization called Nichiren Shōshū. The former is a layperson's organization, while the original has a priestly base.

Shinran (1173–1262)

A tradition of reciting the name of Amitābha began in India. Shinran's lineage traces back to seven Pure Land patriarchs, beginning with two of India's foremost philosophers: Nāgārjuna and Vasubandhu, founders of the Mādhyamika and Yogācāra schools of Mahāyāna thought. But meditation on the Buddha of Boundless Light was never formalized as a separate school there. On the other hand, Pure Land Buddhism became the most prominent of all forms of Buddha-dharma practiced in East Asia.

Shinran was a temple priest on Mount Hiei. In 1201 he joined Hōnen's group of Pure Land seekers for six years. Hōnen had already gone back to lay life, and Shinran took him as a mentor and renounced his monastic vows. Under Hōnen's guidance, Shinran studied the Pure Land sūtras and began the practice of repeating Amida Buddha's name. His period of study ended when both were charged with irreligious behavior and forced into exile. While in exile, Shinran separated from Hōnen, married, and began to raise a family of five or six children. In the midst of this lay life, he came to a new understanding of the Mahāyāna Buddhist notion that "saṃsāra is nirvāṇa." Shinran became convinced that even a family man could attain the peace of nirvāṇa. This was done through Amida's compassion, which brought ordinary people steeped in the suffering of saṃsāra to rebirth in the Western Paradise.

Shinran taught that his was a degenerate age in which there were no buddhas in the world, and people labored heavily under the three poisons of desire, hatred, and ignorance. The age will last until the human life span decreases to ten years, and the best response to this cosmic misfortune is an appeal to Amida's compassion. Shinran had faith that a sincere, faithful hearing of Amida's name, even once, brings rebirth into Amida's Western Paradise. The mantra of Amida's name is like a wish-granting gem that helps everything it touches. Thus, Shinran taught that Jōdo Shinshū (True Pure Land) devotees need not rid themselves of the human passions to be saved. Rather than try to abandon all passions, they should cultivate a sincere heart, deep faith in Amida's bodhisattva vows, and a wish to be reborn into the Pure Land.

In the midst of a fertile period of Japan's religious history, Shinran established the True Pure Land sect, which complemented the Pure Land (Jōdo-shū) sect of his teacher Hōnen. Jōdo-shū and Jōdo Shinshū became the main Amida sects in Japan. To this day, Shinran's True Pure Land teaching inspires a vital practice of Buddhism devoted to the Buddha of Boundless Light. The Pure Land schools of Shinran and Hōnen represent the tariki spiritual orientation whereby adherents rely on the compassion of Amida for salvation from the ills of this world.

Tenzin Gyatso (b. 1935): a Tibetan leader

Tenzin Gyatso, the fourteenth Dalai Lama, is a spiritual leader of the Tibetan people, and head of the Tibetan Government in Exile. He advocates a non-violent solution to the problems of the Tibetan people whose country was invaded and occupied by the Chinese People's Liberation Army in 1950. Tenzin Gyatso, who was 16 years old at the time. fully took up his position as head of state in Tibet, and attempted diplomatic negotiations with Mao Ze-dong on behalf of the Tibetan people. These talks were to little or no avail, because Mao considered religion to be a cultural poison. Dissatisfaction among the Tibetan people grew on account of the severe repression of religious freedom imposed during the 1950s, culminating in mass demonstrations and widespread resistance to Chinese rule. Finally, in March of 1959, the Dalai Lama determined to escape from the country to save his life and continue his work abroad.

The Dalai Lama has become a visible figure on the world stage since escaping from Tibet. He proposed a five-point peace plan for cooperation between the Tibetan autonomous region and China, for which he won the Nobel Peace Prize in 1989. In his acceptance speech, the Dalai Lama bore witness on behalf of the Tibetan people noting, "more than one sixth of Tibet's population of six million died as a direct result of the Chinese invasion and occupation," but he "[did] not wish to dwell on this point" (Piburn 1990: 40). Overall, the Dalai Lama adopts the Buddhist perspective of interdependence and personal responsibility.

Specifically, Tenzin Gyatso takes a bodhisattva's perspective with regard to the Chinese government and the plight of the Tibetan people. Although the Chinese could be considered to be an "enemy" of the Tibetan people, the Dalai Lama daily meditates on compassion for them. He practices a meditation known as the Exchange of Self and Other that involves visualization on the breath. He imagines breathing in the troubles, suffering, and ignorance of even the individuals assigned to torture Tibetans in the prisons. In turn, he imagines breathing out happiness, and sincerely giving it to them. The premise behind this meditation is that all living beings want happiness and do not want suffering. It acknowledges that people often try to achieve their happiness in ways that involve harming others. But according to an optimistic Buddhist view of human nature, the Dalai Lama believes that when people are truly happy, they will act according to their fundamental beneficence. Tenzin Gyatso has been teaching this meditation, along with other aspects of Buddha-dharma, to people in many countries over the past several decades.

Sulak Sivaraksa (b. 1933): a Thai activist

Sulak Sivaraksa is a Thai Buddhist who is working to implement the principles of Buddhist economics. He was educated in England, but returned to his native land to promote prosperity for the downtrodden. Buddhism is Sivaraksa's native tradition, and he finds it suitable to the enterprise of bringing happiness to suffering living beings. He considers that Buddhism provides a sound ethical framework within which sound and socially responsible economic policies can be developed. Sivaraksa works from the conviction that successful economic life is grounded in an active spiritual life. He started the Thai NGO movement, and inspired many socially progressive initiatives.

Plate 9.3 "Two peace activists." Tenzin Gyatso (b. 1935), the fourteenth Dalai Lama and Maha Ghosananda (1913–2007), the Supreme Patriarch of Buddhism in Cambodia are seated here at the Abbey of Gethsemani in Trappist, Kentucky (July 1996). Both monks have done extensive work on behalf of refugees (Tibetan, Cambodian) and world peace. Tenzin Gyatso won the Nobel Peace Prize in 1989 and Maha Ghosananda was a nominee for the prize in 1996. Here Tenzin Gyatso is seated on Maha Ghosananda's right side. Note the similarities between the Tibetan Mahāyāna and Cambodian Theravāda (Nikāya) monks in their mode of dress and facial expressions.

Sivaraksa rejects what he considers an excessive consumerism that tends to arise in Western culture. He feels that small-scale cultures can effectively create economic models based on their indigenous values when rooted in sound ethical principles. Along these lines he instituted two branches of social development, which have potential for wider application beyond Thai society.

- ***Alternatives to Consumerism.*** This is an international network devoted to finding ways based in Buddhist values to develop sustainable economic models that de-emphasize unchecked consumption and emotions of deprivation that motivate people to consume.
- ***The Spirit in Education Movement.*** Sivaraksa is founding a new college in Thailand based in the bodhisattva ethic of working for the sake of suffering beings. The educational mission is to facilitate research on non-violence, and to come up with alternative economic, political, and social policies that are non-violent. Specifically, Sivaraksa wants to understand the impact of violence entrenched at various levels of society on the health, education, and welfare of the people. This involves the development of an alternative model of education.

Sivaraksa has inspired other socially minded Buddhists to apply the Buddha-dharma from below – that is, from the grass roots of Buddhist societies instead of from the elite monastic institutions. Sivaraksa has brought Buddhism back to square one. Buddha himself did not write down his teachings. But if he could have done so, Gautama probably would have spelled Buddhism with a small "b."

PART 2
BUDDHIST TEXTURE

FOUNDATIONAL TEXTURE

Tripiṭaka is the term used for the body of Buddha's teachings in both Nikāya and Mahāyāna Buddhism. These three (*tri*) baskets (*piṭaka*) are the: (1) vinaya that includes training precepts for the order and related stories; (2) sūtras, which are direct teachings from the Tathāgata; and (3) abhidharma texts that systematically present a technical material from the sūtras. The Nikāya (Theravāda) and Mahāyāna canons have the same fundamental teachings, and overlap considerably. However, Mahāyānists have some sūtras which are found unacceptable by Theravādins. As might be expected, their abhidharma commentaries sometimes have a different emphasis, as the slant on commentarial literature reflects the character of the particular school of thought.

Vinaya: Buddhist training for monks and nuns

Rules for the monks

When Buddha's community was still relatively small, training rules were made up as occasions demanded.

They were formulated by a democratic process patterned on tribal customs used by the Śākya and other small clans of the middle Ganges basin where Gautama grew up. The number of rules gradually amounted to some 227 for monks, and the *pratimokṣa* portion of the vinaya basket classifies these rules according to their importance. Four rules if broken bring "defeat" or expulsion from the spiritual community. According to the Buddha-dharma, killing a human being is the worst thing any person can do.

The rules of less consequence instruct a monk (and most of these also apply to nuns) on how to comport himself. A monk may not raise his fist, should not urinate standing up, not speak with his mouth full, not laugh loudly in places that are inhabited, and so forth. Even the color of the mendicant's robe is specified in the training rules: "When a bhikkhu has acquired a new robe, one of three kinds of discolouring must be applied by him, that is, green or mud or dark brown" (Thera 1969: 108).

Eight special rules for nuns

About a year after Gautama attained enlightenment, his aunt requested that an order for nuns be established. Buddha complied with this request, but on the condition that eight special rules be observed by women mendicants.

1 Monks are senior to nuns, regardless of when they entered the order.
2 Nuns must not spend the rainy season in a place without monks.
3 Nuns must do their bimonthly service under the direction of monks.
4 Nuns must report to both monks and nuns after the rains retreat.
5 Nuns who break a rule must be disciplined by both monks and nuns.
6 Both monks and nuns must be present to ordain new nuns.
7 Nuns must never admonish monks.
8 Monks may admonish nuns.

All together bhikṣunīs have 311 rules. Truly, some rules were intended to protect women from being exploited by men. For example, a monk cannot ask a nun to repair his robe for him if she is not a blood relative.

Buddhist texts acknowledge that there is ultimately no difference between women and men. Women can attain enlightenment. But due to cultural conditions, it may be more difficult in many cases for women to gain the leisure and opportunity to lead an ascetic or monastic life. Indeed, a number of training precepts developed for nuns had to do with the overall position of women in ancient Indian society.

An early bhikṣunī named Soma attained enlightenment. But she had to tell Māra off when this personification of negativity appeared to try to dissuade her from gaining deep realization. Māra said:

> That which sages may attain,
> the Firm State [steady mind] very hard to reach,
> a woman with two fingers' worth
> of wisdom cannot win.

In response to this put-down, Soma answered snappily:

> What's it to do with a woman's state
> when the mind is well-composed
> with knowledge after knowledge born
> sees into Perfect Dhamma clear?
> For who indeed conceives it thus:
> a woman am I, a man am I
> of what indeed then am I –
> it's worthwhile Māra's speech.
>
> (*Samyutta Nikāya* verse 2: Khantipalo 1979: 143)

Naturally Māra, the lord of illusion whose job is to keep living beings on the wheel of rebirth, might advertise the differences between a woman and a man. But any enlightened being knows for sure that the mind is free of the body's accidental properties. Being a woman or a man is due to karma, and perhaps has relevance in the world. But as for enlightenment, wisdom has no sexual orientation and is not tied to bodily form.

Gautama is said to have declined twice his aunt's request to establish a saṃgha for nuns. He agreed only the third time Mahaprājapatī made her request. To some, the first two refusals make Buddha appear to be negative toward women. In recent times with the challenge from women's movements, Buddhists are coming to terms with this apparent misogyny. At the First International Conference on Buddhist Nuns the

Fourteenth Dalai Lama spoke of the cultural conditioning of Buddhist texts, and feels that women should not be discriminated against in the tradition.

> [I]n certain Buddhist texts, for example in the Vinaya texts, bhikshus are accorded a higher position than the bhikshunīs. Similarly, if one has created a certain fruitional karma and is sure to remain as a bodhisattva, it is taught that one must necessarily take a male body. Many of these explanations came about in relation to the times, the place, and the social conditions, and most probably were not the original thought of the Dharma itself.
>
> (Tenzin Gyatso, Fourteenth Dalai Lama: Tsomo 1988: 42)

Gautama's discourses: the poisoned arrow

Over forty-five years Gautama gave many discourses. One of them includes the parable of the poisoned arrow, which shows that Buddha was an intensely practical teacher. The sūtras normally tell a story, and set the context in a specific location in north India. An anthropologist reading about Gautama's conversation with Mālunkyaputta would be thrilled to know the many details it provides about bows and arrows in ancient India. In fact, most of the earliest historical evidence pertaining to life during the period of Gautama's mission is taken from the Buddhist scriptures. Presumably they were transmitted orally from Gautama's own mouth through his disciples for some three centuries. And as might be expected – when the oral tradition was committed to writing, views of the current religious climate may have entered into the texts. Nevertheless, historians rely heavily on the Buddhist scriptural materials for insights about life in the centuries surrounding Gautama's life. In any case, the conversation between Buddha and Mālunkyaputta gives insight into what kind of teacher Buddha was.

One day Buddha's disciple Mālunkyaputta was alone in meditation and seemed to become a little annoyed with the lack of information he was getting from the Tathāgata. It struck him that Buddha should answer certain questions. Or at least the enlightened one should admit that he did not know their answers, if that was the case. He decided to quit being Buddha's disciple if the Tathāgata did not either answer his questions or admit ignorance. So he approached Buddha in a respectful manner, and said:

> Here, venerable sir, while I was alone in meditation, the following thought arose in my mind: "These speculative views have been undeclared by the Blessed One. . . . If he does not declare these to me, then I will abandon the training and return to the low life." If the Blessed One knows "the world is eternal," let the Blessed One declare to me "the world is eternal"; if the Blessed One knows "the world is not eternal," let the Blessed One declare to me "the world is not eternal." If the Blessed One does not know either "the world is eternal" or "the world is not eternal," then it is straightforward for one who does not know and does not see to say, "I do not know, I do not see."
>
> (*Cūlamālunkya Sutta* 63: Nanamoli and Bodhi 1995: 533–534)

Mālunkyaputta continued in this manner, putting a long list of questions to Buddha: Is the world finite or infinite? Is the soul the same as the body or is it one thing and the body another? After death does a Tathāgata exist or not? After death does a Tathāgata both exist and not exist? After death does a Tathāgata not exist and not not-exist? The Buddhist tradition has since called these questions "unanswerables." No one will ever know whether Buddha could have answered them.

Buddha replied to Mālunkyaputta first by asking if he had ever promised to teach these things. The disciple had to admit that Buddha never promised to address these questions. Then Buddha gave a kind of "answer." He told a parable about a man injured by a poisoned arrow.

> Suppose, Mālunkyaputta, a man were wounded by an arrow thickly smeared with poison, and his friends and companions, his kinsmen and relatives brought a surgeon to treat him. The man would say: "I will not let the surgeon pull out this arrow until I know whether the man who wounded me was a noble or a brahmin or a merchant or a worker." And he would say: "I will not let the

> surgeon pull out this arrow until I know the name and the clan of the man who wounded me.
>
> (*Cūlamālunkya Sutta* 63: Nanamoli and Bodhi 1995: 534)

The Tathāgata continued to elaborate numerous objections brought up by the poor man. Before he would allow the surgeon to remove the arrow he wanted to know if the man was tall, short, or of middle height; dark, brown, or golden-skinned; if the man lived in a village, town, or city; if the bow from which the arrow was shot was a long-bow or a crossbow; whether the bowstring was fiber, reed, sinew, hemp, or bark; whether the shaft was wild or cultivated; what kinds of feathers were on the arrow's shaft, whether vulture, crow, hawk, peacock, or stork; what kind of sinew the shaft had as a binding, whether ox, buffalo, lion, or monkey; and what kind of arrow wounded him, whether hoof-tipped, curved, barbed, calf-toothed, or oleander.

As for the poor man in the parable . . . he would die before having his questions answered. Through the parable, the Tathāgata drew a parallel between the man shot with a poisoned arrow and Mālunkyaputta. Knowing whether an arrow in one's back had the feather of crow would not save the man's life. Just so, knowing whether the world is eternal or not will not save a person from the continual round of rebirth, old age, suffering, and death. Therefore, Buddha left his disciple's questions unresolved. Finally, Buddha simply reminded Mālunkyaputta that he did resolve the problem of suffering. Buddha's refusal to answer Mālunkyaputta's speculative religious questions is known as the Noble Silence.

Abhidharma: karma and its fruits

The subject of **karma** runs throughout Buddha's teachings. Karma is from a Sanskrit root *kṛ*, meaning to do or to make. Any action of body, speech, or mind associated with the mental formation of intention will bear fruit. The fruit matches the deed in kind. Acts of harming bring harm in return. Acts of kindness bring happiness in return. The fruits of karma can come within the same lifetime in which the deed was performed, or in a future lifetime. A person's motivation in committing the act determines the weight of the karma, and the intensity of its fruit. Buddha taught that the law of karma is as much a part of the workings of the universe as the laws governing material things. A mango pit will, under appropriate conditions, produce a mango tree – not a lemon tree. Just so, actions of hatred will produce suffering – never happiness.

The fruit of karma will be heavy or light depending upon how often the act is done, whether the act is completed, who is the object of the action, and the motivation with which the act was committed. For example, the repercussion for killing a human being is greater than for killing an animal. A harsher fruit comes when the act is done with hatred, than when it is done accidentally, and so forth. To lighten the painful effects of negative karma, a person can develop **four opponent powers** by doing the following:

1 Take **refuge** in the **Three Jewels**.
2 Confess one's sins.
3 Counteract the non-virtuous deed with its opposite (called the antidote).
4 Vow to make an effort not to repeat the act.

The Four Noble Truths (Four Great Facts)

- ***The fact of suffering.*** Duḥkha means suffering. It includes physical and emotional distress; the unhappiness of losing things that one likes; and the unease that comes from dealing with the fundamentally impermanent condition of all phenomena, including our bodies. Duḥkha is inherent in existence because birth, old age, sickness, and death are all infused with suffering.
- ***The fact of the cause of suffering.*** Gautama identified three poisons that cause duḥkha: ignorance, hatred, and greed. In any situation where one person inflicts harm on another, one finds one of the three poisons. Hatred and greed are rooted in ignorance about the nature of reality, **tathatā**.
- ***The fact of the end of suffering.*** The end of suffering is called nirvāṇa. Nirvāṇa is the opposite of saṃsāra, and can be attained when the three poisons are removed. The obstacle standing in the way of universal happiness is the fact that each sentient being has the responsibility to eliminate his or her own ignorance.

- *The fact of the path to end suffering.* Buddha prescribed the Noble Eightfold Path to help people free themselves from suffering. Each step on the path is called a "right" activity, indicating that it should be done thoroughly, correctly, and with kind consideration of all other living beings.

Mahāyāna sūtra literature

Mahāyānists accepted a handful of texts that Theravādins found unacceptable. These were originally written in Sanskrit, and appear to have come into India's culture after Buddha passed away. They were

BOX 9.4 A SPIRITUAL PATH: THE NOBLE EIGHTFOLD PATH

Gautama declared the Great Fact that eight steps could be taken to end suffering. The Noble Eightfold Path is divided into three categories: wisdom, mental cultivation, and moral conduct. The path is like a loop, because the practice of one step helps a person to grow stronger in the practice of another step.

Right view (wisdom). A person understands the Four Great Facts, which become the foundation for every act of body, speech, and mind. This wisdom involves right understanding of the nature of reality as characterized by the three marks of existence: non-self, impermanence, and suffering. Right view is the specifically Buddhist step on the path. All other steps are familiar to many religions. But a Buddhist uses the three marks to inform the other activities on the Noble Eightfold Path.

Right aim (wisdom). A person has thoughts of love and non-violence aimed at all living beings. This right thought lacks the selfish motivation involved in all unwholesome mental formations, such as ill-will, jealousy, and hypocrisy.

Right speech (virtue). A person speaks no lies, slander, gossip, or abusive words toward others, including enemies. Words are used to encourage living beings (including animals) to perform helpful activities that bring happiness to oneself and others. Words are used to tactfully speak truthfully and constructively.

Right action (virtue). A person promotes honorable, peaceful conduct that respects all life. Basic aspects of morality are included in right action, such as no sexual misconduct, no destruction of life, and so forth.

Right livelihood (virtue). A person makes a living in a job that brings happiness, education, health, and socially constructive ends. Someone engaged in right livelihood avoids work that involves harming, cheating, or misleading other living beings, such as selling weapons, dealing in harmful drugs, charging inordinate amounts of interest, and so forth.

Right effort (mental discipline). A person is energetic in developing wholesome states of mind, and eliminating unwholesome states of mind. The virtuous attitudes already present are cultivated, and the non-virtuous attitudes are diminished. With right effort, doing things that help other living beings becomes a joy, and is not experienced as troublesome.

Right mindfulness (mental discipline). A person pays close attention to his or her physical and mental condition. This is done so that constructive reactions can be made in response to events that happen. Right recollection is practiced in terms of four Foundations of Mindfulness, namely the body, feelings, states of mind, and mental formations.

Right contemplation (mental discipline). A person keeps attention unwavering on an object, be it a Buddha statue, a virtuous mental state such as patience, the breath, and so on. This concentrated activity – occurring with a center or focal point – naturally leads to eight mental absorptions: four in the Brahmā abodes of pure form, and four in the abstract states of no form. (See Table 9.1.)

never part of the Nikāya Buddhist canon. Here are a few of the most prominent.

Prajñāpāramitā sūtra

The Prajñāpāramitā or Perfection of Wisdom sūtras comprise a set of teachings composed in Sanskrit that have śūnyatā as their fundamental subject matter. When śūnyatā is realized, prajñā (wisdom) is perfect. Prajñāpāramitā is personified as feminine, akin to the gnostic Sophia. There are several Prajñāpāramitā sūtras of various lengths, from 100,000 verses to a single line or word. The date of their composition is uncertain, but sometime early in the history of Mahāyāna Buddhism – between the second centuries BCE and CE – is a likely range.

Vimalakīrti-nirdeśa sūtra

This text is unusual because a householder is the main character, rather than a monk. For this reason it became very popular in Asia. His name is Vimalakīrti, a wealthy businessman from the beautiful Ganges Valley town of Vaiśālī. He had an encounter with Mañjūśrī, the imaginal bodhisattva of wisdom. Mañjūśrī asked a question about the nature of reality to various of Gautama's disciples. Vimalakīrti remained silent while other disciples used many words about non-duality. His silence is interpreted as a profound display of wisdom, as the true nature of reality cannot be spoken. Otherwise, Vimalakīrti comments profoundly on the relationship between emptiness and form – the preferred subject of the text.

Infinite Life Sūtra (Sukhāvatīvyūha sūtra)

This is a key text of Pure Land Buddhism that relates a story told by Gautama Buddha one day on Vulture Peak in India. It is about a person named Dharmakāra who, in the distant past, generated bodhicitta, or the mind of enlightenment intent on relieving the suffering of all living beings. The story incorporates a list of forty-eight vows that Dharmakāra (Jap: Hōzo) spontaneously uttered, which established him as a bodhisattva. Of the forty-eight vows made by Dharmakāra, the twentieth declares his determination that all beings should have access to the Pure Land just hearing his name, and meritoriously wishing for rebirth with him. By the force of the bodhisattva's vows, it became possible for all beings to achieve liberation from saṃsāra through rebirth into the Pure Land. This Pure Land text further declares how Dharmakāra worked for eons to fulfill his vows. Through his efforts a Pure Land was created, and Dharmakāra became the Buddha named for infinite light, Amitābha.

SUPPORTIVE TEXTURE

Nikāya commentary

Buddhaghosa (fifth century CE) is thought to have been a Hindu brāhmaṇa convert to Buddhism. He was ordained as a monk and became a great scholar of Nikāya Buddhism, and was affiliated with the Great Monastery in Anuradhapura in Sri Lanka. In the Pāli language he compiled and translated the Nikāya canon; translated Sinhalese exegetical literature; wrote commentaries on each of the "three baskets" of the Buddhist canon; and drew upon oral and written sources to compose an extensive compendium of Buddhist practice known as the *Path of Purification* (*Visuddhimagga*).

The monumental *Path of Purification* is divided into three parts that represent the standard segmentation of Buddha's Noble Eightfold Path: virtue, mental discipline, and wisdom. Buddhaghosa sprinkled stories and verses into his painstaking description of methods by which practitioners can purify their moral action, meditation, and insight. As a Theravādin, Buddhaghosa emphasized the goal of becoming an arhat. This is attained once the wisdom of non-self is realized. In turn, wisdom depends upon the cultivation of virtue and mental discipline.

On virtue

To illustrate the guarding of the eye faculty in the practice of virtue, Buddhaghosa wrote of an elder who encountered on the road a lovely woman all decked out, running away from her husband. When she laughed out loud, the elder looked up and attained arhatship, because he suddenly saw bare reality. He saw only what was there, and not the signs of a woman, or a man, or beauty, or ugliness. Buddhaghosa says:

He saw the bones that were her teeth,
And kept in mind his first perception
And standing on that very spot
The Elder became an Arhat.

(Buddhaghosa 1976: 22 [I, 55])

When the woman's husband came after her, he asked the elder, "Venerable sir, did you by any chance see a woman?" To this, the now-arhat replied:

Whether it was a man or woman
That went by I noticed not;
But only that on this high road
There goes a group of bones.

(Buddhaghosa 1976: 22 [I, 55])

On mental discipline

Buddhaghosa named forty objects upon which meditators can focus attention to develop calmness. These include fire, water, blue flowers, a Buddha image, a rotting corpse, the Abodes of Brahmā, and the immaterial states in the realm of no form. He specified appropriate objects for meditators of different temperaments, and advised on how to distinguish one type of person from another by their manner of walking, eating, sleeping, and so on. According to Buddhaghosa, the benefits of concentration include various siddhis, such as walking on water; traveling in space like a winged bird while in a seated cross-legged position; gaining knowledge of the passing away and reappearance of beings using the divine eye; and recollecting one's past lives in great detail. To train in recollecting one's past lives, he advised:

> So a bhikkhu [monk] who is a beginner and wants to recollect in this way should go into solitary retreat . . . . [H]e should advert to all the things done during the whole night and day in reverse order. . . . And so, in reverse order too, he should advert to the things done on the second day back, and on the third, fourth and fifth day, and in the ten days, and in the fortnight, and as far back as a year. . . . When by these means he adverts to ten years, twenty years, and so on as far back as his own rebirth-linking in this existence, he should advert to the mentality-materiality occurring at the moment of death in the preceding existence.
>
> (Buddhaghosa 1976: 453–454)

Gautama Buddha recalled his past lives on the night of his enlightenment, and regularly made use of other siddhis, such as traveling through space, to aid in his teaching. As the siddhis are part of the science of yoga, Buddhaghosa included them in his treatise.

On wisdom

The practice of virtue and mental discipline prepare a person for gaining wisdom that realizes non-self and the dependently arising nature of the world. One gains wisdom through analysis of various matters included in Buddha's teaching of the Four Great Facts. This may be done through an analytical **vipaśyanā** meditation. For example, meditating on the five **skandhas** (heaps of conditioning) is a very effective means of realizing non-self. After attaining a certain level of quiescence through śamatha, the meditator can practice mindfulness of mental formations with a focus on these five heaps:

1 *Forms* – includes the five sense organs (for seeing, hearing, tasting, touching, smelling) plus the physical basis of thinking (sometimes considered to be the heart, the brain, or the whole body).
2 *Feelings* – includes the recognition of what is pleasant, unpleasant, or neutral.
3 *Perceptions* – includes the categories used to label our experience.
4 *Mental formations* – includes intention, the five hindrances, seven factors of enlightenment, and other mental contents.
5 *Minds* – includes the consciousnesses associated with each of the forms (eye, ear, tongue, skin, nose, heart/mind/body).

Through contemplating the skandhas that make up a person, it becomes evident that living beings are: (1) not stable, (2) provoke suffering, and (3) ultimately have no inherent existence. With the direct experience of non-self the meditator achieves nirvāṇa or the peace of no more suffering. Nirvāṇa can be attained while the meditator is still alive (nirvāṇa with the body), or at the point of passing away (nirvāṇa without the body). Nirvāṇa in the body can occur for a maximum of seven days at a time, without danger to the meditator. On the other hand, nirvāṇa realized at the moment of death results in no more compulsory rebirth, hence no more duḥkha. Realization of non-self is the crux of Buddhist wisdom. After realizing non-self one can choose no more rebirth (as does an arhat), or choose to return to saṃsāra and be in it, but not of it (as does a bodhisattva).

CROSS-OVER TEXTURE

Songs of the early Buddhist nuns

The earliest known anthology of women's writing in India and possibly in the world is the *Therīgatha* (verses of the Therīs, or elders) written around 80 BCE. The *Therīgatha* is a collection of 522 verses composed by women who were Buddhist renunciates. Thoughts about the Therīs' lives and songs circulated orally for centuries. They were finally compiled in the *Paramatta Dipani*, a commentary dating from the 500s CE (Tharu and Lalita 1990: 68). Generally, the Therīs sang of the sorrow in their lives, and the breakthrough insights that gave them freedom from worldly cares. Joining the Buddhist saṃgha allowed women to move out of the householder stage of life. They could be relieved of the drudgery that the life at home could bring to a woman in India of Buddha's day. But happiness did not come automatically to those who renounced the world. Happiness was guaranteed only after each had realized for herself the import of the Buddha's teachings. The *gāthās* sung by Therīs named Ubbiri, Sungalamata, and Mettika make clear that the sufferings of women came from many sources – loss of a child, an "unscrupulous man," poverty, household drudgery, or old age.

Ubbiri mourned the loss of her daughter, crying heart-broken in the charnel ground for Jiva. At some point in her despair Ubbiri realized the profound truth of impermanence. In these verses the Therīs told how the Buddha's dharma called her back to her senses.

> "O Ubbiri, who wails in the wood
> 'O Jiva! Dear daughter!'
> Return to your senses. In this charnel field
> Innumerable daughters, once as full of life as Jiva,
> Are burnt. Which of them do you mourn?"
> The hidden arrow in my heart plucked out,
> The dart lodged there, removed.
> The anguish of my loss,
> The grief that left me faint all gone,
> The yearning stilled,
> To the Buddha, the Dharma, and the Saṃgha
> I turn, my heart now healed.
>
> (Quoted in Tharu and Lalita 1990: 68–69; translated by Uma Chakravarti and Kumkum Roy)

Sungalamata was the mother of a boy who became a Buddhist monk. After living the householder's life, she too longed to gain the same kind of freedom and insight that was available to her child. She sang:

> A woman well set free! How free I am,
> How wonderfully free, from kitchen drudgery.
> Free from the harsh grip of hunger,
> And from empty cooking pots.
> Free too of that unscrupulous man,
> The weaver of sunshades.
> Calm now, and serene I am,
> All lust and hatred purged.
> To the shades of the spreading trees I go
> And contemplate my happiness.
>
> (Quoted in Tharu and Lalita 1990: 69; translated by Uma Chakravarti and Kumkum Roy)

Mettika had grown old. She had been born to an eminent brāhmaṇa family, but eventually took up the nun's life. As an enlightenend member of the nun's saṃgha, Mettika would have taught other women the Buddha-dharma. Here is her teaching on the Noble Truth of the suffering of old age.

> Though I am weak and tired now,
> And my youthful step long gone,
> Leaning on this staff,
> I climb the mountain peak.
> My cloak cast off, my bowl overturned,
> I sit here on this rock.
> And over my spirit blows

The breath
Of liberty.
I've won, I've won the triple gems.
The Buddha's way is mine.
(Quoted in Tharu and Lalita 1990: 69–70; translated by Uma Chakravarti and Kumkum Roy)

Mettika's verses come from the mind and heart of a woman of India. Yet her sentiments express a Buddhist insight and the happiness of liberation that could easily have been spoken by a Zen Buddhist in Japan centuries later.

Coping with starvation in a Thai village

Food has never been taken for granted by the majority of people on this planet. Some people die of hunger, some flee from famine, and some perform rituals to stave off disaster. The Therī Sungalamata spoke of freedom from the suffering of "empty cooking pots" and the "harsh grip of hunger" that came with Buddhist realization. Wisdom and meditation can combat hunger to some extent. Yet wisdom is not always enough. Recall the famine that drove the early Jain leader Bhadrabāhu in the third century BCE to leave the Ganges basin area (where Sungalamata also lived) with his disciples (see page 182). And even when times are good, religious people remember from where their food comes. In a Thai village, people who call themselves Buddhists perform ceremonies that pre-date the Buddhist religion. A veneer of Buddhist lore is added to something more fundamental – worship of Nang Phrakosob, the goddess of rice.

Nang Phrakosob is the female rice spirit who gave herself for the sake of life and the dharma (religion) from time immemorial. Villagers in Thailand tell a story of the four cosmic ages when four Buddhas came to earth along with rice. As in India, the Thai people believe that with every age (each lasting thousands of years) the spiritual and material condition of humankind degenerates. The present age is the worst of all and everyone awaits the coming of the future Buddha Maitreya to usher in a golden age. At that wonderful time fragrant rice will again be plentiful, and people will have great spiritual capacity to live according to the Buddha-dharma.

A keen sense of the relationship between ecology and spirituality comes through the story of Nang Phrakosob. Thai Buddhists feel that rice is a gift from the worldly gods that helps human beings to sustain their lives and their religious practice. The female rice spirit came to human beings four times; and four times she left. At the start of each age a Buddha partook of the rice, and it is said that the first Buddha actually introduced rice to the region of India where he lived and taught. Yet whenever people mishandled the rice over the ages, Nang Phrakosob became upset and withdrew from the human community. Once it was only through the persuasion of animals (a fish, golden deer, and parrot who were some form of beneficent spiritual beings in disguise) that she agreed to return to human civilization. Another time she was moved to return only because people recited sacred mantras.

In the first age a grain of rice was a bright, silvery color the size of seven human fists. At that time rice carried the amazing fragrance of coconut and cow's milk. In the second age a grain of rice was the size of four human fists. It became smaller in the following two ages having the girth of three fists, and then shrank to half that size. Why? Because human beings acted in a non-virtuous manner and harmed her. The manner in which human beings harmed and insulted Nang Phrakosob tells much about the ethical sensibilities of the Thai Buddhists. People beat the rice and harmed her; they tried to grab her and broke the stalk in two down the middle; and they began to sell her. Eventually human beings had to do the very hard labor of planting and harvesting rice themselves. It was no longer given freely as in the beginning. In addition, the Thai people had rituals they needed to perform to gain the cooperation of the local spirits (*phii*).

The story of Nang Phrakosob has many references to folk beliefs that are in line with an ancient cosmology. It refers to the gods Indra and Brahmā, the snake king, local spirits, and a mythical ruler. According to Buddhist teachings none of these imaginal players knows the path to enlightenment. Yet they are players in the Thai folk religious drama. Buddhist monks do not require the Thai people to give up these ancient agricultural beliefs. Yet Buddhist values have found their way into the story. And in the end the story's message is that a person's very life goes hand in hand with the practice of religion. They see from the reaction of Nang Phrakosob that if people are non-virtuous they will starve. The story makes several references to starvation and enumerates the various kinds of rice that became available over time. Thus it not only gives a moral teaching, but also provides a folk history of the people of northeast Thailand. The final message of the story about rice in Thailand is that people should try to become as patient as Maitreya, the future Buddha himself. The ceremony (called the *sukhwan khaw*) that calls the rice spirits into the fields ends with this blessing:

> Anyone who eats this rice, may he have a long life, may he become as wise as Phraa Chao Mahosot [Gautama Buddha in a former life] and be as patient as Phraa Mettai [Maitreya, the future Buddha]. Let everyone's wished be fulfilled as I have said.
>
> (Tambiah 1970: 364)

PART 3
BUDDHIST PERFORMANCE

MEDITATION

Gautama saw the nature of reality and escaped from the compulsion to be reborn over and over again in saṃsāra. He attained enlightenment while meditating. Thus meditation became the key practice of Buddhism – because the ultimate aim of every Buddhist is to awaken as Buddha did. Consequently, when we think of the backdrop of the stage upon which characters in the Buddhist tradition enact their drama, we think of meditation. The Buddhist tradition adjusted to the society and needs of people as it traveled through South, Central, and East Asia. In this process of cultural transformation, several styles of meditation developed.

Nikāya Buddhist *satipaṭṭhāna* meditation: four applications of mindfulness

The Satipaṭṭhāna Sutta, discourse on the foundation of mindfulness (Pāli: *sati*), is a widely used sūtra (Pāli: *sutta*) from the Nikāya canon. In this lecture Buddha taught four ways to apply mindfulness. Any one of these four foundations of mindfulness can lead the meditator to realize the three marks of existence: non-self, impermanence, and suffering. In modern times such application of mindfulness is often called vipaśyanā meditation. These four topics on which a Buddhist meditates form the basis of all other Buddhist styles of meditation. Here are some typical instructions from the Nikāya scriptures:

- *Mindfulness of the body.* Contemplate the "body in the body." Become aware of the process of breathing, mindful of the continuous alternation of the in breath and out breath. Doing so, notice the impermanence of the breath. Next, apply mindfulness to various small actions involved in sitting, lying down, standing, and walking. In addition to noticing things like the lifting of one's arm or blinking, also become mindful of the hotness or coolness of one's internal organs, and so forth. Thus, becoming aware of the body's condition, notice how pain and pleasure are associated with the body. These observations take one into the next category in which mindfulness is applied to feelings.
- *Mindfulness of feelings.* Be mindful of one's reactions to sense impressions, and note whether they are pleasant, unpleasant, or neutral. Gain a realistic impression of one's likes and dislikes in response to things seen, heard, touched, smelled, tasted, and thought. Now apply awareness of the three types of feelings to better shape actions that stem from them. For example, if responding to a feeling of annoyance (which is unpleasant), make the choice to practice patience and not react with anger. On the other hand, take a pleasant feeling of love for one's cat and extend it to all cats in the universe!
- *Mindfulness of state of mind.* Now become mindful of one's general mental condition be it tense, excited, bored, stressed, balanced, calm, loving, patient, greedy, angry, dull, concentrated, and so forth. Then notice that these conditions do not persist. They change and can be changed. Anger can be transformed into calmness; greed can be transformed into expansiveness; balance can be enhanced; and so forth. The image of eating stew may be helpful here. Being mindful of

one's "state of mind" is like tasting the soup of a stew. Being mindful of "mental formations" (see the next paragraph) is like tasting the carrots, potatoes, onions, etc. in the stew.

- *Mindfulness of mental formations.* Some Buddhist philosophers name fifty-two mental formations. Several of them (such as intention) occur with every mental event, while others are associated with either wholesome or unwholesome attitudes. Some (such as sleep) can even be positive, negative, or neutral. The point is to become aware of them. Then enhance the positive ones and eliminate the negative ones. Two lists of mental formations are often given for contemplation: five hindrances that work against enlightenment, and seven factors that are conducive to enlightenment. Buddha gave suggestions on how all the negative mental formations can be reduced and eliminated. Likewise he taught how to develop and perfect the positive mental formations.

Tibetan Buddhist *lam-rim* meditation: stages of the path to enlightenment

Nyingma, Śākya, Kagyu, and Geluk are the four schools of Tibetan Buddhism. Each composed **lam-rim** (stages of the path) texts that include these basic instructions as a means to attain enlightenment.

- *Take refuge.* Bow down, making offerings, and take refuge with a deep conviction that Buddha taught a suitable path to enlightenment. Refuge is taken in the Three Jewels: Buddha, dharma, and spiritual community.
- *Recognize human potential.* Contemplate the preciousness of human life. Develop a sense of gratitude and urgency by contemplating the lives of less fortunate beings who live in saṃsāra, including animals, hungry ghosts, and hell beings. Consider how human life is favorable for enlightenment because it includes enough suffering to motivate one to end suffering for oneself and others. Think how worldly godlings are less fortunate than human beings in the sense that their lives are almost too privileged.
- *Contemplate death.* Maintain an awareness of death, to feel motivated to use one's precious human life wisely. Think how one's death will certainly come, but the time of that death is uncertain (and could be at any time). Consider how the only thing one can take at the time of death is the mental impact of spiritual practice. Resolve to practice dharma to prepare for death and a favorable rebirth, or freedom from saṃsāra.
- *Remember karma and its fruits.* Consider how one's acts of body, speech, and mind will bear fruit. Think how virtuous action brings happiness, while non-virtuous action brings duḥkha.
- *Generate bodhicitta.* Establish the bodhisattva motivation to meditate for the benefit of all living beings. Think about how kind living beings have been to one. (They are like one's mothers.) Over the course of many lifetimes, all beings have been at one time or another very kind to one. Therefore, generate the feeling to help them.
- *Realize śūnyatā.* Go deeply into consideration about the true nature of reality – tathatā. Do this by analyzing the five heaps, or the impermanent character of various objects.

Zen kōan meditation: does a dog have Buddha-nature?

A famous Zen kōan goes like this:

> A monk once asked Master Joshu, "Has a dog the Buddha Nature or not?" Joshu said, "Mu!"
>
> (Shibayama 1974: 19)

What is the meaning of the case? One commentary goes like this:

> In studying Zen, one must pass the barriers set up by ancient Zen Masters. For the attainment of incomparable satori, one has to cast away his discriminating mind. . . . Now tell me, what is the barrier of the Zen Masters? Just this "Mu" – it is the barrier of Zen. . . . Those who have passed the barrier will not only see Joshu clearly, but will go hand in hand with all the Masters of the past, see them face to face. You will see with the same eye that they see with and hear with the same ear. Wouldn't it be wonderful? Don't you want to pass the barrier? Then concentrate yourself into this

> "Mu," with your 360 bones and 84,000 pores, making your whole body one great inquiry. Day and night work intently at it. Do not attempt nihilistic or dualistic interpretations. It is like having bolted a red hot iron ball. You try to vomit it but cannot.
>
> (Shibayama 1974: 19)

Whoever can give this answer with *complete conviction* passes through the gateless barrier of Zen, because answering in such a way can only be done with an enlightened mind. The peculiar thing about this kōan is the meaning of "NO!" ("MU!")

Supposedly everything has Buddha-nature. Then, why is the answer, "MU!"? Whatever the practitioner decides . . . "MU!" must be delivered with 100 percent certainty. "MU!" contains the whole universe and the whole person. "MU!" is delivered from the hara, and with body–mind not separated by a single iota.

There are some variations of answers recorded in Zen literature. Here the master recited a traditional verse, and waits for an answer.

> MASTER:
>
> The song on "mu," written by Zen master Ryofu, says:
> "Joshu's dog has no Buddha-nature,
> Ten thousand green mountains are hidden in an ancient mirror,
> The one-footed Persian goes into China,
> And the eight-armed Nata carries out administrative orders."
> How about this?
>
> ANSWER:
>
> First the pupil says, "Mu." Then, making a fist, he punches the base of his master's skull. In this case, the master says, "Explain!" and the pupil answers, "This is called the hit-in-the-base-of-the-skull."
>
> (Hoffman 1975: 63)

Chan master Hui-neng, the sixth patriarch of the meditation school, taught that the nature of mind is pure, and that original mind could be suddenly recognized. Hui-neng did not teach ways to attain sudden enlightenment, but the eighth patriarch Ma-zu (709–788) developed tactics of aesthetic shock for doing so. With sudden gestures that involved hitting, shouting, and surprising his disciples, Ma-zu prompted them to recognize the gap in their stream of thought. Ma-zu used the method of direct pointing to lead students to face the non-dual, now-consciousness of their don't know, beginner's mind. This beginner's mind is the Buddha's silence. It is the gap in thought that allows one to recognize the relationship between śūnyatā and forms. It is the key to freedom from suffering. A great Zen master Hakuin (1685–1768) liked to speak of the Great Doubt that kōan meditation generated in the mind. He told disciples that the puzzle should continually intensify, creating greater and greater doubt, through an ever deeper and more pressing question. The question becomes like a red hot iron ball in the belly. The more intense the Doubt becomes, the more explosive the enlightenment experience is when the Doubt is overcome. Awakening comes in a flash of silence.

Pure Land meditation: visualizing Amitābha

Pure Land Buddhists practice a set of visualizations recorded in the *Infinite Life Sūtra* with the aim of being reborn with Buddha Amitābha into the Western Paradise. The text contains instructions that Gautama Buddha gave to Queen Vaidehi who (along with King Bimbisāra) had been imprisoned by their son. After her husband was starved to death, the queen appealed mentally to Buddha who was living nearby at the time. He appeared in a hierophanic vision as a response to her heartfelt prayer, and taught her to meditate on Amitābha and the Pure Land. As the Pure Land tradition evolved, these teachings became known as Settled Mind and Dispersed Mind practices because they include variant guidelines for people of greater and lesser spiritual development. The text instructs Pure Land practitioners to ground their meditation in three pure actions: (1) care for parents, serve elders, and so on; (2) take refuge in the Three Jewels, observe proper decorum, and so on; and (3) generate the mind of enlightenment, believe in the cause and effect of karma, and so forth.

Pure Land meditators should sit facing west and observe the sun "which is like a drum suspended above the horizon" until the image becomes clear with eyes open or closed (Hsiao 1995: 97). Next they imagine

Plate 9.4 "Buddha Amitābha." Pure Land Buddhists visualize Buddha Amitābha with streaming rays of light. This Buddha brings people into his paradise with a hook of compassion that draws their hearts upward toward him. Amitābha is popular in East Asia where Pure Land Buddhism developed.

clear water that becomes bright, transparent ice, which turns into lapis lazuli. Gradually that base is decorated with numerous golden ropes, jewels, colored lights, banners, and musical instruments. Meditators are instructed to be constantly mindful of this visualization, except when sleeping. Upon the lapis lazuli ground more beautiful things are visualized, such as seven rows of tall jeweled trees with flowers and leaves, nets of pearls – all shining with lights, and so forth. After some time, Pure Land practitioners feel they are seeing the Pure Land.

In the course of Pure Land visualizations Buddha Amitābha appears with a bodhisattva on either side. The figures are huge, and so must be mentally entered from a small mark such as a white curl of hair situated between the eyebrows of Amitābha. From a single sign like that, numerous other marks spontaneously emerge. Through this type of concentration the meditator enters a state of samādhi. While in this rarified state of one-pointed concentration, the meditator should aspire to be reborn into the Western Paradise. At this point Pure Land practitioners may feel that their bodies are illuminated with lights of 500 colors. They may feel their spiritual eye opening up. Sometimes the body of Amitābha seems to fill the sky completely. At other times it may be some sixteen or eighteen feet tall. In any case, faithful Pure Land practitioners have faith that their practice of such visualizations will become useful at the moment of death. At that time, they sincerely aim to take rebirth in the Western Paradise and be drawn up by Amitābha's hook of compassion. The experience of being reborn will feel as quick as the snapping of one's fingers.

KEY POINTS

- Gautama was born in what is today Nepal, in the sixth century BCE during a speculative period of Indian history when new questions were being asked about karma, rebirth, and escape from saṃsāra.
- After waking up to the nature of reality – thus meriting the title Buddha – Gautama spent forty-five years teaching four Great Facts or Noble Truths about suffering, its origin, its cessation, and the Noble Eightfold Path to freedom from suffering.

- Gautama rejected the absolute authority of the Vedic scriptures; denied the validity of the Āryan caste system (although he was born into it); discounted the tradition mandating the procreation of sons (although he had a son); and overrode the Āryan āśrama system that reserved intensive spiritual practice for the elderly (by starting early). Besides that, he rejected the dearly held notion of an eternal, unchanging ātman.
- The Buddhist tradition is divided into two main branches that have the same philosophical foundation: (1) Nikāya, which spread through South Asia, emphasizes the goal of the arhat who gains freedom from rebirth. (2) Mahāyāna, which spread through Central and East Asia, emphasizes the goal of the bodhisattva who continually returns to the world for the sake of living beings.
- Buddhist scripture is divided into three "baskets" including (1) stories and training rules, (2) Gautama's discourses, and (3) systematic discussions of the key teachings. Beyond that, many commentaries have been written on these three baskets.
- Gautama was a practical man who did not confirm or deny the existence of God. He did not discuss abstract cosmology, or spell out points of doctrine for others to believe. Everything the Buddha taught is said to be "interpretable" – except for his observation on the emptiness of persons and phenomena.
- Although Buddhism disappeared from India for over six centuries (from about 1200 to 1800 CE) it adapted to new cultural circumstances. Several styles of meditative practice developed among practitioners of the Nikāya, Tibetan, Pure Land, and Zen schools of Buddhism.

STUDY QUESTIONS

1. List the various kinds of imaginal and exceptional players according to whether they are more involved in Nikāya or Mahāyāna Buddhism.
2. Distinguish mythic, historical, and philosophical elements in the story of Buddha's life. Why do you think the Buddhist tradition mixes these elements?
3. Name several historical persons, and state their contribution to the development of Buddhist ideas and practices.
4. What are the basic teachings of Buddha-dharma? (Hint: See the Four Great Facts with the Noble Eightfold Path, and the six perfections.)
5. Describe the realms of saṃsāra according to Buddhist cosmology. What is the relationship between mental states of meditation and places that exist?
6. Identify some styles of meditation that developed in the Buddhist tradition.
7. Contrast the life and aspirations of Buddhist monks and nuns with those of laypeople such as villagers in Thailand.

GLOSSARY

Abodes of Brahmā Four levels of meditation or dhyāna in the realm of pure form of saṃsāra in Buddhist cosmology; each abode is associated with a boundless social emotion: love, compassion, sympathetic joy, and equanimity; where the god Brahmā dwells.

Ādi Buddha (Sanskrit) Mahāyāna Buddhist concept of the ground of awareness personified through this metaphor.

aniconic Not involving figural representations (icons) of extraordinary persons, such as prophets, buddhas, and so forth.

arhat (Sanskrit) Person who has realized non-self and need not take rebirth after passing away; goal of Theravāda Buddhist practice.

ātman the soul or eternal self; some Hindus strive to realize that ātman is none other than Brāhmaṇa (i.e., the living essence of the universe).

bhikṣu (Sanskrit) Buddhist monk.

bhikṣunī (Sanskrit) Buddhist nun.

bodhicitta (Sanskrit) Mind of enlightenment; compassionate mental decision to bring all living beings out of suffering; with this in mind the practitioner starts along the bodhisattva path.

bodhisattva (Pāli: bodhisatta) Theravādins typically use the word *bodhisatta* with reference to Gautama Buddha before he became enlightened – including past lifetimes from the time he was an ascetic named Sumedha. Mahāyānists use the word with reference to practitioners (at different levels of spiritual development) who seek enlightenment and vow to return to the world endlessly to free sentient beings from suffering.

buddha bodies Buddhist concept referring to the forms in which an enlightened being can appear to people. (1) The form body is a flesh and blood person, such as the human Gautama who lived in India. (2) The communion body is the subtle form body that appears in the dreams and contemplative visions of skilled meditators and faithful people. (3) The dharma body is the mind of an enlightened being, seen when someone realizes the deepest point of Buddha's teachings. Theravāda Buddhists do not discuss the communion body.

dharma (Sanskrit) Duty (Hinduism); Buddha's teaching, as in Buddha-dharma. From a Sanskrit root *dhṛ*, meaning to bear or uphold. This represents the law of the universe that upholds or maintains existence.

dhyāna (Sanskrit) Meditation; any of eight high states of consciousness within saṃsāra reached through śamatha meditation; jhāna in Pāli; basic term used for Buddhist meditation school (see Zen).

duḥkha (Sanskrit) Suffering, dissatisfaction, alienation; Buddha's first Great Fact says this characterizes life before enlightenment.

four opponent powers Four Buddhist ways to minimize the effects of negative karma: take refuge, confess, apply an antidote, and vow not to repeat the act.

hwadu (Korean) Buddhist meditation practice involving focus on the question or key point of a kōan.

***Jātaka* tales** Birth tales about Buddha's past lives.

jiriki (Japanese) Self-power; refers to Buddhist practice in which personal discipline and effort plays a major role, as in Zen. (See also tariki.)

karma (Sanskrit) Actions of body, speech, or mind that bear fruit of similar type; a key tenet in the liberation traditions of India.

kōan (Japanese) Mental puzzle based on enlightened words and actions of Buddhist masters of the meditation schools, especially Chan masters who lived during the Tang dynasty (ca. 600–900) in China.

lam-rim (Tibetan) Stages of the path; genre of Tibetan Buddhist literature outlining meditations according to topics designed to lead to realization of emptiness and generation of compassion.

Mahāyāna Northern Buddhism. Culturally progressive branch of Buddhism found primarily in East and Central Asian countries: Taiwan, Korea, Japan, and Vietnam (which has both Mahāyāna and Theravāda), as well as pre-Communist China and Tibet; holds bodhisattva ideal.

mandala (Sanskrit) Mystic diagram representing the universe as a microcosm correlated with a mental state of spiritual value such as compassion, peace, and so forth; used in tantric Buddhism.

mantra (Sanskrit) Mystic syllables whose vibration facilitates perception of beings in the imaginal realm; used in religions from India.

mudra (Sanskrit) Mystic hand gestures that symbolize various spiritual states, such as freedom from fear; many correlate with beings in the imaginal realm; used in religions from India; important to Jain, Buddhist, and Hindu iconography.

Nikāya Term for the Theravāda Buddhist tradition or any of about 18 early Buddhist schools (all of which are now extinct except Theravāda); term brought into use by contemporary scholars of Buddhism to replace the negative-sounding "Hīnayāna" ("lesser vehicle") found in classic Mahāyāna texts with reference to the early Buddhist schools including Theravāda.

nirvāṇa (Sanskrit) Blown out, Buddhist enlightenment whereby rebirth into saṃsāra stops.

Noble Eightfold Path The eight steps which Buddha recommended as the way to attain enlightenment; these constitute the fourth Great Fact (Noble Truth); divided into three categories: wisdom, moral conduct, and mental cultivation.

non-self Lack of intrinsic self; translation of *anātman* (Sanskrit) or *anatta* (Pāli); term Buddhists use to indicate that sentient beings have a dynamic stream of consciousness rather than an eternal soul (ātman); Buddhist tradition names non-self as one of the three marks of existence.

parinirvāṇa (Sanskrit) A Buddha's final nirvāṇa, which occurs at the time of death.

prajñā (Sanskrit) Wisdom; in Buddhism realization of śūnyatā or anātman.

refuge Standard prayer that orients a Buddhist's mind toward the Three Jewels: Buddha, dharma, saṃgha.

śamatha (Sanskrit) quiescence, calmness; a branch of Buddhist meditation leading to the dhyānas, but not to enlightenment.

saṃsāra (Sanskrit) The cycle of birth and death characterized by suffering; until one attains nirvāṇa (Buddhism), moksha (Hinduism), or *kevala* (Jainism) one is reborn into saṃsāra.

saṃgha (Sanskrit) Buddhist fourfold spiritual community; monks, nuns, laymen, and laywomen; typically refers to monks and nuns.

satori (Japanese) Zen Buddhist term for enlightenment.

shikan-taza (Japanese) Just sitting; represents the highest form of meditation for Zen Buddhists of Dōgen's Sōtō school.

siddha (Sanskrit) Indian yogī who practices tantra.

siddhis (*iddhi*: Pāli) Supernormal powers such as: traveling in space like a winged bird, while in a seated, cross-legged position; gaining the divine eye, whereby one gains knowledge of the passing away and reappearance of beings; and recollecting one's past lives in great detail.

six perfections Buddhist spiritual path of a bodhisattva, involving the practice of: generosity, morality, patience, joyous effort, calm abiding, and wisdom.

skandhas (Sanskrit) Five heaps of conditioning making up the person, according to Buddhist theory: forms, feelings, perceptions, mental formations, and minds.

śramaṇa (Sanskrit) Wandering ascetic.

śūnyatā (Sanskrit) Emptiness, lack of inherent existence; deepest nature of reality as dependently arising according to Buddhist philosophy.

supreme buddha Specialized term with reference only to buddhas who come into the world to show the path to enlightenment when it has become defunct; examples are Dīpaṃkara, Gautama, and Maitreya (the future Buddha).

tantra (Sanskrit) Form of yogīc practice involving mantras, mudras, and maṇḍalas; called Vajrayāna Buddhism in India and Tibet, and Shingon in Japan.

tariki (Japanese) Other power; refers to Buddhist practice in which reliance on the compassion of Amida Buddha plays a key role, as in the Pure Land schools. (See also jiriki.)

Tathāgata (Sanskrit) Thus-gone One; title that Gautama Buddha liked to apply to himself.

tathatā (Sanskrit) Thusness; reality as it is; Buddhist concept telling how things appear when a person is enlightened: just so.

Theravāda Southern Buddhism. Culturally conservative branch of Buddhism found primarily in South Asian countries: Sri Lanka, Kampuchea, Laos, Myanmar, and Vietnam (which has both Theravāda and Mahāyāna). Holds arhat ideal, and emphasizes historical Buddha.

Three Jewels Buddhist way of talking about the three complementary aids to spiritual transformation: Buddha, dharma, and saṃgha.

three marks of existence Non-self, impermanence, and suffering (Sanskrit: anātman, anitya, duḥkha). Buddhist teachings typically involve a discussion of these.

three poisons Three mental afflictions that cause suffering and rebirth into saṃsāra, according to Buddhist theory: ignorance, greed, hatred.

tripiṭaka (Pāli) Three baskets of Buddha's teaching: vinaya (including the monastic saṃgha training precepts), sūtras (discourses), and abhidharma (systematic commentaries).

Tuṣita heaven A realm of existence in Buddhist cosmology, where Maitreya, the future Buddha, waits to descend to earth. Buddha's mother was reborn here.

vipaśyanā (Sanskrit) Branch of Buddhist meditation leading to insight into the three marks of existence. (See also śamatha.)

zazen (Japanese) Discipline of sitting meditation, emphasized by Zen Buddhists.

KEY READING

Conze, Edward, Horner, I. B., Snellgrove, David, and Waley, Arthur (ed. and trans.) (1995) *Buddhist Texts through the Ages*, Oxford: Oneworld Publications.

Digha Nikāya (1997) *The Long Discourses of the Buddha: A Translation of the Digha Nikāya*, trans. M. Walshe, Boston, MA: Wisdom Publications.

Gross, Rita M. (1993) *Buddhism After Patriarchy*, Albany, NY: State University Press of New York.

Jones, K. (1989) *The Social Face of Buddhism: An Approach to Political and Social Activism*, Boston, MA: Wisdom Publications.

Majjhima Nikāya (1995) *The Middle Length Discourses of the Buddha: A New Translation of the Majjhima Nikāya*, trans. B. Nanamoli and B. Bodhi, Boston, MA: Wisdom Publications.

Rahula, Walpola (1974) *What the Buddha Taught*, New York: Grove Press.

Suzuki, D. T. ([1958] 1973) *Zen and Japanese Culture*, Princeton, NJ: Princeton University Press.

CHAPTER 10

Hindu tradition

TIMELINE

	BCE	
	ca. 3100–1500 (from radiocarbon dating)	Indus Valley/Sindhu Sarasvatī Civilization
	ca. 1500–1000	Āryan migration (disputed)
	CE	
12 Āḻvārs and 63 Nāyaṉārs	ca. 600s–900s	
Śaṅkara	ca. 800	
Rāmānuja	1056–1157	
Madhva	1238?–1317?	
Jñāneśvara	1275–1296?	
Vallabha	1475–1531	
Caitanya	1485–1533	
Mīrābaī	Early sixteenth century	
Tulsī Dās	1532–1623	
	1525–1857	Mughal rule in India
Rāmprasād Sen	1718–1775	
Rām Mohan Roy	1772–1833	
	1857–1947	British rule in India
Bāl Gangādar Tilak	1856–1920	
Mohandās Gāndhī	1869–1948	
	1875	Ārya Samāj founded
	1893	Vivekānanda in Chicago
A. C. Bhaktivedānta Swāmī Prabhupāda	1896–1977	
Ānandamayī Mā	1896–1981	
	1947	Creation of Pakistan
	1949	Indian constitution outlaws caste discrimination
Maharishi Mahesh Yogī	b. 1917	
B. K. S. Iyengar	b. 1918	

"Hinduism" is an umbrella term that covers an almost bewildering array of religious expressions, including "330 million gods" . . . which are actually just One. Yet in spite of the great variety of ideas and practices encompassed by the term, Hindus generally hold these four assumptions in common: (1) The universe has no beginning and no end, but goes through regular cycles of creation, maintenance, and destruction. (2) Living beings go through a cycle of rebirths propelled by their karma until they attain liberation. (3) Ascetic practice is effective in bringing human beings to liberation from the cycle of rebirth. (4) The core Vedic scriptures were revealed, and specially trained people of the priestly class preserve their authoritative content.

The history of migration in ancient India is much disputed nowadays. Yet it appears that people carrying two distinct religious cultures interacted over millennia to produce modern Hinduism. Āryan Vedic traditions (where Āryan is a cultural, not a racial term) co-mingled with traditions of the Harappāns who developed the Indus Valley Civilization. Additional influences from India's various indigenous peoples must also be considered in the mix. Much is known about Vedic religion, and almost nothing is known about the older Indus Valley culture. Even the relationship between the Indus Valley people and other indigenous Indians is not clear. People holding Āryan traditions seem to have politically overpowered inhabitants of the Indus River Valley in the second millennium BCE. Thereafter the Āryans produced a body of sacred literature that became the foundation of Vedic religion. These Vedas still form the core of modern Hindu scripture. On the other hand, cultural influences from the people who lived along the Indus River (ca. 3100–1500 BCE) are more difficult to trace because they left no literature, and the inscribed seals found in their settlements have yet to be deciphered. But clearly many non-Vedic elements filtered into an ever-growing body of religious worship and literature over the generations.

The Vedic religion is based on the teachings of Āryan **ṛṣis** whose 1,028 surviving hymns comprise the *Ṛgveda.* The seers' hymns appear comparable in age to hymns attributed to Zarathushtra in the *Avesta.* Both date from the second millennium BCE. Linguistic and literary analyses suggest that the *Ṛgveda* and the *Avesta* belonged to people related by language and culture. Zarathushtra and the Vedic ṛṣis shared a common religious foundation derived from the Āryans. Scholars estimate that the Āryans split into two groups before Zarathushtra lived – and certainly before the hymns of the *Ṛgveda* and the *Avesta* were written down. But regardless of their common origin, religion in Iran and India developed quite differently. The mingling of Indus Valley and Indian folk traditions with Āryan culture produced a multi-faceted Hindu tradition the like of which never developed in Iran or elsewhere.

PART 1 HINDU PLAYERS

THE ULTIMATE PRINCIPLE

Brahman

The Vedic seers of ancient India thought of the universe as being set in order by a force called Ṛta. The seasons were associated with the principle of Ṛta, and hymns of the *Ṛgveda* spoke of Ṛta as the law. This law of the universe was a principle of order independent of any **deva** (divine being). Ṛta came to be thought of as the force that protected truth and order in the universe. The ṛṣis sang:

> The laws of Ṛta are firm and resistless. For the good of living beings Ṛta assumes forms infinite and beauteous. Because there is Ṛta, men hope for long-lasting food. The Vedas enshrine eternal Truth within themselves by the grace of Ṛta.
>
> (*Ṛgveda* IV.23.9)

Ṛta allowed the eternal Truth to be enshrined in the Vedas. Yet even as the ṛṣis sang in praise of Ṛta, they became increasingly interested in the very power of the speech through which those praises became manifest. The ṛṣis identified the speech that came through them as **brahman** (great power), and felt an immediacy and protective power associated with their sacred speech. For example, Ṛṣi Viśvāmitra claimed that brahman (i.e., as powerful speech) protected his Bhārata clan (*Ṛgveda* 3.53).

BOX 10.1 CULTURE CONTRAST: WHO WERE THE ĀRYANS AND HARAPPĀNS?

The original homeland of the ṛṣis who sang hymns recorded in the *Ṛgveda* is a topic of heated debate. Most scholars contend that the ṛṣis were Āryan priests who migrated with their communities to India, Iran, and Europe from one of three areas in Central Asia (see Bryant 2001: 38–43). They generally agree that Āryans came to the Indus River Valley, probably in a couple of waves, between 1500 and 1000 BCE. But they disagree as to whether the influx should be called an *invasion* or a *migration.* One scholar of Iranian archeology calls for "a change of concern from trying to identify the date and direction of movement of an 'event' like an invasion to the complexities of the processes of cultural change and adaptation" (Dyson 1993: 577).

Edwin Bryant coined the term Indigenous Āryan "school" with reference to scholars who claim that the Āryans were native to India (Bryant 2001: 7). Indigenous Āryanists contend that Āryans neither "invaded" nor "migrated to" India *because they already lived in India* around the Sarasvatī and Sindhu (= Indus) rivers. (The Sarasvatī was an ancient river in northwest India whose dried-up bed is perceptible in satellite images.) Thus the Indigenous Āryan "school" prefers to call the Indus Valley Civilization by either of two alternate designations: Sindhu Sarasvatī Civilization or Indo-Sarasvat Civilization.

The idea that the Āryans were native to India lends new urgency to the question of race: Did the Āryans designate themselves as noble (*ārya*) because of their distinctive and exclusive ritual practices and beliefs? Or were the Āryans a "race" of light-skinned people as opposed to the dark "race" of Dravidians indigenous to India (as many nineteenth- and twentieth-century scholars believed)? The Āryan heritage remains an open question – and one that is quite political. European colonialists who believed themselves to be of ancient Āryan stock never entertained the notion that they should trace their heritage to indigenous Indians. They preferred to think of the Āryan race as having brought a superior culture to India as well as to Old Europe. But whether or not race is a basis for distinguishing Āryans from other people, it is fair to say that the Āryans distinguished themselves *at least* on the basis of religion.

After surveying the Āryan invasion–migration debate, Edwin Bryant concluded:

> [O]ne has almost no grounds to argue for a South Asian Indo-European homeland from where other speakers of the Indo-European language departed, but one can argue that much of the evidence brought forward to document their entrance into the subcontinent is problematic.
>
> (Bryant 2001: 11–12)

Archeological remains from the Indus Valley shed some insight into the Harappān culture. According to the results of carbon dating techniques, the Indus ancient river valley civilization probably existed as far back as 3100 BCE, and ended mysteriously around the time the Āryans arrived. People may have lived in Harappā (a city unearthed in 1920) between 2600 and 1700 BCE. The Harappān pictographic script is being studied, and researchers continue to work on Harappā, Mohenjo Daro, Kalibangan, and other cities in the area between the Indus and the dried-up Sarasvatī River – with a keen interest in analyzing plant and animal material for more clues about the ancient people who lived there (see Possehl 1979: esp. 253–283, 329–360). Several "non-Vedic" elements found in the Hindu tradition seem to have come from the Indus Valley peoples – for example, ritual bathing and feminine imagery. The Harappāns used brick, built well-planned cities with wide streets with drainage, and used rectangular pools (possibly) for ritual purposes. They also created figurines of bulls and what researchers think of as mother goddesses. "What happened to the Harappāns?" is still a hot issue.

The ṛṣis considered their manifest speech as just one-quarter of the incantation, and felt that three-quarters of every sound was always hidden. Brahman encompassed the whole of speech, manifest and unmanifest. Thus Brahman became associated with AUṀ – the all-encompassing sound of the universe. According to the *Chāndogya Upaniṣad*: "As all leaves are held together by a stalk, so is all speech held together by AUṀ" (II.23.3). The syllable AUṀ covers the entire gamut of sound vibrations utterable by the human voice. The *A* begins deep in the chest with an open jaw. Modulation to the *U* involves gradually closing the jaw to allow the sound to ascend through the throat. Gradually the sound vibrates the upper palate as the mouth closes to utter Ṁ. The *bindu* (dot) is the resulting vibration at the highest point in the nasal cavity from where the sound trails into its most subtle form. As Vedic tradition evolved, brahman as all-powerful speech took on the sense of the great, indestructible, all-pervasive power that pervades the entire universe. Brahman as AUṀ came to be experienced as the living essence of the universe.

IMAGINAL PLAYERS

As Hindu tradition emerged out of Vedic religion the number of imaginal players multiplied. The "oldest" deities are the subject of hymns in the *Ṛgveda*. The stories of later deities were told in the Hindu epics and a group of "ancient tales" (*Purāṇas*).

Vedic devas and devīs

The *Ṛgveda* is full of songs to what the ṛṣis called "shining ones" (devas). Some devas were associated with natural phenomena, such as: Agni (fire), Uṣas (dawn), and the Maruts (wind). Others were personified entities with specific cosmic functions. For example, Mitra and Varuṇa were the main guardians of Ṛta (cosmic order), while Indra protected warriors. Indra, himself a warrior, drank a concoction made from sacred cow's milk that was mixed with a plant-deva called Soma. In the course of a Vedic ritual the Soma drink was offered to Indra. The officiants and warriors who attended the ceremony also partook of the liquor, which may have had a hallucinogenic effect. The ṛṣis sang to Soma:

> Golden-hued Hari (Soma), unconquerably valiant, who infuses strength into all, who upholds Heaven and Earth, loves to indwell the holy heart, even as one who has built a new house is all eager to occupy it.
>
> (*Ṛgveda* IV.23.9)

For some three hundred years starting around 1000 BCE the Āryans pushed their settlements eastward into the valley between the Ganges and Yamunā rivers. The area between the Himālaya and Vindhya mountain ranges came to be known as Āryavārta, "land of the Āryas." During this time, Agni (the fire deva) became a predominant figure in Vedic worship as brāhmaṇas elaborated the fire sacrifice (*agni hotra*). Vedic priests built fire altars with great precision because an orderly altar corresponded to an orderly cosmos. They sang numerous hymns to Agni who was the fire that cooked food, brought light and warmth, and carried offerings through smoke from the sacrificial fire from humans to the other devas.

The Hindu trimūrti

Gradually Vedic tradition conceived of Brahman as manifesting as the **trimūrti**, a trinity of deities who are associated with Hindu cosmology: Brahmā, Viṣṇu, and Śiva. Hindus portray the world as endlessly going through cycles (*yugas*) in which Brahmā creates, Viṣṇu sustains, and Śiva destroys. As Hindu tradition developed, Viṣṇu and Śiva became the most popular, while worship of Brahmā developed relatively less.

Viṣṇu: the sustainer

Viṣṇu is the divine force that maintains the world as long as feasible. To this end, Viṣṇu manifested in the form of nine **avatāras**, each of which came into the world to prevent destruction at a time of great need (Table 10.1). A tenth avatāra is now waiting to descend. **Vaiṣṇavas** are committed to all the avatāras of Viṣṇu. For the most part they worship Rāma and Kṛṣṇa along with their consorts Sītā and Rādhā. Traditional Hindus regard them as real people from India's ancient past. Approximately two out of three Hindus in the world today are Vaiṣṇavas.

Table 10.1 Viṣṇu's avatāras

Form	*Name*[1]	*Activity*[2]
Fish	Matsya	Rescued the first man Manu in his ark during the Great Flood.
Tortoise	Kūrma	Helped obtain the water of life during the Great Flood.
Boar	Varāha	Fought for 1,000 years to slay the giant demon Golden Eye who had drowned the earth in the ocean.
Man-lion	Narasiṁha	Slew the demon Golden Dress who ruled all the worlds for a million years.
Dwarf	Vāmana	Recovered heaven and earth by taking three "giant" steps.
Rāma with an ax	Paraśu-Rāma	Preserved the well-being of his mother and brothers, while cleverly respecting the wishes of his father (an evil king).
Charming Rāma	Rāma-Candra	Obedient prince who became king, and is beloved for his exemplary conduct. His story is told in the *Rāmāyaṇa.*
Dark One	Kṛṣṇa	Famous for many activities, as a child, cow herder, and charioteer. Widely worshiped by Hindu devotees.
Awakened One	Buddha	Founder of Buddhism who inspired Indians to clarify the Hindu beliefs and ideals.
Impure One	Kalki	Will arrive on a white horse with a blazing sword at the end of the world cycle to destroy the wicked and restore purity.

Notes
1 Sanskrit name.
2 Cosmic adventures are described extensively in the *Purāṇas.*

Śiva: the destroyer

Śiva ("the Auspicious One") is the divine force that destroys the world when it can no longer be maintained. Knowing Śiva, one knows liberation from duality and becomes free from the snare of rebirth. Hindus who worship Śiva are called **Śaivas** (Table 10.2).

Śākti: feminine power

Śākti ("energy") is the divine female in Hindu tradition, and those who worship her are called **Śāktas** (Table 10.3). She is often called by the generic term **Devī** (goddess). Hindus tell many stories about Devī – and her various manifestations are known by specific names, including Durgā, Kālī, Lakṣmī, and Sarasvatī. Sometimes Śākti accompanies Śiva or Viṣṇu (as himself and in his incarnations as Rāma and Kṛṣṇa). But Śāktas tend to see the goddess as a powerfully independent figure. Some forms of Devī are widely known in India, while others are fairly localized. Hindus in the eastern area of the Indian subcontinent (Bengal) seem to have been particularly interested in the goddess, both in her local and pan-Indian forms.

Plate 10.1 "The goddess Kālī (Bhadrakālī)." "Auspicious" Kālī presents the fierce aspect of cosmic power. Here she wears a necklace of human heads and stands on a corpse that represents defeat of selfish thinking. In front of Kālī is the trimūrti: Brahmā with many heads (left), Śiva with long hair (right), and Viṣṇu (middle). Śāktas worship Kālī.

Table 10.2 Depictions of Śiva

Role	*Iconographic description*	*Symbolic meaning*
Lord of the Dance: Naṭarāja	• Four-armed, two-legged figure dances in a circle of flames. • Upper arms: left and right hands hold a drum. • Lower arm: left hand. • Lower arm: right hand. • Upraised right leg. • Left foot crushes a demon.	• Transcendence of birth and death because untouched by flames. • Drum beats the rhythm of creation, and the fire of destruction. • Gestures "fear not." • Points to upraised right leg. • Refuge and divine mercy. • Power to destroy wickedness.
Śiva the Ascetic	• Naked with long, matted hair and body smeared with ashes.	• Non-attachment to the material world.
Śiva, husband and father	• Shown with wife Parvatī and sons Skanda and Gaṇeśa.	• Male and female cosmic complementarity; Gaṇeśa's trunk removes obstacles.
Śiva *liṅgam*	• Phallic object that is coupled with the circular *yoni* form.	• The paradox of male and female; destruction and creation.
Half-woman Lord: Ardhanārīśvara	• Human figure: female on the left side; male on the right side.	• Complex nature of reality that embodies and transcends duality; dynamic co-existence of Śiva–Śākti.

Table 10.3 Depictions of Śākti (Devī)

Name	*Iconographic description*	*Symbolic meaning*
Sarasvatī	• Four-armed, two-legged lovely seated figure. • Two lower hands play the *vīna*, a stringed instrument. • Upper right hand holds a crystal rosary. • Upper left hand holds a book.	• A beneficent manifestation of Devī as the patron of Hindu culture. • The arts, including sacred speech and aesthetics. • Mind purified through recitation of sacred mantras. • Learning, including all forms of intellectual study.
Lakṣmī. Also Rādhā, Sītā.	• Lovely consorts of Viṣṇu (who are also depicted as avatāras Kṛṣṇa and Rāma).	• Beneficent manifestation of Devī; the goddess of fortune (wealth) is Lakṣmī.
Durgā. Also Pārvatī, Kālī.	• Sixty-four-plus forms; often rides lion or tiger (many fierce). • Around four to twenty arms that carry: bow, dagger, rosary.	• Goddess of the material world; fierce forms destroy evil and bring power. • Keeps the world under control and metes out punishment as necessary with many arms.
Śītalā	• Smallpox disease (Śītalā becomes merciful when worshiped. Devotees may be blessed with a direct vision of Śītalā upon seeing someone afflicted by smallpox.)	• The pox marks signal both human frailty and divine mercy. The disease presents an opportunity to encounter the goddess. Śītalā is present throughout time and space, but people need to see her in manifest form. Śītalā appears as disease in her divine play (*līlā*).

EXCEPTIONAL PLAYERS

Four major types of religious specialists made a lasting impact on Hindu religious life in India: (1) the ṛṣi, (2) the priest, (3) the renunciate, and (4) the **bhakta** (devotee). All but the divinely inspired Vedic seers may be found in India today, though some people use the term ṛṣi for holy person.

Ṛṣis

A ṛṣi is a divinely inspired poet. Tradition names seven ṛṣis to whom the songs of the *Ṛgveda* were revealed. The *Śatapatha Brāhmaṇa* lists them as: Gotama, Bhāradvāja, Viśvāmiṭra, Jamad-agni, Vasiṣṭha, Kaśyapa, and Atri. Other ṛṣis mentioned in later texts include: Marīchi, Angiras, Pulaha, Kratu, Pulastya, Bḥrigu, Daksha, Kaṇwa, Vālmikī, Vyāsa, Manu, and Vibhāṇḍaka (Dowson 1974: 268). Ṛṣis tended to pass down their knowledge orally through the family line from father to son. The ṛṣis seem to have been involved in a deep search for knowledge.

> The Rishi was not the individual composer of the hymn, but the seer (*draṣṭā*) of an eternal truth and an impersonal knowledge. The language of the Veda itself is śruti, a rhythm not composed by the intellect but heard, a divine Word that came vibrating out of the Infinite to the inner audience of the man who had previously made himself fit for the impersonal knowledge.
>
> (Aurobindo 1956, 1982: 8)

The words *śruti* (hearing) and *dṛṣṭi* (sight) from their Vedic hymns suggest that the ṛṣis had profound experiences of seeing and hearing. Tradition calls them "poets endowed with divine inspiration, with vision of universal truths, poets to whom the finest poetry came in perfect and lovely form" (Gopalacharya 1971: 9).

Priests

Over the generations the Āryan ṛṣis orally transmitted their sacrificial hymns. Eventually these were memorized by brāhmaṇas who were members of the priestly class. These Vedic priests took excruciating care to repeat the ancient ṛṣis' exact words with precise intonation, and to re-enact ritual gestures the seers had used in sacrifices to Agni, Soma, and other devas. As the Āryan community settled and grew, the sacrificial process evolved and 1,028 Vedic hymns were compiled into the *Ṛgveda*. As the Āryans adopted a settled lifestyle and began to construct brick fire altars, Agni became more important than Indra who was the patron of warriors. Agni was involved in three fires: (1) fire lit in a round area that cooked food for the sacrifice, (2) fire lit in a square area in which offerings were made to the devas, and (3) fire lit in a semi-circular area in which offerings were made to the ancestors. Vedic ritual gradually became more intricate, and key material from the *Ṛgveda* was included in two new texts used by brāhmaṇas – the *Sāmaveda* and the *Yajurveda*. The original *Ṛgveda* with its 1,028 divinely revealed hymns was used by hotar priests who loudly chanted hymns from the collection. The *Sāmaveda* contained a selection of especially potent words from the *Ṛgveda* that were sung by *udgātar* priests. The *Yajurveda* was used by *adhvaryu* priests to guide them in the technical performance of the ritual. The *adhvaryu* priests also uttered sacred words (but in a low voice) to make their ritual gestures more powerful. The *Ṛgveda, Sāmaveda,* and *Yajurveda* came to be known collectively as the "triple knowledge" (*trayī vidyā*). Eventually a fourth text, the *Atharvaveda*, was counted as a Vediç scripture. Some of its 731 hymns derive from the *Ṛgveda*, while most of the text is devoted to medicine, magical incantations, and material from India's folk traditions.

Renunciates

Gradually the sense developed among Āryans that priests were not the only members of society who had a solemn duty. The ṛṣis had sung about Puruṣa, the Great Person, whose body parts had been distributed through a primordial cosmic sacrifice. And in the process of settling Aryāvārta this hymn was used to provide the archetype for a brāhmaṇical society. Of Puruṣa the ṛṣis had said:

> His mouth became the Brahmin; his arms were made into the Warrior, his thighs the People, and from his feet the Servants were born.
>
> (*Ṛgveda* 10.90)

By the 500s BCE the concept of *varṇa-dharma* (class duty) was crystallizing among the Āryans living in their fertile "land of the Āryas" (Aryāvārta) between the Gangā and Yamunā rivers. A sense developed among the Āryans that to maintain cosmic order, social life should be structured according to four *varṇas* (literally "colors") (see Box 10.2). The system worked something like this. Males of the upper three varṇas would study the Vedas, with brāhmaṇas becoming Vedic specialists. Members of all classes would marry and become householders. After the couple became grandparents to a male child from a son, they were free to retire to the forest. As "forest dwellers" they observed such austerities as "constantly subsist[ing] on flowers, roots, and fruit alone, which have been ripened by time and have fallen spontaneously" (*Manu* VI.21). Gradually forest dwellers were to increase the intensity of their renunciation by living under the open sky exposed to heat and rain, dwelling at the foot of trees, and so forth. Finally, the man should sever his ties completely to family and society. The *Laws of Manu* specifies:

> Having studied the Vedas in accordance with the rule, having begat sons according to the sacred law, and having offered sacrifices according to his ability, he may direct his mind to (the attainment of) final liberation.
>
> (*Manu* VI.36)

The man who became a complete renunciate was called a ***saṁnyāsī***. But not everyone who wanted to renounce the world wound up going through the three earlier stages of life.

As the profession of priest was crystallizing into a highly distinctive social caste, some religious seekers began to question their growing authority. In fact, they questioned the validity of the entire **varṇa-āśrama-dharma** system, and even the authority of Vedic scriptures themselves. **Heterodox** leaders such as Vardhamāna Mahāvīra and Gautama Buddha posed alternative ideas about how **dharma** was to be upheld, and how rebirth was to be escaped. (1) They did not reject the notion of cosmic order, but disagreed about how dharma was to be observed in human society. (2) They did not reject the notion of saṃsāra, but had different interpretations about the nature of action (karma). Thus Mahāvīra and Buddha established alternative spiritual communities in the Ganges basin (where Āryan tradition was less strong than at points west). They attracted people from every varṇa to their Jain and Buddhist saṃghas. Yet it appears that the majority of brāhmaṇas stayed within the Vedic tradition – but they too were asking questions. This period of India's religious history is sometimes called "speculative" due to the intensive striving of the saṃnyāsīs to know more and to question their assumptions. The word for such a renunciate "striver" is *śramaṇa*. During the speculative period many strivers wandered around the Ganges River Valley, including those of Vedic, Jain, and Buddhist persuasion.

Bhaktas

A style of worship known as *bhakti* (devotion) emerged in India at the beginning of the Common Era (100s BCE to 100s CE). This marked the beginning of the Hindu religion as most Indians practice it today. While Manu and others were detailing the particular duties of each varṇa, Indian philosophers were speculating anew on the nature of Brahman. They asked whether Brahman as the living essence of the universe might somehow manifest in the world in the form of different deities. New rituals developed in contrast to those done by Vedic priests. Coming on the scene was a type of theistic literature that focused on the divine-with-form (*saguṇa*). Whereas the Vedic devas were not envisioned during the ritual sacrifice, the new Hindu bhaktas began worshiping anthropomorphic (of human shape) and theriomorphic (of animal shape) images of the divine. The path of devotion (bhakti-mārga) centered on **pūjā**, which involved offering to Viṣṇu, Śiva, or Devī a variety of articles that were pleasing to the senses: water, flowers, incense, fire (light), music, and food. The desire to worship deities with form spurred the development of two new religious arts in India: (1) creation of images, and (2) temple building. A magnificent effort at temple building was made between 800 and 1200 CE. Thus, besides making offerings to the gods on home altars or outdoors, Hindus could worship magnificent portrayals of the divine in a spacious environment filled with sacred art.

BOX 10.2 A SPIRITUAL PATH: THE VARṆA-ĀŚRAMA-DHARMA

The varṇa-āśrama-dharma provides the framework for leading a righteous life in India. It outlines the appropriate duty (dharma) for each person according to his or her social class (varṇa) and stage of life as allowed by gender (āśrama).

In a profound sense, the ancient varṇa-āśrama-dharma system still provides an ideal model for Hindu life. Mohandās Gāndhī said, "Hinduism is nothing without the law of Varna and of Ashrama" (Gāndhī 1962: 5). He was convinced that with proper observance of the varṇa-āśrama-dharma the world would be peaceful – even free from starvation, suffering, and disease. Gāndhī's confidence was based on an ancient notion about dharma that is summed up in one phrase: "Protected, it protects."

One step toward the Gāndhian ideal was taken in 1949 (a year after Mohandās Gāndhī's assassination) when the Indian constitution outlawed caste discrimination. Presently Indian laws are supposed to assure educational and employment opportunities for all people regardless of their varṇa. Some Hindus want India's constitution to be a modern form of the *Laws of Manu* to eliminate the validity of tribal and Muslim laws that still operate. Activist Dalits oppose this position, and argue that "the Laws of Manu are a prime example of high-caste Hindus' oppression of lower castes" (Rinehart 2004: 75). Dalits, formerly known as Untouchables, are low on the social scale – even low within the śūdra class or beneath it. Thus they may be particularly sensitive to the needs of the "oppressed."

Table 10.4 Varṇa-āśrama-dharma

Varṇa	*Vocation*	*Vedic image*	*Dharma (duty)*	*Āśrama required*
Brāhmaṇa	Priests and their wives; intellectuals	Puruṣa's head	Preserve sacred knowledge (the Vedas); advise; perform rituals	Celibate student,* married couple, retired "forest dweller," wandering mendicant*
Kṣatriya	Rulers, warriors; administrators	Puruṣa's arms	Maintain an orderly society whose members are well protected	Celibate student,* married couple, retired "forest dweller," wandering mendicant*
Vaiśya	Businessmen; herders; farmers	Puruṣa's thighs	Sustain society by generating wealth	Celibate student,* married couple, retired "forest dweller," wandering mendicant*
Śūdra (with many sub-castes beneath)	Servants and laborers	Puruṣa's feet	Serve upper three varṇas; perform menial jobs	Married couple

* Males only

HISTORICAL PLAYERS

Sūtra writers of "sacred science"

Hindus typically speak of six orthodox darśanas. The Sanskrit word **darśana** literally means view, point of view, or perspective. (Darśana has been translated as philosophy, theology, system, and sacred science; but the *practical* sense of the darśanas is hard to capture.) Although many of the ideas expressed in the darśanas percolated among Indian thinkers for generations, their foundational texts arose during the same time period in the history of Indian thought. The encounter with Jain and Buddhist thinkers around 300 BCE prompted Hindus to clarify their ideas and methods of spiritual realization. The six Hindu darśanas were "orthodox" statements linked to the Vedas. Many proponents of one or another point of view explicitly counteracted positions put forth by heterodox thinkers such as Jains and Buddhists who rejected the authority of the Vedas.

Authors of the core texts of the six darśanas summarized the basic tenets of their "perspective" in pithy sūtras (aphorisms). Striving for clarity, accuracy, and focus, they pared down key ideas to the bare essentials. The potent verses, memorized by students, served as the basis for direct realization of their jam-packed meaning. Traditionally a commentary (oral or written) was used to unpack subtleties of the arguments and levels of signification in the concepts. A typical listing of the six darśanas is made in terms of three complementary sets: (1) Nyāya-Vaiśeṣika, (2) Sāṃkhya-Yoga, and (3) Mīmāṃsā-Vedānta. Hindu tradition gave names to the authors of the sūtras that serve as the darśanas' foundational texts, but historical data on those writers is generally lacking. Table 10.5 gives an approximate account of the subject matter of each darśana. The Sāṃkhya-Yoga darśanas are treated in Part 2 (see page 250).

The six darśanas are fundamentally "developments of a single doctrine according to different points of view, and in various, but by no means incompatible, directions" (Guénon 1928, 2001: 14). In common they: (1) accept the Vedas as authoritative, (2) counter what they see as Buddhist skepticism, (3) posit an ultimate objective reality that is not impermanent (versus the Buddhist viewpoint), (4) accept the notion of an endless cosmic cycle of creation, maintenance, and dissolution (as do Buddhists), (5) use a common vocabulary (with particular twists), and (6) have the goal of liberation from cyclic existence.

Three Vedānta commentators

The sacred sciences traditionally were studied as part of an oral tradition, and over generations the key texts of each darśana accumulated layers of commentary that shaped the course of Hindu worship and belief. Śaṅkara, Rāmānuja, and Madhva are key commentators of the Vedānta darśana. Each gave a distinctive slant to the *Brahmā Sūtra* – a foundational text that distilled the essential teachings of the Upaniṣads.

Śaṅkara (ca. 800 CE)

Śaṅkara played a key role in defining the darśana known as Advaita Vedānta. Typically Advaita Vedānta is paired with Mīmāṃsā because the two darśanas approach the Vedas from complementary perspectives.

Table 10.5 Six Hindu sacred sciences

Darśana	*Sūtra author**	*Subject matter***
Nyāya	Gautama	Logic; science of right reasoning; epistemology
Vaiśeṣika	Kaṇāda	Physics (atomism); ontology
Sāṃkhya	Kapila	Cosmogony (creation theory); psychology
Yoga	Patañjali	Science of attaining samādhi
Mīmāṃsā	Jaimini	Theory of language (re: scriptural injunctions)
Vedānta	Vyāsa	Science of realizing Brahman

** Traditional names; historicity in question. ** Approximate.*

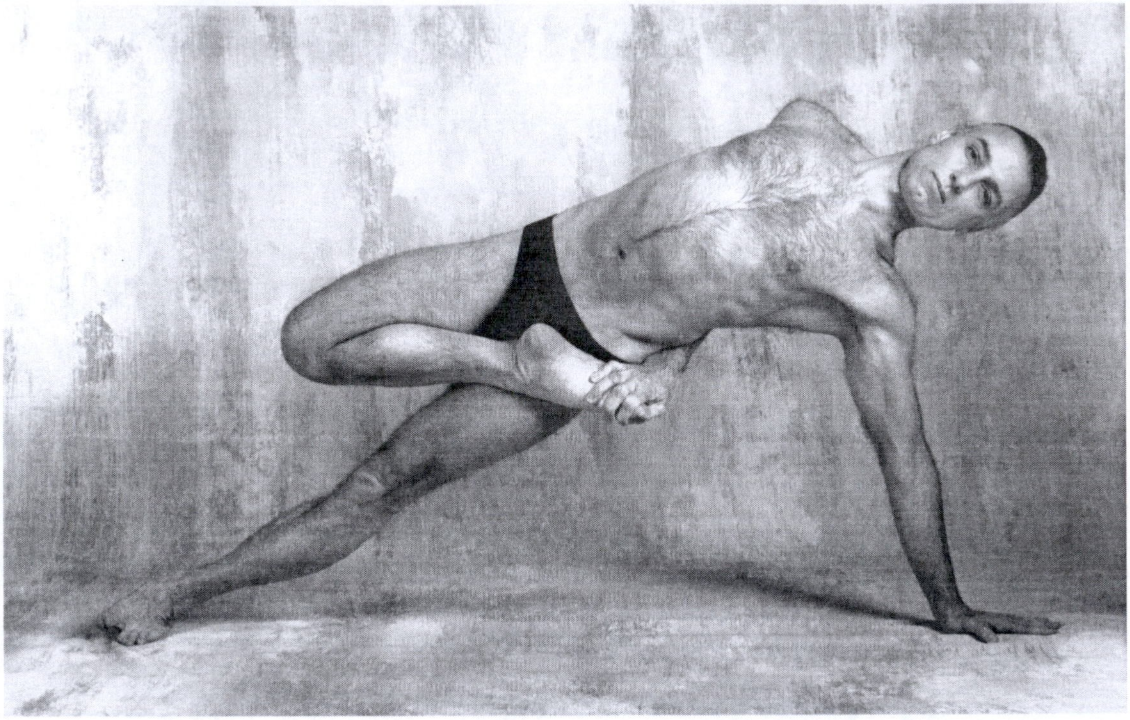

Plate 10.2 "Kaśyapa's pose (*Kaśyapāsana*)." In studios and health clubs the world over, the ancient Indian tradition of oral commentary continues whenever a teacher corrects a student's yoga pose. The sacred science of yoga (*yoga-darśana*) includes various *āsanas* such as the one exhibited here by the American teacher John Schumacher. The legacy of the Vedic ṛṣis shines through the poses after thousands of years. This pose is named after a Vedic ṛṣi named Kaśyapa, who must have enjoyed spending his time like this. Other āsanas are named after the ṛṣis Viśvāmitra, Vasiṣtha, Bhāradvāja, and Marīchi.

Śaṅkara focused on the essential wisdom contained in the Vedas, while Mīmāṃṣā philosophers sought to clarify the Vedic teachings on proper social and ritual conduct. From Śaṅkara's perspective, injunctions presented in the Mīmāṃṣā literature are appropriate for people who have only a conventional understanding of the world and do not know that the world is ***māyā*** (illusion). Māyā is cosmic illusion experienced as ignorance (*avidyā*). By contrast, his Advaita Vedānta teachings point to reality as *Tat Tvam Asi* (That Art Thou). Tat Tvam Asi means that one's soul (ātman) is none other than Brahman. Śaṅkara's *a-dvaita* (non-dual) perspective is based on teachings of the Upaniṣads, revealed scriptures that are supposed to present the essence of the Vedic hymns (see page 247).

Śaṅkara spoke of two truths: (1) practical (*vyavahāra*), and (2) ultimate (*pāramārthika*). Practical knowledge is based on experience that accords with everyday conventional reality. Such knowledge is not mistaken in the worldly sense. On the basis of empirical knowledge great technological progress can be made. But practical knowledge does not recognize māyā, and works from the assumption that things in the world are separate entities. To move from such conventional knowledge to the ultimate view of reality one must go beyond sense activity. The Advaita Vedānta darśana allows a person to make such a move by way of jñāna (knowledge) instead of ritual action. In a state of consciousness known as samādhi the delusion of māyā is penetrated. Liberation from saṃsāra involves ridding oneself of ignorance through transformative jñāna. Thus Advaita Vedānta is called a path of knowledge (jñāna-mārga). Those who reach the highest state of knowledge realize the truth that their ātman (soul) is not separate from Brahman, the living essence of the universe. To attain this transformative *advaita* experience of identity, a person must have: (1) the ability to discern between what is eternal and what is not, (2) disinterest in worldly pleasures, and (3) a desire for complete liberation (even from heavenly rebirths) accompanied by highly developed personal qualities such as: self-restraint, patience, and mental concentration.

Rāmānuja (ca. 1016 to ca. 1137)

Rāmānuja pondered Śaṅkara's claim that the path of knowledge (*jñāna-marga*) brought a-dvaita – the complete merging of the soul with Brahman. He conceded that Brahman is the only substantial reality. But he went on to discuss three aspects of reality: (1) non-sentient matter (*acit*), (2) numerous finite sentient beings (*cit*), and (3) one all-pervasive Īśvara (Supreme Lord). According to Rāmānuja, the Supreme Lord is not ultimately distinguished from matter and sentient beings. Yet out of ignorance sentient beings associate themselves heavily with their material bodies – although they are *sat-cit-ānanda* (truth-consciousness-bliss) like Īśvara. Laboring under the influence of karma, people perceive the world through secondary consciousnesses. Thus they do not recognize the essential nature of the all-powerful Īśvara.

BOX 10.3 SYMBOLS: THE FIVE SHEATHS

Advaita Vedānta presents a path of knowledge (jñāna-mārga) through which a person can become liberated from saṃsāra. Contemplating deeply the teachings of the Upaniṣads brings a kind of transformative jñāna. One teaching that opens the way to realizing the union of ātman and Brahman is the theory of the body's five sheaths. Words used to describe the "position" of the five sheaths sound ambiguous. At times it appears that the sheath of bliss is "outside" the body. But paradoxically to get to this "outside" a person must penetrate to the innermost core of himself or herself.

Sheath of the body (annamaya kośa). This is the gross physical body that is most apparent to the senses. It is the material body created by food. This body sustains the others, and provides a vehicle for moving through the others. It is least susceptible to change, and is altered through diet, drink, and exercise including yoga postures.

Sheath of breath or vital force (prāṇamaya kośa). This is the body of prāṇa (breath) that energizes the gross material body. When the breath is regulated and becomes calm and subtle, the gross body calms down. Vital energy is inhaled with the breath, and with mindful breathing obstructions in the gross body are cleared.

Sheath of mind (manomaya kośa). This is the mentality of a person based on sense impressions, emotions, and thoughts including dreams. This sheath reacts to the outside world through the filter of duality that discriminates between this and that, self and others.

Sheath of intellect (vijñanamaya kośa). This is a higher function of mentality that transcends the senses, thoughts, and emotions. Karma or the impact of past actions regulates our experience from here, including sickness. The practice of chanting in kīrtan purifies this sheath.

Sheath of bliss (ānandamaya kośa). This is associated with realization of the divine. This is a human being's true nature. Ultimately, the adept contacts the unstruck sound, the *śabad* here. Coming to this sheath is necessary for liberation from the cycle of transmigration. This may be considered the most subtle sheath that enwraps what some call the soul.

The body sheaths may be thought of like the layers of an onion – both as moving outward from the physical body, and moving inward to the center of the heart. There (at the innermost or the outermost area) the yogī discovers that self (ātman) and cosmos (Brahman) are not-two (advaita).

Rāmānuja taught that people could become free of the bondage of rebirth through bhakti (devotion). A devotee of Īśvara was to contemplate divine qualities (defined by sense perceptions) vividly without a break in awareness. The contemplation should be continuous and steady like the flow of oil out of its vessel. Such awareness of the Lord purifies a human being of ignorance about the all-pervading substantial reality of the Supreme Lord. Devotees who contemplate Īśvara's qualities express a semblance of divine qualities in their own actions. They feel an emotionally encompassing sense of Īśvara's presence. They feel desperate at losing touch with the divine qualities when the Supreme Lord is obscured in times of forgetfulness or because of karma. Rāmānuja also taught that mysteriously the Lord bestows grace that moves devotees to bestow their love. Thus there is a dialectic of devotion creating a tension between the bhakta and the Supreme Lord.

Śaṅkara had acknowledged that worship of Īśvara was a legitimate spiritual path, but only as a prelude to non-dual knowledge of Brahman. Rāmānuja disagreed. He argued that an individual sentient soul never completely loses its identity in a non-dual state. On the contrary, salvation comes through the creative devotional tension between Īśvara and the sentient being. Along these lines Rāmānuja established an alternative Vedānta point of view in reaction to Śaṅkara's Advaita perspective. He used the term "viśiṣṭa-advaita" to suggest that reality is non-dual (a-dvaita) – but in a distinguished or qualified (viśiṣṭa) sense. Rāmānuja's disciples came to be known as Qualified Non-dualist (Viśiṣṭa Advaita) persuasion. They were Vaiṣṇava bhaktas who worshiped the divine in the form of Viṣṇu.

Madhva (1238?–1317? CE)

A few generations after Rāmānuja another Vaiṣṇava bhakta pushed the Qualified Non-dualist Vedānta perspective a step further. Madhva introduced the perspective of Dual (Dvaita) Vedānta. He conceded that the world and its creatures depend upon Brāhmaṇ. Yet, based on his reading of the Upaniṣads, Madhva posited two uncreated principles in the universe: (1) Īśvara, and (2) matter (*prakṛti*). Matter was composed of: (1) sentient matter (jīva) and (2) insentient matter. Madhva claimed that Īśvara and human souls (as subtle forms of matter) are separate uncreated eternal principles. They are always "two" (*dvaita*) because they are fundamentally distinct. Īśvara governs the law of karma, and liberation from saṃsāra comes through devotion. Sentient beings depend upon Īśvara's grace, and Īśvara's grace is limited by the bhakta's capacity to receive it. Devotion is correlated with recognition of dependence upon the Supreme Lord. Yet the fact of whether or not a person recognizes this dependence is predestined. The tension between devotion and recognition of dependence is embedded in the bhakta's relationship of servitude with the Supreme Lord. Liberation comes in abiding as the slave of the Supreme Lord. Madhva conceived of the Supreme Lord as Viṣṇu.

The new Hindu saints

Rāmānuja and Madhva paved the way for a thriving bhakti-mārga that rivaled Śaṅkara's impersonalist jñāna-mārga. Their teachings provided the Hindu devotional movement with a highly developed point of view that posited at least some measure of separation between sentient beings and the Supreme Lord. Both Rāmānuja's Viśiṣta Advaita and Madhva's Dvaita perspectives on the Vedānta indicated that devotion to God was the best means of gaining final liberation from rebirth. Thus after Rāmānuja and Madhva established the notion that God must be encountered, a whole new area of study opened up. Śaṅkara's jñāna-mārga had involved intensive study of the Upaniṣads with their teachings on ātman and Brahman. On the other hand, the bhaktas embraced a whole new body of literature that included sacred stories of Viṣṇu, Śiva, and Śākti. Beyond that, new rituals, fine arts, and methods of meditation grew up in response to the devotional fervor that sprang up all over India. Hindus could worship numerous gods as expressions of the one Brahman. These include the family's **iṣṭa-devatā** (chosen deity), the village deity, and other deities whose worship is required by caste and so forth. Hindu housewives play a key role in worship by maintaining a home altar for family use. Altars contain images of the family iṣṭa-devatā as well as the personal chosen deities of various family members.

The devotional movement was percolating in south India among the Tamils some two centuries before Śaṅkara wrote his great Advaita Vedānta commentaries. Between 600 and 900 CE a number of poet-saints spread the spirit of devotion among the people – even causing a fair number to leave their Buddhist and Jain traditions. Specifically, twelve devotees of Viṣṇu are known as the Āḷvārs, and sixty-three devotees of Śiva are known as Nāyaṇārs. The Tamil poets, along with Rāmānuja (himself from south India), spurred the Hindu bhakti movement. These bhaktas believed that ordinary people could attain liberation (mokṣa) by relating to a manifestation of the divine-with-form. Their notion that the divine could be *seen* was well received by an increasing number of Hindus. Thus the word darśana as "view" took on a vital new meaning for Hindus on the path of devotion. The classic darśanas had offered six "perspectives" on the Veda by making use of logic, physics, yoga, non-dual experience, and so forth. However, among bhaktas a sense emerged that a profound "view" of reality could be obtained by "seeing" a holy person or catching a glimpse of the deity through the eyes of an idol. This is because simultaneously the deity "sees" the devotee.

> The prominence of the eyes in Hindu divine images also reminds us that it is not only the worshiper who sees the deity, but the deity sees the worshiper as well. The contact between devotee and deity is exchanged through the eyes. It is said in India that one of the ways in which the gods can be recognized when they move among people on this earth is by their unblinking eyes.
>
> (Eck 1998: 7)

All over India devotees of Viṣṇu (as Kṛṣṇa or Rāma), Śiva, and Śākti had transformative religious experiences while viewing idols of their iṣṭa-devatās. This process has two aspects: (1) the deity or holy person "gives darśana" while the devotee "takes darśana" (namely *darśan denā* and *darśan lenā* in Hindi) (Eck 1998: 6). Among the many remarkable Hindus treading the bhakti-mārga were three Vaiṣṇavas whose work further defined the notion of what it meant to worship a personal God. Jñāneśvara as his name suggests combined a knowledge path (jñāna-mārga) with devotion to Īśvara. Vallabha inspired an extensive form of **pūjā** in which the image of the deity was treated like a living person to whom food was offered in worship. And Mīrābāī was among the first female Hindu saints in the devotional tradition. Her life exemplifies challenges faced by women bhaktas who traditionally were dependent upon their fathers in youth, their husbands as householders, and their sons as widows.

Jñāneśvara (1275–1296? CE)

Jñāneśvara was born in western India, and became a leader in the Sant ("saint") tradition. Jñāneśvara was the second son in a family with four children who grew up as social outcasts, due to a scandal caused by his father. The man had been married without children, and so went to Banaras to take up the life of *śramaṇa*. His former wife eventually persuaded the ascetic to return; and he did so. Afterwards, the reunited couple began to have children. The orthodox brāhmaṇa community excommunicated him because a person who renounced the world was never to return to it as a brāhmaṇa. The harsh rejection from brāhmaṇa society drove the 9-year-old Jñāneśvara's parents to drown themselves in a holy river. Afterwards he requested and received from the brāhmaṇas a certificate of purity. Jñāneśvara's elder brother became his gurū. They both practiced fasting and meditation in a forest hermitage, and developed many siddhis as a result. Jñāneśvara was initiated into the Nāth cult whose lineage traces back to Gorākhnāth, the alchemist and *haṭha* **yogī** (see page 269). As a Nāth he worshiped Śiva, but as a Vaiṣṇava he was devoted to Kṛṣṇa. As a teenager he composed a devotional commentary on the *Bhagavadgītā* in the Marathi language known as the *Jñāneśvari*. It combined both threads of his spiritual life (*haṭha yoga* and bhakti) and became a major holy book for the yogīc tradition in medieval India. Today this commentary on the *Bhagavadgītā* is considered to be among the greatest works of Hindu spirituality. At the age of about 20, Jñāneśvara had himself sealed into a stone room near Pune to fast and meditate. (It is said that this impenetrable room has never been opened.) There, he attained samādhi, and passed away. Jñāneśvara's form of combined Śaiva–Vaiṣṇava worship was practiced by a group of Sants from Mahārāṣṭra who worshiped Viṭṭhala, a divine manifestation with characteristics of both Śiva and Kṛṣṇa. To this day, Viṭṭhala devotees trace their lineage through Jñāneśvara back to Gorākhnāth.

Vallabha (1479–1531 CE)

A teacher named Vallabha elaborated the pūjā ritual that influenced bhaktas throughout India. He founded a Vaiṣṇava spiritual community called the Way of Nourishment (*Pushtī Marg*). His disciples developed the art of cooking to feed the idols. As one would nourish a child, so they wished to interact with the divine through the preparation of a sacred meal. Thus Hindu bhaktas added food to their standard pūjā offering. The use of idols in the new Hindu style of worship sparked a theological debate as to whether a deity inhabited an image (*mūrti*) or actually becomes the image. The problem arose as to whether an idol could ever be destroyed – reasoning that if an image was the own form (svarupa) of the deity it should never be destroyed. Vallabha taught that a *mūrti* could be animated and then deanimated: (1) During the pūjā a deity's image is animated. (2) After the ritual it becomes deanimated and can be destroyed. Vallabha was a proponent of idol worship, even though his view of reality was based in pure non-dualism (*a-dvaita*). He taught that Kṛṣṇa was accessible to human beings through use of idols. In daily life, Vallabha's disciples maintained a sense of the deity-with-form by visualizing themselves as Kṛṣṇa's companions while walking, eating, taking cows for grazing, and so forth. Thus Vallabha taught that ultimate reality was personalized as Kṛṣṇa. However, he said that the highest stage of spiritual experience involved eliminating all separation between the bhakta and God. The bhakta's goal was to attain unqualified union with Kṛṣṇa as an unlimited, formless divine being.

Mīrābāī (early sixteenth century CE)

The Rajputs are a cultural group based in north and west India who identify with an ancient lineage that traces back to Viṣṇu's avatāras Rāma and Kṛṣṇa. They claim descent from Rāma, and the ancient custom of **satī** strongly resonates among them. In some versions of Rāma's story (told in the *Rāmāyaṇa*) his wife Sītā committed satī to demonstrate her purity after being abducted by the demon Rāvaṇa. The custom of satī is outlawed in India today, but cases of it are still reported from time to time, and five centuries ago it appears that a Rajput woman was expected to commit satī. In the case of Mīrābāī, only her devotion to Kṛṣṇa saved her from death on her husband's funeral pyre. She lived during the period of Mughal rule in India, and it is said that Emperor Akbar heard about Mīrābāī and wished to see her. Akbar presumably disguised himself among his musicians so that he could be blessed by touching her feet.

Mīrābāī's love of Kṛṣṇa was awakened when she was a child. The path of devotion had become an option for young and old, men and women, and people of all social classes. One day when she was just a girl, Mīrābāī saw a wedding party and asked her mother whom she would marry. Her mother told Mīrābāī that for the time being she should contemplate a little statue of Kṛṣṇa when she thought of marriage. Mīrābāī held that thought for her whole life. Thus, although she married a king, Mīrābāī never had conjugal relations. When her husband died, Mīrābāī's loyalty as a Rajput wife would have required her to commit satī. Multiple views about Mīrābāī's death circulate among Vaiṣṇavas. One version of her story says that she lived to an old age, while another gives an extraordinary account claiming that Kṛṣṇa rescued Mīrābāī when she tried to commit sati. In the way of bhaktas, Mīrābāī sought Kṛṣṇa on another plane of existence, and his statue opened up to receive her. It is said that the widow promptly disappeared inside an idol of Kṛṣṇa.

Modern Hindu social activists

In the modern period Hindus were subject to Western colonialism. The British rule began in the mid-eighteenth century and ended in 1947. In response an Independence Movement grew. Freedom fighters tried various methods to make the British "quit India." After two hundred years the British left India. In the wake of their departure – and to the anguish of many Indians – their land was divided. The nation of Pakistan was formed from the western portion of India's Punjab. In a massive and bloody population transfer, Muslims moved to Pakistan and Hindus retreated to India. Hindu nationalism began to emerge in response to cultural and political pressures under British rule. And even after half a century of independence, it continues to grow.

Rām Mohan Roy (1772–1833)

When the British colonized India they introduced a Western style of education. Many Bengalis were receptive to a British education and other aspects of Western culture. Among them was a Bengali brāhmaṇa Rām Mohan Roy. Rām Mohan led a social reform movement known as the Brāhmo Samāj in 1828. The father of poet Rabindranath Tagore wrote a covenant for the organization. Although at first it was a small, purely religious organization, its influence on the Indian social and political agenda became significant. The Brāhmo

Samāj forbade the social customs of sati, polygamy, and sought to improve the status of women. Moreover, it supported the rationality and humanism promoted in Western education. Rām Mohan Roy was eclectic. He learned Persian and Arabic, and seems to have been greatly influenced by Islam as well as Christianity. He opposed idolatry and spoke ardently in favor of monotheism. Rām Mohan believed that all spiritual traditions have the same essence. He believed that if Hindu idolatry were eliminated, the monotheistic essence of the Vedas and Upaniṣads would become evident. When Rām Mohan Roy died in 1833, he left a legacy that was developed by a series of leaders. As it matured, the Brāhmo Samāj came to stand for certain ideals still felt in India today, including: (1) the sovereignty of human reason over religious faith, and (2) democratic government. To promote the Brāhmo Samāj ideals, an inexpensive newspaper for the lower classes was published by the organization.

Svāmī Dayānanda Sarasvatī (1824–1883)

Svāmī Dayānanda Sarasvatī was a Sanskrit scholar who made a deep study of the *Ṛgveda.* He grew up in a religious Śaiva household, but turned from worship using idols. He thought that the many gods of Hinduism were an aberration of true Vedic teachings, and advocated that Hindus return to the monotheism of the Vedas. Dayānanda considered that the multiple deities named in the Vedas were intended as descriptive names for aspects of a single God. Moreover, he thought that the hymns of the ancient Vedic ṛṣis contained scientific truths, whose insights could inform further modern scientific research. To bring study of the Vedas back to prominence, Dayānanda established the Ārya Samāj in 1875.

Bāl Gangādar Tilak (1856–1920) and Mohandās Gāndhī (1869–1948)

Bāl Gangādar Tilak and Mohandās Gāndhī were two leaders of India's Independence Movement who defined a Hindu ethic of social activism. They wished to clarify ethical standards that should be maintained in the fight against British rule of India. And like so many Hindus throughout the centuries, Tilak and Gāndhī turned to the *Bhagavadgītā* for guidance, and each wrote a commentary on it. A major teaching of the *Bhagavadgītā* is that an act done for God is pure if one does not hanker after the fruits of the act. Both Tilak and Gāndhī agreed that actions performed with devotion and without self-interest are pure, but they disagreed as to whether or not Hindu ethics permits violent action. They interpreted the warrior Arjuna's predicament as to whether or not he should take up arms to fight a righteous battle in different ways. Based on their understanding of the *Bhagavadgītā's* message, the two modern freedom fighters came to radically different conclusions about a Hindu's duty to resist British colonialism.

Tilak considered violence as an acceptable tool in India's fight for independence. He "believed in truth, non-violence and such other moral virtues as absolutely and invariably binding *in a perfect society only* . . . but that exceptions were necessary in the interest of public good" (Gosvai 1983: 46). Tilak's judgment was based on the assumption that an evil-doer must pay all consequences for sinful acts, and one who fights for justice incurs no bad karma.

> [I]t is clearly stated in our religious treatises, that when a saint is thus compelled to perform some unsaintly Action, the responsibility of such unsaintly Action does not fall on the pure-minded saint, but that the evil-doer must be held responsible for it, as it is the result of his evil doings (*Manu* 8.19 and 351).
>
> (Tilak 1935: 554)

Gāndhī promoted non-violent Hindu ethics based on the *Bhagavadgītā.* He viewed the text as symbolic. Thus although Arjuna entered into battle against his cousins, Gāndhī thought the fight should be interpreted as an inner struggle.

> [W]hen I first became acquainted with the *Gita*, I felt that it was not a historical work, but that, under the guise of physical warfare, it described the duel that perpetually went on in the hearts of mankind, and that physical warfare was brought in merely to make the description of the internal duel more alluring. . . . The author of the *Mahābhārata* has not established the necessity of physical warfare; on the contrary he has proved its futility. He has made the victors shed tears of sorrow and repentance, and has left them nothing but a legacy of miseries.
>
> (Desai 1984: 127–128)

Thus regardless of the opponent's activity, Gāndhī "would in no case initiate or support any untruthful or violent action in retaliation even in self-defence. He followed and recommended only non-violent action involving suffering by oneself even unto death" (Gosavi 1983: 46). It is an open question as to how far apart Tilak and Gāndhī really stand in their formulation of Hindu ethics. Gāndhī outlined a hierarchy of action in which an act of violence was superior to an act of cowardice – but violence was worse than non-violence.

Modern Hindu gurūs

Hindu gurūs seriously began to teach Western students starting in the days of British rule in the mid-eighteenth century, and continuing through today. Some identified with the ancient darśanas of Yoga and Vedānta; others were devotional theists; and still others were charismatic self-initiated personalities with less precise affiliations.

Rāmakrishna (1836–1886)

Rāmakrishna was born in Bengal. He spent many years living at the Kālī temple near Calcutta, serving as priest there. Although Rāmakrishna was a devotee of the goddess Kālī, he had a variety of experiences of the divine with and without form. These shaped his view that many religious paths led to the same divine presence. In 1893 his disciple Vivekānanda (1863–1902) attended the World's Parliament of Religions in Chicago, and thus became the first Hindu missionary in the West. To promote the teachings of his gurū (as well as his own) Vivekānanda founded the Rāmakrishna Mission based on the Advaita Vedānta perspective.

A. C. Bhaktivedānta Swāmi Prabhupāda (1896–1977)

A. C. Bhaktivedānta Swāmi Prabhupāda was born in Bengal, and was initiated into Kṛṣṇa devotion as a young adult. He became a pharmacist, but at age 58 was instructed by his gurū to teach Kṛṣṇa consciousness in the West. He was initiated as a renunciate in the lineage of Madhva (founder of Dvaita Vedānta) and Caitanya (founder of the Gauḍīya Vaiṣṇavas). Bhaktivedānta's works of translation and commentary amount to over sixty volumes, including the *Bhagavadgītā*, and the *Śrīmad-Bhāgavatam Purāṇa*. He also established the International Society for Krishna Consciousness (ISKCON), whose members are known as Hare Krishnas. Their worship – involving chant, scriptural study, mantra recitation, and dance – is modeled on Caitanya's devotion to Kṛṣṇa.

Ānandamayī Mā (1896–1981)

Ānandamayī Mā was born in Bengal (now Bangladesh) into a family of Kṛṣṇa devotees. From an early age she showed signs of spontaneous religious experience. Increasingly she attracted attention by healing people, and manifesting unusual physical contortions in which her body would seem to shrink, or stretch. She had a calling to self-initiation in the name of a personal, unspecified form of God. These words of the saint reflect her direct and poignant teaching: "Many feel the urge to create a new and better world. Rather than let your thoughts dwell on such matters, you should concentrate on That by the contemplation of which there is hope of perfect peace. It is man's duty to become a seeker after God or Truth" (Yogānanda 1981: 442, n.2). A shrine dedicated to Ānandamayī Mā is on the outskirts of Hardwār at the āśram (devotional center) she had established.

Maharishi Mahesh Yogī (b. 1917)

Maharishi Mahesh Yogī was born in central India (Madhya Pradesh) and was educated as an engineer. Upon meeting a teacher in the lineage of Śaṅkara he became inspired by the Advaita Vedānta teachings. After twelve years with his gurū, he spent two years in silence. He founded the International Transcendental Meditation Society, which teaches students to meditate with a mantra, and develop siddhis. Maharishi promotes organic agriculture, traditional Vedic medicine (*Āyurveda*), and the practice of meditation. After 11 September 2001 he began broadcasting weekly satellite press conferences, family Internet chat, and other Internet programs to encourage world peace.

B. K. S. Iyengar (b. 1918)

B. K. S. Iyengar was born in southwest India (Karnataka) to a large, poor family. He overcame serious child illnesses (tuberculosis, typhoid, and malaria) by studying yoga – first with his brother-in-law Sri T. Krishnamacharya, and then intensively on his own. He teaches in the lineage of Patañjali, and developed a style of practice known as Iyengar Yoga. He pioneered the use of props, at first making use of various items found cast off, such as bricks and chairs. His daughter Geeta and son Prashant carry on the Iyengar Yoga tradition, which emphasizes precision in the practice of āsana and prāṇayama.

PART 2 HINDU TEXTURE

FOUNDATIONAL TEXTURE

Hindus divide their literature into two main groups: śruti (= heard, i.e., revealed) and *smṛti* (= remembered). The śruti texture is based on words directly "heard" by the ancient ṛṣis as recorded in the *Ṛgveda*. The smṛiti texture treats matters not directly connected to Vedic ritual. In its broadest sense, Hindus use the term "Veda" with reference to all the śruti texts. This body of Vedic śruti literature includes the *Ṛgveda*, *Yajurveda*, *Sāmaveda*, and *Atharvaveda* (see page 236). These four collections of hymns are known as the Saṃhitās (things "joined" or "connected"). Appended to each of the four Saṃhitās are Brahmānas, Āraṇyakas, and Upaniṣads. These three additional layers of text were added gradually as types of commentary on the Saṃhitā material. The Brahmānas discussed largely the ritual aspect of the Saṃhitās, while the Āraṇyakas and Upaniṣads commented on the inner meaning of the hymns. Collectively the four Saṃhitās plus their Brahmānas, Āraṇyakas, and Upaniṣads are called the Sanātana Dharma (Eternal Law). Sanātana Dharma is the term Hindus use for their religion. Beyond the śruti literature is a large body of smṛti literature that includes epics, law books, and numerous collections of stories about the gods.

The *Ṛgveda*

The core of śruti texture is the *Ṛgveda*. Basically all śruti literature relates back to this work. The 1,028 hymns of the *Ṛgveda* were revealed to the ancient ṛṣis. They were passed down orally for generations, and most likely committed to writing at some point between 1300 and 1000 BCE. These hymns were collated for ritual purposes into two further collections, the *Sāmaveda* and the *Yajurveda* (see page 236). The hymns speak of ritual offerings made for material wealth in the form of cows, horses, and gold – as well as for success in the form of victory in battle, the birth of children, and physical strength. The rituals were aimed not only at the production of an orderly world, however. Some interpreters insist that the ṛṣis were profoundly interested in their own spiritual transformation. These were not competing interests. The Vedic worldview recognized correspondences among various levels of reality: personal, social, natural, and cosmic.

The Upaniṣads

The latest addition to the Vedic corpus was a series of teachings known as the Upaniṣads. Ṛṣis named Āruṇi, Yājñavalkya, Bālāki, Śvetaketu, and others transmitted their knowledge to disciples living in the forests of north India starting around 800 BCE. Hindus have 108 Upaniṣads, the oldest thirteen of which have taken on the most importance. The Upaniṣads are considered śruti material because the ṛṣis experienced "without their effort" an "independent reality" that impinged on their consciousnesses (Radhakrishnan 1992: 23). The word "upaniṣads" refers not only to the Upaniṣads texts themselves, but also to certain "mysterious words, expressions and formulas, which are only intelligible to the initiated" (Deussen 1966: 16). For example, the *Chāndogya Upaniṣads* uses the term "upanishads" to mean "hidden teachings" that produce honey from the flower of Brahman (here understood as AUṀ) (III.5.1). This suggests that the Upanishads tell of what has been heard directly (śruti) by the sages. AUṀ as Brahman is the eternal sound of the universe. The ṛṣis heard it and composed texts with hidden words (upaniṣads) to pass on the secret of AUṀ to others.

The 108 Upaniṣads are about a special kind of knowledge (jñāna) that allows a person to experience the vast greatness of Brahman. This experience is difficult to convey in everyday speech. Thus the ṛṣis

BOX 10.4 INTERPRETATIONS: THE MEANING OF "COW" AND "HORSE"

Aurobindo Ghose (1872–1950) was a freedom fighter like Tilak and Gāndhī (see page 245) and a prolific writer. He was also a poet, yogī, and philosopher with an interest in the dimensions of meaning packed into verses from the *Ṛgveda* and Upaniṣads. He compared the Upaniṣads to "secret teachings such as those of the Greek [Orphic and Eleusinian] mysteries, and explored key terms in light of their esoteric meaning" (Aurobindo [1956] 1982: 4). For example, Aurobindo suggests that the words for cow (*go*) and horse (*ashva*) in the ṛṣis' hymns refer beyond the two animals to a meditator's inner light and subtle energy.

> [For the ṛṣis] the two chief fruits of Vedic sacrifice, wealth of cows and wealth of horses, were symbolic of richness of mental illumination and abundance of vital energy. . . .
>
> [T]he word *ashva*, usually signifying horse, is used as a figure of the Prana, the nervous energy, the vital breath, the half-mental, half-material dynamism which links mind and matter. Its root is capable, among other senses, of the ideas of impulsion, force, possession, enjoyment, and we find all these meanings united in this figure of the Steed of Life to indicate the essential tendencies of Pranic energy.
>
> (Aurobindo [1956] 1982: 42, 46)

It is impossible to properly translate the hymns of the *Ṛgveda* due to the richness of their meaning. How would one translate the word *go* or *ashva* and keep both the sense of animal and subtle energies? Their meanings go far beyond what one thinks of in English as a "cow" or "horse." Translation of the ṛṣis' verses is also problematic because any change in the original sounds heard directly by the ṛṣis would disturb the specific pattern of vibrations established in the verses. Thus according to traditional Hindu thinking, translations cannot preserve the cosmic and spiritual impact of the hymn.

and commentators often used the poetic language of metaphor, paradox, and symbol to speak of Brahman. For example, the final verse of the *Taittirīya Upaniṣad* conveys the experience of merging ātman (self) and Brahman with this paradoxical verse:

> I am food, I am food, I am food. I am the food-eater. I am the foodeater. I am the foodeater. I am the combining agent. I am the combining agent. I am the combining agent. I am the first born of the world-order, earlier than the gods, in the centre of immortality. Whoso gives me, he surely does save thus. I, who am food, eat the eater of food.
>
> I have overcome the whole world. I am brilliant like the sun. He who knows this. Such is the secret doctrine [ya evaṁ veda ity upaniṣat].
>
> (III.10.5)

When the above verse is chanted, the meditator aspires to become illumined and directly realize the import of the "secret doctrine" (upaniṣad). Pithy verses from the Upaniṣads were collected into the *Brahmā Sūtra*, which became a key text for Hindus following the Vedānta darśana. Vedāntins explored the inner aspects of the ancient ṛṣis' teachings, while those who studied Vedic ritual developed the Mīmāṃṣā darśana.

SUPPORTIVE TEXTURE

The *Bhagavadgītā* in the *Mahābhārata*

The *Mahābhārata* is a Sanskrit poem based on ancient Indian oral history. Its 110,000 or so couplets were composed between ca. 400 BCE and ca. 400 CE. A brief section called the *Bhagavadgītā* (Song of God) was inserted into the epic between ca. 200 and ca. 100 CE. This short text earned such high status among Hindus that some call it a work of śruti. Its content centers on the ethical issue of social duty (varṇa-dharma) prompted by the warrior Arjuna's horrific quandary: To kill or not to kill my relatives in warfare? The *Bhagavadgītā* opens with these Sanskrit lines followed by a literal translation (adapted from Sargeant 1984: 39).

Dhṛtarāṣṭra uvāca	[The blind king] Dhṛtarāṣṭra spoke:
dharma-kṣetre	On the dharma field, on
kuru-kṣetre	the Kuru field
samavetā yuyutsavaḥ	assembled, ready to fight
māmakāḥ pāṇḍavāś	mine and the sons of
caiva	Pāṇḍu
kim akurvata saṁjaya	what they did? Samjaya?

"Dharma" is the first word spoken by King Dhṛtarāṣṭra. This fact suggests that righteous duty (i.e., virtue) takes precedence over everything else in battle. Arjuna was poised for battle, standing in a chariot in the middle of Kurukṣetra. All commentators agree that Kurukṣetra (the Kuru field) is a large field in the Punjab where the battle between rival factions of the Bhārata clan presumably fought. But not everyone is clear about Arjuna's proper duty. For example, Bāl Gangādar Tilak and Mohandās Gāndhī came to opposite conclusions (see page 245).

Arjuna, the pre-eminent Hindu warrior, is poised on the battlefield to fight against a faction of his family that has perpetrated an injustice. He must do his dharma – his righteous duty – to correct *a*-dharma (injustice) in the world. Or must he? Apparently Arjuna had a conflicting set of duties: (1) a warrior's duty to set *a*-dharma right and protect his people, and (2) duty to his family elders. When Arjuna saw his teachers and others in the opposing camp on the battlefield he became weak with grief, and appealed to his charioteer for help. (The charioteer was his cousin the avatāra Kṛṣṇa.) Desperate and despondent, Arjuna said to Kṛṣṇa:

> My limbs sink down
> And my mouth dries up
> And my body trembles
> And my hair stands on end.
>
> (I.29)
>
> Gāṇḍiva [Arjuna's bow] falls from [my] hand,
> And my skin burns,
> And I am unable to remain as I am,
> And my mind seems to ramble,
>
> (I.30)
>
> And I perceive inauspicious omens,
> O Handsome-haired One,
> And I foresee misfortune
> In destroying my own people in battle.
>
> (I.31)
>
> If the armed Sons of Dhṛtarāṣṭra
> Should kill me in battle
> While I was unresisting and unarmed,
> This would be to me a greater happiness.
>
> (I.46)

After setting the stage with Arjuna's refusal to fight, the *Bhagavadgītā* presents a religious discourse by Kṛṣṇa about the necessity for people to observe the dharma proper to their varṇa. Upon seeing his teachers and other family members on the enemy side of the battlefield, Arjuna was tempted to renounce his duty as a warrior and head for the forest to meditate. His duty as a warrior to fight for a righteous cause conflicted with his duty to respect teachers and protect his family. Kṛṣṇa resolved Arjuna's dharma conflict by notifying him that a deed that is in accord with one's social dharma would not accrue sin if it were done for the Lord without attachment to its fruits. Moreover, Kṛṣṇa taught that it was always better to do one's own dharma (even if poorly) than to attempt to do the dharma proper to another social station (even if that act were done well). Doing the dharma of another social class even "invites danger," Kṛṣṇa warned (*Bhagavadgītā* III.35). Thus the *Bhagavadgītā* reinforced dharma texts such as the *Laws of Manu*, which were being written at roughly the same time.

There is not much "action" in the *Bhagavadgītā*. Viewed from the outside, warriors on the battlefield within close range of Arjuna would have seen only this: (1) Arjuna drops his bow. (2) Arjuna sits down. (3) Arjuna converses with Kṛṣṇa. (4) Trembling, Arjuna bows to Kṛṣṇa. (5) Arjuna retrieves his bow and arises. From the inside much, much more happens: Kṛṣṇa reviews the rudiments of the Sāṃkhya darśana, introduces the notion of bhakti yoga, and temporarily opens Arjuna's divine eye (*divya-cakṣu*). With his divine eye opened, Arjuna saw Kṛṣṇa with uncounted arms, bellies, thighs, feet, faces, gaping mouths, and eyes blazing. He saw the universe burning with God's radiance, and the bloody course of battle ahead. He saw Kṛṣṇa as Time itself. The vision was utterly terrifying, and Arjuna asked for mercy – begging Kṛṣṇa to stop (XI.45). Shortly after the kratophany, Arjuna was resolved to fight. So he retrieved his bow, and stood ready for battle. He would fight out of devotion to the Lord because it was his duty. And he would not be attached to the fruits of his actions, as Kṛṣṇa had taught.

The *Rāmāyaṇa*

The *Rāmāyaṇa* is the shorter of India's two epics. The earliest of these "adventures of Rāma" is probably the oldest Sanskrit poem. The historical core of the story's action may have taken place around 1900 BCE in India and Śrī Lanka. Hindu tradition attributes the first written *Rāmāyaṇa* to the sage Vālmīki whose version has around 24,000 verses, composed (ca. 400 BCE) in a high style of Sanskrit known as *kāvya*. The story involves the exploits of the avatāra Rāma, his wife Sītā, his brother Lakṣmana, and their dear monkey friend Hanumān. These heroic characters typify moral excellence for Hindus. They are emulated and beloved by Vaiṣṇavas to this day. Hindus say that Viṣṇu manifests as a fully human avatāra due to the nature of the work he had planned. As a deity of the Hindu trimūrti, Viṣṇu's cosmic function is to sustain the world. In this instance, he had to vanquish the demon Rāvaṇa. Since Rāvaṇa had a boon that gave him protection from supernatural beings, only an ordinary mortal could kill him. It was feared that Rāvaṇa would wreak excessive havoc, because no ordinary person could stand up to him. Thus Viṣṇu came in the form of Rāma to do the job.

The *Purāṇas*

The *Purāṇas* or "ancient stories" are books of Hindu mythology. They have become immensely popular over the generations, and shaped the religious culture of modern India. The *Purāṇas* contain sacred stories of devas and devīs in luxurious detail. Also found in these popular texts are tales of cosmic creation and destruction, ritual instructions, and sacred histories of places of pilgrimage. Individual *Purāṇas* tend to contain material associated with one or another of the deities worshiped on the Hindu path of devotion: Viṣṇu, Śiva, or Devī. A series of comic books in modern times tells stories from these texts. This is just one way the *Purāṇas* continue to sustain the Hindu religious heritage.

Patañjali's *Yoga Sūtras*

Patañjali's work on the sacred science of yoga is the foundational text of the Yoga darśana. The *Yoga Sūtras* go hand in hand with ancient concepts developed in the Sāṃkhya darśana (except that Yoga adds reliance on Īśvara for its practice). Sāṃkhya described the evolution of the world from Prakṛti (primal matter), and Yoga is involved with a practical course of human devolution to reach the point of creative origin. In the course of material evolution all aspects of the human being manifest from most subtle to least subtle in this order: (1) consciousness (*buddhi*), (2) ego (*ahaṃkāra*), (3) mind (*manas*), (4) sensory organs (*jñāna-indriyas*), and (5) motor organs (*karma-indriyas*). Correspondingly the world perceived by human beings evolved from subtle to gross: (1) an energy mass that corresponds to consciousness (*mahat*), (2) gross physical elements (*bhūtas*), and (3) subtle physical essences (*tanmātras*). Practitioners of the Yoga darśana trace a course of devolution step-by-step starting with awareness of the function of the motor organs and moving backwards. Finally they realize pure consciousness (*buddhi*) at the point where it evolved from prakṛti. At that point buddhi perceives the cosmos as pure matter in which all three **guṇas** are perfectly equilibrated in a state of suspended production. This means that the three guṇas – light (*sattva*), movement (*rajas*), and inertia (*tamas*) – are in their quiescent state of utmost unmanifested dynamism. In this quiescent state (*pralaya*) the buddhi functions in mirror-like fashion to reflect puruṣa (pure spirit). According to the Sāṃkhya darśana, prakṛti and Puruṣa are forever distinct. Thus the yogī can never move from even the most quiescent state of matter to become pure spirit. Yet liberation from rebirth (hence the compulsion to return to a material form for future lives) is attained upon clear recognition that reality comprises prakṛti and Puruṣa.

Patañjali's teachings have traditionally been practiced under the guidance of a gurū. And according to the Hindu way of thinking, a gurū will appear when the

Plate 10.3 "Viṣṇu sleeps on the serpent of eternity." This classical Indian dance posture depicts Lord Viṣṇu reclining on the serpent of eternity. The giant coiled cobra supports Viṣṇu on the cosmic ocean, and shelters the deity with his many hoods. The *Purāṇas* explain that Lord Viṣṇu rests like this in dreamless sleep throughout the Night of Brahmā. During this period of inactivity the entire universe is absorbed in Brahman. After 4.32 billion years a lotus grows from Viṣṇu's navel. From the lotus Brahmā the Creator emerges to re-create the world, thus starting another world cycle.

student is ready. Commenting on the *Yoga Sūtras*, a contemporary teacher suggests how a student can become ready:

> [O]nce we have purity of mind, no doubt someone will come to tell us what the true meaning of these things are and what is to be done. "When the disciple is ready, the *Guru* comes," is a well-known Hindu saying. When the receiver is well-tuned, the music comes. We need not send out invitations. All that is necessary is for us to tune ourselves. Then without even a second's delay, the *Guru* will come in some form. If we are not ready though, even with a hundred *Gurus* around we can't be benefited. For a *Guru* can't force anything into us. We must be ready to receive. Similarly, the music is within the radio but it cannot force the speaker to vibrate and bring it out. That is why preparation – developing virtues like *yama* and *niyama* – is very important.
>
> (Rāma 1985: 170)

Study of the Yoga darśana begins with moral restraint (*yama*) and physical discipline (*niyama*). To complement this purification of mind and body, the yogī practices various postures (*āsana*) and breathing exercises (*prāṇayama*). These prepare the yogī to sit unmoving for long periods of time with extended inhalations and exhalations. Such pacification allows the yogī to perceive ever subtler aspects of the body–mind. This perception deepens through three stages (*dhāraṇā*, *dhyāna*, and *samādhi*). At the point of samādhi-without-form the yogī becomes liberated from compulsory rebirth. Patañjali calls the final state *dharmamegha samādhi*. One who reaches it is a **jīvan-mukta**, one who lives (*jīvan*) while liberated (*mukta*) from compulsory rebirth. That person knows intuitively how to deal with all kinds of people by means of what Patañjali calls the four keys: friendliness, compassion, delight in the virtue of others, and equanimity. Many teachers in Hindu tradition speak of the jīvan-mukta.

Limb 1 Yamas *(moral restraints)*

- *Ahiṃsā* (Non-violence) Hostilities cease around a person who is firmly established in non-violence.
- *Satya* (Truthfulness) Fear leaves one who refrains from falsehood and sees things as they are.
- *Asteya* (Non-stealing) Wealth comes to a person who is firmly established in non-stealing.
- *Brahamchārya* (Non-sensuality) This involves maintaining equilibrium with respect to needs, passions, and relationships.
- *Aparigraha* (Non-grasping) This involves not accumulating beyond the capacity to use things properly.

Limb 2 Niyamas *(personal discipline)*

- *Śauca* (Cleanliness) This involves purification of the body (inside and outside), thoughts, and subtle energies.

- *Samtoṣa* (Contentment) To be content means to achieve freedom from desires.
- *Tapas* (Inner heat) This is related to intensity of effort and spiritual striving amidst inner and outer obstacles.
- *Svādhyāya* (Self-study) This involves jñāna, including penetration of subtle levels of AUṀ, and contemplation of the meaning of religious scriptures.
- *Īśvara Praṇidhāna* (Surrender to Īśvara, the Supreme Lord) This involves self-surrender when the yogī is motivated to experience Īśvara.

Limb 3 Āsanas (body postures)

There are hundreds of postures named after sages, animals, and objects including: tortoise, dog, wheel, and staff. Postures are performed to achieve physical one-pointedness (*ekagrata*). This limb is associated with haṭha yoga. Practice of the āsanas promotes mental concentration and physical health. Hindus tell stories about the sages whose names are associated with certain postures.

Limb 4 Prāṇayama (regulated breathing)

The breath (*prāṇa*) becomes subtle to the point where no physical effort is made to breathe and it is not felt. The yogī achieves four states in turn: waking, sleep, dreamless sleep, and "the fourth" (*turīya*). A person's thoughts are moved by prāṇa, but thoughts can be circumvented by dealing directly with the flow of prāṇa through the body and universe. Guiding the prāṇa at first should be gentle, like leading a child by the hand.

Limb 5 Pratyhāra (sense withdrawal)

The five senses (taste, touch, sight, hearing, and smell) are withdrawn from the sense objects, as a turtle withdraws its head and four limbs. The yogī senses things, but maintains equilibrium. The mind mirrors objects without using the senses. Instead of knowing through forms (*rūpa*) and mental states (*citta vṛtti*) the yogī directly contemplates what the Sāṃkhya philosophers call the essence of objects. This is a superior knowledge. The yogī is not afraid of anything.

Limb 6 Dhāraṇā (fixed attention)

Dhāraṇā is the step of training oneself to meditate. Practice is successful when the mind settles, not wandering from the object. The yogī prolongs the time it takes for one breath. The mind becomes steady through unwavering attention to an object such as the navel, a "lotus" flower in the heart, light at the brow, tip of the nose, or an external object.

Limb 7 Dhyāna *(meditation)*

Dhyāna is attained when the breath lasts 12 × 12 seconds. This is the continuous flow of cognition toward the object without stray associations or images. Mental flow is smooth and uninterrupted like oil poured from one vessel to another. When dhāraṇā turns into dhyāna some signs may appear, such as hearing beautiful music, a flute, a gong, a roaring ocean, or feeling like being bathed in beautiful moonlight, and so on. One's sense of having a body is absent.

Limb 8 Samādhi *(union)*

Samādhi is attained when one breath lasts 12 × 12 × 12 seconds. Samādhi with form gives rise to samādhi without form in which the subject–object distinction is lost. This highest state of union is called *kaivalya*, also known as *dharmamegha*, the cloud of dharma. Making effort in dhāraṇā leads to effortless dhyāna, which leads to spontaneous samādhi. Finally there is so much motion that the yogī appears as a motionless top spinning very fast. Even "desire" for union with the divine drops away here.

CROSS-OVER TEXTURE

Poems of a Śākta bard

The Śākta poet Rāmprasād Sen (1718–1775) felt that no religious practice was ultimately worth anything. There was no meaning to ritual, and there were no caste boundaries for a true devotee. He wrote (Sen 1999: 49):

> You'd better not touch me,
> Death – I've just lost caste
> On the very day
> The kind Mother was kind to me.

Rāmprasād claimed that all devotion was within the bhakta's heart, and nowhere else. Thus worship involving ritual gestures and offerings at shrines was unnecessary. For salvation (mokṣa) the Śākta cried out, and thought of the feet of the goddess. He depicted himself as a hurt child appealing to the Mother who is at times tender, and at times angry and negligent. This dual nature of the Mother – typical of the goddess in India – is not bothersome to Śākta devotees. Whatever they experience from the Mother they welcome as a sign of her love. Sometimes Rāmprasād and other Śāktas poets challenged the Mother for imposing hardships upon them, but this was taken as a sign of the depth of their love for her. Here Rāmprasād speaks of his poverty (Sen 1999: 18):

> I've got a bone to pick with you, Mother.
> You've trapped me in a family
> And seen to it I stay poor. . . .
>
> So where is Your fortune? I know You've got
> The Lord of Wealth in Your pocket.
> Why do You hold out on Rāmprasād?
>
> At Your feet I can defeat
> Every evil every foot of the way.

That visual impression based on the thinking of the Mother gave the Śāktas darśana. And a glimpse of the Holy Mother could bring spiritual transformation. By uttering the Mother's name, the bhakta could gain release from saṃsāra at the time of death. This sense of a name's power runs so deep in Indian culture that parents name their children by God's names, so that as they die the parents will be uttering the name of God.

PART 3
HINDU PERFORMANCE

ENCOUNTERING THE DIVINE THROUGH "PILGRIMAGE"

Pilgrimage is a mainstay of Hindu life. Hindus criss-cross Bharat Māta (Mother India) to visit places identified in the sacred lore of the *Purāṇas*. Some Hindus may go on pilgrimage to sites where pieces of Śākti's body were scattered. Others may go to Vṛndāvana where Kṛṣṇa played the flute for the **gopīs**. Then again many Hindus visit Vārāṇasī to immerse themselves in Gangā, the goddess who is a river. From one point of view, the land of India is the Holy Mother, whose sacred sites continually bring spiritual benefit to millions of devotees. From another point of view, it is not necessary for a Hindu to *go* anywhere on pilgrimage in India because the body is known to be a temple of God. Thus some Hindus sit unmoving for hours and days on end to lead their subtle breath along the thousands of rivers within their bodies. Others just think of the Mother in their hearts and they find themselves with the goddess. Yet others read or hear a story and are transported to the place of the deity. In other words, Hindus can go on inner and outer "pilgrimages" to encounter the divine. Hindus may access the divine through these four sacred sites: (1) the land, (2) the body, (3) the story, (4) the emotions. Each of these focal points interpenetrates the others in Hindu tradition. And they all open up to energies of the spiritual realm.

Sacred land: Bharat Māta

The *Purāṇas* speak of 108 Mother goddesses whose sacred sites are scattered around Bharat Māta or Mother India (the number 108 is sacred in India). A nice round list of 108 includes some mythical places not seen on the ground or water. Other sacred sites are said to exist in remote places such as in: (1) the solar orb, (2) the heart, (3) among beautiful girls, and (4) among Divine Mothers (Bhattacharyya 1999: 241). But even places of pilgrimage that *are* found on Indian soil or water interpenetrate other levels of existence. In Hindu tradition *all* things have their gross and subtle aspects. This point is a foundational teaching in the Sāṃkhya darśana, which identifies a subtle aspect of every material element. Hindus visit holy places to participate in the spiritual power of pilgrimage sites that channels divine energy into the material world. These places of power are called *tīrthas* (doorways) between the material and spiritual realms of existence. Many sites are associated with parts of Śākti's body. According to one story, a grieving Śiva carried his lover's corpse all over Bharat, and bit by bit a piece dropped off – here and there – making the land sacred. The city of

Vārāṇasī stands out among all other sacred sites as the Mahāshmashāna, the Great Cremation Ground (Eck 1998: 32). Normally a cremation ground where the Hindu dead are cremated is considered a ritually polluted place. But the power of the ancient Kāśī (the city of light, Vārāṇasī) is so great that Hindus pray to have their ashes scattered in the Ganges River there.

Sacred body: the inner landscape

The writings of Gorākhnāth (ca. 1000 CE) on yoga in the Nāth tradition complemented Patañjali's *Yoga Sūtras*. Nāths trace their spiritual lineage to the deity Śiva who is called the Ādi Nāth (Primordial Nāth) because wisdom and inspiration flow through him to yogīs of his lineage. Gorākhnāth described an inner geography of the body complete with sun and moon, wind, rivers, and places where lotus flowers bloom. Nectar associated with the life essence is said to drip from the moon at the top of the head, while the sun abides in the lowest cakra or energy center. The feminine power of Śākti is identified with the sun at the base of the spine. Tantric yogīs know her as **kuṇḍalinī**, the thrice-coiled snake. Once awakened, kuṇḍalinī-śākti ascends the central channel (the *suṣumṇā nāḍī*) of the spine. Upon reaching the crown cakra at the top of the yogī's head, she unites with Śiva who sits immobile there. Through such a process Nāth yogīs seek control over death and attain the status of jīvan-mukta.

Sacred story: *The Holy Lake of the Acts of Rāma*

Tulsī Dās wrote a bhakti version of the *Rāmāyaṇa* in Hindi. He structured the poem as a kind of pilgrimage to a Holy Lake where devotees immerse themselves in the ultimate reality of Rāma and Sītā. Through his narration Tulsī Dās symbolically constructed a rectangular pool. He built four *ghāṭs* (stairways) leading down into the lake through four dialogues, each of which presents a distinctive perspective on the acts of Rāma: (1) a crow speaks to a Garuḍa bird, (2) Śiva speaks to Pārvatī, (3) two sages speak to each other, and (4) Tulsī Dās speaks to devotees. And though the dialogues overlap, each can be distinguished according to the words used to address characters within the text. Tulsī Dās organized his poem into seven chapters, symbolized as seven steps for each ghāṭ. Thus each chapter includes the four dialogues. Devotees are led closer to the holy lake as they descend from one step to the next. Arriving at the holy lake after the seventh chapter, those who engage themselves in the story are purified in the sacred water. Reaching the pool, bhaktas become immersed in the absolute because the water is Rāma himself – who is inseparable from Sītā.

Tulsī Dās was inspired to write a new version of the *Rāmāyaṇa* because in a hierophanic experience he had found himself in places where Sītā had been. Thus he believed that through hearing his story of the *Holy Lake of the Acts of Rāma*, others could also come face-to-face with the divine. Also based on experience, he believed in the power of Rāma's name. For example, Tulsī Dās became infected when the plague hit Vārāṇasī. He attributed the illness to momentarily forgetting the name of Rāma. In that moment of forgetfulness, he opened himself up to the plague. Afterwards Tulsī Dās recovered. He was convinced then that Rāma not only hears the prayers of human beings, but also loves and protects those who worship him. Thus the single word that seems to run through everything for Tulsī Dās is "Rāma." Devotees of Rāma are inspired by Tulsī's story and repeat with devotion the name "Rāma." By so doing, the deity becomes established within their heart/mind. And by invoking Rāma, bhaktas attain darśana of their Lord. Vaiṣṇavas who worship Rāma believe that chanting Rāma's name has a purifying effect upon them. Thus when a devotee repeats the syllables "Rāma" many times the mantra comes out as "*marā*" and "*amarā*" as well as "*rāma*." The devotee thus knows that Rāma (*rāma*) is the power that overcomes death (*marā*) to bring the undying (*amarā*) transcendence of rebirth.

Sacred emotions: *bhāvas* and the *rasa* of spiritual love

According to Indian aesthetic theory, the audience of an effective Indian drama should experience a mood or **rasa** (literally, "taste"). Works of dramatic art should be created to have one rasa that predominates. The challenge of both dramatists and performers is to evoke that rasa in the audience by stirring up various bhāvas (emotions). The bhāvas work synergistically to re-create the appropriate rasa in each member of the audience. The primary bhāvas are supplemented by secondary bhāvas. This double dose of emotion generates a deeper experience of the bhāvas and gives the audience a profound aesthetic "taste." The bhāvas are basic emotions that fluctuate in a person, largely beyond their control. However, a rasa is a sustained aesthetic mood deliberately cultivated in the course of a performance on the basis of various fleeting emotions. Performers go through elaborate training to master the canon of external signs that are meant to convey a spectrum of emotions. They learn gestures, postures, and words to evoke specific bhāvas in the audience to convey the rasa of the artistic piece. Hand and facial gestures are among the most powerful carriers of meaning in Hindu performance. They make up a performative language that has been standardized in Indian aesthetics.

The Vaiṣṇava bhakti tradition elaborated on the theory of bhāva and rasa from a spiritual point of view. It speaks of several bhāvas that become transformed into *bhakti-rasa*, which is the "sweet mellow of devotional service" (Caitanya 1991: 60). Thus both the audience of an Indian drama and the devotee of Kṛṣṇa attain a sustained taste (or "mellow") through the cultivation of their emotions. But the devotee of Kṛṣṇa cultivates spiritual emotions that lead to the most sublime taste that is humanly possible – the taste of *prema*. Prema is a "spontaneous and unalloyed love" of

Plate 10.4 "Gopīs search for Kṛṣṇa." On the banks of the Yamunā River in Vṛndāvana Kṛṣṇa plays his flute. The transcendental music attracts the cowherd girls and they dance. As Kṛṣṇa shows his love for Rādhā and the other gopīs they generate greater love for him. The Lord's response is yet more love. A gopī may feel the bhāva of jealousy if Kṛṣṇa seems to pay special attention to Rādhā. But the Lord will suddenly disappear the moment any gopī thinks, "This is mine!" with a possessive feeling toward Kṛṣṇa. Here the gopīs are seen looking for Kṛṣṇa who has disappeared.

the Lord (Caitanya 1991: 96) that can be understood as follows:

> *Bhāva-bhakti* [which involves rendering spontaneous service to the Lord] . . . so excessively affects the heart that it melts and becomes a sublime slave of love, bringing the highest feelings of divine bliss within easy reach, and generates an intense desire for Kṛṣṇa. The fully perfected souls term this over-vaulting ecstasy as *prema.*
>
> (Śrīla Rupa Gosvami quoted in Caitanya 1991: 61)

To experience prema a person must continually cultivate the spiritual bhāvas in daily life. Thus the bhakta chants the Lord's name, remembers Kṛṣṇa's pastimes, seeks self-knowledge, and so forth. But it is not enough merely to practice. One must practice with true humility, said Caitanya Mahāprabhu (1486–1533 CE), founder of the Gaudiya Vaiṣṇava community:

> One who thinks of himself lower than the grass, who is more tolerant than a tree, and who does not expect personal honor but is always prepared to give all respect to others, can very easily always chant the holy name of the Lord.
>
> (Caitanya 1991: 31)

The practice of cultivating the spiritual bhāvas with humility brings an evolution of the personality. A bhakta with highly developed bhāvas: (1) becomes tolerant and unperturbed even in difficult situations, (2) does not want to waste time, (3) is interested only in what links directly to Kṛṣṇa, (4) has a taste for chanting the holy name, (5) loves the places of Kṛṣṇa's pastimes, and so forth. Thus there is a difference between being a member of the audience in an Indian drama and being a devotee of Kṛṣṇa. Members of an audience leave the theater once the performance is done, but devotees are always engaged in spiritual practice. Vaiṣṇavas may choose among several forms of Kṛṣṇa as the object of devotion: (1) Kṛṣṇa of the *Bhagavadgītā* who presents himself as Arjuna's charioteer, (2) Bala Kṛṣṇa who is seen as a mischievous and mysterious child, or (3) Kṛṣṇa of the *Purāṇas* who is a blue, two-armed cowherd. A devotee worships the form of Kṛṣṇa that best accords with his or her temperament and experiences the rasa of God that corresponds to that particular form.

Vaiṣṇava bhaktas aspire to become servants, of the servants of the gopīs, who are considered the purest devotees of Lord Kṛṣṇa. The *Śrīmad-Bhāgavatam Purāṇa* tells of the cowherd Kṛṣṇa and his relationship with the gopīs (milkmaids). Rādhā is named as his favorite, but there are many gopīs whose various personalities show a full spectrum of responses to God's presence and absence. Rādhā and the other milkmaids cultivate the rasa of love for Kṛṣṇa, but experience a range of emotions in the process of relating to their Lord. The cowherd form of Kṛṣṇa plays a flute, and its spiritually transcendent sound entices the milkmaids to come to the groves of Vṛndāvana seeking him. The gopīs love to dance with Kṛṣṇa, but their joy in this encounter is transformed into longing when he suddenly disappears. Thus the gopīs experience a range of bhāvas from the ecstatic joy of being with God to the profound longing that comes when they want him back.

Caitanya was often moved to dance from a deep devotion to the cowherd form of Kṛṣṇa. His intense devotion to Kṛṣṇa outwardly looked like a kind of madness. However, according to Caitanya's devotional tradition his acts were a result of deep spiritual bhāvas:

> Blood came out of the pores of his hair, his teeth chattered, his body shrank in a moment and at the next appeared to swell up. He used to rub his mouth against the floor and weep, and had no sleep at night. . . . [S]ometimes the joints of his body seemed to contract. The only burden of his songs was that his heart was aching for Kṛṣṇa, the Lord.
>
> (Dasgupta 1969: 227)

Gauḍīya Vaiṣṇava bhaktas believe that inwardly Caitanya found himself in Vṛndāvana, dancing among the gopīs as he went into such spells of devotional fervor. Normally people cannot see the subtle manifestation of Vṛndāvana because their minds are subject to **māyā** (illusion). But great devotees such as Caitanya were able to access the transcendent realm where Kṛṣṇa abides. Indeed, Gauḍīya Vaiṣṇavas identify Caitanya with Kṛṣṇa himself because Caitanya was so profoundly in tune with the Lord.

Gauḍīya Vaiṣṇava bhaktas dance, sing, and tell stories about Kṛṣṇa to deepen their devotion. They recite mantras based on the names of the Lord. Extensive recitation of sacred sounds cultivates a spontaneous outflow of their heart's spiritual love for Kṛṣṇa. Among the many symptoms of ecstatic love (called *sattvika bhāva*) that may manifest in a gopī devotee are spontaneous dancing, rolling on the ground, singing or crying loudly, stretching, yawning, and laughing (Prabhupāda 1985: 219).

The experience of Kṛṣṇa becomes increasingly profound in the course of a gopī's worship, depending on his or her level of devotion. Sometimes bhaktas see themselves "in Vṛndāvana" with Kṛṣṇa.

> Vṛndāvana is the transcendental place where Kṛṣṇa enjoys His eternal pastimes as a boy, and it is considered the topmost sphere in all existence. When this Vṛndāvana is exhibited in the material world the place is called Gokula, and in the spiritual world it is called Goloka, or Goloka Vṛndāvana.
>
> (Prabhupāda 1985: 46n)

There is a mysterious relationship between Gokula and Goloka. Both are in some way associated with the physical place in India called Vṛndāvana. Yet a devotee need not be in that physical place to abide with Kṛṣṇa in Vṛndāvana. Kṛṣṇa exhibits his pastimes in Gokula Vṛndāvana. Beyond that, Goloka Vṛndāvana appears to be a higher plane. Yet once the purest devotion is achieved Gokula and Goloka are not seen to differ.

"MAKING PERFECT" THIS LIFE

In the *Bhagavadgītā* Kṛṣṇa told Arjuna about three paths that lead to liberation from rebirth: (1) the path of knowledge (jñāna-mārga), (2) the path of devotion (bhakti-mārga), and (3) the path of action (karma-mārga). For example: Hindus who follow Śaṅkara's teachings of Advaita Vedānta are on the jñāna-mārga; Gauḍīya Vaiṣṇava devotees who lovingly worship Kṛṣṇa are on the bhakti-mārga; and when Arjuna determined to fight as a warrior on the battlefield of Kurukṣetra he was on the karma-mārga.

The karma-mārga involves not only faithful performance of one's class duty, but also engagement in **saṃskāras** (life cycle rituals) that perfect everyday life in this world for eligible Hindus. Hindu tradition typically names sixteen rituals aimed at "making perfect" (saṃskāra) life in this world for people of the "twice-born" varṇas. Of the sixteen saṃskāras, eleven are concerned with children – including three for the unborn child and one at birth. Śūdras and untouchables traditionally participated in few if any of the saṃskāras. The relationship between the śūdras and members of the upper three classes is complex – and may go back to an early division between Āryans and other people in India. The question of whether the distinction between the "twice-born" Āryans and the others was racial or cultural causes heated debate today among scholars. In modern times, many of the traditional saṃskāras are simplified or may even be neglected by the "twice-born" classes. Some Hindus call for the return of traditional values and more thorough attention to details of the saṃskāras.

Hindus of the upper three varṇas are called "twice born" (*dvi-ja*). Brāhmaṇa, kṣatriya and vaiśya boys of around 12 years of age symbolically become "twice-born" persons by going through the *upanāyana* ritual of receiving a sacred thread. Their first birth is by way of a mother's womb. Their second birth is by way of the Vedas. In modern times mostly brāhmaṇa boys go through the *upanāyana* ceremony. They acquire a sacred thread that is to be worn (except while bathing) until the moment of complete renunciation in the last stage of life (āśrama). Nowadays the majority of Hindu males who acquire a sacred thread never take up the life of complete renunciation. Hindu women do not go through the sacred thread ceremony. They are presumed to share in the spiritual status of their husbands and thus become a legitimate part of the "twice-born" system. Women of the upper three varṇas participate in the childhood rites, and pick up again at marriage. The marriage ceremony remains highly significant – and for a woman marriage takes the place of the *upanāyana* ritual.

A key moment of the sacred thread initiation is the transmission of the Gāyatrī mantra – an invocation to the sun from the *Ṛgveda* (3.62.10). The Gāyatrī mantra asks for illumination.

OṂ BHŪR BHUVAH SVAH
TAT
SAVITUR VARENYAM
BHARGO DEVASYA DHĪMAHI
DHĪ YO YONAH
PRACHODAYAT

Throughout all of existence
"That" essential nature
illuminating existence is the
Adorable One.
May all beings perceive with subtle intellect
the magnificent brilliance of enlightened
awareness.
(Shanti Mayi translation 2007:
http: //www.shantimayi.com/gayatri_sm.html)

All who receive the Gāyatrī transmission should recite it each morning and evening. But whether or not a person is given the Gāyatrī mantra, there is always one word that runs throughout the lives of Hindus: AUṀ. The mantra AUṀ found its way from the ancient *Ṛgveda* into all levels of classical and popular Hindu tradition. AUṀ is called the root mantra because it reflects the underlying sound of the universe. According to one popular Hindu interpretation A (the first letter of the Sanskrit alphabet) represents the world's creation by Brahmā, *U* represents the world's maintenance by Viṣṇu, and Ṁ represents the world's destruction by Śiva. The dot (*bindu*) above the *M* represents the world in its nascent form between periods of manifestation. Thus AUṀ represents the sound flowing into silence beyond all form back to Brāhmaṇ, the primordial energy of the universe.

KEY POINTS

- "Hinduism" flowed from Vedic religion, the Indus Valley Civilization, and indigenous folk traditions. The foundational texture is based on 1,028 hymns sung by the Vedic ṛṣis. Beyond that, many non-Vedic elements found their way into Hindu thought and practice. These are presumed to derive from the Indus Valley people and other indigenous Indians.
- Hindus generally hold these four assumptions in common: (1) The universe has no beginning or end, but goes through regular cycles of creation, maintenance, and destruction. (2) Living beings go through a cycle of rebirths propelled by their karma until they attain liberation. (3) Ascetic practice is effective in bringing human beings to liberation from the cycle of rebirth. (4) The core Vedic scriptures were revealed, and specially trained people of the priestly class preserve their authoritative content.
- Hindu devotional worship is directed at three main manifestations of God: Viṣṇu, Śiva, and Śākti. Beyond the Vaiṣṇava, Śaiva, and Śākta forms of devotion one finds the worship of numerous local godlings throughout India – especially among women villagers. Many of the local godlings are female.
- Seers, priests, renunciates, and devotees are four major types of religious specialists that made a lasting impact on Hindu religious life in India. All but the divinely inspired Vedic seers may be found in India today.
- Six sacred sciences (darśanas) form the basis of Hindu philosophy. In common they: (1) accept the Vedas as authoritative, (2) counter what they see as Buddhist skepticism, (3) posit an ultimate objective reality that is not impermanent (versus the Buddhist viewpoint), (4) accept the notion of an endless cosmic cycle of creation, maintenance, and dissolution (as do Buddhists), (5) use a common vocabulary (with particular twists), and (6) have liberation from the cycle of existence as their goal.
- Rāmānuja and Madhva established the notion that God must be encountered. This notion paved the way for new rituals, fine art, methods of meditation, and literature. The worship of God with form brought the concept of the iṣta-ḍevatā (chosen deity) whereby amidst the numerous divine beings Hindus tend to have one "chosen deity" on which to focus their attention.
- Hindus recognize three religious paths to liberation from the cycle of rebirth: (1) the path of knowledge (jñāna), (2) the path of devotion (bhakti), and (3) the path of action (karma). In

practicing these paths Hindus use symbols to evoke an experience of different levels of reality – whether meditating on a sacred text, receiving a life cycle initiation, or going on pilgrimage.

STUDY QUESTIONS

1. Distinguish between the early Vedic and the later Hindu concepts of the universal principle and the deities.
2. Define these terms: ṛṣi, brāhmaṇa, *śramaṇa*, and bhakta. What is the difference between a Śākta, a Vaiṣṇava, and a Śaiva in terms of their object of worship?
3. Describe the main teachings of these two classical Hindu darśanas: Yoga and Vedānta. What new sense did the term *darśana* take on in the Hindu bhakti movement?
4. Name three developments of Indian culture that were associated with the emergence of the Hindu religion from the older Vedic tradition. (*Hint*: These have to do with ritual, art, and architecture.)
5. Name some prominent figures who helped develop Hindu devotional theism (bhakti). Name other prominent figures who responded to India's encounter with the West (social activists and gurūs).
6. Distinguish between śruti and smṛiti in Hindu religious literature. Name some major texts from each category.
7. Name several ways of going on inner and outer "pilgrimage" in Hindu tradition. What different methods do Hindus use to encounter the divine?

GLOSSARY

avatāra One descended from on high; one of ten incarnations of the Hindu deity Viṣṇu.

bhakta Devotee. A Hindu on the path of devotion (bhakti-mārga).

Brahman The ultimate principle of Hindu tradition, thought of as the living essence of the universe.

darśana View, perspective. One of six schools of Hindu sacred science; in Hindu devotional theism "taking darśana" means seeing and being seen by a holy person or deity.

deva Shining one. General term for a god of the ancient Vedic religion, used later in Hindu tradition.

Devī Goddess. General term for goddess in Hindu tradition; name of a goddess when capitalized.

dharma Law. Duty. In Hindu thought, associated with caste duty.

gopī Milkmaid. Hindu devotee of Kṛṣṇa from the Gauḍīya Vaiṣṇava tradition.

guṇa One of three dynamic qualities of the material world, according to the Hindu Sāṃkhya darśana: light (*sattva*), movement (*rajas*), and inertia (*tamas*). These have a wide range of associations including foods, social classes, and colors.

heterodox Not adhering to the orthodox or authoritative views of a tradition.

iṣṭa-devatā The "chosen deity" of a Hindu who focuses worship on one among many gods and goddesses. Typically a person worships the family's chosen deity, the village deity, and others in addition to his or her personal deity.

jīvan-mukta One who is liberated while living; the goal of many Hindus.

kuṇḍalinī A form of the Hindu goddess imagined as a snake thrice-coiled at the base of the spine to be awakened in meditation by Śākta yogīs.

māyā Illusion. Term used in Hindu tradition, especially in the Advaita Vedānta school.

pūjā Homage. Hindu ritual that involves offerings to deities who are treated as honored guests.

rasa The "taste" conveyed through performance (e.g., dance) in both Hindu aesthetic and devotional traditions. The highest taste is love for God.

ṛṣi Seer. In Hindu tradition, sages to whom words (hymns) of the *Ṛgveda* were revealed.

Śaiva Hindu devotee of Śiva.

Śākta Hindu devotee of Śākti, the goddess.

saṃskāra One of sixteen rites of the Hindu life cycle.

saṃnyāsī Renunciate in the traditional Hindu fourth stage of life; also called śramaṇa (striver) or sadhu.

satī Ancient custom (now outlawed) in India of a woman burning herself on her husband's funeral pyre.

trimūrti Hindu divinity portrayed as three-in-one: Brahmā the creator, Viṣṇu the sustainer, and Śiva the destroyer of the world.

Vaiṣṇava Hindu devotee of Viṣṇu, most often in his incarnations as Kṛṣṇa or Rāma.

varṇa-āśrama-dharma Duty according to the caste, life stage, and gender of a person in Hindu society.

yogī Practitioner of yoga in Indian religious culture. Yoga refers not only to physical postures but also to practice on the path of knowledge (jñāna-mārga), path of devotion (bhakti-mārga), and path of action (karma-mārga).

KEY READING

* Scriptual citations are noted according to verse numbers. English renderings were taken from these texts: *Rigveda* from Gopalacharya (1971), *Upanishads* from Radhakrishnan (1992), *Laws of Manu* from Buhler (1886), *Bhagavadgītā* from Sargeant (1984).

Bryant, Edwin (2001) *The Quest for the Origins of Vedic Culture: The Indo-Aryan Migration Debate*, Oxford and New York: Oxford University Press.

Doniger, Wendy ([1975] 2004) *Hindu Myths: A Sourcebook Translated from the Sanskrit*, London: Penguin.

Goodall, Dominic (1996) *Hindu Scriptures* (based on an anthology by R. C. Zaehner), London: J. M. Dent.

Klostermaier, Klaus K. (1994) *A Survey of Hinduism* (2nd edn), Albany, NY: State University of New York Press.

Kumar, Nita (1994) *Women as Subjects: South Asian Histories*, Charlottesville, VA: University Press of Virginia.

Lochtefeld, James G. (2002) *The Illustrated Encyclopedia of Hinduism*, 2 vols, New York: The Rosen Publishing Group.

Rinehart, Robin (ed.) (2004) *Contemporary Hinduism: Ritual, Culture, and Practice*, Santa Barbara, CA: ABC-CLIO, Inc.

CHAPTER 11

Sikh tradition

TIMELINE

	CE	
Kabīr	1398–1448; 1398–1518 (traditional)	
Nānak (Gurū 1)	1469–1539	
Amar Dās (Gurū 3)	1479–1574	
Bābā Siri Chand	1494–1643	
Aṅgad (Gurū 2)	1504–1552	
	1526–1530	Bābur reigns
	1530–1540	Humāyūn reigns
Rām Dās (Gurū 4)	1534–1581	
	1540–1545	Sher Shāh reigns
Dādū Dayāl	1544–1603	
	1545–1554	Islam Shāh reigns
	1555–1556	Humāyūn's rule restored
	1556–1605	Akbar reigns
Arjan Dev (Gurū 5)	1563–1606	
Hargobind (Gurū 6)	1595–1644	
	1603–1604	*Ādi Granth* compiled
	1605–1627	Jahāṇgīr reigns
	1606	Arjan Dev martyred
Tegh Bahādur (Gurū 9)	1621–1675	
	1627–1658	Shāh Jahān reigns
Har Rāi (Gurū 7)	1630–1661	
Har Krishan (Gurū 8)	1656–1664	
	1658	Earliest *janam-sākhī*
	1658–1707	Auraṇgzeb reigns
Gobind Siṅgh (Gurū 10)	1666–1708	
	1675	Tegh Bahādur martyred
	1699	Khālsā formed
	1707–1712	Bahādur Shāh I reigns
	1707–1857	Period of successor states in Mughal Empire
Rañjīt Siṅgh (mahārājā)	1780–1839	
	1849	British annex the Pañjāb
	1873	Siṅgh Sabhā founded
Amrita Pritam	1919–2005	
	1947	Partition of Pañjāb
	1962–1964	*Śrī Gurū Granth Sāhib Darapan*
	1984	Operation Blue Star

The word "Sikh" means disciple or learner. Sikhs are disciples of the ultimate **Gurū** who is God. This tradition of God's disciples emerged from the spiritually charged atmosphere of medieval north India in the Pañjāb. There in the land of many rivers a 30-year-old Hindu had a hierophanic experience, and declared, "There is no Hindu and no Muslim." The year was 1499, and the man became known as Gurū Nānak, the first Sikh. After Nānak, the spiritual succession of learners ran through nine more humans before culminating in a holy book.

The life spans of the ten human Gurūs coincide with the era of Muslim Mughal rule in India, which flowered into one of the world's most magnificent empires from the sixteenth to the eighteenth centuries. The Sikh founder lived during the invasion of the first Mughal emperor, and the tenth Gurū passed away the year after the death of the last great Mughal emperor. The Mughals imported their government from the Muslim world to enforce a centralized despotism. The Mughal ruler was the temporal leader of non-Muslims, and the temporal and spiritual leader of Muslims. Mughal rulers exhibited an extreme range of attitudes toward non-Muslims, and during certain periods a strict Islamic theocracy was enforced. Thus on one hand, Akbar and his great-grandson Dārā Shikōh (who never ruled) were receptive to the Hindu and Sikh faiths. On the other hand, the fifth and ninth Gurūs were martyred under orders from Akbar's son, and his great-grandson, who were highly conservative Muslim rulers.

Many medieval Hindu bhaktas and Muslim Sūfīs in north India belonged to the Sant I Bhagat tradition. Devotees tended to be poor peasants and artisans who sang God's praises in the vernacular language using imagery from everyday life, and to ignore rituals that reinforced caste barriers. They did not dwell on the Vedas or the Hindu avatāras, and had little interest in asceticism. At the same time that these Bhagats (later called Sants) were pouring their hearts into devotional hymns, poets of the Mughal court at Agra were composing some of the finest Persian verses in the history of world literature. Both of these cultural rivers influenced the religious expressions of the Sikh Gurūs. Their holy scripture is a rich literary cache that includes verses composed in local dialects and Pañjābī — wrought through with Persian literary details.

PART 1 SIKH PLAYERS

THE ULTIMATE PRINCIPLE

Sat Nām

Sikhs are monotheistic. There is One God who is considered **Sat Nām**, the True Name. This divine force is called Akāl Purakh, the Timeless Being. The Sikh scripture begins with the **Japjī**, a prayer written by Nānak that illustrates the Sikh understanding of God. It calls on people to meditate (*jap*) and find God's True Name. Sikhs recite it each morning.

> There is but one God.
> Truth Incarnate.
> The Master Creator.
> Unafraid.
> Disdains none.
> Image Eternal.
> Beyond Incarnation.
> Self-existent, True.
> Realised through the grace of the Gurū.
>
> Jap [Meditate]
>
> He was true in the primal time.
> Before the time primal, true.
> True today.
> Ever would He be true, so does Nānak say.
> (*Ādi Granth*, p. 1: Duggal 2004: 1)

Beyond this, Sikhs describe God in terms of people precious to human beings, such as: Father, Beloved, Master, Giver, and Teacher. God is also called by names familiar to Hindus (Rām, Govinda, Hari), as well as Muslims (Rahīm). Yet in spite of such numerous characterizations of God, Nānak said, "By thinking, He cannot be reduced to thought, even by thinking hundreds of thousands of times" (*Ādi Granth*, p. 6: Khālsā, online). This is because Sikhs feel that there is always more to be said. This limitless sense of the divine is conveyed through the gender-neutral expression **Wāhegurū**, a modern Sikh term that captures both the *mysterium tremendum* and *mysterium fascinans*.

IMAGINAL PLAYERS

The *Gurū Granth Sāhib*

The ***Gurū Granth Sāhib*** is the Sikh scripture. It is a physical representation of the divine Name. Sikhs feel that its verses became holy through God's mercy, not through the doings of any human being. Originally, the divine Name was Nānak's Gurū. Nānak began a human lineage when he passed the Gurūship to Aṅgad, who gave it to Amar Dās, and so on down to the tenth Gurū. Coming full circle, Gobind Siṅgh returned the Gurūship to the divine Name with no outer form to gaze upon except letters of an alphabet especially created for it. The alphabet is known as **Gurmukhī**, the Gurū's mouth. The tenth human Gurū transmitted the spiritual lineage of the **panth** to the *Ādi Granth* with the idea that no human would ever again fill the role of Gurū. Thus the Sikh scripture came to be called Gurū.

EXCEPTIONAL PLAYERS

The traditional life stories of the first Sikh Gurūs are called janam-sākhīs, meaning birth stories. A devotional attitude pervades these janam-sākhīs, which contain accounts of hierophanic events alongside historical details. Material for Nānak's life is contained in about half a dozen janam-sākhīs, the earliest of which was not composed until half a century after the Gurū passed away. Even then, when people were still alive who had known Nānak, they seem not to have been consulted for the sake of an accurate historical record. Yet the fact that the janam-sākhīs contradict one another on points of chronology and detail does not seem to impair their religious value. The legendary texts about Nānak are widely used today by Sikhs.

The Gurūs sometimes spoke about their lives, but much of the material pertains to their devotional life in connection with God. Thus the accounts given here about the ten Sikh Gurūs include historical details (derived from outside sources) as well as mythic elements (derived from the janam-sākhīs and oral tradition). From tone and context, the two types of events can be distinguished readily. In addition, as with accounts of the lives of exceptional persons from other traditions treated in this textbook, when matters are ambiguous a comment is made to situate the event into its proper context.

Gurū 1: Nānak (1469–1539)

Nānak was born as a Hindu in the Pañjāb, India. He was of the Khatrī (merchant) class, married a merchant's daughter, and had two sons. Nānak became one of the most successful spiritual leaders of his day, and was retroactively recognized as the first Sikh Gurū. He built up a following by singing devotional hymns, accompanied by Mardāna, a Muslim musician who played the Arab fiddle (rabab). The fate of Nānak's panth may have stayed tied to the Bhagat tradition of Hinduism if not for an unusual incident. Early one morning in 1499 at age 30, Nānak went with Mardāna to bathe in the Bain River. But seemingly due to some mishap Nānak did not surface from where he had dipped into the river. Villagers dragged the river to search for his body, but to no avail. After three days, Nānak emerged from the place where he was thought to have drowned. His body was radiant, but he remained silent. When Nānak finally spoke, he made a radical and powerful declaration: "There is no Hindu and no Muslim." Sikh tradition says that during his mysterious absence Nānak visited a sacred place where he drank an immortal nectar – the Divine Name. He was also ordered to devote himself to **Nām simaran**, remembrance of that True Name. Thus on 20 August 1507 Nānak began reciting the True Name. Renouncing his belongings and job, Nānak began two decades of travel with Mardāna to sing praises of the God who had no form but a Name. And it is through this Name that a person ends rebirth (*Ādi Granth*, p. 940).

Nānak taught that all human beings were equal under God regardless of gender, social class, and religion. Even in his manner of dress, Nānak rejected sectarianism by wearing articles marking both Hindu and Muslim styles. He brought devotees from different social classes together for meals without observing divisive ritual taboos. He promoted **sevā**, community service, which ultimately meant service to the one, unique, formless creator God. In line with Muslim values, Nānak rejected the celibate, reclusive life of the saṃnyāsī that was idealized by Hindus. He favored

Table 11.1 Sikh Gurūs: contexts and contributions

	Name	*Quality*	*Gurūship*	*Lived under Mughal ruler*	*Contributions/ activities*	*Relation to successor*
1	Nānak	Humility	1499–1539	Bābur/Humāyūn	Founds Sikh faith – Nām simaran	None
2	Aṅgad	Obedience	1539–1552	Humāyūn/Sher Shāh/ Islam Shāh	Teaches gurmukhī script	None
3	Amar Dās	Equality	1552–1574	Islam Shāh/Humāyūn/ Akbar	Institutes laṇgar, defends religious freedom	In-law
4	Rām Dās	Service	1574–1581	Akbar	Excavates tank, founds Amritsar	Father
5	Arjan Dev	Self-sacrifice	1581–1606	Akbar/Jahāṇgīr	Compiles *Ādi Granth* – starts building Harimandir – martyred	Father
6	Hargobind	Justice	1606–1644	Jahāṇgīr/Shāh Jāhān	Built Akal Takht – wore *mīrī* and *pīrī*	Grandfather
7	Har Rāi	Mercy	1644–1661	Shāh Jāhān/Auraṇgzeb	Frees animals from chase, maintains Sikh army	Father
8	Har Krishan	Purity	1661–1664	Auraṇgzeb	Shows that Gurū is not limited by age – heals people of smallpox	Nephew
9	Tegh Bahādur	Calmness	1664–1675	Auraṇgzeb	Defends Hindu, Sikh religious freedom – martyred (beheaded)	Father
10	Gobind Siṅgh	Royal courage	1675–1708	Auraṇgzeb d. 1707	Founded khālsā – scholar, writer	None

family life in which husband and wife respect each other as equals.

After Nānak and Mardāna had traveled widely for about two decades, Bābur began his conquest of the Pañjāb to establish the Mughal Empire (1526–1857). Today Nānak is remembered as "the first person . . . to strongly protest and to address Bābur in 1528 as *jabar* (oppressor) and declared his rule as butcher's rule" (Grewal 1991: 22). Nānak and Mardāna were imprisoned for a time at Saidpur (Eminabad in Pakistan). The trouble between Nānak and Bābur marked the start of a long series of encounters between Sikh Gurūs and Mughal emperors. Bābur began the Islamization of India. This transformation from Hindu to Muslim culture continued with more or less intensity throughout the duration of the Mughal Empire, which was not completely defunct until the British came to India (late eighteenth and early nineteenth centuries). Some Mughal policies were antithetical to India's indigenous traditions. For example, Bābur built mosques over sacred Hindu sites, as in Ayodhya where a temple to Rāma was overtaken. On the other hand, the Muslim mystics enriched Indian spirituality as Sūfis offered a *nirguṇa* perspective to the people wherever the iconoclastic Mughals advanced.

Nānak made the first transmission of the Sikh lineage on 7 September 1539 about two weeks before he passed away. He placed five paise (an Indian currency) and a coconut in front of his most worthy disciple, Bhāī Lehna. Nānak bowed to him and bestowed the name Aṅgad, meaning "part of me," or "my limb." Nānak declared that the Gurū merely changed his body. A Sikh Gurū is not identified by the body (*deh*), but by the **jot** that shines through that body. Subsequently, Gurū Aṅgad, the second "Nānak," chose another Nānak – and so it went down through the tenth Gurū. Each subsequent Gurū was a Nānak because there was no differentiation among them: the jot was the same.

Although the first Gurū Nānak had two sons, he did not transfer the Sikh lineage through his family line. The eldest son, Bābā Siri Chand (1494–1643), had strong spiritual inclinations. He lived the unmarried ascetic life of a sannyasin, and gathered his own disciples, known as the Udāsīs. Bābā Siri Chand died at the age of 149, midway through the sixth Gurū's term. And though he was not leading the Sikh lifestyle, the Sikh Gurūs respected Bābā Siri Chand. The eldest sons of Gurū Amar Dās and Gurū Hargobind joined his Udāsī order. Bābā Gurditta, the sixth Gurū's son, even became Bābā Siri Chand's spiritual successor. Under their leadership the Udāsīs took effective steps to preserve the Sikh tradition, especially in the difficult years of Mughal rule. Although he disavowed the family life for himself, Bābā Siri Chand raised his nephew and encouraged householders to live meaningful spiritual lives. It is said that Nānak's son appears in visions to disciples to this day. Among the Udāsīs were a number of spiritually accomplished and educated female teachers.

Plate 11.1 "Gurū Nānak visits Lalo's house." Lalo was a low-caste carpenter. Nānak's visit to his house showed that the Gurū dismissed caste distinctions and valued the honesty and hard work of simple people. Mardāna, the Muslim musician, was Nānak's companion through many travels. Whenever Nānak felt moved by the shabad (spiritual word) in his heart, he asked Mardāna to play his *rabab* (stringed instrument). Gift of the Kapany Collection, 1998.58.14. © Asian Art Museum of San Francisco. Used by permission.

Gurū 2: Aṅgad (1504–1552)

Aṅgad (Bhāī Lehna) was born into a Hindu family with the goddess Durgā as his chosen deity. At age 27 he experienced an aesthetic shock on hearing a recitation of Nānak's Japjī. Inspired by this, he went to the town where Nānak was staying, and became his disciple. Nānak sent Lehna back to his village to help the poor and sing God's True Name. Eventually Lehna returned to Nānak. After Nānak died, Lehna went into solitary meditation for six months. Once persuaded to return to society, he followed the routine that Nānak had established for the panths. This second Nānak was a capable organizer, and expanded the number of Sikh centers. As part of the move to consolidate the new tradition, the Udāsī disciples of Bābā Siri Chand were turned away from the Sikh panth. Aṅgad required strict discipline, which meant awakening at dawn for **kīrtan**, beginning with a recitation of Nānak's Japjī. After morning prayers disciples generally engaged in physical fitness activities. Each day the **laṅgar** was served free of charge to people who ate together regardless of social standing or caste. The main portion of the day was spent working, and the community gathered again for evening prayers.

Aṅgad educated a new generation of Sikhs. To make young Sikhs literate in their mother tongue Pañjābī, he commissioned a biography of Nānak, and had Nānak's hymns transcribed into Gurmukhī, which is a simplified version of the Pañjābī script. Thereafter, the script became standard for the *Ādi Granth*, and all other hymns used in kīrtan. A few days before passing away four days prior to his forty-eighth birthday, Aṅgad passed the Sikh lineage down to Amar Dās. Despite the ambitions of Aṅgad's two sons, the second Gurū chose the 73-year-old Amar Dās because of his deep spiritual constitution.

Gurū 3: Amar Dās (1479–1574)

Amar Dās, the son of a farmer and trader, was a devout Vaiṣṇava Hindu before he became Aṅgad's disciple. His mind was turned toward the Sikh panth after hearing Gurū Aṅgad's daughter reciting Nānak's Japjī. He felt moved to meet Aṅgad, and became a deeply devoted disciple. Although Amar Dās was twenty-five years older than the second Nānak, he carried water for his Gurū. Each year Aṅgad distributed a turban to his close disciples. People made fun of Amar Dās, because he wore one turban on top of the other, refusing to discard any of his Gurū's gifts. When Aṅgad passed the spiritual lineage to Amar Dās, one of Aṅgad's sons was jealous. He kicked the old man, and pushed him from the Gurū's seat. In response, Amar Dās cradled the young man's foot, saying that his old bones were hard and must have hurt him. After the incident Amar Dās sealed himself off in a hut, but was persuaded to come out and serve as Gurū. Aṅgad's son proved unable to gather a following, and left the area.

Gurūs Amar Dās, Rām Dās, and Arjan Dev (during twenty-five years as Gurū, prior to his martyrdom) were at liberty to openly develop the Sikh tradition while Akbar (1556–1605) reigned as Mughal emperor. Akbar was a tolerant Mughal ruler who came to power in Amar Dās' lifetime. He promoted a religion he called the Divine Faith (Dīn i-Ilāhī) that combined fire-centered worship, monotheism, vegetarianism, and religious tolerance. He built a Hall of Worship at his capital, and rebuilt some Hindu temples as well. Akbar's son Jahāṇgīr (1605–1627) testified in his journal to the wide-ranging interest in religions held by his father:

> But in his character one prominent feature was, that with every religion he seems to have entered, through life, into terms of unreserved concord, and with the virtuous and enlightened of every class, of every sect and profession of faith, he did not scruple to associate, as opportunities occurred; for the most part devoting the life-long night to this species of social enjoyment.
>
> (Price 1829: 49)

Amar Dās contributed to the development of the Sikh tradition in three ways. He (1) clarified Sikh ethics, (2) institutionalized the tradition, and (3) solidified the Sikh identity. Specifically, the third Gurū spoke out for social justice, and tended the needy. He approved of widow remarriage, and opposed satī (widow burning) and purdah (veiling). Amar Dās compiled a collection of hymns that became the seed of the Sikh scripture, including his own poems in addition to those by Nānak, Aṅgad, Kabīr, and others. He established twenty-two Sikh community centers (*manjis*), each with a panth leader in charge. Furthermore, he trained a group of 146 devotees to travel around teaching and performing kīrtan. Some of these devotees may have been women. Amar Dās developed special Sikh celebrations, namely a festival that parallelled the Hindu Festival of Lights (Dīwālī), and a ceremony for births and funerals. He also reformed the laṅgar, emphasizing the element of social equality. Thus it is said that when Akbar visited Amar Dās in 1567, the emperor joined the laṅgar, and ate among people of all social stations before seeing the Gurū.

On the day of his death at age 95, tradition says that Gurū Amar Dās passed the Gurū's jot to his son-in-law Jetha. He gave the name Rām Dās, Servant of God, to the 40-year-old successor. Amar Dās' eldest son did not attend the ceremony. Meanwhile, Amar Dās bequeathed to his daughter Bhani (Jetha's wife) lands and villages donated by Emperor Akbar.

> Bhani alone was singled out as his [Amar Dās'] economic successor. Bequeathing lands and villages to a female heir would have been inconceivable in even the later social and cultural milieu of ensuing chroniclers. Clearly, even the inclusion of Bibi Bhani as a possible leader points to an imagination which, given the Gurū's estimation of his daughter and the possible inclusion of females among the elite devotees, envisioned a central place of leadership for women in the Sikh world view.
>
> (Jakobsh 2003: 31)

Gurū Amar Dās' gift of inheritance to his daughter Bibi Bhani suggests that a woman may have come close to being a Sikh Gurū. But the Sikh tradition typically presents an all-male spiritual lineage from the first down through the tenth Gurūs, and says little about their wives.

Gurū 4: Rām Dās (1534–1581)

Rām Dās (Jetha) had heard about Gurū Amar Dās, and became curious about meeting the old man. When they met, Jetha was so moved by the encounter that he stayed with the third Nānak and worked devotedly by his side. In turn, Amar Dās was impressed by the young man, and gave his daughter Bibi Bhani in marriage to Jetha. The couple had three sons. The first had aspirations to become the fifth Nānak, while the second preferred to live as a recluse. But Arjan Dev, the youngest (who shared a birthday with Nānak), was Rām Dās' favorite due to his humility and devotion. Little did anyone know that this youngster would become the first Sikh martyr.

Rām Dās' entire tenure as Gurū was conducted under the reign of the tolerant Akbar. He was free to deepen the panth's Sikh identity, but only after Akbar resolved some charges accusing Sikhs of defaming Hindus and Muslims. Rām Dās expanded the pool that the Gurū Nānak loved to visit, and founded a village there, which Bābā Siri Chand called Amritsar. This village was to become the center of Sikh religious life. While Rām Dās headed the Sikh panth, there seems to have been an increase of women's participation in the community. Rām Dās even composed a four-stanza ceremonial hymn used for Sikh weddings in which the man and woman circumambulate the *Ādi Granth*, once for each stanza.

On the day Rām Dās died he passed the Gurūship on to his youngest son Arjan Dev. According to the Sikh custom of lineage transmission, the Gurū marked Arjan Dev on the forehead with saffron paste. When Arjan Dev became the fifth Gurū on 1 September 1581 exactly seven years had passed since Amar Dās died and initiated Rām Dās into the Gurūship.

Gurū 5: Arjan Dev (1563–1606)

As the son of a Gurū, Arjan Dev was steeped in the religious life. He became a prolific poet, and compiled the *Ādi Granth*. He dictated numerous original compositions to the scribe Bhāī Gurdās. Then he arranged the hymns of all the Gurūs in order of their succession beginning with the first Nānak, and ending with his own. Arjan Dev pronounced the authority of the *Ādi Granth*, and meanwhile declared as heretical another collection compiled by his brother. Emperor Akbar learned of the *Ādi Granth* from advisors who considered it an infidel work that was contrary to Muslim teachings. But after hearing some readings, the emperor felt the Sikh scripture was not dangerous, and went to visit Arjan Dev.

Gurū Arjan Dev laid the foundation for the **Harimandir** in Amritsar, putting it in the middle of the holy tank where it stands to this day. When Arjan Dev installed the newly compiled scripture in the Harimandir, Akbar offered fifty-one gold coins. To raise funds for its construction and future projects, Arjan Dev set up the masand system from the twenty-two centers founded by Amar Dās. Masands were heads of Sikh centers, charged with collecting a tithe from Sikhs that amounted to one-tenth of their earnings. They also initiated people into the panth. Thus the Sikh tradition had the means to grow in size, wealth, and influence in the Pañjāb.

Arjan Dev was the third Gurū to live under Emperor Akbar's tolerant rule. But Akbar's reign ended in 1605, a year after the *Ādi Granth* was installed in the Harimandir. A year later Arjan Dev was dead. He was martyred under Akbar's son, Jahāṇgīr. Akbar had prayed to have a son, and after some time Prince Muḥammad Salim (Jahāṇgīr) was born. Akbar had the prince tutored from age 4 so that he learned four languages (Persian, Arabic, Turkish, Hindi) along with arithmetic, geography, and other subjects. But despite the love bestowed by his father, Jahāṇgīr was quite different from Akbar in temperament, ideology, and rule. While Akbar took an interest in the spiritual diversity of north India, Jahāṇgīr aimed to deepen the influence of Islam through the Mughal Empire. He thus abolished the ecumenical Divine Faith that his father instituted.

While still prince, Jahāṇgīr arranged to have the historian Abul Fazzel killed for insinuating that the Prophet Muḥammad was eloquent, but not divinely inspired. He felt the scholar was poisoning Akbar's mind against Islam, but noted in his journal that his father eventually "shewed himself once more an orthodox believer" (Price 1829: 33). Akbar was displeased with this murder, and declared that Jahāṇgīr's son Khusrau should succeed to the Mughal throne in place of Jahāṇgīr. But the prince remarked after earning his father's displeasure, "I solemnly appealed to the Prophet's sacred name, and ventured to proclaim that, with his assistance, I should still make my way good to the throne of Hindustaun" (Price 1829: 33). In fact, Akbar passed the rulership to his son Jahāṇgīr in 1605.

In 1606, five months after Jahāṇgīr came to power, Prince Khusrau led a revolt against his father. He was caught and thrown into prison. Gurū Arjan Dev had blessed Prince Khusrau. As a repercussion, Ajrun was fined, but would not pay it or admit to treason. Arjan Dev's property was confiscated, and he was taken into custody. Even aside from resenting Arjan Dev's encouragement of the rebel prince, Jahāṇgīr had it in mind to take care of the annoyance that the Sikh Gurū's popularity brought him – even to the point of converting Hindus and Muslims to the Sikh panth. Jahāṇgīr had written of Arjan Dev:

> They called him Gurū and from all sides. . . . *Many times, it occurred to me to put a stop to this vain affair or to bring him into the assembly of the people of Islam.*
>
> (Jahāṇgīr, quoted in Mahajan 1964: 199)

Arjan Dev encouraged horse trading among Sikhs, and had assembled large numbers of horses and elephants. He also had bodyguards, wore rich clothes, and was training his son Hargobind in the art of swords and hunting to take up a leadership position. Thus beyond the Gurū's association with his rebel son, Jahāṇgīr was uneasy about Arjan Dev's military organization, which had a regular source of funding and a centralized authority. Whatever the motive, Sikhs say that Jahāṇgīr presented Arjan Dev with the ultimatum: convert to Islam or die.

Arjan Dev had a deep conviction that the Sikh religion was meant to exist in this world as a separate spiritual lineage. Thus, he refused to remove any hymns from the *Ādi Granth*, and would not convert to Islam. Historically speaking, the precise circumstances of Arjan Dev's death are still not resolved as to whether he was executed, tortured, or drowned in the Ravi River (McLeod 2005: 20). Nevertheless, Sikh tradition counts Arjan Dev as the first Sikh martyr, and states that Arjan Dev remained calm as he was forced to sit on an iron hotplate set over flames, with burning sand poured over his head and body. During a period of respite Arjan Dev went into the cool river and died of shock. His body was carried downstream – never to be found. Five days before he died Arjan Dev had passed the Gurūship to his only child Hargobind. Knowing that Hargobind would live under Jahāṇgīr's rule, Arjan Dev told his son to sit fully armed on the Gurū's seat, and maintain a Sikh army.

BOX 11.1 CULTURE CONTRAST: RELIGIOUS DEVOTION IN MEDIEVAL NORTH INDIA

Gurū Nānak lived in a time of intense cross-fertilization of religious ideas. Nāths, Bhagats (later called Sants), and Sūfīs all expressed love of the divine in slightly different but intermixing ways.

A Nāth yogī: Gorākhnāth (ca. 1000 CE). The Nāths claim a spiritual lineage that came directly from the Hindu god Śiva, who is the Ādi Nāth or Primal Nāth. Śiva bestowed the spiritual lineage on Matsyendranāth. He passed it on to Gorākhnāth who brought disparate yoga lineages back to their roots in haṭha yoga. Gorākhnāth was interested in supernormal powers (siddhis), and aimed to become a liberated sage freed from future rebirths (a jīvan-mukta). In Sikh art, Nānak is seen meeting with Gorākhnāth – though this encounter seems to be a mythical rather than historical comment on reality. Nāth spirituality directly inspired the Sant (or saint) tradition. Some Sants even claim that Gorākhnāth mystically appears to initiate them, even to this day. Yet, while Nāths concentrate on haṭha yoga, Sants practice bhakti, devotional worship.

A nirguṇa Bhagat/Sant: Kabīr (b. 1398). Sants are Hindus who conceive of the divine either with qualities, such as form and color (saguṇa), or without qualities (nirguṇa). Saguṇa bhaktas worship the incarnations of Viṣṇu, mostly Kṛṣṇa or Rāma. Nirguṇa bhaktas resemble Sūfīs in their iconoclasm or shyness with regard to images, and worship the divine through the Word. The poet-saint Kabīr had both Hindu and Sūfī spiritual teachers. Like a Sūfī and many Hindu Bhagats, he related to the divine as nirguṇa or formless, without attributes. Kabīr clearly exemplifies the interpenetration of traditions found in north India around the time the Sikh tradition was born.

Kabīr was from a Muslim family that belonged to the weaver caste in Banaras, India. He called his father by a name signifying Nāth, which suggests that weavers had converted to Islam from Nāthism. Kabīr criticized Nāths for seeking immortality, and claimed that the only antidote to the power of death is Nām, God's name. His own name Kabīr, meaning Great, is one of the ninety-nine Islamic names of God in Arabic. Some of Kabīr's poetry is included in the *Ādi Granth*.

An eclectic Ṣūfī: Dādū Dayāl (1544–1603). Muslims leaving Persia for India abandoned the libraries, taking only their mental wealth. They transported specialized knowledge and traditional cultural lore that was not encased in books: architecture, music, poetry, epics, art, and the Sūfī mystic path. Among these treasures, Persian music, poetry, and mysticism most impacted upon religious life in north India. Both the Sants and Sikhs are beholden to Sūfī spirituality along with its music and poetry. Among the Sūfīs was Dādū Dayāl, one of the three earliest nirguṇa bhakti Sants, along with Kabīr and Nānak.

Dādū Dayāl embodies the syncretistic north Indian medieval culture. He was a Muslim with Nāth connections who promoted Muslim–Hindu interaction. He called God Alakh, meaning "one with no qualities." And though the Muslim Dādū Dayāl worshiped the divine in its formless state, today's saints in his lineage are Hindu saguṇa bhaktas who worship Rāma.

Gurū 6: Hargobind (1595–1644)

Hargobind was the only son of the martyred Arjan Dev, and was thrust into the position of Gurū at the age of 11. He built up a Sikh army with a thousand horses, and recruited many Hindus to defend religious freedom threatened by Mughal rule. Hargobind laid the foundation for the **Akal Takhat** near the Harimandir to balance the spritual function of the temple with a political seat for the military. The sixth Gurū added a second kirpān (sword) to his dress code, calling the first *pīrī* and the second *mīrī* to signify two kinds of justice – spiritual and temporal (see Box 11.2). *Pīrī* was the insignia of Gurūship, and *mīrī* was to defend the faith.

Besides the sword, Hargobind began using other symbols of royalty, including a tuft of plumes on his headdress, an umbrella, and a hawk. Sometimes he was challenged for departing from the custom of Nānak's humble dress. It is said that when a hermit asked him about this, the Gurū replied that he showed royal aspect only on the exterior. Inside, he had already renounced attachment to this world. Although the Sikh flag was hoisted from the time of the third Gurū, Hargobind changed the cloth color from white to saffron. He raised this new flag at the Akal Takht for the first time in 1609.

Hargobind was arrested and imprisoned by Jahāṇgīr. A year or so later the Gurū was released, and developed a friendly relationship with the emperor. However, the relationship between Sikhs and the Mughal court would sour again fifteen years later when Jahāṇgīr's successor Shāh Jahān began to rule. All together Hargobind led the panth for thirty-eight years. During that time, the influence of women in the panth seems to have declined. Even earlier under Gurū Arjan Dev, the formality of the masand system, and its connection with the Sikh economy seems to have distanced women from leadership positions. Masands collected tithes, managed monies, and performed Sikh initiations. Culturally speaking, these would be institutional functions less open to women's participation. And after Arjan Dev's martyrdom, a prominent role for women was less likely with the new Sikh commitment to the double-edged sword used in defense of the faith.

At the time of Hargobind's death several prominent Sikhs had ambitions to succeed him. The Gurū bestowed the spiritual lineage upon his grandson, the 14-year-old Har Rāi who was both pious and trained in the martial arts. (Meanwhile Hargobind's youngest son, Tegh Bahādur, would mature, and come into the leadership position as the third Gurū to succeed his father exactly two decades later.)

Gurū 7: Har Rāi (1630–1661)

Har Rāi was born to Hargobind's eldest son. He had a gentle disposition, and freed many animals from the chase to protect their lives. He hunted, but kept the animals in his personal zoo. Yet on the advice of his grandfather, Har Rāi maintained a Sikh army of around two thousand soldiers. However, fearing retaliation from the Mughals on account of his grandfather's activism, Har Rāi lived mostly in seclusion. He came into no major conflicts with the Mughal army; and he died just three years after Shāh Jahān's son Auraṇgzeb came to power.

Auraṇgzeb had felt that his father was becoming incompetent, and far too extravagant in building the Taj Mahal for his burial place – along with a smaller version for his wife. Thus Auraṇgzeb imprisoned Shāh Jahān, seized power, and forbade anyone to make his own grave into anything but a simple, unenclosed mound of dirt. He regulated life according to a strict regimen in which public singing and music was forbidden (except in the case of a popular Sūfī saint, Shaikh Yahya Chisti), the length of a man's beard was fixed (and cut by special people hired to enforce the regulation), and placing lamps at the tombs of saints was forbidden. Auraṇgzeb ordered the destruction of Hindu temples, and was intent on ruling India according to a highly conservative interpretation of the sharī'a. Meanwhile Gurū Hargobind had befriended Auraṇgzeb's brother Dārā Shikōh, who had the ecumenical religious leanings of his great-grandfather Akbar. (He even translated the Upaniṣads into Persian.) This association put him out of favor with the Mughal court when Auraṇgzeb became emperor following the fierce struggle for succession between the brothers.

On the day of his death, Har Rāi chose his 5-year-old son as successor in the Sikh spiritual lineage. He would not consider his eldest son Rām Rāi to be the eighth Gurū because he befriended Auraṇgzeb. Rām Rāi had appeased the emperor by changing a word of Nānak's hymn to mean "faithless" instead of "Muslim." It is said that Nānak intended the passage to indicate that only God knows who burns in hell, with neither Hindu nor Muslim being exempt.

Gurū 8: Har Krishan (1656–1664)

Har Krishan was not only the youngest Gurū, but also his tenure was by far the shortest. He received the spiritual transmission at age 5 and died two years later of smallpox, while trying to heal people with the disease. Har Krishan's youth reminds Sikhs that the form of a person's body (deh) is not to be identified with the divine light (jot) that manifests through the body. The jot flowed through the human vessel of the 5-year-old Har Krishan, the 95-year-old Amar Dās.

The jot also continues to illumine through the book, the *Gurū Granth Sāhib*. Thus Sikhs are left to wonder why the jot never flowed through a female Gurū.

As he lay dying, Har Krishan chose his uncle Tegh Bahādur to carry on the Sikh lineage. Performing the ritual of succession instituted by the first Nānak, Har Krishan requested five coins and a coconut for the transmission exercise. The sick child waved his hand over these objects and uttered, "Bābā Bakala." People interpreted these words to mean that Tegh Bahādur who was living as a recluse in Bakala village was to be the ninth Nānak. Tegh Bahādur was the youngest son of the sixth Gurū Hargobind, and was called out of seclusion to serve in the role of Gurū at age 43.

Gurū 9: Tegh Bahādur (1621–1675)

Tegh Bahādur was raised as the only child of the sixth Gurū. Hargobind had trained his son in swordsmanship and horse riding. From a young age Tegh Bahādur fought alongside his father. But at age 13 he became disenchanted with violence after a bloody battle, and leaned toward the contemplative life. At age 35, Tegh Bahādur went to live as a recluse in the isolated village of Bakala. But some eight years later he was called to serve as the ninth leader of the panth, amidst controversy as to who should succeed Har Krishan, the child Gurū. Rām Rāi (Har Rāi's son who had been co-opted by Auraṇgzeb) had Tegh Bahādur arrested as an impostor and disturber of the peace. And though the charges were dropped, much trouble was in store for the Gurū.

Tegh Bahādur traveled throughout the Pañjāb, actively promoting the Sikh way of life among the disenfranchised. He had wells dug around the countryside for those without easy access to water, and set up communal kitchens where laṇgar could be served. He reached out more widely to gain new disciples across north India through Delhi and Agra (Mughal seats of power), and eastward to Allāhābād, Banaras, Gayā, and Patna. He pushed onward but without his family further east, into Bangladesh and Assam. Among the Gurūs, only Nānak had gone into these areas, and traveled so widely. Tegh Bahādur's message was based on the foundational values promulgated by Nānak: honest work and sevā. Whatever donations came to his cause he channeled back to the communities.

Tegh Bahādur actively resisted the anti-Hindu policies of Emperor Auraṇgzeb who forbade Kashmiri brāhmaṇas to wear their sacred threads, forced conversions to Islam, imposed taxes on sites of pilgrimage, and destroyed Hindu temples. Some sources claim that Tegh Bahādur laid waste areas of the Pañjāb. Whatever the case, in 1675 Auraṇgzeb summoned Tegh Bahādur to Delhi. When he did not show up, he was apprehended, and imprisoned. The emperor presented Tegh Bahādur with the choice of embracing Islam, or preparing himself for death. Tegh Bahādur refused to convert to Islam. Like his grandfather Arjan Dev, the Gurū believed that Sikhism was meant to be a tradition distinct from Hinduism or Islam. It is said that he was confined to an iron cage, deprived of food, and made to watch other Sikhs being tortured. Finally, he was beheaded. Thus Tegh Bahādur became the second Sikh martyr. On the day of his death Tegh Bahādur passed the jot to his son Gobind Rāi who was 9 years old.

Gurū 10: Gobind Siṅgh (1666–1708)

Gobind Rāi (who later adopted the name Siṅgh) was an answer to the prayers of his parents. He was born in Bihār rather than the Pañjāb because Tegh Bahādur was in the midst of extensive travels when his wife went into labor. At age 5 the family returned to the Pañjāb, where Gobind Rāi learned to read and write in Pañjābī, Braj, Sanskrit, and Persian. But despite his poetic skills, the young man became deeply involved in the military aspect of the panth in reaction to the martyrdom of his father, and the challenges of living under Auraṇgzeb's conservative Islamic rule.

In 1679 the Rajputs revolted against Emperor Auraṇgzeb. Other revolts occurred among the militant Hindu Satnamis, the Jaṭ peasants, and others. In response to the politically unstable situation, Gobind Rāi dissolved the twenty-two official Sikh positions established by Amar Dās, the third Gurū. Gobind Rāi had reason to question the loyalty of the agents (masands) who were mainly drawn from the urban Khatrī caste, and had built up their own small seats of power through years of handling the Sikh tithe. Instead, Gobind Rāi built a new standing army of mercenaries by instituting a Sikh organization that he called the **khālsā** on New Year's Day of 1699 (1 Vaisakh of the lunar calendar or March 30 of the solar calendar).

Plate 11.2 "The Sikh Gurūs." Every religion that came out of India used the word "gurū" with reference to spiritual teachers. But Sikhs focused the word's meaning on the ten human Gurūs seen in this painting. From the tenth Gurū, the Sikh spiritual lineage passed into the *Gurū Granth Sahib* (the holy scripture) where it remains. Those who have faith in this lineage call themselves Sikhs (literally, "disciples"). In the most profound sense every Sikh is a disciple of the ultimate Gurū – namely God.

He asked for volunteers among the Sikhs to come up and sacrifice their heads. One dedicated male disciple responded, and was taken into a tent. The Gurū came out with a bloody sword, and asked for another volunteer. One by one, four more male disciples offered their heads. And one by one Gobind Rāi (soon to take the name Siṅgh) appeared with a bloodied sword. Finally when no one else volunteered the Gurū brought out the five men and blessed them with a two-edged sword dipped in a vessel of sugar water. Gobind Rāi asked for such a blessing in return. Thus, the khālsā was instituted with the baptism of the first five members, plus the Gurū himself. In principle, Sikhs now say that both women and men are entitled to the very same baptism. History will never know how Gobind Rāi would have responded if a woman disciple had offered her head.

Men of all social classes could be initiated into the khālsā, which was perceived as a new kṣatriya caste. Thousands of Jaṭ peasants joined and populated what amounted to a Sikh army. After instituting the khālsā, Sikhs entered into open conflict with the Mughal army. Gobind Siṅgh lost his two elder sons in battle, the younger two were executed shortly thereafter, and his mother passed away (presumably of a broken heart). Gurū Gobind Siṅgh wrote a letter to Auraṇgzeb, appealing to the emperor's sense of justice and commitment to qur'ānic principles. He challenged the emperor to fight face to face. In response, Auraṇgzeb invited Gobind Siṅgh for an audience. However, the meeting never took place, because the Mughal emperor died before it could occur. Afterwards Auraṇgzeb's two sons vied for power. Gobind Siṅgh militarily supported the elder son Bahādur Shāh who

BOX 11.2 SYMBOLS: THE FIVE "K" SYMBOLS

The first five members of the khālsā are called the Panj Piare, the Five Beloved Ones. Among them were a kṣatriya, a Jaṭ peasant, and three low-caste workers (a barber, washer, and water carrier). Members of the khālsā had to renounce the use of tobacco, alcohol, meat slaughtered according to Islamic custom, and sexual contact with Muslims. Men who were baptized into the khālsā took the name of Siṅgh. (Later on women would be granted baptism and take the name Kaur.) Every Siṅgh adopted the custom of wearing five articles. In the Pañjābī language these begin with the letter K. The **Five Ks** have symbolic as well as practical value.

Keś (uncut hair). This represents the natural appearance of saintliness, and is the first token of the Sikh faith. The head hair is kept under a turban or veil, while the body hair remains unshaved. The head hair is gathered into a knot worn on the top of the head by men, and slightly back by women. These spots correspond to the place of the sun and the moon, respectively. Uncut hair indicates the acceptance of God's will.

Kanghā (comb). A comb is normally kept on the person, as the hair is combed several times each day. The hair is unbound and combed for sleeping. The hair must be kept well groomed. This is in contrast to the matted hair of some Indian yogīs that represents their renunciation of the world. It stands for hygiene and discipline.

Kacch (short breeches). This is an undergarment used by male members of the khālsā, which covers the body from above the knees to the waist. It symbolizes chastity and self-control. Its loose-fitting form allows freedom of movement in battle. Wearing this undergarment contrasts with the nakedness of some ascetics who completely renounce the world.

Kaṛā (steel bracelet). This is a steel bracelet worn on the right wrist at all times. The circular form symbolizes the wheel of dharma and universal emperor, indicating spiritual and temporal realms of life. It stands for restraint, and servitude to God.

Kirpān (sword, dagger). This weapon is meant for self-defense, and is carried at all times, even if only as a small insignia. It symbolizes having the dignity to fight for spiritual and temporal justice. It only becomes a weapon as a last resort when protection of oneself or others is required.

was successful in claiming the throne. In the midst of this political confusion, two Pathans stabbed Gobind Siṅgh below the heart. The Gurū was healed, but the wound reopened as he pulled his bow to fight in defense of the new ruler. As he lay dying, Gobind Siṅgh summoned a loyal Sikh named Banda Bahādur (1670–1716) from seclusion to lead the Sikh army. But he passed the spiritual lineage down to no one. At this point the balance of power in the panth was tipped in favor of the Jaṭ peasants rather than the urban Khatrī merchants.

Gobind Siṅgh transmitted the jot to the Sikh scripture as he lay dying. With the customary act of taking five coins and a coconut, the tenth Gurū named the *Ādi Granth* as his successor. Thus the human line of Sikh Gurūs came to an end on 7 October 1708.

HISTORICAL PLAYERS

Gobind Siṅgh's successors

Māta Sundri

Gurū Gobind Siṅgh had three wives, one of whom was named Māta Sundri (?–1747). Although little is said of her (or any other Gurū's wife) in the Sikh literature, it is probable that Māta Sundri led the Sikh panth for thirty-nine to forty years after Gobind Siṅgh's death. Her four decades of leadership represent a tenure longer than that of any of the ten Gurūs except Nānak. Little is known of Māta Sundri.

Bandha Siṅgh Bahādur

Gurū Gobind Siṅgh appointed Bandha Siṅgh Bahādur to lead the charge against the Mughals. He roused many Sikhs to action, and led a peasant uprising that stirred up bloody battles. After some Sikh successes, the Mughal army crushed the peasant uprising. Bandha Siṅgh Bahādur was tortured to death as his flesh was ripped with red-hot pincers. Sikhs remember him as a warrior who inspired future Sikhs to resist tyrannical rule. However, the legacy of the peasant uprising was alienation between Muslims and Sikhs from the village level up.

Guerrilla fighters and the Sikh misls

After the death of Bandha Siṅgh Bahādur in June 1716, the Sikh army surrendered to the Mughals. Thereafter the panth regrouped into roving guerrilla bands, which eventually consolidated into roughly a dozen misls (Arabic = equal). The misls were local confederations centered on villages, each headed by a chief. Twice a year, on traditional days for Sikh gatherings, leaders of the misls assembled to discuss their plans of action. They based resolutions known as *gurmattās* (literally, Gurū's advice) on their deliberations. The misl structure consolidated the Sikhs' influence in local affairs, but competition among the chiefs of these small confederacies led gradually to their weakness. Finally, the Sukachakya Misl annexed the others. It was headed by Charat Siṅgh, whose son Rañjīt Siṅgh would become the head of an independent Sikh territory. Thus, between the demise of Mughal rule and the arrival of British colonialists, Mahārājā Rañjīt Siṅgh provided the panth not only with a Sikh cultural identity, but also with political integrity. He fended off the Afghans who tried to move in to fill the power vacuum created by the deterioration of the Mughal Empire.

Rañjīt Siṅgh (1780–1839)

Rañjīt Siṅgh was born in a Pañjābī village in what is now Pakistan. From a young age he showed considerable military talent. In 1798 he responded to the political chaos in the Pañjāb that threatened the Sikhs when the Afghans overtook Lahore (then in India, now in Pakistan), and were set to attack Amritsar, the site of the Sikh Harimandir. Rañjīt Siṅgh mobilized an army, and pushed the Afghans out of Lahore. At first he hesitated, but then took the title of mahārājā in 1801. Thus Rañjīt Siṅgh came to rule a Sikh state known as Sarkar Khālsā with its seat in Lahore. This independent Sikh kingdom extended into Kashmir and Peshawar. The mahārājā governed for forty years over a populace that was 15 percent Sikh, 25 percent Hindu, and 60 percent Muslim. He was religiously tolerant and ruled a secular state, allowing freedom of expression and worship – though he listened to recitations from the *Ādi Granth* every day.

Mahārājā Rañjīt Siṅgh personally observed the sacred customs of each group, fasting during Ramaḍān, participating in the Hindu Holī festival, and making regular trips to Amritsar to dip in the holy tank at the Golden Temple. He supported religious institutions by giving gold to Hindu temples, grants to Muslim schools, and covering the Sikh Harimandir in gold. Under Rañjīt Siṅgh's rule, Muslims were allowed to follow their religious law. By contrast, he denied the Christian missionaries permission to establish convent schools, and insisted that they teach Sikh scripture. He abolished capital punishment. He was known as a benevolent ruler who cared for farmers and soldiers alike. He was humane, with an inquisitive mind and a sense of humor. Rañjīt Siṅgh ordered his armies never to deface holy books, sacred sites, places of learning, standing crops, or women.

Respondents to British colonial rule

A decade after Mahārājā Rañjīt Siṅgh died, the British annexed the Pañjāb. Thus in 1849 the independent Sikh state came to an end. Rañjīt Siṅgh had not made clear provisions for his succession, and the weakness and confusion that ensued upon his death left the Sikhs vulnerable to the British who had already colonized other parts of India.

Siṅgh Sabhā

In response to the activity of Christian missionaries who entered India, a group of Sikhs created the Siṅgh Sabhā (Lion Society) of Amritsar. The Society began as a local response to the pressures of conversion to Christianity on four Sikh students at the Amritsar Mission School in 1873. Soon a second Siṅgh Sabhā was created in Lahore. These initial centers formed the core of a Siṅgh Sabhā movement that spread through the Pañjāb. There was a spectrum of views in the Siṅgh Sabhā from conservative members who considered the Sikh tradition to be an outcropping of Hinduism, to radical members who pushed for the reformation of a Sikh state that was religiously and politically divorced from Hindu influence. The Siṅgh Sabhā movement consolidated into the Lahore line known as the Tat Sabhā in 1902, and is still somewhat active today under that name. The latest scriptural commentary produced by the Siṅgh Sabhā was the *Śrī Gurū Granth Sāhib Darapan* by Sāhib Siṅgh, published between 1962 and 1964. The mission of the Siṅgh Sabhā movement began by clarifying Sikh doctrine, attitudes, and practices. The result has been a strengthened religious identity, and a sense of cultural uniqueness among Sikhs. Through the movement the panth was reconstituted with the value of a casteless society in contrast to Hindu neighbors. In 1898 Kahn Siṅgh Nabha wrote a text called *Ham Hindu Nahin* ("We are not Hindus"). Even so, years later in 1947 when the time came for partition of the Pañjāb following the successful fight for independence from Britain, the Sikhs chose to live on the Indian side of the Pañjāb with Hindus, rather than in the west Pañjāb that became Pakistan.

Akālī Dal (Akālī Army)

Akālī Dal was founded in 1920 as a reform movement directed at maintaining Sikh control by members of the khālsā over the **gurdwārās** after the Pañjāb came under British control. It grew out of the Tat Khālsā branch of the Siṅgh Sabhā movement in Lahore. Originally Akālī Dal referred to soldiers, but this "Timeless Army" (Akālī = timeless, dal = army) became a political party, and is at the forefront of political activity to this day. In 1961 the party split. Certain factions within the Akālī Dal tried to move the Sikh tradition from a religion of resistance to a religion of revolution. They called for a separate state to be known as Khālistān, land where the khālsā rules. When India was on the brink of gaining independence from British rule most Sikhs were dismayed at the plan to carve up the Pañjāb. But as the Muslim League was being promised the western portion of the Pañjāb to create the nation of Pakistan, the separatist Sikhs wanted their own nation to be called Khālistān.

In 1984 Jarnail Siṅgh Bhindravale (1947–1984), leader of a radical Sikh portion of the Akālī Dal party, took up residence in the Akāl Takht with his followers. He had quickly risen as a popular fundamentalist leader calling for Sikh independence from India to form the nation of Khālistān. Tensions between the Akālī Dal party and the Hindu Congress party mounted, and Prime Minister Indira Gāndhī sent soldiers from the Indian army to remove them. In the course of their attack on 5 June 1984 Bhindravale and others were killed, and the building complex was badly damaged. This sacrilegious event known as Operation Blue Star stirred deep feelings of resentment among Sikhs, and two of the Prime Minister's bodyguards retaliated by assassinating her in October of that year. In the following days Sikhs in Delhi and in the Pañjāb were murdered by raging mobs of Hindus. Thereafter, the Indian government killed a number of militant Sikh leaders, and has brought a kind of peace to the nation once again. In 2004 after all-India elections, Dr. Manmohan Siṅgh, a Sikh, became Prime Minister after Sonia Gāndhī, leader of the Congress Party, declined the office.

Modern Sikhs

The 1925 Gurdwārās Act defined Sikhs as a separate religion. Furthermore, publication of the *Sikh Rahit Maryādā* in 1950 clarified for Sikhs the specific discipline that their unique tradition entailed. The document is based on the prescriptions for conduct given by Gurū Gobind Siṅgh. The Shiromaṇī Gurdwārā Prabandhak Committee (SGPC) is the Sikh body that governs from the Akāl Takht. Its SGPC website contains a link to the *Sikh Rahit Maryādā*, which defines a Sikh as:

> Any human being who faithfully believes in
> i. One Immortal Being,
> ii. Ten Gurūs, from Gurū Nānak Sāhib to Gurū Gobind Siṅgh Sāhib,
> iii. The *Gurū Granth Sāhib*,
> iv. The utterances and teachings of the ten Gurūs and
> v. The baptism bequeathed by the tenth Gurū, and who does not owe allegiance to any other religion, is a Sikh.
>
> (*Sikh Reht Maryada*. Available online: <http: //www.sgpc.net/rehat_maryada/ section-one.html>)

According to the SPGC a Sikh must be baptized. Not all male Sikhs joined the khālsā in the time of Gurū Gobind Siṅgh. Even today not all Sikhs elect to be baptized into this branch of the Sikh community. Thus from a cultural point of view, which is less conservative than the official definition provided by the *Sikh Rahit Maryādā*, there are several kinds of Sikhs:

- ***Amritdhārī.*** A Sikh man or woman who has received amrit (has been initiated into the khālsā). These Sikhs use the names Siṅgh for men, and Kaur for women. They wear the 5Ks.
- ***Keśadhārī.*** One who keeps long hair. A Sikh who does not cut his hair (keś), but who does not formally join the khālsā through baptism. (This typically refers to male Sikhs.)
- ***Mona Sikh.*** Sikh men with cut hair. Many of these Sikhs were born into Amritdhari families, and retain the name Siṅgh.
- ***Sahajdhārī.*** A Sikh who is a gradual adopter. There is a tendency among these Sikhs to identify with the panth of its early days prior to formation of the khālsā.

Cross-cultural Sikhs

The Sikh tradition is becoming better known and appreciated due to increased worldwide communication, and through the Sikh diaspora. Yogī Bhajan and Bābā Virsa Siṅgh are two Sikhs of our times who have shared aspects of their tradition that dovetail with Western interests in medicine, social work, and inter-religious dialogue.

Yogī Bhajan (1929–2004)

Harbhajan Siṅgh Puri (Yogī Bhajan) was born in what is now Pakistan. He began the study of yoga at age 8 with a teacher named Sant Hazara Siṅgh, and mastered the practice of Kuṇḍalinī yoga in less than a decade. Yogī Bhajan's practice of tantric yoga is a modern expression of the Nāth practice derived from Gorākhnāth who standardized the tantric theory of the chakras and nadis. Yogī Bhajan introduced the practice of Kuṇḍalinī yoga into North America in 1968. The following year he established 3HO, the Healthy, Happy, and Holy Organization. Under its auspices, many Kuṇḍalinī yoga students started businesses that have proved to be successful, including the line of health foods that produced items such as "Yogī Tea," and "Peace" cereal. Members of 3HO also created a drug rehabilitation program called 3HO SuperHealth that was used as a model in both Russia and India. In 1974 Harbajan Siṅgh Yogī was honored at the Akāl Takht in Amritsar for his contributions to the American Sikh movement.

Yogī Bhajan designed yoga sadhanas to remedy illness derived from imbalances in the material, mental, and spiritual aspects of life, squarely within the context of a Sikh spiritual practice. His Sikh disciples typically live a disciplined life in āśrams, adopt a vegetarian diet, and practice kuṇḍalinī yoga. According to traditional Sikh values, they are encouraged to live a wholesome married life, awake before sunrise each day, and serve society. Their religious life encapsulates aspects of standard Sikh devotion including Nām simaran, gurbāṇī, and kīrtan. Members of 3HO maintain the traditional 5K dress code of the khālsā instituted by Gurū Gobind Siṅgh, and adopt the names Kaur and Siṅgh.

Bābā Virsa Siṅgh (ca. 1934–2007)

The story of Bābā Virsa Siṅgh told by his disciples carries the flavor of a traditional spiritual biography with its mixture of historical and hierophanic events. Bābā Virsa Siṅgh grew up in a north Indian Pañjābī village. At a young age he turned to meditation and the path of devotion. It is said that as a child he prayed to be spared a life of farming after cutting a plant, and being upset at the green sap oozing out. As if in answer to his wish not to hurt any plants, which were like living beings to him, the bottom of the child's feet broke out in painful sores. That meant he was relieved of his work. A figure then appeared mysteriously in a vision to provide Bābā Virsa Siṅgh with instruction both in meditation and sevā. It was Bābā Siri Chand, the oldest son of Gurū Nānak who had renounced the world some four centuries earlier. After his hierophanic encounter with the saint Bābā Virsa Siṅgh manifested healing powers. Gobind Siṅgh, the tenth Sikh Gurū, also appeared to instruct Bābā Virsa Siṅgh. This experience further established the boy on the Sikh spiritual path.

Bābā Virsa Siṅgh transformed several wastelands into productive farms that provide food and services for their regions. In 1968 he created Gobind Sadan, an egalitarian establishment where the *Gurū Granth Sāhib* is recited continuously. Members of the spiritual community follow a traditional Sikh regimen of rising early in the morning to remember God's name. To promote interreligious understanding, he founded the Gobind Sadan Institute for Advanced Studies in Comparative Religions, housed in Delhi, India. The Institute promotes the diffusion of knowledge about the world's religions, with special attention to their common principles and spiritual foundations. Bābā Virsa Siṅgh has become an international spokesperson for conflict resolution. It is said that Bābā Virsa Siṅgh saw a manifestation of Jesus, and created a shrine at the Institute known as Jesus' Place where some people claim to have been healed.

PART 2
SIKH TEXTURE

FOUNDATIONAL TEXTURE

Poetry was in the air throughout north India in the sixteenth century when the Sikh holy scripture was compiled. The majority of Safavid Persian poets of the era were to be found in India, attracted by the great wealth of the Mughal court. Although it was a time of great prosperity in Persia, lucrative and prestigious positions were available to them through Mughal patronage. But it was not only those with a great sophistication and learning who spoke words of beauty and devotion. Enthusiasm for attempting to give earthly expression to divine beauty seemed to be lost on no one from the poorest peasant to the wealthiest ruler. In this creative environment, it is as though the Sikh holy scripture captured the spirit of devotion to God that wafted through the hearts of devotees in medieval India wherever it could be found.

Gurū Granth Sāhib

The *Ādi Granth* is a compendium of works that reflect deep and authentic expressions of bhakti spoken by saints from about 1100 to 1600 CE. It contains poetic compositions of more than forty artists, including fifteen north Indian Sants. Languages represented in the work include Pañjābī, Sanskrit, Persian, and Arabic as well as the medieval vernacular forms of Hindi and Marathi. Altogether there are 5,894 hymns in the sacred book. About half of them are hymns that Nānak sang during kīrtan. Most – but not all – hymns in the *Ādi Granth* were composed by the Sikh Gurūs: 974 hymns are by Nānak, 62 by Aṅgad, 907 by Amar Dās, 679 by Rām Dās, and 2,218 by Arjan Dev, the initial

Plate 11.3 "Sikh elder reciting gurbāṇī from *Gurū Granth Sāhib.*" The *Gurū Granth Sāhib* has been standardized into a printed format of exactly 1,430 pages. Thus the Sikh scripture can be easily cited by page number.

compiler. Hymns by Gurū Tegh Bahādur (115) were added after the initial compilation. Hymns by Gurū Gobind Siṅgh were made into a separate collection known as the ***Dasam Granth***, or Book of the Tenth (Gurū).

The *Gurū Granth Sāhib* has three main sections, covering exactly 1,430 pages in its contemporary printed format, with eighteen or nineteen lines per page. (This standardized format means that citations can be made by page number.) The text is divided into three parts: (1) pages 1–13 provide an introduction comprising four standard daily prayers (one morning, two evening, and one bedtime), including Nānak's Japjī; (2) pages 14–1353 are the ragas (including the introductory material set into context) divided into thirty-three sections; and (3) pages 1354–1430 contain miscellaneous works that do not fit into the other categories, including verses by Kabīr and some later additions to the text, such as verses by the ninth Gurū, Tegh Bahādur. Hymns in the middle section are arranged by length, theme, and author: short hymns come before long hymns, writings of the Gurūs precede hymns of other saints, and hymns are arranged in the order that the Gurūs appeared historically. Because they embodied the same jot, the Gurūs all call themselves Nānak.

Sikh teachings

Values pervading the *Gurū Granth Sāhib* guide Sikhs to maximize their human potential for living a truthful, pure, and just life. The *Ādi Granth* speaks of many divine qualities to be emulated by Sikhs in acts of body, speech, and mind. Above all, devotion to God fulfills the human capacity to perform any and all activities.

- *Oneness of God.* Sikhs are thoroughly monotheistic. God is One, with no incarnations. Unlike Hindus who believe in avātaras such as Rāma and Kṛṣṇa, Sikhs do not think of God as saguṇa, with qualities apprehended by the five senses. They worship God through the word. Sikhs participate in kīrtan to praise the True Name.
- *Divine mercy.* Sikhs believe that people and all living beings go through many rebirths. In this, Sikhs are like Hindus, and unlike Muslims on this point. And though a person can make an effort to follow the spiritual path, ultimately God frees a person from transmigration through divine mercy. Sikhs keep Nām in their hearts, and are freed through grace.
- *Divine justice.* As God exercises justice, so Sikhs are committed to protecting the downtrodden and defending their faith. The early decades of the tradition transpired while Mughals ruled north India. Due to the sometimes hostile reception of Muslim rulers to their faith, and the martyrdom of two Gurūs at the hands of Mughal emperors, Sikhs grew to value mīrī, the sword of justice.
- *Personal devotion.* There is no intermediary between human beings and God. There are no Sikh priests. The ten Gurūs emanated Divine Light, and transmitted this jot through the Sikh spiritual lineage. Yet Sikhs do not worship the Gurūs. The *Gurū Granth Sāhib* provides a living link to Divine Light.
- *Personal discipline.* Sikhs minimize ritual. As the tradition developed, some rituals came into play, such as marriage rites, the manner of recitation of holy scripture, and baptism into the khālsā. The main focus of ritual activity is a focus on personal spiritual discipline regarding the divine Word through Nām simaran, gurbāṇī recitation, and kīrtan.
- *Service.* Sikhs should not renounce the world. The ideal is for Sikhs to marry, and not live the celibate and reclusive life of mendicants. Although seeking freedom from rebirth, Sikhs should work hard in an honest way, practice sevā within society, and share their earnings with the needy.
- *Social equality.* Human beings are all equal in the light of the divine. This means one should eliminate gender bias, social class distinctions, and prejudice of faith. To abide by this, the Sikhs established sangat or congregation as a democratic social and spiritual community. Members of this sangat share meals in the laṅgar or community kitchen.
- *Spiritual equality.* Nānak came out of his hierophanic experience and declared, "There is no Hindu and no Muslim." God is One, and God is in every genuine prayer. No prayer becomes the Word without God's Mercy, and no single spiritual tradition owns Truth. God is without religious lineage, and grants mercy to those who understand the manifestation of this divine example in the world.

SUPPORTIVE TEXTURE

Dasam Granth

Only the *Ādi Granth* has the status of Gurū. But portions of the *Dasam Granth* that have been authenticated as the tenth Gurū's writings are often used in prayer. The *Dasam Granth* is a collection of writings attributed to Gobind Siṅgh, the tenth (dasam) Sikh Gurū – though not all Sikhs and scholars today agree on the authorship of every piece. The text (comprising 1,428 pages in modern standard editions) was complied about three decades after the Gurū passed away by Bhāī Mani Siṅgh, custodian of the Harimandir. The *Dasam Granth* contains meditations, sayings of wisdom, and Hindu mythic material. Some verses are used in the Sikh baptism ritual, and in daily prayer. A key prayer is the Ardās, which is recited during Sikh ceremonies in gurdwārās, and to open the day in Sikh schools. The *Dasam Granth* also contains the Zafarnameh (Letter of Victory) that Gobind Siṅgh wrote to Emperor Auraṇgzeb. Gobind Siṅgh's mastery of language and poetics is evidenced in the letter. He composed the 135 verses in Persian (the literary language of the Mughal Empire) using the meter of the *Shāhnameh* by Firdowsī, a tenth-century Persian poet. Gobind Siṅgh praised God in terms that a conservative Muslim like Auraṇgzeb could not reject.

Sikh collections

The reading of four collections of Sikh writings is permitted in the Golden Temple: The *Gurū Granth Sāhib*, the *Dasam Granth* by Gobind Siṅgh, and two collections of hymns by the Sikh writers Bhāī Gurdās Bhallā (1551–1633) and Nand Lāl Goyā (d. 1712). Bhāī Gurdās Bhallā was a nephew of the third Gurū, Amar Dās. Not only was he very close to his uncle, but he also became the disciple of the two succeeding Gurūs, Rām Dās and Arjan Dev. He wrote down the original *Ādi Granth* by hand as dictated by Gurū Arjan Dev, and became the second official reader of the holy scripture in the Harimandir. In addition to being a scribe, Bhāī Gurdās Bhallā was a poet and commentator. He wrote 39 long poems (*vars*) in Pañjābī, and 556 shorter works in the Braj Indian dialect. His are among the most prized of Sikh writings. Nand Lāl Goyā was among the disciples of Gurū Gobind Siṅgh. He wrote 61 odes (*ghazals*) and 510 couplets in Persian, emphasizing meditation on the Divine Name as the means to salvation.

CROSS-OVER TEXTURE

Voices of women in Gurū Nānak's life

Amrita Pritam (1919–2005) was a prolific Sikh poet and novelist who wrote in the Pañjābī language. On the anniversary of Gurū Nānak's 300th birthday she wrote the poem "Nine Dreams and the Annunciation." But the poem's ten stanzas contain no mention of Nānak. The first nine stanzas relive the months of pregnancy before delivery of a child. The final stanza announces a birth. The first word of the poem is "Tripta," Nānak's mother's name. Thus the whole poem is about Nānak – reflected through his mother's experience of bearing him in her womb. The poem begins with an account of a dream about the conception. It contains several allusions to the hierophanic experience that Nānak had in mention of the river and milk:

> Tripta woke up with a start,
> arranged the bedcover,
> covered her shoulders with a veil,
> looked at her husband
> and said, . . .
> "On this January night
> I put my legs in the river.
> On this chilly night the river is warm.
> It's strange, the water turned into milk
> with the touch of my limbs.
> And I bathed in milk: the river is magical."
>
> (Pritam 1979: 26)

The poem ends with lines spoken by Tripta that honor the future Gurū's birthday:

> "The fire of my womb burst into flames,
> brightens the lamp of the body.
> Oh send for the earth's maid:
> This is my first birth pain."
>
> (Pritam 1979: 28)

Amrita Pritam followed the women in Gurū Nānak's life. Thus she wrote verses not only about his mother, but also about Sulakhni, Gurū Nānak's wife. Pritam was aware of problems that Sulakhni faced as the wife of a religious man. She wrote a monologue giving voice to the experience of a woman who was left with the task of bringing up two sons after the Gurū had gone on His life's mission. Sulakhni found strength in the Sun when "being put through the test" which was the "Sun-test to which there was no end" (Pritam 1989: 117). In the eyes of the twentieth-century poet, Gurū Nānak's wife had a deep spirituality of her own. Pritam expressed this through the symbol of the Sun, the source of illumination who gave Sulakhni strength to endure life's trials.

> I was a shadow and am one still
> I've travelled with the Sun on His course:
> Have drunk of His glory
> And bathed in a stream full of His light.
>
> (Pritam 1989: 116–117)

Amrita Pritam herself experienced a keen affinity with the sun. To her the sun in the sky belonged to no single religion, but symbolized a vital force for all those who rise early in the morning. Beyond that, for Pritam the sun had an immediacy that spoke of life – and death.

BOX 11.3 INTERPRETATIONS: "FINDING" WOMEN IN HISTORY

How can we "find" the women whose stories have not been told? Three concepts used by scholars interested in bringing the situation of South Asian women to light are: agency, protest, and alternative discourse (Jakobsh 2003; Kumar 1994).

Agency. Agency refers to the power of people to act and have an impact on society. Often women have not been thought of as "actors" in history because they did not have access to knowledge, hence power. The agent in South Asian culture would not necessarily operate under the same value system as the agent as defined by European culture. Thus a student of religions should notice the qualities of people who seem to have the most and least power in any given society.

Protest. Protest refers to the way people who lack power try to gain a share of influence in society, and determine the course of their lives. Because men tend to be the key "actors" in patriarchal societies, women (and other subordinates) express resistance to subjugation. Just as religions that are not of the status quo often become "religions of resistance," so people can lead a lifestyle of resistance, protesting through small details of everyday living, such as using sarcasm, wearing distinctive clothing, and so forth.

Alternative discourse. Alternative discourses (means of expression) are various ways that subordinate people in society resist the status quo. The discourses are "alternative" because subalterns (underprivileged people) do not have access to elite channels of education and power. Examples of non-mainstream discourse are diaries, correspondence, and autobiographical accounts, as well as expressive texts from oral tradition such as folktales, jokes, and so forth.

These three concepts help identify and put into context people whose voices are difficult to hear. Autobiographies are one form of *alternative discourse* that women have effectively used as *protest* against inequitable social pressures. One example of alternative discourse in the Sikh tradition is Sharan-Jeet Shan's *In My Own Name: An Autobiography*. The author begins by saying, "I am not a writer by the furthest stretch of imagination, as this is my first attempt at writing anything." Shan wrote not "as a case against the arranged marriage" as such. Rather the life story was "a statement of a very personal mental anguish, on behalf of hundreds of women . . . Asian women in particular" for whom an arranged marriage became a source of physical and emotional trauma (Shan 1985: i). Sharan-Jeet's work is of great value not only because it gives visibility to Sikh women in history, but also because it strengthens the *agency* of women caught in the net of cultural constraints.

Its fire moved beyond being a symbol on the written page. In her autobiography, *Life and Times* Amrita Pritam described circles of fire that appeared to her in prognostic visions of Prime Minister Indira Gāndhī four days before she was assassinated by two Sikh bodyguards in October 1984, as well as on the day of the tragedy. With such sensitivity, Amrita Pritam became a voice for women in Pañjābī society – keenly aware of the challenges faced by Tripti and Sulakhni all the way down to the late Prime Minister Indira Gāndhī.

PART 3 SIKH PERFORMANCE

CONTEMPLATING THE DIVINE NAME

Sikh tradition says that during the period of three days when Nānak disappeared in a river, he drank heavenly nectar, and received a **hukam** (divine order) to remember the True Name. Following this divine injunction, Sikhs developed three ways of remembering the divine

Gurū: Nām simaran, gurbāṇī recitation, and kīrtan. And no matter which way they recite, Sikhs believe that only out of mercy for human beings did the Lord make the words of the saints into the Divine Name.

Remembering the Divine Name: Nām simaran

Nām simaran means remembrance of the Divine Name. It is the Sikh form of what is called dhikr in Sūfīsm. Nām simaran is the basic form of individual worship in Sikhism. Proper remembrance of Nām occurs in a mental state of intuitive balance. Nām simaran may be done by tongue or by breath in the heart. At an advanced stage of remembrance the practice becomes effortless, and the Nām vibrates through every pore of the devotee's body – whether the devotee is walking, sitting, or standing.

Two expressions of the Divine Name are Sat Nām and Wāhegurū. These divine names are key examples of shabad, or the Word. A devotee gains access to the shabad through breaking down the Nām into **nād**, seed syllables with particular vibrational qualities and meanings. For example, the word "Gurū" combines the nād "gu" (meaning darkness) and the nād "rū" (meaning light). Thus, the word "Gurū" indicates one who brings devotees from darkness to light.

BOX 11.4 A SPIRITUAL PATH: TAKING HUKAM

The *Rahit Maryādā* is a modern text based on Gurū Gobind Siṅgh's prescriptions for leading the Sikh life. According to this formulation, a Sikh should rise three hours before dawn, bathe, and begin to pray. The daily prayers begin with recitation of Gurū Nānak's Japjī, which stands as the initial prayer of the *Gurū Granth Sāhib*. After the prayers, a Sikh prepares to carry out the day in accordance with God's Will. As a method of contemplating God's Will, Sikhs follow a custom known as "taking hukam." A hukam is a command or divine order. In the Japjī Nānak said that a person strips away illusions by following the hukam.

> By remaining silent, inner silence is not obtained, even by remaining lovingly absorbed deep within. The hunger of the hungry is not appeased, even by piling up loads of worldly goods. Hundreds of thousands of clever tricks, but not even one of them will go along with you in the end. So how can you become truthful? And how can the veil of illusion be torn away? O Nanak, it is written that you should obey the Hukam of His Command, and walk in the Way of His Will.
>
> (*Ādi Granth*, p. 1)

The method of taking hukam is to open the *Gurū Granth Sāhib* "at random." The divine order for the day is the first hymn revealed at the top of the left-hand side of the page (the *Ādi Granth* is read from left to right as you are now reading this book). If the hymn at the top of the page begins on the previous page, the devotee turns back the exposed page and reads the hymn from its starting point. Every Sikh should take the day's hukam in the early morning hours prior to eating, if possible.

Whenever a Sikh opens the holy scripture a hukam should be taken. Hukam is taken at the start of every day at the Harimandir. This daily hukam is now made public over the Internet. This allows Sikhs to take hukam if they are not able to do so personally with their own copy of the scripture. However, Sikhs should have a copy of the *Gurū Granth Sāhib*, and read it from start to finish (completing one reading every two months or so). The Sikh practice of taking hukam began when the *Gurū Granth Sāhib* was first installed within the Harimandir in 1604. In addition to providing material for daily contemplation, taking hukam guides the choice of names for Sikh children, and provides personal advice.

Reciting sacred verses: gurbāṇī

Continuous remembrance of the Divine Name prepares the Sikh disciple for **gurbāṇī**, which is recitation of prayers (bāṇis) from the *Gurū Granth Sāhib.* Whereas Nām simaran is done by repeating a divine name, gurbāṇī involves recitation of whole verses. Gurbāṇī recitation enhances the impact of the verses as their meaning is conjoined with the effect of their sound vibrations. Gurū Aṅgad developed a script based on the Sanskrit alphabet whose letters are each sounded one after the other in adjacent parts of the oral cavity to produce a full gamut of vibrational effects. He called it Gurmukhī, meaning "from the Gurū's mouth" because it recorded the bāṇis, which were holy verses uttered in the midst of God consciousness. Recitation of the bāṇis thus reproduces in a devotee the conditions under which the verses were originally uttered as different energetic pressure points of the oral cavity are activated.

The Gurmukhī alphabet captures permutations of nād sound syllables associated with the elements of ether, air, fire, water, and earth. According to the spiritual technology of the Sikh scripture, the gurbāṇīs are variously balanced in terms of these elements. For example, the daily bāṇis include one from each element: Japjī is associated with ether, Jaap Sāhib with air, Anand Sāhib with fire, Rehiras with water, and Kīrtan Sohilā with earth.

Although letters of the alphabet are the divine form visible to the outer eye, the Sikh scriptures convey forms of the universe through its sounds. What has been said about the *Jaap Sāhib* composed by Gurū Gobind Siṅgh applies as well to verses of the *Ādi Granth.*

> These forms [created by the sounds of the words] are constituted in the universe of imagination which becomes the basis of a new cosmology, a cosmology that goes beyond any conceivable cosmos of the physical as well as metaphysical world. . . .
>
> This Cosmic Word . . . is a coordinating link between the body and the soul, between the physical and the spiritual, between nature and culture.
>
> (Gill 1989: 4, 13)

Singing God's praises: kīrtan

Kīrtan is the Sikh form of what is called bhajan in Hinduism. It is the practice of singing verses based on Sikh religious texts, principally the *Ādi Granth* and *Dasam Granth.* Kīrtan is typically performed with musicians playing the tabla drum and harmonium to accompany the singing of a group of devotees. Nānak used to perform kīrtan twice a day; but nowadays kīrtan has become part of Sunday congregational worship at a gurdwārā, along with kaṭha (sermons, scriptural readings). The elderly Gurū Amar Dās said:

> That which is sung intuitively is acceptable; without this intuition, all chanting is useless. . . . With intuitive ease, embrace Samaadhi. In the state of intuitive balance, chant His Glories, lovingly absorbed in devotional worship.
>
> (*Ādi Granth*, p. 68)

Kīrtan is the central act of communal worship for Sikhs. Nānak even said that when he died, he wanted no ritual – but only kīrtan, the singing of Gurū's hymns praising God. From early days in the Sikh tradition, the Harimandir became the central site in which God's praises were sung.

> Sujan Rāi of Batala, writing about Sikhs in 1696, says in his *Khulasatut-Twarikh*: "The only way of worship with them is that they read the hymn [*sic*] composed by their Gurūs and sing them sweetly in accompaniment with musical instruments. In the Golden Temple, Amritsar, up to this day, nothing but continuous singing of hymns day and night by relays of singers is allowed."
>
> (Siṅgh 1985: xiii)

Cognizant of the spiritual technology of sound, the fifth Gurū arranged the hymns of the *Ādi Granth* according to musical measures. His aim was to cultivate in his disciples a kind of spiritual illumination that had the quality of steadiness (*Sahj*). Arjan Dev did not use keys that encourage the extremes of uplift or depression. Thus he omitted use of *Hindol* and *Megh* (which promote ecstasy), as well as *Deepak* and *Jog* (which promote melancholy) by themselves. But Arjan Dev artfully used those musical measures to modify others. For example, "*Hindol* was combined with *Besant* to vivify serene contentment, and *Deepak* was used to heighten the seriousness of *Gauri* and to make it more vigorous" (Siṅgh 1985: xviii). Moreover, musical keys are related to themes. Thus "each piece, within itself, is polytechnically well-constructed, its component parts being interconnected and evolving the growth of the inner idea" (Siṅgh 1985: xx).

The sound of silence: anahat śabad

The works enshrined in the *Gurū Granth Sāhib* outwardly express the Divine Word or Nām. The corollary to this sacred Nām is the **anahat śabad**. If Nām is the manifest sound, anahat śabad is the unmanifest sound beyond speech that is experienced within silence. Nām is struck sound. Anahat śabad is unstruck sound. Through reciting Nām, the unstruck sound of śabad can be realized. The Kīrtan Sohilā presents this anahat śabad cosmic sound current metaphorically as a drum. In this verse, it portrays metaphorically the inner experience that comes from remembering God's name:

> Upon that cosmic plate of the sky, the sun and moon are the lamps. The stars and their orbs are the studded pearls. The fragrance of sandalwood in the air is the temple incense, and the wind is the fan. All the plants of the world are the altar flowers in offering to You, O Luminous Lord.
>
> What a beautiful Aartee, lamp-lit worship service this is! O Destroyer of Fear, this is Your Ceremony of Light. The Unstruck Sound-current of the Shabad is the vibration of the temple drums.
>
> (*Ādi Granth*, p. 13)

Contemplation of the Divine Name through Nām simaran, gurbāṇī, or kīrtan evokes a profound experience of the word that is not simply outward. The body of the devotee becomes a kind of temple. Gurū Nānak explains that the cosmic sound current becomes apparent at the Tenth Gate, which is distinct from the other nine body orifices.

> Where is that Gate, and where is that Dwelling in which You sit and take care of all? The Sound-current of the Naad vibrates there, and countless musicians play on all sorts of instruments there. . . . The sound current of the Naad vibrates in each and every heart.
>
> (*Ādi Granth*, p. 6)

Sikh recitation of the Divine Name involves a spiritual technology. But according to the Sikh view, proper utterance of holy words never occurs without the Gurū, through whom God's Grace flows.

KEY POINTS

- The Sikh tradition is monotheistic, with an understanding that God has no physical form, but manifests to human beings as Sat Nām, the True Name.
- Nānak founded the Sikh panth over a period of four decades. Although he traveled widely, as far as Iraq in the west to Assam in the east, the new tradition only flourished in the Pañjāb until modern times.
- The historical time frame for the ten Sikh Gurūs coincides with the start and decline of the Mughal Empire. The Sikhs Gurūs had a mixed relationship with the Mughal emperors. Akbar was tolerant of the new faith, while Jahāṇgīr and Auraṇgzeb martyred the fifth and ninth Gurūs.
- Gurū Nānak prescribed three main principles by which disciples should guide their lives: (1) remember God's Name, (2) make an honest living without renouncing the world, and (3) share with others and serve them.
- There were ten human Gurūs, who are each called "Nānak" because they transmit the same jot or divine light while they serve in the capacity of Gurū. The Gurūship was transmitted to the *Ādi Granth* (*Gurū Granth Sāhib*) by the tenth Nānak. God is the ultimate Gurū, and Sikhs are "disciples."
- The *Ādi Granth* is the Sikh holy scripture, which is considered as a living Gurū. It is composed of over five thousand hymns written principally by the first five Gurūs; but it also contains over nine hundred hymns by saints who pre-date the Sikh tradition.
- The Sikh scripture is a magnetic text in the sense that it is structured to form a nexus of spiritual energy that conveys God's Name. Sikhs from the

time of the initial compilation of the *Ādi Granth* have been aware of the value of realizing the intricacies of its structure.

STUDY QUESTIONS

1 How do Sikhs describe the divine?
2 Name the ten Gurūs along with one or two main contributions of each.
3 Why were Gurūs Arjan Dev and Tegh Bahādur killed?
4 Name three main developments in Sikh history during the 300 years after the death of Gurū Gobind Siṅgh.
5 List the key Sikh teachings.
6 What is the role of women in the Sikh tradition?
7 Name and describe the three main ways that Sikhs remember God's Name.

GLOSSARY

Akal Takhat (Pañjābī) Throne of the Timeless (Persian: takhat = throne). Seat of the Sikh panth's legal, political, and military authority. Located in Amritsar near the Harimandir.

anahat śabad (Pañjābī) Unstruck sound corresponding to the Nām or Word of God in Sikhism. If Nām is the manifest sound, anahat śabad is the unmanifest sound beyond speech apprehended within.

Dasam Granth (Pañjābī) Sikh holy book attributed to the tenth Gurū, Gobind Siṅgh. (Scholars debate the authorship of portions of it.)

Five Ks Five articles worn by members of the Sikh khālsā, all beginning with the letter K in Pañjābī: keś (uncut hair), kanghā (comb), kaccha (men's undergarment), kaṛā (steel bracelet), kirpān (sword, dagger).

gurbāṇī (Pañjābī) Recitation of prayers (bāṇis) from the Sikh holy scripture, whose effect is conveyed through meaning conjoined with sound vibration.

gurdwārā (Pañjābī) Sikh temple.

Gurmukhī (Pañjābī) Gurū's mouth. Script in which the Sikh holy scripture is written. The second Gurū, Aṅgad, commissioned the writing of Nānak's biography and hymns transcribed into this simplified Pañjābī script.

Gurū The notion of gurū is pan-Indian. The Sikh tradition magnifies it to call God the ultimate Gurū. Ten human Gurūs and the holy scripture are called Gurū because they embodied the jot, the Gurū's divine light.

Gurū Granth Sāhib (Pañjābī) Sikh holy scripture. The *Ādi Granth* collection of inspired poetry became the final Gurū after the tenth human Gurū passed the lineage out of the human sphere, investing it into the Primal (Ādi) Book (Granth).

Harimandir (Pañjābī) Temple of God (Harī) in Amritsar, India. Main Sikh temple in the world. Also called the Golden Temple.

hukam (Pañjābī) Divine order. Reading from the *ādi granth* chosen at random, which applies to one's situation in life that day or at that time. Hukam means divine order, based on a Persian word meaning royal decree.

Japjī (Pañjābī) Morning prayer by Gurū Nānak. First prayer in the *Gurū Granth Sāhib.*

jot (Pañjābī) Divine light embodied by the ten human Sikh Gurūs, and holy scripture, the *Gurū Granth Sāhib.*

khālsā (Pañjābī) Order of Sikhs who wear the Five Ks instituted by Gurū Gobind Siṅgh on 30 March 1699. It is often thought of as being the order of the "pure ones" because khalis in Persian means unsullied. The word also relates to a term from the Mughal administration meaning oversight of lands or revenues.

kīrtan (Pañjābī) Sikh communal singing based on scriptural verses.

laṇgar (Pañjābī) Sikh free community meal where all devotees eat together without divisive ritual taboos.

nād (Pañjābī) Seed syllables in Sikh holy scripture, with particular vibrational qualities and meanings.

Nām simaran (Pañjābī) Remembrance of God's True Name. Preferred form of individual worship in Sikhism.

panth a religous group founded by a spiritual teacher.

Sat Nām (Pañjābī) True Name. Sikh name for God.

sevā (Pañjābī) Service for the sake of others. A key value in Sikhism.

Wāhegurū (Pañjābī) Sikh term used to express God's ineffable nature – that which is beyond description.

KEY READING

Ādi Granth. Several versions of the Sikh scripture are available in English. Beyond the online translation by S. S. Khalsa, and that of K. S. Duggal are the following: Siṅgh, Gopal (trans.) (1962) *Sri Gurū Granth Sahib* (4 vols), Delhi: Gur Das Kapur and Sons; and Siṅgh, Manmohan (1969, 1982) *Sri Gurū Granth Sahib* (7 vols), Amritsar: Shiromani Gurdwara Parbandhak Committee.

Cole, W. Owen and Samghi Piara Siṅgh (1998) *The Sikhs: Their Religious Beliefs and Practices* (2nd edn), Portland, OR: Sussex Academic Press.

Jakobsh, Doris R. (2003) *Relocating Gender in Sikh History: Transformation, Meaning and Identity*, New Delhi: Oxford University Press.

McLeod, W. H. (1989) *The Sikhs: History, Religion, and Society*, New York: Columbia University Press.

McLeod, W. H. (trans.) (1984) *Textual Sources for the Study of Sikhism*, trans. and ed. W. H. McLeod, Totowa, NJ: Barnes and Noble.

Siṅgh, Kushwant (2004) *A History of the Sikhs* (2 vols) (2nd edn), New Delhi: Oxford University Press.

CHAPTER 12

Chinese traditions

TIMELINE

	BCE	
Culture heroes and sage kings	Third millennium (traditional)	
	ca. 2205–1600	Xia dynasty
	ca. 1600–1045	Shang dynasty
	[ca. 1300]	[archeological data]
Three virtuous founders	Third millennium (traditional)	
	1045–771	Western Zhou dynasty
Lao-zi (Lao-tzu)	Sixth century (traditional)	
Confucius (Kong fu-zi)	551–479	
	ca. 475–221	Warring States period
Mo-zi (Mo-tzu)	468?–376?	
Mencius (Meng-zi, Meng-tse)	372?–289?	
Zhuang-zi (Chuang-tzu)	360?–280?	
Xun Zi (Hsün-tzu)	330?–227?	
Wang Bi (Wang Pi)	226–249	
	221–207	Qin (Ch'in) dynasty
	200s	First unified Great Wall built
	206	Han dynasty begins
	CE	
	ca. 65	Buddhism in China
	184–205	Yellow Turban revolt
	184	Celestial Masters theocracy established
Ge Hong	284–364	
Guo Xiang	d. 312	
	220	Han dynasty ends
	618–906	Tang dynasty
	960–1279	Song dynasty
Zhu Xi (Chu Hsi)	1130–1200	
Wang Yang-ming	1472–1529	
Mao Ze-dong (Mao Tse-tung)	1893–1976	

Writing in Chinese civilization goes back more than 3,000 years (to at least 1300 BCE). In the course of a long and often turbulent history Chinese literacy was preserved such that people unable to understand each other's dialects could communicate through writing. From the old days, when writing was used to record divinations on bones and tortoise shells, until 1912 of our Common Era, a Chinese Imperial tradition was carried on. The amount of territory rulers controlled varied according to the age – and at times even heads of small principalities called themselves "king" (*wang*). But the ancient title "Son of Heaven" was reserved for those who strictly maintained all the Imperial Rites. Sons of Heaven were obliged to keep the world in order by responding to seasonal changes and to perform the Sacrifice to Heaven in winter and the Sacrifice to Earth in summer. Simultaneously Chinese peasants working the land were concerned about the seasons. And so it was that the folk traditions of peasants ran alongside the Chinese Imperial tradition. As time passed certain segments of a growing population became more wealthy, literate, and sophisticated. Thus some traditions (that might be called philosophical or religious depending on the period of their development) emerged among the elite who felt the influence of both the Imperial and folk traditions.

Two main traditions emerged from native Chinese soil – generally called Daoism and Confucianism. In general, Daoists were heavily steeped in Chinese folk traditions while Confucians defined themselves in relation to the Chinese Imperial tradition. Yet Chinese religion is not so clear-cut. At times Daoism eclipsed Confucianism as the official Chinese tradition with its elite philosophers and priests. On the other hand, the Confucian concern for ancestral rites and proper social relationships filtered down from the scholars and officials to the common people. An intensive cross-fertilization among the strands of tradition in Chinese life occurred over countless generations. This meant that in the midst of people's lives, aspects of the Confucian and Daoist traditions intricately overlapped. Thus it is useful to think collectively of "Chinese traditions" to counteract the cut-and-dried sense carried by the Western terms typically used, namely: (1) Confucianism and neo-Confucianism on one hand, and (2) philosophical Daoism and religious Daoism on the other. In fact, only in the late 1800s were Chinese terms for "religion" and "philosophy" invented (i.e., *zong jiao* and *zhe xue*). If needs be, the development of Chinese religions can be defined in three critical moments that produced: (1) a classic form of Confucian and Daoist traditions, (2) a religious Daoist form (running for a while alongside a new philosophical form), and (3) a Confucian revivalist form (see Box 12.1).

PART 1 DAOIST AND CONFUCIAN PLAYERS

THE ULTIMATE PRINCIPLE

The high powers

Early Chinese history involved a rivalry between the Shang people and the Zhou (Chou) people. The Shang people lived in north central China and were ruled by a warrior clan. Their economy ran on an agricultural base largely involving the harvest of wheat and millet. They lived in fortified towns, and knew the use of writing and metalworking. Meanwhile the Zhou farmed land around the Wei River some 300 miles southwest of Shang territory. They were influenced by Shang culture – and adopted much of it wholesale after the year 1122 BCE (traditional Zhou date) when Zhou militants overthrew the Shang ruler and installed their own lineage. Both the Shang and the Zhou rulers revered a supreme power, known respectively as Shang-di and **Tian** (T'ien).

- Shang-di, the supreme High (*shang*) Lord (*di*), was associated with the sky and heaven. Shang diviners used oracle bones, tortoise shells, and later dried stalks of the yarrow plant to do three things: (1) determine whether the Lord on High approved of certain activities, such as going to war, (2) get indications of future events, and (3) find out what Shang-di expected of them. The earliest Chinese writing (ca.1400 BCE) was on oracle bones used to communicate with Shang-di.
- Tian originally meant the sky. Tian (like Shang-di) had a will that was to be discerned by ritual specialists. The Zhou interpreted violent weather

as a bad omen through which Tian Ti, the Heavenly Lord, warned that rulers were acting against its will. Zhou leaders claimed the support of Tian in ousting the Shang ruler, saying they had received the Mandate of Heaven to found a new dynasty. Thus Zhou emperors felt obliged to act according to the will of Heaven to fulfill the Mandate.

Dao

In the Chinese language **dao** means way, road, or path. Confucians and Daoists both consider dao as the ultimate way to live that should be pursued by every human being. Yet they teach about the dao with different emphases.

- ***The Dao of Heaven.*** Confucians speak of the Way of Heaven (Tian). They believe that the basic structures of Heaven and human beings are identical, and teach that humans should cultivate the way through education. One who cultivates the dao through learning comes to know the will of Heaven. Knowing the will of Heaven, one acts according to the way. "When the Way prevails in a country he [a wise person] can rise to official position through his words. When the Way does not prevail in the country, he can preserve himself through silence" (*Doctrine of the Mean* 27 in Chan 1963: 110).
- ***The unspeakable Dao.*** Daoists observed that the dao about which anyone can speak is not the actual dao. The dao is formless, with no beginning and no end. It is potentially one **yin** and one **yang** existing prior to all manifestations. The Ten Thousand Things (i.e., everything in the cosmos) arise from the dao. One grasps the dao by letting it go. One cultivates the dao through actionless action (**wu-wei**). A person on the dao knows when he or she has enough (*Dao De Jing* 44). "The green stalk, the tower, the leper and the giant, the elegant and the grotesque – we pass through them all on the Tao, and they are all part of the whole" (*Chuang Tzu* in Horwitz 2003: 133).

IMAGINAL PLAYERS

Culture heroes

Traditional accounts trace the start of Chinese civilization back to the early part of the third millennium (3000–2500) BCE when three culture heroes each had a share in promoting technological revolutions: (1) Fu Xi taught fishing with nets and trapping. (2) Shen Nong introduced agriculture and commerce. (3) Huang-di was the patron of shamans who invented the compass and the pottery wheel. He also taught human beings how to breed silkworms and wrote the first book on medicine. Huang-di is the "Yellow Emperor" whose teachings Daoists sometimes claim to propound. The legendary contributions of Fu Xi, Shen Nong, and the Yellow Emperor outline the course of the ancient Chinese economy. A society whose livelihood was based on fishing and hunting turned to the development of agriculture. It gained complexity through commerce and writing.

Stories of culture heroes besides the standard three (Fu Xi, Shen Nong, and Huang-di) are scattered through China's vast folklore culture. Among them is Pan-gu who appears in a myth (ca. third century BCE with later versions) as the creator of the world. According to the Pan-gu story, the universe began in the form of a chicken's egg. The egg separated into a heavy yin portion that became Earth, and a light yang portion that became Heaven. The yin and yang portions continued to separate for 13,000 years at a rate of ten feet per day. Pan-gu took the space between them, and when he died the parts of his body turned into the Earth's geological formations. Pan-gu's head became the four sacred mountains; his eyes became the sun or lightning; his fatty tissue became the oceans; his hair and beard became the grasses and trees; and his breath became the wind.

Sage kings

Yao, Shun, and Yu are three sages who are considered to be the divine ancestors of the Chinese people. Tradition situates the sage rulers in the latter part of the third millennium (2500–2000) BCE, in a period following the culture heroes. The sage kings stand as models of benevolent and righteous rule. Confucius said of Yao that "Heaven alone is truly majestic . . . and only Yao could equal it" (*Analects* 8:19; Hinton 1998: 86). The *Book of History* provides this image of the revered Yao:

> He was kind and benevolent. . . . His radiance was like a shining cloud, rich without ostentation and regal without luxuriousness. The eaves of his thatch were not trimmed; the rafters were unplanned, while the beams of his house had no ornamental ends. He ate simply, his person unadorned and his clothes without embroidery, simple and without variety. . . . In summer he wore simple garments, and in winter he covered himself with skins. Yet he was the richest, wisest, longest-lived and most beloved of all that ruled.
>
> (Höchsmann 2001: 13)

Yü is considered to be the founder of the Xia dynasty (2205–1176 BCE, traditional). He instituted the principle of hereditary rule in the Chinese Imperial tradition. And while Emperor Yü is remembered as a virtuous ruler, the name of the tyrant Jie who ended the Xia dynasty became synonymous with evil.

Daoist immortals (xian, hsien)

An immortal is a human being who never dies. In Chinese art immortals are often portrayed ascending to Heaven riding on a crane. The crane symbolized longevity because presumably a crane can live for 1,000 years or more. Daoist alchemists practiced exercises involving circulation of **qi** (life energy) to attain immortality. They believed that immortals sometimes lived in the mountains or forests as hermits for hundreds of years, while others floated away in their physical bodies to a heavenly realm at the time of their earthly death. In such cases they may leave only their clothes behind, or their bodies may appear not to decay. Celestial immortals live in the Daoist Heaven (Tian), on the Isles of the Immortals, or in the Western Kun Lun Mountains. The Eight Immortals (*ba-xian*) dwell in the Western Kun Lun Mountains where the Queen Mother of the West (Xiwang mu) oversees cultivation of the Peaches of Immortality. Many Daoists aspired to abide with the Queen Mother of the West because future earthly cataclysms of flood and fire will not reach her domain.

Folk deities

The Jade Emperor is a widely known figure in religious Daoism. Abiding in a heavenly palace he administers a bureaucracy that parallels the Imperial bureaucracy on Earth. Among the Jade Emperor's officials are: (1) the deity of Mount T'ai, (2) city godlings, (3) Lord of the Hearth, and (4) local godlings. All the officials in this hierarchy look after the spiritual and material welfare of human beings and present reports to the Jade Emperor at the start of each calendar year. They work for the Jade Emperor, using their power and goodwill to benefit the people. Such godlings are promoted, demoted, or transferred depending upon how well they perform their duties. In 1115 CE the Song (Sung)

Plate 12.1 "Reverence to Lord of the Hearth." The Lord of the Hearth is the kitchen deity whose picture is set above the hearth so he can listen to family gossip. He is the family protector and is pictured surrounded by children. Every New Year the Lord of the Hearth reports to the Jade Emperor about goings-on in families such as this one (of the 1800s). Chinese families worship him on full moon and new moon days. Just before the New Year honey is spread on the Lord of the Hearth's mouth so he will speak sweet words about the family when he reports to the Jade Emperor.

Emperor bestowed the title Shang-ti upon the Jade Emperor and built the first temple to honor him.

Confucian ancestors

The Chinese concept of family includes the living and those who have passed away. The Confucian virtue of **xiao** (filial piety) requires that children (generally eldest sons) celebrate ancestral rites that prescribe specific gestures, offerings, and prayers. Ancestors are more powerful than living human beings in some ways, yet they depend on the rites. In general the more power and status a person has in life, the more power and status the ancestor has in death. Thus ancestor worship in high-status families is more complex and lasts for more generations than ancestor worship of families with less social status. When ancestors are properly respected they contribute to family prosperity; otherwise they cause havoc. Thus even Buddhist altars in Confucian society contain ancestor tablets to maintain social harmony. Ancestor tablets are erected on home altars for recently deceased family members, and important family matters still require their consent. Thus decisions pertaining to marriage, travel, business, education, and so forth involve divination rituals. More formal Confucian ancestral halls contain rows of tablets that span generations. Elaborate rites in these halls focus on ancestors representing a family lineage. The practice of ancestor worship spread throughout East Asia under the influence of the deep Confucian regard for filial piety.

EXCEPTIONAL PLAYERS

Emperors

Traditionally in China emperors were thought of as beings of tremendous power (*de*), connected to their ancestral lineages through **li** (the ancient rites). Imperial rites were conducted to channel ancestral power through the living emperor to keep the world in order. Ceremonial acts performed by the emperor (as a microcosm) made a comparable impact on the Imperial realm (as a macrocosm) due to the laws of sympathetic magic. Emperors were like human calendars who measured time and reflected the seasons in their gestures. Corresponding to each season of the year an emperor's comportment was ritually specified to include: garment color, direction faced, food consumed, music heard, and so on. Based on the notion that Li ordered the world, Confucius claimed that Emperor Shun governed simply by following Li. He identified the Sage King as a ruler who had perfected wu-wei.

> The Master said: "If anyone has managed to rule by doing nothing [*wu-wei*], surely it was Shun. And how did he do so much by doing nothing? He just sat reverently facing south [the ceremonial position of the emperor], that's all!"
>
> (*Analects* 15:5; Hinton 1998: 172)

From a traditional Chinese point of view, affairs of state were matters of cosmic consequence. An emperor was blamed for earthquakes and plagues as well as for social unrest. If an emperor failed to perform the required ceremonial duties the whole culture or **wen** was disturbed. Chinese culture was based on the pattern of Heaven, and the rites were designed to maintain order based on that pattern. The emperor was responsible for enacting the will of Heaven by living according to the dictates of Li and thus keeping order in the realm.

HISTORICAL PLAYERS

The 100 scholars (600–200 BCE)

Kong fu-zi (latinized as Confucius) lived amidst a lingering cultural tension between members of the Shang and Zhou lineages. Although he may have been born to Shang ancestry Confucius always said, "I follow the Zhou!" Zhou leaders had overthrown the Shang ruler some five hundred years earlier. Yet over the generations remnants of Shang aristocratic families maintained among themselves an almost futile sense of superiority. The ancient Zhou rulers were supported by a military social class of knights (*shi*); but because they lacked administrative experience the Zhou had retained highly trained Shang aristocrats in government to perform ritual and administrative functions. These educated Shang aristocrats of the Zhou court were known as *ru* – taken to mean weak or yielding in

BOX 12.1 CULTURE CONTRAST: THE DEVELOPMENT OF CHINESE RELIGIONS

New religious orientations in China emerged as three glorious dynasties fell – the Zhou, Han, and Tang. The following diagram, drawn in the form of a hexagram, represents the cultural alternation between times of relative political stability and times of social instability. The Zhou, Han, and Tang periods of stability are represented as unbroken "yang" lines, while the times of disturbance in which people sought new ways to solve their problems are represented as broken "yin" lines (on yin–yang symbolism see Box 12.3).

CONFUCIAN REVIVAL (ca. 900–1200 CE)
The late Tang Confucian revival culminated in the work of Zhu Xi (1130–1200) within the School of Principle (*li xue*). His interpretations eventually became the new orthodoxy. Buddhist texts were removed from the civil service curriculum as the Five Classics and Four Books (assembled by Zhu Xi) formed a new basis for the Imperial examination.

SONG DYNASTY (960–1279) RELIGIONS
Daoist, Buddhist (Pure Land and Chan), and non-affiliated community temples exist. After the Tang religious persecution of 845 CE:
(1) Pure Land and Chan Buddhism survived,
(2) Zoroastrianism was destroyed, and
(3) Nestorian Christianity drastically declined.
Confucians worked in government and ran institutes of higher learning.

TANG DYNASTY (618–906 CE)
The "three teachings" (*san jiao*) flourished in the dynamic interaction among Confucians, Daoists, and Buddhists. Daoist and Buddhist traditions matured. Arts (especially poetry) and science were fertilized through trade in goods and ideas from the Tang capital at Chang'an across Central Asia to India and to Mediterranean ports. The glory ended in economic and political disarray that prompted growing anti-Buddhist sentiment. A 20-month religious persecution of Buddhists (which officially included Zoroastrians and Nestorian Christians) began in 845 after the Daoist emperor Tang Wu-zong said: "Should any temple in a prefectural city be an edifice of beauty and art, let it be preserved; otherwise let it be destroyed" (Goodrich 2002: 129).

DARK LEARNING PHILOSOPHY (ca. 200–500 CE)
The Dark Learning (*xuan xue*) philosophers emphasized metaphysics in their commentaries on the *Book of Changes*, *Dao De Jing* and *Zhuang-zi*. Scholars such as Wang Bi (226–249 CE) saw Confucius as a sage and explored aspects of Confucian texts that went beyond rectification of names (focused on proper ritual and social relationships).

BEGINNING OF DAOIST CHURCHES (ca. second century CE)
In 184 CE the Celestial Masters Sect (Way of Five Pecks of Rice) established a Daoist theocracy in Sichuan. Their sect absorbed the Yellow Turbans (Way of Great Peace) and an alchemical tradition focused on methods of becoming an immortal. Daoist sects revered the heavenly Lao-zi and got revealed scriptures. Other Daoist churches gradually grew.

HAN DYNASTY (206 BCE–220 CE)
Art and science advanced in the Han Imperial age. (1) The first attempts at developing porcelain were made. (2) In astronomy eclipses were understood as regular occurrences and not due to the emperor's failures. (3) Agricultural improvements included development of drought-resistant rice, improved crop rotation. (4) In music the lute and mandolin were new instruments. (5) History was linked to perceptible events, not mythic themes. (6) In literature a common script was used, and a national bibliography contained some 677 works (see Goodrich 2002: 46 ff.). Buddhism first enters China via the Silk Roads. Chinese still call themselves "people of the Han." The glorious Han dynasty ended with peasant (e.g., Yellow Turbans) revolts and the redistribution of power to small warlord "kings."

DAOSITS OF THE 100 SCHOOLS (ca. 600–300 BCE)
The Daoist school was called dao. Only in the first century CE did it become associated explicitly with the *Dao De Jing* and the *Zhuang-zi*. In their present form those works date from the third century BCE. The *Dao De Jing* is attributed to Lao-zi (who lived in the sixth century BCE, according to traditional dating) and Zhuang-zi (360?–280? BCE), who wrote the *Zhuang-zi*.

CONFUCIANS OF THE 100 SCHOOLS (bai ja) ERA
In the "100 schools" Confucians were within the school called ru (classicists). The two key Confucian figures were Confucius (551–479 BCE) and Mencius (372?–289? BCE). Classicists studied the ancient Zhou documents. Other schools included Mohists (mo) and Legalists (fa), founded by Mo-zi (468?–376? BCE) and Xun-zi (330?–227? BCE).

WESTERN ZHOU DYNASTY (1045–771 BCE)
Confucians idealized the "Way of the Ancients" shown by the Zhou rulers, especially the Duke of Zhou. Zhou culture provided a body of myth with its culture heroes (Fu Xi, Shen Nong, Huang-di), sage kings (Yao, Shun, Yu), and virtuous founders (King Wen, King Wu, King Zhen). The Zhou Rites included annual sacrifices to: Heaven (yang) and Earth (yin). The Chinese Imperial tradition was based on the Zhou odes, documents, rites, and divination studies. These texts formed the core of what became four of five Confucian classics: *Book of Odes*, *Book of History*, *Book of Changes*, and *Book of Rites*. The glorious Western Zhou dynasty ended after 800 years when what remained was "a neglected family of priest-kings with scarcely the vestiges of power" (Morton and Lewis 2005: 25).

contrast to the powerful shi, knights. As heirs of a defeated dynasty the Shang *ru* tried to maintain the ancient Shang traditions. During the years of Western Zhou decline and into the Warring States period (ca. 475–221 BCE) the position of the shi became less and less relevant. As Zhou power waned, a handful of problem-solvers began to propose incisive views on politics, religion, and society. The Chinese call this the age of 100 scholars. And though 100 is a poetic number there were a handful of thinkers between 600 and 200 BCE whose impact on East Asian culture is felt strongly even today. Among the 100 scholars were Confucians, Mohists, and Daoists – plus others known as Legalists whose practical bent led them to stray from the Confucian mean (middle way).

Lao-zi (604–531 BCE, traditional)

Daoists call Lao-zi (604–531 BCE, traditional) their founder. His *Dao De Jing* (Book of the Way and Virtue) is the foundational text of their tradition. A legend says that Lao-zi was conceived by a shooting star, and remained in his mother's womb for sixty-two years before being born. An official second-century BCE account says that Lao-zi was an archivist at the Zhou court whom Confucius consulted on matters of li. Biographer Sima Qian (ca. 145–86 BCE) wrote: "Laoxi cultivated Dao and virtue . . . and his learning was devoted to self-effacement and not having fame. He lived in Zhou for a long time; witnessing the decline of Zhou, he departed" (Chan 2000: 2). Disillusioned with society the Old Master headed for the mountains – or even for India as some later Daoists have claimed. When Lao-zi arrived at the northwest border separating China from the barbarians, the official at the gate requested a written record of his thoughts. Thus Lao-zi produced some 5,000 characters about the dao and **de** (power, virtue). His work became known as the *Lao-zi* or the *Dao De Jing*, and over the generations some 700 commentaries were written on it. The text in its present form dates from around 300 BCE, and thus some scholars date Lao-zi to that time. Other scholars suspect that Lao-zi is a purely legendary figure and prefer to speak only of the book. Regardless of *when or whether* Lao-zi lived, these verses of *Dao De Jing* are meant to express Lao-zi's description of himself:

> People are wreathed in smiles
> As if at a carnival banquet.
> I alone am passive, giving no sign,
> Like an infant who has not yet smiled.
> Forlorn, as if I had no home. . . .
>
> Others have plans,
> I alone am wayward and stubborn,
> I alone am different from others,
> Like a baby in the womb.
>
> (*Dao De Jing*, verse 20 in Addiss and Lombardo 1993: 20)*

The image of the baby captured the Daoists' imagination. They see a connection between sages and infants, as the spontaneous acts of a baby are reminiscent of the actionless action (wu-wei) of a sage. Sometimes Lao-zi is called Old Baby.

Confucius (551–479 BCE)

Toward the end of his life Confucius assessed his own moral-intellectual development:

> At fifteen my mind was set on learning. At thirty my character had been formed. At forty I had no more perplexities. At fifty I knew the Mandate of Heaven (*T'ien ming*). At sixty I was at ease with whatever I heard. At seventy I could follow my heart's desire without transgressing moral principles.
>
> (*Analects* 2:4, Chan 1963: 22)

Confucius used words that reflected things he valued: learning, character, the Mandate of Heaven, moral principles, and so forth. Thus the following review of the Master's life correlates six core Chinese ideas with the time-frames Confucius outlined in reflecting upon his life: (1) filial piety (xiao, hsiao), (2) the genuine human (jun-zi, chün-tzu), (3) ritual propriety (li, li), (4) Heaven (Tian, T'ien), (5) benevolence (**ren**, jen), and (6) the five social relationships. An account of his moral-intellectual development becomes understandable in terms of key Chinese ideas because Confucius lived to embody high cultural values. And though Confucius did not speak of his childhood, this account ties his early years to the ancient Chinese concept of cultural patterns (wen). In the course of this discussion, the chronology of Confucius' professional life should also be kept in mind: (1) From birth to age 15 Confucius lived with a poor family in Lu; (2) from age 15 to 30 he was a student and filial son in Lu; (3) from age 30 to 55 he pursued his professional life in Lu; (4) from age 55 to 68 he traveled in self-imposed exile through various neighboring states; (5) from age 68 to 72 he was a scholar and teacher in Lu (Nansen 1997: 535–537).

On wen: childhood

Confucius was born in the state of Lu (presently Qufu, Shandong province). Tradition says that his ancestors were Shang nobles from the state of Song. Confucius' father, Shulianghe, was a minor official who worked as head of a county in Lu. Confucius was just one among many of his generation whose families had little real status, though they were from old aristocratic lines.

High-paying jobs were passed down within prestigious families and many boys grew up with little prospect of applying their talents. When Confucius was 3 years old Shulianghe passed away, and without the patriarch his family became impoverished. With no father as head of the household, Confucius engaged in various forms of physical labor for a livelihood as he grew up.

Confucius was born into a patriarchal society where men and women had specific duties ascribed to them. His mother would have been in a difficult position without Shulianghe, for according to tradition her place was strictly in the home.

> The wife must always be guided by the will of the master of the house, be he father, husband, or grown son. Her place is within the house. There, without having to look for them, she has great and important duties. She must attend to the nourishment of the family and to the food for the sacrifice. In this way she becomes the center of the social and religious life of the family, and her perseverance in this position brings good fortune to the whole house.
>
> (*I Ching* comment on **hexagram** 37 in Wilhelm and Baynes 1950, 1971: 145)

Confucius grew up holding the view that people should perform their proper social duties to create a harmonious culture in accord with Heaven's will. He seemed to have a particular sensitivity to disorder and noticed a lack of propriety among people in high places. Confucius seemed disturbed by irregularities in the pattern of Chinese culture and began thirsting for knowledge of how to live correctly.

On xiao: "At fifteen my mind was set on learning"

Confucius spent most of his life near Lu. Although he grew up in meager circumstances, the fatherless boy was able to study the six skills mastered by educated boys of aristocratic families: ceremonies, music, archery, carriage driving, calligraphy, and calculation (Nansen 1997: 535). Over time he also studied works that were later designated as Confucian classics. When Confucius was 17 years old his mother passed away. The practice of filial piety (xiao) called for a period of three years' mourning (where a "year" is calculated at nine months) following the death of a parent. For twenty-seven months a proper filial son was to refrain from: work, sexual relations, eating refined foods, wearing fine clothes, playing music, and so forth. Thus, upon the death of this mother, Confucius observed the rites of mourning as a filial son. Confucian tradition says that *after the three-year mourning period was officially concluded* Confucius could not bring himself to play the lute for three more days. This hesitancy suggests that his xiao was sincere. Traditionally the practice of xiao involved pious obligations toward the spirits, one's ancestors, and one's deceased parents. Confucius would later recalibrate the focus of xiao to underplay the relationship with spirits and emphasized something new: filial piety in relation to one's living parents.

On jun-zi: "At thirty my character had been formed"

No information has been preserved about Confucius' wife, but it is likely that they had a boy and a girl. Confucius established a private school (said to be the first in Chinese history) when he was around 30 years old. He observed that many young men from prestigious families took their official positions for granted and were lax in fulfilling their duties. Confucius believed that boys should be educated to think clearly and develop their moral character. He argued that the most intellectually qualified and morally upright candidates for government positions should be awarded jobs so that social problems could be solved. Thus Confucius stressed that each man in his school should become a **jun-zi**. At that time the word jun-zi meant prince, but Confucius often used the word to mean gentleman. He taught that a person was not a jun-zi merely because he came from a noble line. To Confucius, being princely was a matter of moral character. It was a matter of de. A jun-zi was noble in mind and heart. Therefore, someone could be a jun-zi without noble birth. On the other hand, even a person of aristocratic lineage might not be a true jun-zi.

On Li: "At forty I had no more perplexities"

In ancient China the ritual of sacrifice was paramount. The Shang emperors were buried with human beings who were to serve as attendants in the afterlife. The early Zhou rulers continued to practice human sacrifice, but people were gradually replaced by substitutes, real material wealth was replaced by paper money, and so forth. In the sixth century BCE the attitude toward sacrifice appeared to be changing, and Confucius did much to reform the practice of the ancient rites. Confucius served as a Master of Ceremony (Li) in his home state of Lu and lobbied for high ethical standards. The corruption of traditional values among the social elite disturbed Confucius, who said: "As for what follows the opening libation at the Imperial Sacrifice, I'd rather not see how they do it these days" (*Analects* 3:10 in Hinton 1998: 24). Yet Confucius would never consider abandoning the ancient rituals – even though he thought they were being performed without the proper decorum and moral authority.

> As the ceremony had fallen into neglect, Adapt Kung wanted to do away with sacrificing sheep to announce a new moon to the ancestors. The Master said: "You love sheep, Kung, but I love Ritual."
>
> (*Analects* 3:17 in Hinton 1998: 25)

Confucius thought of Li not merely as formal ritual, but also as the way of proper conduct in society. He insisted that both state rituals and acts of daily life be done with propriety. Confucius aimed to restore the inner dimension of de (virtue, power) to ceremony that he believed the ancients possessed. He believed that proper performance of ritual should bring the people in harmony within their families, villages, states, and the cosmos. Heaven would be pleased and all would go well under the great bowl of the sky if rulers performed the Imperial Sacrifices at the altars of Heaven and Earth in a timely manner with precision and sincere decorum. Their example would trickle down through society and their moral authority would please the ancestors and – above all – Heaven. Thus Confucius revolutionized the notion of Li.

On Tian: "At fifty I knew the Mandate of Heaven"

Confucius wanted to follow the Mandate of Heaven in his own life. He studied the Rites to understand what actions align human beings with the will of Heaven. He also studied history to figure out how social, natural, and political events correlated with each other. He could deduce that in times of social disarray the will of Heaven was being thwarted. And by identifying times of harmony Confucius could learn what Heaven required of human beings. Between the ages of 30 and 55 Confucius pursued his professional life in Lu and worked to reform society to conform to the ancient ways. At age 51 Confucius was appointed as the head of a county in Lu. This was a minor post akin to the job his father had before passing away. For the next four years Confucius climbed the social ladder becoming, in turn, Minister of Industry, Minister of Public Security, and acting Prime Minister of Lu (Nansen 1997: 536). He taught that the way of the Former Kings was in concert with the will of Heaven. However, by advocating the ancient ways Confucius was both reactionary and progressive. His teachings threatened the status quo. It cut into the practice of nepotism whereby people simply inherited jobs through family connections. The radical nature of Confucius' teachings apparently did not go unnoticed. After twenty-five years of professional work in Lu, Confucius' career was cut short when he offended one of Lu's powerful noblemen. Thus at age 55 Confucius left Lu. He went into exile in 497 BCE.

On ren: "At sixty I was at ease with whatever I heard"

Confucius traveled through six states in self-imposed exile for thirteen years. At times he and his disciples went hungry. Confucius approached princes and dukes to promote his political agenda. Some listened with caution as the former minister from Lu taught that rulers should govern by moral authority. However, Confucius and his band of wandering scholars sometimes met with suspicion and hostility. Once Confucius was mobbed and thrown into prison, and another time he needed armed protection. Confucius had to escape on foot from Song, the place of his ancestors.

Despite the hardships that Confucius encountered, he counseled his disciples always to cultivate ren (humaneness) and not to aim for position or profit. He said, "The Humane master the difficult parts before expecting any rewards" (*Analects* 6:21 in Hinton 1998:

Plate 12.2 "Confucius." Confucius hearkened back to ancient Chinese culture and upheld the Duke of Zhou as a ruler because he had sympathy for peasants and did not abuse hereditary power. Confucius popularized the Duke of Zhou and called for a restoration of government based on his example. The Duke of Zhou introduced the Mandate of Heaven concept to justify the Zhou takeover of Shang rule. Confucius extended the concept, asking people to live every day in accord with the Mandate of Heaven.

60). Confucius spoke often of ren as an ideal toward which a person should aim over the course of a lifetime. He never admitted that anyone had actually achieved the profound humaneness of ren. Yet ren was not an exaggerated moral virtue beyond the reach of a human being. Ren was *humanity* – being human. Ren had to do with being unselfish and yet doing things in the proper measure. From the age of 55 to 68 Confucius traveled giving counsel but received no government position. Yet he said, "At sixty, I could hear the truth with equanimity." If Confucius is taken at his word, he maintained equanimity in the midst of his difficulties in exile, and counseled his disciples to do likewise.

> The Master said: "Don't worry if you have no position: worry about making yourself worthy of one. Don't worry if you aren't known and admired: devote yourself to a life that deserves admiration."
>
> (*Analects* 4:14 in Hinton 1998: 36)

Yet it came to pass that many of Confucius' students did receive positions in government over the years.

On the five relationships: "At seventy I could follow my heart's desire without transgressing moral principles"

In 484 BCE a new Prime Minister of Lu invited Confucius to return home – though he had no interest in creating a Confucian government. Thus at the age of 68 Confucius began to consolidate his life's work and spent the final four years of his life teaching and writing. He wrote a history of the state of Lu known as the *Spring and Summer Annals*, and edited (with commentary) key texts he considered essential for the education of a jun-zi. These included the *Book of Odes*, *Book of Rites*, *Book of History*, and *Book of Changes*. Confucius also established a new group of disciples in Lu. Traditional accounts say that Confucius had 3,000 students, seventy-two of whom became particularly well qualified. Certain disciples wrote down the teachings they received from Confucius. The collection of pithy anecdotes and advice became known as the *Lun-yu* (*Analects*). From the *Analects* it appears that Confucius had fifteen or twenty regular students, four of whom seem to have been the most important. He died at the age of 72 within five years of returning to Lu.

Confucius' life was devoted to a study of the ancient Chinese classics, and he saw time and again that these always pointed to the necessity for human beings to cultivate their moral character. He also saw that such moral cultivation took place in the context of proper social interactions. Thus the five social relationships stood as the legacy of Confucius. Throughout East Asia Confucians would always contemplate the nature of these five relationships: (1) ruler–subject, (2) father–son, (3) husband–wife, (4) elder brother–younger brother, and (5) friend–friend. They are based on a hierarchical family model.

> Three of the five social relationships are to be found within the family – that between father and son, which is the relation of love, that between husband and wife, which is the relation of chaste conduct, and that between elder and younger brother, which is the relation of correctness. The loving reverence

> of the son is then carried over to the prince in the form of faithfulness to duty; the affection and correctness of behavior existing between the two brothers are extended to a friend in the form of loyalty, and to a person of superior rank in the form of deference. The family is society in embryo; it is the native soil on which performance of moral duty is made easy through natural affection, so that within a small circle a basis of moral practice is created, and this is later widened to include human relationships in general.
>
> (*I Ching* comment on hexagram 37 in Wilhelm and Baynes 1950, 1971: 144)

From the Confucian point of view, one's country is an extension of the family, like an extended clan. The ruler is like one's father, officials are like parents, and common people are like children. Responsibility to the family is threefold: (1) continue the family lineage, (2) bring prosperity to the family, and (3) gain positive acknowledgment of the family in society. Xiao requires absolute obedience to the older generations, and solemn responsibility for raising the younger generation properly according to the way of Heaven. In the Confucian hierarchy one fulfills responsibility to one's superior by extending kindness toward one's inferior. A human being exists in a hierarchy of relationships that are patterned according to nature. The lower is responsible to the higher – and thus must still care for the lower. The five relationships became so important to Confucian society that the Confucian tradition is sometimes called "family-ism."

Mo-zi (468?–376? BCE)

Mo-zi was probably born soon after Confucius died. He was schooled in classical thought, but rejected the fundamental lynchpin of Confucian society – the five social relationships. Mo-zi was a utilitarian who said the government should forbid all Confucian customs that served no purpose in society. He propounded an anti-Confucian view that he called universal love. This was not an emotional love but a dispassionate concern for human welfare across the board. Mo-zi taught that people should extend their love to everyone equally because it was useful for society. He also wanted to eliminate the three-year mourning period observed by Confucian filial sons. To him the practice of filial piety foolishly removed productive members of society from the workforce and thus hurt the country's economy. Mo-zi argued against the practice of many traditional rites, and was against music and all the unnecessary and costly finery of court life. Mo-zi and his disciples wandered about wearing coarse garments and sandals. They spoke out against violence in society and against war. Yet he was a staunch authoritarian. He advocated a widespread system of spying, whereby even family members would inform on one another about deviance from the political program. Under the auspices of universal love a person's love of family members should be no more intense than love of strangers. Mo-zi insisted that a person's loyalty be directed at the state.

Mencius (372?–289? BCE)

Meng-zi (latinized as Mencius) was the first great thinker to elaborate upon Confucius' teachings. He was taught by a man who studied under the grandson of Confucius. Mencius made advances in Confucian thought with regard to ren, methods of education, and social policy. Confucius thought that any person could become noble of character, even a peasant. Extrapolating from Confucius' views Mencius stated outright that human nature was fundamentally good. However, this did not mean that all human beings acted well. He said, "The great man is one who does not lose his [originally good] child's heart" (4B12 in Chan 1963: 76). This meant that people needed education to protect their innate goodness. Mencius believed in destiny (*ming*) and felt that without teachers a person of intelligence could easily lose the child's heart and turn into a criminal. He clarified common misconceptions about destiny in these terms:

> Everything is destiny (*ming*). A man should accept obediently what is correct [in one's destiny]. Therefore, he who knows destiny does not stand beneath a precipitous wall. Death sustained in the course of carrying out the Way to the limit is due to correct destiny. But death under handcuffs and fetters is not due to correct destiny. (7A2)
>
> (Chan 1963: 79)

For Mencius, living properly in the light of destiny involved learning how to live according to the dao. He believed that without an education, misfortune would be a person's lot in life. Thus Mencius established public education in China. He was particular about which books were edifying and favored teaching a range of subjects including music.

Zhuang-zi (360?–280? BCE)

Zhuang-zi was born soon after Mencius. Like Mencius, he wrote essays. But Zhuang-zi wrote as a Daoist. With humor and irony he provided a social critique of the Confucian and Mohist traditions as they were practiced in his day. For example, Confucius spoke much of the jun-zi who refined his character with a proper education and observation of the rites. Yet for Zhuang-zi the *true* gentleman was one who could anticipate the ill-effects of his own actions. His disapproval of scandalous Confucians of his day was couched in this story of an encounter between the Daoist Lao-zi and Confucius. Lao-zi said this to Confucius who had been "peering around at everything" as if he were in charge of it all:

> Put away that officious look and that all-knowing expression of yours, and you might become a real gentleman. . . . You can't endure the wounds of your own times . . . but you're oblivious to your own running rampant over the next ten thousand generations. Are you so crude on purpose, or have you just lost the capacity to recognize consequences? You run rampant in a quest for men's favor. Your whole life is a *shame*. This is the behavior, the 'advancement' of mediocre men drawn together by mean secrets, joined in praise of Yao, in blame of Chieh. Better to forget them both. Better to do away with praise. What goes against things is always wounded. Everything that moves goes wrong. The sages [i.e., the truly wise people] shuffle their feet and wait, embarrassed, at the beginning of things – so that *all* may take part and gain merit in accomplishment. But everything *you* undertake is arrogance and affectation.
>
> (*Chuang Tzu*, ch. 26 in Hamill and Seaton 1998: 135)

Zhuang-zi taught that rulers should refrain from meddling. They should not be like the marquis of Lu who coveted a highly prized bird and killed it with grand court music and a sumptuous banquet, instead of letting it live a bird's life. He also took aim at government corruption. In one vignette, Zhuang-zi wrote of himself appearing before the king of Wei. When the king expressed sorrow for his distress upon seeing Zhuang-zi's coarse, patched clothes and dilapidated shoes, Zhuang-zi retorted, "It is poverty, not distress! . . . Tattered clothes and old shoes indicate only poverty and not distress. Only when I live, as I do now, under a benighted ruler, and seditious ministers, then it is possible for me to be in distress" (Höchsmann 2001: 5).

Xun-zi (300–238 BCE)

Xun-zi was born while Mencius and Zhuang-zi were getting on in years. Like Mencius, Xun-zi engaged in classical studies. But he and Mencius came up with opposite views on human nature. Xun-zi was convinced that people were innately bad. Thus he rejected the political freedom that Mencius advocated. Xun-zi used the conduct of newborn babies to make his case for the innately evil nature of human beings. He observed that babies are consumed with self-interest: they want to be warm; they demand to be fed; and they insist on sleeping when tired. Even as children become adults they want to fill their needs above and beyond all else. Seeing this, Xun-zi taught that people needed strict guidance because there was no guarantee they would act in a way that was beneficial to others. Just as crooked wood had to be steamed and pressed into shape, so human beings needed to be forced into civil conduct. Xun-zi specified the course of education, allowing little freedom of choice. He advocated classical studies to promote knowledge of the ancient kings – but not for the common person. Xun-zi approved of the traditional rites, but not when done with respect to the spirits. In his view, the rites were strictly to establish social order and compensate for the self-centered tendencies of human beings. Two of Xun-zi's students were highly influential in the Legalist movement: Han Fei (d. 233 BCE) and Li Si (fl. 221–207). Li Si instituted Legalism as the basis for governance in the Qin Empire (221–207 BCE). And though Qin rule lasted for only one decade, Legalism fundamentally changed the course of Chinese politics from that day forward. For example, the Han ruler who replaced the second Qin emperor officially supported the Confucian tradition, but had Legalists as his key advisors. And so it went through four centuries of Han rule and beyond.

"Religious" Daoists

Han rule disintegrated after four centuries. Natural disasters occurred and men traveled in search of work and food, leaving their households devastated. Peasant revolts grounded in the Daoist tradition led to the demise of the Han dynasty. This politically unstable and economically depressed environment provoked a new cultural tendency for people to identify with groups that cut across family lines. Two influential Daoist groups that emerged in the late Han era were the: (1) Way of the Five Pecks of Rice and (2) Way of Great Peace. In the short term they played an important role in uniting peasants against Han oppression; and in the long term the Way of the Five Pecks of Rice established the foundation for a Daoist church that persists as the Celestial Masters sect on the island of Taiwan and elsewhere to this day.

The Way of the Five Pecks of Rice

The Way of the Five Pecks of Rice was the first organized Daoist church in Chinese history. The group was so-called because people paid five pecks of rice per year as a membership fee or as payment for healing. Zhang Daoling was a mountain dwelling hermit who became the first patriarch of the group after he claimed that Lao-zi appeared in a vision (in 142 CE). The heavenly Lao-zi indicated that those who followed him would be saved from catastrophe as the world came to an end. Zhang Daoling was called a Celestial Master (*Tian-shi*) – and the title was passed to his son and grandson, in turn. When Zhang Daoling passed away, believers thought that he had become an Immortal. To this day he is called the Ancestral Celestial Master. The third Celestial Master, Zhang Lu, led a rebellion against the Han ruler, and in 184 CE established an independent theocratic state in Sichuan. Heading what was now called the Way of the Celestial Masters, Zhang Lu had the notion that "the celestial bureaucracy should be replicated on earth by a hierarchy of priests who were responsible not just to one or two initiates, but to a larger body of the faithful, and, through them, to the society as a whole" (Bokenkamp 1997: 14). The Celestial Masters sect was socially progressive in bringing religion to people of all social classes. It gave more opportunity to women than was typical in Chinese patriarchal culture where women were subject to male authority (particularly of their husbands) and socially pressured to bear sons.

The Way of Great Peace (Tai Ping Dao)

Zhang Jiao (d. 184), along with his two younger brothers, led a group known as the Way of Great Peace. All three brothers were healers and worked with poor peasants whose sickness they attributed to social ills. They saw local officials abusing peasants, and people starving due to a heavy tax burden. Thus, discontent with Han rule, they organized a band of guerrilla fighters who lived in mountain retreats. Word spread about their practice of faith healing, and the group came to have around 360,000 fighters known as Yellow Turbans after their headgear. The color yellow represented Heaven, whose support they sought in overthrowing the Han ruler. The Yellow Turbans revolted in 184 CE and spoke of social harmony that would come after the evil of the world was swept away through violence. They proclaimed equal rights among people and redistribution of land. Followers of the Way of Great Peace expected an era of Great Peace following the overthrow of the Han, but the movement ended in 205 CE when the revolutionaries were defeated. After the Yellow Turbans were defeated, remnants of their Way of Great Peace were absorbed into the Way of the Celestial Masters. Zhang Lu was ruling as Celestial Master in Sichuan when the Way of Great Peace broke up, and the two sects had a common interest in the heavenly Lao-zi and faith healing. Zhang Lu wrote a commentary (ca. 190–220 CE) on the *Dao De Jing* that dealt with the preservation and nourishment of qi within one's body. As the Celestial Masters Sect evolved, several methods of working with qi developed that involved herbal medicine, ritual music, dieting, and meditation. Great emphasis was placed on repentance as an aspect of healing meditation because members of the church believed that illness was caused by sin. The ultimate goal of practitioners was to become purified enough to live on air and be transformed into immortals.

Proponents of Dark Learning

After the break-up of the Han Empire, China was divided for some 350 years. In this Period of Disunity (220–589 CE) states changed both hands and boundaries a number of times. Barbarians moved into the north of China, which had been the traditional seat of the cultured Han people. Wishing to preserve their power and culture, the elite Han families migrated southward and set up weak states in their newly colonized territory. Their interest was turning from Confucian toward Daoist teachings, and in the south the northern émigrés encountered an alchemical tradition that enriched their developing interests. One thinker they encountered was Ge Hong (284–364) who had military training as well as a keen interest in alchemy. Ge Hong believed that immortality was not restricted to members of powerful families, but was available to anyone who practiced proper methods.

From about 200 to 600 CE a group of scholars became interested in what they called Dark Learning (xuan xue). The expression "dark, profound or mysterious" learning comes from the *Dao De Jing* where Lao-zi said the dao is "darker than dark" (*xuan zhi you xuan*). These philosophers contrasted their "xuan xue" with the rectification of names studied by Confucian officials interested in how people must live according to their "name" in the five social relationships as "ruler," "subject," "filial son," and so forth. A key thinker in the Dark Learning movement was Wang Bi (226–249 CE) who wrote commentaries on the *Dao De Jing*, *Book of Changes*, and *Analects*. Wang Bi and others reacted against the popular Daoist practice that was sweeping the countryside under the directives of the Celestial Masters and other groups. Their new Daoist pantheon, immortalization of Lao-zi, revealed scriptures, and collective yearning to become immortal did not accord with the conservative approach of Dark Learning, which concentrated on subtle states of mind hinted at in the *Dao de jing*, *Zhuang-zi*, *Book of Changes*, and *Analects*, for example. Dark Learning is sometimes called neo-Daoism, but that term is misleading. Xuan xue involved the study of both Confucian and Daoist classic works, and proponents were not enthusiastic about the growing movement of church Daoists with their belief in a heavenly bureaucracy. As a movement xuan xue lasted into about the sixth century CE, but its influence continued to filter through Chinese thought. It can even be felt among practitioners of the martial art of Tai-ji quan today.

Zhu Xi (1130–1200)

At the mid-point of Han rule in the first century CE some Buddhist texts, monks, and statues had begun to filter into China by way of the Silk Roads used for international trade by Han merchants. Gradually over several centuries the Buddhist tradition became a considerable economic and intellectual force in Chinese culture. Both Confucians and Daoists found themselves influenced by Buddhist thought and the monastic system of life and education. For their part, Chinese peasants were impacted by the Mahāyāna Buddhist teachings about bodhisattvas who would help them through troubled times. By the Tang era (618–906) Confucian, Daoist, and Buddhist traditions were interacting in profoundly creative ways through the arts and philosophy. Yet toward the end of Tang rule a fierce anti-Buddhist sentiment was growing. The eloquent essayist and Tang official Han Yu (768–824) reminded his Daoist emperor that Buddha was a barbarian, and urged him not to honor the foreigner's religion. Twenty-six years later, in 845 CE, under economic pressure to generate funds, Emperor Tang Wu-zong (814–846) conducted a twenty-month religious persecution. According to a report of the Board of Worship, 4,600 monasteries and 40,000 hermitages were destroyed, while 260,000 Buddhist monks and nuns were returned to lay life. Zoroastrians and Nestorian Christians were counted as heretical Buddhists and targeted as well. The Buddhist monasteries had been tax-exempt, and clergy were exempt from work – and this had caused resentment. Afterwards, during the Song dynasty (960–1279), the Pure Land and Chan Buddhist sects recovered because they had not been dependent on large libraries. On the other hand, the highly philosophical brands of Buddhism basically perished, the Zoroastrian tradition did not recover, and the Christians suffered a serious setback. In this atmosphere of national pride and economic hardship, a Confucian revival began. Confucians took another look at their philosophy and aimed to infuse it more thoroughly with native Confucian values – and purge it of Buddhist elements.

Zhu Xi (1130–1200) worked to reclaim elements of the Confucian tradition that were blending too much with Buddhist and Daoist thought. Zhu Xi's work was in line with thinkers in the School of Principles (*li xue*) branch of neo-Confucian thought. Generally he is credited with bringing the School of Principle to its high point and extending neo-Confucian influence in Korea and Japan with his remarkable analyses. He made the notion of principle (*li*) central to his analyses and insisted that principle was not merely an intellectual abstraction. He argued that principle extends throughout the universe and governs all things as the self-evident, self-sufficient source of goodness. A thing comes into being only because there is already a principle of that thing. But neither the principle nor the material thing is prior to the other. To account for this paradox Zhu Xi reshaped the Daoist concept of Supreme Ultimate (*Tai-ji*). He considered the Supreme Ultimate as the "reservoir of infinite potentiality" that embodied yin and yang, as the "operation of myriad things" (Chan 1987: 115). Zhu Xi called Tai-ji the single principle that was the sum total of all particular principles, and said that Tai-ji was present not only throughout the universe as the ultimate principle but also within every human being.

In classical times Mencius had claimed that human nature was good, and Confucian revivalists such as Zhu Xi were interested in further defining the nature of human beings. They aimed to identify what goes beyond the instincts to distinguish human beings from other animals. They recognized that human beings had desires (as Xun-zi had pointed out), but argued that it was only inappropriate desire that made people act evilly. Immoral conduct was action done selfishly "for private," and was to be countered by moral conduct "for public." The Neo-Confucians named four virtues that reduced selfishness: humaneness (ren), righteousness (yi), propriety (li), and intelligence (zhi). Among the four virtues they tended to see ren as all-inclusive and primary. Zhu Xi's teaching on how to actualize Tai-ji within each person centered on the notion of ren. He revolutionized the key Confucian concept of benevolence to fit with his concept of principle. He spoke of ren as both "the character of the mind" and "the principle of love" (Chan 1987: 120). With this double character ren embodied all four Confucian virtues while being one of them. Zhu Xi said that humaneness (ren), righteousness (yi), propriety (li), and intelligence (zhi) are all part of the "character of mind." By cultivating the principle of love human beings can manifest the Supreme Ultimate, which is the benevolent character of mind latent within them. Zhu Xi also taught that intelligence (like ren) embodied all four virtues, while being one of them. He was convinced that gaining a clear knowledge of things set the other virtues in motion. Zhu Xi viewed the list of four Confucian virtues as circular. Thus the means of actualizing Tai-ji involved cultivation of all the virtues in a synergistic manner.

Wang Yang-ming (1472–1529)

Wang Yang-ming is often considered to be the fourth great Confucian after Confucius, Mencius, and Zhu Xi. He lived at a time when Pure Land and Chan Buddhist traditions had revived in China, and anti-Buddhist sentiment had died down. Thus rather than purge his philosophy of Buddhist elements, Wang Yang-ming's thinking was highly compatible with Chan practice. In fact, *practice* was the key to Wang Yang-ming's neo-Confucian philosophy. His School of Mind (*xin xue*) defined itself as an intuitive alternative to the School of Principle, which was highly rational. In 1492 at the age of 20, Wang Yang-ming spent a full week meditating in front of a bamboo grove to discover the principle (li) in things because Zhu Xi had written that the ultimate principle was discoverable in particular principles (which would include objects such as a bamboo tree). Still unenlightened after seven days, Wang Yang-ming concluded that to know the world a person must look within the mind, not to external objects as was advocated by the School of Principle. He extended Mencius' notion of the goodness of human nature to speak of a primordial awareness that was the source of all goodness and the embodiment of all things in the cosmos. Yet as a Confucian, Wang Yang-ming was concerned with the world and public life. He felt that knowledge and action were inseparable. Thus primordial awareness was discoverable through social action and human involvement. And while other Confucians tended to focus on the rectification of names in terms of correcting social behavior, Wang Yang-ming argued that troubles in the world were caused by a failure to know oneself. Thus he advocated rectifying troubles in the world by means of intuitive self-knowledge coupled with practical action. Wang Yang-ming's philosophy was enthusiastically received in Japan where both Shintō and Chan Buddhists related to its intuitive and engaging outlook.

Mao Ze-dong (1893–1976)

Politics in modern China during the last half of the twentieth century had a devastating effect on religion. The last emperor of China was deposed in 1911, and in 1919 the May Fourth Movement introduced the New Cultural Movement that brought the concepts of Mr. Democracy and Mr. Science. The New Culture Movement exposed modern Western ideas to the Chinese. These were based in the European Enlightenment, and carried the idea of personal rights and the role of reason and independent thinking, and self-determination. On 1 October 1949 Mao Ze-dong stood at Tienanmen Square in Peking (Beijing) and proclaimed the People's Republic of China. He continued to build his power base and eventually fomented the Great Proletarian Cultural Revolution in 1966. Then for an intensive decade (1966–1976) Mao Ze-dong was bent on destroying all remnants of religion in China. Chairman Mao claimed to have liberated the Chinese people from the Confucian tradition. He exercised authoritarian rule, enacting policies that hearken back to both Mo-zi (470–391 BCE) and Qin Shi Huang-di, the first emperor of "China" (r. 221–210). Yet in the interest of destroying the old order Mao Ze-dong moved beyond his debt to Chinese history. He felt that Marxism-Leninism was unique, and that the Communist Party held the key to destroying old ideas, old culture, old customs, and old habits. Beyond attacking the "Four Olds" Mao Ze-dong wanted China to recover from the more recent oppression of colonialism.

Perhaps the Marxism of the Great Proletarian Cultural Revolution in China replaced – or attempted to replace – the old religions of China. Mao Ze-dong provided his people with a doctrine (communism), a scripture (the *Sayings of Chairman Mao*, known as the Little Red Book), rituals (meetings to study the scripture, share a symbolic meal and pledge allegiance), and a culture hero (Chairman Mao). After the opening years of the communist revolution Robert J. Lifton puzzled over the tremendous psychological hold that Chairman Mao had over his followers.

> This is by no means the first time that a political leader has been made into a divinity. But few in the past could have matched Mao in the superlatives used, the number of celebrants, or the

Plate 12.3 "Restored Confucian tablet." During the Chinese Cultural Revolution instigated by Mao Ze-dong symbols of Confucianism were targeted for destruction. For example, stone tablets dedicated to various Confucian scholars at the Temple of Confucius in Beijing were broken. In the new millennium many Chinese appear to be seeking a restoration of Confucian values. This look back at the "old" is reflected in the reconstitution of the scholars' tablets – one of which is seen here.

> thoroughness with which the message of glory has been disseminated. Even more unique has been the way in which the leader's words have become vehicles for elevating him, during his lifetime, to a place above that of the state itself or of its institutional source of purity and power, in this case the Party.
>
> (Lifton 1968: 63)

After the Great Proletarian Cultural Revolution freedom of religious belief was instituted as government policy. Lei Zhengchang, a staff member of the Institute for World Religions in Beijing, explained the official rationale for why China must allow religion – even though in theory religion should disappear by itself under optimal social conditions.

> Some people point out: China is a Socialist country with Marxism-Leninism-Mao Zedong Thought as its guide. Communists are atheists. Why has China adopted the policy of allowing freedom of religious belief?
>
> . . . Opposing theism is the elementary principle for all materialists and Marxists. However, the existence of religion is caused by ideological understanding, in addition to economic factors. The viewpoint which holds that religion will disappear by itself very quickly with the development of economic construction, science, and technology is unrealistic. For this reason, it is necessary to lay down correct principles and policies.
>
> (MacInnis 1989: 38–39)

Currently China is in the midst of culture change in the aftermath of Marxism-Leninism-Mao Ze-dong Thought that was its guide.

> One of the great surprises of China after Mao has been the efflorescence of religious belief and practice. It is a surprise not only for many Chinese Communists, whose scientific materialist ideology teaches them that religion is destined to wither away with the advance of history, but also for many Western observers of China. . . .
>
> Yet with the death of Mao and the end of the Cultural Revolution era, all kinds of religious practices are springing back to life. Throughout the countryside, peasants are reviving the old marriage and funeral rites, celebrating traditional festivals, sometimes calling on the services of sorcerers and shamans, and even in some places rebuilding local shrines and temples. On a more formally organized level, Buddhist temples and Islamic mosques are being refurbished and a surprising number of young people are entering training to become monks, nuns and imams. Despite enormous obstacles, the Catholic and Protestant churches have survived and are growing. Enough Communist Party and Youth League members are forsaking atheism for religious belief that the Party has had to issue anxious directives about how to stem this tide.
>
> (MacInnis 1989: xv)

Contemporary Daoists

Taiwan is the seat of most religious Daoist ritual in modern times. There is a vast range of practices among the various sects due to periods of historical separation as well as different founding lineages. Daoist ritual specialists lead elaborate rituals that have an inner component of visualization involving travel to other realms. The ceremonies include other ritualists who do such things as perform acrobatics to symbolize such travel and sing hymns. On behalf of the community, the Daoist priest journeys to the Astral Court of the Jade Emperor to bow down and present a memorial that clarifies the reason for the ritual, such as requiem services, healing exorcisms, and communal prosperity.

> [The priest] summons the gods and attendants within his own body to merge with their counterparts in the astral places. He transforms his body into the cosmic body of the Most High Laozi. . . . But his most important meditation involves the reversal of time: he visualizes himself as an infant, escorted on a long voyage through his microcosmic body to the cranium, the palace of the Jade Emperor, where he presents a memorial outlining the purposes of the ritual. Upon his descent back into his abdomen, the inner infant ages again.
>
> (Dean 2000: 672–673)

While the priest performs the complex inner and outer ritual (involving specific gestures, symbolic objects, and so forth) representatives in the Daoist community engage in their own ritual activities timed to correspond to the great moments of the priest's astral journey. They make offerings (food, drink, incense) to the gods at the temple altar, march in processions, and participate in communal festivities that may take the greater part of many days. And regardless of their association with Daoist ritual, people influenced by Chinese culture throughout East Asia are heavily imbued with Confucian values that emphasize education and the five family relationships.

PART 2 THE RELIGIOUS TEXTURE OF CHINESE TRADITIONS

Ancient Chinese books were collections of various writings most of which were preserved on pieces of bamboo, including songs, ritual instructions, anecdotes, interpretations, lectures, government records, and so forth. Eventually these materials were linked together in the form of scrolls. The diverse body of texture dates from different eras, and the books grew fuller over the centuries with additional documents, commentaries, and so forth.

FOUNDATIONAL TEXTURE: CONFUCIAN TRADITION

The classics

The Chinese term for a classic book is *jing*. The **Five Classics** came to form the core of the Confucian curriculum: *Book of Odes*, *Book of Rites*, *Book of History*, *Spring and Autumn Annals*, and *Book of Changes*. (*A Book of Music* was once included among the classics, and surviving portions were incorporated into the *Book of Rites*.)

Book of Music (mostly lost)

Emperors enacted prescribed ritual movements, music, and songs to regulate the world and settle the hearts of beings in the empire. This regulation and movement occurred according to wen, the network of subtle correspondences between the inherent pattern of Heaven and specific cultural forms in Chinese civilization.

> Music was looked upon as something serious and holy. It fell to music to glorify the virtues of heroes and thus to construct a bridge to the world of the unseen. In the temple men drew near to God with music and pantomimes (out of this later the theater developed). . . . The ancestors were invited to these divine services as guests of the Ruler of Heaven and as representatives of humanity in the higher regions. . . . The ruler who revered the Divinity in revering his ancestors became thereby the Son of Heaven, in whom the heavenly and the earthly world met in mystical contact.
>
> These ideas are the final summation of Chinese culture. Confucius has said of the great sacrifice at which these rites were performed: "He who could wholly comprehend this sacrifice could rule the world as though it were spinning on his hand."
>
> (*I Ching* commentary to hexagram 16 in Wilhelm and Baynes 1950, 1971: 68–69)

Book of History

The *Book of History* includes pieces used in ritual dance performances at the Zhou royal court. For example, it contains the libretto for a war dance that celebrated the Zhou victory over Shang rule. The time-frame covered by the documents ranges from about 3000 BCE to 700 BCE. There are speeches and reports on the deeds of emperors, including a description of the character of the legendary Sage King Yao. Its "Announcement on Alcohol" claims that the last Shang rulers lost the Mandate of Heaven on account of their degenerate behavior and fondness for alcohol. This underscores the fundamental notion that the behavior of an emperor has wide-ranging consequences for the people and the cosmos. Heaven grants its mandate to rulers who care for the needs of their subjects. This teaching became central to the Confucian worldview.

Book of Rites

The *Book of Rites* contained detailed rules for all the rites concerning public life, as well as aspects of private life. There is a discussion of the three-year period of mourning to be undertaken by the filial son at the death of a parent. Other subjects include what is to be done, worn, at what time, and so forth on the occasion of weddings, funerals, court receptions, and sacrifices. A portion of this book was an ancient musical text. These matters were known through the oral tradition in Confucius' day, and were committed to writing around 200 BCE. Rituals are specific to a person's social standing and place in the family hierarchy. Any educated gentleman should have been conversant with these many rules.

Book of Odes

The *Book of Odes* has 305 poems on topics including love, war, eulogies, and lamentations. Many were used during ritual sacrifice at the Zhou royal court, accompanied by dances, music, and bells. Confucians studied the songs to contemplate their moral implications, and sometimes understood them allegorically. Some comments by Confucius make clear how precious he considered the *Book of Odes.*

> Adept Hsia asked: "What does it mean when the Songs say
>
> *Dimpled smile so entrancing,*
> *glancing eyes so full of grace:*
> *purest silk so ready for color?"*
>
> "For a painting," replied the Master, "you need a ground of pure silk."
>
> "And for Ritual – what ground do you need?"
>
> "How you've lifted my spirits, Hsia!" exclaimed the Master. "With you, I can truly discuss the *Songs*!"
>
> (*Analects* 3:8 in Hinton 1998: 23)

Confucius expected that the poetry would mold the character and behavior of his students who took up government jobs.

> The Master said: "A man may be able to chant all three hundred *Songs* from memory and still falter when appointed to office or waver when sent on embassies to the four corners of the earth. What good are all those *Songs* if he can't put them to use?"
>
> (*Analects* 13:5 in Hinton 1998: 141)

Book of Changes

The *Yi Jing* (*I Ching*) or *Book of Changes* is an ancient book of divination. It symbolically encompasses every situation possible in the world with sixty-four hexagrams. Each hexagram is made up of a different combination of broken and unbroken lines. According to Chinese tradition, the culture hero Fu Xi first made the trigrams (two of which make a hexagram). At the very least, the notion of whole and divided lines goes back well beyond Zhou times, probably into the Xia (2205–1766 BCE, traditional) and Shang (1766–1150 BCE) times. The core of the *Book of Changes* is attributed to King Wen, father of the founder of the Zhou dynasty (1150–249 BCE). King Wen is thought to have arranged the hexagrams and written short verses (called Judgments) on each one. Presumably he was held captive by the last Shang ruler when he did this work on the divination manual.

Spring and Autumn Annals

The *Spring and Autumn Annals* is a chronicle of events from 242 years in Lu, the state in which Confucius was born. To say that Confucius "made" rather than "wrote" the book conveys the fact that this Lu chronicle was basically a compilation of old government records – with what seems to have involved only minimal editorial judgments. Confucius added no interpretative comments. The *Annals* are classified into sections covering the rule of various dukes. Typically events are identified in terms of the day, month, and season of the year in which it occurred. For example, a chapter in the book on Duke Chaou reads as follows:

1. In the [duke's] twenty-fifth year, in spring, Shuh-sun Shay went to Sung.
2. In summer, Shuh E had a meeting with Chaou Yang . . . and Little Choo in Hwang-foo.
3. Grackles came to Loo and built nests in trees.
4. In autumn, in the seventh month, on the first Sin day there was a great sacrifice for rain. On the last Sin day, we sacrificed for rain again.
5. In the ninth month, on Ke-hai, the duke retired to Ts'e. He halted at Yang-chow.
6. The marquis of Ts'e came to condole with the duke in Yay-tsing.
7. In winter, in the tenth month, on Mow-shin, Shuh-sun Shay died.

8. In the eleventh month, on Ke-hae, Tso, duke of Sung, died in K'euh-keih.
9. In the twelfth month, the marquis of Ts'e took Yun.

(*Spring and Autumn Annals* X.25 in Legge 1960, 1970: 707)

The *Spring and Autumn Annals* became a model for historical summations in Chinese Confucian culture. Mencius praised the *Spring and Autumn Annals*, which Confucius undertook to write on his own private authority without an order from his ruler. Confucius prized his book as an instructive piece of history from

BOX 12.2 INTERPRETATIONS: HOW HONEST AND THOUGHTFUL WAS CONFUCIUS?

Despite the praise Confucius received for the rectification of names, his historical work seems to be characterized by concealment. James Legge (1815–1897) read with care the *Spring and Autumn Annals*, which is traditionally attributed to Confucius. And though he said it pained him to criticize Confucius, Legge was forced to conclude the following about the author of the Confucian classic:

> First, he had no reverence for truth in history, – I may say no reverence for truth, without any modification. . . . Second, he shrank from looking the truth fairly in the face. It was through this attribute of weakness that he so frequently endeavoured to hide the truth from himself and others, by ignoring it altogether, or by giving an imperfect and misleading account of it. . . . Third, he had more sympathy with power than with weakness, and would overlook wickedness and oppression in authority rather than resentment and revenge in men who were suffering from them. He could conceive of nothing so worthy of condemnation as to be insubordinate.
>
> (Legge 1960, 1970: 49)

Legge discussed several cases of suppression, concealment, and misrepresentation found in the *Spring and Autumn Annals*. For instance: (1) Confucius ignored the deaths of two dukes who had renounced allegiance to the Zhou emperor, probably because their death notices would have called them "kings" while the Zhou only acknowledged them as "viscounts." (2) Confucius used the same word "died" to describe several very different deaths, as by murder, poison, and natural, and thus glossed over vicious political ambition and intrigue. (3) Confucius simply stated that a certain duke's widow "retired" to another state, whereas she actually fled for her life – having been an accomplice to her husband's murder and guilty of incest with her half-brother (see Legge 1960, 1970: 40–49).

James Legge criticized the author of the *Spring and Autumn Annals* not only because he suppressed truth, but also because he lacked originality. Confucius is known for demanding that his students think for themselves by extrapolating upon ideas. Thus the lack of any interpretation in the *Spring and Autumn Annals* disappointed Legge, who said this about the text:

> The paragraphs are always brief. Each one is designed to commemorate a fact; . . . [I]t can hardly be said that there is anything in the language to convey to us the shadow of an idea of the author's feeling about it. The notices, for we cannot call them narratives, are absolutely unimpassioned. A base murder and a shining act of heroism are chronicled just as the eclipses of the sun are chronicled. So and so took place; – that is all. No details are given; no judgment is expressed.
>
> (Legge 1960, 1970: 3)

So how might concealment and the absence of interpretation in the *Spring and Autumn Annals* be reconciled with Confucius' commitment to intellectual curiosity and the rectification of names? What might be the reasons for Confucius' style of writing history?

which future rulers could learn. Yet many times Confucius concealed the truth in presenting such a lean text (see Box 12.2). For example, in the above account of the duke's twenty-fifth year a reader does not know without a commentary or historical background that when the duke "retired" to Ce, he was actually *fleeing for his life* after rebelling against the minister who had kept him in a miserable state of subjection (Legge 1960, 1970: 43).

SUPPORTIVE TEXTURE: CONFUCIAN TRADITION

The Four Books

Beyond the Five Classics, the **Four Books** stand as the core Confucian texts: (1) *Analects*, (2) *Great Learning*, (3) *Doctrine of the Mean*, and (4) *Mencius*. Tradition holds that these represent a succession in the transmission of Confucian philosophy from the Master through the disciple Zeng-zi (Tseng-tzu) to Confucius' grandson Zi Si (Tzu-ssu) – and down to Zi Si's disciple's student Mencius. Zeng-zi's *Great Learning* and Zi Si's *Doctrine of the Mean* were originally chapters in the *Book of Rites*, but were excerpted due to their seminal value in summarizing Confucian ethics and metaphysics. The Four Books were used for civil service examinations in China from 1313 to 1905, along with the Song Confucian Zhu Xi's commentaries.

Analects

Confucius did not write down his teachings, but notes were collected by his disciples and assembled in a collection of sayings known as the *Analects*. Confucius claimed that he transmitted what was taught to him, and was faithful to the Ancients. So, if we take Confucius at his word, he has left us with a most traditional teaching. The creativeness of the *Analects* comes in the application of ancient Chinese wisdom to the circumstances of his day. The wisdom of the Ancients had been corrupted, and Confucius tried to teach the cultivation of character and reinstate tradition as exemplified by the legendary sage kings and early Zhou rulers. In the *Analects* Confucius emphasized the importance of clear speech. He said:

> If names are not rectified, then language will not be appropriate, and if language is not appropriate, affairs will not be successfully carried out. If affairs are not successfully carried out, rites and music will not flourish, and if rites and music do not flourish, punishments will not hit the mark. If punishments do not hit the mark, the people will have nowhere to put hand or foot. Therefore the names used by the noble person must be appropriate for speech, and his speech must be appropriate for action. In regard to language, the noble person allows no carelessness, that is all.
>
> (*Analects* 13:3 in deBary and Bloom 1999: 56)

This teaching came to be known as the **rectification of names**, meaning the principle of living up to one's prescribed social role (e.g., the ruler should live up to the name "ruler); making the meaning of names (words) clear and consistent. Confucius thought that rulers of his day were not living up to the name "ruler."

Great Learning

Zhu Xi divided the *Great Learning* into a "text" with ten chapters of commentary, and then added another layer of commentary. Zhu Xi claimed that Confucius' student Zeng-zi wrote the ten commentaries and recorded Confucius' words in the "text." The book sums up key aspects of three Confucian concerns: education, morality, and politics. It teaches eight steps intended to lead adult learners to actualize the Confucian moral and social agenda: (1) the investigation of things, (2) extension of knowledge, (3) sincerity of will, (4) rectification of the mind, (5) cultivation of the personal life, (6) regulation of the family, (7) national order, and (8) world peace (Chan 1963: 84). The *Great Learning* shows the application of ren through a balance of individual and social concerns. The title indicates the core value of education in the Confucian tradition – learning. And these words from the "text" (which is under 500 words in translation) capture Confucius' concern for development of one's character: "From the Son of Heaven to ordinary people, all, without exception, should regard cultivating the person as the root" (deBary and Bloom 1999: 331).

Doctrine of the Mean

A tradition states that Confucius' grandson Zi Si wrote this metaphysical text. It treats two subjects about which Confucius was fairly silent: (1) the way of Heaven and (2) human nature. Some passages reflect material in the *Book of Mencius*, which tends to be more mystical than the *Analects*. The opening lines of the *Doctrine of the Mean* give a taste of its subtle content:

> What Heaven (*T'ien*, Nature) imparts to man is called human nature. To follow our nature is called the Way (Tao). Cultivating the Way is called education. The Way cannot be separated from us for a moment. What can be separated from us is not the Way. Therefore the superior man is cautious over what he does not see and apprehensive over what he does not hear. There is nothing more visible than what is hidden and nothing more manifest than what is subtle. Therefore the superior man is watchful over himself when he is alone.
>
> (Chan 1963: 98)

The *Doctrine of the Mean* emphasizes moderation (i.e., the "mean") as a prescription for harmony between human beings and the cosmos. The idea that a person should not act according to extremes captures Confucius' attitude in everything from hunting (fish, but not with a net) to emotion (experience joy without abandon, grief without self-injury). Both Daoist and Buddhist scholars were drawn to the *Doctrine of the Mean* for its intuitive appeal.

The Mencius

Mencius is counted as the second great Confucian thinker after Confucius. He composed the brief essays collected in the *Mencius*. The book advances Confucian thought in asserting definitively that human nature was good. Mencius extended the notion of humaneness (ren) to government as a whole, and made recommendations as to how Government by Goodness should be applied in practical political terms. Mencius advised rulers to cultivate virtue as well as attend to nitty-gritty matters such as instituting the well-field system (whereby land is divided up into a 3 × 3 square with a well in the center that is shared by eight family farms). The *Mencius* also contains profound passages on the nature of life and death. A couple of passages from the *Mencius* may give a sense of the depth and range of Mencius' thought:

> Mencius said, "When Heaven is about to confer a great responsibility on any man, it will exercise his mind with suffering, subject his sinews and bones to hard work, expose his body to hunger, put him to poverty, place obstacles in the paths of his deeds, so as to stimulate his and, harden his nature, and improve wherever he is incompetent."
>
> (6B15)
>
> Mencius said, "All things are already complete in oneself. There is no greater joy than to examine oneself and be sincere. When in one's conduct one vigorously exercises altruism, humanity is not far to seek, but right by him."(7A4)
>
> Mencius said: "It would be better to have no *Book of History* than to believe all of it. In its 'Completion of War' section [for example], I accept only two or three passages. A man of humanity has no enemy in the world."(7B3)
>
> (Chan 1963: 78, 79, 81)

FOUNDATIONAL TEXTURE: DAOIST TRADITION

Dao De Jing (Tao Te Ching)

Three key concepts from the ***Dao De Jing*** came to pervade Daoist thought: dao (way), de (power, virtue) and wu-wei (actionless action). Each word has layers of meaning that relate to the Daoist experience of being in the world. Beyond the literal translations the words convey great intuitive meaning for a Daoist.

Dao: the Way

The opening line of the *Dao De Jing* warns that the Dao cannot be known through words. The book starts with a paradox about the way. Lao-zi said, *Dao ke dao fei chang dao*. Three of the six opening words are simply "dao." In English this line has been rendered in many ways, and most do not keep all three instances of the word "dao."

Table 12.1 Opening line of the *Dao De Jing* in English translation[1]

TAO called TAO is not TAO.**
The Tao that can be expressed is not the eternal Tao.
The Tao that can be told is not the eternal Tao.
The Tao that can be talked about is not the true Tao.
The way that can be spoken of is not the constant way.
Tao that can be spoken of / Is not the Everlasting (*ch'ang*) Tao.

Notes [1]Translations are from Addiss and Lombardo (1993: 1); Ch'u Ta-Kao (1976: 11); Feng and English (1972: 1); Kwok, Palmer and Ramsay (2002: 27); Lau (1963: 57).
[2] Unless otherwise noted, all other translations from the *Dao De Jing* in this chapter are from Addiss and Lombardo.

Table 12.2 Verse 4 of the *Dao De Jing* in English translation[1]

TAO is empty – Its use never exhausted. Bottomless – The origin of all things. It blunts sharp edges, Unties knots, Softens glare, Becomes one with the dusty world. Deeply subsistent – I don't know whose child it is. It is older than the Ancestor.	The Tao is an empty vessel; it is used, but never filled. Oh, unfathomable source of ten thousand things! Blunt the sharpness, Untangle the knot, Soften the glare, Merge with dust. Oh, hidden deep but ever present! I do not know from whence it comes. It is the forefather of the emperors.

Note: [1] The translation on the left is from Addiss and Lombardo (1993: 4); the translation on the right is from Feng and English (1972: 4).

Although dao cannot be known through words, Lao-zi speaks poetically about it. A sense of the profound meaning of the word dao may be gotten from this verse, which begins by saying "empty dao" (*Tao ch'ung*).

De: power, virtue

The second word of Lao-zi's book's title adds tremendous value to the first. To the inexpressible dao is added de with its two worlds of meaning. De can be translated as power or virtue. Historically virtue and power have been closely associated in Chinese philosophy. To capture the meaning of de a reader should think of both power *and* virtue – even though a translation choice must be made. De is a spontaneous and inconspicuous power that flows through a person who comprehends the dao. This power is associated with true virtue, which has little to do with conventional morality. Lao-zi suggests that conventional morality arises only after people have lost their connection to the dao. Here the Daoist turns the Confucian virtues of ren (benevolence), yi (righteousness), and xiao (filial piety) on their heads.

Ta tao fei
Great TAO rejected:
Benevolence and righteousness appear.

Learning and knowledge professed:
Great hypocrites spring up.

Family relations forgotten:
Filial piety and affection arise.

The nation disordered:
Patriots come forth.

(*Dao De Jing* 18)

The fourth Confucian virtue is zhi (intelligence). From a Daoist point of view, De is virtue grounded in knowledge of reality that goes beyond concepts. Daoist intelligence involves knowing how to act without acting.

Wu-wei, actionless action

The actionless action of a sage is in tune with the way of Heaven. Wu-wei is the human expression of dao. A sage "acts and expects nothing, accomplishes and does not linger, [and] has no desire to seem worthy" (*Dao De Jing* 77).

> Heaven's TAO does not contend
> But prevails,
> Does not speak
> But responds,
> It is not summoned
> But arrives,
> Is utterly still
> But plans all actions.
>
> Heaven's net is wide, wide,
> Loose –
> But nothing slips through.
>
> (*Dao De Jing* 73)
>
> Act and you ruin it.
> Grasp and you lose it.
> Therefore the Sage
> Does not act
> *Wu wei*
> And so does not ruin
> *Ku wu pai*
> Does not grasp
> And so does not lose. . . .
>
> The Sage
> Helps all beings find their nature,
> But does not presume to act.
>
> (*Dao De Jing* 64)

Zhuang-zi (Chuang-tzu)

The second Daoist classic is the ***Zhuang-zi.*** Its author Zhuang-zi was not only a social critic but also a mystic dedicated to knowing the dao through actionless action. He puzzled over the nature of reality and played with the notion of transformation. Zhuang-zi often wrote himself into little vignettes, as in this exploration of change.

> Long ago, Chuang Chou [Zhuang-zi] dreamed he was a butterfly fluttering among trees, doing as he pleased, completely unaware of a Chuang Chou. A sudden awakening, and there, looking a little out of sorts, was Chuang Chou. Now I don't know whether it is Chou who dreamed he was a butterfly, or whether a butterfly dreams he's Chuang Chou. But between Chuang Chou and the butterfly, we ought to be able to find some sort of distinction. This is what's known as Things Changing.
>
> (*Chuang Tzu*, ch. 2 in Hamill and Seaton 1998: 18)

Zhuang-zi provided Daoist instructions on how to become an immortal through the practice of inner alchemy. According to Zhuang-zi's story the Yellow Emperor met Master Guang Cheng-zi on Mount Kong-tong. The master gave these instructions for actualizing "the primordial integrity of matter," and controlling the disintegrators of matter (*Zhuang Zi* XI in Giles 1974: 126).

> See nothing; hear nothing; let your soul be wrapped in quiet, and your body will begin to take proper form. Let there be absolute repose and absolute purity; do not weary your body nor disturb your vitality – and you will live forever. . . . Cherish that which is within you and shut off that which is without; for much knowledge is a curse. Then I will place you upon that abode of Great Light, which is the source of the positive Power [yang], and escort you through the gate of Profound Mystery, which is the source of the negative Power [yin].
>
> (*Chuang Tzu* XI in Giles 1974: 127)

Zhuang-zi was not systematic in his explanations and mostly just hints at details of meditation practice in his writing. Later proponents of Daoist Dark Learning went much further in writing down methods designed to bring immortality. Texts of the canon include esoteric matters such as: (1) alchemical prescriptions for medicines that bring immortality, and (2) meditation instructions on "creating the embryos of perfection within the body through the absorption of lunar and solar essences" (Bokenkamp 1997: 7).

SUPPORTIVE TEXTURE: DAOIST TRADITION

Guo Xiang's commentary on *Zhuang-zi*

Guo Xiang (d. 312 CE) examined the paradoxical nature of wu-wei in his commentary on the *Zhuang-zi*. He correlated wu-wei with knowledge of the dao. To be able to act without acting, Daoists must: (1) preserve their vital spirit, and (2) act in harmony with nature. A profound knowledge of the nature of reality is needed to do both of these things.

- ***Preserving qi.*** To preserve one's qi a person must not feel regret. But to avoid regret a person needs to penetrate the meaning of destiny.

  > Every one is in some situation, but not every one knows that every situation is destined. Therefore those [archers, for example] who are no[t] hit, consider themselves as specially skillful, and are thus much delighted. But at other times when they are hit, they regret their mistakes and thus hurt their spirit. That is because they know nothing about destiny.
  >
  > (Fung 1975: 101)

- ***Acting harmoniously.*** To act in harmony with nature a person must carefully observe the activity of various things that exist in the world. True understanding of the nature of things leads to action that respects their nature. Action that respects the nature of things is wu-wei, actionless action. Guo Xiang said, "Nonaction does not mean nothing doing [*sic*]. Let everything do what it does, and then its nature will be satisfied" (Fung 1975: 152). Wu-wei involves the recognition of one's own nature as well as the nature of other things. And as one acted out of respect for the nature of other things, so one must act out of respect for one's own nature. For Guo Xiang such self-respect meant allowing oneself to develop spontaneously without hankering after another's position.

  > With conscious effort some people try to be great artists, but they can never succeed. Yet without knowing how, the great artists spontaneously become artists. With conscious effort some people try to be sages, but they can never succeed. Yet without knowing how, the sages spontaneously become sages. Not only that the sages and artists are difficult to be imitated, we cannot even be fools, or dogs, by simply wishing and trying to be.
  >
  > (Fung 1975: 101)

The spontaneous action of wu-wei is not equivalent to acting irresponsibly according to one's instincts. To act spontaneously a person must have a free flow of vital energy through the body and a mind that is not obstructed. Knowing this, Daoists developed a method of spontaneous action involving psychophysical exercises (see Box 12.4).

CROSS-OVER TEXTURE

Xun-zi's *Art of War*

During the Warring States period (479–221 BCE) Xun-zi observed that as the various states of Lu, Qin, Song, and others were contending for power, great resources were expended. A single conflict could involve half a million casualties, representing 50 percent of a standing army. Thus Xun-zi wrote *The Art of War* as counsel to rulers who were involved in such massive and disruptive conflicts. He viewed war as a last alternative and said that war should involve the least possible loss of life and resources. For example, to "*preserve resources and minimize their expenditure* . . . he advocated a preference for *capturing the whole target intact* rather than destroying it" (Wee 2003: 80).

> *Sūn Zi* clearly favored capturing the whole intact rather than destroying it. To him, winning is not only about destroying the enemy. Rather, it is about *getting stronger*. This means minimizing the expense of resources. It would be even better if one could win without even raising an army! For this reason, he focused a lot of attention on using non-direct confrontation strategies (including the use of diplomacy) and on winning the "heart" of the enemy. Clearly he did not favour an all-out conflict. In fact, he termed the assault of walled cities as the lowest of all strategies.
>
> (Wee 2003: 80)

He said that every effort should be made to bring war to as quick an end as possible, and warned against inappropriate interference of rulers in warfare when they are ignorant of military matters. The interference of rulers in war who lack military knowledge and experience creates disaster for the state.

Xun-zi's ideas on the virtues of a Master of War reflect Mencius' notion of Government by Goodness. He noted that soldiers are drawn to the generals who possess ren, while Mencius said people would naturally want to come under the dominion of a ruler who governed with humaneness (ren). Along those lines Xun-zi advocated treating prisoners-of-war well so that they could be won over (2.34–35). Consistent with the Confucian concern for keeping the best people in political office, Xun-zi named five acts that harm the people: (1) using public office for personal benefit, (2) promoting inequality before the law, (3) toleration of crime and violence and hiding the truth, (4) monopolizing government administration by favoring friends, using taxation to reap profit, enriching themselves and their families, and (5) extensively tailoring welfare projects and general expenditures resulting in loss of jobs. Xun-zi insisted that a person who commits any of these five acts should be dismissed from office (see Cleary 2003: 238).

PART 3 PERFORMANCE IN CHINESE TRADITIONS

DIVINATION IN THE *BOOK OF CHANGES*

The *Book of Changes* is probably the oldest of the Chinese classics. It is a divination text that has been in use for about 3,000 years. Tradition holds that around 1000 BCE King Wen wrote a series of short verses called Judgments that form the core of the text. Layers of commentary were added over a period of a thousand years. In his old age Confucius made a deep study of the *Book of Changes*, and though he did not edit or change the form of this classic, tradition says that he wrote a commentary on it. "The most plausible assumption is that he discussed this book with his disciples, just as he did other classics, and told them his thoughts about it. Then disciples of a later generation must have gathered these opinions together as commentaries or introductory chapters" (Wilhelm 1960: 12).

Symbolism of the sixty-four hexagrams

The meaning of "change" in the *Book of Changes* indicates that every situation in the world is dynamic. And though any given situation is represented by a hexagram, it is in the process of changing into something else. The movement through the sixty-four hexagrams occurs within a fixed pattern as everything in the cosmos changes within certain patterns. As day and night, the movement of heavenly bodies, and the seasons display a pattern, so the change from one hexagram to the next is not haphazard or arbitrary. By knowing the quality of the moment as represented by the hexagram that comes up in the divination, a person can think of how to respond according to the dao to overcome danger, weakness, and so forth. By contemplating the nature of the moment, one also knows how best to act in accordance with it and maximize its benefits.

Sixty-four hexagrams embodied in the *Book of Changes* represent all the possible combinations of six lines that are either yang (whole) or yin (divided). Thus the content represents a totality that covers all situations in the cosmos. Each hexagram is named according to what the unique pattern of lines symbolizes. The sixty-four hexagrams are named after many types of situations.

> We find images representing the primary needs of man – for instance, The Corners of the Mouth, symbolizing nourishment – and also images that picture the evolution of the personality: Youthful Folly, Molting, Biting Through, Possession, Return (The Turning Point), The Obstacle, Oppression, Standstill, Waiting, Decrease, Retreat; then Break-Through, Pushing Upward, Development, Increase, Abundance, and (the two last images) After Completion and Before Completion. Then there are situations taken from social life: The Marrying Maiden, The Clan, The Well, Fellowship with Men, Holding Together, Approach, Wooing,

BOX 12.3 SYMBOLS: YIN AND YANG

The meaning of yin and yang evolved over generations of use. Originally the Chinese character for yin was "cloud," meaning it was something that shadowed or made dark. The image of the cloud is also of water that brings nature to life. The character for yang was a yak tail or banner flying in the sun. It was something bright. The signifier for "mountain slope" was added to each. Thus yin was the north side of a hill (which was shady) or the southern bank of a river. By contrast, yang was the south side of a hill (which was sunny) or the north side of a river. Yin came to represent darkness and yang came to represent light. Gradually many sets of opposites were associated with yang and yin. The image of a circle divided into two drop-like shapes (each containing a seed of the other) symbolizes the dynamic interaction of yin and yang.

Table 12.3 Symbolism of yin and yang

	Yang symbolism	**Yin symbolism**
———	sunny side	shady side
YANG LINE	warm	cold
— —	dry	wet
YIN LINE	bright	dark
— —	masculine	feminine
— —	active	passive
———	procreative	receptive
TRIGRAM	positive	negative
("THUNDER")	mythic animal: dragon	mythic animal: phoenix
— —	breath	blood
— —	creative	receptive
———	heaven	earth
———	head	abdominal cavity
———	round, expansive	square, flat
———	energy	form
HEXAGRAM	red	black
("GREAT POWER")	spiritual soul	physical soul

Coming to Meet, Following, The Power of the Great, Peace; but also Opposition and conflict. Further, individual character traits are singled out: Modesty, Grace, Innocence, Enthusiasm, Inner Truth. Finally, we find images of suprapersonal significance: The Clinging, The Arousing, Holding Still, The Gentle, The Joyous, and, above all (the first two hexagrams), The Creative and The Receptive.

(Wilhelm 1960: 4–5)

The hexagrams become meaningful based on the relationship between the six yin or yang lines. The meaning of the combination of lines is developed with respect to: (1) polarity, (2) the seasons, and (3) manifestations of the natural world. A polar opposite is expressed through a single line; each season is expressed through a combination of two lines; and natural manifestations are expressed through a series of trigrams. When used in divination the form of a hexagram "grows" like a plant from the ground up – the first line appearing at the bottom. The entire schema is derived from combinations of whole and divided lines (see Table 12.4).

Levels of meaning in the *Book of Changes*

Understanding the deeper meaning of hexagrams that come up in a divination session takes years of study. It could happen that the meaning remains obscure. A traditional Confucian saying indicates the depth of the *Book of Changes*, whose symbols take time to penetrate.

> First take up the words,
> Ponder their meaning,
> Then the fixed rules reveal themselves.
> But if you are not the right man,
> The meaning will not manifest itself to you.
>
> (Wilhelm 1960: 65)

The Daoist commentator Wang Bi from the Dark Learning movement identified four levels of meaning in the *Book of Changes*: (1) words, (2) images, (3) meaning, and (4) precepts. He said: (1) once the image was grasped, one could dispense with the words; (2) once the meaning was grasped, one could dispense with the image; and (3) once the precept was grasped, one could dispense with the meaning. Wang Bi explains this poetically as follows:

> It is like following a trail to catch a hare. Once one has the hare, one forgets the trail. Or it is like putting out wicker traps to catch fish. Once one has the fish, one forgets the traps. Now, the words are the trails of the images, and the images are the traps of the meaning. The images arise from the meaning, but if one retains only the images then what is retained are not the right images. The words arise from the images, but if one retains only the words then what is retained are not the right words. Thus only by forgetting the images can one grasp the meaning, and only by forgetting the words can one grasp the images. In fact, grasping the meaning consists in forgetting the images, and grasping the images consists in forgetting the words. . . . Only when one forgets images and studies the meaning do the precepts emerge.
>
> (*Chou I Lüeh-li* in Wilhelm 1960: 87–88)

A sample coin toss

Divination with the *Book of Changes* involves a method of selecting yarrow stalks or tossing coins. The coin method is simpler as the hexagram is built from six tosses of three coins. The coin's head could represent the yang number 3, in which case its tail would represent the yin number 2. (Yang numbers are always

Table 12.4 Evolution of the eight trigrams in the *Book of Changes*

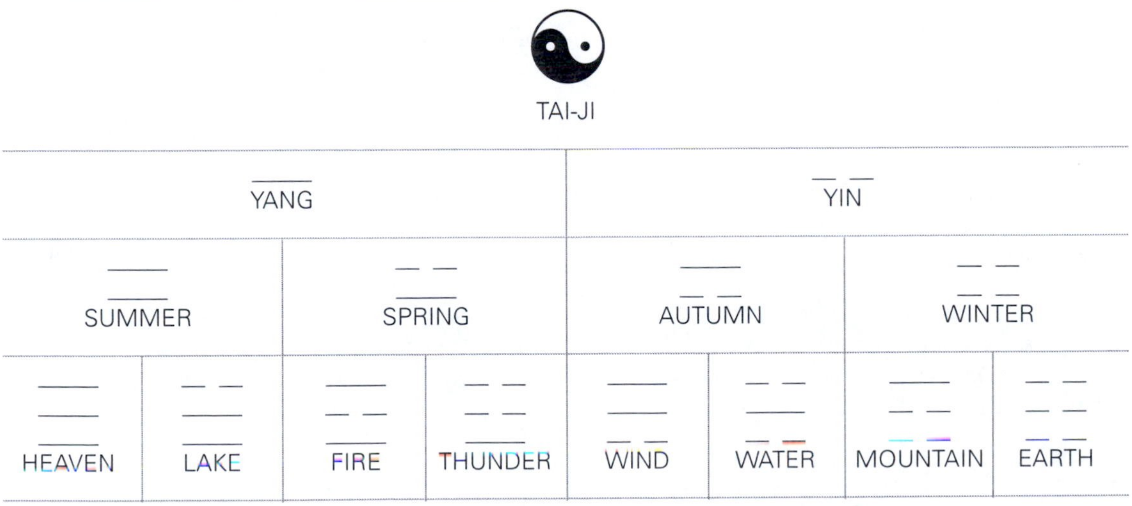
TAI-JI
YANG
YIN
SUMMER
SPRING
AUTUMN
WINTER
HEAVEN
LAKE
FIRE
THUNDER
WIND
WATER
MOUNTAIN
EARTH

BOX 12.4 A SPIRITUAL PATH: TAI-JI QUAN

Plate 12.4 "Gathering the qi of Heaven." Daoists developed several forms of psychophysical movement based on the absorption and circulation of environmental energy through the human body. The foundation of movement was opening up to universal energy, and circulating that energy according to various patterns through psychophysical movement. Qi-gong was the basic discipline on which the martial art of Tai-ji quan developed. Both work with the basic Chinese insight regarding the complementarity of yin and yang forces.

ADVICE ON THE PRACTICE OF TAI-JI QUAN

Toong Ying-kit, a modern master of Tai-ji quan, had many insights on the practice of his art. Eleven key points about the practice of Tai-ji quan, based on Master H. H. Lui's translation of Toong Ying-kit's "Experience Talk" are highlighted here (Lui ca. 1978: 1–10).

Point 1. Toong Ying-kit points out that Tai-ji quan is an "inner" as opposed to an "outer" school boxing system. While an outer system draws strength "from the bones," an inner system stores strength (called *gin*) in the sinews. He says that Tai-ji quan involves "no tense muscles or rigid joints" or "jumping up and down and other physical exertions."

Point 2. Toong Ying-kit advises the student of Tai-ji quan to focus on spirit, mind (will), and form (posture). Thus the practice involves seeking "excellence" in one's spiritual, mental, and physical dimensions.

Point 3. Toong Ying-kit says, "If your posture is not correct and your spiritual and mental aspect are not in harmony, then it will be like cooking an empty pan over a fire; regardless how long you hold it there, nothing can be cooked."

Point 4. Toong Ying-kit advises the student of Tai-ji quan to "inhale and exhale naturally" without exertion. He says that eventually, when one's "movement is in good shape," breathing becomes naturally "very calm and even."

Point 5. In the practice of Tai-ji quan one should "relax the shoulders and drop the elbows." Toong Ying-kit says that "one must not gather his strength into the area between the shoulder and upper back." Rather strength must be relocated "to the area between the shoulder and the elbow."

Point 6. The correct posture in Tai-ji quan involves raising one's head and lifting one's inner thighs upward. This way the head can "relax and become straight and central," while the *chi* (energy) is encouraged to rise upwards from the "lower part" of the spine.

Point 7. A student of Tai-ji quan can train and improve while "merely walking or sitting down." Movement will improve through learning to "heighten the sensitivity" of the body and exercising the "mind to mobilize the 'chi'." Toong Ying-kit gives this example: "[S]uppose unconsciously you pick up a teacup. If you hold it tightly then you feel one thing, and if you relax your fingers, you feel something else. . . . By varying your movement you will feel how the 'chi' works in your body."

Point 8. Toong Ying-kit says the Tai-ji quan classics teach that "inner strength is rooted in the feet, developed through the legs, controlled by the waist, and expressed through the fingers."

Point 9. Toong Ying-kit reminds students that "[o]ne yin and one yang is called Tao," and says by way of explanation, "[o]ne yin, one yang; one emptiness, one solidness." He advises students to "pay attention to this yin-yang theory" when they move an arm or a foot. In this context he relays Lao-zi's mysterious comment "I am good at the art of concealing." About this famous phrase Toong Ying-kit says: "This has very deep meaning."

Point 10. Toong Ying-kit quotes Mencius as saying, "When one puts his heart into something, he is able to understand his own nature. When one is able to understand his own nature, he is able to understand heaven." This comment is food for thought.

Point 11. Toong Ying-kit observes that Tai-ji quan brings great strength when practiced properly. He says, "Once a man returns to nature, back from the acquired stage to original nature, his strength is unlimited. It's amazing."

odd, while yin numbers are always even.) Three heads yield 9, which is a changing yang line. Three tails yield 6, which is a changing yin line. Any other combination of heads and tails does not yield a changing line. A changing line means that after the hexagram is produced it will "change" into a second hexagram. The form of the second hexagram depends on which of its six lines are changing lines. A hexagram without changing lines does not lead to another hexagram in the divination reading. Here is an example of two hexagrams that came from six tosses of three coins. T = tail with a value of 2; H = head with a value of 3.

> Toss 1: H, H, H (3 + 3 + 3 = 9) yields a changing YANG line.
> Toss 2: T, T, H (2 + 2 + 3 = 7) yields an unchanging YANG line.
> Toss 3: H, H, T (3 + 3 + 2 = 8) yields an unchanging YIN line.
> Toss 4: H, H, T (3 + 3 + 2 = 8) yields an unchanging YIN line.
> Toss 5: T, T, H (2 + 2 + 3 = 7) yields an unchanging YANG line.
> Toss 6: H, H, T (3 + 3 + 2 = 8) yields an unchanging YIN line.

This coin toss produces the two hexagrams shown in Table 12.5.

The Judgment on hexagram 60 given by King Wen says:

> LIMITATION. Success.
>
> Galling limitation must not be persevered in.

The commentary on King Wen's Judgment explains:

> A lake occupies a limited space. When more water comes into it, it overflows. . . . Limitations are troublesome, but they are effective. If we live economically in normal times, we are prepared for times of want. Limitations are also indispensable in the regulation of world conditions. In nature there are fixed limits for summer and winter, day and night, and these limits give the year its meaning. In the same way, economy, by setting fixed limits upon expenditures, acts to preserve property and prevent injury to the people.
>
> (Wilhelm and Baynes 1971: 231)

About the changing line, the *Book of Changes* says that Confucius made this comment:

> Where disorder develops, words are the first steps. If the prince is not discreet, he loses his servant. If the servant is not discreet, he loses his life. If germinating things are not handled with discretion, the perfecting of them is impeded. Therefore the superior man is careful to maintain silence and does not go forth.
>
> (Wilhelm and Baynes 1971: 232–233)

Table 12.5 Reading from sample coin toss

Hexagram 60 Limitations (Water over Lake) changes to #29 Danger (Water over Water)

— —		8: unchanging yin	→	— —		The trigram image of Water derives from the fact that water is soft (yin) outside and hard (yang) on the inside. It is also associated with danger and the second son.
———	WATER	7: unchanging yang	→	———	WATER	
— —		8: unchanging yin	→	— —		
— —		8: unchanging yin	→	— —		The trigram image of Lake derives from the fact that a lake is hard at the bottom (two yang lines) and softer at the top (yin). It also means joy and the third daughter.
———	LAKE	7: unchanging yang	→	———	WATER	
———		9: changing yang	→	— —		

Note: The hexagram Limitation changed into the hexagram Danger because the first toss produced a changing line. When interpreting the coin tosses, special attention is paid to the symbolism of the changing line, which moved from yang to yin.

This interpretation of number 9 at the bottom of the hexagram comes from the fact that within the hexagram is the further symbolism of a gate. Thus seeing locked doors, the person represented by the changing yang line at the bottom of the hexagram does not move ahead.

The entire hexagram of Limitation changes to the hexagram of Danger. Hexagram 29 is called Danger because it is a doubling of the trigram of Water which stands for the abysmal or danger. The commentary says that in the human sphere of action the trigram of Water also "represents the heart, the soul locked up within the body, the principle of light enclosed in the dark – that is, reason" (Wilhelm and Baynes 1971: 115). This is because yang (light) is surrounded by yin (dark). King Wen's Judgment on hexagram 29 reads:

> The Abysmal repeated.
> If you are sincere, you have success in your heart,
> And whatever you do succeeds.

The commentary on the Judgment explains that if a person is sincere when confronted with difficulties, he or she succeeds.

> Water sets the example for the right conduct under such circumstances [of danger]. If flows on and on, and merely fills up all the places through which it flows; it does not shrink from any dangerous spot nor from any plunge, and nothing can make it lose its own essential nature. It remains true to itself under all conditions. Thus likewise, if one is sincere when confronted with difficulties, the heart can penetrate the meaning of the situation. And once we have gained inner mastery of a problem, it will come about naturally that the action we take will succeed. In danger all that counts is really carrying out all that has to be done – thoroughness – and going forward, in order not to perish through tarrying in the danger.
>
> (Wilhelm and Baynes 1971: 115)

The *Book of Changes* sheds an optimistic light on every situation in the world. Each of the sixty-four hexagrams represents a basic circumstance in life – and images derived from the arrangement of yin and yang lines in the hexagram indicate how a jun-zi might best approach the situation at hand. The ancient Chinese text is based in the confidence that a person who understands his or her circumstances can act appropriately according to the dao.

KEY POINTS

- Chinese religions hearken back to culture heroes and sage kings who are supposed to have lived in the third millennium BCE. Yet the earliest archeological evidence (oracle bones with writing on them) dates from ca. 1300 BCE when divination was practiced at the Shang court.
- The two early Chinese concepts of supreme power were Shang-di and Tian, revered by Shang and Zhou rulers respectively. The notion of the formless dao with its yin and yang manifestations became a key philosophical expression of the ultimate principle used by both Daoist and Confucian thinkers.
- The sixth through third centuries BCE are known in China as the era of 100 scholars. The most important thinkers of that era included: Lao-zi, Confucius, Mo-zi, Mencius, Zhuang-zi, and Xun-zi. Politically the Legalist disciples of Xun-zi exerted tremendous influence, even at times when the Confucian tradition was considered official.
- Confucians viewed society as an extended family that included ancestors. Personal responsibility was outlined in terms of five social relationships: ruler–subject, father–son, husband–wife, elder brother–younger brother, and friend–friend. Filial piety (xiao) is a core value to this day in East Asian countries (such as Vietnam, Korea, and Japan) that were influenced by the Confucian tradition.
- The concepts of dao, de (power, virtue), and wu-wei (actionless action) discussed in the *Dao De Jing* and *Zhuang-zi* provided a foundation for later Daoist Dark Learning which involved a quest for health and even immortality. The Celestial Masters sect is the first group to found a Daoist church (second century CE) and their tradition still flourishes today in Taiwan.
- The five ancient books known as the Confucian classics are: *Book of History*, *Book of Rites*, *Book of Odes*, *Book of Changes*, and the *Spring and Autumn Annals*. King Wen whose son founded the Zhou dynasty (ca. 1000 BCE) was supposed to have written the core text of the *Book of Changes*, which attracted much attention from both Daoist and Confucian thinkers over the ages.
- The Confucian revivalist Zhu Xi was the first to present these four books in one volume: *Analects*, *Great Learning*, *Doctrine of the Mean*, and *Mencius*. These became the basic texts used for civil service examinations in China from 1313 to 1905. In 1949 Mao Ze-dong's *Red Book* replaced Confucian classics, and a Chinese religious crisis culminated in the Great Proletarian Cultural Revolution of 1966 to 1976.

STUDY QUESTIONS

1. What was the Mandate of Heaven, and under what circumstances did the concept of a mandate develop?
2. Define these five key Confucian notions: cultural patterns (wen), filial piety (xiao), the genuine human (jun-zi), ritual propriety (li), Heaven (Tian), benevolence (ren), and the five social relationships.
3. Name the Five Classics and Four Books of the Confucian tradition. Describe their contents.
4. Define the three Daoist concepts as used in the *Dao De Jing* and the *Zhuang-zi*: dao, de, and wu-wei. Note how they were applied in the martial art of Tai-ji quan.
5. Compare the writings of Mencius and Xun-zi. Why were Confucians reluctant to consider Xun-zi a true Confucian?
6. Name the cultural progress made during the Qin and Han dynasties. Contrast their official ideologies.
7. Describe the symbolism of the *Book of Changes* in terms of agricultural imagery, harmony, and balance.

GLOSSARY

Two main systems of romanizing Chinese characters are: (1) pinyin and (2) Wade-Giles. This book follows the pinyin system. However, in the timeline, glossary and index the Wade-Giles form is printed in parentheses. In cases where a latinized name is used (as with Confucius and Mencius), the pinyin form is given in parentheses. Direct quotes from outside sources and bibliographic entries preserve the romanization used by the source.

dao (tao) Way, road, path; term used in Chinese traditions for the way of the universe.

Dao De Jing (*Tao Te Ching*) Chinese Daoist classic attributed to Lao-zi, also known as the *Lao-zi* (*Lao-tzu*).

de (te) Power or virtue; term used in Chinese traditions for the moral force that brings social and cosmic influence.

Five Classics Five ancient texts that became foundational texts in the Confucian tradition: *Book of Odes*, *Book of Rites*, *Book of History*, *Spring and Autumn Annals*, and *Book of Changes*.

Four Books Four texts that became the basis for the Chinese Confucian civil service examination from 1313 to 1905: *Analects*, *Mencius*, *Great Learning*, and *Doctrine of the Mean*.

hexagram A figure made up of six lines (whole or divided) stacked on top of each other. The Chinese *Book of Changes* is based on sixty-four hexagrams.

jun-zi (chün-tzu) Princely person, gentleman; word for prince in ancient China; Confucius used it to mean someone of sound moral character.

li Ancient Chinese rituals as prescribed in the *Book of Rites*; Confucius added the sense of propriety; in the neo-Confucian School of Principle it is the principle (archetype, law) that governs the form of all material things.

qi (ch'i) Chinese term for subtle life energy that runs through both the body and the cosmos; in the yogīc traditions of India it is called by the Sanskrit term prāṇa, meaning subtle breath.

rectification of names Chinese (especially Confucian) principle of living up to one's prescribed social role (e.g., the ruler should live up to the name "ruler"); making the meaning of names (words) clear and consistent.

ren (jen) Benevolence, humaneness; a key Confucian virtue.

Tai-ji Supreme Ultimate; in Chinese thought the reservoir of infinite potentiality that embodies yin and yang.

Tai-ji quan Supreme Ultimate Fist; Chinese martial art based on concepts in the *Dao De Jing* and *Book of Changes*.

Tian (T'ien) Chinese term for Heaven introduced by ancient Chinese Zhou rulers in the second millennium BCE.

wen (Chinese) Pattern; culture; civilization.

wu-wei (wu-wei) Actionless action; in Chinese thought (especially Daoist) the paradox of doing nothing, and leaving nothing undone.

xiao (hsiao) Filial piety; reverence in ancient China for spirits, one's ancestors, and one's deceased parents. Confucius underplayed the spirits, and emphasized living parents.

yin/yang In Chinese thought, the complementary principles that manifest in all things in the universe, such as female, dark, receptive (which are yin), and male, light, creative (which are yang).

Zhuang-zi (*Chuang-tzu*) Chinese Daoist classic attributed to Zhuang-zi.

KEY READING

Bokenkamp, Stephen R. (1997) *Early Daoist Scriptures*, Berkeley, Los Angeles, and London: University of California Press.

Chan, Wing-tsit (trans. and comp.) (1963) *A Sourcebook in Chinese Philosophy*, Princeton: NJ: Princeton University Press.

Gernet, Jacques ([1972] 1982) *A History of Chinese Civilization*, trans. J. R. Foster, Cambridge: Cambridge University Press.

MacInnis, Donald E. (comp.) (1989) *Religion in China Today: Policy and Practice*, Maryknoll, NY: Orbis Books.

Morton, W. Scott and Lewis, Charlton M. ([1980] 2005) *China: Its History and Culture*, New York: McGraw-Hill.

Robinet, Isabelle (1997) *Taoism: Growth of a Religion*, trans. Phyllis Brooks, Stanford, CA: Stanford University Press.

Yang, C. K. (1967) *Religion in Chinese Society*, Berkeley and Los Angeles: University of California Press.

CHAPTER 13
Shintō tradition

TIMELINE

	BCE	
Jimmu Tennō	660 (traditional)	
	250 BCE–250 CE	Yayoi (Bronze-Iron) period
	CE	
Pimiku	?201–?269	
Shōtoku Taishi	574–622	
	712	*Kojiki* complete
	720	*Nihongi* complete
	710	Nara established as capital
	794	Heian established as capital
	618–907	Tang dynasty in China
	960–1279	Song dynasty in China
Murasaki Shikibu	b. 978?	
	1192–1867	15 shōguns rule
	1192–1333	Kamakura era
	1603–1867	Tokugawa era
	1614	Christianity banned
	1650	First Thanksgiving pilgrimage to Ise (others 1705, 1771, 1830)
Motoori Norinaga	1730–1801	
Nakayama Miki	1798–1887	
	28 March 1868	Official separation of Buddhism from Shintō
	1870–1945	State Shintō
Emperor Hirohito	1901–1989	
	1945–1952	Japan under Allied forces
	1 January 1946	Emperor Hirohito declares his humanity
Emperor Akihito	b. 1933 (r. 1990–present)	
	1996	2000th anniversary of Ise

The indigenous religion of Japan is known as **Shintō**. The Japanese archipelago comprises four main islands: Hokkaidō, Honshū, Shikoku, and Kyūshū. Early migration patterns to and from these islands are not well understood. The distant ancestors of the Japanese people are Mongols from Korea, Malayo-Polynesians from China and the South Pacific, and the Caucasian-like "hairy" **Ainu** peoples who seem to have been the first inhabitants of the islands. By the time the Japanese were first recorded in history in the 200s CE the immigrant groups were already an ethnically unified people – except for pockets of Ainu who today are found far to the north on Hokkaidō. Although the physical distance between the Japanese islands and the mainland is not great, until modern times travel proved to be difficult and the political will to engage with Korea and China varied with the times. In general there was no continuous contact between Japan and the mainland until the mid-1800s.

Early Shintō was fundamentally an expressive religion that focused on purification and communion with the **kami**. Over time Shintō went through several key changes – particularly as it interfaced with Buddhist and Confucian traditions from China. The various Shintō traditions include folk elements, Shintō-Buddhist variations, and Shintō as an imperial cult. Yet through the transformations Shintō kept its expressive character with a focus on ritual. The earliest Shintō writings existing today are two extensive chronicles: the *Kojiki* (Record of Ancient Matters) and the *Nihongi* (History of Japan), both issued in the eighth century CE. They begin with creation stories and continue into what amounts to a fairly reliable history of events that occurred after 400 CE. The main character in the stories is **Amaterasu**, who is the divine energy of the sun. She is said to be the ancestor of Japan's imperial family whose line continues unbroken from the first human emperor Jimmu until today. Historians place Jimmu's reign somewhere between 550 and 800 CE, while Shintō tradition situates him in the seventh century BCE. The Japanese people have often practiced Shintō along with other traditions. This remains true today in Japan where the **Kami Way** permeates Japanese culture regardless of other religious influences.

PART 1
SHINTŌ PLAYERS

THE ULTIMATE PRINCIPLE

Mysterious – nature – life – creative energy

Kami are vast myriads of mysterious entities that form the focal point of indigenous Japanese religion. Some modern Japanese interpreters translate the term "kami" (which is used in both singular and plural) as "high," "above," and "lifted up." Kami as an ultimate principle may be thought of as life energy and may be described as mysterious. Japanese people have felt the mysterious kami presence in powerful and unusual objects or situations including storms, sprouting rice, animals, ancestors, heroic humans, work, trees, minerals, rocks, heavenly bodies, and more. In general, kami are associated with mysterious life-giving energies. Sometimes kami are specifically linked to dynamic powers involving growth and reproduction. For example, the sprouting of rice first signals that creative (*musubi*) kami are at work.

Kami have been distinguished in terms of the way natural objects express themselves. With their subtle aesthetic sense the Japanese have perceived many fine aspects of nature. For example, Shintō tradition speaks of a "soft and fast sun," "long, soft continuous breezes such as those which rustle the leaves of trees," winds that "disperse the morning mists," and so forth (Herbert 1967: 465, 490). It may not be too far-fetched to call the Mysterious Creative Life Energy of Nature the ultimate principle of Shintō.

> Since every feature of Nature is either a child of the greatest Kami or at least under the special care of a Kami who is their child, it is not surprising to find that every beauty and power of Nature is the object of a respect which may amount to worship. This is true of practically every one of them, from celestial bodies to the very herbs and stones, from rivers and mountains to wind and thunder.
>
> (Herbert 1967: 465)

Kami are not solidly associated with the mere physicality of objects. Kami are an energetic life presence that manifests here and there. Not all trees, for example, would be automatically recognized as kami. Rather, kami energy might be recognized in an unusual tree with a triple-trunk or a tree with branches all bending in the same direction.

IMAGINAL PLAYERS

The mysterious life current that is Shintō's ultimate principle manifests in innumerable ways. General categories into which kami might be divided to understand their many workings are: (1) nature kami and (2) mythic kami.

Nature kami

- ***Trees.*** Trees seem to have been among the earliest kamis to be revered by the Japanese people. Among trees the *sakaki* (Cleyera japonica; pine) is most precious. The sakaki is found around many Shintō shrines and its branches are used in Shintō rituals.
- ***Food.*** Kami of growth come down from the mountains into the rice fields. Key Shintō agricultural rites are addressed to the creative kami of growth and food. Among the most popular kamis is Inari who is associated with the harvest, food, and fertility.
- ***Animals.*** Some wild animals have been recognized as kami, such as the wolf, tiger, hare, wild white boar, white deer, and snake. The fox is thought to be a kami messenger and came to be associated with Inari whose shrines have many fox statues, big and small.
- ***Mountains.*** Mountains were among the earliest natural objects to be perceived as kami by the Japanese people. Visiting mountain shrines is a common form of Shintō pilgrimage. Mountains are revered especially by hunters, woodcutters, and charcoal-makers whose livelihood depends upon them.
- ***Geological entities.*** Shintō includes recognition of various kami associated with the earth and cosmos. Some of these are clay, stones, lightning, metals, minerals, gemstones, stars, sun, and moon. Many forms of water are also recognized to have a kami presence, including springs, wells, rivers, the ocean, rain, and storms.
- ***Human constructions.*** Crossroads and houses are among the human constructions that are protected by kami. Many of these kami are deeply embedded in age-old Japanese folk traditions and remain unnamed. Often flowers are offered with reverence to the many household kami who protect the gate, kitchen, cooking stove, lavatory, well, and so forth.

Mythic kami

Many kami of nature came to be associated with Shintō stories relating how they came into existence or their role in various events of sacred history. Two Japanese chronicles (the ***Kojiki*** and ***Nihongi*** compiled in the eighth century CE) tell stories about several nature kami, including the kami of the sun, storms, and the moon (see page 336).

Amaterasu

Amaterasu, the sun kami, became especially important to the Japanese identity. Her magnificence becomes apparent in this passage where she prepares herself for a confrontation with her brother:

> And she forthwith, unbinding her august hair, twisted it into august bunches; and both into the left and into the right august bunch, as likewise into her august head-dress and likewise on to her left and her right august arm, she twisted an augustly complete [string] of curved jewels eight feet [long] of five hundred jewels; and slinging on her back a quiver holding a thousand [arrows], and adding [thereto] a quiver holding five hundred [arrows], she likewise took and slung at her side a mighty and high [-sounding] elbow pad and brandished and stuck her bow upright so that the top shook; and she stamped her feet into the hard ground up to her opposing thighs, kicking away [the earth] like rotten snow and stood valiantly like unto a mighty man.
>
> (deBary *et al.* 2001: 22, adapted from Chamberlain, *Ko-ji-ki*, pp. 45–59)

Clan kami

Some mythic kami are revered as *uji-gami* (tutelary clan deities). The social status of a clan was reflected in the authority and power of its kami protector. The Imperial Clan claimed unique and superior status among all humans due to their exclusive descent from Amaterasu through Jimmu Tennō, the first emperor manifesting as a human. Of lesser status were members of Divine Clans, whose members claimed descent from mythic kami through Jimmu Tennō 's companions or through noble families who ruled Japan prior to Jimmu Tennō's reign. Uji-gami shrines distributed throughout Japan served as a political bond. Eventually Shintōists used the tutelary clan kami system to protect not only families but also their extended alliances in villages and districts.

Guild kami

Many Japanese professions are linked to tutelary kami named in the *Kojiki* and *Nihongi*. Traditional guilds traced their tutelary kami back to episodes involving Amaterasu. For example: (1) mirror makers revere the kami who made the mirror that enticed Amaterasu to come out from hiding in a cave, (2) jewelers revere the kami who made the eight-foot-long string of 500 jewels worn by the sun kami, and (3) dancers and **geisha** have as their tutelary kami Ame-no-uzume who danced to entertain Amaterasu. There is a sense that these tutelary guild kami not only protect, but also enable (*yosasu*) human beings to act in this world on their behalf.

EXCEPTIONAL PLAYERS

From time to time Shintōists regard a human being as a living kami. This is always the case with the Japanese emperors, and occasionally true of heroic or uncommonly powerful people such as shamans. Thus in the Shintō context, the most exceptional players in the drama of religions are the emperors and the charismatic people mentioned above.

Emperors

Japan's emperors all belong to the Yamoto clan, which traces back to Amaterasu. She sent her grandson Ninigi down from the High Plain of Heaven to the Luxuriant-reed-plain land-of-fresh-rice-ears (i.e., Japan). The sun kami presented Ninigi with a troupe of entertainment kami, and three objects that would serve as imperial regalia: (1) a mirror, (2) a jewel, and (3) a sword. Ninigi ruled and passed the imperial regalia down the line. Jimmu, his great-grandson, became the first emperor to gain control over the region of Yamoto. Thus the Yamoto clan traced its imperial line from Emperor (Tennō) Jimmu who was the first ruler in Amaterasu's line to serve in the form of a human being. Modern historians place Jimmu Tennō's reign somewhere in the Asuka and Nara periods (552–794 CE), while the

Plate 13.1 "Japan – a straw culture." Japan has been called a straw culture (*wara no bunka*) linked to 2,000 years of rice cultivation. Villagers store rice straw on poles or slim trees creating a tent-like effect (seen here in a refined and stylized form). Japanese folk culture introduced numerous items made of rice straw, such as sandals, hats, coats, mats, utensils, ropes, masks, and even tree protectors – shown in this picture as they appeared in winter at Nijo Castle in Kyōto. Would one be wrong to detect a kami presence here?

traditional date for his accession to the throne is given as 660 BCE, based on symbolic calculations from the Chinese calendar. All members of the Imperial Clan family are high-born, but only the one who becomes emperor is associated with the quality of kami.

Charismatic humans

Shintō tradition demarcates no hard and fast division between humans and kami. Thus ritual specialists or individual charismatic individuals who commune with the kami are occasionally identified as kami themselves. Here are some examples of human beings who keep close contact with the kami:

- ***Miko.*** Ritual specialists known as miko (female shamans) typically entered a state of kami possession to seek protection for the community, fruitful harvests, and communication with the dead.
- ***Shrine priestesses.*** For generations, young women of the Yamoto ruling families served as shrine priestesses (*saiō*) in Amaterasu's shrine at Ise. There they could commune with the kami.
- ***Spirits of the dead.*** War heroes or people with unusual faith and commitment who served the emperor (hence Japan) have occasionally been recognized as kami. Sometimes restless spirits of people who die by accident or in some other unfortunate way are also placated.

HISTORICAL PLAYERS

Shintō tradition shifted its focus several times in the course of Japanese history – often in response to key changes in Japan's political-cultural environment. The following six players represent these turning points:

- *The Yayoi cultural period*: Queen Pimiku (?201–?269 CE) lived when the Japanese people practiced early Shintō.
- *About 300 years later*: Crown-prince Shōtoku (574–622) was born when Japan adopted the Buddhist tradition and centralized power under the emperor on a Confucian model.
- *About 400 years later*: Murasaki Shikibu (b. ?978 CE) was born when Japanese culture was distinguishing itself in the midst of Chinese influences.
- *About 200 years later*: The first shōgun was appointed by the emperor as general of the army (in 1192), which ushered in a feudal style of rule in the midst of new Chinese influences.
- *About 700 years later*: The Imperial House of Japan restored its absolute power through the Meiji regime that began with the defeat of the fifteenth shōgun in 1867 and the establishment of Shintō, the official state cult.
- *About 100 years later*: The **Tenrikyō** sect started by Nakayama Miki (1798–1887) blossomed into one of the most successful "newly arisen religions" after the fall of the Meiji government in World War II.

Queen Pimiku (?201–?269 CE)

The Japanese people made a great economic transition after many generations of fishing, hunting, and gathering. During the Yayoi period (250 BCE–250 CE) they adopted the technology of wet rice agriculture from Korea and China. Around the same time they developed metalworking skills in bronze, copper, and iron. The new rice-growers revered kami who descended from the mountains for their planting festivals (*matsuri*) and returned to the mountains after grateful farmers offered first fruits to them. Late in this Bronze-Iron period there lived a woman called Pimiku (?201–?269 CE). According to Chinese historians of the third century CE, Pimiku ruled a region of Japan known as Yamatai (possibly on Kyushu, but this location is disputed by present-day scholars). It appears that Pimiku was a miko (female shaman), for their *Record of Wei* said of this unmarried woman, "She occupied herself with magic and sorcery, bewitching the people" (Tsunoda 1951: 13). The chronicle goes on to say that following some political turmoil after Pimiku passed away, order was restored when Iyo (a 13-year-old female relative of Pimiku) became ruler. Subsequently it appears that leaders coming from the Yamoto plain began to rule the queen's land. This was the Imperial Family who traced their descent from Amaterasu. The Chinese historians fill out the picture of life on the queen's land by describing a number of practices that seem to represent early Shintō customs:

Men, great and small, all tattoo their faces and decorate their bodies with designs. . . . The Wa [i.e., Japanese], who are fond of diving into the water to get fish and shells, also decorated their bodies in order to keep away large fish and waterfowl. Later, however, the designs became merely ornamental. Designs on the body differ in the various countries – their position and size vary according to the rank of the individual. . . .

When death occurs, mourning is observed for more than ten days, during which period they do not eat meat. The head mourners wail and lament, while friends sing, dance, and drink liquor. When the funeral is over, all members of the whole family go into the water to cleanse themselves in a bath of purification.

When they go on voyages across the sea to visit China, they always select a man who does not arrange his hair, does not rid himself of fleas, lets his clothing [get as] dirty as it will, does not eat meat, and does not approach women. This man behaves like a mourner and is known as the fortune keeper. . . .

Whenever they undertake an enterprise and discussion arises, they bake bones and divine in order to tell whether fortune will be good or bad. First they announce the object of divination, using the same manner of speech as in tortoise shell divination; then they examine the cracks made by the fire and tell what is to come to pass.

In their meetings and in their deportment, there is no distinction between father and son or between men and women. They are fond of liquor. In their worship, men of importance simply clap their hands instead of kneeling or bowing.

(Tsunoda 1951: 10–13)

This *Record of Wei* points out religious customs of the early Japanese people that persist today in Shintō. Remnants of Pimiku's political system and reverence for miko are found today in Okinawa. Moreover, the *kami no michi* makes use of water purification, divination, *sake* as a sacred drink, shamanism, and simple reverential handclaps. Meanwhile, tattoos lost relevance for the Japanese. In the early days of Shintō there seem to have been no fixed shrines. Kami were thought to dwell only for a short time in the human world – but in natural surroundings far from human habitation. The kami manifested spontaneously and rites were performed where the kami presence had been felt. This was likely to have been around a special tree, grove, forest, rock, cave, mountain, river, seashore, or similar. Before conducing a rite, a temporary square space (*himorogi*) was set up. This might have a sacred pine tree with a shoulder-high rope around it. The kami was invoked and thought to leave afterwards. Gradually more permanent shrines were set up where the kami were thought to dwell on a semi-permanent basis – or at least be closely associated with a **goshintai** (symbolic body) that was ceremoniously placed in the inner sanctum of the shrine to represent them or embody their mysterious presence.

Crown-prince Shōtoku Taishi (574–622 CE)

Shōtoku Taishi was born just when China was on the verge of entering its highly creative Tang era (618–906 CE) in which Buddhist, Confucian, and Daoist traditions had ongoing productive literary and artistic encounters. Empress Suiko (r. 592–628) appointed Shōtoku as regent, giving him virtually complete authority to govern. Soon after the Japanese received their first Buddhist teachings through Korea (traditionally in either 538 or 552 CE), they made a prolonged and intensive effort to import nearly every available aspect of Chinese culture. In this connection Shōtoku was a key influence in promoting the Buddhist tradition in Japan. He also paved the way for the Japanese to adopt Tang-era fine arts, orchestral court music and dance, literature, technology (weaving, metal working, lacquer ware), social ethics, law codes, a landholding and tax system, architecture, town planning, philosophy, and a system of political governance.

Shōtoku strengthened Japan's cultural link to China. He sent a large embassy of monks and scholars to China in 607 CE. When they returned (some after his death) they patterned the Yamoto court after the Tang Chinese model. This was accomplished by a group of Chinese-educated Japanese in the Taika Reform (645–646). Following Shōtoku's lead, embassies to China continued for the next two and a half centuries, spanning the whole Tang era in China. Shōtoku is credited with first calling the Japanese ruler *Tennō* (emperor, heavenly sovereign) instead of *daio* (great king). This ideologically presented the Japanese ruler according to a Chinese model, whereby government was justified according to Heaven's mandate (see page 289). Calling the first emperor Jimmu Tennō gave assurance that the heavenly sovereign was not mortal, but a living kami. In connection with the title Tennō, Japanese emperors were called Aketsu-mikami (manifestation of kami) or Arahito-gami (kami appearing as human). This added a Shintō religious value to the Chinese concept.

Shōtoku introduced seventeen moral guidelines to the Yamoto court in 604 CE. His "constitution" included a mixture of practical matters and religious counsel that reflected Confucian and Buddhist influences. It calls for officials to do things such as: revere the Three Jewels (of Buddhist tradition); avoid class prejudice, gluttony, covetousness, and anger; engage in the consultative process; and (perhaps most significant) recognize a single sovereign of the entire country. Contemporary historian George B. Sansom noted that the "interest [of the seventeen articles] lies in the fact that they represent not a new system of administration but a turning point in the ideals of government, inspired by the new learning, both religious and secular, from abroad" (Sansom 1962: 72). And though he personally seemed to have become a Buddhist, Shōtoku maintained all Shintō imperial rites, agricultural festivals, and so forth.

Just under a century after Shōtoku passed away, the Imperial Family built their capital in 710 CE at Nara on the Yamoto plain. Nara was built (on a smaller scale) according to the Chinese model of the Chinese Tang capital. Buddhist monasteries grew so quickly around Nara that after less than a century a new ruler thought it prudent to extract the imperial palace from its surroundings. An attempt to move the capital nearby to Nagaoka (near Heian) proved troublesome due to internal intrigue, violence, and what were perceived as resultant illnesses and deaths. Thus the new capital (also built on the Chinese model) was finally constructed not far away at Heian in 794 CE. The city is part of today's Kyōto. In the year 838 CE the last great embassy left Japan for China. It returned the following year. After that Japan shifted its focus. The years between 900 and 1200 marked a transformative time during which the Japanese defined their newly enriched culture. Many centuries later the Tokugawa-era scholar Motoori Norinaga (1730–1801) reflected back upon this time of cultural redefinition. He noted that the native Japanese sentiment at times was obscured in the process of assimilating so many elements of Chinese civilization. But Motoori remarked on one woman whose extraordinary work of Japanese literature managed to sustain and capture the quintessential Japanese sensibility toward life – its pathos. The woman was Murasaki Shikibu (b. ?978 CE), a lady-in-waiting to the Heian Empress Akito at the Heian court.

Murasaki Shikibu (b. ?978 CE)

Murasaki Shikibu was among the ladies of the Heian court who wrote in Japanese because they were not educated in Chinese. They learned the new *kana* syllabary that was developed out of Chinese characters for use in recording the Japanese tongue. And with enthusiasm women of the Heian court developed a whole new form of literature. The contemporary historian Edwin O. Reischauer explained the phenomenon this way:

> For the most part, educated men, much like their counterparts in medieval Europe, scorned the use of their own tongue for any serious literary purpose and continued to write histories, essays, and official documents in Chinese; but the women of the imperial court, who usually had insufficient education to write in Chinese, had no medium for literary expression other than their own language. As a result, while the men of the period were pompously writing bad Chinese, their ladies consoled themselves for their lack of education by writing good Japanese, and created, incidentally, Japan's first great prose literature.
>
> (Reischauer 1970: 34–35)

Thus the Japanese women's intuitive writing became what later nativists like Motoori Norinaga recognized as the genuine feature of the Japanese mindset. Around the year 1000 CE Sei Shōnagon wrote the Pillow Book (*Makura no Sōshi*) and Murasaki Shikibu wrote the ***Tale of Genji*** (*Genji Monogatari*). Together they provide a picture of court life among Heian nobles of the day.

Murasaki lived right in the middle part of the Heian era (794–1185) at the height of the power and

BOX 13.1 CULTURE CONTRAST: THE JAPANESE SHINTŌ IDENTITY

In spite of the massive adoption of cultural elements from China, it is important to bear in mind that the Chinese never invaded Japan. The Japanese tended to modify what did not suit them and maintained their cultural identity. The persistence of a Japanese worldview and culture may be seen in the following examples:

Adoption. Contrary to Confucian ideals, the Japanese continued to maintain hereditary government posts, as inheritance was deeply embedded in their aristocratic society. The automatic nature of inheritance was somewhat tempered by the long-standing Japanese custom of adoption, which allowed a man to choose his successor. When there was no male heir the Japanese adopted the husband of a daughter, a young relative, or even someone who was not related by blood.

Bushidō. The Japanese rejected the Chinese-style draft army, as they did not need a large army. Beyond that they maintained the military as an aristocratic profession. In medieval Japan the Shintō military tradition developed the **Bushidō** (way of the warrior-knight) code. These eight attitudes that characterize a warrior were: (1) loyalty, (2) gratitude, (3) courage, (4) justice, (5) truthfulness, (6) politeness, (7) reserve, and (8) honor. There is the flavor of the Confucian tradition running through these, as well as the Zen Buddhist focus of mind and fearlessness. Yet the product was something with a native Japanese flavor that seems to have continued to the present day.

Japanese language. The Japanese initially adopted Chinese characters for writing and chose Chinese as their literary language. Yet they continued to speak Japanese, which was quite a distinctive language. Moreover, during the 800s CE they adapted the Chinese ideograms to the Japanese language with two syllabaries (known as *kana*) that used simplified characters to phonetically represent Japanese syllables. For example, they wrote the "Collection of Myriad Leaves" (*Manyōshū*) whose 4,516 native poems were copied syllable by syllable in Chinese characters used in a phonetic manner to represent the Japanese words.

influence of the famous Fujiwara family. In fact, she married a Fujiwara lieutenant who was in the Imperial Guard. The Heian government amounted to a Fujiwara oligarchy and the rise of a court aristocracy. In Murasaki's day the nobles generally regarded country people as uncivilized. The gentlepersons of the court developed the Japanese language of politeness, and a culture of luxury with its ceremony, elegant pastimes, cosmetics for men and women, attention to penmanship, and so forth. Perhaps the most distinctive cultural development of the Heian era was in the realm of Japanese literature. Neglecting the thirty-one-syllable poem that was popular at the court, Murasaki wrote what is counted as the world's first novel. It records court life centered on the figure of Prince Genji and his family circle. The book shows psychological sensitivity, but also records elements of the emerging Japanese culture. Murasaki observed this scene, for example:

> A number of grey-haired old ladies were cutting out and stitching, while the young girls were busy hanging out quilts and winter cloaks over lacquered clothes-frames. They had just beaten and pulled a very handsome dark-red under-robe, a garment of magnificent colour, certainly unsurpassed as an example of modern dyeing – and were spreading it out to air.
>
> (Murasaki 1993: 624)

The very object of a Heian book was counted as part of its artistry – as the paper and perfume conveyed a particularly Japanese sense of aesthetics. But while the upper crust of Heian society were busy developing their highly refined blend of Chinese and Japanese influences, some religious specialists living in the mountains were blending foreign and native influences as well. These were the **yamabushi** (mountain priests or hermits). They can be distinguished from miko (female shamans) and Shintō priests (*onshi* or *oshi*) by their particular functions, which combine Buddhist practice with folk Shintō elements.

The yamabushi were ascetics with uncut hair who lived in the mountains conducting physical and spiritual practices to acquire power over spirits of the dead. The order of yamabushi that survives today is the Shugen-dō, founded by a priest of the En family in the mid-600s CE. For a while their numbers declined, but the sect was revitalized and reorganized by a Shingon Buddhist monk named Shōbō (832–909). The yamabushi worked as a team with miko as assistants. (Sometimes they also married these miko.) The yamabushi used special techniques to help the miko go into a trance to find out for a client what grudge a spirit of the dead was holding. After interpreting the miko's announcement the yamabushi would remedy the problem. Thus the miko diagnosed and the yamabushi exorcised. The yamabushi would go from one mountain to another and from one village to another. Some were ballad singers or musicians as well. And though Shugen-dō was affiliated with the Tendai and Shingon Buddhist traditions, it shows considerable Shintō influence in its connection with sacred mountains, the service of the miko, and so forth. Some yamabushi even became Shintō priests. Nowadays the yamabushi still exist in Japan, meeting villagers to pray for good harvests, exorcise negative spirits from houses, conduct healings, and so forth. They seem to resemble the characters noted by the third-century CE Chinese historians who observed that on voyages across the sea to China the Japanese always have a man with them "who does not arrange his hair" (see page 327).

Fifteen shōguns (1192–1867)

Culturally, with the decline of the Heian court, **samurai** warriors replaced the Fujiwara courtiers. This was due to economic changes as the military leaders gained more local influence in the countryside. The rise of a samurai class represented the militarization of Japanese society. The emperor still maintained the position as ruler seated in Heian. But from a practical point of view the leaders of various semi-independent estates came to control Japanese political life. Finally in 1192 these estates came under a single leader's control. This was Minamoto Yorimoto – the first man appointed by the emperor as shōgun ("generalissimo"). This meant that he was given command of the emperor's army. Thus began the Kamakura era (1192–1333). The shōgunate settled in Kamakura, some 300 miles from Heian (Kyōto), and kept their political liaison intact.

The downfall of the Tang dynasty in China had come after a major persecution of Buddhism in 845 CE. In response to the chaotic atmosphere on the mainland, Japan had discontinued its envoys to China and went through 300 years of isolation. Now, with the emergence of the first shōgun, that isolation was about to end (only to be imposed again in 1600 for about 300 years by the Tokugawa regime!). Medieval Japanese history can be measured between the moment the first shōgun took power in 1192 and the moment the fifteenth and final shōgun was deposed in 1867. The fifteen military chiefs stand like bookends encompassing a whole new orientation toward life flowing from a second period of intensive contact with China. But what the Japanese encountered in 1200 was not a China of the Tang dynasty with its flowering of three traditions – Buddhist, Daoist, and Confucian. Rather the Japanese encountered the Song dynasty (960–1279) in China. There, Pure Land and Chan Buddhist traditions percolated in the midst of a growing neo-Confucian Chinese cultural pride. Japanese Buddhist teachers of the Kamakura era who were disillusioned with the state of Buddhism in their country enthusiastically embraced the Buddhist traditions that Song China had to offer. Hōnen, Shinran, and Nichiren promoted Pure Land, True Pure Land, and Nichiren Buddhist practices that began filtering through all levels of Japanese society. Eisai and Dōgen promoted Rinzai and Sōtō Zen (Chan) Buddhist practices that appealed to the samurai (see page 210).

Throughout this medieval period the Japanese people distinguished Buddhist and Shintō traditions as the Buddha Way (*butsu-dō*) and the Kami Way (*kami no michi* or *shen-dao*). Shintō shrines (*jinja*) were distinguished from Buddhist temples (*tera*) but both were contained in religious complexes to serve complementary functions. A tera would be built within the precinct of a jinja so that the Buddhist priest could perform rituals propitiating the kami. The reverse was also done, whereby kami were enshrined in Buddhist temples. Sometimes the kami were thought of as buddhas or bodhisattvas. As in the community, so both Shintō and Buddhist religious practices were observed in Japanese homes. Some people maintained both **kamidanas** (Shintō altars) and **butsudans** (Buddhist altars) for their households.

In time the Kamakura power base weakened. After several more generations of decline in the effectiveness of the Japanese feudal system, a talented member of the Tokugawa family was poised to take a firm grip on Japan. In the interest of creating unity in Japan Tokugawa Ieyasu (1542–1616) became shōgun in 1603. He instituted a far-reaching bureaucracy that lasted until 1867 with the fall of the Tokugawa regime. Under Tokugawa rule there was no class mobility, no intermarriage, and each family was required to register at the local Buddhist temple. Temple officials kept census records, while Zen Buddhist monasteries became centers for the arts and neo-Confucian studies. The presence of the kami no michi is felt strongly in medieval Japan through the arts. And though the arts of tea, the sword, flower arranging, and so forth are often called Zen arts, a Shintō influence thoroughly pervades them (see Box 13.3).

The Tokugawa regime instituted a new government based on neo-Confucian ideas and political practices derived from interpretations of Confucian literature by Zhu Xi (1130–1200) (see page 301). The neo-Confucian ideology was well suited to monarchic rule because it gave a strong sense that everything under heaven is governed by a single principle (li), which is embodied in the ruler. Hayashi Razan (1583–1657), the first official Japanese neo-Confucian, promoted the Chinese doctrine of five social relationships in these terms:

> Heaven is august, Earth is ignoble. Heaven is high, Earth is low. Just as there is a distinction of high and low between Heaven and Earth, in the society of men, a prince is noble while the subject is common. Proper decorum calls for a hierarchy between the noble and the common, the elder and the younger persons. . . . Unless the distinction between the prince who is noble and the subject who is common is maintained, the land cannot be governed. . . . If the Way that distinguishes the prince as the subject, and the father and the son is followed, and the principle of distinguishing the high and the low, the exalted and the vulgar is upheld, the Way of Heaven will prevail above, and human relationships will be clear below.
>
> (quoted in Hane 1972: 165)

The Tokugawa rulers maintained a strict isolationist policy, and closed Japan in reaction to a century of Christian influences. Christianity first came with the Portuguese traders in 1542. At first Christianity was welcomed along with Portuguese guns. But Christians experienced a backlash when Tokugawa Ieyasu realized that their loyalty to God's authority was greater than their loyalty to the state. In 1614 the shōgun gave all foreign priests one month to leave Japan. Two years later he ordered all Japanese Christians to renounce their religion and become Buddhist on pain of death. At this point the Japanese Christians (some of whom were already second and third generation) were either martyred, recanted, or began to practice secretly. By 1640 most traces of the **Kirishitan** religion were gone. Throughout the Tokugawa era, people had to undergo a yearly ritual of "treading pictures" (*fumi-e*) at the Buddhist monasteries. This involved stepping on images of Jesus Christ or the Virgin Mary to prove their rejection of the Christian tradition.

The Imperial House of Japan

Crown-prince Shōtoku's Japan with its three complementary traditions transformed in the course of 1,300 years into a society apparently dominated by Buddhist and Confucian traditions. By the late Tokugawa era, some nationalistic activists became adamant about removing foreign elements from Shintō and restoring it to the center of Japanese life. They bemoaned the fact that the emperor had become little more than a figurehead through 600-plus years of powerful military rule under the fifteen shōguns from the year 1192. The Japanese effort toward a Shintō restoration was crystallized by two nativist Japanese movements that emerged in the late 1700s and continued to grow in influence until Japan was defeated by the Allies in World War II: (1) **kokugaku** (nativism or national learning) sought to define, restore, and nurture the native Japanese mindset; (2) **kokutai** (national essence or national spirit) aimed to wrest power from the Tokugawa shōgun and restore full authority to the Imperial House of Japan, which traced back through Jimmu Tennō to Amaterasu. The nationalistic ideology of kokutai was fed by the literary and philological work of kokugaku (see Box 13. 2).

In 1868 the Meiji government replaced the Tokugawa regime and restored full authority to the Imperial House of Japan. The Meiji government replaced the Tokugawa state sponsorship of Buddhism with state sponsorship of Shintō and identified thirteen

BOX 13.2 INTERPRETATIONS: THE KOKUGAKU WAY TO READ

Motoori Norinaga (1730–1801) was a Japanese literary scholar of kokugaku (nativism, national learning). As a nativist he wanted to discover the core spirituality-mentality of the Japanese people. Motoori felt that in ancient times when words were conveyed through the mouths of people and heard by the ears of people (i.e., through oral transmission) there was an accord between meaning (*kokoro*), an event (*koto*), and a word (*kotoba*). To get a better sense of the oral tradition, Motoori wrote in the antique style and favored words in contemporary Japanese usage that hearkened back to the Nara period (710–794) when the Japanese still used much of their antique language. He noticed that old words are not necessarily strange sounding. Yet he found that word choice and word order were significant cultural markers. Thus Motoori taught nativist readers to adjust Chinese phrases that were alien to the Japanese people (e.g., illegitimate elder brother, legitimate wife, national polity). He also noted that the Chinese expressions "day and night" and "mountains and sea" should be corrected to the Japanese wording of "night and day" and "sea and mountains." Motoori felt that authentic Shintō values were reflected in the ancient songs preserved in the *Kojiki* and the *Nihongi* where "one will find that things are not stated to excess, and that the ways of the world and the inner thoughts of people are known by intuition" (Motoori 1997: 146–147).

Motoori further identified *mono no aware* (the pathos of things, the sorrow of human existence) as a characteristic feature of a Japanese understanding of the world. He identified Murasaki Shikibu's *Tale of Genji* (ca. 1000 CE) as a prime example of such pathos. Motoori saw in her novel an emotional truth steeped in the melancholy of the human condition. He observed that Murasaki's work was not riddled with Buddhist and Confucian morality that would judge Genji's adultery. Rather, with true Japanese sensibility she wrote a work that was:

> simply a tale of human life that leaves aside and does not profess to take up at all the question of good and bad and that dwells only on the goodness of those who are aware of the sorrow of human existence (*mono no aware*). . . . [The] illicit love affairs described in the tale [are] there not for the purpose of being admired but for the purpose of nurturing the flower of the awareness of the sorrow of human existence (*mono no aware*).
>
> (deBary *et al.* 2005: 485)

According to his Shintō intuitive belief (based particularly on the *Kojiki*) Motoori said the world was created by kami, and the Japanese people were descended from Amaterasu. He felt that a debt of gratitude is owed to the sun kami whose radiance continues to sustain the world. He claimed that the proper way to live was the ancient way in accord with how the kami established life on earth. With a universalistic outlook Motoori said that the Way of the Sun Goddess was "the true Way that permeates all nations within the four seas" (deBary *et al.* 2005: 500)

groups as non-Shintō religions officially designating them as Sect Shintō. These sects were considered as separate religions and their places of worship were called churches (*kyokai*) as opposed to shrines (*jinja*). During this time the Meiji government supervised Buddhists, Christians, and **New Religions** (Shinkō Shūkyō, literally "newly arisen religions") and other sects. They all dedicated themselves to the Imperial House. In 1882 a Bureau of Shrines was established and a legal distinction between Shrine Shintō (*jinga Shintō*) and Sect Shintō (*kyoha Shintō*) was made. This did not involve the construction of new shrines. Rather it awarded a new status to shrines that qualified as Shintō shrines, as opposed to those whose affiliations were regarded as other. In the midst of this reform, the hereditary Shintō priesthood was abolished and priests became government appointees. Beneath the government officials were priests of the Shintō shrines appointed by the government who maintained the state rituals. The people themselves continued to worship kami at their local shrines.

The Meiji government undertook an imperial campaign on the mainland. Victories in the Sino-Japanese war (1894–1895) and Russo-Japanese war (1904–1905) were part of a Japanese strategy to become a world stage player instead of capitulating to the forces of European colonialism. Japan focused on strengthening Japan against Western powers. During these Japanese wars of aggression parents often traveled to Shintō shrines (on what was known as the 100-shrine pilgrimage, for example) to appeal to the kami to protect their sons doing military duty. Japan's emperors of the twentieth century rode white horses and donned military uniforms. Imitating the ancient style of government, they served in both a political and religious capacity. Thus the emperors performed Shintō rituals at the Grand Shrines of Ise to commune with Amaterasu. After 1890 education of Japanese students was permeated with nationalistic ideas, with an ethic of filial piety toward the emperor who was to be viewed as a father figure. Japanese schools had shrines with a picture of the emperor and upon hearing the emperor's name they jumped to attention. History was taught beginning with the divine ancestry of the emperor and the Japanese people. Obedience to one's superior was required and self-sacrifice came to be regarded as a key virtue. This nationalistic education came to a halt

Plate 13.2 "Long-legs and Long-arms watch the sunrise." Living on the seashore of north China facing Japan are two mythical beings: Ashinaga (Long-legs) and Tanaga (Long-arms). They like to go fishing together. Ashinaga carries Tanaga far from shore – and there in the deep water Tanaga scoops up fish. Shibata Zeshin (1807–1891) painted this scene with the symbol of his native Japan (the sun) on the horizon. What religious or political meaning might the artist have intended in doing so?

suddenly when on 1 January 1946 Emperor Hirohito (1901–1989) was forced to declare that he was not divine. Japan lost to the Allies in World War II and was obliged to forgo having an army. The existence of Shintō as a state institution had lasted for about seventy years in all.

Nakayama Miki (1798–1887)

A popular theistic movement led by individual charismatic teachers sprouted up in the late Tokugawa era (mid-1800s) in the midst of depressed social and economic conditions. The Meiji government later designated these various groups by the term New Religions. At the start, the New Religions attracted followings mainly among poor farmers and urban laborers. Their leaders obtained their authority through personal experience of the divine, based on the traditional Shintō notion that kami manifest themselves through exceptional people. Most of these groups "derived their inspiration from occult practices prevalent among the mountaineer priests [yamabushi]" (Anesaki 1930: 310). Some New Religions sprang from Buddhist roots and some had undertones of Kirishitan (i.e., Christian) belief. However, most of the New Religions were grounded in Shintō and recognized the traditional kami of the *Kojiki* and *Nihongi*, such as Amaterasu, Izanagi, and Izanami (see Table 13.1).

Characteristic features of the New Religions include: (1) charismatic, shamanic leadership, (2) an emphasis on spiritual healing and purification, (3) reverence for ancestors, and (4) an expectation of happiness and

Table 13.1 Japanese New Religions: a sample

Sect name/Founder[1]	*Social status of parents*	*Conversion experience*[2]
KUROZUMI Kurozumi Munetada (M)	Shintō priest	(35) Union with Amaterasu Ōmikami, the Sun Kami
TENRIKYŌ Nakayama Miki (F)	Ruined landowner	(41) Possession by 10 kami, organized by Tenri Ō no mikoto (Supreme Kami of Divine Wisdom)
KONKŌ Kawate Bunjirō (M)	Poor farmer	(45) Inspired, possessed by Konjin or Konkō-Daijin (Great Kami of Gold)
ŌMOTO Deguchi Nao (F) Deguchi Onisaburō (M)	Poor carpenter; poor peasant	(56) Chosen, possessed by Konjin (Great Kami of Gold); (27) Entranced, called by Ko-matsu-no-mikoto (Kami of a Small Pine Tree)
HITONO-MICHI Kaneda Tokumitsu (M) Miki Tokuchika (M)	Small-scale merchants	(52) Inspired by the Rising Sun and came to the view that kami is one, not many
REIYŪ-KAI Kotani Kimi (F)	Poor peasant	(25) Chosen, possessed by kami and spirits; Related to Nichiren Buddhist tradition
RISSHŌ-KŌSEI-KAI Naganuma Myōko (F)	Poor laborer	(50) Chosen, possessed by spirit of Nichiren and other Buddhist figures
SŌKA-GAKKAI Makiguchi Tsunaburō (M) Toda Jōsei (M)	Farmer; fisherman	(59) Preach monotheistic theology based on Nichiren's teachings. (Toda Jōsei organized the Sōka-Gakkai sect.)

Notes [1] Male (M) or female (F).
[2] Age when converted is in parenthesis.
Source: Adapted from Hori (1968: 230–231).

success in this world (see Picken 1994: 260–263). In general, women tend to play a more prominent role in the New Religions than in traditional Shintō or Buddhist communities, and participation is geared toward the lay community.

The earliest Shintō-derived New Religion is Tenrikyō (Religion of Divine Wisdom) founded by Nakayama Miki (1798–1887). She was a peasant from Yamoto who practiced the Pure Land Buddhist tradition that focused gratitude toward Amida (Amitabha) Buddha for his universal compassion. One day Nakayama's son became ill and she hired a healer. Because the healer's assistant could not attend the consultation, he asked Nakayama to serve as a channel of healing energy. In doing so, she became possessed by a kami – and continued to have experiences of kami possession from that day forward. A kami called Tenri Ō no Mikoto (Lord of Divine Wisdom) spoke through Nakayama. The kami presented itself also as Oyagama (God the Parent) and began working healing miracles through her. The kami asked that Nakayama's family dedicate all their belongings to the poor, and she took this message to heart. Nakayama's daughter had faith in the mission and together they spread teachings that urged people to recover their original nature of sincere piety (*makoto-shinjitsu*) by cleansing themselves of eight dusts: grudge, covetousness, hatred, selfish love, enmity, fury, greed, and arrogance. Nakayama's fame spread. Disciples regarded her as the Kami no Yashiro (living shrine of the kami) whose message of healing and charity was a prescription for realization of God's kingdom as harmonious life on earth.

Nakayama was imprisoned on several occasions, but managed to write down messages from Oyagama that came through her in two books, the *Mikagurauta* and the *Ofudesaki*. Among her revelations were songs of thirty-one syllables and deliberate physical movements. The shaman's poetic utterances and dance steps became the basis for Tenrikyō liturgy whose central rite is the Kagura Zutome (salvation dance service). In a revelation Nakayama identified a site (the *jiba*) as the sacred place from where human beings originally came. At that spot she later passed away in the midst of a liturgical performance. Nakayama's disciples worked with profound enthusiasm to build a great temple at the jiba, which they called "Terrace of Nectar" (*Kanrodai*). Tenrikyō adherents believe that the founder never died, but continues to exist as a powerful spiritual presence in the temple sanctuary from where she helps do away with social ills and prepare for the *kanrodai sekai* (perfect divine kingdom) – a new world order in which human beings will live joyous and blissful lives. Along with Sōka Gakkai (of Buddhist derivation) Tenrikyō has proved to be the most popular and successful among the Japanese New Religions. More than 200 churches are spread throughout the world, mostly for the sake of Japanese emigrants.

In modern times Shintō has gone through two major upheavals. During the Meiji era the institution of hereditary Shintō priesthood became defunct as the rulers officially appointed priests. In the early 1900s Japan had some 200,000 shrines that were nationalized by the Meiji government. In 1945 the Allies abolished the Imperial Cult after their victory that ended World War II. Shintō shrines suddenly lost all state sponsorship. Stranded with no funding and no organization, priests became ordinary citizens and many did not continue to practice their Shintō vocation. After Shintō shrines were made private their numbers diminished to around 80,000. The New Religions finally gained complete freedom of organization and practice in 1945. In 1946 the Association of Shintō Shrines was formed as an affiliation of local shrines. Priests and committees drawn from among worshipers managed these shrines. Ownership of the land and buildings was privatized and fundraising became a key aspect of support. In the face of this regrouping Japanese New Religions have become very popular, especially these two: (1) Sōka Gakkai, a Buddhist offshoot of Nichiren teaching from Kamakura era, and (2) Tenrikyō, a Shintō offshoot from the Tokugawa era (1603–1867). At the same time the number of Shintōists seems to be dropping annually (see Table 0.1). Nowadays there are over 2,000 New Religions whose membership ranges from a mere one hundred all the way to Sōka Gakkai's estimated sixteen million (on Tenrikyō and other religions that emerged on the world stage in this era see Box 7.4 on page 174).

PART 2
SHINTŌ TEXTURE

FOUNDATIONAL TEXTURE

The Record of Ancient Matters (*Kojiki*) and the History of Japan (*Nihongi* or *Nihon-Shoki*) are the earliest Shintō writings still in existence (dating from 712 CE and 720 CE). They gave names to several of the myriad kami. Among those named, Amaterasu became the most famous due to her standing as ancestor of the Yamato clan. The Emperor Temmu (r. 673–686) was interested in having a record of Japan's history. Thus the scribes began to record stories that had been transmitted orally over generations by a guild of *kataribe* who may have been kami-possessed. The books contain myths, poems, and historical statements. These formed the foundation for Shintō rituals. They also provided the classic references on various tutelary kami of the clans and guilds. The two texts contain material from what may have been independent mythic cycles. For instance, different versions of creation are told in each book.

- The *Kojiki* tells of steaming mud and water out of which grew a plant with seven branches. Each branch held two kami who were brother and sister. These seven pairs of twins were dispersed throughout the cosmos and after an undetermined span of time a brother–sister team was born. They were called Izanagi (He-Who-Invites) and Izanami (She-Who-Invites).
- The *Nihongi* begins with a Chinese-style myth of creation in which the cosmos was formed from an egg-like mass that separated into a male (yang) heavenly portion and a female (yin) earthly portion.

Regardless of such differences, the content of the two texts overlaps considerably. Both contributed to Shintō lore about the kami and Japan's sacred history.

Stories in the *Kojiki* and *Nihongi*

The Record of Ancient Matters and History of Japan both describe the creation of the islands of Japan as follows: Izanagi and Izanami stood on a cloud bridge that spanned the sky. Izanagi stirred the muddy water with jeweled spears given to them by the other kami. Islands formed where the mud splashed. Izanagi and Izanami descended to the new land and engaged in a primordial union that made them husband and wife.

Thereafter, Izanagi and Izanami created waters, winds, fire, fields, substances that could be eaten, mountains, and other things. Izanami made fire but was badly burnt in the process. She turned her skull and ribs into caves and other bones to rocks. After she perished Izanagi sought her in Yomi (= darkness), the underworld. There he saw Izanami putrefying with maggots. Izanagi escaped from his underworld pursuers and purified himself in a stream.

Izanagi needed to be purified after escaping from Yomi due to his contact with death. Thus he purified himself. This became the prototype for the Great Purification of Shintō tradition. To become free from pollution Izanagi washed three parts of his body, and from each a kami child was born: (1) from his left eye was born the sun, (2) from his nose, the storms and thunder, and (3) from his right eye, the moon. The sun was Amaterasu, the Heaven-Shining-Great-August-Deity, who came to rule the High Plain of Heaven. The storm was her elder brother Susano-o, His-Swift-Impetuous-Male-Augustness. He came to rule the earth. The moon was Takamagahara, the sun's younger brother who became her consort and helped her rule.

The *Nihongi* says that Izanagi and Izanami together as a couple created the three children. After making the land, they consulted, saying, "We have now produced the great-eight-island country, with the mountains, rivers, herbs, and trees. Why should we not produce someone who shall be lord of the universe?" (deBary *et al.* 2001: 21; adapted from Aston, *Nihongi*, I:18–20). They then produced Amaterasu. After that came the moon kami, a "leech child which even at the age of three years could not stand upright" whom they therefore abandoned to the winds, and then Susano-o. This last kami would figure largely in the cultural memory of the Japanese people. The *Nihongi* describes Susano-o as follows:

> This god has a fierce temper and was given to cruel acts. Moreover he made a practice of continually

weeping and wailing. So he brought many of the people of the land to an untimely end. Again he caused green mountains to become withered. Therefore the two gods, his parents, addressed Susa-no-o no Mikoto, saying, "Thou art exceedingly wicked, and it is not meet that thou shouldst reign over the world. Certainly thou must depart far away to the Nether-land." So they at length expelled him.

(deBary *et al.* 2001: 21; adapted from Aston, *Nihongi*, I:18–20)

Susano-o committed several polluting acts for which he was fined and banished from the High Plain of Heaven, including: (1) damaging Amaterasu's rice fields, (2) defiling her house by voiding excrement in her New Palace at the time of celebrating the Feast of First Fruits, and (3) intending to go to see his mother in the polluted place of Yomi. After his banishment Susano-o carried out several deeds that helped restore him to the good graces of the other kami. He slew a serpent that had eight heads and eight tails. In one tail of the serpent Susano-o came upon a great sword that was to become one of the three imperial regalia. Eventually he came back into the good graces of all the kami.

On one occasion Susano-o startled his sister as she was weaving. The *Nihongi* says:

Then Amaterasu started with alarm and wounded herself with the shuttle. Indignant of this, she straightway [*sic*] entered the Rock-cave of Heaven and, having fastened the Rock-door, dwelt there in seclusion. Therefore constant darkness prevailed on all sides, and the alternation of night and day was unknown.

(deBary *et al.* 2001: 24; adapted from Aston, *Nihongi*, I:40–45)

The series of acts performed by various kami to persuade the Heavenly Shining One to come out again have lived for centuries in Shintō ritual. After this disaster, eighty myriad kami met at the Tranquil River of Heaven. They made a plan to persuade the sun to come out. They brought roosters to call each other outside the cave, and replanted a 500-branched *sakaki* tree taken from Mount Kagu in Yamoto. They decorated the upper branches with strings of jewels and an eight-hand mirror, and the lower branches with blue and white offerings. Some recited a liturgy. A troupe of kami danced and made music while kami Ame-no-uzume, the Terrible Female of Heaven, displayed herself with elegant gestures.

[She] took in her hand a spear wreathed with Eulalia grass and, standing before the door of the Rock-cave of Heaven, skillfully performed a mimic dance. She took, moreover, the true Sakaki tree of the Heavenly Mount Kagu and made of it a head-dress; she took club-moss and made of it braces; she kindled fires; she placed a tub bottom upwards and gave forth a divinely inspired utterance.

(deBary *et al.* 2001: 25; adapted from Aston, *Nihongi*, I:40–45)

This inspired utterance piqued Amaterasu's curiosity. The Heavenly Shining One asked herself, "Since I have shut myself up in the Rock-cave, there ought surely to be continual night in the Central land of fertile reed-plains. How then can Ame no Uzume no Mikoto be so jolly?" (deBary *et al.* 2001: 25; adapted from Aston, *Nihongi*, I:40–45). Attracted by the music, roosters, glimpses of light glancing off the jewels, and the sacred speech, Amaterasu peeked out of the Rock cave, and then emerged from hiding. To prevent the world from again suffering in darkness the kami placed a **shimenawa** (a huge rope) across the cave's mouth.

Myth, history, and ritual

Shintō tradition says that Susano-o went to Korea and then to Izumo on the western coast of the Japanese island of Honshū. There his descendant Ōkuni-nushi (Great Land Master) ruled the earth for some time. Eventually Amaterasu noticed the unruly conduct under the governance of his descendants, and decided to send her grandson to rule. Shintōists revere Susano-o as a protector. He is enshrined at the Yasaka Jinja in Kyōto, among other places. From a historical point of view it appears that stories about Susano-o derive from a cult centered at Izumo that historically was filtered into the Yamoto cult, which derived from Amaterasu's grandson Ninigi (Ruddy-Plenty). Amaterasu's clan set up their government on the Yamoto plain across the mountains from Izumo on the eastern side of Honshū.

Amaterasu's shrine was set up at Ise, near the east coast of the island. Amaterasu is enshrined at other locations but the Ise shrine contains the sacred mirror as her goshintai (symbolic body) and continues to be her main dwelling place. In the Edo period (1615–1868) Amaterasu become a popular object of worship as a few million Shintō pilgrims visited the Grand Shrines of Ise.

SUPPORTIVE TEXTURE

Modern Shintō theology

Until modern times, Japanese thinkers tended not to establish any Shintō doctrines. The social ethics and philosophical views of Confucian and Buddhist traditions seem to have occupied them instead. Yet with an interest in defining the Shintō contribution to Japanese thought, some philosophers are working to clarify the principles of Shintō ethics. Hiraï Naofusa identified the "life-attitude of **makoto**" as the "source" of Shintō ethics:

> *Makoto* is a sincere approach to life with all one's heart, an approach in which nothing is shunned or treated with neglect. It stems from an awareness of the Divine. It is the humble, single-minded reaction which wells up within us when we touch directly or indirectly upon the workings of the Kami, know that they exist, and have the assurance of their close presence with us.
>
> While on the one hand we sense keenly our baseness and imperfection in the presence of the Kami, on the other hand, we will be overwhelmed with ineffable joy and gratitude at the privilege of living within the harmony of nature.
>
> (Quoted in Herbert 1967: 71–72)

Other Shintō ethical values related to makoto are said to be: righteousness, individual and community harmony, cheerfulness of heart, thankfulness to nation, society, and family, effort to be a good citizen and member of society and family, devotion to the common interest, tolerant generosity that involves a "mental search for variety," benevolence, propriety and reverence, filial piety, industriousness, exercise of a strong will, and consciousness of shame. Many of these Shintō values are reminiscent of basic Confucian ethics (see Herbert 1967: 72ff.). Yet Shintō thinkers feel that the overriding value of makoto (as sincerity, cleanliness, honesty, and conscientious) gives Shintō ethics a Japanese quality. The Shintō sensibility also includes a subtle and personal feeling for nature, coupled with a sense of the pathos of things (*mono no aware*).

Some conservative Shintōists object to philosophizing, which amounts to an apologetic response to modern Western attitudes that fault religions with no explicit moral rules. They say that an authentic Shintō ethic is spontaneous and intuitive. This alternative view of Shintō ethics holds that human beings need freedom and become paralyzed by needless rules. Jean Herbert, a modern interpreter of Shintō, reported the gist of such a conservative viewpoint:

> From a purely practical angle, if a man follows the pattern of life which has been bequeathed to him by his ancestors the Gods, what need is there to codify rules of conduct for various arbitrary groups of occasions? It is only when the man should fall so low as to be divorced from the life which children of the gods should live that he must resort to principles of morality – which otherwise would have a paralyzing effect and infringe upon the freedom which is his heirloom and which he needs.
>
> (Herbert 1967: 69)

They believe that as children of Amaterasu the Japanese have an innate capacity to act properly when guided by the principles of purity demonstrated by the kami. They recognize that rules are created in times of alienation from the way of the kami, and find a solution in reconnecting with the kami no michi. One approach of going back to traditional Shintō principles is through *misogi* (purification). The process of purification starts with the outer cleansing and culminates in an understanding that the deepest level is "pacifying the soul" (*chin-kōn*).

CROSS-OVER TEXTURE

Japanese poetry

Many early Japanese poets wrote in the Chinese language, in the Chinese style – and even took on

BOX 13.3 SYMBOLS: THE PRESENCE OF KAMI IN JAPANESE LIFE

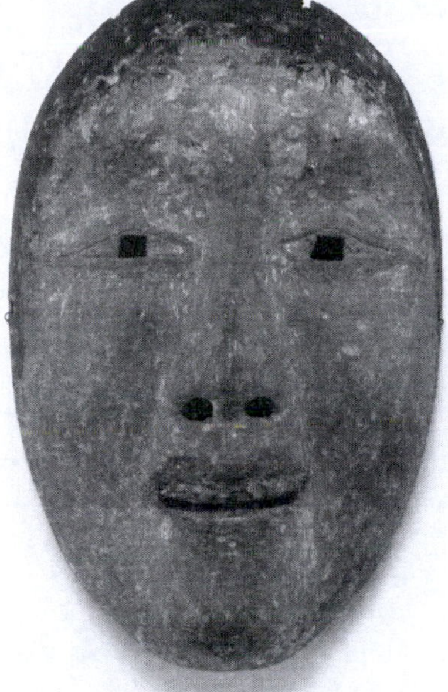

Plate 13.3 "Shintō mask: a young woman's face." Through the history of Shintō performance many styles of mask evolved to carry a rich array of symbolic meanings. One convention used the shape of eye openings to indicate the age of female characters portrayed by the mask: square openings for young women and half circles for older women. Note the eyes of this mask worn during the 1500s or 1600s. Masks are used in many types of Shintō performances including dance and processions, as well as court and religious rituals.

The stories of Izanagi, Izanami, Amaterasu, Susano-o, and other kami impacted the development of Japanese culture through many centuries, and give meaning to the life of Japanese people to this day. Here are some examples of stories that expressed themselves through ritual, art, and politics.

The three imperial regalia. Amaterasu bestowed three objects upon her grandson Ninigi before sending him down to Japan from the High Plain of Heaven: mirror, jewel, and sword. According to archeological evidence, the Japanese had used spears, swords, and mirrors made of bronze at least 500 years before the sacred stories about the imperial regalia were written down. They became imperial regalia that were passed down through generations of emperors. An enthronement transmission with these three imperial regalia was televised in 1989 with the accession of Emperor Akihito (Heisei).

The shimenawa rope. The shimenawa is a specially braided straw rope that demarcates the sacred space of Shintō shrines in memory of the time Amaterasu retreated to the Rock-cave after being shown disrespect by her brother Susano-o.

The troupe of kami. The dance and music created by the kami to entertain Amaterasu became the seed of Japanese theater. During the late 1300s and 1400s in the courts of the shōgun traditional Japanese dance was used in Nō drama. Nō performance involved a handful of actors who portrayed Shintō myths (such as Amaterasu being coaxed out of the cave by kami) and historical episodes through chant and dance movements. Ame-no-uzume, whose elegant gestures made Amaterasu joyful, is popular in the geisha tradition.

The sun. Amaterasu as the sun appears on a white background at the center of the Japanese flag. The connection between the ruler and the sun kami may indicate the early presence of a solar cult in Japan. The Yamoto ancestor cult used beads, mirrors, and items related to the horse. Scholars interpret the custom of keeping white imperial horses as another indication of connections between the ruling family and a solar cult.

Ninigi. The ancestral connection between Amaterasu's grandson Ninigi and his descendant Jimmu was taken to mean that every Japanese emperor was a living kami. Prior to World War II no ordinary person could even look at the emperor and no one could look down at him from above. These taboos pertained to the notion that the emperor was semi-divine.

Chinese pen-names. But poetry is one aspect of culture that the Japanese soon made to suit themselves. The radical differences between the Chinese and Japanese languages motivated new explorations into the possibilities of poetic expression. The development of pivot words (*kake-kotoba*) and the later **haiku** form seems to have captured the Japanese sentimentality.

Pivot words

In the Japanese language each syllable generally has one consonant followed by one vowel. Many words contain other words within them. There are also many homonyms. These are words that sound the same but have different meanings embedded within other words which makes for rich possibilities of layers of expression. Thus in Japanese poetry the feature of word association is called the "pivot word" around which several meanings are linked. In his study of Japanese literature Donald Keene said, "The function of the 'pivot-word' is to link two different images by shifting in its own meaning" (Keene 1955: 4–5). Keene provided the following double translation of this poem by Shin Kokinshū (dated 1205 CE) based on his understanding of the pivot words and alternate meanings of the sounds:

> *Kie wabinu, utsurou hito no, aki no iro ni,*
> *mi wo kogarashi no, mori no shita tsuyu.*
>
> (1) Sadly I long for death.
> My heart tormented to see how he, the inconstant one,
> is weary of me, I am weak as the forest dew.
>
> (2) See how it melts away,
> that dew in the wind-swept forest,
> where the autumn colors are changing!
>
> (Keene 1955: 6)

Tanka

A twenty-volume collection of Japanese poems called the *Manyōshū* (Collection of Myriad Leaves) dates from the eighth century CE. Many of its 4,516 poems are *tanka* or "short poems" with a 5-7-5-7-7 syllable structure. The tradition ordinarily calls for a natural scene to be expressed in the first three lines, with their five, seven, and five syllables. The last two lines bring a wave of emotion that reveals a parallel between nature and the human condition. Here is an example:

Haru tateba	When spring comes
kiyuru koori no	the melting ice
nokori naku;	leaves no trace;
Kimi ga kokoro mo	Would that your heart too
ware ni tokenan.	melted thus toward me.

(Reischauer and Craig 1978: 27)

Haiku

Haiku is a Japanese art form of three poetic lines in a 5-7-5 format that was based on the older tanka form. Here subtle connections between nature and aspects of life are compressed into a mere seventeen syllables. Among the most famous haiku artists was Matsuo Bashō (1644–1694) who was born as a low-ranking samurai. He gave up that social position in 1672 and moved to the city of Edo, whose population was approaching one million. He began to concentrate on writing poetry, and focused on the lowly side of city life. Although Bashō became accomplished as a professional poet in the city, he turned to a life of lonely wandering during the ten years before he passed away. Consider these translations of Bashō's haiku by James H. Foard:

Yuku haru ya	Spring departs –
Tori naki uo no	Birds cry; fishes' eyes
Me wa namida.	Fill with tears.
Toshi toshi ya	Years and years –
Saru ni kisetaru	The monkey keeps wearing
Saru no men.	A monkey's mask.
Samidare ya	Constant rain –
Kaiko wasurau	The silkworms are sick
Kuwa no hata	In the mulberry fields.

(Foard 1976: 381, 385, 384, 379)

Bashō and other great haiku poets captured the double sense of Japanese aesthetics as they expressed both **wabi** (loneliness) and **sabi** (poverty). Wabi is reflected in the sense of the person as but a small, humble part of the vast mysteriousness of nature. Sabi is reflected in the simplicity of haiku whose three lines are lean and minimal.

BOX 13.4 A SPIRITUAL PATH: JAPANESE AESTHETICS

Wabi-sabi. Wabi and sabi are two notions central to Japanese aesthetics. Wabi is an experience characterized by longing, tearfulness, nostalgia, aesthetics appreciation, loneliness, and sincerity. Sabi refers to things that are weathered, rustic, stark, or imperfect – which convey a sense of poverty, leanness, chilliness, or simplicity. Often an encounter with something sabi brings up a feeling of wabi.

Wabi and sabi intermingle in the purity of living apart from society in the heart of nature where one lives purified by nature (wabi) without pretense (wabi) in a simple way (sabi) in poverty (sabi). Wabi and sabi also intermingle in the Japanese arts, including: (1) martial arts (archery, self-defense, the sword), (2) literary arts (poetry, calligraphy), and (3) arts of sacred spaces (flower arrangement, tea). The way of tea (cha-do) shows how even drinking a cup of tea can serve as a kind of spiritual path that leads to deeper awareness of reality.

The way of tea. Tea seeds were brought to Japan from China by the Zen Buddhist Eisai (1141–1215) during the Kamakura period. It was the age of the samurai who increasingly went to study the arts in Zen monasteries and drink tea. The way of tea developed into a Japanese art form that reflects Shintō sensibilities to nature and the Buddhist contemplative attitude and awareness of interdependence. The tea ceremony takes place in silence in a small thatched tea hut, ideally placed in a beautiful natural setting. Powdered green tea is spooned into boiling water in a pot situated low in the floor of the tea hut where a fire burns. Scrolls with single-line poems hang on the walls. Each tea bowl is unique with its own flaw. Tea-drinkers listen to the sounds of nature outside the hut and hear them reflected in the tea preparation. The sound of the boiling water echoes the sound of the wind flowing through the pine trees outside the tea hut. The whisking of tea mimics the rustling of leaves outdoors. In the midst of the loneliness of wabi and the simplicity of sabi those practicing the way of tea gain a deep sense of the mysterious presence of kami – perhaps in the wind, in the trees, in the boiling water, and in the tea itself. Ultimately, tea is no-tea. Zen master Seisetsu (1746–1820) said that whoever enters into the realm of no-tea realizes: No-tea is no other than the Great Way (*ta-tao*) itself (Suzuki 1970: 310).

PART 3
SHINTŌ PERFORMANCE

PURITY AND COMMUNION IN SHINTŌ RITUAL

Shintō rituals from archaic times until today have been concerned with two things: (1) removing impurities, and (2) maintaining communion with the kami. **Tsumi** is impurity or pollution. It is associated with disasters, sickness, and errors. Impurities that happen to human beings include injury, death, immodest behavior, contagious disease, wounds, and other ill things. Tsumi is not considered necessarily within the control of a human being, but all states of pollution must be purified. Sometimes whole groups of people must be purified. A person cannot exist in the right relationship with the kami in a polluted condition. Therefore at the very least all those who approach the Shintō shrine wash their mouth and hands at the "water purification place" (ablution pavilion). There are three basic Shintō means of removing impurities: (1) *harai* (purification through rites), (2) *misogi* (purification with water), and (3) *imi* (avoidance of the sources of pollution). Beyond the ritual ways of removing pollution are three means of maintaining a close relationship with the kami to develop the proper attitude toward life: (1) keeping a kamidana in the home, (2) visiting local shrines and making pilgrimages to Ise or other prominent shrines, and (3) participating in festivals.

Harai (purification through rites)

Shintōists call priests to ritually purify situations in which pollution has become or may become a problem. People may go to festivals, visit shrines, or call priests to travel to a site to perform a harai (ritual purification). Shintōists generally seek to be purified through rites performed by a priest at times of: (1) groundbreaking, (2) misfortune, (3) travel, (4) home cleaning, (5) marriage, and (6) communal purification. A few examples should suffice to give a sense of these rites: (1) On the occasion of groundbreaking a priest is called in to pacify kami in the area where a new building is to be erected. (2) Japanese tradition considers special times in people's lives when they are more likely to encounter misfortune than usual, such as in a woman's thirty-third year and a man's forty-second year. On these years purification is sought. (3) Someone who is going on a trip will seek safe travel and request protection from the kami through ritual purification. (4) On many occasions a Shintōist will want a house or business establishment freed from pollution, such as for home cleaning at New Year, after a death, at the start of an election campaign, and upon opening a new business. (5) A Shintō wedding ceremony is called a Shinzen Kekkon. It involves purification of the couple and their families, and concludes with a drink of sake to commune with the kami. (6) At times an entire community wants to be rid of pollution and seeks purification.

Misogi (purification with water)

Misogi involves water purification done by pouring water over oneself by hand, by buckets or ladles, crouching in a river or ocean, or standing beneath a waterfall. Misogi Shuhō or waterfall purification is among the key Shintō rituals. People are led through the ritual by a priest who performs ritual movements that include esoteric mudras (hand gestures) for purification. The leader directs some physical exercises, pours sake into the waterfall and throws salt both into the falls and on to the participants. Entering the waterfall first, the leader then directs each person to follow and informs him or her of the proper time to exit the falls. Men wear a loincloth and headband, while women wear a headband and usually a white *kimono*, a formal divided skirt, and wide-sleeved outer robe that reaches the knees. They allow the rushing sacred mountain water to fall on the backs of their necks and shoulders, saying, "Harae tamae kiyome tamae rokonshōjo," ("I beg for removal of impurity. I beg for cleansing. Make pristine all six elements"). Misogi Shuhō usually takes place late at night or at the crack of dawn. Some people undertake the ritual often.

Imi (avoidance of pollution)

Imi is the avoidance of pollution incurred by using taboo words (such as saying the word for "cut" at weddings) or doing taboo acts (like getting married on "Buddha's death" day). Imi is required of people who have been polluted by contact with a corpse, snakebite, incest, leprosy, tumors, and so forth. Anyone who is ritually unclean may be cursed as he or she approaches a Shintō shrine. Thus Shintōists practice imi to avoid pollution whenever possible.

Keeping a kamidana (home altar)

Each morning offerings of food (e.g., cooked rice) and drink (e.g., water) are set on the altars. The kamidana has representations of local and national kami, and homage is paid to the kami morning and evening. Many Japanese make an annual pilgrimage to a major shrine. From those sites (especially Ise, which is Amaterasu's shrine) they bring back sacred objects (which may simply be blessed paper) to place on their home shelves (kamidana) or attach to doors, put in stables, and so forth. Kami are also asked to bless people's homes during construction. Ritual specialists invoke them when the threshold, central pillar, kitchen, and bathroom are built. By contrast, the butsudan has representations of Buddhas, ancestor tablets, and ashes of the deceased. Tablets are inscribed with a new Buddhist name, and are generally kept for thirty-three or fifty years. On the Buddhist altar are ancestors of the main family of the oldest son in the father's line. Special offerings are made in conjunction with Buddhist memorial masses and particularly during forty-nine days of mourning.

Visiting a Shintō shrine

Common Shintō practitioners (not priests) go to the Shintō shrine and walk on foot beyond the point where the **torii** stands as a gateway. This walk has a purifying effect. Someone with an illness, open wound, flowing blood, or who is in mourning should not approach the shrine (though this practice may be somewhat relaxed in the present day). It is appropriate to remove hats, scarves, and coats. Ritual actions include several instances of bowing, handclapping, bell ringing, and kneeling to make an offering. It is common for people to go to Shintō shrines on important occasions of their personal lives such as: (1) when new business is conducted, (2) when a soldier goes to war, or (3) when children are born, start school, get married, and so forth.

Participating in shrine festivals (matsuri)

Festivals are an aspect of Shintō that goes back to the earliest days of planting and harvesting rice, and today matsuri is the heart of all Shintō activities. The shrine festivals follow a four-part sequence: (1) invoking the kami, (2) making offerings to the kami, (3) entering into communion with the kami, and (4) sending the kami back. A Shintō priest, having undergone a personal purification ritual, makes a ritual invocation that calls the kami to the shrine and opens the doors of the shrine's inner sanctum. Offerings such as rice, salt, water, sake, rice cakes, fish, seaweed, vegetables, grain, and fruit are present for the kami. In village festivals the Shintō participants carry a portable shrine (*mikoshi*) and march in procession. Young men dressed in festive clothing shout and act in ways reminiscent of ecstatic kami-possession and sometimes rush through the streets. The ceremony involves dancing, drumming, and singing in addition to contests. Performances may include ritual Japanese dances by shrine maidens (called miko), a lion dance, a Nō performance, or a Sumo wrestling contest. All performances are meant as entertainment for the kami, and the contests serve as forms of divination. For example, the outcome of tug-of-war, Sumo wrestling, horse-racing, archery, and swordsmanship competitions indicates the kami's will. The heart of a festival is entering into communion with the kami. For this a feast is prepared. Wooden casks of sake are broken open and consumed as a means of communing with the kami. The feast may end with silent meditation. Finally the kami formally are sent back and the doors of the inner sanctum are closed.

KEY POINTS

- Kami are the mysterious presences revered in Shintō tradition. They are mainly understood either as aspects of nature or as divine figures from the *Kojiki* and *Nihongi*. Various kami function as tutelary (guardian) kami for clans, guilds, and locations.
- Shamanism has been a long-standing aspect of Shintō. According to Chinese historians of the third century CE, a Japanese ruler called Pimiku was a shaman. Japanese women shamans are called miko, and they sometimes work together with yamabushi to contact spirits of the dead.
- Throughout China's Tang era (618–907 CE) the Japanese deliberately imported elements of Chinese civilization, forming (among other things) their basic model for imperial rule. Late in the Chinese Song era (960–1279) the Japanese were deeply impacted by neo-Confucian ideology as well as Pure Land and Chan (Zen) Buddhist traditions.
- One of the most striking ways that the Japanese culturally distinguished themselves was through literature. Nativist interpreters such as Motoori Norinaga (eighteenth century CE) claim that the authentic Japanese sentiment is the "pathos of life," which can be felt clearly in Murasaki Shikibu's *Tale of Genji*.
- The Tokugawa shōgunate unified Japan and oversaw a period of nearly 300 years of peace. This was achieved through a strict isolationist policy and government based on a neo-Confucian ideology of a highly stratified society, and a widespread network of Buddhist monasteries to which families officially were attached.
- The Shintō tradition continued to impact daily life throughout various political and cultural transformations in Japan. A strong sense of nationalism developed among the Japanese people as they were affected by State Shintō from 1868 until 1945 when Japan was defeated by the Allies in World War II.
- Since the end of World War II the New Religions in Japan have gained tremendous popularity – especially Sōka Gakkai (derived from the Nichiren

Buddhist tradition) and Tenrikyō (based in part on the Shintō belief in kami-possession).

STUDY QUESTIONS

1 Define the term "kami" and name two types of kami recognized in the Japanese Shintō tradition. Review stories about the kami given in the *Kojiki* and *Nihongi*.
2 Describe the religious life of the early Japanese people and reflect on connections between early forms of worship and religious practice today.
3 What impact did the import of Chinese civilization (sometimes through Korea) have on Japanese religious and political life? When were the periods of most intensive contact between Japan and China?
4 Name two Japanese contributions to world literature, and identify a couple of great authors. (Hint: Think of the novel and haiku.)
5 Define kokutai and kokugaku. What was their impact on life and thought in Japan in the century or so prior to World War II?
6 Describe the rise of the New Religions in Japan, with specific reference to the origins and beliefs of Tenrikyō.
7 Describe Shintō ethics and practices today in terms of: (1) the importance of makoto, (2) removal of impurities, and (3) maintaining communion with the kami.

GLOSSARY

Ainu Early Caucasian-like people living in Japan with a distinctive culture.

Amaterasu The kami of the sun, from whom all Japanese emperors are said to be descended according to Shintō belief.

Bushidō Way of the warrior-knight; code of conduct for samurai that appeared earlier but was formalized around 1600 in the Tokugawa era.

butsudan Household Buddhist altar in Japan.

geisha A professional group of women entertainers in Japan, trained from childhood in singing, dancing, and the art of conversation.

goshintai A sacred object used in a Shintō shrine to represent or embody a kami presence.

haiku Seventeen-syllable poem in three lines of 5-7-5 format that developed in Japan.

kami (singular or plural) (literally, high, above, lifted up) Mysterious creative life energies that form the focus of Shintō worship.

Kami Way (Japanese: kami no michi) Another name for Shintō.

kamidana (literally, kami shelf) Shintō home altar for use in kami worship.

Kirishitan A Japanese Christian.

Kojiki (Record of Ancient Matters) Earliest surviving Shintō book (completed in 712 CE).

kokugaku Nativism or national learning; a literary-philological cultural movement from the Tokugawa era (1603–1867) dedicated to understanding and restoring the kokutai (national essence) of Japan.

kokutai (literally, national essence or national polity) Ideology promoted during the Meiji era (1868–1912) in Japan to justify the establishment of State Shintō.

makoto The life-attitude of sincerity that is the core value of Shintō tradition.

New Religions (Japanese: Shinkō Shūkyō) The "newly arisen religions" that developed in Japan starting in the late Tokugawa era, including Tenrikyō and Sōka Gakkai.

Nihongi (***Nihon-Shoki***) (History of Japan) Second oldest Shintō book (completed in 720 CE).

sabi (Japanese) Principle in Japanese art indicating an objective simplicity (poverty). See wabi.

samurai (literally, men who serve) Members of the military class in medieval Japan.

shimenawa (literally, enclosing rope) Ceremonial rope braided with rice straw displayed in Shintō sacred places.

Shintō Japan's indigenous religion; Shintō is the Chinese pronunciation of the Japanese term *kami no michi*, Kami Way; it comprises the Chinese characters for *shen* (spirit) and *dao* (way).

Tale of Genji (*Genji Monogatari*) First novel in world literature, written by Murasaki Shikibu around 1000 CE about life in the Heian court.

Tenrikyō (literally, Religion of Divine Wisdom) A Japanese New Religion founded by Nakayama Miki (1798–1887) after being possessed by a kami.

torii (literally "bird-perch") Gateway to a Shintō shrine; also symbols marking places associated with kami.

tsumi Pollution in Shintō. Harai is purification. Thus a Shintōist removes sumi by means of harai.

uji-gami A tutelary clan kami in the Shintō tradition.

wabi (Japanese) Principle in Japanese art indicating a subjective loneliness. See sabi.

yamabushi Mountain ascetics who combine elements of Shintō and Buddhist traditions in their practices of healing and exorcism.

KEY READING

deBary, W. Theodore, Keene, Donald, Tanabe, George, and Varley, Paul (2001) *Sources of Japanese Tradition*, 2nd edn, vol. 1, New York: Columbia University Press.

deBary, W. Theodore, Gluck, Carol, and Tiedemann, Arthur E. (2005) *Sources of Japanese Tradition*, 2nd edn, vol. 2, New York: Columbia University Press.

Herbert, Jean (1967) *Shintō: At the Fountain-head of Japan*, New York: Stein & Day.

Hori, Ichiro (1968) *Folk Religion in Japan: Continuity and Change*, ed. Joseph Kitagawa and Alan Miller, Chicago, IL: University of Chicago Press.

Kitagawa, Joseph M. ([1966] 1990) *Religion in Japanese History*, New York: Columbia University Press.

Picken, Stuart D. B. (1994) *Essentials of Shintō: An Analytical Guide to Principal Teachings*, Westport, CT: Greenwood Press.

Sansom, George B. (1962) *Japan: A Short Cultural History*, revised edn, New York: Appleton-Century-Crofts (first published in 1943).

CHAPTER 14

The challenge of religion

A CHALLENGE FROM YOUR AUTHOR

Ideas, arts, rituals, and social customs fill the world's religions with things of beauty, insight, and value to human beings. *Introducing World Religions* brought you many of these. Yet it would be dishonest to ignore the fact that in the name of religion, many human acts of violence or inconsideration were done and continue to be done. Religious teachings may even encourage acts of inhumanity or folly. Noticing such negative potential, thoughtful people sometimes approach their religions creatively. In the course of history, such creativity has brought a full spectrum of responses from excommunication to reform, from scorn to applause, from misunderstanding to acceptance.

Dealing creatively with discomfort

Areas of religion that sometimes disturb people are exclusivity, prejudice, and culturally opaque materials. Of course, one person does not always agree with another person's religious assessment. Yet it may be worthwhile to consider a few examples of what people have considered problematic in their traditions. New insights often come from looking at things from unfamiliar vantage points. No doubt, upon further consideration you will think of numerous other individuals who have made creative efforts to make their religion meaningful and responsive to their life and times.

- ***Exclusivity.*** Some people are troubled by the boundaries that religions appear to set up between one group of human beings and another. Mahatma Gāndhī (1869–1948), leader of the non-violent struggle for India's independence from Britain, exemplifies this creative response to discomfort.
- ***Lack of meaning.*** Some people are worried about elements of their religions that lack meaning for them. Material can seem irrelevant or appear inauthentic for any number of reasons, including culture-boundedness. Thomas Jefferson (1743–1826), the third president of the United States of America, exemplifies this creative response to discomfort.
- ***Prejudice.*** Some people are disturbed by apparent systemic prejudices within their scriptures against a group or people based on gender, belief, social class, and so forth. Elizabeth Cady Stanton (1815–1902), principal in the fight for a woman's right to vote in the United States of America, exemplifies this creative response to discomfort.

Gāndhī's *Āśram Bhajanavali*: counteracting exclusivity

Mohandās Gāndhī was the central figure who engineered a non-violent satyagraha protest movement leading India to independence from British rule. In Gāndhī's āśram twice each day a prayer service was held based on the *Āśram Bhajanavali* – a hymnal he compiled over a period of four decades. The prayer-book contained verses from five religious traditions that he felt spoke to the heart: Hindu, Jain, Sikh, Christian, and Muslim. In 1930 he prepared a version of this prayer-book in the English language, which is available today under his name with the title *Book of Prayers*.

As a Hindu, Gāndhī was probably already predisposed to openness regarding various spiritual paths – because Hinduism itself comprises so many religious options. Yet it took courage to bring together prayers from different traditions into his āśram's prayer-book. Some Muslims criticized Gāndhī for combining words from the Qur'ān with other prayers. And ultimately,

Gāndhī's consideration across cultural and religious boundaries may have cost him his life. A nationalist Hindu assassinated Gāndhī for apparently being too sympathetic to the Muslim cause. (Some say Gāndhī endorsed the plan for a separate Muslim state, which became Pakistan – but there is historical disagreement on this point.)

The US Congress published Jefferson's collation of gospel passages in 1904 – a full century after he had begun to work on it while stationed in the White House. This work, later known as the *Jefferson Bible*, is available today.

The *Jefferson Bible*: seeking authenticity

Thomas Jefferson, key author of the *Declaration of Independence* was the third president of the United States of America from 1801 to 1809. With a concern for the place of religion in society, he wrote the *Bill for Establishing Religious Freedom* that established the separation of church and state in Virginia. In 1804 President Jefferson began to compile for himself a version of the Christian Gospels that suited his intellect. He brought to his desk a blank book, a razor, his bible – and the wish to discover the authentic Jesus of Nazareth. He proceeded to cut out all gospel passages regarding Jesus that he thought must reflect the true Jesus. These he assembled in a volume he called *The Philosophy of Jesus.* President Jefferson did not speak publicly about his personal faith, although detractors labeled him as a deist. He was born into an Anglican household, but donated to each Christian denomination in his town. Overall, Jefferson favored the Unitarian commitment to a historically plausible, rational human figure of Jesus.

President Jefferson continued his biblical editing project into his late seventies. He compared translations of the Gospels of Mark, Matthew, Luke, and John. In four columns he listed Greek, Latin, French, and English translations of passages that he considered authentic. Left behind were the miracles, the angels, and the resurrection of Christ. Whether or not such events have truth-value, they were not meaningful to Jefferson with his European Enlightenment mentality. Thus, the president eliminated from his version of the Gospels whatever seemed to be accretions from the classical Greek tradition, and neo-platonic metaphysics. After all the cutting and pasting, Jefferson found a rational Jesus with sound ethical views. In 1820 he completed the project, entitling his text *The Life and Morals of Jesus of Nazareth Extracted Textually from the Gospels in Greek, Latin, French, and English.*

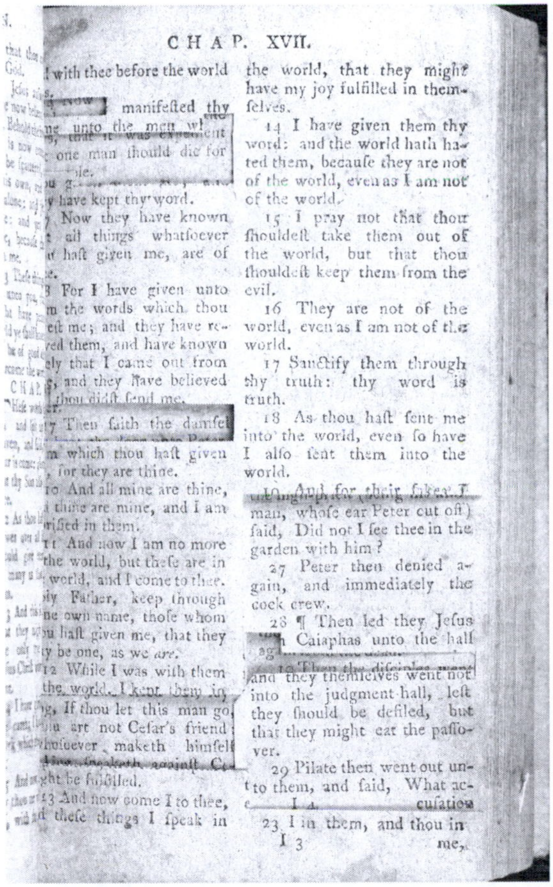

CHAP. XVII.

with thee before the world
manifeſted thy
unto the men wh
one man ſhould die for
have kept thy word.
Now they have known
all things whatſoever
haſt given me, are of
For I have given unto
the words which thou
me; and they have re-
ved them, and have known
that I came out from
and they have believed
thou didſt ſend me.
Then ſaith the damſel
which thou haſt given
for they are thine.
10 And all mine are thine,
thine are mine, and I am
ified in them.
11 And now I am no more
the world, but theſe are in
world, and I come to thee.
Father, keep through
own name, thoſe whom
haſt given me, that they
be one, as we *are*.
12 While I was with them
the world, I kept them in
If thou let this man go,
art not Ceſar's friend:
whoſoever maketh himſelf
might be fulfilled.
13 And now come I to thee,
theſe things I ſpeak in

the world, that they might
have my joy fulfilled in themſelves.
14 I have given them thy
word: and the world hath ha-
ted them, becauſe they are not
of the world, even as I am not
of the world.
15 I pray not that thou
ſhouldeſt take them out of
the world, but that thou
ſhouldeſt keep them from the
evil.
16 They are not of the
world, even as I am not of the
world.
17 Sanctify them through
thy truth: thy word is
truth.
18 As thou haſt ſent me
into the world, even ſo have
I alſo ſent them into the
world.
man, whoſe ear Peter cut off)
ſaid, Did not I ſee thee in the
garden with him?
27 Peter then denied a-
gain, and immediately the
cock crew.
28 ¶ Then led they Jeſus
Caiaphas unto the hall
and they themſelves went not
into the judgment hall, leſt
they ſhould be defiled, but
that they might eat the paſſo-
ver.
29 Pilate then went out unto them, and ſaid, What ac-
cuſation
23 I in them, and thou in
me,

Plate 14.1 "Jefferson's handiwork." Thomas Jefferson (the third US president) created his own version of the New Testament Gospels. In 1804 at his desk in the White House – razor in hand – Jefferson began cutting out portions of the Christian Gospels that he considered authentic. He left passages that seemed like exaggerations, such as miracles and the story of Christ's resurrection. Here you see a page of what was left after Jefferson razored out his favorite parts to make what became known as the *Jefferson Bible*.

The *Woman's Bible*: attacking prejudice

Elizabeth Cady Stanton, proponent of a woman's right to vote in the United States of America, recited her *Declaration of Sentiments* at the first Woman's Rights Convention, convened in Seneca Falls, New York in 1848. The text consciously echoed Thomas Jefferson's *Declaration of Independence.* Jefferson had declared in 1776:

> We hold these truths to be self-evident; that all men are created equal, that they are endowed by their Creator with certain unalienable Rights, among these are Life, Liberty and the pursuit of Happiness. – That to secure these rights Governments are instituted among Men.

Elizabeth Cady Stanton declared in 1848:

> We hold these truths to be self-evident; that all men and women are created equal; that they are endowed by their Creator with certain inalienable rights; that among these are life, liberty, and the pursuit of happiness. . . . The history of mankind is a history of repeated injuries and usurpations on the part of man toward woman, having its direct object the establishment of an absolute tyranny over her. To prove this, let facts be submitted to a candid world.

In an attempt to submit facts to a candid world, Stanton and other contributors to the *Woman's Bible* sought to expose gender prejudice stemming from scriptures that impacted upon the views of a Judeo-Christian nation. In this context they also set out guidelines for the comparative study of religions. Antoinette Brown Blackwell suggests that students of religions must be even-handed – but not complacent – in approaching the problem of the emancipation of women. She says the old texts cannot be authoritative, because they are culture-bound.

> If the suggestions and teachings of the various books of our Bible, concerning women, are compared with the times in which severally they were probably written, in general they are certainly in advance of most contemporary opinion. The hurtful blunder of later eras has been the setting up of early, cruder standards touching the relations of man and of women, as moulding influences and guides to broader civilizations. They cannot be authoritative. . . .
>
> I believe that the Bible's Golden Rule has been the real substratum of all religions, *when fairly applied from their own point of view.* But the broader and more discriminating applications of the rule theoretically both to men and to women in every relation of life have made, and necessarily must have made, most of the earlier practical regulations and teachings, beneficent perhaps in their day, pernicious in ours when regarded as still authoritative. . . .
>
> Turn on the light and so change the point of view. But criticism of ancient creeds, literatures or morals, to be entirely fair and just, must be comparative criticism. To be broadly comparative it must virtually include contemporary and intermediate as well as existing creeds, literatures or morals.
>
> (Blackwell in Stanton [1898] 1974: 185–186)

The *Woman's Bible* represents an early attempt in biblical criticism to examine the position of women in a society infused with biblical values. It also gives a strong endorsement for comparative studies in religions based on awareness of cultural bias. Elizabeth Cady Stanton and other contributors to the *Woman's Bible* would not tolerate gender prejudice – whether coming from the mouth of Thomas Jefferson or the foundational texts of their faith. In this they set an example of individuals who attempted to make their religion meaningful for their life and times.

THE WHEEL OF FAITHS

Our times call for special efforts at inter-religious communication. Each religion has unique strengths. These underlie valuable perspectives that can enrich our conversations on the world stage. Cross-fertilization of ideas does not call for mixing of faiths. It calls for mutual understanding and respect. To begin the conversation, we might start by recognizing one basic strength per religion. The Wheel of Faiths pictured and discussed

BOX 14.1 ATHEISM AND MYSTICISM

The Americans Thomas Jefferson and Elizabeth Cady Stanton were influenced by the European Enlightenment. The legacy of Enlightenment thinkers gave them room for openly critiquing their religion – within the bounds of monotheistic belief. Was there any room for atheism in their thought? Many works of Enlightenment thinkers were published anonymously or posthumously due to the religiously sensitive nature of their subject matter. Open expressions of atheism cost authors a high price in terms of social acceptance. Many of the groundbreaking thinkers who explored religion from the perspective of reason did not associate themselves with atheism. Many presumably found a personally rewarding way to think about God. Still, it is hard to know how various Enlightenment thinkers might have developed their theories in an environment that easily allowed a person to declare himself or herself as an atheist. A book entitled *Traite des trios Inposteurs* (*Treatise of the Three Impostors*) was circulated anonymously and secretly in 1777 both in print and handwritten manuscript form. It argued that revelation was a fictional product of the imagination, using arguments developed by Spinoza and Hobbes. It also claimed that the Abrahamic religions were instituted to gain political power, making reference to Moses, Jesus, and Muḥammad. The *Treatise* extols the use of reason as a tool for debunking false notions perpetrated by religions, and to throw off the bondage of institutions that control people through appeals to religious authority.

While many Enlightenment thinkers believed in God (conceived in various ways as universal intelligence, and so forth) their heavy emphasis on rationality tended to make them disbelieve in the imaginal realm of existence. They did not distinguish between the faculty of spiritual imagination that perceives beings of the imaginal realm, and fantasy of a bewildered imagination. This materialistic Enlightenment attitude persists among students of religions to this day. And though belief in angels persists as an article of faith in Islam, it tends to be de-emphasized in mainstream Judaic and Christian traditions. Angels may even be ridiculed among modern secular people. Thus one is likely to find a great contrast between reactions – even among readers of this textbook – to these two statements from the *Treatise of the Three Impostors*. By observing our reactions, it is possible to understand much about our own culture in this historical moment.

- ***First statement.*** "The fear which made the Gods also made Religion, and ever since men have got it into their heads that there were invisible Angels which were the cause of their good or bad fortune, they have renounced good sense and reason, and they have taken their chimeras for so many Divinities which were in charge of their conduct" (Anderson 1997: 14).
- ***Second statement.*** "One can judge from all that we have said that Christianity like all other Religions is not more than a crudely woven imposture, whose success and progress would astonish even its inventors if they came back to the world" (Anderson 1997: 31).

Thus with the championing of reason, certain Enlightenment thinkers discounted miracles and established a radical outside position in their view of religion. Some historians of religions hold such a far outside position to this day. Their perspective helps maintain balance in the field of study. But this does not mean that the exercise of reason necessarily discounts the use of the spiritual imagination. Enlightenment thinkers were interested in establishing a perspective whereby human beings through their rational powers could free themselves and others from blind faith, fundamentalism, and authoritarianism. Enlightenment thinkers did not take into account the creative imagination as a legitimate category of cognitive activity. Yet, other thinkers in the history of religions who explore the function of the creative imagination provide a perspective that allows a student of religions to appreciate a far inside position – in which angels, for example, are neither seen as objects of the senses, nor discounted as hallucinations of the fantastical imagination. For example, Henry Corbin distinguished between physical and imaginal perceptions according to Islamic mystic theology:

> It is quite evident that the mental vision of the Angel of the Earth, for example, is not a sensory experience. If, by logical habit, we classify this fact as imaginary, the question nonetheless remains as to what can justify an identification of what is imaginary with what is arbitrary and unreal, the question as to whether representations deriving from physical perception are the only ones to be considered as *real* knowledge, whether physically verifiable events alone can be evaluated as facts.
>
> (Corbin 1977: 11)

The two poles represented by atheism and mysticism are present in modern studies of world religions to this day. The differences in outlook can prove to be highly creative when people of different opinions engage with one another.

Plate 14.2 "The Visitation." This carving (ca. 1310) was from a Dominican convent in Central Europe. Here stand the Virgin Mary and her kinswoman Elizabeth – both of whom had their pregnancies announced by Angel Gabriel (Luke 1:11–38). Each figure is inset with a crystal-covered cavity through which images of their infants (Jesus and John the Baptist) may originally have been visible. What meaning does this piece of sacred art have if the miraculous story behind it is taken away? (What is left of religion if the sacred is removed?)

here (Figure 14.1) highlights a great contribution of each religion conceived in terms of individual and collective: discipline, balance, and care. Naturally, each religion has something to contribute to every category. And no religion provides the perfect example of a category. This schema – though imperfect – is offered simply as a starting point for inter-religious discussion.

Discipline: orderly society

The notion of an orderly society may strike people as both favorable and oppressive. It is important to appreciate the underlying motivation for the creation of a religious society. At their root, such motives might be fundamentally noble. Yet at times societies based on religious values may become distorted by motives of political ambition. What can we learn of benefit from two traditions grounded in the impulse to create a perfect society: Islam and Hinduism?

Muslim discipline

The Muslim tradition promotes a society devoted to Allāh's will through consistency of belief and ritual. The Six Articles of Faith and the Five Pillars serve as the foundation for an Islamic society whose members

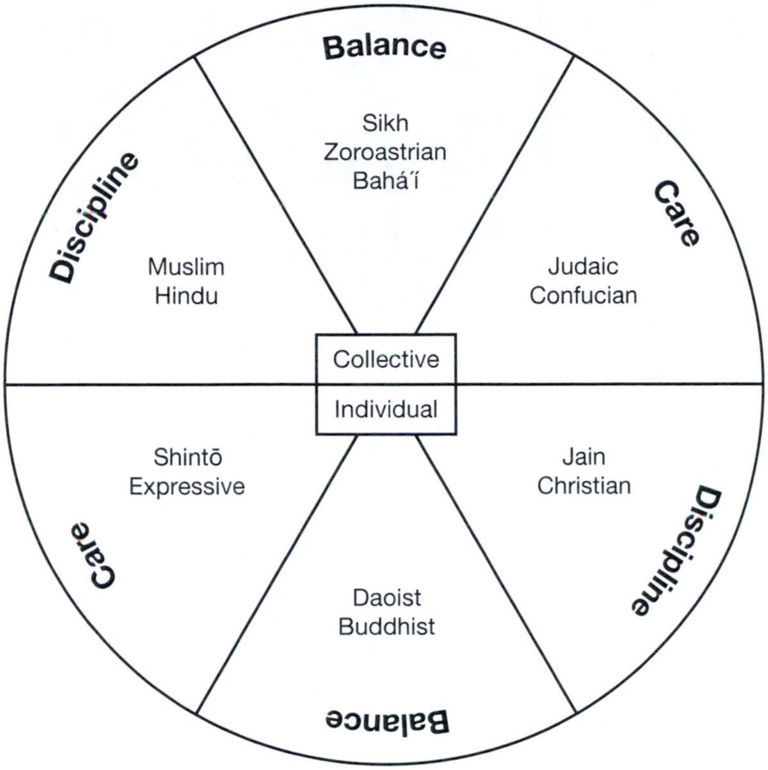

Figure 14.1
Wheel of Faiths: What can we learn from each other?

ideally act according to the sharī'ạ based principally in the Qur'ān and ḥadīth. The beauty of having a whole population devoted to spiritual development – praying five times per day, among other things – can become obscured if institutions become heavy-handed in imposing a narrow perspective on life.

Hindu discipline

The Hindu tradition is grounded in a system of four basic social castes produced according to the profound metaphysical law of karma. People are born to parents of the caste appropriate to his or her spiritual make-up based on past life actions. This system makes for an orderly society in which every person is allowed a prescribed range of activity that is presumed to be suited to their temperament and spiritual needs. Some argue that over time the caste system became increasingly rigid, oppressive, and unjust – allowing for too little personal discretion and social mobility.

Discipline: personal

Jain discipline

The Jain tradition takes as its central focus the practice of non-violence in thought, word, and deed. This imposes a tremendous personal responsibility on each and every Jain practitioner. It is incumbent upon laymen and laywomen as well as monks and nuns to minimize the amount of violence committed at any given moment. The personal discipline required to avoid harming any living being in diet, job, daily habits, and attitude is tremendous.

Christian discipline

The Christian tradition emphasizes becoming Christ-like in one's actions. This involves personally adhering to a high moral code that includes not only personal attitudes, but also social actions. The personal discipline ranges from praying without ceasing in one's heart, to living among the poorest of the poor to care for them in their time of need.

Balance: cultural attitudes toward gender and race

A tradition that acknowledges more than one seat of creativity tends to achieve a kind of creative balance. In quite different ways, the Sikh, Zoroastrian, and Bahá'í traditions provide lessons in balance.

Sikh attitudes

The Sikh tradition offers a model for gender balance reflected in Arjan Dev's sense of the divine: "Thou O Lord, art my Father and Thou my Mother" (*Gurū Granth Sāhib*, p. 1144). Aṅgad encouraged women to be educated along with men, and Gobind Siṅgh admitted both sexes to the Khālsā on equal terms. Although all the Gurūs were male, the tradition memorializes many strong women including Mai Bhago who led deserters in battle.

Bahá'í attitudes

The Bahá'í tradition recognizes prophets from many of the world's religions. Beyond that they sanctify inter-cultural and interracial marriage, seeing all humans as equal in the eyes of God.

Zoroastrian attitudes

The Zoroastrian tradition sees the world as presenting a choice between the Truth and the Lie. While there is no sense that people should give any weight to the Lie, the dualistic perspective nevertheless introduces a kind of cultural balance. The faithful weigh circumstances, and make an effort to balance out negativity with positivity.

Balance: personal states of mind

Personal balance and cultural balance interact. For instance, rituals can promote a balanced state of mind. Yet some religions – such as the Daoist and Buddhist traditions – focus directly on cultivating balanced states of mind.

Daoist balance

The Daoist tradition encourages realization of the balance between yin and yang – the receptive and progressive tendencies that occur in all things. Recognizing these feminine and masculine forces at play in themselves and in the world, Daoists respond in complementary ways to maintain harmony. In winter they remember that summer will come; in sadness they recall happier times. They become soft to mitigate hardness; they listen as well as speak, and so forth. Thus, in balance, they counteract harm and become intelligent.

Buddhist balance

The Buddhist tradition seeks personal balance between wisdom and compassion. Wisdom allows a clear perspective on the world and oneself. Seeing reality as it is prompts compassion for all living beings, who seek happiness often in disastrous ways. Wisdom and compassion are thought of as two wings of a bird, which cannot fly without a balance of the two.

Care: cultural preservation

Judaism and Confucianism have excelled in caring for their cultural traditions through thick and thin. These two traditions are very different in terms of their histories. One has stayed put geographically and has a strong sense of itself as the center of the world, while the other has been forced to uproot itself geographically and move its people time and again. Yet, both teach us about maintaining cultural identity.

Judaic cultural preservation

Over the course of their history as a people, the group faithful to the Torah has endured numerous trials and tribulations. Yet, the Jewish people preserved texts, rituals, and family connections. And when rituals (such as temple sacrifice) were no longer feasible, they were adapted while preserving the integrity of the faith.

Confucian cultural preservation

Chinese Han tradition typically takes a long-term perspective on political-cultural development, and generally holds the value of preserving itself. Thus, Han culture seems to have survived the onward march of history over millennia as well as two radical cultural revolutions (under the rule of both the Ch'in dynasty and Mao ze-dong). Reformers of both cultural revolutions bolted in reaction to China's traditional reverence for the "old" – but the old seems to have resilience. Indeed, while suggesting his own reforms, Confucius insisted that he was merely hearkening back to traditional culture.

Care: personal sense of responsibility for nature

These days many people are becoming increasingly aware of threats to the ecology of our planet. Traditionally, animistic traditions and Shintō have taken care of their physical outdoor environments. This is due to a deep personal respect for nature. This personal sense translates into integration of the natural world into religious rituals and stories.

Shintō sense of responsibility

Natural forces such as wind and sprouting rice are recognized as Shintō kami. The Japanese sensitivity to natural forces and the energy of natural objects teaches us to pay attention to the energy of growth, life, and fertility.

Expressive sense of responsibility

Expressive traditions are closely tied to specific localities. Their rituals and stories allow people to attune the properties of plants, animals, natural objects, and seasons of their locales.

PARTING WORDS

We live in a shrinking world. Here on this lonely planet people of various traditions are in a position to encounter each other more than ever before in the course of history. Yet every day the news carries ample evidence that people with different religious beliefs misunderstand each other. Lack of familiarity with world religions contributes to these misunderstandings, which often lead to negative impressions and outright conflict. One pressing example of mutual misappreciation is the case of people of the Abrahamic faiths: Judaism, Christianity, and Islam. There seems to be increasing intercultural alienation between Muslims and Westerners (Jews and Christians) in our world at the present time. A survey put out in 2006 by the Pew Global Attitudes Project indicates that "Muslims" and "Westerners" are plagued with negative stereotypical views of each other:

> Many in the West see Muslims as fanatical, violent, and as lacking tolerance. Meanwhile, Muslims in the Middle East and Asia generally see Westerners as selfish, immoral and greedy – as well as violent and fanatical.
>
> (Pew Global Attitudes Project 2006)

Here it would be appropriate to take up the insider–outsider challenge. In spite of what may appear to be a great divide between the Islamic and Western cultural domains, there is a place for communication and diplomacy. In 1983 Willard G. Oxtoby examined the issue of interfaith dialogue and concluded:

> Christian–Islamic dialogue has probably undergone more change during the 1970s than any other area of interfaith dialogue. . . . The surprising thing is that as the now "resurgent" Islamic world has gained political and economic power, many of its community leaders have become more willing to talk, not less.
>
> (Oxtoby 1983: 87)

Oxtoby felt that the increased willingness of Muslim community leaders to engage in dialogue with Christians was a result of being respected "after centuries of Crusader polemic followed by centuries of patronizing colonial disdain" (Oxtoby 1983: 88).

The European colonial legacy is still with us – for better or for worse. For the better we can appreciate a hidden irony in the history of European colonialism. As one taproot of the modern study of world religions it helped open the way for cross-cultural understanding. It also united many people with a common language.

Glossary

Abodes of Brahmā Four levels of meditation or dhyāna in the realm of pure form of saṃsāra in Buddhist cosmology; each abode is associated with a boundless social emotion: love, compassion, sympathetic joy, and equanimity; where the god Brahmā dwells.

aboriginal One who was there "from the beginning;" term refers to native peoples of a region, used interchangably with the term indigenous.

Abram (=Abraham) Patriarch of Jews, Christians, and Muslims. The Lord renamed him "Abraham" upon giving the command to circumcise all males of the covenant.

Ādi Buddha (Sanskrit) Mahāyāna Buddhist concept of the ground of awareness personified through this metaphor.

Adonai (Hebrew) Term for "Lord" spoken out loud in places where YHVH appears in the Hebrew Bible.

agency Term used by social scientists to emphasize the element of will (or political deprivation of will) in the lives of human actors who comprise and create society.

aggadah (pl. aggadot) Narrative. A Jewish legend, parable, joke, sermon, historical tale, or other narrative. Helps interpret biblical material, often by suggesting why something is or how it happened to become so.

ahiṃsā (Sanskrit) Non-violence. The core value of Jain tradition, which involves minimizing harm to oneself or other beings through acts of body, speech, and mind.

Ahura Mazdā Wise Lord. The ultimate principle in the Zoroastrian (Mazdean) religion that is associated with sacred fire.

Ainu Early Caucasian-like people living in Japan with a distinctive culture.

Akal Takht (Pañjābī) Throne of the Timeless (Persian: takht = throne). Seat of Sikh panth's legal, political, and military authority. Located in Amritsar near the Harimandir.

Allāh (Arabic from *al-ilah*, the deity) Primary name for God in Islam.

Amaterasu The kami of the sun, from whom all Japanese emperors are said to be descended according to Shintō belief.

Amesha Spentas Holy Immortals. Beneficent entities in Zoroastrian religion that protect the physical world, and inspire good thoughts, good words, and good deeds.

anekānta (Sanskrit) Not one-sided. Non-bias. The ideal perspective in Jain tradition, which involves seeing all sides of an issue or situation.

Angra Mainyu The hostile spirit in Zoroastrian religion who battles the "twin" spirit Spenta Mainyu in this physical world.

anahat śabad (Pañjābī) Unstruck sound corresponding to the Nām or Word of God in Sikhism. If Nām is the manifest sound, anahat śabad is the unmanifest sound beyond speech apprehended within.

aniconic Not involving figural representations (icons) of extraordinary persons, such as prophets, buddhas, and so forth.

aparigraha (Sanskrit) Non-grasping. A form of non-violence in Jain tradition that entails not clinging to material things, or opinions.

apocalypse (Greek: *apokalypsis* = unveiling) A revelation that professes to reveal the future. The New Testament's *Apocalypse of John* predicts a cataclysmic struggle between good and evil at Armageddon bringing the end of the world.

apostle (Greek: *apostolos* = messenger) A handful of disciples appointed by Jesus of Nazareth to heal and spread his message, plus other prominent early Christians such as those who witnessed Jesus' resurrection, Paul, and early missionaries.

Arab Nomadic Bedouin tribes of Arabia and their descendants; people whose language is a dialect based on Arabic; people who use Arabic as a ritual language, i.e., Muslims.

Aramaic Ancient Semitic family of languages. Widely used by Jews and non-Jews in Palestine (mixed with Greek words) and Babylon (mixed with Persian words). Language of the Talmud.

arhat (Sanskrit) Person who has realized non-self and need not take rebirth after passing away; goal of Theravāda Buddhist practice.

Ark A chest made of acacia wood overlaid with gold that was housed in a special shrine in Solomon's temple in Jerusalem (ca. 1000 BCE), but was lost that temple was destroyed by the Babylonians in 587 BCE.

Ashkenazim (pl.) Diaspora Jews who lived in Germany and France, and their descendants. Many migrated to Eastern Europe or America. They speak Yiddish, a Germanic language, mixed with Semitic words.

ātman The soul or eternal self; some Hindus strive to realize that ātman is none other than Brāhmaṇ (i.e., the living essence of the universe).

avatāra One descended from on high; one of ten incarnations of the Hindu deity Viṣṇu.

Avesta The Zoroastrian scripture; the ancient ritual language from eastern Iran used by worshipers of Ahura Mazdā.

axis mundi (Latin) World pole. Term used by historians of religions for any symbol that vertically connects the realms of existence, and represents the center of the world.

ba'alim (sing. *ba'al*) Canaanite gods, the worship of whom was forbidden by Mosaic Law.

babalawô "Father of the secret," a priest of Ifá divination practiced among the Yoruba ethnic peoples of West Africa and people elsewhere (e.g., the Caribbean, America) who practice Yoruba-based traditions. Also known as *bokónô*, those who "repel" danger.

barzakh (Arabic) A (hidden) barrier between two things. Describes the imaginal realm in Islamic cosmology where angels abide.

bhakta Devotee. A Hindu on the path of devotion (bhakti-mārga).

bhikṣu (Sanskrit) Buddhist monk.

bhikṣunī (Sanskrit) Buddhist nun.

bodhicitta (Sanskrit) Mind of enlightenment; compassionate mental decision to bring all living beings out of suffering; with this in mind the practitioner starts along the bodhisattva path.

bodhisattva (Pāli: bodhisatta) Theravādins typically use the word bodhisattva with reference to Gautama Buddha before he became enlightened – including past lifetimes from the time he was an ascetic named Sumedha. Mahāyānists use the word with reference to practitioners (at different levels of spiritual development) who seek enlightenment and vow to return to the world endlessly to free sentient beings from suffering.

bokónô A ritual specialist (among the Fon people of West Africa) trained in sacred lore, medicine, and divination techniques.

Brāhmaṇ The ultimate principle of Hindu tradition, thought of as the living essence of the universe.

brāhmaṇa (Sanskrit) A member of the priestly class of ancient India, according to Vedic teachings. The caste persists today among Hindus.

buddha bodies Buddhist concept referring to the forms in which an enlightened being can appear to people. (1) The form body is a flesh and blood person, such as the human Gautama who lived in India. (2) The communion body is the subtle form body that appears in the dreams and contemplative visions of skilled meditators and faithful people. (3) The dharma body is the mind of an enlightened being, seen when someone realizes the deepest point of Buddha's teachings. Theravāda Buddhists do not discuss the communion body.

Bushidō Way of the warrior-knight; code of conduct for Japanese samurai, formalized around 1600 in the Tokugawa era.

butsudan Household Buddhist altar in Japan.

cabbala (kabbala) Jewish mystical tradition.

Candomblé A Yoruba-based tradition in Brazil, related to other African diaspora traditions including Santería, Umbanda and others. The West African spiritual system is known as Vodún, which incorporates the Ifá tradition of divination.

Christ (Greek: *christos* = anointed one) Christian term meaning Messiah. From the early days of Christianity used to qualify the name of Jesus: Jesus Christ.

companions Early Muslims who saw or heard Muḥammad speak at least once.

conversos Jews forcefully converted to Roman Catholic Christianity in Spain and Portugal mainly during the 1400s.

Council of Nicea (I) A Christian council held in Nicea (Turkey) in 325 CE that affirmed the Incarnation, composed the Nicene Creed, and condemned Arius as a heretic for denying the divinity of Jesus.

Covenant Bahá'í term for God's assurance of continuing guidance to humanity based on divine guidance that came through Bahá'u'lláh.

creative imagination A human way of perceiving beings or forms in mystical visions of the imaginal realm. In Hindu and Buddhist yoga this is called the "divine eye" (Sanskrit = *divya-cakṣu*). In Islamic mysticism the term in Arabic for this imagination is *quwwat al-khayāl.*

crucifixion Death by hanging on a cross, used as a form of capital punishment in the Roman Empire. Christians invested great meaning tin the death of Jesus on the cross as atoning for the sins of humankind.

cultural imperialism The cultural domination that results from the spread of values, customs, and so on associated with a politically or economically powerful nation or civilization – often accompanied by an attitude of triumphalism.

dao (tao) Way, road, path; term used in Chinese traditions for the way of the universe.

Dao De Jing (*Tao Te Ching*) Chinese Daoist classic attributed to Lao-zi, also known as the *Lao-zi* (*Lao-tzu*).

darśana View, perspective. One of six schools of Hindu sacred science; in Hindu devotional theism "taking darśana" means seeing and being seen by a holy person or deity.

Dasam Granth (Pañjābī) Sikh holy book attributed to the tenth Gurū, Gobind Siṅgh. (Scholars debate the authorship of portions of it.)

de (te) Power or virtue; term used in Chinese traditions for the moral force that brings social and cosmic influence.

definition of religion A religion is a dynamic cultural complex with positive or negative impacts that stake a claim to legitimacy based on a foundational connection to reports of hierophany.

deva Shining one. General term for a god of the ancient Vedic religion, used later in Hindu tradition.

Devī Goddess. General term for goddess in Hindu tradition; name of a goddess.

dharma (Sanskrit) Duty (Hinduism); Buddha's teaching, as in Buddha-dharma. From a Sanskrit root *dhṛ*, meaning to bear or uphold. This represents the law of the universe that upholds or maintains existence.

dhimmī (Arabic) Protected people. People of the book (typically Jews, Christians, and Zoroastrians) who may practice their faith in a Muslim country, under certain restrictions.

diaspora Dispersion. Used with reference to Jews forced into exile following the destruction of the Jerusalem temple in 70 CE, and more broadly to Jews living outside the land of Israel.

dhyāna (Sanskrit) Meditation; any of eight high states of consciousness within samsara reached through śamatha meditation; jhāna in Pāli; basic term used for buddhist meditation school.

Digambara (Sanskrit) The "sky-clad" community of Jains whose monks take a vow of nudity.

disciple In a general sense, a follower of Jesus of Nazareth, past or present. In a narrow sense, only Jesus' closest male followers are called disciples in the Christian scriptures.

divination Fortelling future events or interpreting current circumstances through ritual methods that make use of signs and frequently involve supernatural communications

divyadhvani (Sanskrit) Literally, divine sound. Sound emitted from a Jain who attains to the highest knowledge. Digambaras believe it is inarticulate sound that can only be interpreted by special disciples. Śvetāmbaras believe it is divine because certain non-humans (such as godlings) can understand it.

duḥkha (Sanskrit) Suffering, dissatisfaction, alienation; Buddha's first Great Fact says this characterizes life before enlightenment.

East–West diptych A metaphor that emphasizes the orientalist view of the world as divided into two opposing flat plates (a diptych) with the West on one side and the East on the other.

'el A common word used in the Torah with reference to the Israelite God; General Semitic term for a god. The Hebrew Bible speaks of *'el shaddai*, *'el roi*, *'el olam* and *'el bethel* with reference to a mountain, seeing, eternity, and a house of a god.

emancipation The acquisition of equal legal status for Jews in eighteenth-century Europe, starting with US and French citizenship following the American and French Revolutions.

epistle (Greek = letter) Twenty-one letters in Greek attributed to Jesus' apostles written to Christian communities threatened by loss of faith and organizational difficulties. The earliest New Testament writings.

eschatology (Greek: *eschatos* = last) Refers in general to the "last things" or the final condition of humanity and the cosmos.

Eternal Beings of the Dreaming Supernatural beings discussed in the sacred lore of the Australian Aboriginal peoples.

Eucharist (Greek: *eucharistia* = thanksgiving) [*yoo*'kah'rist] The central ritual of Christian worship, based on the last meal shared by Jesus with his disciples prior to the crucifixion. Also known as Holy Communion, or the Lord's Supper.

European colonialism Europeans in modern times (sixteenth to twentieth centuries) taking political and economic charge of foreign territories to gain control of maritime trade and to spread Christianity. This began with Portugual and Spain, followed by the Dutch, British, and French.

European Enlightenment A European cultural movement spanning the late 1600s to the late 1700s that emphasized the role of human reason in thinking about religion, and championed intellectual freedom and tolerance.

Evangelical Christians Protestant Christians whose spirituality centers on experience of personal conversion and salvation through Jesus Christ, with an emphasis on millenarian expectations.

existential value The intellectual or emotional weight of an experience that bears on a person's very existence. Term taken from existentialist philosophy.

Exodus Exit. Name of the Torah scroll that tells of the Israelite escape from bondage in Egypt (ca. thirteenth century BCE or later).

expressive traditions Performance-based traditions that rely on oral transmission of sacred lore, and many non-verbal expressions to build religious meaning.

Fá Fon term for the orisha associated with divination, who is known also as Ifá, Orunmila, and Orunla. Fá refers to the Fon divination system.

Five Classics Five ancient texts that became foundational texts in the Confucian tradition: *Book of Odes*, *Book of Rites*, *Book of History*, *Spring and Autumn Annals*, and *Book of Changes*.

Five Ks Five articles worn by members of the Sikh khālsā, all beginning with the letter K in Pañjābī: keś (uncut hair), kanghā (comb), kaccha (men's undergarment), kaṛā (steel bracelet), kirpān (sword, dagger).

Five Pillars of Islam Five key rituals performed by Muslims: proclaiming the creed, prayer, social welfare tax, fasting, and pilgrimage.

Four Books Four texts that became the basis for the Chinese Confucian civil service examination from 1313 to 1905: *Analects, Mencius, Great Learning,* and *Doctrine of the Mean.*

four opponent powers Four Buddhist ways to minimize the effects of negative karma: take refuge, confess, apply an antidote, and vow not to repeat the act.

frashkard In the Zoroastrian religion, the restoration or freshening of the cosmos after 12,000 years of finite time.

Fravahar A key Zoroastrian symbol of a figure whose upper body is a bearded man, and whose lower body is a bird with outstretched wings.

fravashi A spiritual being in the Zoroastrian religion who serves as a feminine guardian spirit.

Gate (*báb*) Religious name for the founder of the Bábí Faith (from which came the Bahá'í Faith).

Gāthās Five songs (comprising 17 sections) attributed to Zarathushtra that form the oldest portion of the Zoroastrian *Avesta.*

geisha A class of women in Japan who are trained from childhood in singing, dancing and the art of conversation.

Gemara' Two collections of commentary on the Mishnah. When combined with the Mishnah, they form the Palestinian Talmud and the Babylonian Talmud.

Glory of God Translation of the name of the Bahá'í founder, Bahá'u'lláh.

Good Religion Term for the Zoroastrian religion found in the *Avesta.* The religion is also called Zarathushti or Zoroastrian, after its founder.

gopī Milkmaid. Hindu devotee of Kṛṣṇa from the Gauḍīya Vaiṣṇava tradition.

goshintai A sacred object used in a Shintō shrine to represent or embody a kami presence.

gospel (translated from Greek: *euaggelion* = good news) A New Testament narrative of the life of Jesus. Those written under the names Mark, Matthew, Luke, and John are officially part of the Christian scriptures.

Greatest Name Term in the Bahá'í Faith for the Name of God, which is "Bahá" (Glory, Splendor, Light).

griot A storyteller or oral historian among the Dogon people of Mali in West Africa

guṇa One of three dynamic qualities of the material world, according to the Hindu Samkhya darśana: light (*sattva*), movement (*rajas*), and inertia (*tamas*). These have a wide range of associations including foods, social classes, and colors.

gurbāṇī (Pañjābī) Recitation of prayers (bāṇis) from the Sikh holy scripture, whose effect is conveyed through meaning conjoined with sound vibration.

gurdwārā (Pañjābī) Sikh temple.

Gurmukhī (Pañjābī) Gurū's mouth. Script in which Sikh holy scripture is written. The second Gurū, Angad, commissioned the writing of Nānak's biography and hymns transcribed into this simplified Pañjābī script.

Gurū The notion of gurū is pan-Indian. The Sikh tradition magnifies it to call God is called the ultimate Gurū. Ten human Gurūs and the holy scripture are called Gurū because they embodied the jot, the Gurū's divine.

Gurū Granth Sāhib (Pañjābī) Sikh holy scripture. The *Ādi Granth* collection of inspired poetry became the final Gurū after the tenth human Gurū passed the lineage out of the human sphere, investing it into the Primal (Ādi) Book (Granth).

ḥadīth (Arabic = narrative) Traditional report that relates Prophet Muḥammad's words, deeds, or silent approval under various circumstances. Narrative presentation of Sunnah.

ḥajj (Arabic) Muslim pilgrimage to Mecca, Minā, 'Arafāt, and Muzdalifah. One of the Five Pillars of Islam.

haiku Seventeen-syllable poem in three lines of 5-7-5 format that developed in Japan.

halachah Legal material from the Talmud, Midrash, and later rabbinical writings; the sum total of religious law that defines the Jewish way of life.

Hands of the Cause of God People appointed by Bahá'u'lláh, 'Abdu'l-Bahá, and Shoghi Effendi to protect and propagate the Bahá'í message.

Harimandir (Pañjābī) Temple of God (Har) in Amritsar, India. Main Sikh temple in the world. Also called the Golden Temple.

Ha-Shem Name for the Lord used in the Tanakh.

Hebrew Members of early Jewish tradition; Semitic language in which Jewish scriptures are written.

Hellenic (adjective) Refers to the culture of the Hellenes (Greeks), as opposed to "Hellenistic," which refers to cultures influenced by Hellenic culture (e.g., fourth-century CE Persian culture).

Hellenistic era Three centuries from the time of Alexander the Great to the end of the Roman Republic (336–31 BCE) covering lands influenced by Alexander's conquest where culture mixed Hellenic (Greek) and West Asian (e.g., Persian) traditions.

hermeneutics The discipline of interpretation, often of scripture.

heterodox Not adhering to the orthodox or authoritative views of a tradition.

hexagram A figure made of six lines (whole or divided) stacked on one another. The Chinese *Book of Changes* is based on sixty-four hexagrams.

hierophanic history Accounts of religious experiences of hierophany, as opposed to accounts based in conventional history. Many spiritual (auto)biographies may be considered as such.

hierophany (Greek: *hieros* + *phainein* = sacred + to manifest) Manifestation of the sacred. Hierophanic events are unique, but people attempt to recapitulate them in the ritual arena of space–time using power objects.

hijra (Arabic) Migration. Muḥammad's migration from Mecca to Yathrib (Madīna) on Friday, 16 July 622 CE. This marks the formation of the Muslim community, and the start of the Islamic calendar as year 1 AH (*Anno Hegirae*)

Holy Trinity Christian mystery of three divine persons in one: God the Father, Jesus Christ the Son, and the Holy Spirit.

homology (n.) A likeness between two or more things that have the same structure; e.g., Mircea Eliade speaks of the moon, the snail, and the bear as homologous because they all appear and disappear (Eliade 1996: 157).

hukam (Pañjābī) Divine order. Reading from the *Ādi Granth* chosen at random, which applies to one's situation in life that day or at that time. Hukam means divine order, based on a Persian word meaning royal decree.

hwadu (Korean) Buddhist meditation practice involving focus on the question or key point of a kōan.

icon (Greek = image, portrait) A two-dimensional visual representation of a saintly figure which introduces the viewer to that figure in the imaginal realm. Used in Orthodox Christianity.

iconoclastic controversy Arguments over whether or not icons should be used. The debate first occupied the Christian world (especially Byzantium) for over a century starting in 730 CE.

Ifá System of divination that originated among the Yoruba peoples of West Africa, and is practiced by related groups including diviners among the Fon people of Dahomey (Benin), Candomblé diviners in Brazil, and others.

iḥrām (Arabic = making forbidden or sacred) A state of ritual purity adopted by Muslim pilgrims before entering Mecca and circling the Ka'ba.

imaginal realm (Arabic: *'alam al-khayāl*; Latin: *mundus imaginalis*) The ahistorical realm of "reality" where immaterial beings abide. Most religions make reference to such beings, whether or not they accept these figures.

imām (Arabic) Leader. Honorific title for a Muslim who leads the daily prayers. Refers to divinely sanctioned spiritual-political leaders in Shī'ī Islam.

incarnation (Latin = made flesh) A physical body through which an immaterial body of another being comes into this world. Most Christians consider Jesus to be an Incarnation of God (God born into the flesh), and thus call Jesus the Son of God.

indigenous peoples Early inhabitants of a place who have a longstanding cultural association to their geographical region prior to its colonization or annexation as a modern nation-state

indulgences Certificates representing acts of penance sold through the Roman Catholic Church. Martin Luther criticized them for representing transactions with God, and diverting funds to Rome.

insider–outsider challenge The challenge for people to adopt both inside and outside positions in their study of religions. This means to empathize with a religious worldview while maintaining a critical (analytic, not hostile) perspective.

Iranis Zoroastrians who remained in Persia following the Arab conquest in 636+ CE; also known as Zardushtis.

Israel Name used collectively for Jews as a people; name of modern nation-state established in May 1948; name of the northern kingdom taken from the Hebrews by the Assyrians in 722 BCE.

Israelites (Hebrew: *benei Yisra'el* = children of Israel) People of Jewish tradition named after the patriarch Jacob who was called Israel.

iṣṭa-devatā The "chosen deity" of a Hindu who focuses worship on one among many gods and goddesses. Typically a person worships the family's chosen deity, the village deity, and others in addition to his or her personal deity.

Japjī (Pañjābī) Morning Prayer by Gurū Nānak. First prayer in the *Gurū Granth Sāhib.*

***Jātaka* tales** Birth tales about Buddha's past lives.

Jew (=Judean) Term for Jewish people based on the name of the southern kingdom of Judah, whose capital Jerusalem was destroyed by the Babylonians in 586 BCE.

jihād (Arabic *jahada* = "he made an effort") Struggle. The inner (personal) and outer (political) effort to overcome threats to the practice of Islam. Both are of equal importance, but the inner jihād is more difficult.

Jina (Sanskrit) Conqueror, Victor. Title given to Jain tīrthaṅkaras because they are victorious over the suffering of saṃsāra.

jiriki (Japanese) Self-power; refers to Buddhist practice in which personal discipline and effort plays a major role, as in Zen. (See also tariki.)

jīva (Sanskrit) Life force or soul. Used by Jains to describe any living being with one to five senses, including earth bodies, human beings, godlings, and so forth.

jīvan-mukta One who is liberated while living; the goal of many Hindus.

jot (Pañjābī) Divine light embodied by the ten human Sikh Gurūs, and holy scripture, the *Gurū Granth Sāhib.*

jun-zi (chün-tzu) Princely person, gentleman; word for prince in ancient China; Confucius used it to mean someone of sound moral character.

Ka'ba (Arabic = cube) Cube-shaped shrine in Mecca, Arabia that is the focal point of Muslim pilgrimage and daily prayer.

kami (singular or plural) (literally, high, above, lifted up) Mysterious creative life energies that form the focus of Shintō worship.

Kami Way (Japanese: kami no michi) Another name for Shintō.

kamidana (literally, kami shelf) Shintō home altar for use in kami worship.

karma (Sanskrit) Literally, action. Actions of body, speech, and mind that bring effects in line with their causes. Jains, Buddhists, and Hindus have slightly different interpretations on the nature of such action.

kevala-jñāna (Sanskrit) Literally, unique knowledge. The highest realization according to Jain teachings, after which a person becomes a siddha upon dying.

khālsā (Pañjābī) Order of Sikhs who wear the Five Ks instituted by Gurū Gobind Singh on 30 March 1699. It is often thought of as being the order of the "pure ones" because khalis in Persian means unsullied. The word also relates to a term from the Mughal administration meaning oversight of lands or revenues.

Kirishitan A Japanese Christian.

kīrtan (Pañjābī) Sikh communal singing based on scriptural verses.

kōan (Japanese) Mental puzzle based on enlightened words and actions of Buddhist masters of the meditation schools, especially Chan masters who lived during the Tang dynasty (c. 600–900) in China.

Kojiki (Record of Ancient Matters) Earliest surviving Shintō book (completed in 712 CE).

kokugaku Nativism or national learning; a literary-philological cultural movement from the Tokugawa era (1603–1867) dedicated to understanding and restoring the kokutai (national essence) of Japan.

kokutai (literally, national essence or national polity) Ideology promoted during the Meiji era (1868–1912) in Japan to justify the establishment of State Shintō.

kratophany (Greek: *kratos* + *phainein* = power + manifest) Manifestations of power that have yet to be counted as sacred, such as a terrific tsunami storm.

kṣatriya (Sanskrit) A person of the warrior or ruling class in ancient India according to Vedic teachings. Contemporary Hindus still abide by such notions of caste.

kufr (Arabic) Disbelief; denial of God. A major offense in Islam because it shows ungratefulness to Allāh.

kuṇḍalinī A form of the Hindu goddess imagined as a snake thrice-coiled at the base of the spine to be awakened in meditation by Śākta yogīs.

La Chingada Culturally packed (nearly unspeakable) term meaning the violated woman, used by Mexicans with reference to La Malincha, the mother Martín Cortés (16th century CE) who is considered to be the first *mestizo*.

lam-rim (Tibetan) Stages of the path; genre of Tibetan Buddhist literature outlining meditations according to topics designed to lead to realization of emptiness and generation of compassion.

laṇgar (Pañjābī) Sikh free community meal where all devotees eat together without divisive ritual taboos.

li Ancient Chinese rituals as prescribed in the *Book of Rites*; Confucius added the sense of propriety; in the neo-Confucian School of Principle it is the principle (archetype, law) that governs the form of all material things.

liberation theology A branch of Christian theology that promotes the social values of peace, justice, and equality. It emerged in Latin America in the 1960s, and spread worldwide.

liminal beings Beings that move betwixt-and-between two realms of existence or experience. Players in the drama of world religions that inhabit the imaginal realm.

magi (sing: *magus*) Zoroastrian priests (now called *mōbads*).

Mahāyāna Northern Buddhism. Culturally progressive branch of Buddhism found primarily in East and Central Asian countries: Taiwan, Korea, Japan, and Vietnam (which has both Mahāyāna and Theravāda), as well as pre-Communist China and Tibet. Holds bodhisattva ideal, and includes dhyāni buddhas.

makoto The life-attitude of sincerity that is the core value of Shintō tradition.

malakhey elohim Angels; messengers of God.

mandala (Sanskrit) Mystic diagram representing the universe as a microcosm correlated with a mental state of spiritual value such as compassion, peace, and so forth; used in tantric Buddhism.

Manifestation Bahá'í term for one of God's messengers or universal prophets. Each perfectly reflects God's attributes on earth, but is not God. Bahá'ís consider that Bahá'u'lláh is God's messenger for this age.

manna A sweet, flaky food that the Israelites believed was provided by the Lord to sustain them in the desert after leaving Egypt.

mantic (adj.) General term for practices related to divination.

mantra (Sanskrit) A set of sacred words whose vibrations have a purifying effect on the person who recites them. For Jains and Hindus the most inclusive sacred word is AUṀ.

māyā Illusion. Term used in Hindu tradition, especially in the Advaita Vedānta school.

Mazdean A person who worships Ahura Mazdā; also called Zoroastrian or Zardushti, and more specifically Irani or Parsi.

messiah (Hebrew: *mesiach*) An anointed one from the line of David, the ancient Israelite king. Christians accept Jesus as the Messiah.

mestizo Term of Spanish origin for a person of mixed blood, used with reference to Mexicans of Spanish and Indian descent, for example.

midrash A story *about* a story in the Hebrew Bible. A literary form filling a gap between two words – different from a commentary, which elaborates on one word or point.

millenarianism, millennialism Christian belief in the future millennium during which Christ will come again to reign over a new world (for 1000 years), based on Revelation 20.

minyan Ten adult Jews needed for worship. Women are included in Reform, Reconstructionist, and Conservative, but not Orthodox Jewish sects.

Mishnah A compilation of Jewish instruction written in Hebrew from oral tradition that forms the early layer of the two Talmuds.

Mithra One of the chief *yazatas* in Zoroastrian religion, associated with the sun and contracts; became the focus of a religious sect that spread throughout the Persian and Roman Empires during the Parthian era (250 BCE–226 CE).

mitzvoth (sing. mitzvah) Commandments: 613 religious duties to be observed by Jews.

moko Term used by the indigenous Maori people of New Zealand for tattoo.

mokṣa (Sanskrit) Liberation from the cycle of rebirth. Jains, and Hindus aspire to this. Buddhists (and sometimes Jains) call it nirvāṇa.

mudra (Sanskrit) Mystic hand gestures that symbolize various spiritual states, such as freedom from fear; many correlate with beings in the imaginal realm; used in religions from India; important to Jain, Buddhist, and Hindu iconography.

Muslim One who "surrenders" (to Allāh's will). A person of the Islamic faith. Words "Muslim" and "Islam" stem from the Arabic root *salam*, meaning peace, surrender.

mysterium fascinans (Latin) A mystery that draws people toward it because it evokes the emotion of religious fascination.

mysterium tremendum (Latin) A mystery that frightens people away because it evokes the emotion of religious awe.

nād (Pañjābī) Seed syllables in Sikh holy scripture, with particular vibrational qualities and meanings.

Nām simaran (Pañjābī) Remembrance of God's True Name. Preferred form of individual worship in Sikhism.

native (n., adj.) Used with reference to indigenous, aboriginal people (i.e., people are native whose family line is traced to a certain place). No value judgment should mark this word, although in the past it (as also the word primitive) carried connotations suggesting that the native was uncultured, hence inferior.

New Religions (Japanese: Shinkō Shūkyō) The "newly arisen religions" that developed in Japan starting in the late Tokugawa era, including Tenrikyō and Sōka Gakkai.

New Testament The portion of Christian scripture that complements the Old Testament. It contains twenty-one epistles, four gospels, a history of the early church, and a prophecy about the end of the world.

Nihongi **(*Nihon-Shoki*)** (History of Japan) Second oldest Shintō book (completed in 720 CE).

Nikāya Term for the Theravāda Buddhist tradition or any of about 18 early Buddhist schools (all or which are now extinct except Theravāda); term brought into use by contemporary scholars of Buddhism to replace the negative-sounding "Hīnayāna" ("lesser vehicle") found in classic Mahāyāna texts with reference to the early Buddhist schools including Theravāda.

Nineteen Day Feast A monthly gathering among all local groups of Bahá'ís, held on or about the first day of each of the nineteen months of the Bahá'í calendar.

nirvāṇa (Sanskrit) Blown out, Buddhist enlightenment whereby rebirth into saṃsāra stops.

Noble Eightfold Path The eight steps which Buddha recommended as the way to attain enlightenment; these constitute the fourth Great Fact (Noble Truths); divided into three categories: wisdom, moral conduct, and mental cultivation.

non-self Lack of intrinsic self; translation of anātman (Sanskrit) or anatta (Pāli); term Buddhists use to indicate that sentient beings have a dynamic stream of consciousness rather than an eternal soul (ātman); Buddhist tradition names non-self as one of the three marks of existence.

Old Testament The portion of Christian scripture that was adopted from Judaism, basically equivalent to the Hebrew Tanakh.

orientalism A racist attitude running through Western scholarship and politics (leaking to the general public) that lumps all peoples of the "Orient" (East) together without distinguishing their specific characteristics. Concept developed by Edward Said, postcolonial theorist.

orisha The spiritual beings of the indigenous Yoruba tradition of West Africa, and related traditions such as Candomblé, Santería, Umbanda, Vodoun, and others.

Pahlavi Persian language (also called Middle Persian) in which most Zoroastrian theological texts and religious commentaries are written, especially in the 800s and 900s CE; name of the secular dynasty that ruled Iran from 1925 to 1979.

panth A religious group founded by a spiritual teacher.

parinirvāṇa (Sanskrit) A Buddha's final nirvāṇa, which occurs at the time of death.

Parsis Zoroastrians ("Persians") who migrated to India in search of religious freedom starting in 936 CE.

pbuh Letters standing for "peace be upon him" that Muslims write after the name of a prophet. In Arabic, "alaihi as-salam" abbreviated "as" instead of pbuh.

People English translation of the term in various Native American languages, used with reference to themselves.

Pentecost A Christian holiday fifty days after Easter that commemorates the experience of glossolalia by a group of Christians in which they began speaking in tongues.

Persians A tribe of western Iranians; a name for Iran because the Achaemenids and Sassanids ruled from the southwestern province of Persia (Fārs); all Persians are Iranian, but not all Iranians are Persian.

phenomenology A philosophical school that originated in the early 1900s with Edmund Husserl in Germany. Applied to religion, it becomes a field of study that aims to describe and understand the religious experience of sacred phenomena, especially through sense experience that occurs prior to rational thought.

play Term used by anthropologists with reference to the activity of *Homo ludens* (the human player) whose creative, spontaneous activity is central to the creation of culture.

postcolonial turn Phase of modern cultural criticism that can involve a wide range of issues including: challenging western ethnocentrism, exposing the nation state mentality established by colonialists for ease of subjugation, and deconstructing feminine identity in light of colonialism.

prajñā (Sanskrit) Wisdom; in Buddhism realization of śūnyatā or anātman.

principle Term for the highest, greatest, or deepest aspect of the cosmos conceived by a human being. A word such as "God" is often used with reference to (in the words of Christian Saint Anselm) "that greater than which nothing can be conceived."

progressive revelation Bahá'í belief that God's revelation is never final, and that Manifestations of God revealed God's teachings and laws according to the needs of the times in which they lived.

pūjā Homage. Hindu ritual that involves offerings to deities who are treated as honored guests.

Q (German: *Quelle* = source) Name given by German biblical scholars to a hypothetical *quelle* (source) from which Synoptic Gospel authors drew their material.

qi (ch'i) Chinese term for subtle life energy that runs through both the body and the cosmos; in the yogic traditions of India it is called by the Sanskrit term prāna, meaning subtle breath.

Qur'ān (Arabic) Recital. The Muslim holy scripture.

rabbi Teacher. A scholar of Jewish scripture.

rasa The "taste" conveyed through performance (e.g., dance) in both Hindu aesthetic and devotional traditions. The highest taste is love for God.

rectification of names Chinese (especially Confucian) principle of living up to one's prescribed social role (e.g., the ruler should live up to the name "ruler); making the meaning of names (words) clear and consistent.

reductionist In the context of religious studies, scholars rejecting the *sui generis* view of religions, and therefore working largely in the social sciences; they explain religious data without presuming the existence of anything irreducibly religious.

refuge Standard prayer that orients a Buddhist's mind toward the Three Jewels: Buddha, dharma, saṃgha.

religionist A term coined by contemporary scholar Robert A. Segal with reference to scholars in religious studies who hold a *sui generis* view of religions, including both theologians and historians of *religions* who claim that something irreducibly *religious* exists.

Religious Impression The experience of a Religious Subject being deeply moved (impressed) in the moment when an object is perceived as religiously meaningful, which gives rise to a creative act called a Religious Expression that tends to have symbolic meaning.

Religious Subject A person (the subject) who attains religious faith or understanding through an encounter with something experienced as sacred. Religious Subject and Religious Object come into existence at the same existential moment, and give rise to Religious Impressions and Religious Expressions.

religious symbol An object that represents or reconstitutes a sacred entity. The stand-in for a hierophany, which is its ultimate expression. The term is ambiguous, and needs more scholarly attention.

ren (jen) Benevolence, humaneness; a key Confucian virtue

resurrection Rising up after death. In Christianity the term for Jesus rising up on the third day after dying on the cross and being placed in a tomb. Easter celebrates this event.

revalorization The attribution of new meaning or value to a religious symbol.

ṛṣi Seer. In Hindu tradition, sages to whom words (hymns) of the *Ṛgveda* were revealed.

Sabbath (Hebrew: *shabbat*) The last day of creation according to the Torah, celebrated weekly by Jews from before sundown Friday to after sundown Saturday.

sabi (Japanese) Principle in Japanese art indicating an objective simplicity (poverty). See wabi.

sacrament A ritual that mediates divine grace (normally from the Holy Spirit). Typically it recalls a hierophany. Roman Catholic and Orthodox Christians recognize seven sacraments, while many Protestant Christians recognize two.

Śaiva Hindu devotee of Śiva

Śākta Hindu devotee of Śākti, the goddess.

Salafism (Salafiyyahs in Arabic = predecessors) General term for the Islamic fundamentalist movement that includes Muslims who strive to return to the disciplined ways of their predecessors in the early days of Islam.

śamatha (Sanskrit) Quiescence, calmness; a branch of Buddhist meditation leading to the dhyānas, but not to enlightenment.

saṃgha (Sanskrit) Buddhist fourfold spiritual community; monks, nuns, laymen, and laywomen; typically refers to monks and nuns.

saṃlekhanā (Sanskrit) Jain ritual of holy death in which consumption of food gradually is curtailed, until nothing is eaten or drunk.

saṃnyāsī Renunciate in the traditional Hindu fourth stage of life; also called śramaṇa (striver) or sadhu.

saṃsāra (Sanskrit) The cycle of rebirth. Literally, wandering around.

saṃskāra One of sixteen rites of the Hindu life cycle.

samurai (literally, men who serve) Members of the military class in medieval Japan.

Saoshyant Zoroastrian Savior who will come to usher in the end of time.

satī Ancient custom (now outlawed) in India of a woman burning herself on her husband's funeral pyre.

Sat Nām (Pañjābī) True Name. Sikh name for God.

satori (Japanese) Zen Buddhist term for enlightenment.

scholasticism A movement among medieval theologians of the Abrahamic traditions who aimed to resolve apparent contradictions between faith and reason.

Seder Ritual meal taken on the first night or two of Pesach (Passover), following steps prescribed in the *Haggadah.*

Sephardim Diaspora Jews who lived in Spain, Portugal, or Islamic Mediterranean lands, and their descendants. Many migrated to North Africa or the Middle East. They speak Ladino, a language akin to medieval Spanish.

sephiroth Ten emanations of divine light contemplated by Jewish mystics in the cabbala tradition. They comprise the Tree of Life.

sevā (Pañjābī) Service for the sake of others. A key value in Sikhism.

shahāda (Arabic) Muslim creed: "There is no God but God; Muḥammad is his Prophet." One of the Five Pillars of Islam.

sharī'ạ (Arabic) Body of sacred law in Islam.

Shī'a (Arabic) Branch of Islam concentrated in Iran, Iraq, Lebanon, Bahrain, parts of Afghanistan, and Pakistan (adjective: Shī'ī) (about one-fifth of Muslims are Shī'a).

shikan-taza (Japanese) Just-sitting; represents the highest form of meditation for Zen Buddhists of Dōgen's Sōtō school.

shimenawa (literally, enclosing rope) Ceremonial rope braided with rice straw displayed in Shintō sacred places.

Shintō Japan's indigenous religion; Shintō is the Chinese pronunciation of the Japanese term *kami no michi*, Kami Way; it comprises the Chinese characters for *shen* (spirit) and *dao* (way).

shirk (Arabic) Polytheism, or associating someone or something with God's power. A major offense in Islam because it disregards Allāh's unity.

Sho'ah The Holocaust during which an estimated six million Ashkenazi Jews were systematically harassed or put to death under policies of genocide instituted by the German Nazi Third Reich between 1933 and 1945.

siddha (Sanskrit) The disembodied jīva (soul) of a Jain who has attained liberation. These beings abide at the apex of the universe.

siddhi (Sanskrit) A supernormal power such as clairvoyance or telepathy that comes as a side-product of meditation. Discussed in Jain, Buddhist, and Hindu texts.

six perfections Buddhist spiritual path of a bodhisattva, involving the practice of: generosity, morality, patience, joyous effort, calm abiding, and wisdom.

skandhas (Sanskrit) Five heaps of conditioning making up the person, according to Buddhist theory: forms, feelings, perceptions, mental formations, and minds.

Spenta Mainyu The Holy Spirit in Zoroastrian religion who battles the "twin" spirit Angra Mainyu in this physical world.

śramaṇa (Sanskrit) Literally, a striver. A renunciate mendicant of India who seeks liberation from saṃsāra.

Sūfī Muslim mystic.

sui generis (Latin) "Belong to its own kind," or in a class of its own.

Sun Dance Native American ceremonial including a dance in which participants face the hot sun for several days, and offer their flesh to the divine for the sake of their community.

Sunnah (Arabic) Tradition, or path. The body of Muslim tradition about Prophet Muḥammad including legal perspectives, orders, matters of worship, sayings, habits, and so on.

Sunnī (Arabic) Branch of Islam whose members refer to themselves as people of the tradition (Sunnah) and community (about four-fifths of Muslims are Sunnī).

śūnyāta (Sanskrit) Emptiness, lack of inherent existence; deepest nature of reality as dependently arising according to Buddhist philosophy.

supreme buddha Specialized term with reference only to buddhas who come into the world to show the path to enlightenment when it has become defunct; examples are Dīpamkara, Gautama, and Maitreya (the future buddha).

sūra (Arabic) Chapter of the Qur'ān. There are 114 altogether.

Śvetāmbara (Sanskrit) The "white-clad" community of Jains, who wear clothes.

symbol (n.) An object or act that effectively represents something else because it has a common structure; a symbol is the visible form that stands in for – or makes present – an invisible or abstract entity in need of a concrete representation. Religious symbols are distinguished from signs because they are associated with spiritual power and are generally created on the basis of hierophanic events.

syncretism (n.) The combining of elements from different traditions. Syncretism implies a thorough fusion, but the extent to which each element is destroyed in the process of syncretism remains a matter of debate. A "syncretic" culture might better be called "mixed" or "varied."

Synoptic Gospels The Greek term *synoptic* (*optics* = seen and *syn* = together) describes the Christian gospels of Matthew, Mark, and Luke because they contain much common material.

Tai-ji Supreme Ultimate; in Chinese thought the reservoir of infinite potentiality that embodies yin and yang.

Tai-ji quan Supreme Ultimate Fist; Chinese martial art based on concepts in the *Dao De Jing* and *Book of Changes.*

Tale of Genji (*Genji Monogatari*) First novel in world literature, written by Murasaki Shikibu around 1000 CE about life in the Heian court.

Talmud Commentary on the Tanakh (one from Palestine, one from Babylon) comprising collections called the Mishnah and the Gemara'.

Tanakh Name for the Hebrew Bible (Christian Old Testament) made from the first letters of Torah, Nevi'im, and Ketuvim.

tantra (Sanskrit) Form of yogīc practice involving mantras, mudras, and maṇḍalas; called Vajrayāna Buddhism in India and Tibet, and Shingon in Japan.

tapu (taboo) Term used by the Maori of New Zealand with reference to powerful (hence dangerous) things or situations that must only be encountered through ritual

tariki (Japanese) Other power; refers to Buddhist practice in which reliance on the compassion of Amida Buddha plays a key role, as in the Pure Land schools. (See also jiriki.)

Tathāgata (Sanskrit) Thus-gone One; title that Gautama Buddha liked to apply to himself.

tathatā (Sanskrit) Thusness; reality as-it-is; Buddhist concept telling how things appear when a person is enlightened: just so.

tawḥīd (Arabic) Belief in the unity of God.

Tenrikyō (literally, Religion of Divine Wisdom) A Japanese New Religion founded by Nakayama Miki (1798–1887) after being possessed by a kami.

Theravāda Southern Buddhism. Culturally conservative branch of Buddhism found primarily in South Asian countries: Sri Lanka, Kampuchea, Laos, Myanmar, and Vietnam (which has both Theravāda and Mahāyāna). Holds arhat ideal, and emphasizes historical Buddha.

thick description Complex description that suggests the significance of an action or thing, as opposed to the "thin" portrayal of its obvious outward aspect; term coined by English philosopher Gilbert Ryle, and applied to the interpretation of culture by anthropologist Clifford Geertz .

Three Jewels In Jain tradition: Right Thought, Right Faith, Right Conduct. All these hearken to the princple of ahiṃsā (non-violence). In Buddhist tradition, this is the Buddhist way of talking about the three complementary aids to spiritual transformation: Buddha, dharma, and saṃgha.

three marks of existence Non-self, impermanence, and suffering (Sanskrit: anātman, anitya, duḥkha). Buddhist teachings typically involve a discussion of these.

three poisons Three mental afflictions that cause suffering and rebirth into saṃsāra, according to Buddhist theory: ignorance, greed, hatred.

Tian (T'ien) Chinese term for Heaven introduced by ancient Chinese Zhou rulers in the second millennium BCE.

tīrtha (Sanskrit) Literally, ford or crossing-place. Metaphorically, a ford that enables one to cross the river of saṃsāra. Refers to Jain holy places and the fourfold spiritual community that includes monks, nuns, laymen, and laywomen.

tīrthaṇkara (Sanskrit: *tīrtha* = ford, crossing-place, *kara* from *kri* = to make) Human beings born into the world to show living beings how to cross the ford (stream) of saṃsāra. They reintroduce the Jain path, and inspire disciples to establish *tīrthas*. Twenty-four appear in each phase of an endless cosmic cycle.

torii (literally, "bird-perch") Gateway to a Shintō shrine; also symbols marking places associated with kami.

towosi Ceremonial gardener of the indigenous people of theTrobriand Islands (Papua New Guinea).

transubstantiation Actual transformation of the inner essence of the bread and the wine of the Eucharist into the body and blood of Jesus Christ. Belief held by Roman Catholics since the Council of Trent (1545–1563), but rejected by other Christians.

trickster A type of mythic character who plays on the border between the world of humans and the unseen world of the spirits or godlings; often a messenger; known for playing tricks, hence the name trickster.

trimūrti Hindu divinity portrayed as three-in-one: Brahmā the creator, Viṣṇu the sustainer, and Śiva the destroyer of the world.

tripitaka Three baskets of Buddha's teaching: vinaya (including the monastic saṃgha training precepts), sūtras (discourses), and abhidharma (systematic commentaries).

tsaddik (m.; f. tsaddeket) "Pious one." A learned, saintly person among Ḥasidic Jews, usually addressed as "rebbe."

tsumi Pollution in Shintō. Oharai is purification. Thus a Shintōist removes sumi by means of harai.

Tuṣita heaven A realm of existence in Buddhist cosmology, where Maitreya, the future Buddha, waits to descend to earth. Buddha's mother was reborn here.

uji-gami A tutelary clan kami in the Shintō tradition.

'ulamā (Arabic, plural of *'ālīm* = one with knowledge) Scholars involved in research on any of the Islamic sciences based in the Qur'ān, Sunnah, and sharī'ạ, such as jurisprudence or theology.

Universal House of Justice The supreme administrative body of the Bahá'í community, ordained by Bahá'u'lláh. Nine members are elected by the membership of the National Spiritual Assemblies.

Vaiṣṇava Hindu devotee of Viṣṇu, most often in his incarnations as Kṛṣṇa or Rāma.

varṇa-āśrama-dharma Duty according to the caste, life stage, and gender of a person in Hindu society.

vipaśyanā (Sanskrit) Branch of Buddhist meditation leading to insight into the three marks of existence. (See also śamatha.)

vision quest A form of prayer used by Native Americans in which an individual spends time alone, fasting, in an isolated place to appeal to the cosmic powers for guidance, protection, and greater personal ability.

vodú (vodoo, vodoun) West African term for spirit.

wabi (Japanese) Principle in Japanese art indicating a subjective loneliness. See sabi.

Wāhegurū (Pañjābī) Sikh term used to express God's ineffable nature – that which is beyond description.

Wakan-Tanka Sioux term for "Great Mystery." It pervades and energizes the cosmos.

wen (Chinese) Pattern; culture; civilization.

wu-wei (wu-wei) Actionless action; in Chinese thought (especially Daoist) the paradox of doing nothing, and leaving nothing undone.

xiao (hsiao) Filial piety; reverence in the ancient China for spirits, one's ancestors, and one's deceased parents. Confucius underplayed the spirits, and emphasized living parents.

yamabushi Mountain ascetics who combine elements of Shintō and Buddhist traditions in their practices of healing and exorcism.

YHVH Tetragrammaton of the Lord's name. Jews do not speak this aloud, but substitute "Adonai" (Lord) in its place.

yin/yang In Chinese thought, the complementary principles that manifest in all things in the universe, such as female, dark, receptive (which are yin), and male, light, creative (which are yang).

yogī Practitioner of yoga in Indian religious culture. Yoga refers not only to physical postures but also to practice on the path of knowledge (jñāna-mārga), path of devotion (bhakti-mārga), and path of action (karma-mārga).

zazen (Japanese) Discipline of sitting meditation, emphasized by Zen Buddhists.

Zhuang-zi (*Chuang-tzu*) Chinese Daoist classic attributed to Zhuang-zi.

Bibliography

Adamson, Hugh C. and Hainsworth, Philip (1998) *Historical Dictionary of the Baha'i Faith*, Lanham, MD; London: The Scarecrow Press.

Addiss, Stephen and Lombardo, Stanley (trans.) (1993) *Tao Te Ching*, introduced by Burton Watson, Indianapolis: Hackett Pub. Co.

Ahmed, L. (1999) *A Border Passage: From Cairo to America – A Woman's Journey*, New York: Farrar, Straus and Giroux.

Al-Faruqi, M. J. (2000) "Women's Self-identity in the Qur'ān and Islamic Law," in G. Webb (ed.) *Windows of Faith: Muslim Women Scholar-Activists in North America*, edited by G. Webb, Syracuse, NY: Syracuse University Press, pp. 72–101.

Ali, A. Y. (1938) *The Meaning of the Glorious Qur'ān*, Cairo: Dar al-Kitab al-Masri.

Allen, Thomas G. (ed.) (1960) *The Egyptian Book of the Dead: Documents in the Oriental Institute Museum at the University of Chicago*, Chicago, IL: University of Chicago Press.

Altmann, Ruth V. (1985) *The Jewish Way of Life*, Jerusalem: Nezer David.

Anderson, A. (1997) *The Treatise of the Three Impostors and the Problem of Enlightenment: A New Translation of the* Traite des trois Inposteurs *(1777 Edition) With Three Essays in Commentary*, Lanham, MD: Rowman and Littlefield.

Anesaki, Masaharu (1930) *History of Japanese Religion: With Special Reference to the Social and Moral Life of the Nation*, London: Kegan Paul, Trench, Trubner and Co.

Asad, M. (trans.) (1980) *The Message of the Qur'ān*, Gibraltar: Dar al-Andalus. (Quotes from the Qur'ān used in this textbook are from Asad's English rendering unless otherwise noted.)

'Aṭṭar (Farid al-Din 'Aṭṭar) (1966) *Muslim Saints and Mystics: Episodes from the Tadhkirat al-Auliya'* ("Memorial of the Saints"), trans. A. J. Arberry, London: Routledge and Kegan Paul.

Aurobindo, Śrī ([1956] 1982) *The Secret of the Veda*, Pondicherry: Śrī Aurobindo Ashram.

Bahá'u'lláh (1975) *The Seven Valleys and the Four Valleys*, trans. Marzieh Gail in consultation with Ali-Kuli Khan, Wilmette, IL: Bahá'í Publishing Trust.

—— (1979) *Epistle to the Son of the Wolf*, trans. Shoghi Effendi, Wilmette, IL: Bahá'í Publishing Trust.

Barrett, David, K., George, T. and Johnson, Todd M. (eds) (2001) *World Christian Encyclopedia: A Comparative Survey of Churches and Religions in the Modern World*, New York: Oxford University Press.

Bashier, S. H. (2004) *Ibn al-'Arabi's* Barzakh*: The Concept of the Limit and the Relationship between God and the World*, Albany, NY: State University of New York Press.

Bashō, M. (1986) *The Narrow Road to the Deep North, and Other Travel Sketches*, trans. N. Yuasa, New York: Viking Penguin.

Bhattacharya, B. C. ([1939] 1974) *The Jaina Iconography*, Delhi: Motilal Banarsidass.

Bhattacharyya, N. N. (1999) *The Indian Mother Goddess*, 3rd edn, New Delhi: Manohar.

Bible (1993) *The Complete Parallel Bible: New Revised Standard Version, Revised English Bible, New American Bible, New Jerusalem Bible*, New York: Oxford University Press. (Translations in this book are from the New Jerusalem Bible, unless otherwise specified.)

Bokenkamp, Stephen R. (1997) *Early Daoist Scriptures*, Berkeley; Los Angeles; London: University of California Press.

Bowker, John (ed.) (1997) *The Oxford Dictionary of World Religions*, Oxford: Oxford University Press.

Boyce, Mary (ed. and trans.) (1984) *Textual Sources for the Study of Zoroastrianism*, Chicago, IL: University of Chicago Press.

—— (1996) *A History of Zoroastrianism*, vol. 1, Leiden; New York; Cologne: E. J. Brill.

Brown, Joseph E. (1953) *The Sacred Pipe: Black Elk's Account of the Seven Rites of the Oglala Sioux*, recorded and edited by Joseph E. Brown, Norman; London: University of Oklahoma Press.

Bryant, Edwin (2001) *The Quest for the Origins of Vedic Culture: The Into-Aryan Migration Debate*, Oxford; New York: Oxford University Press.

Buddhaghosa, B. (1976) *The Path of Purification (Visuddhimagga)*, trans. B. Nyanamoli, Berkeley, CA: Shambhala Press.

Buhler, G. (trans.) (1886) *The Laws of Manu, with Extracts from Seven Commentaries*, Oxford: Clarendon Press.

Caitanya, Mahāprabhu Śrī (1990) *Śrī Śikṣāṣṭaka: Eight Beautiful Instructions*, with commentary by Śrīla Bhaktivinoda Thākura, and purports by Śrīla Bhaktisiddhānta Sarasvatī Gosvāmī, translated by Śrī Sarvabhāvana dāsa, edited by Riktānanda dāsa, Bombay: Prospect Printing and Publishing, Pvt. Ltd.

Carybé, Jorge A. (1993) *Os Deuses Africanos no Canbomble da Bahia* (African Gods in the Candomble of Bahia), 2nd edn, Salvador: Bigraf.

Chan, Alan K. L. (2000) "The *Daode jing* and Its Tradition," in Livia Kohn (ed.) *Daoism Handbook*, Leiden; Boston; Cologne: Brill, pp. 1–29.

Chan, Wing-tsit (trans. and comp.) (1963) *A Sourcebook in Chinese Philosophy*, Princeton, NJ: Princeton University Press.

—— (1987) *Chu Hsi: Life and Thought*, Hong Kong: The Chinese University Press, and New York: St. Martin's Press.

Chang, G. C. C. (trans.) (1962) *The Hundred Thousand Songs of Milarepa*, 2 vols, Secaucus, NJ: University Books.

Chitrabhanu, Gurudev S. (1980) *Twelve Facets of Reality: The Jain Path to Freedom*, ed. Clare Rosenfield, New York: Dodd, Mead and Co.

Ch'u Ta-kao (trans.) (1976) *Tao Te Ching*, London: Unwin Paperbacks.

CIA World Factbook, Available online at http://geography.about.com/library/cia/blcindex.htm/ (accessed 17 September 2007).

Cleary, Thomas (trans.) (2003) *The Art of War: Complete Texts and Commentaries*, Boston; London: Shambhala.

Corbin, H. (1977) *Spiritual Body and Celestial Earth: From Mazdean Iran to Shi'ite Iran*, trans. from French by Nancy Pearson, Princeton, NJ: Princeton University Press.

Dasgupta, S. N. (1969) *History of Indian Philosophy*, abridged by R. R. Agarwal and S. K. Jain, Allahabad: Kitab Mahal.

Davies, Lisa (2000) "Monstrous Mothers and the Cult of the Virgin in Rosario Castellanos' *Oficio de tinieblas*," New Readings, Vol. 6, Cardiff, Wales: Cardiff University.

deBary, William T. and Bloom, Irene (eds) (1999) *Sources of Chinese Tradition*, vol. 1, 2nd edn, New York: Columbia University Press.

Dean, Kenneth (2000) "Daoist Ritual Today," in Livia Kohn (ed.) *Daoism Handbook*, Leiden; Boston; Cologne: Brill, pp. 659–682.

Desai, Mahadev (1984) *The Gospel of Selfless Action, or The Gita According to Gandhi*, Ahmedabad: Navajivan Publishing.

Deussen, Paul ([1906] 1966) *The Philosophy of the Upanishads*, translated by Rev. A. S. Geden, New York: Dover Publications, Inc.

Dowson, John (1974) *A Classical Dictionary of Hindu Mythology and Religion, Geography, History, and Literature*, 12th edn, Ludhiana: Lyall Book Depot.

Drewes, G. W. J. and Brakel, L. F. (1986) *The Poems of Hamzah Fansuri*, Dordrecht, Holland: Foris Publications.

Duggal, Kartar Singh (trans.) (2004) *The Holy Granth: Sri Gurū Granth Sahib*, 4 vols, New Delhi: Hemkunt Publishers (P) Ltd.

Dumoulin, H. (1979) *Zen Enlightenment: Origins and Meaning*, trans. J. Mardalo, New York: Weatherhill.

Dyson, Robert H. (1993) "Paradigm Changes in the Study of Indian Civilization," in Gregory L. Possehl (ed.) *Harappan Civilization: A Recent Perspective*, New Delhi; Oxford: IBH Publishing, pp. 571–581.

Eck, Diana (1998) *Darśan: Seeing the Divine Image in India*, 3rd edn, New York: Columbia University Press.

Ehrman, B. (2004) *The New Testament: A Historical Introduction to the Early Christian Writings*, New York: Oxford University Press.

—— (2005) *Misquoting Jesus: The Story Behind Who Changed the Bible and Why*, New York: HarperSanFrancisco.

Eliade, Mircea (1964) *Shamanism: Archaic Techniques of Ecstasy*, New York: Bollingen Foundation.

—— (1978) *A History of Religious Ideas: From the Stone Age to the Eleusinian Mysteries*, vol. 1, Chicago, IL: University of Chicago Press.

—— ([1958] 1996) *Patterns in Comparative Religion*, trans. Rosemary Sheed, Lincoln; London: University of Nebraska Press.

Feng, Gia-fu and English, Jane (trans.) (1972) *Tao Te Ching* by Lao Tsu, photography by Jane English, calligraphy by Gia-fu Feng, New York: Vintage Books.

Fletcher, Alice C. (1883) "The Sun Dance of the Oglalla Sioux," in *Proceedings of the American Association for the Advancement of Science*, 31st meeting, August 1882, Salem: Published by the Permanent Secretary, pp. 580–584.

Florensky, P. (1996) *Iconostasis*, trans. D. Sheehan and O. Andrejev, Crestwood, NY: St. Vladimir's Seminary Press.

Foard, James H. (1976) "The Loneliness of Matsuo Bashō," in Frank E. Reynolds and Donald Capps (eds) *The Biographical Process: Studies in the History and Psychology of Religion*, The Hague: Mouton, pp. 363–391.

Fung, Yu-lan (1975) *Chuang Tzu: A New Selected Translation with an Exposition of the Philosophy of Kuo Hsiang*, New York: Gordon Press. First published in 1933, Shanghai, China: The Commercial Press.

Gāndhī, M. K. (1962) *Varṇashramadharma*, compiled by R. K. Prabhu, Ahmedabad: Navajivan Publishing House.

Ghazali, al- (1979) *On the Duties of Brotherhood*, trans. M. Holland, Woodstock, NY: Overlook Press.

Giles, Herbert A. (trans.) ([1926] 1974) *Chuang Tzu: Taoist Philosopher and Chinese Mystic*, New York: AMS Press.

Gill, H.S. (1989) *Jaap Sāhib: The Cosmology of Guru Gobind Singh*, trans. and intro. H. S. Gill, New Delhi: Gobind Sadan Institute for Advanced Studies in Comparative Religion.

Goodrich, L. Carrington (2002) *A Short History of the Chinese People*, Mineola, NY: Dover Publications.

Gopalacharya, Mahuli R. (1971) *The Heart of the Rigveda*, Bombay: Somaiya Publications.

Gopalan, Subramania (1973) *Outlines of Jainism*, New York: Halsted Press.

Gosavi, D. K. (1983) *Tilak, Gandhi and Gita*, Bombay: Bharatiya Vidya Bhavan.

Grewal, Gurdial S. (1991) *Freedom Struggle of India by Sikhs and Sikhs in India*, 2 vols, Ludhiana: Sant Isher Singh Rarewala Education Trust.

Guénon, René ([1928] 2001) *Man and His Becoming according to the Vedānta*, trans. Richard C. Nicholson, Ghent, NY: Sophia Perennis.

Gulick, Robert L. (1975) "Preface," in Bahá'u'lláh's *The Seven Valleys and the Four Valleys*, trans. Marzieh Gail, in consultation with Ali-Kuli Khan, Wilmette, IL: Bahá'í Publishing Trust, pp. vii–xiii.

Gyatso, J. and Havnevik, H. (eds) (2005) *Women in Tibet*, New York: Columbia University Press.

Haile, Berard (1947) *Prayer Stick Cutting in a Five Night Navaho Ceremonial of the Male Branch of Shootingway*, Chicago, IL: Syracuse University Press.

Hakeda, Y. S. (1972) *Kukai: Major Works*, New York: Columbia University Press.

Halevi, S. (1997) *The Life Story of Adam and Havah: A New Targum of Genesis 1:26–5:5*, Northvale, NJ: Jason Aronson.

Hamill, Sam and Seaton, J. P. (trans.) (1998) *The Essential Chuang Tzu*, Boston; London: Shambhala.

Hane, Mikiso (1972) *Japan: A Historical Survey*, New York: Charles Scribner's Sons.

Hauptman, Judith (1998) *Rereading the Rabbis: A Woman's Voice*, Boulder, CO: Westview Press.

Helminski, C. A. (2003) *Women of Sufism: A Hidden Treasure – Writings and Stories of Mystic Poets, Scholars, and Saints*, Boston; London: Shambhala.

Herbert, Jean (1967) *Shintō: At the Fountain-head of Japan*, New York: Stein and Day.

Herskovitz, Melville Jean (1967) *Dahomey: An Ancient West African Kingdom*, 2 vols, Evanston: Northwestern University Press.

Hinton, David (1998) *The Analects: Confucius*, Washington, DC: Counterpoint.

Höchsmann, Hyun (2001) *On Chuang Tzu*, Belmont, CA: Wadsworth.

Hoffman, Y. (trans.) (1975) *The Sound of the One Hand: 281 Zen Koans with Answers*, New York: Basic Books.

Hori, Ichiro (1968) *Folk Religion in Japan: Continuity and Change*, edited by Joseph Kitagawa and Alan Miller, Chicago, IL: University of Chicago Press.

Horwitz, Tem (2003) *Tai Chi Ch'uan: The Technique of Power*, USA: Cloud Hands.

Hsiao, I. with Stewart, H. (1995) *The Three Pure Land Sutras*, Berkeley, CA: Numata Center for Buddhist Translation and Research.

Hultkrantz, Ake (1981) *Belief and Worship in Native North America*, ed. Christopher Vecsey, Syracuse, NY: Syracuse University Press.

Jakobsh, Doris R. (2003) *Relocating Gender in Sikh History: Transformation, Meaning and Identity*, New Delhi: Oxford University Press.

Iqbāl, M. ([1934] 1962) *Reconstruction of Religious Thought in Islam*, Lahore: Ashraf Press.

Iran-Constitution [ICL Document status 1992] Available online: <http://www.oefre.unibe.ch/law/icl/ir00000_.html> (accessed 10 July 2006).

Jacobi, Hermann (trans.) (1968a, b) *Jaina Sutras*, parts 1 and 2, New York: Dover Publications.

Jaini, Padmanabh S. (1979) *The Jaina Path of Purification*, Berkeley; Los Angeles: University of California Press.

—— (1982) "Is There a Popular Jainism?" Paper presented at the XIth Annual Conference on South Asia, 5–7 November, 1982.

Jeyifo, Biodun (2001) *Conversations with Wole Soyinka*, Jackson: University Press of Mississippi.

Jorgensen, Joseph G. (1972) *The Sun Dance Religion: Power for the Powerless*, Chicago, IL; London: University of Chicago Press.

Karp, Abraham J. ([1962] 1981) *The Jewish Way of Life and Thought*, New York: Ktav Publishing House, Inc.

Keene, Donald (1955) *Japanese Literature: An Introduction for Western Readers*, New York: Grove Press.

Kennedy, Paul (1987) *The Rise and Fall of the Great Powers: Economic Change and Military Conflict from 1500 to 2000*, New York: Random House.

Khalsa, Sant S. (trans.) *Ādi Granth*. Available online at: <http://www.sikhs.org> (accessed 28 July 2006). [All quotes from the *Ādi Granth* are from this translation except the first by Duggal.]

Khantipalo, B. (1979) *Banner of the Arhats: Buddhist Monks and Nuns from the Buddha's Time till Now*, Kandy, Sri Lanka: Buddhist Publication Society.

Kierkegaard, S. (1985) *Fear and Trembling: Dialectical Lyric by Johannes* de silentio, trans. A. Hannay, New York: Penguin.

King, R. (1999) *Orientalism and Religion: Postcolonial Theory, India and "The Mystic East"*, New York: Routledge.

Klein, Isaac (1979) *A Guide to Jewish Religious Practice*, New York: The Jewish Theological Seminary of America.

Kohli, S.S. (1975) *Sikh Ethics*, New Delhi: Munshiram Manoharlal Publishers.

Kwok, Man-Ho, Palmer, Martin and Ramsay, Jay (trans.) (2002) *Tao Te Ching*, calligraphy by Kwok-Lap Chan, London: Vega.

Kumar, Nita (1994) *Women as Subjects: South Asian Histories*, Charlottesville, VA: University Press of Virginia.

Kurzman, Charles (ed.) (1998) *Liberal Islam: A Source Book*, New York: Oxford University Press.

Kushner. L. (2000) *The River of Light: Jewish Mystical Awareness*, Woodstock, VT: Jewish Lights Publishing.

Lalwani, K. C. (n.d.) *Jaina Namokara: Obeisance to the Enlightened*, The Late Rawatmal Lalwani Commemoration Series, no. 1, Calcutta: Kamala Lalwani Prajñānam.

Lau, D.C. (trans.) ([1963] 1985) *Lao Tzu: Tao Te Ching*, New York: Penguin Books.

Leaman, O. (1996) "Orientalism and Islamic philosophy," in S. H. Nasr and O. Leaman (eds) *History of Islamic Philosophy, Part II*, London: Routledge, pp. 1143–1148.

Leclerq, J. ([1957] 1985) *The Love of Learning and the Desire for God: A Study of Monastic Culture*, trans. C. Misrahi, New York: Fordham University Press.

Legge, James ([1960] 1970) *The Chinese Classics:* The Ch'un Ts'ew *with* The Tso Chuen, vol. 5 of 5, Hong Kong: Hong Kong University Press. (Originally published by Oxford University Press in 1893.)

Levinson, David (2000) *The Wilson Chronology of the World's Religions*, with contributions from John Bowman, C. Roger Davis, Michael Golay, and Eva Weber, New York; Dublin: The H. W. Wilson Company.

Lifton, Robert J. (1968) *Revolutionary Immortality: Mao Tse-Tung and the Chinese Cultural Revolution*, New York: Random House.

Lui, Hubert H. (trans.) (n.d.) "Experience Talk" – Experience of Learning Tai Chi Chuan, by Toong Ying-kit Published in Hong Kong, 1958, Manuscript from *c.* 1978.

Lincoln, B. (1985) "Notes toward a Theory of Religion and Revolution", in Lincoln (ed.) *Religion, Rebellion, and Revolution*, New York: St. Martin's Press, pp. 266–292.

Lundin, E. G. and Lundin, A. H. (1996) *Contemporary Religious Ideas: Bibliographic Essays*, Englewood, CO: Libraries Unlimited, Inc.

McArthur, H. (1969) "Basic Issues, A Survey of Recent Gospel Research," in H. K. McArthur (ed.) *In Search of the Historical Jesus*, New York: Charles Scribner's Sons, pp. 139–144..

McCutcheon, R. T. (2001) *Critics Not Caretakers, Redescribing the Public Study of Religion*, Albany, NY: State University of New York Press.

McGeveran, William A. (2005) *The World Almanac and Book of Facts 2005*, New York: World Almanac Books.

McLeod, W. H. (2005) *Historical Dictionary of Sikhism*, 2nd edn, Lanham, MD: The Scarecrow Press, Inc.

Mahajan, V. D. (1964) *Mughal Rule in India*, New Delhi: S. Chand and Co.

Male, E. (1958) *The Gothic Image: Religious Art in France of the Thirteenth Century*, trans. D. Nussey, New York: Harper and Row.

Malinowski, Bronislaw ([1935] 1966) *Coral Gardens and Their Magic: Soil-tilling and the Agricultural Rites in the Trobriand Islands*, vol. 1, 2nd edn, introduction by Edmund R. Leach, London: George Allen and Unwin.

Maneri, S. (1974) *Letters from a Sufi Teacher*, trans. B. Singh, New York: Samuel Weiser.

Marrone, S. P. (2003) "Medieval Philosophy in Context," in A. S. McGrade (ed.) *The Cambridge Companion to Medieval Philosophy*, Cambridge: Cambridge University Press, pp. 10–50.

Martin, B. (1974) *A History of Judaism: Europe and the New World*, New York: Basic Books.

Meier J. P. (1991, 1994, 2001) *A Marginal Jew: Rethinking the Historical Jesus*, 3 vols, New York: Doubleday.

Modi, Jivanji J. (1922) *The Religious Ceremonies and Customs of the Parsees*, Bombay: British India Press.

Morton, W. Scott, and Lewis, Charlton M. ([1980] 2005) *China: Its History and Culture*, New York: McGraw-Hill.

Motoori, Norinaga (1997) *Kojiki-den, Book 1*, introduced, translated, and annotated by Ann Wehmeyer, with a preface by Naoki Sakai, Ithaca, NY: Cornell University East Asia Program.

Murasaki, Shikibu (1993) *The Tale of Genji*, trans with an intro. by Arthur Waley, New York: Modern Library.

Murata, S. and Chittick, W. C. (1994) *The Vision of Islam*, New York: Paragon House.

Nanamoli, B. and Bodhi, B. (trans.) (1995) *The Middle Length Discourses of the Buddha: A New Translation of the Majjhima Nikāya*, Boston, MA: Wisdom Publications.

Nansen, Huang (1997) "Confucius and Confucianism," in Brian Carr and Indira Mahalingam (eds) *Companion Encyclopedia of Asian Philosophy*, London; New York: Routledge, pp. 535–552.

Nascimento, Abdias do (1995) *Os Deuses Vivos da Africa* (Orishas: The Living Gods of Africa in Brazil), Rio de Janeiro: IPEAFRO/Afrodiaspora.

Nasr, Seyyed H., with Aminrazavi, Mehdi (1999) *An Anthology of Philosophy in Persia*, vol. 1, New York; Oxford: Oxford University Press.

Ohnuma, R. (2006) "Debt to the Mother: A Neglected Aspect of the Founding of the Buddhist Nuns' Order," *Journal of the American Academy of Religion*, 74 (4): 861–901.

Olson, James S. (ed.) (1991) *Historical Dictionary of European Imperialism*, New York: Greenwood Press.

Otto, Rudolph (1931) *Religious Essays*, trans. Brian Lunn, London: Oxford University Press.

—— ([1923] 1970) *The Idea of the Holy*, trans. John W. Harvey, London: Oxford University Press.

Ouspensky, L. (1978) *Theology of the Icon*, Crestwood, NY: St. Vladimir's Seminary Press.

Oxtoby, W. G. (1983) *The Meaning of Other Faiths*, Philadelphia, PA: The Westminster Press.

Paz, Octavio (1961) *The Labyrinth of Solitude: Life and Thought in Mexico*, trans. Lysander Kemp, New York: Grove Press. First published in 1950; expanded and revised in 1959.

Pernoud, R. (1966) *Joan of Arc: By Herself and Her Witnesses*, trans. E. Hyams, New York: Stein and Day.

Pew Global Attitudes Project (2006) (released 22 June 2006) *The Great Divide: How Westerners and Muslims View Each Other*. Available online at <http://pewglobal.org/reports/display.php?ReportID=253> (accessed 18 July 2006; 8 September 2006).

Piburn, S. (1990) *The Nobel Peace Prize and the Dalai Lama*, Ithaca, NY: Snow Lion Publications.

Picken, Stuart D. B. (1994) *Essentials of Shintō: An Analytical Guide to Principal Teachings*, Westport, CT: Greenwood Press.

Possehl, Gregory L. (ed.) (1979) *Ancient Cities of the Indus*, Durham, NC: Carolina Academic Press.

Powell, M. A. (1998) *Jesus as a Figure in History: How Modern Historians View the Man from Galilee*. Louisville, KY: Westminster John Knox Press.

Prabhupāda, A. C. Bhaktivedānta (1985) *The Nectar of Devotion: The Complete Science of Bhakti-yoga*, London: The Bhaktivedānta Book Trust.

Price, David (trans.) (1829) *Memoirs of The Emperor Jehāngueir, written by himself* (translated from Persian), London: Oriental Translation Committee.

Pritam, Amrita (1979) *Alone in the Multitude*, trans. and ed. Suresh Kohli, New Delhi: Indian Literary Review Editions.

—— (1989) *Life and Times*, New Delhi: Vikas Publishing House Pvt Ltd.

Pritchard, James B. ([1950] 1955) *Ancient Near Eastern Texts Relating to the Old Testament*, Princeton, NJ: Princeton University Press.

Rādhākrishnan, S. (1992) *The Principal Upaniṣads*, Atlantic Highlands, NJ: Humanities Press.

Rāma, Swami (1985) *Perennial Psychology of the Bhagavad Gita*, Honesdale, PA: Himalayan Institute.

Razvi, M. A. (1997) *Suhrawardi and the School of Illumination*, London: Curzon Press.

Reischauer, Edwin O. ([1946] 1970) *Japan: The Story of a Nation*, London: Duckworth.

Reischauer, Edwin O. and Craig, Albert M. (1978) *Japan: Tradition and Transformation*, Boston, MA: Houghton Mifflin.

Rinehart, Robin (2004) "Hearing and Remembering," in Robert Rinehart (ed.) *Contemporary Hinduism: Ritual, Culture, and Practice*, Santa Barbara, CA: ABC-CLIO, Inc., pp. 67–97.

Roberts, D. S. (1982) *Islam: A Concise Introduction*, New York: Harper and Row.

Robinson, J. M. (ed.)(1996) *The Nag Hammadi Library in English*, 4th edn, trans. and intro. by members of the Coptic Gnostic Library Project, Leiden: E. J. Brill.

Robley, H. G. (2003) *Maori Tatooing*, Mineola, NY: Dover Publications. First published in 1896 by Chapman and Hall, London.

Robson, J. (1965) *Mishkat al-masabih vol. 1 part 5* of (1963–65) *Mishkat al-masabih: English Translation with Explanatory Notes*, 4 vols, Lahore: Sh. Muḥammad Ashraf.

Root, Martha ([1981] 2000) *Táhirih the Pure*, Los Angeles, CA: Kalímát Press.

Said, Edward W. (1978) *Orientalism*, New York: Pantheon Books.

Sangave, Vilas A. (1997) *Jaina Religion and Community*, compiled and edited by B. Srinivasa, Murthy, Long Beach, CA: Long Beach Publications.

Sansom, George B. (1962) *Japan: A Short Cultural History*, revised edn, New York: Appleton-Century-Crofts (first published in 1943).

Sargeant, Winthrop (trans.) (1984) *The Bhagavad Gita*, revised edn, ed. Christopher Chapple, foreword by Swami Samatananda, Albany, NY: State University of New York Press.

Sen, Rāmprasād (1999) *Grace and Mercy in Her Wild Hair: Selected Poems to the Mother Goddess*, trans. Leonard Nathan and Clinton Seely, Prescott, AZ: Hohm Press.

Shah, Natubhai (1998) *Jainism: The World of Conquerors*, Vol. 1 of 2 vols, Brighton; Portland: Sussex Press.

Shan, Sharan-Jeet (1985) *In My Own Name: An Autobiography*, London: The Woman's Press.

Shanti Mayi (2007) Gāyatrī Mantra available online at http://www.shantimayi.com/gayatri_sm.html (accessed 8 August 2007).

Shibayama, Z. (1974) *Zen Comments on the Mumonkan*, trans. S. Kudo, New York: Signet.

Sikh Reht Maryada. Available online: http://www.sgpc.net/rehat_maryada/section-one.html (accessed 26 February 2007).

Singh, Teja (trans.) (1985) *The Holy Granth: Śrī Rag to Majh*, Patiala: Pañjābī University Publication Bureau.

Sivaraksa, S. (1992) *Seeds of Peace: A Buddhist Vision for Renewing Society*, Berkeley, CA: Parallax Press.

Smith, Jonathan Z. (1978) *Map is Not Territory: Studies in the History of Religions*, Chicago: University of Chicago Press.

—— (2004) *Relating Religion: Essays in the Study of Religion*, Chicago IL: University of Chicago Press.

—— (gen. ed.) (1995) *The HarperCollins Dictionary of Religion*, San Francisco, CA: HarperSanFrancisco.

Smith, M. ([1928] 1977) *Rabi'a the Mystic AD 717–801 and Her Fellow Saints in Islam*, London: Cambridge University Press.

Smith, Wilfred C. ([1963] 1991) *The Meaning and End of Religion*, Minneapolis, MN: Fortress Press.

Solomon, Norman (2006) *Historical Dictionary of Judaism*, 2nd edn, Lanham, MD: The Scarecrow Press.

Somé, Malidoma (1994) *Ritual: Power, Healing and Community*, Portland, OR: Swan/Raven and Co.

Soyinka, Wole (ed.) (1975) *Poems of Black Africa*, introduction by Wole Soyinka, New York: Hill and Wang.

Stanton, Elizabeth Cady and the Revising Committee ([ca. 1895–8] 1974) *The Woman's Bible*, Seattle: Coalition Task Force on Women and Religion.

Suzuki, Daisetz T. (1970) *Zen and Japanese Culture*, Princeton, NJ: Princeton University Press.

Tambiah, S. J. (1970) *Buddhism and the Spirit Cults in North-east Thailand*, Cambridge: Cambridge University Press.

Taraporewala, Irach J. S. ([1947] 1977) *The Gāthās of Zarathushtra: Text with a Free English Translation*, first published Bombay: Dr. Irach J. S. Taraporevala. New York: AMS Press.

Tharu, Susie and Lalita, K. (eds) (1990) *Women Writing in India: 600 BC to the Present*, vol. 1, *600 BC to Early 20th Century*, New York: The Feminist Press at The City University of New York.

The Oxford English Dictionary, Available online at http://www.oed.com.

Thera, N. (trans.) (1969) *Patimokkha: 227 Fundamental Rules of a Bhikkhu*, Bangkok: King Maha Makuta's Academy.

Thobhani, Akbarali (1998) *Mansa Musa: The Golden King of Mali*, Dubuque, IA: Kendall/Hunt Publishing.

Tilak, Bāl Gangādhar (1935) *Srīmad Bhagavadgītā Rahasya or Karma-yoga-shāstra*, 2 vols, trans. Bhalchandra Sitaram Sukthankar, Bombay: R. B.Tilak, Bombay Vaibhav Press.

Tsomo, K. L. (ed.) (1988) *Sakyadhita: Daughters of the Buddha*, Ithaca, NY: Snow Lion Publications.

Tsong-kha-pa (2000, 2002, 2004) *The Great Treatise on the Stages of the Path to Enlightenment*, 3 vols, trans. The Lamrim Chenmo Translation Committee, editor-in-chief, J. W. C. Cutler, ed. G. Newland, Ithaca, NY: Snow Lion Publications.

Tsunoda Ryūsaku (trans.) (1951) *Japan in the Chinese Dynastic Histories: Later Han Through Ming Dynasties*, ed. L. Carrington Goodrich, Perkins Asiatic Monographs, No. 2, South Pasadena: P. D. and Ione Perkins.

Tukol, T. K. (1976) *Sallekhanā is not Suicide*, Ahmedabad: L. D. Institute of Indology.

Verger, Pierre F. (1993) "The Orishas of Bahia," in Jorge A. Carybe, *Os Deuses Africanos no Canbomble da Bahia*, Salvador: Bigraf, pp. 235–261.

Warlukurlangu Artists (1987) *Kuruwarri: Yuendumu Doors*, Canberra: Australian Institute of Aboriginal Studies.

Wee, Chow-Hou (2003) *Sun Zi Art of War: An Illustrated Translation with Asian Perspectives and Insights*, Singapore: Prentice Hall.

Weissler, Chava (1998) *Voices of the Matriarchs: Listening to the Prayers of Early Modern Jewish Women*, Boston, MA: Beacon Press.

Whittstock, Laura Waterman and Salinas, Elaine J. (2007) "A Brief History of the American Indian Movement," available online at http://www.aimovement.org/ggc/history.html (accessed 7 February 2007).

Wilhelm, Hellmut (1960) *Change: Eight Lectures on the* I Ching, trans. Cary F. Baynes, New York: Harper Torchbooks.

Wilhelm, Richard and Baynes, Cary F. (trans.) ([1950] 1971) *The I Ching or Book of Changes*, The Richard Wilhelm Translation rendered into English by Cary F. Baynes, based on the *Chou I Chê Chung*, a Chinese edition from the K'ang Hsi period (1662–1722 CE), Princeton, NJ: Princeton University Press.

Wyman, Leland C. (ed.) (1957) *Beautyway: A Navajo Ceremonial*, commentaries, New York: Pantheon Books.

Yogananda, Paramahansa ([1946] 1981) *Autobiography of a Yogi*, 12th edn, Los Angeles, CA: Self-Realization Fellowship.

Yule, Henry (1875) *The Book of Ser Marco Polo*, vol. 1, London: John Murray.

Zuesse, Evan M. (1985) *Ritual Cosmos: The Sanctification of Life in African Religions*, Athens: Ohio University Press.

—— (1995) "Divination," in Mircea Eliade (ed.) *The Encyclopedia of Religion*, vol. 3, New York: Simon and Schuster Macmillan, pp. 375–382.

Index

*An asterisk (*) indicates that the Glossary contains a full entry for the term. Page numbers indicate discussion of the topic within the chapters, study questions and other glossed terms. Boldfaced numbers refer to plates.

Related titles from Routledge

Introduction to the Study of Religion

John Harding and Hillary Rodrigues

Why do people study religion? How have they studied it in the past? How do we study religion today? Is the academic study of religion the same as religious education? These and many other questions are addressed in this engaging introduction to the discipline of religious studies, written by two experienced university teachers. The authors have crafted this book to familiarize novice students with key concepts and terminology in the study of religion. More advanced students will find a varied array of theoretical perspectives and methodological approaches to the field. Topics include:

- Definitions of religion
- How religion began to be studied: traditional perspectives – philosophical and theological
- How people experience religion: perspectives in the study of religious consciousness and perception – phenomenological and psychological
- Studying religion within communities: social and cultural perspectives – anthropological, sociological, political and economic
- Judging religion: critical perspectives – feminist approaches, the interaction of popular literature and religion
- Contextual perspectives – historical and comparative

The book encourages students to think critically about the perspectives and methods presented and they will find arguments for the strengths and limitations of these. Summary boxes, a timeline, a glossary and other pedagogic aids help students readily grasp key concepts.

John S. Harding is a member of the Religious Studies Department at the University of Lethbridge, Canada.

Hillary Rodrigues is chair of the Religious Studies department at the University of Lethbridge, and recipient of that institution's Distinguished Teaching Award (2000). He is also a former chair of the Department of Anthropology.

ISBN13: 978–0–415–40888–2 (hbk)
ISBN13: 978–0–415–40889–9 (pbk)

Related titles from Routledge

Religion: The Basics

Malroy Nye

How does religion fit in with life in the modern world? Do you have to 'believe' to be a part of one?

From televangelism in the American South to the wearing of the hijab in Britain and Egypt; from the rise of paganism to the aftermath of 9/11, this accessible guide looks at the ways in which religion interacts with the everyday world in which we live. It is a comprehensive introduction to the world of religion, and covers aspects including:

- Religion and culture
- How power operates in religion
- Gender issues
- The role of belief, rituals and religious texts
- Religion in the contemporary world

Religion: The Basics offers an invaluable and up-to-date overview for anyone wanting to find out more about this fascinating subject.

> 'Finally, a book written for the general reader that communicates clearly and authoritatively the many advances that have taken place in the academic study of religion over the past generation.'
> Russell T. McCutcheon, *University of Alabama*

ISBN10: 0–415–26379–4
ISBN13: 978–0–415–26379–5

Related titles from Routledge

Religions in the Modern World: Traditions and Transformations

Edited by Paul Fletcher, Hiroko Kawanami, Linda Woodhead and David Smith

'An excellent textbook and essential reading for anyone who wishes to be up to date with major religious traditions in the modern era.'

Bill Parsons, *Santa Clara University*

This is an unrivalled guide to contemporary religions. It brings together the methods of both the humanities and the social sciences to offer a cutting-edge introduction to the latest work in the study of religion. *Religions in the Modern World* is comprehensive in its coverage. It considers the main religious traditions of both Asia and the West, as well as new forms of religion and spirituality such as New Age. In addition to providing an historical introduction to each religion, the volume offers detailed and original analysis of their interactions with modernity.

Topics covered include:

- religion, colonialism and postcolonialism
- religious nationalism
- women and religion
- secularization and sacralization
- religion and authority
- the rise of new spiritualities

User-friendly and written by practising and specialist teachers, it includes case studies and anecdotes, text extracts, chapter menus and end-of-chapter summaries, glossaries and annotated further reading sections.

The editors: **Linda Woodhead**, **Paul Fletcher**, **Hiroko Kawanami** and **David Smith** are all members of the Religious Studies Department at Lancaster University, one of the leading international institutions in the study of religion.

ISBN13: 978–0–415–21783–5 (hbk)
ISBN13: 978–0–415–21784–2 (pbk)